JOSEPHUS' ACCOUNT OF THE EARLY DIVIDED MONARCHY

BIBLIOTHECA EPHEMERIDUM THEOLOGICARUM LOVANIENSIUM

CVIII

JOSEPHUS' ACCOUNT OF THE EARLY DIVIDED MONARCHY (*AJ* 8,212-420)

REWRITING THE BIBLE

BY

CHRISTOPHER BEGG

DS
121.6
.B34
1993
seab

1425

LEUVEN
UNIVERSITY PRESS

UITGEVERIJ PEETERS
LEUVEN

1993

THE UNITED LIBRARY
2121 Sheridan Road
Evanston, IL 60201

age 0817

CIP KONINKLIJKE BIBLIOTHEEK ALBERT I, BRUSSEL

ISBN 90 6186 536 0 (Leuven University Press)
D/1993/1869/12
ISBN 90-6831-506-4 (Uitgeverij Peeters)
D. 1993/0602/58

No part of this book may be reproduced in any form,
by print, photoprint, microfilm or any other means without written
permission from the publisher

Leuven University Press/Presses Universitaires de Louvain
Universitaire Pers Leuven
Krakenstraat 3, B-3000 Leuven-Louvain (Belgium)

© Uitgeverij Peeters, Bondgenotenlaan 153, B-3000 Leuven (Belgium)

FOREWORD

To the memory of my mother,
Joan Vessa Begg (1920-1962)

Duty and pleasure do not invariably coincide. In terminating this project it is, however, a pleasant duty to cite the many persons who, directly or indirectly, have assisted me in carrying it through to completion.

I am conscious in first place of the great debt of gratitude I owe to my past and present Ordinaries, William Wakefield Cardinal Baum and James Cardinal Hickey. It has been their sustained support which enabled me to pursue my scholarly interests through the years.

I am likewise deeply aware at this moment of all I have received from the various communities with which I have been or am associated. Of these, I am especially grateful to my family, my father and step-mother, George and Catherine Begg, in particular, for their generous financial backing and unfailing interest in the progress of my work. Equally deserving of recognition in this context is my brother Joseph W. Begg, who with enormous patience and perseverance inducted me into the world of the word processor; without Joe's help I could never have completed this work. On this occasion I have as well warm memories of the staff and students of the American College, Leuven, Belgium, which offered me a "a home away from home" during my Sabbatical, 1989-1990. Another European *Zuhause* has been provided for me through the years by my dear friends, Ida and Edna Fecker of Sigmaringen, Germany, who so often overwhelmed me with their kindness. Still another cherished community for me during the last decade has been the parish family of St. Joseph's Church, Washington D.C., where I have the privilege of serving as weekend assistant.

Colleagues and library personnel on both sides of the Atlantic have also had a substantial hand in the realization of this project. Space considerations do not allow me to name them individually, but I do wish, at least, to express a word of collective gratitude to the professors of the Faculty of Theology, Katholieke Universiteit te Leuven, my revered *alma mater*, to the members of the Department of Theology, the Catholic University of America, Washington D.C., where I have taught since 1982 and to the library staffs in both Leuven and Washington. I am likewise deeply grateful to Prof. Louis Feldman, the world's premier Josephus scholar, who has displayed such wonderful courtesy and helpfulness in responding to a beginner's queries.

Finally, these acknowledgements would not be complete without mention of two long-time, loyal priest friends, Rev. Michael Murray and Msgr. Paul Langsfeld. Their solicitude, humor and availability have given me the impetus to persevere.

I pray God's blessing on all the above persons who, in their varied ways, have been the channels of his goodness to me.

Washington D.C., October, 1992   Christopher BEGG

ACKNOWLEDGMENTS

The text and translation of Josephus, *Jewish Antiquities*, Book 8, §§ 212-420, are used by the permission of the publishers and the Loeb Classical Library from H. St. John THACKERAY and Ralph MARCUS (trans.), *Josephus*, Vol. V, Cambridge, MA, Harvard University Press, 1967.

The Greek text of this edition is reprinted on pp. 287-326. The critical apparatus is not included there; variant readings are discussed in the course of my commentary.

TABLE OF CONTENTS

INTRODUCTION

My purpose in this study is a modest and limited one. I wish to examine in some detail a segment of Josephus' *Antiquitates Judaicae* (hereafter *AJ*), i.e. his account of the early divided monarchy from the breakup of the nation following Solomon's death through the demise of Ahab in the second half of Book 8 (§§ 212-420)[1]. I chose this passage for investigation first of all because it constitutes a rather well-delimited sequence within *AJ* as a whole. The preceding first half of Book 8 (§§ 1-211) is a self-contained account of the reign of Solomon[2]. It is true that

---

1. For the text and translation of Josephus' writings I base myself primarily on: H.St.J. THACKERAY, R. MARCUS, A. WIKGREN, L.H. FELDMAN, *Josephus* (LCL), Cambridge, MA - London, 1926-1965 (for *AJ* 8,212-420, see Vol. V, pp. 685-797 where the translation and notes are by Marcus [hereafter Mar]). For purposes of comparison I have likewise consulted the following editions and/or translations of Josephus: J. HUDSON and S. HAVERCAMPUS, *Flavii Josephi Opera Omnia*, Amsterdam, 1726 (hereafter Hud); G. DINDORF, *Flavii Josephi Opera*, Paris, 1845-1847 (hereafter Df); I. BEKKER, *Flavii Josephi Opera Omnia*, Leipzig, 1855-1856 (hereafter Bk); B. NIESE, *Flavii Josephi Opera. Editio maior*, Berlin, 1885-1895 (hereafter N); idem, *Flavii Josephi Opera. Editio minor*, Berlin, 1888-1895 (hereafter N*); S.A. NABER, *Flavii Josephi Opera Omnia*, Leipzig, 1888-1896 (hereafter Na); T. REINACH (ed.), *Œuvres complètes de Flavius Josèphe*, Paris, 1900-1932 (translation of and notes on *AJ* 8,212-420 by J. WEILL [hereafter W] are found in Vol. II, 1926, pp. 204-245); A. SCHALIT (trans.), *Joseph ben Mattijjahu Kadmoniot ha-jehudim*, Jerusalem, 1944-1963 (hereafter Sc); E. NODET, *Flavius Josèphe, Antiquités Juives*, Paris, 1990- .

The extant witnesses for our segment of *AJ* consist in first place of seven medieval codices (hereafter designated collectively as codd), i.e.:

R	Regius Parisinus	(14th century)
O	Oxoniensis	(15th century)
M	Marcianus (Venetus)	(13th century)
S	Vindobonensis	(11th century)
P	Parisinus Gr. 1419	(11th century)
L	Laurentianus	(14th century)
V	Vaticanus	(13th-14th centuries)

In addition, the following witnesses (excerpts, translation, printed edition) are also available for *AJ* 8,212-420:

Exc	Excerpta Peiresciana	(10th century)
E	Epitome	(10th-11th centuries)
Zon	Zonaras' *Chronicon*	(12th century)
Lat	Latin translation	(original, 6th century)
Ed.pr.	Editio princeps	(Basel, 1544)

For an up-to-date discussion concerning groupings and characteristics of these witnesses, see E. NODET, *Le texte des Antiquités de Josèphe (1.1-10)*, in *RB* 94 (1987) 323-375; idem, *Flavius Josèphe* I, pp. xiii-xxii.

2. On this segment, see L.H. FELDMAN, *Josephus as an Apologist to the Greco-Roman World: His Portrait of Solomon*, in E. SCHÜSSLER FIORENZA (ed.), *Aspects of Religious Propaganda in Judaism and Early Christianity*, Notre Dame, 1976, pp. 69-98; H.E. FABER

Josephus' treatment of Jehoshaphat of Judah, introduced by him in 8,315, continues on into Book 9 (see 9,1-44). On the other hand, the episode with which Book 8 ends, i.e. the death of Ahab (8,398-420)[3], is clearly a climatic moment in Josephus' history of the divided monarchy as is indicated, e.g., by the extended reflection he appends to the narrative proper, see 8,418-420. That episode may then be appropriately regarded as the conclusion to the period of the early divided monarchy in Josephus' presentation. More important for my choice, however, was the consideration that *AJ* 8,212-420 represents relatively "uncharted" scholarly territory, which has not hitherto received the systematic, paragraph-by-paragraph examination I envisage.

A study like the one I project immediately confronts the question: what source(s) did Josephus use for his story of the early divided monarchy? To that question the ready and obvious answer is that, throughout *AJ* 8,212-420, Josephus' dominant source is the "Bible", 1 Kings 12-22 and its parallel 2 Chronicles 10-18 in particular[4]. Things become much more problematic, however, when one goes on to ask: which specific "Bible(s)" did Josephus use in composing 8,212-420 (and more generally the "scriptural portion" of *AJ*, i.e. 1,1-11,296 as a whole): was it Hebrew (proto-MT)[5], Greek (LXX)[6], an Aramaic "Targum"[7], or

VAN DER MEULEN, *Das Solomo-Bild im Hellenistisch-Jüdischen Schriftum*, Kampen, 1978, passim.

3. Of course, the very fact that a new "book" of *AJ* begins following this episode in our MSS is another indication that the episode does constitute something of a conclusion. For the subscriptions which mark the end of Book 8 in the various witnesses, see N, II, p. 266.

4. That Josephus utilized both Kings and Chronicles in composing *AJ* 8,212-420 is clear from the fact that his presentation draws on material peculiar to both books. E.g., in 8,230-245 he retells the story of the Bethel confrontation found only in 1 Kings 13, whereas in 8,274-286 he relates the conflict between Jeroboam and Abijah of Judah in obvious dependence on the Chronistic *Sondergut* narrative, 2 Chronicles 13. On Josephus' utilization of both Kings (the Deuteronomistic History) and Chronicles as sources, see in general E. BEN ZWI, *The Authority of 1-2 Chronicles in the Late Second Temple Period*, in *JSP* 3 (1988) 59-88, esp. pp. 73-76. Compare the (odd) passing remark of E. NODET, *Pourquoi Josèphe?*, in *Naissance de la méthode critique. Colloque du centenaire de l'École biblique et archéologique française de Jérusalem* (Patrimonies: Christianisme), Paris, 1992, 99-106, p. 100: "... l'on peut... se demander s'il [Josephus] a vraiment connu les Chroniques...".

5. That Josephus in Book 8 of *AJ* was relying primarily on a Hebrew Biblical text *à la* MT Kings is advocated, e.g. by A. RAHLFS, *Septuaginta-Studien. III. Lucians Rezension der Königsbücher*, Göttingen, 1911, pp. 92-111; A.T. OLMSTEAD, *Source Study and the Biblical Text*, in *AJSL* 30 (1913) 1-35, p. 29, n. 2.

6. The prevailing scholarly view of long-standing is that Josephus knew the "Later Historical Books", i.e. Samuel – 2 Maccabees, primarily in their "LXX" (as opposed to "MT") form, see L.H. FELDMAN, *Josephus and Modern Scholarship (1937-1980)*, Berlin-New York, 1984, pp. 166-170. The authors in question – some of whom do admit Josephus' subordinate use of a Hebrew text of these books – further typically hold that the historian's Greek text of (Samuel-)Kings (and Chronicles) was closer to that of the so-called "Lucianic recension" (see n. 11) than to the "Old Greek" represented by Codex

did Josephus, in fact, know the "Bible" only second-hand, through the medium of learned Alexandrian Jewish midrash(im)[8]?

As I begin my study of *AJ* 8,212-420, I wish to leave open the possibility of Josephus' utilization, for this sequence at any rate, of all three of the "Bibles" just cited. I do this on several grounds: First, as L. H. Feldman points out, *a priori* considerations do favor the likelihood that Josephus would both have been in a position to and had reasons to consult the Biblical text in the above three linguistic forms[9]. In addition, there is the above-mentioned fact that our segment of *AJ* has yet to be examined in any systematic way — a lacuna that extends also to the matter of the nature of its Biblical source(s). In view of these considerations, I intend to compare *AJ* 8,212-420 with its Biblical parallel material as found in the following major textual witnesses: MT[10], Codex Vaticanus (hereafter B) as representative of the "Old

Vaticanus. They include: A. MEZ, *Die Bibel des Josephus untersucht für Buch V-VII der Archäologie*, Basel, 1895; H.ST. J. THACKERAY, *Josephus. The Man and the Historian*, New York, 1929, p. 85; G. RICCIOTTI, *Il testo della Bibbia in Flavio Giuseppe*, in *Atti del XIX Congresso Internazionale degli Orientalisti*, Roma, 1938, 464-470, p. 465; P.E. KAHLE, *The Cairo Geniza*, London, 1941, pp. 154-155 (he explains the affinities between Josephus and "Lucian" in terms of a secondary assimilation of the former to the latter effected by Christian scribes); S.P. BROCK, *The Recensions of the Septuagint Version of 1 Samuel*, Diss. Oxford, 1966; E.C. ULRICH, *The Qumran Text of Samuel and Josephus* (HSM, 19), Missoula, MT, 1978; idem, *Josephus' Biblical Text for the Books of Samuel*, in L.H. FELDMAN and G. HATA (eds.), *Josephus, the Bible and History*, London, 1989, pp. 81-96; S. PISANO, *Additions or Omissions in the Books of Samuel* (OBO, 57), Freiburg-Göttingen, 1984; V. SPOTTORNO, *Some Remarks on Josephus' Biblical Text for 1-2 Kings*, in C. COX (ed.), *VI Congress of the International Organization for Septuagint and Cognate Studies* (SBLSCS, 23), Atlanta, 1987, pp. 277-285. It should be kept in mind that the above view is based above all on findings of a comparison of the text of Josephus with that of Samuel (MT and LXX). Hitherto, a detailed textual comparison has not been carried out between Josephus and Kings (or Chronicles).

7. That Josephus throughout *AJ* 1-11 made major use of an Aramaic prototype of the Targumin known to us from later times is advocated by S. RAPPAPORT, *Agada und Exegese bei Flavius Josephus*, Wien, 1930, pp. xx-xxiv and E.L. DIETRICH, in his recension of Rappaport's work in *Philologische Wochenschrift* 51 (1931) 465-470, c. 467. See also Mar in his preface to *Josephus*, vol. V (covering *AJ* 5-8), p. viii who calls attention to the "new instances", cited by him in the footnotes of his translation, "of Josephus's use of an Aramaic translation of Scripture practically identical with the traditional Targum of Jonathan...".

8. This position is propounded in particular by G. HÖLSCHER, *Josephus*, in *PW* 9[2] (1916) 1934-2000, cc. 1955,1959,1961. Hölscher's position involves the difficulty that it invokes a third, unknown quantity to explicate the relationship between Josephus and the Bible; see RAPPAPORT, *Agada*, p. XVII. (Curiously, however, in his recension of THACKERAY, *Josephus* [see n. 6] in *REJ* 92 (1932) 107-112, p. 111, Rappaport seems to align himself with Hölscher's view.)

9. L.H. FELDMAN, *Use, Authority and Exegesis of Mikra in the Writings of Flavius Josephus*, in M.J. MULDER and H. SYSLING (eds.), *Mikra* (CRINT, 2,1), Assen, 1988, 455-518, pp. 456-460.

10. For this I use BHS. It might be noted here that, in contrast to the case, e.g., of Samuel, Qumran has not yielded significant Hebrew MSS of either Kings or Chronicles.

Greek"[11], the (proto-) Lucianic (or Antiochene) recension of the LXX (hereafter L)[12] with whose text in the historical books from Samuel on Josephus is claimed to have a particular affinity (see n. 6), as well as the

11. I use the text of B printed by A.E. BROOKE, N. MACLEAN, H.ST. J. THACKERAY, *The Old Testament in Greek According to the Text of Codex Vaticanus*, II:II *I and II Kings*, Cambridge, 1930; II:III *I and II Chronicles*, 1932.

It should be pointed out here that 3 Reigns (hereafter Rgns) 12-21 constitutes part of one of the two so-called "non-kaige" segments in the B text of 1-4 Rgns, i.e. 3 Rgns 2,12-21,43 (MT 21, 29) (the other is 1 Rgns 1-2 Rgns 11,1). The B segments so denominated are those which have not been conformed to (proto-) MT to the same extent as its "kaige" portions (i.e. 2 Rgns 11,2-3 Rgns 2,11; 3 Rgns 22-4 Rgns 25). For this distinction, see: D. BARTHÉLEMY, *Les devanciers d'Aquila* (VTSup, 10), Leiden, 1963, pp. 34-41, 91-143. As such then B, for most of its Kings material that is of interest for our purposes (i.e. 1 Kings 22 excepted), is somewhat closer to the (proto-) Lucianic text (see next note) which likewise escaped (thorough-going) assimilation to a text *à la* MT than are its "kaige" segments, see J.D. SCHENKEL, *Chronology and Recensional Development in the Greek Text of Kings* (HSM, 1), Cambridge, MA, 1968, pp. 10-11.

In Greek Chronicles (hereafter Par), L.C. ALLEN, *The Greek Chronicles* I (VTSup, 25), Leiden, 1974, pp. 67, 137-141 concludes that the textual family represented by B is consistently closest to the original LXX, having undergone less systematic assimilation to MT than any of the other families distinguished by him. Conversely, the "Lucianic group" (see next note) is the family which has been most affected by that process.

12. For the L text in Kings I use the recent edition of N. FERNÁNDEZ MARCOS and J.R. BUSTO SAIZ, *El texto antioqueno de la Biblia griega. II. 1-2 Reyes* (TECC, 53), Madrid, 1992. In 1-2 Kings L is represented by six MSS which Fernández and Busto denote as 19, 108 (these two MSS almost invariably coincide), 82, 93, 127, and Z (the corresponding sigla in Brooke, MacLean and Thackeray [see n. 11] are b', b [collectively b], o, e₂, c₂ and Z). Additional witnesses to the L text in 1-2 Kings are "the Questions on Kings and Chronicles" of Theodoret of Cyrrhus († 466) and the Vetus Latina (hereafter VL) itself attested especially by the Scriptural quotations of Lucifer of Caligri († 370). On the characteristics and relationships of all these witnesses, see the introduction of Fernández's and Busto's edition.

For L Chronicles (of which a new edition is in preparation under the direction of Fernández), I use the text of P. DE LAGARDE, *Librorum V.T. Canonicorum Graece pars prima*, Göttingen, 1883 together with the apparatus of Brooke, MacLean and Thackeray. In Chronicles L is attested by e.g.: the MSS b', b (collectively b), e₂, Theodoret, Lucifer as well as the 10th century VL MS Complutensis (for this see R. WEBER, *Les anciennes versions latines du deuxième livre des Paralipomènes*, Rome, 1945).

On L see: R.S. HAUPERT, *The Relationship of Codex Vaticanus and the Lucianic Text in the Book of Kings from the Viewpoint of the Old Latin and Ethiopic Versions*, Philadelphia, 1930; B.M. METZGER, *Chapters in the History of New Testament Textual Criticism* (NTTS, 4), Leiden, 1963, pp. 1-41; S. JELLICOE, *The Septuagint and Modern Study*, Oxford, 1968, pp. 157-171; E. TOV, *Lucian and Proto-Lucian. Towards A New Solution of the Problem*, in *RB* 79 (1972) 101-113; ALLEN, *Chronicles* I, pp. 65-75; N. FERNÁNDEZ MARCOS, *The Lucianic Text in the Books of Kingdoms: From Lagarde to the Textual Pluralism*, in A. PIETERSMA and C. COX (eds.), *De Septuaginta*. FS J.W. Wevers, Mississauga, Ontario, 1984, pp. 161-174; idem, *Literary and Editorial Features of the Antiochene Texts in Kings*, in C. COX (ed.), *VI Congress of the International Organization for Septuagint and Cognate Studies* (SBLSCS, 23), Atlanta, 1987, 287-304; J.R. BUSTO SAIZ, *On the Lucianic Manuscripts in 1-2 Kings*, in COX (ed.), *Congress*, pp. 305-310; idem, *El texto Lucianico en el Marco del Pluralismo textual. Estado de la Cuestion y Perspectivas*, in *EstEcl* 65 (1990) 3-18; B.A. TAYLOR, *The Lucianic Manuscripts of 1 Reigns*. Vol. I: *Majority Text* (HSM, 50), Atlanta, 1992.

Targum (Pseudo-) Jonathan on the Former Prophets (hereafter TJ)[13] and the Targum on Chronicles (hereafter TC)[14]. My comparison will entail then regular reference to the distinctive readings of these witnesses with a view to ascertaining where Josephus' affinities lie in any given instance. Such a multi-sided comparison may sound complicated and confusing (and it is to a certain extent). It should, however, be kept in mind that substantive differences in content among the above witnesses are relatively infrequent in 1 Kings 12-22 and 2 Chronicles 10-18, just as all these witnesses are closer to each other than Josephus is to any of them. Ultimately then one might speak, with due qualification, of a common Biblical storyline available to Josephus in composing 8,212-420.

I am not, however, concerned simply with tracing the similarities and differences between Josephus and the various witnesses to the text of Kings and Chronicles. In addition, I wish to examine the "what" and the "why" of Josephus' rewriting of the Biblical source story in *AJ* 212-420. Under the former heading I shall investigate, e.g., Josephus' deletions, additions, and rearrangements as well as his contentual and terminological modifications of the Biblical data. I shall likewise look to his integration of the material of Kings and Chronicles with their sometimes marked differences of content and sequence into a single presentation as also the use made by him of extra-Biblical traditions, both Jewish and pagan. Finally, I shall attempt to ascertain the reasons for and the effects of Josephus' "retelling procedures" in dealing with the Biblical record (the "why question")[15].

With regard both to Josephus' Biblical text(s) and his various re-writing techniques, I wish to recognize here at the start my debt to R. Marcus (Mar), J. Weill (W) and A. Schalit (Sc) for the many helpful observations furnished by them in the notes to their respective trans-lations of our segment of *AJ*[16]. My aim in this study is to systematize and expand their individual observations by integrating these within a comprehensive comparison between Josephus and his source(s).

By way of conclusion to this introduction, I should say a brief word concerning my procedure in what follows. In order to facilitate my comparison, I have divided up the material of *AJ* 8,212-420 into 18 longer or shorter sections corresponding to the chapter divisions (or other contentual units) within Kings and/or Chronicles. I discuss each of the 18 Josephian sections in turn with special attention to the textual

13. I use the text of A. SPERBER (ed.), *The Bible in Aramaic* II, Leiden, 1959 and the translation of D.J. HARRINGTON and A.J. SALDARINI, *Targum Jonathan on the Former Prophets* (The Aramaic Bible, 10), Wilmington, DE, 1987.

14. I use the text and translation of R. LE DÉAUT - J. ROBERT, *Targum des Chroniques* I-II (AnBib, 51), Rome, 1971.

15. On the notion of retelling/rewriting as exemplified in the Biblical portion of *AJ*, see T.W. FRANXMAN, *Genesis and the "Jewish Antiquities" of Flavius Josephus* (BibOr, 35), Rome, 1979, pp. 24-27.

16. For these see n. 1.

affinities and rewriting techniques it evidences. A conclusion will attempt to bring together the findings of the previous analysis.

The following table offers an overview of my 18 sections along with the parallel passages of Kings and/or Chronicles[17]:

1 Kings (MT)	AJ	2 Chron (MT)
12,1-24	I. The Split (8,212-224)	10,1-11,4
12,25-31	II. Jeroboam's Initiatives (8,225-229)	—
12,32–13,34	III. Bethel Confrontation (8,230-245)	—
(14,21-31)	IV. Rehoboam's Reign (8,246-264)	11,5-12,16*
14,1-18	V. Abijah's Death (8,265-273)	—
(15,1-8)	VI. Jeroboam vs. Abijah (8,274-286)	13,1-23*
14,19-20;15,25-32	VII. Baasha's Coup (8,287-289)	—
(15,9-23)	VIII. Asa's Victory (8,290-297)	14,1-15,19*
15,33–16,4;15,16-22	IX. Baasha vs. Asa (8,298-306)	16,1-6
16,5-28;15,24	X. North/South Contrast (8,307-315)	(16,7-17,1a)
16,29-34	XI. Ahab Introduced (8,316-318)	—
17,1-24	XII. Elijah's Initial Ministry (8,319-327)	—
18,1-46	XIII. Elijah on Carmel (8,328-346)	—
19,1-21	XIV. Elijah at Sinai (8,347-354)	—
21,1-29	XV. Naboth's Murder (8,355-362)	—
20,1-43	XVI. Ahab's Syrian Wars (8,363-392)	—
(22,41-46)	XVII. Jehoshaphat's Early Reign (8,393-397)	17,1b-19*
22,1-40	XVIII. Ahab's Death (8,398-420)	18,1-34

---

17. In several instances the above table cites a passage from Kings or Chronicles within parentheses. Thereby, I indicate that the passage so marked has been used only minimally by Josephus, whereas the parallel text (designated with an *) clearly represents his main source for the particular episode.

I

THE SPLIT
(8,212-224)

1 Kings 12,1-24 // 2 Chron 10,1-11,4[18] relates the circumstances surrounding the breakup of the united monarchy following Solomon's death. The Biblical presentation(s) might be divided up as follows:

1) The Preliminaries   (12,1-3aα // 10,1-3aα)
2) King-People Exchange   (12,3aβ-5 // 10,3aβ-5)
3) Rehoboam's Consultation   (12,6-11 // 10,6-11)
4) Rehoboam's Decision   (12,12-15 // 10,12-15)
5) Split Consummated   (12,16-20 // 10,16-19)
6) Split Confirmed   (12,21-24 // 11,1-4)

I shall now examine in turn the corresponding segments of Josephus' version of the happening, 8,212-224.

1. *The Preliminaries* (8,212). Josephus introduces the "Shechem affair" with the following temporal indication: "After the death of Solomon, his son Roboamos ('Ροβοάμου)[19], who was borne to him by an Ammanite woman named Nooma (Νοομᾶς)[20], succeeded to his kingdom (διαδεξαμένου... τὴν βασιλείαν)[21]...". Josephus derives the

---

18. On the contrasts between the Chronistic and Kings' versions of the episode, see G.N. KNOPPERS, *Rehoboam in Chronicles: Villain or Victim?*, in *JBL* 109 (1990) 423-440.

19. Cf. MT Rehoboam; 3 Rgns // 2 Par 'Ροβοάμ. Here, as regularly elsewhere, Josephus "declines" the invariable name-forms of MT/LXX. See his statement concerning his procedure in this regard in *AJ* 1,129: "With a view to euphony and my readers' pleasure these names (i.e. of Noah's descendants) have been Hellenized. The form in which they here appear is not that used in our country, where their structure and termination remain always the same; thus Nochos [Noah] in Hebrew is Noe, and the name retains this form in all the cases".

20. In 1 Kings 14,21 and 2 Chron 12,13 she is called "Naamah". B 3 Rgns 14,21 has Μααχὰμ, L Ναανά, while B 2 Par 12,13 reads Νοομμά (Codex Alexandrinus [hereafter A] 2 Par 12,13 has a form corresponding to that used by Josephus above). A. SCHLATTER, *Die hebräischen Namen bei Josephus* (BFCT, 16:3), Gütersloh, 1913, p. 81, s.v. נַעֲמָה and A. SCHALIT, *Namenwörterbuch zu Flavius Josephus*, in K.H. RENGSTORF (ed.), *A Complete Concordance to Flavius Josephus*, Supplement I, Leiden, 1969, p. 88, s.v. Ναααμά propose Νααμά as the original form of the name here in line with the "Naama" of Lat.

21. Elsewhere this expression occurs in *Bellum Judaicum* (hereafter *BJ*) 1,490; *AJ* 7,117.244.334.337.371; 8,50.144.264.286; 9,27.172.215; 10,23.37.81.98; 13,253.366; 19,362; *Contra Apionem* (hereafter *Ap*) 1,117.121. All my "statistics" concerning Josephus' word usage are drawn from: K.H. RENGSTORF (ed.), *A Complete Concordance*

content of his indication concerning Rehoboam's[22] accession from 1 Kings 11,43b // 2 Chron 9,31b where it rounds off a series of closing notices concerning Solomon's reign[23]. He anticipates his notice on Rehoboam's mother, in turn, from a later point in the sequence of the Biblical narrative(s), i.e. 1 Kings 14,21 (= 14,31, MT) // 2 Chron 12,13 where she is mentioned, exceptionally, among the closing notices for Rehoboam. In so doing, Josephus aligns himself with the standard practice of the Bible itself where mention of a king's mother normally constitutes part of the opening notices for a given (Judean) ruler.

To appreciate what now follows in *AJ* 8,212, it is necessary to look first at the textual situation in 1 Kings 12,1-3aα // 2 Chron 10,1-3aα. In all witnesses of both Kings and Chronicles the sequence begins with Rehoboam coming to Shechem where "all Israel" had assembled to make him king. Thereafter, however, divergencies set it. MT 1 Kings 12,2-3aα reads: "and when Jeroboam... heard, he was still in Egypt, where he had fled from before king Solomon, and Jeroboam dwelt (יֵּשֶׁב) in Egypt. And they sent and called to him..."[24]. Notably different is 3 Rgns (BL)[25] which passes directly from 1 Kings 12,1 to v. 3aβ with no equivalent to MT's vv. 2-3aα. 3 Rgns does, however, give a faithful rendition of MT's 12,2 (including its [self-evident] "and Jeroboam dwelt in Egypt") at another point in its sequence, i.e. following the notice on Solomon's burial in 11,43aβ. Conversely, 3 Rgns follows its rendering of 12,2 in that context with a further item which diverges completely from MT's 12,3aα ("and they sent and called to him"), namely, "he (Jeroboam) straightaway comes to his own city into the land of Sareira on the mount of Ephraim"[26].

to Flavius Josephus, Leiden, 1973-1983. In them I leave aside readings bracketed by Rengstorf (on these see the remarks in *Concordance*, I, p. xv).

22. In referring to Biblical figures when not actually citing the text of Josephus, I shall generally employ the familiar English renderings of their names rather than the Grecizied forms utilized by him (on these see n. 19). Exceptions are occasionally made when there is a marked difference between the Josephian and Biblical forms of a name.

23. Following his mention (*AJ* 8,21la) of Solomon's death and burial (// 1 Kings 11,43a) at the point where Kings (MT) then gives its notice on Rehoboam's succession (11,43b), Josephus (8,211b) has rather an encomium on Solomon and a *Vorausschau* on the later-to-be narrated consequences of the king's apostasy both of which lack a Biblical parallel as such.

24. For my Biblical translations I use RSV (with occasional [more literalistic] adaptations).

25. In what follows I will use the siglum 3 Rgns (or 2 Par) to designate the combined witness of B and L to a given reading. Where the two witnesses diverge, this will be indicated by a separate citation of their readings.

26. Before thereafter giving its equivalent to MT's 11,43b (Rehoboam's accession) 3 Rgns recapitulates the notice on Solomon's death from 11,43aα. This was necessary because otherwise, after its preceding sequence treating of Jeroboam, the phrase "his son" of 11,43b would seem to make Rehoboam Jeroboam's rather than Solomon's progeny.

The above difference between Kings[27] and 3 Rgns seems to go together with an additional, more comprehensive divergence regarding the moment at which Jeroboam begins to play a role in the Shechem affair. In MT he does so right from the start, arriving from Egypt just as the parley begins (note the explicit references to Jeroboam's approaching Rehoboam along with the people in its 12,3aβ and 12). In 3 Rgns 12, by contrast, the first mention of Jeroboam – who there is earlier said to go, not to Shechem, but to "Sareira" (see above) – is in v. 20 (i.e. it does not mention Jeroboam in its vv. 3 or 12, see below). There has been much controversy as to which of the two presentations has the better claim to originality. I cannot enter into this discussion here[28]. For our purposes it is, however, important to note that Josephus' account is definitely closer to MT Kings (and 2 Chron/ 2 Par) than it is to 3 Rgns. In particular, Josephus has no parallel to the latter's placing of 1 Kings 12,2 (MT) following 11,43a or to its attached notice on Jeroboam's going to Sereira. Conversely, he does speak, as 3 Rgns does not, of a "summoning" of Jeroboam à la MT's 1 Kings 12,3aα.

At the same time, however, Josephus freely rearranges and condenses the elements of 1 Kings 12,1-3aα (// 2 Chron 10,1-3aα) as I shall now show in detail. Josephus' rearrangement of the Biblical sequence is already evident from the fact that he starts off his version with a rendition of 1 Kings 12,3aα. In other words, upon Rehoboam's accession what happens first, in his presentation, is not Rehoboam's going to Shechem (so 12,1 // 10,1), but the summoning of Jeroboam. In wording this item, Josephus further introduces several specifications into the rather indeterminate Biblical formulation. The summoning comes "immediately" (εὐθὺς) upon Rehoboam's accession. Those calling Jeroboam are not the unidentified Biblical "they", but rather the authoritative "leaders of the (common) people" (οἱ τῶν ὄχλων ἄρχοντες)[29]. Finally, Josephus likewise specifies, as the Bible does not, whither Jeroboam's summons was dispatched, i.e. "to Egypt" (cf., however, 12,2aβ // 10,2aβ which speaks of Jeroboam as being "still in Egypt"

27. Both 2 Chron and 2 Par 10,2-3aα basically reproduce the wording of 1 Kings 12,2-3aα: 2 Chron 10,2b states that Jeroboam "returned (וַיָּשָׁב) – note that the difference between this form and 1 Kings 12,2b's וַיֵּשֶׁב, "he dwelt" is only a matter of vocalization), whereas 2 Par 10,2b has the conflate reading "Jeroboam *dwelt* in Egypt and Jeroboam *returned* from Egypt" (in addition, B 2 Par 10,3aα reads a sg. as opposed to the pl. verbs of 1 Kings 12,3aα // 2 Chron 10,3aα, i.e. "and he sent and called to him...").

28. On the whole question see J.C. TREBOLLE BARRERA, *Salomón y Jeroboan. Historia de la recensión y redacción de 1 Reyes 2-12;14*, Jerusalem, 1980, pp. 49-82; S.L. MCKENZIE, *The Source for Jeroboam's Role at Shechem (1 Kgs 11:43-12:3,12,20)*, in *JBL* 106 (1987) 297-300; T.M. WILLIS, *The Text of 1 Kings 11:43-12:3*, in *CBQ* 53 (1991) 37-44.

29. This precise construction occurs only here in Josephus, cf. *AJ* 11,11 ἄρχουσι τοῦ πλήθους.

just prior to the Shechem parley)[30]. Having thus begun with his version of 12,3aα, Josephus next proceeds to give his parallel to 12,2bβ // 10,2bβ. In so doing, the historian leaves aside 12,2abα // 10,2abα whose content (Jeroboam's "hearing", his being still in Egypt where he had fled from Solomon) appears superfluous in light of his earlier mention of Jeroboam's flight to Egypt (see 8,210 // 1 Kings 11,40), as well as his immediately preceding notice about Jeroboam's summons going "to Egypt". Josephus' parallel to 12,2bβ // 10,2bβ reads "when he (Jeroboam) came to them at the city of Sikima (Σίκιμα)[31]...". Here, Josephus aligns himself with the reading "he returned" of 2 Chron 10,2bβ (see 2 Par) as opposed to the "he remained (in Egypt)" of 1 Kings 12,2bβ, *vide supra*. He further specifies, with 12,1 // 10,1 in view, that it was "at Shechem" that Jeroboam met his summoners. Only after thus relating the content of 12,3aα,2bβ // 10,3aα,2bβ, does Josephus introduce the notice of 12,1 // 10,1: once the leaders and Jeroboam have come together at Shechem, Rehoboam "arrived" (παραγίνεται)[32] there

30. Josephus prepares his reference to the leaders of the people sending "to Egypt" to summon Jeroboam here in 8,212 in what precedes: under Solomon Jeroboam "attempted to persuade the people (τὸν λαὸν) to turn away from Solomon" (*AJ* 8,209, no Biblical parallel); subsequently, Jeroboam "fled to Isakos, the king of Egypt, and remained with him until Solomon's death" (8,210 // 1 Kings 11,40).

31. This form of the city's name corresponds to that found in 3 Rgns 12,1. 2 Par 10,1 has Συχὲμ.

32. Josephus' use of the historic present (hereafter h.p.) here corresponds to the πορεύεται of B 3 Rgns 12,1, contrast the past forms of L 12,1 (ἐπορεύθη) and 2 Par 10,1 (ἦλθεν). The h.p. of παραγί(γ)νομαι occurs some 73 × in the Josephan corpus (7 × in our segment: 8,212.231.310.320.328.346.349).

Over the course of *AJ* 8,212-420 Josephus employs the h.p. some 60 ×. Of these uses, most pertain to one of four categories: 1) verbs of motion (coming, going, sending, 19 ×); 2) verbs of seeing and saying (9 ×); 3) descriptions of military initiatives/acts of violence (13 ×); and 4) notices on royal deaths, burials, and accessions (10 ×).

How does Josephus' relatively high use of the h.p. in *AJ* 8,212-420 compare with that of the parallel material in 3 Rgns and 2 Par? In B 3 Rgns where 12,1–21,29 constitute part of the "non-kaige" section 2,12–21,29 (see n. 11), which as H.St.J. THACKERAY, *The Septuagint and Jewish Worship*, London, 1923, pp. 20-22 notes, is characterized precisely by its preference for the h.p., that form occurs 35 × (8 × in two passages, i.e. 12,24a-z and 16,28a-h which have no parallel in Josephus [or MT]). Most of these uses pertain to three categories distinguished above in the Josephan use of the h.p.: verbs of motion (8 ×), (death-)burial-succession notices (17 ×), verbs of perceiving (3 ×). Some or all of the L MSS of 3 Rgns 12,1–21,29 read a past form in six instances where B has the h.p.: 12,1.24k; 15,24; 16,6; 18,40; 21,36. Finally, 2 Par 10,1-18,34 exhibits no uses of the h.p., consistently reading a past form where the 3 Rgns parallel has a h.p. (6 ×).

It thus appears that Josephus in *AJ* 8,212-420 displays a clear tendency to favor the h.p. vis-à-vis the Greek of his Biblical sources (Hebrew, of course, lacks an equivalent form). Similarly, as A. PELLETIER, *Lettre d'Aristée à Philocrate* (SC, 89), Paris, 1962, p. 216 notes, Josephus, in his rewriting of the *Letter of Aristeas* (hereafter *LA*), several times introduces the h.p. where the source has an aorist, compare, e.g., ἀντέγραψεν (*LA* 5,41) // ἀντιγράφει (*AJ* 12,51); προσέταξεν (*LA* 11,294) // κελεύει (*AJ* 12,102). The above findings correspond to the more general conclusion of K. ERIKSSON, *Das Präsens Historicum in der nachklassischen griechischen Historiographie*, Lund, 1943, p. 77, i.e. that

too since this was the site that had been "decided on (δέδοκτο)[33] by the Israelites" (τοῖς Ἰσραηλίταις)[34] to "proclaim him king" (ἀποδεῖξαι βασιλέα)[35]. In contrast to the Bible Josephus thus ascribes the initiative to the Israelite leaders (and Jeroboam) rather than to Rehoboam; he reacts to their assembling at Shechem by going there himself[36].

How is Josephus' re-arrangement/reworking of 1 Kings 12,1-3aα // 2 Chron (Par) 10,1-3aα to be explained? I suggest that he took his cue from might seem like a lack of logical order in the Biblical presentation(s). In particular, the Bible has Jeroboam "hear" and "return" (12,2 // 10,2) before he is "sent and called for" (12,3aα // 10,3aα). Josephus reverses this "unlogical" sequence: Jeroboam, in his account, is first summoned, then comes. Why though does Josephus also diverge from

of all the Hellenistic historians studied by him, it is precisely Josephus who makes most use of the form (1014× in *BJ*, 2,640× in *AJ* according to Eriksson's calculations). He (ibid.) attributes Josephus' heavy use of the form to his dependence both on classicizing (Atticizing) authors like Dionysius of Halicarnassus and Nicolaus of Damascus who revived the form and the earlier historians Herodotus and Thucydides who employ it with some frequency (to these "inspirations" for Josephus' use of the h.p. one should add the LXX itself). See Eriksson's summary discussion of the various categories within Josephus' use of the h.p., ibid., pp. 77-82.

From the above it thus appears that also in his use of h.p., Josephus evidences his characteristic tendency to go his own way vis-à-vis the sources. For the rest, Josephus' use of the h.p. in *AJ* 8,212-420 does not seem to follow readily recognizable principles which would explain why he employs it rather than a past form in a particular instance. On the other hand, it does seem to be the case that he favors the h.p. with certain specific verbs, e.g., παραγίνομαι (7× in 8,212-420) and πέμπω (5×). Otherwise, his usage appears inspired by the (occasional) urge to give a heightened vividness to his narration.

On the phenomenon of the h.p. in Greek literature, see further J.M. STAHL, *Kritisch-historische Syntax des griechischen Verbums der klassischen Zeit*, Heidelberg, 1907, pp. 90-92; K. BRUGMANN and A. THUMB, *Griechische Grammatik*, München, 1913[4], pp. 555-556.

33. Thus NN*Mar; Na reads ἐδέδοκτο with MSP.

34. Josephus uses the designation "the Israelites" with a variety of referents over the course of *AJ*: 1) for the unitary chosen people in the period from the oppression in Egypt down to the death of Solomon (c. 90× ; this would likewise seem to be the referent here at 8,212 at a moment just prior to the split). In this period "the Israelites" serves as a synonymn for the preferred designation, i.e. "the Hebrews" (for this synonymity, see, e.g., *AJ* 2,201-202); 2) as the name of the Northeners following the split (c. 80×); on occasion, however, Josephus denotes this population as "Hebrews" as well (see, e.g., 8,381;9,62); 3) of the Judean survivors of the 587 catastrophe (see, e.g., 10,164-165); and 4) of the (lay) retournees from Babylon (9× in *AJ* 11). On Josephus' various designations for the chosen people, see A. ARAZY, *The Appellations of the Jews (Ioudaios, Hebraios, Israel) in the Literature from Alexander to Justinian*, Diss. New York University, 1973, pp. 170-181. See also n. 198.

35. This construction occurs also in *BJ* 1,117.225.343.346.458.632.646.665.668; 2,3; *AJ* 6,35.40.91.131; 7,8.9.24.55.71.197.289.338.351.355.356.363.372.382; 8,204.310.352; 9,113.125.149.282; 10,102; 11,3.5.31; 12,212.361; 14,446.465; 16,133; 17,53.

36. With this Josephian sequence in which Rehoboam is the last to arrive at Shechem, compare 3 Rgns' opening of its alternative account of the Shechem parley which stands within its great plus following 1 Kings 12,24 in 12,24n: "Then Jeroboam went to Shechem... and there he assembled the tribes of Israel. And Rehoboam went up there also".

the Biblical order in placing these items prior to mention of Rehoboam's coming to Shechem (see 12,1 // 10,l)? Here, I propose that Josephus was motivated by the consideration that Jeroboam, living in Egypt, would need more time getting to Shechem than would Rehoboam coming from Jerusalem. Consequently, in assembling the parties at Shechem, the first thing needing to be done was to summon Jeroboam from his far-off exile – see Josephus' extra-Biblical specification that the leaders sent for him "immediately". But then, commencing with that summons, Josephus naturally relates Jeroboam's response to it before, finally, noting Rehoboam's coming to Shechem. His procedure in this instance attests to the historian's sensitivity to problems posed by the source account(s) and the freedom with which he acts in resolving those problems.

2. *King-People Exchange* (8,213-214). The Biblical account of our episode's opening interaction comprises four "moments": the Israelites' approach to Rehoboam (12,3aβb // 10,3aβb), their word to him (12,4 // 10,4); his response (12,5a // 10,5a); and the people's withdrawal (12,5b // 10,5b). In recounting the first of these moments, Josephus once again aligns himself with Kings and Chron/Par against 3 Rgns in his explicit mention of Jeroboam among those approaching Rehoboam, see above. In contrast, however, to the former witnesses' reference to "all (+ the assembly of, 1 Kings 12,3 and 2 Par 10,3) of Israel" coming to Rehoboam, Josephus (8,213) specifies that it was the same representative group who had previously summoned Jeroboam, i.e. the "leaders of the people" (οἱ... ἄρχοντες... τοῦ λαοῦ)[37] who now approach the king-designate.

The word addressed to Rehoboam by the Israelites in 12,4 // 10,4 comprises three juxtaposed components, i.e. an accusatory statement concerning Solomon, an appeal to Rehoboam, and a (conditional) promise by the people. Each of these elements has its pendant in Josephus' version[38]. For the rest, however, Josephus notably reworks

37. This same phrase occurs in *AJ* 7,341. Compare οἱ τῶν ὄχλων ἄρχοντες in 8,212. The juxtaposition of the two phrases in 8,212 and 213 suggests that λαός in the latter simply means "crowd" as it often does in *BJ* (see e.g., 1,22.550;2,l). On Josephus' varying (non-)use of λαός in its LXX sense as *the* designation for the chosen people, see H. STRATHMANN, λαός, in *TWNT* 4 (1942) 29-39, esp. p. 38.

38. As he does repeatedly throughout *AJ* 8,212-420, Josephus recasts the Biblical direct address ("they said to Rehoboam, 'your father made our yoke heavy. Now therefore lighten the hard service of your father... upon us'...") as indirect discourse here ("the leaders... urged [Rehoboam] to lighten..."). Josephus' use of these two forms of "quotation" (as well as their mixture) has been studied by B. THÉROND, *Discours au style indirect et discours au style direct dans la Guerre des Juifs de Flavius Josephus*, in A. CAQUOT *et al.* (eds.), *Hellenica et Judaica*. FS V. Nikiprowetzky, Leuven-Paris, 1986, pp. 139-152 and P. VILLALBA I VARNEDA, *The Historical Method of Flavius Josephus* (ALGHJ, 19), Leiden, 1986, 89-117. What emerges from the discussion of these authors is

the Biblical source(s). First of all, he reverses the *Vorlage*'s sequence of appeal and "accusation", turning the latter into an explicit motivation for the former. In doing this, I suggest, Josephus was guided by the consideration that to begin a petitionary address with an an accusation of the addresse's father is not an effective *captatio benevolentiae*. Again, in Josephus the Israelites do not simply, like their Biblical counterparts, request Rehoboam "to lighten their bondage somewhat" (ἀνεῖναί τι τῆς δουλείας αὐτοῖς, compare 3 Rgns 12,4αβ κούφισον [2 Par 12,4αβ ἄφες] ἀπὸ τῆς δουλείας τοῦ πατρός σου)[39]. They invoke as well the underlying stance they are asking Rehoboam to adopt towards them, i.e. "to be more lenient (χρηστότερον)[40] than his father". With this additional appeal, focussed on what Rehoboam is to be rather than simply to do for the people, Josephus makes a first reference to the inner states of his characters which will be highlighted by him in what follows and which distinguishes his version from the more "objective" Biblical one(s).

As noted, Josephus appends the people's charge concerning Solomon as a motivation to their previous appeal: "*for* (γὰρ)... the yoke they had borne under him (Solomon) had been heavy indeed (βαρὺν...

first that while *BJ* tends to favor – in this like both LXX and NT (see N. TURNER, *A Grammar of New Testament Greek*, III. *Syntax*, Edinburgh, 1963, pp. 325-326) – *oratio recta*, in *AJ* overall it is rather *oratio obliqua* which comes to the fore. It further appears that not all the motivations for the use of indirect discourse in *BJ* as these have been identified by Thérond are operative in *AJ* 8,212-420. Specifically, while (according to Thérond) the former work utilizes this style to "devalorize" characters (Josephus' opponents in particular) to whom it denies the right to "speak for themselves" (*op. cit.*, pp. 141-142), in *AJ* 8,212-420 at least Josephus seems to employ indirect discourse with "good" and "bad" characters indiscriminately (just as he does his occasional direct discourse). On the other hand, another factor, cited by Thérond in connection with *BJ* (*ibid.*, pp. 140-141), i.e. use of indirect discourse allows for/signals a freer reproduction of a speaker's words than does direct discourse does seem operative also in our segment. Given the fact that throughout the segment Josephus takes considerable liberties with the wording of Scripture, his constant recourse to such a device is readily understandable (in this connection it may be noted that also in his [verbally quite free] rewriting of *LA*, the historian repeatedly substitutes indirect for that document's direct discourse, compare e.g., *AJ* 12,13-15 // *LA* 2,10; *AJ* 12,25 // *LA* 3,19b; *AJ* 12,91-93 // *LA* 10,177-180; *AJ* 12,102 // *LA* 11,293-294; *AJ* 12,108.110a // *LA* 12,310.312, cf. PELLETIER, *Lettre*, pp. 27, 36, 170, 171, 179 and VILLALBA I VARNEDA, *Method*, pp. 111-115). On the occasional use of direct discourse and the shift from indirect to direct discourse within a given speech in *AJ* 8,212-420, see nn. 175, 772.

39. Josephus uses the above genitival phrase "lighten bondage" also in *BJ* 4,402. On the phrase's term δουλεία (which Josephus has in common with 3 Rgns 12,4 // 2 Par 10,4, see above in the text) and its *Wortfeld*, see J.G. GIBBS and L.H. FELDMAN, *Josephus' Vocabulary for Slavery*, in *JQR* 76 (1986) 281-310.

40. Josephus uses the adjective χρηστός 52 ×. On the term, see L.R. STACHOWIAK, *Chrestotes. Ihre biblisch-theologische Entwicklung und Eigenart* (SF N.F., 17), Freiburg, 1957, esp. pp. 38-39; K. WEISS, χρηστός, in *TWNT* 9 (1973) 472-488, esp. pp. 475-476; C. SPICQ, *Notes de lexicographie néo-testamentaire* II (OBO, 22/2), Freiburg-Göttingen, pp. 971-976.

ζυγὸν... ὑπενεγκεῖν)⁴¹". In 12,4bβ // 10,4bβ the people's word closes
with a brief (conditional) promise: "we will serve (3 Rgns // 2 Par
δουλεύσομέν) you". Josephus expatiates, once more focussing attention
on his personages' inner state: "they would be better disposed (εὐνούστεροι)⁴² towards him and accept servitude more willingly (ἀγαπήσειν τὴν
δουλείαν)⁴³ if treated with kindness (ἐπιείκειαν)⁴⁴ than if made to fear
him".

In 1 Kings 12,5 // 2 Chron 10,5 the scene closes with Rehoboam's
injunction to the people to go and return in three days and the notice
that they did so. In Josephus Rehoboam's response becomes a promise
explicating what is implicit in the source's version of his word: "he said
that in three days he would give them an answer (ἀποκρινεῖσθαι)⁴⁵ to
their request". Josephus who thus passes over Rehoboam's actual
dismissal of the people, likewise omits mention of their departure as
something self-evident. In place of the latter item, he introduces the
following comment concerning the emotional affects of Rehoboam's
response upon his hearers:

41. Compare B 3 Rgns 12,4 ὁ πατήρ σου ἐβάρυνεν [L ἐσκλήρυνε] τὸν κλοιὸν ἡμῶν; 2
Par 10,4 ὁ πατήρ σου ἐσκλήρυνεν τὸν ζυγὸν (so Josephus, see above) ἡμῶν.
The above is Josephus' only use of the phrase "bear a yoke"; only here too does he
employ the expression "heavy yoke".
42. Josephus uses the adjective εὔνους 39 × . On the term and the related substantive
εὔνοια in Hellenistic inscriptions and kingship literature as designating "loyal(ty)", see:
W. SCHUBERT, Die hellenistische Königsideal nach Inschriften und Papyri, in APF 12 (1937)
1-26, esp. pp. 8-9, 16-17; idem, Das Gesetz und der Kaiser in griechischen Urkunden, in Klio
30 (1937) 54-66, esp. pp. 63-64; P. HERRMANN, Der Römische Kaisereid (Hypomnemata,
20), Göttingen, 1968, pp. 23-25; M. WEINFELD, The Loyalty Oath in the Ancient Near
East, in UF 8 (1977) 371-414, esp. pp. 383-384; SPICQ, Lexicographie, Supplément (OBO,
22/3), 1982, pp. 316-321.
43. With this construction, compare AJ 3,20 where Moses informs the Hebrews that
God is testing them to see whether they "prefer slavery" (δουλεύειν ἀγαπᾶτε) and 8,4
where Adonijah tells Bathsheba that he is "... happy to serve (ἀγαπᾷ ... τὴν δουλείαν)
under him (Solomon)...".
The reference which Josephus, following the Bible, attributes here to the Israelites
concerning their "servitude" under Solomon stands in a certain tension with his earlier
affirmation (AJ 8,161 = 1 Kings 9,22 // 2 Chron 8,9) that under Solomon "no one of the
Hebrews was a slave (ἐδούλευεν)... they all bore arms and served in the field... rather
than lead the lives of slaves (δουλεύοντες)...". On the other hand, it should also be noted
that elsewhere too Josephus does portray the monarchy as a potential source of
"servitude" for the people, see AJ 6,42 (// 1 Sam 8,16) (Samuel tells the people demanding
a king): "ye with all yours will be bondservants (δουλεύσετε) to the king..."; 14,41 (the
would-be kings Hyrcanus and Aristobulus) are charged by the Jews with "seeking to
change their form of government in order that they may become a nation of slaves
(δοῦλον)".
44. Josephus uses this substantive 17 × . On it see SPICQ, Lexicographie I (OBO, 22/1),
1978, pp. 263-267.
45. Thus the conjecture of N (cf. Lat responsum se), followed by N*MarNa for the
ἀποκρίνασθαι of ROE and MSP's ἀποκρίνεσθαι.

he immediately roused their suspicions (ὕποπτος... γίνεται)⁴⁶ by not
assenting to their wishes (μὴ... ἐπινεύσας... τὰ πρὸς ἡδονήν)⁴⁷ on the
spot, for they held kindness (χρηστὸν)⁴⁸ and friendliness (φιλάνθρωπον)⁴⁹ to be an easy matter, especially for a young man. Nevertheless,
the fact of his deliberating (τὸ βουλεύσασθαι)⁵⁰ and not refusing them on
the instant (τῷ⁵¹ μὴ παραυτίκα ἀπειπεῖν)⁵² seemed to offer some ground
for good hope (ἀγαθῆς ἐλπίδος)⁵³.

The whole above sequence has no basis in the Bible which limits itself
to what characters do and say; it reflects rather Josephus' preoccupa-
tion with the psychological dimensions of the affair.

3. *Rehoboam's Consultation* (8,215-218a). 1 Kings 12,6-11 // 2 Chron
10,6-11 relate Rehoboam's taking counsel, first with a set of older
advisers (12,6-7 // 10,6-7) and then with a group of younger ones (12,8-
11 // 10,8-11). In narrating Rehoboam's consultation with the former
group, Josephus first introduces the explicit mention of the king's
"calling them together". He substitutes (see, however, below) the
designation "his father's friends" (τοὺς πατρῴους φίλους)⁵⁴ for Bibli-

46. The above construction "become suspicious" occurs also in *AJ* 1,263; 5,112;
15,131.
47. This is the only instance of the above construction "not assenting to wish(es)" in
Josephus, cf., however, the related phrase in *AJ* 6,5. The phrase πρὸς ἡδονήν itself recurs
in *BJ* 1,30.515; 2,347.650; 6,315; 7,71; *AJ* 1,46.61.64.129.232; 2,66,80; 4,141 (5,179);
7,195; 8,236.277.418; 11,11.178; 12,398; 13,4; 14,367; 15,27.238; 16,402. With Rehoboam's "not assenting to the wishes (πρὸς ἡδονήν) of the people" here in 8,214, contrast
7,195: Absalon "spoke ingratiatingly (πρὸς ἡδονήν)" to those who had lost their suits.
Absalom's action leads to his being acclaimed king by the people, whereas Rehoboam's
contrary posture will result in his being denied kingly recognition by the Israelites.
48. Compare χρηστότερον, 8,213. See also n. 40.
49. Josephus uses this substantivized adjective (= "humaneness") also in *BJ* 5,334;
6,324.340 as well as 27× elsewhere in its adjectival sense. On the term and its cognate
noun φιλανθρωπία, see C. SPICQ, *La Philanthropie hellénistique, virtu divine et royale*, in
ST 12 (1958) 169-191; idem, *Lexicographie* II, pp. 922-927; R. LE DÉAUT, *φιλανθρωπία
dans la littérature grecque jusqu'au Nouveau Testament (Tite III,4)*, in *Mélanges
E. Tisserant* I (Studi e Testi, 231), Vatican City, 1964, 255-294; FELDMAN, *Mikra*, p. 49;
idem, *Josephus' Portrait of David*, in *HUCA* 60 (1989) 129-174, pp. 150-153.
Note that in *AJ* 10,64 (cf. Tit 3,4) Josephus collocates the nominal forms of the two
substantivized adjectives of 8,214 in reference to Gedaliah. See further SPICQ, *Philanthropie*, p. 176, n. 1 for combinations of the same two terms elsewhere in Greek literature.
In this connection it might be noted that the various terms used of the "benignity"
which is asked of the would-be ruler Rehoboam in 8,213-214 and subsequently rebuffed
by him, i.e. ἐπιείκεια, χρηστός, φιλάνθρωπος are all cited by Josephus as qualities of
David, see 7,391 where he calls David ἐπιεικῆς χρηστός... φιλάνθρωπος. In his refusal to
adopt these qualities of his grandfather, Rehoboam thus appears in Josephus as a kind of
"anti-David" with all the disastrous consequences for national unity that entails.
50. N conjectures βουλεύεσθαι (the conjecture disappears in N*).
51. Thus the conjecture of NN* followed by Mar for codd's τοῦ which Na adopts.
52. The above expression "refuse immediately" occurs only here in Josephus.
53. The phrase "good hope" occurs also in *AJ* 1,325; 5,222; 13,201.
54. The above expression "father's friends" occurs also in *BJ* 2,104; *AJ* 8,264; 9,95;
13,422.

cal "the old men (3 Rgns 12,6 πρεσβυτέροις) who stood before
Solomon...", thereby assimilating them to the well-known Hellenistic/
Roman court grouping, "the king's friends".

In 1 Kings 12,7 // 2 Chron 10,7 the senior advisers' response follows
immediately on Rehoboam's question to them. Josephus, on the
contrary, prefaces his version of their response with the comment "and
they, as was to be expected (ἅπερ εἰκὸς)[55] of men of kindly disposition
(εὔνους)[56] and acquainted with the nature of crowds, advised him...".
This Josephan insertion both carries forward his psychologizing of the
episode and provides an advance evaluation of the "friends'" actual
counsel. The wording of the response given Rehoboam differs somewhat in 1 Kings 12,7 and 2 Chron 10,7. The former reads "if you will
be a servant to this people today *and serve them* and answer them (> 3
Rgns) and speak good words to them, then they will be your servants
for ever", whereas the latter has "if you will be kind to this people and
please them and speak good words to them, then they will be your
servants for ever"[57]. Josephus' version of the reply is more reminiscent
of the Chronicler's, lacking as it does mention (so 1 Kings) of a
"serving" of the people by the king. At the same time he attributes a
more expansive response to the "friends", once again highlighting the
psychological element:

> (they advised him) to speak to the people in a friendly spirit (φιλο-
> φρόνως)[58] and in a more popular style (δημοτικώτερον)[59] than was usual

On the category of the royal "friends", see SPICQ, *Lexicographie*, II, pp. 940-943 with
reference to older literature. Also elsewhere Josephus frequently (some 75 ×) introduces
an (anachronistic) reference to "(royal) friend(s)" where the Bible lacks this. See, e.g., the
following instances where, *à la* his substitution of "paternal friends" for "old men who
stood before (i.e. served) Solomon" here in 8,215, Josephus replaces Biblical mentions of a
king's "servants" with references to royal "friends": *AJ* 6,250 (Saul's "friends and
chieftains" // 1 Sam 22,6 "servants"); 8,367 (Ahab's "friends and kinsmen" // 1 Kings
20,6 "servants"). 379 (Ben-hadad's "friends" // 1 Kings 20,23 "servants"); 9,81 (Joram's
"friends" // 2 Kings 7,12 "servants"). 171 (Joas' "friends" // 2 Kings 12,21 = 2 Chron
24,25 "servants"); 11,195 (Ahasureus' "friends" // Est 2,2 "servants").

55. Only here in Josephus.

56. Cf. εὐνούστεροι, 8,213. H. SCHRECKENBERG, *Einige Vermutungen zum Josephustext*, in *Theokratia* 1 (1967-1969) 64-75, p. 69 conjectures εὖ voῦv here.

57. On the Chronicler's reformulation of Kings here, see M. WEINFELD, *The Counsel of
the "Elders" to Rehoboam and its Implications*, in *Maarav* 3 (1982) 27-52, esp. pp. 27, 33.

58. Josephus uses this adjective/adverb 33 ×. Note especially *AJ* 7,30 where he applies
it to David, just as he qualifies that king with a whole series of other terms for the
"benignity" asked of Rehoboam, but eventually refused by him, see n. 49.

59. Josephus uses this adjective/adverb 23 ×. Compare DIONYSIUS OF HALICARNASSUS,
The Roman Antiquities (hereafter *RA*) (LCL; tr. E. CARY), London-Cambridge, MA,
1937-1950, 7.45.4 where Marcius is urged to "descend... to a more democratic (τὸ
δημοτκώτερον) behaviour". On the contacts and contrasts between Josephus and Dionysius in general, see: R.J.H. SCHUTT, *Studies in Josephus*, London, 1961, 92-101;
F.G. DOWNING, *Redaction Criticism: Josephus' Antiquities and the Synoptic Gospels (1)*,
in *JSNT* 8 (1980) 46-55; T. RAJAK, *Josephus and the "Archaeology of the Jews"*, in *JJS* 33

for the royal dignity (κατὰ βασιλείας ὄγκον)⁶⁰, for in this way he would secure their goodwill (χειρώσεσθαι⁶¹... εἰς εὔνοιαν)⁶², since subjects naturally (φύσει)⁶³ liked affability (τὸ προσηνὲς)⁶⁴ in their kings and to be treated by them almost as equals (ἰσότιμον)⁶⁵.

1 Kings 12,8a // 2 Chron 10,8a makes the transition to Rehoboam's second consultation noting, without comment, that he "forsook" the elders' counsel. Josephus elaborates this item in two respects. First, he provides an explicit evaluation of their counsel as "good and beneficial (ἀγαθὴν... καὶ συμφέρουσαν)⁶⁶, perhaps (ἴσως)⁶⁷ for all occasions, or, if not for all, at any rate (πρός γε)⁶⁸ for that particular occasion (when he was to become king, ὅτ' ἔδει γενέσθαι βασιλέα)⁶⁹". He then proceeds to offer a "theological" explanation of Rehoboam's "rejecting the advice" (γνώμην ἀπεστράφη)⁷⁰ of the "friends": "it was God, I believe, who caused him to condemn what should have been of benefit (κατακριθῆναι τὸ συμφέρον)⁷¹ to him". With this interjected remark, of the sort that occurs also elsewhere in his presentation (see, e.g., 8,409), Josephus anticipates the sources' invocation of divine causality at a later point in the episode, see 1 Kings 12,15 // 2 Chron 10,15.

Josephus now relates, in parallel to 12,8b-9 // 10,8b-9, Rehoboam's assembling his contemporaries and asking their advice. Whereas, however, in 12,9 // 10,9 Rehoboam quotes them the words of the people's appeal (12,4 // 10,4), in Josephus he informs "the young men who had been brought up with him" (μειράκια τὰ συντεθραμμένα)⁷² of the advice of the "elders" (τῶν πρεσβυτέρων)⁷³. With this substitution

---

(1982) 465-477; G.E. STERLING, *Historiography and Self-Definition. Josephos, Luke-Acts and Apologetic Historiography* (NovTSup, 64), Leiden, 1992, 284-290.

60. This is Josephus' only use of the above expression "royal dignity". He employs ὄγκος elsewhere in *BJ* 3,2; 4,319; 7,443; *AJ* 8,63; 18,222.

61. Thus the emendation of Ed. pr., followed by NN*NaMar, for the codd's χειρώσασθαι.

62. This is the only occurrence of the phrase "secure goodwill" in Josephus. With its εὔνοιαν, compare the cognate adjectival forms εὐνούστεροι (8,213) and εὔνους (8,215).

63. See Josephus' reference to the advisers' "knowing the nature (φύσιν) of crowds", 8,215a.

64. Elsewhere *BJ* 3,507; 4,472; *AJ* 8,394; 11,234.

65. Josephus uses the substantivized adjective (τὸ) ἰσότιμον also in *BJ* 4,319.389, cf. *BJ* 1,71; 4,393; *AJ* 12,119.

66. The collocation "good and beneficial" occurs only here in Josephus.

67. So NN*Mar. Na reads ἴσως μεν with SP.

68. Thus Ed.pr., followed by NN*NaMar, for the codd's πρός τε.

69. Mar's translation lacks an equivalent to this Greek phrase, see W, *ad loc.*: "où il s'agissait de prendre le pouvoir".

70. The above construction "reject advice" occurs only here in Josephus.

71. This is Josephus' only use of the above construction "condemn the beneficial".

72. Josephus' other uses of συντρέφω are in *AJ* 18,191; *Ap* 2,204.

73. Note Josephus' use of this term from 1 Kings 12,6 // 2 Chron 10,6 for which he had earlier (8,215) substituted "(his father's) friends".

Josephus avoids repeating the language of 12,4 // 10,4. That Rehoboam, as Josephus has it, should tell his second set of advisers what the first group had said likewise makes psychological sense; having already rejected the latter's advice (see above), he wishes thereby to provoke the former into giving a contrary, rival opinion. Just as he does in the case of the "elders", Josephus precedes the young men's counsel with an inserted characterization of them, i.e. "whom neither their youth nor God permitted[74] to discern a better course (νοεῖν τὰ κρείττω)[75]". By means of this notice he both evaluates and accounts for the ill-conceived advice they will give. In 12,10bα // 10,10bα there is yet another repetition of the language of 12,4 // 10,4 (see 12,9 // 10,9), this time as part of the young men's reference to the people in their response. Josephus, avoiding this verbal repetition as well, proceeds immediately to the core of their advice. The young men's proposal as found in 12,10bβ-11 // 10,10bβ-11 consists of three figurative comparisons between Rehoboam and his father. Of these, Josephus reproduces the first (Rehoboam's "little [βραχύτατον][76] finger [δάκτυλον][77] is thicker than his father's loins [τῆς τοῦ πατρὸς ὀσφύος... παχύτερον][78]") and third (in place of the "whips" [μάστιξιν, so 2 Par] with which Solomon "chastised" [ἐνουθέτει][79] the people, Rehoboam will do the same with "scorpions" [σκορπίοις, so 3 Rgns // 2 Par]). For the intervening Biblical image of a (still heavier) "yoke", he substitutes, however, a prosaic equivalent: "if they found his father excessively harsh (σκληροῦ)[80], they would experience much more unpleasant treatment (λήψεσθαι πεῖραν[81] δυσκόλου[82]) from himself".

The Bible makes as such no mention of Rehoboam's reaction to the

74. See the (likewise interjected) remark of 8,216 "it was God... who caused him (Rehoboam) to condemn...".

75. Only here in Josephus.

76. This is the reading found in the L witness Theodoret (see n. 12); it is adopted by NN*NaMar in preference to the βραχύτερον of codd E.

77. Josephus' specification "finger" here is lacking in 1 Kings 12,10 // 2 Chron 10,10 as well as in 3 Rgns 12,10, all of which read (literally) "my littleness". It does, however, stand in 2 Par 12,10 (Theodoret [see previous note] notes the equivalence between 2 Par and Josephus on this point) as well in the margin of the L MS 82/o. In TJ and TC the image is transposed into a prosaic "my weakness is stronger than the strength of my father". On all these readings, see further F. VATTIONI, *3 (1) Re 12,10; 2 Par (Cr) 10,10 e Teodoreto di Ciro*, in *Aug* 31 (1991) 475-477.

78. Compare 2 Par 10,10 παχύτερος τῆς ὀσφύος τοῦ πατρός μου.

79. Josephus uses νουθετέω 15 ×. Cf. 3 Rgns 12,11 // 2 Par 12,11 ἐπαίδευσεν.

80. On this term, see SPICQ, *Lexicographie*, Supplément, pp. 606-610. Josephus perhaps found inspiration for his use of the term here in 3 Rgns 12,13a // 2 Par 10,13a which states that upon the people's return Rehoboam answered them "harshly" (σκληρά).

81. Josephus uses the expression "experience treatment" also in *BJ* 2,340; *AJ* 2,6; 4,1.191; 8,166; 15,367; *Vita* 126.160.

82. Josephus employs the term δύσκολος 25 ×. On it, see SPICQ, *Lexicographie*, I, pp. 218-220.

young men's counsel (contrast 12,8 // 10,8), proceeding directly – and rather abruptly – to the people's return (12,12 // 10,12). Josephus (8,218) provides a transition with his reference to the affect of their counsel on him: "with this advice the king was pleased (ἡσθεὶς)[83], thinking such an answer proper to the royal dignity (προσήκειν τῷ τῆς ἀρχῆς ἀξιώματι)[84]". With this addition, Josephus leaves readers in no doubt how Rehoboam will answer the crowd. At the same time, the addition sets in ironic perspective the description of the crowd's mood which Josephus appends to the Biblical (12,12 // 10,12) mention of their return to Rehoboam: "all the people were excited (μετεώρου τοῦ λαοῦ παντὸς ὄντος)[85] and anxious to hear (ἀκοῦσαι... ἐσπουδακότος)[86] what the king might say, supposing it would be something friendly (φιλάνθρωπον, see 8,214)".

4. *Rehoboam's Decision* (8,218b). Josephus' notice on the crowd's return ("the multitude [τὸ πλῆθος, cf. 1 Kings (3 Rgns) 12,12 "all Israel", 2 Chron 10,12 "all the people (2 Par λαὸς)] assembled on the third day...") does not explicitly mention Jeroboam among those approaching Rehoboam. In this he diverges from 1 Kings 12,12 // 2 Chron (Par) 10,12, but agrees with 3 Rgns 12,12 (see above). It should, however, be kept in mind that, in contrast to 3 Rgns, Josephus (8,212) does cite Jeroboam's participation in the Shechem parley right from the start. Given that earlier mention, he perhaps thought it unnecessary to single out Jeroboam by name here in 8,218. In other words then it need not be supposed that his non-mention of Jeroboam at this point reflects his utilization of a text à la that of 3 Rgns 12,12.

1 Kings 12,12-14 // 2 Chron 10,12-14 narrates the second exchange between Rehoboam and the people with considerable circumstantiality, repeating, e.g., Rehoboam's injunction to the crowd (12,12b= 12,5) and an extended portion of the young men's advice to him (12,14b= 12,11). Josephus is markedly shorter: "ignoring the counsel of his (older) friends (φίλων)[87], he answered them as the young men had advised (see 12,13b-14aα // 10,13b-14aα)".

1 Kings 12,15b // 2 Chron 10,15b pauses within the flow of the narrative to offer a first, explicit theological commentary upon what has transpired: "... it was a turn of affairs brought about by the Lord

---

83. Na conjectures πεισθεὶς here with reference to *AJ* 8,277 where Abijah refers to his father's having been "persuaded (πεισθεὶς) by the advice of wicked men".

84. The above construction "proper to the royal dignity" occurs also in *AJ* 4,216. Recall the elders' (rejected) counsel to Rehoboam that he speak to the people "in more popular style than was usual for the royal dignity (κατὰ βασιλείας ὄγκον)", 8,215.

85. Compare μετεώρου τοῦ πλήθους ὄντος, *AJ* 4,36.

86. Compare σπουδαζόντων... ἀκοῦσαι, *AJ* 9,111 (of Jehu's officers).

87. Once again (see 8,215) Josephus substitutes this designation for the Biblical "elders".

(Chron God) that he (Chron the Lord) might fulfill his word (3 Rgns ῥῆμα, 2 Par λόγον) which the Lord spoke by Ahijah... to Jeroboam... [see 1 Kings 11,31-39]." Josephus, who has already twice cited God's influence on characters' initiatives (see above), words this notice as follows: "This came about in accordance with the will of God (κατὰ τὴν τοῦ θεοῦ βούλησιν)[88], in order that what Achias (Ἀχίας)[89] had prophesied (προεφήτευσεν)[90] [see AJ 8,206-208] might be accomplished (λάβῃ τέλος)[91]".

5. *Split Consummated* (8,219-221a). Once again, (see 8,218), Josephus goes beyond the Bible in prefacing reference to the crowd's words/ actions with mention of the emotions animating them: "struck a cruel blow by these words[92] and hurt (ἀλγήσαντες)[93] as though actually experiencing what he had spoken of doing, they became indignant (ἠγανάκτησαν)[94] and all cried out in a loud voice...". As in 1 Kings 12,16aβ // 2 Chron 10,16aβ, Josephus first has the crowd declare their association with the Davidids dissolved: "they no longer had any common tie with David (οὐδὲν... εἶναι συγγενὲς πρὸς Δαυίδην)[95] and his descendants from that day on". Whereas, however, in 12,16bα // 10,16bα the crowd ends up with the cry "to your tents, O Israel. Look now (2 Par βλέπε; 3 Rgns reads βόσκε, 'pasture') to your own house (3 Rgns // 2 Par οἶκον), David", he has the Israelites state rather: "they would leave to Roboamos only (αὐτῷ μόνον)[96] the temple (τὸν ναὸν)

---

88. This phrase, with slight variations, occurs some 30 × in Josephus (never in *BJ*). On the concept "will of God" in Josephus, see: A. Schlatter, *Wie sprach Josephus von Gott?* (BFCT, 14:1), Gütersloh, 1910, p. 26; H.A. Attridge, *The Interpretation of History in the Antiquitates Judaicae of Flavius Josephus* (HDR, 7), Missoula, MT, 1976, pp. 74-75, n. 2.

89. Compare MT "Ahijah"; 3 Rgns // 2 Par Ἀχειά.

90. The verb προφητεύω occurs 58 × in Josephus (only once in *BJ*, i.e. 1,69). Josephus consistently avoids, as here, both terms, i.e. ῥῆμα (see 3 Rgns 12,15) and λόγος (see 2 Par 12,15) LXX uses so frequently to designate a divine "utterance", substituting a variety of equivalent formulations (including "prophesy"). Of the two LXX terms, ῥῆμα occurs only 6 × in the Josephan corpus, never designating God's "word", while according to Schlatter, *Gott*, p. 69 the historian's only use of λόγος in this sense is *BJ* 7,343 where Eleazar invokes "the ancestral and divine precepts (λόγοι, note the pl.)". Schlatter (ibid.) attributes Josephus' avoidance of the LXX (and NT) "word of God language" to his highlighting rather the divine "law(s)" as constitutive for Judaism. See further n. 128.

91. Josephus employs the above phrase "receive accomplishment" elsewhere in *BJ* 2,529; *AJ* 2,73; 4,125; 5,7.53; 9,73; 10,67; 11,180; 12,55.107; 13,173.187; *Vita* 107.152.308.393.414.

92. At this point MSP have the plus ὡς ὑπὸ σιδήρου which Na adopts, cf. Lat's plus "velut opere".

93. The verb ἀλγέω occurs 15 × in Josephus.

94. The verb ἀγανακτέω occurs 55 × in Josephus.

95. Compare the words of Mariam to Pharoah's daughter in *AJ* 2,226 "(it was lost labour... to summon to feed the child [Moses] those who) μηδὲν πρὸς αὐτὸ συγγενὲς ἔχουσιν.

96. Thus Ed.pr. followed by NN*NaMar; codd E have μόνῳ agreeing with αὐτῷ.

which his grandfather (πάππος)⁹⁷ had built". Here, Josephus apparently takes the Biblical mention of David's "house" (i.e. dynasty) as a reference to the Temple⁹⁸. He likewise has the people (only) "threaten to desert him (Rehoboam)" rather than actually "dispersing to their tents" (so 12,16 // 10,16) since in what follows they still seem to be assembled in proximity to Rehoboam.

Like B 3 Rgns Josephus has no parallel to the (disruptive) 1 Kings 12,17 (also read by L 3 Rgns) // 2 Chron (Par) 10,17 "but Rehoboam (B 2 Par reads Jeroboam) reigned over the people of Israel who dwelt in the cities of Judah". One need not, however, conclude that Josephus' source text(s) lacked the verse. Given its disruptive character, as well as its duplication of 1 Kings 12,20 (see below), Josephus could very well have decided on his own to leave the verse aside.

1 Kings 12,18 // 2 Chron 10,18 laconically relates the Israelites' stoning of Rehoboam's envoy "Adoram" (MT) and the king's resultant hasty retreat to Jerusalem. Josephus amplifies this account in three ways. First, he provides a motivation for Rehoboam's dispatch of "Adōramus" ('Aδώραμον)⁹⁹, "the overseer" (τὸν ἐπὶ τῶν φόρων)¹⁰⁰, i.e. "to appease (καταπραύνῃ)¹⁰¹ them and soften their mood (ποιή-σῃ¹⁰² μαλακωτέρους)¹⁰³ by persuading them to forgive (συγγνόν-τας)¹⁰⁴ what he (Rehoboam) had said if there had been in it anything rash (προτετὲς)¹⁰⁵ or ill-tempered (δύσκολον, see 8,217) owing to his youth (ὑπὸ νεότητος)¹⁰⁶". Josephus likewise invokes the feelings

97. On Mar's rendering of his reading, i.e. πάππος here, the reference would be to David, whereas it was Solomon, of course, who actually built the Temple. If Mar's reading/rendition be accepted, it might be accounted for as due to the influence of the mention of "David" in 1 Kings 12,16 // 2 Chron 10,16 (reproduced by Josephus in the phrase "they no longer had any common tie with David", see above; note further that in AJ 1,227 Josephus explicitly designates David as the one who erected the Temple [τὸ ἱερόν]). To be noted, however, is that E does read πατήρ (= Solomon) here in 8,219 (see too Lat pater), a reading adopted by Na and W, ad loc. ("son père").

98. So Mar, Josephus, V, p. 690, n.a.

99. Josephus' form of the name represents a declined equivalent of MT "Adoram". Compare B 3 Rgns 12,18 Ἀράμ, L 3 Rgns 12,18 // 2 Par 10,18 Ἀδων(ε)ιράμ. Josephus has already made mention of this personage in AJ 7,293;8,59.

100. Josephus has already used this title for Adoramos in AJ 7,293. Compare 3 Rgns // 2 Par τὸν ἐπὶ τοῦ φόρου.

101. Josephus uses the verb καταπραΰνω elsewhere in AJ 2,159; 3,310; 7,191.333; 10,93; 20,121.

102. Thus the conjecture of NN*NaMar for the ποιήσειν of ROMS.

103. Josephus' only other use of the above idiom (= "to make soft") is BJ 6,21.

104. Elsewhere Josephus uses συγγινώσκω as here in the sense "to pardon" in BJ 1,167;AJ 6,93 (subject: God); 8,278 (vide infra). On the term and its nominal form συγγνώμη, see K. METZLER, Der griechische Begriff des Verzeihens. Untersucht am Wortstamm συγγνώμη von den ersten Belegen bis zum vierten Jahrhundert n. Chr. (WUNT, 2/44), Tübingen, 1990, esp. pp. 231, 254-259.

105. Josephus uses this adjective 17 × ; on it, see SPICQ, Lexicographie, II, pp. 756-757.

106. This phrase, read by NaMar, is lacking in RO which NN* as well as WSc follow.

underlying the people's action: "so bitter did they feel (ἔσχον πικρῶς)[107] and so great was the anger they nourished (τὴν ὀργὴν ἐτήρησαν)[108] that... they did not let him (Adoramus) speak but threw stones
at him and killed him (βάλλοντες αὐτὸν λίθοις ἀπέκτειναν)[109]".
Finally, he also makes reference to the emotional impact of Adoram's
murder on Rehoboam himself: "seeing this and imagining himself the
target of the stones with which the crowd had killed his minister
(ὑπηρέτην)[110], he was afraid that he might actually suffer (δείσας μὴ...
πάθη)[111] this dreadful fate (τὸ δεινὸν)[112] and immediately mounted
his chariot (ἐπιβὰς... ἐπὶ ἅρματος)[113] and fled to Jerusalem".

1 Kings 12,19-20 (2 Chron (Par) 10 lacks a parallel to 12,20) recounts
the culmination of the split with the accession of the two rival kings,
first Jeroboam (12,19-20a), then Rehoboam (12,20b). In his version,
which follows the more expansive account of Kings, Josephus reverses
the Biblical sequence. Similarly, in line with 3 Rgns 12,20 but against 1
Kings 12,20, he specifies that not only Judah but also Benjamin
designated Rehoboam as king (χειροτονοῦσιν αὐτὸν βασιλέα)[114]. A la
1 Kings 12,19 // 2 Chron 10,19, Josephus prefaces mention of Jeroboam's reception of the Northern rulership (see 1 Kings 12,20a) by
stating that "the rest of the populace (πλῆθος)[115] revolted (ἀπο-

107. This same construction recurs in *AJ* 12,122 (of Vespasian's and Titus' "bitter-
ness" towards the Jews).
108. This is Josephus' only use of the above phrase "keep anger".
109. With the above phrase "throw stones (at him)", compare *AJ* 7,207 λίθοις...
ἔβαλλεν αὐτὸν, cf. *BJ* 1,550; 2,11.492; 3,524; 4,200; 5,111; *AJ* 20,176.180. 3 Rgns 12,18 //
2 Par 10,18 read ἐλιθοβόλησαν... αὐτὸν (ἐν) λίθοις ... καὶ ἀπέθανεν.
110. This noun ὑπηρέτης occurs 25 × in Josephus.
111. The above expression "fearing lest one suffer" occurs also in *BJ* 1,211; *AJ* 7,82;
14,11; 18,352; *Vita* 404.
112. The above phrase "suffer (no) harm" occurs also in *BJ* 3,202;5,337;*AJ* 3,413
(with genitive); 6,255.316; 7,7 (300, genitive); 9,91(genitive).96.100 (genitive).161.258.260;
11,327; 12,252.364.395.403; 14,134; 15,69.204.
113. Compare ἐπιβὰς ἅρματος, *AJ* 9,117. Josephus' explicit mention of Rehoboam's
"mounting his chariot" here corresponds to 1 Kings and L (ἀναβῆναι ἐπὶ τὸ ἅρμα) 12,18
// 2 Chron (Par) 10,18, whereas B 3 Rgns 12,18 ("he hastened to go up to flee to
Jerusalem") lacks it.
114. The above expression "elect king" recurs in *AJ* 6,39.43.54.81.143.311;
8,10.27.53.206.260.350; 9,108; 13,219.
Note that in its 1 Kings 12,21 also MT refers to Rehoboam's convoking both Benjamin
and Judah. Josephus' mention of the former tribe in his version of 12,20 does not then
necessarily prove his dependence on the 3 Rgns as opposed to the MT form of that verse.
Rather, he might readily have taken over the name "Benjamin" from 1 Kings (3 Rgns)
12,21 with a view to explaining how it was that Rehoboam was in a position to convene
that tribe along with Judah. See further Mar, *Josephus*, V, p. 691, n.e who points out that
already twice previously in his presentation Josephus substitutes a reference to the *two*
tribes Rehoboam is to rule where the Bible itself speaks of only one, see *AJ* 8,198 (// 1
Kings 11,13) and 207 (// 1 Kings 11,32 MT [3 Rgns does read "two" here]).
115. Compare Biblical "all Israel" which seems somewhat misleading in that it could
be understood as referring to the twelve tribes in their entirety.

στὰν)[116]... from the sons of David and proclaimed Jeroboam head of the state (τῶν πραγμάτων κύριον)[117]". Whereas, however, 1 Kings 12,19 // 2 Chron 10,19 speaks of that rebellion as perduring "*to* this day", Josephus, conscious that both Israel and the Davidic dynasty itself have long since ceased to exist, refers to the North's revolting "*from* that day" (ἀπ᾽ ἐκείνης τῆς ἡμέρας)[118]. He likewise leaves unutilized 1 Kings 12,20aα which cites Israel's hearing of Jeroboam's (B 3 Rgns reads Rehoboam) return from Egypt and summoning him to its assembly (where he is then elected king, 12,20aβ). In so doing, Josephus contrives to avoid the apparent discrepancy between this item and 1 Kings 12,2-3a // 2 Chron (Par) 10,2-3a (see 8,212) according to which Jeroboam had already "returned" from Egypt to Shechem in reponse to the Israelite summons.

6. *Split Confirmed* (8,222-224). 1 Kings 12,21-24 // 2 Chron 11,1-4 constitutes an appendix to the foregoing. It recounts how Rehoboam's projected military suppression of Israel's rebellion was frustrated by a prophetic intervention. In relating Rehoboam's preparatory marshalling of his forces (see 12,21aβb // 11,1aβb), Josephus omits the notice of 12,21aα // 11,1aα on Rehoboam's "coming to Jerusalem" which appears superfluous after the mention of the king's flight to the capital, 8,221 (= 12,18 // 10,18). Rather, he proceeds directly to the following account:

> Roboamos... held an assembly (ἐκκλησίαν ποιήσας)[119] of the two tribes which remained subject to him[120], and was prepared to take from their number an army of a hundred and eighty thousand[121] chosen men (ἐπιλέκτους)[122] and march out against Jeroboam and his people (λαόν)[123] in order to force (ἀναγκάσῃ) him by war to be (δουλεύειν, cf. δουλεία, 8,213)[124] his servant. (8,222)

116. Compare 3 Rgns 12,19 // 2 Par 10,19 ἠθέτησεν. Josephus employs the same verb, i.e. ἀφίστημι of Jeroboam's earlier, aborted effort to persuade the people to "turn away" (ἀφίστασθαι) from Solomon in *AJ* 8,209.

117. Elsewhere Josephus uses the pl. form of this phrase in reference to Aristobulus and Antigonus in *BJ* 1,69 // *AJ* 13,300.

118. This phrase echoes the Israelites' previous statement that they are disassociating themselves from the Davidids "from that day on" (μετ᾽ ἐκείνην... τὴν ἡμέραν), 8,219.

119. Compare 3 Rgns // 2 Par ἐξεκκλησίασεν. Josephus uses the above idiom "hold an assembly" also in *AJ* 6,86; 8,358.

120. 1 Kings 12,21 // 2 Chron 11,1 name these as Judah and Benjamin. Josephus, who has just (8,221) cited Judah and Benjamin by name as those who elected Rehoboam king, naturally avoids repeating the names here in 8,222.

121. This figure agrees with that given in 1 Kings 12,21 and 2 Chron (Par) 11,1. 3 Rgns 12,21 reads 120,000.

122. The adjective ἐπίλεκτος occurs 37 × in Josephus.

123. In the Bible the reference is to Rehoboam's intention of warring against "(the house of, so Kings) Israel".

124. Elsewhere Josephus uses the above phrase "force to serve" in *AJ* 2,345 of the Egyptians compelling the Hebrews to work for them.

In 1 Kings 12,22-24a // 2 Chron 11,2-4a there now occurs a characteristic prophetic "complex" consisting of: 1) a *Wortereignisformel*[125]; 2) a commissioning formula directing "Shemaiah" to speak to king and people; and 3) the divine word itself comprising a triple directive to the hearers together with a motivation. In accord with his practice elsewhere, Josephus compresses and reformulates this complex. Thus, his own introduction to the divine command runs simply "(Rehoboam) was prevented by God through the prophet (κωλυθεὶς δ᾽ ὑπὸ τοῦ θεοῦ διὰ τοῦ προφήτου)[126] from undertaking the campaign (ποιήσασθαι τὴν στρατείαν)[127]". Several features in this formulation should be noted. First, once again, Josephus avoids a Biblical mention of a divine "word" here, *in casu*, a *Wortereignisformel*[128]. He likewise, as consistently elsewhere, substitutes the designation "prophet" for 1 Kings 12,22 // 2 Chron 11,2's "man of God"[129]. Oddly, given his penchant

125. On this formula, see R. THEN, *"Gibt es denn keinen mehr unter den Propheten?" Zum Fortgang der alttestamentlichen Prophetie in frühjüdischer Zeit* (BEAAJ, 22), Frankfurt/Main, 1990, pp. 45-107.

126. Compare the very similar wording used by Josephus in David's statement in *AJ* 7,371 (where, as in 8,223, it substitutes for the *Wortereignisformel* of the source, i.e., 1 Chron 22,8): ὁ δὲ θεὸς ἐκώλυσέ με διὰ τοῦ προφήτου Νάθα (i.e., from building the Temple). Compare *RA* 9.55.2 (Valerius) "was prevented by the gods" (ἐκωλύθη ὑπὸ τοῦ δαιμονίου) from storming the enemy camp; 9.60.7 "heaven forbade" (τοῦ δαιμονίου κωλύοντος) the Romans from sending out an army (note the parallelism with the situation here in 8,222-223).

Josephus' other uses of the verb κωλύω with God as subject are: *BJ* 2,539; *AJ* 4,1.177; 6,303; 7,337; 8,239; 20,48.

127. ROM read στρατίαν. The construction as read above by Mar occurs also in *AJ* 8,400; 10,188; 11,335; 13,250; *Ap* 1,206.

128. Josephus eliminates the formula consistently in his rewriting of the Biblical sources throughout our segment. In 1 Kings 12-22 // 2 Chron 10-18 MT contains 12 instances of the formula (3 Rgns paraphrases three of these, i.e. 16,7; 18,31; 21,17, eliminating the reference to the "word of the Lord"). Josephus lacks a contentual parallel to three of these 12 uses (i.e. those of 1 Kings 16,7; 17,2; 18,31). In the remaining 9 cases, he invariably replaces the Biblical *Wortereignisformel* with various alternative phrases which allude to God's communicating to or through a prophet without mentioning "the word of the Lord": 8,223 (// 1 Kings 12,22 = 2 Chron 11,2; "he [Rehoboam] was prevented by God through the prophet"). 240 (// 1 Kings 13,20; "God appeared to Jadōn and said"). 256 (// 2 Chron 12,17; "the prophet Shemaiah told them [the Judeans] that God threatened to abandon them"). 299 (// 1 Kings 16,10; "[God] sent to him [Baasha] the prophet Jēūs and warned him..."). 320 (// 1 Kings 17,8; Elijah "goes at the command of God"). 328 (// 1 Kings 18,1; "Elijah goes to Ahab at the command of God"). 351 (// 1 Kings 19,9; Elijah "again hearing [a voice]").360 (1 Kings 21,17; God "sends the prophet Elijah to Ahab").362 (// 1 Kings 21,18; God "said to the prophet [Elijah]"). Also elsewhere in the Biblical portion of *AJ*, Josephus consistently substitutes alternative language for the source's *Wortereignisformel*, see 1,183a (// Gen 15,1).183b (// Gen 15,4); 6,142 (// 1 Sam 15,10); 7,92 (// 2 Sam 7,4 = 1 Chron 17,3).321 (// 2 Sam 24,11).337 (// 1 Chron 22,8); 9,208 (//Jon 1,1); 10,27 (// 2 Kings 20,4 = Isa 38,4). See further n. 215.

129. Josephus shares this tendency with TJ and TC which make the same substitution in their versions of 1 Kings 12,22 and 2 Chron 11,2, respectively. In the MT material paralleling *AJ* 8,212-420 the designation "man of God" occurs 20 ×. In none of these

for introducing proper names where the Bible lacks such, Josephus (apparently) leaves the "prophet" here without a name[130].

In next citing – here too in indirect discourse – the prophet's message (see 1 Kings 12,24a // 2 Chron 11,4a), Josephus transposes the Biblical injunction "you shall not fight against your kinsmen (LXX ἀδελφῶν)" into a statement of principle: "(the prophet said) that it was not right (οὐ... εἶναι δίκαιον)[131] to make war (πολεμεῖν)[132] on one's countrymen (ὁμοφύλους)[133]". He leaves aside the Biblical prophet's further directive "return every man to his home". Conversely, Josephus elucidates the "theological motivation" of 12,24ba // 11,4ba, "this thing is from me (the Lord)": "especially as the revolt of the multitude (τῆς τοῦ πλήθους ἀποστάσεως)[134] had taken place in accordance with the purpose of God (κατὰ τὴν τοῦ θεοῦ προαίρεσιν)[135]".

cases does Josephus reproduce the title. In 10 instances he substitutes the term "prophet": 8,223 (// 1 Kings 12,22 = 2 Chron 11,2, Shemaiah).230 (// 1 Kings 13,1, Jadōn).233 (bis // 1 Kings 13,4, Jadōn).234 (// 1 Kings 13,7, Jadōn).236 (// 1 Kings 13,11, Jadōn).238 (// 1 Kings 13,12, Jadōn).241 (// 1 Kings 13,28, Jadōn).325 (// 1 Kings 17,18, Elijah).382 (// 1 Kings 20,28, the anonymous figure who approaches Ahab). In the remaining 10 instances he either replaces "man of God" with proper names, pronouns and/or verbal expressions, or simply has no contentual parallel to the Biblical verse within which the expression stands.

Elsewhere in the Biblical portion of AJ Josephus makes the substitution of "prophet" for "man of God" a total of 12× : 6,47 (// 1 Sam 6,9, Samuel).48 (// 1 Sam 9,8, Samuel); 9,23 (// 2 Kings 1,10, Elijah).24 (// 2 Kings 1,11, Elijah).49 (// 2 Kings 3,7, Elisha).51 (// 2 Kings 6,10, Elisha).54 (// 2 Kings 6,15, Elisha).73 (// 2 Kings 7,2, Elisha).87 (// 2 Kings 8,7, Elisha).189 (// 2 Chron 25,7, anonymous figure).190 (// 2 Chron 25,9, anonymous figure); 10,67 (// 2 Kings 23,16, Jadōn).

130. The name as found in 1 Kings 12,22 // 2 Chron 11,2, i.e. "Shemaiah" is lacking in codd, although it does stand in Lat ("Samean") and Zon. According to W, Josèphe, II, p. 206, n. 3 it should be restored in the text of 8,223, whereas N, I, p. lviii denies this. N*MarNaSc likewise all omit the name in their texts/translations. For a similar case, see on 8,319.

131. Elsewhere Josephus has a character affirm that some act is not "right" also in AJ 2,127;4,233 (same phrase as above).266; 6,284;7,132.332;12,226;16,125;18,254.280.

132. Compare 3 Rgns 12,24 // 2 Par 11,4 οὐ (δὲ) πολεμήσετε.

133. Josephus uses this term c. 100 × , exclusively in reference to Jews, see RENGSTORF, Concordance, s.v. The sentiments Josephus here attributes to the ancient prophet doubtless reflect his own experiences of the horrors of civil war and cohere with formulations elsewhere in his writings, compare, e.g., his notice on the Israelites' intended attack on the people of Gibeah in AJ 5,151 "But they were restrained by the elders who urged that they ought not so hurriedly to make war on their brethren (πρὸς τοὺς ὁμοφύλους ἐκφέρειν πόλεμον)". See too BJ 4,276 where Josephus has the general Simon use the phrase "we are hurrying... to make war on our fellow-countrymen (... τὸν κατὰ τῶν ὁμοφύλων πόλεμον)"; Vita 171 (Josephus) ἀποκτεῖναι... οὐχ ὅσιον ἡγούμενος ὁμόφυλον ἄνδρα. 321 πρὸς ... τοὺς πολίτας ἐξάπτειν πόλεμον οὐκ ἐνόμιζον εὐσεβὲς εἶναι. 377 (Josephus reminds his troops who are ravaging Sepphoris) ... τοιαῦτα δρᾶν ὁμοφύλους οὐκ ἔστιν ὅσιον.

134. Cf. τὸ... ἄλλο πλῆθος... ἀποστάν, 8,221.

135. Compare 8,218 κατὰ τὴν τοῦ θεοῦ βούλησιν. The above phrase of 8,223, which speaks of an event happening according to God's "purpose", occurs also in AJ 4,24 (Aaron's obtaining the priesthood).109 (the recalcitrance of Baalam's ass; note in the same paragraph the use of the phrase "according to the will of God" of 8,218).

1 Kings 12,24bβ // 2 Chron 11,4bβ concludes the "Shemaiah episode" with the rather repetitious notice "so they hearkened to the word of the Lord and returned (3 Rgns ceased) from going according to the word of the Lord (this second reference to the 'word of the Lord' is absent in Chron)". Josephus, again avoiding reference to the divine "word", merely states "so he did not march out (οὐκέτ᾽ ἐξῆλθε)¹³⁶". To the preceding Biblical narrative he does, however, append the following transitional note: "I shall now relate, first (διηγήσομαι δὲ πρῶτον)¹³⁷ the acts of Jeroboam, the king of Israel [lit. Israelites] (ὁ τῶν Ἰσραηλιτῶν βασιλεύς)¹³⁸, and then in what follows we shall tell what happened in the reign of Roboamos, the king of the two tribes (τοῦ τῶν δύο φυλῶν βασιλέως)¹³⁹. For in this way an orderly arrangement (τὸ εὔτακτον)¹⁴⁰ can be preserved throughout the history (ἱστορίας)¹⁴¹". Such notices, whereby Josephus, e.g., rounds off one episode, prepares what follows, or resumes the thread of his narrative after a digression, are a characteristic feature of the historian's *ars narrandi*, being frequently introduced by him into his retelling of the Biblical story¹⁴².

136. So NN*Mar following the majority of codd (cf. ἐξελθεῖν, 8,222). Na conjectures οὐκ ἐπεξῆλθε, cf. M οὐ κατεξῆλθε.
In MT 1 Kings there is an apparent discrepancy between 12,21-24 (in obedience to Shemaiah Rehoboam refrains from attacking Jeroboam) and 15,6 (> 3 Rgns) which states "there was war between Rehoboam and Jeroboam all their days". Josephus, who has no equivalent to the latter verse, circumvents the difficulty.
137. With reference to Lat where the rendition of the above phrase is preceded by the words "diviso siquidem regno", N, II, p. 225 affirms that there is a lacuna in the Greek text at the opening of 8,224.
138. This is Josephus' standard designation for the Northern kings, in contrast to the Bible's "king of Israel" (see, e.g., 1 Kings 15,9). He uses the designation in reference to Northern rulers 24× in *AJ* 8-9, cf. the verbal equivalent in 9,17. Compare the alternative title "king of the ten tribes" in 8,287 and its related verbal formulation in 8,264.393.
139. Josephus uses this designation for Biblical "king of Judah" (see, e.g., 1 Kings 15,28) also in 8,246.298.314 (+ "of Jerusalem").398; 10,1, cf. 8,274;9,142.216. Elsewhere, he speaks of "the king of Jerusalem": 8,314 (+ "and of the two tribes").393.411.412; 9,17.95; 10,229, cf. 9,42 and "king of the Jerusalemites": 9,31.112.117.130.161.177. 246.278.
140. Elsewhere *BJ* 1,348; 6,141; *AJ* 17,314.
141. Josephus employs ἱστορία 81×.
142. On the feature, see VILLALBA I VARNEDA, *Method*, p. 159. Within *AJ* 8,212-420 one may note the following major examples: 8,229 ("but of these things [the eventual overthrow of the Northern kingdom] we shall write in the proper place"). 245 ("So much concerning Jeroboam it may suffice us, for the present, to have written"). 262 ("but concerning these matters [Herodotus' historical inaccuracies] everyone may speak as he sees fit"). 265 ("This then was the end of Roboamos' history. But now in what follows we have to relate the events of Jeroboam's reign and how he ended his life"). 274 ("But Jeroboam took no thought of these things [the death of his son in accordance with Ahijah's prophecy]"). 282 ("such was the speech which Abias made to the people"). 287 ("Such then is the account we have received concerning Abias..."). 289 ("Thus did the house of Jeroboam suffer fitting punishment for his impiety and lawlessness"). 298 ("Such was the state of affairs under Asanos... I shall now return to the people of Israel and their

Summary. Josephus' version of the breakup of the united monarchy already illustrates the difficulty of determining which of the two parallel Biblical sources (Kings and Chronicles) he was using as well as which text-form(s) of those sources he had before him. The question arises particularly in view of the fact that 1 Kings and 3 Rgns 12,1-24 evidence a variety of differences. In the case of such differences, Josephus' presentation agrees sometimes with the former, sometimes with the latter. With 1 Kings (as also 2 Chron [Par]) he has Jeroboam summoned prior to the Shechem parley (see 12,3aα), and cites him by name in recounting the Israelites' first approach to Rehoboam (see 12,3aβ). He likewise reads 1 Kings 12,21 (= 2 Chron/Par 11,1)'s figure for the size of Rehoboam's army against the smaller number cited in 3 Rgns. Noteworthy too is the lack of any Josephan parallel to the long plus of 3 Rgns following 12,24 (12,24a-z)[143]. In all these cases it does, however, need to be kept in mind that 1 Kings corresponds for its distinctive readings with 2 Chron/ Par. Accordingly, the above items do not constitute incontrovertible evidence for Josephus' use of "MT" 1 Kings in this episode; he might just as well have been working from a text of Chronicles, whether "MT" or LXX.

Conversely, the historian's account does align itself with 3 Rgns 12 for several particulars: non-mention of Jeroboam at the Israelites' return to Rehoboam (compare 1 Kings 12,12= 2 Chron (Par) 10,12), lack of parallel (so B 3 Rgns) to 1 Kings 12,17 (= 2 Chron (Par) 10,17), reference to Benjamin as well as Judah recognizing Rehoboam as king (compare 1 Kings 12,20). As was noted above, however, all these items are ones which Josephus on his own might well have eliminated from (or added to) a source text having (or lacking) them. Thus, clear-cut indications of Josephus' utilization of a text *à la* 3 Rgns 12 likewise seem to be lacking in 8,212-224. On the other hand, it is clear that he used (whether in Hebrew or Greek form) the more

king Basanēs"). 315 ("But there is no great necessity to speak of this king [Jehoshaphat] just now"). 324 ("This, then, is what Menander wrote..."). 325 ("Now the woman of whom we spoke above, who gave food to the prophet..."). 354 ("Such, then, is the history of this prophet [Elijah]"). 363 ("at the same time as this state of affairs [his confrontation with Elijah concerning the murder of Naboth] existed for Achab..."). 388 ("So ended the expedition of Abados..."). 393 ("Such was the condition of Achab. But I shall now return to Josaphat..."). As will be noted, these notices all serve, in their varying ways, to more closely tie together the parts of Josephus' presentation in contrast to the disjointedness which often characterizes the Biblical account.

143. On this conglomeration of notices paralleling portions of 1 Kings 11-12;14 but with many peculiar features, see: Z. TALSHIR, *The Duplicate Story of the Division of the Kingdom (LXX 3 Kings XII 24 a-z)* (Jerusalem Bible Studies), Jerusalem, 1989 (Hebrew); idem, *Is the Alternate Tradition of the Division of the Kingdom (3 Kgdms 12,24a-z) Non-Deuteronomistic?*, in G.F. BROOKE and B. LINDARS (eds.), *Septuagint, Scrolls and Cognate Writings* (Symposium Papers, Manchester, 1990; SBL SCS, 33), Atlanta, 1992, 598-621 and S.L. MCKENZIE, *The Trouble with Kings. The Composition of the Book of Kings in the Deuteronomistic History* (VTSup, 42), Leiden, 1991, pp. 21-40.

expansive text of 1 Kings 12,19-20 with its reference to the installation of both Jeroboam and Rehoboam as kings rather than the shorter version of 2 Chron (Par) with lacks a parallel to 12,20, see above.

As to Josephus' rewriting techniques in our episode, the following summary remarks are in order. Among "re-arrangements", his reproduction of the sequence 1 Kings 12,1-3aα // 2 Chron 10,1-3aα in the order 3aα, 2bβ, 1 is the most notable (see also his reversal of 1 Kings 12,20b and 19-20a). In the category of "omissions" (i.e. of items common to both MT and LXX Kings and Chronicles), Josephus, we have seen, avoids the sources' frequent repetitions of wording and content, see, e.g., 1 Kings 12,4 and 9-10, 5 and 12, 10 and 14, 18b and 21aα. He likewise (so B 3 Rgns) leaves aside 12,17 // 10,17 with its problematic relationship to 12,2bβ-3aα.20b. Especially noteworthy, however, are Josephus' recurring amplifications of the Biblical account. Several of these additions serve to underscore the divine involvement in the outcome of the Shechem parley (God is responsible both for Rehoboam's failure to heed the elders [8,216] and for the ill-conceived advice of the young men [8,217]). This feature is of particular interest in view of L.H. Feldman's observation that, in many contexts, AJ evidences a certain "detheologizing" tendency vis-à-vis the Bible[144]. The bulk of Josephus' amplifications are, however, rather what might be called "politico-psychological" in character. They seek, in other words, to elucidate the internal factors operative in the interplay between Rehoboam, the Israelites and the royal advisers at a moment of critical national decision. Josephus' stress on this dimension- which, as noted, is virtually absent in the Bible's "exteriorized" account- is an instance of what Feldman designates as the historian's "catering to the political interests" of his Hellenistically-schooled readers[145]. In particular, Josephus' attention to the psychology at work in the above "triangle" has points of contact with the vast body of Greco-Latin material, both literary and inscriptional, concerning the qualities of the good/popular ruler and their converse[146]. That Josephus was indeed acquainted with this material is shown by his extended paraphrase (AJ 12,11-118) of LA which in its "banquet scene" (§§ 187-292) contains a series of questions and answers revolving precisely around the problem of the ideal king[147]. Given then Josephus' utilization of LA elsewhere in AJ, it is of interest to note the various terminological affinities between the

144. FELDMAN, Mikra, pp. 504-506.

145. See ibid., pp. 496-498.

146. On this material, see: E.R. GOODENOUGH, The Political Theology of Hellenistic Kingship, in YCS 1 (1928) 55-102; SCHUBERT, Ideal; idem, Gesetz; L. DELATTE, Les traités de la royauté d'Ecphante, Diotogène et Sthénidas, Paris, 1942.

147. On this sequence, see O. MURRAY, Aristeas and Ptolemaic Kingship, in JTS 68 (1967) 337-371, esp. pp. 355-361.

former's treatment of kingship and the "politico-psychological" matter introduced by him in his version of the "Shechem episode". Thus with the ἐπιείκεια and τὸ φιλάνθρωπον which the Israelites hope to be shown by Rehoboam (8,213-214), compare *LA* § 290 where king Ptolemy is praised as preeminent in ἐπιεικείᾳ καὶ φιλανθρωπίᾳ (see also §§ 188.218)[148]. In 8,215 Rehoboam's older advisers remind him that subjects like to be treated on terms of virtual "equality" (ἰσότι-μον). In *LA* (see §§ 191.257.263.282) the effective king is repeatedly depicted as one who continues to regard himself as "equal" (ἴσος) to all. Josephus likewise has Rehoboam being promised that his acceding to the crowd's wishes will secure their "goodwill" (εὔνοια), 8,215. Similarly, in *LA* (§ 215) Ptolemy hears that a king's benignity attracts the "goodwill" (εὔνοιαν) of his subjects, see also § 265 which speaks of the "indissoluble bond of goodwill" that should link king and people[149]. Likewise the people's affirmation (8,213) that they would "love" (ἀγαπήσειν) their servitude if treated kindly by Rehoboam has its pendant in *LA* (§ 265) where the speaker avers that what a king most needs to acquire is the "love" (ἀγάπησις) of those he rules[150]. *LA* and Josephus' "Shechem episode" also evidence terminological links in their allusions to the "bad" ruler. *AJ* 8,217, e.g., uses the term σκληρός ("harsh") in reference to Solomon; *LA* (§ 289) employs the same word of tyrannical monarchs. Via such a use of the terminology of Hellenistic kingship literature, then, Josephus accentuates the episode's interest for his educated Gentile audience.

148. See too the reflection which Philo places on the lips of his wise ruler in *De specialibus legibus* 4.165-166: Tullius is enjoined to "win the affections of the people by kindly affability" (ὁμιλίαις τε φιλανθρώπιας).

149. Compare also the "Treatise on Kinship" of Ecphantes, 276, 11-13 (DELATTE, *Traités*, p. 50): "Il faut qu'une bienveillance (εὔνοιαν) complète soit établie d'abord par le roi envers ses sujets et, en second lieu, par ceux-ci envers le roi...".

150. With the wording of 8,213 where the people ask Rehoboam to be more "lenient" (χρηστότερον) than Solomon so they, in turn, will "love" their service of him, compare Diotogenes' "Treatise on Kingship", 267, 6-7 (DELATTE, *Traités*, p. 42) who speaks of the king's "benignity" (χρηστότας) evoking his people's "love" (ἀγαπαζόμενον).

II

JEROBOAM'S INITIATIVES
(8,225-229)

1 Kings 12,25-31 relates a series of measures undertaken by Jeroboam at the start of his reign[151]. Jeroboam's first such initiative according to 12,25 was his "building" Shechem (his residence) and Penuel. Josephus too records this double construction, omitting, however, both the Biblical localization of Shechem ("in the hill country of Ephraim") and the (obvious) statement "he went from there"[152] that comes between mention of Jeroboam's dwelling in Shechem and his building Penuel in 12,25. He likewise introduces the specification that Jeroboam built "a palace" in Shechem (Σικίμη)[153] and "Phanūēl" (Φανουήλ, so 3 Rgns) in order to obviate, as W[154] and Mar[155] point out, the difficulty that the Bible seems to speak of the king's "building" already existing cities.

1 Kings 12,26-31 next focusses on Jeroboam's reprobate cultic innovations. 12,26a introduces the king's self-reflections in rather abrupt fashion. Josephus takes care to adduce an occasion prompting the royal musings: "not long after (μετ᾽ οὐ πολὺ)[156], when the festival of Tabernacles was about to take place (τῆς σκηνοπηγίας ἑορτῆς ἐντίστασθαι μελλούσης)[157]...". In 1 Kings 12,26b-27 the sequence of Jero-

---

151. 1 Kings 12,32-33 continues this enumeration while also making the transition to the following scene; Josephus' version associates the content of these two verses still more closely with the subsequent narrative as its introduction. Accordingly, I will treat them in the context of my next section.

152. On the import of this phrase, see the conjectures of N. ALLEN, *Jeroboam and Shechem*, in *VT* 24 (1974) 353-357.

153. N (but not N*) conjectures Σικίμων (Σικήμων) here with reference to Lat "Sicimorum".

154. *Josèphe*, II, p. 207, n. 2.

155. *Josephus*, V, pp. 692-693, n. c.

156. This chronological indication occurs 28 × in Josephus, see the listing in VILLALBA I VARNEDA, *Method*, p. 111, n. 271.

157. Josephus uses some variant of the above expression "the festival of Tabernacles taking place" also in *AJ* 4,209; 13,46.241; 15,50. With this indication Josephus anticipates (his version of) the notice of 1 Kings 12,32 in 8,230 according to which Jeroboam instituted his feast at Bethel "in the seventh month", i.e. the date of Tabernacles according to Lev 23,33; Num 29,12 (as well as *AJ* 8,100; 11,154). Josephus' specification of "Tabernacles" here as the moment at which Jeroboam institutes his rival cult likewise serves to introduce the parallelism, which Josephus will work out *in extenso*, between Jeroboam's words inaugurating his cult (see below) and those of Solomon on the dedication of the Temple in that, following 1 Kings 8,2 // 2 Chron 5,3, he has the latter event take place precisely at Tabernacles, see *AJ* 8,100.

boam's actual reflection runs as follows: "Now the kingdom will turn back (3 Rgns ἐπιστρέψει) to the house of David. If this people go up to offer sacrifices in the house of the Lord at Jerusalem, then the heart of this people will turn again (3 Rgns ἐπιστραφήσεται) to their lord(s) [B 3 Rgns + 'to the Lord and'], to Rehoboam, king of Judah, and they will kill me [> L*] and return to Rehoboam king of Judah [> 3 Rgns]". In these one-and-a-half verses Jeroboam speaks (so MT) no less than three times of the possibility of the Israelites' "returning" to the Davidids. Moreover, his initial reference to this eventuality (v. 26b) stands, unmotivated, prior to the condition on which it depends in v. 27aα. How then does Josephus deal with the repetitious and somewhat "illogical" sequence of his source? Leaving aside v.26b, he has Jeroboam immediately formulate his parallel to the conditional clause of v. 27aα: "(he reflected [λογισάμενος][158] that) if he permitted the people (ἐπιτρέψῃ τῷ πλήθει) to go to Jerusalem to worship God (προσκυνῆσαι τὸν θεὸν)[159] and to celebrate the festival (τὴν ἑορτὴν διαγαγεῖν)[160] there...". With this formulation Josephus underscores the royal authority (the people will go to Jerusalem (only) if Jeroboam "permits" them to do so)[161], just as he specifies that they would be going there to "celebrate *the* feast", i.e. the just-mentioned Tabernacles. In next articulating the anticipated outcome of the people's pilgrimage, Josephus has Jeroboam allude, not only to the political, but also, and in first place, to the religious affects this would have on them, i.e. "they might perhaps repent (μετανοῆσαν)[162] and be captivated (δελεασ-

158. In 1 Kings 12,26a Jeroboam "says in his heart", the typical OT idiom meaning "think".

159. This accusatival construction with "(the) God" as object occurs also in *AJ* 6,2 (object: Dagon).154; 8,228; 9,269; 10,211(263); 11,333; 20,164. A. SCHLATTER, *Der Evangelist Matthäus*, Stuttgart, 1929, p. 31 points out that Josephus, in contrast to LXX and NT, favors the accusative rather than the dative with προσκυνέω (note the juxtaposition of both constructions in *AJ* 6,154). On Josephus' varied uses of προσκυνέω (i.e., for both legitimate and illegitimate "worship" as well as for profane "homage"), in relation to other terms of the *Wortfeld*, see: J. HORST, *Proskynein. Zur Anbetung im Urchristentum nach ihrer religionsgeschichtlichen Eigenart* (Neutestamentliche Forschungen, 2), Gütersloh, 1932, esp. pp. 92-93, 112-116, 126-127.

Finally, with the whole above formulation "... (Jeroboam) permitted the people... to worship God...", compare *AJ* 9,139 "(Jehu) permitted (ἐπέτρεψε) the Israelites to bow down before (προσκυνεῖν) the golden heifers".

160. The above construction "celebrate the festival" occurs only here in 8,225 in Josephus.

161. Josephus shows a similar concern with "royal prerogatives" at many other points in his reworking of the Biblical account. Additional examples will be cited at subsequent points in this study.

162. Note the irony of this reference to an Israelite "repentance" with its implication that Israel's current status as a breakaway nation is a sinful one- a curious admission on the part of the ringleader of the split. Josephus' use of the term "repent" here likely reflects the repeated use of "return terminology" in 12,26-27, see above. On Josephus' terms for "repent(ance)", see: SCHLATTER, *Theologie*, p. 147; E.K. DIETRICH, *Die Umkehr*

θὲν)¹⁶³ by the temple (τοῦ ναοῦ) and the ceremonies performed in it (τῆς θρησκείας τῆς ἐν αὐτῷ τοῦ θεοῦ)¹⁶⁴". Only in second place does Josephus' Jeroboam then articulate the "political" implications of his allowing access to Jerusalem: this would lead, negatively, to the Israelites' "deserting" (καταλείψει)¹⁶⁵ him, and positively, to their "going over to their former (πρώτῳ)¹⁶⁶ king" (cf. 12,27aβ, bβ). Should this happen, Jeroboam reasons, he himself "would be in danger of losing his life" (τὴν ψυχὴν ἀποβαλεῖν)¹⁶⁷, see MT B 12,27ba. On this note of urgency for Jeroboam Josephus terminates the royal reflection, i.e. like 3 Rgns he has no equivalent to MT's (redundant) additional reference to an Israelite "return" to Rehoboam, 12,27bβ.

1 Kings 12,28 begins the description of the measures undertaken by Jeroboam in response to the threat he perceives to be facing him. The description opens by noting that Jeroboam "took counsel" (3 Rgns ἐβουλεύσατο + "and he went")–with whom is not said. Josephus reformulates with the transitional phrase "he (Jeroboam) devised the following plan" (ἐπιτεχνᾶται)¹⁶⁸. In parallel to 12,28aβ he next speaks of Jeroboam's "making two golden heifers" (δύο ποιήσας δαμάλεις χρυσᾶς)¹⁶⁹. According to the Biblical sequence, Jeroboam, immediately after making the calves, briefly addresses the Israelites concerning them (v. 28b); only thereafter (v. 29) is mention made of his placing these objects in Bethel and Dan, respectively. Josephus reverses this sequence, thereby eliminating the "interruption" in the Biblical enumeration of Jeroboam's measures with the calves. Specifically, he begins

---

(Bekehrung und Busse) im Alten Testament und im Judentum, Stuttgart, 1936, pp. 306-313; and J. BEHM and E. WÜRTHWEIN, μετανοέω, μετάνοια, in TWNT 4 (1942) 972-1004, esp. pp. 990-991.

163. The only other occurrence of the verb δελεαζέω in AJ is 13, 220 (Tryphon "leads on" the multitude). In BJ it occurs 5 × : 1,519; 2,468; 3,22.100; 5,120.

164. Compare the translation of W, ad loc.: "le culte qu'y recevait Dieu". The above term θρησκεία (= "cult", etc.) is frequent in Josephus (+ 90 ×). On it see SPICQ, Lexicographie, I, pp. 379-382.

165. There is–again–a certain irony to Josephus' use of this term here in that just previously (8,220) he employs the same word when noting that the Israelites "threatened to desert (καταλείπειν)" Jeroboam's rival Rehoboam. Having "deserted" Rehoboam for himself, the Israelites are now ready, in Jeroboam's mind, to reverse the process by "deserting" him for Rehoboam.

166. P lacks the term. Na conjectures ἑτέρῳ.

167. The above construction "lose one's life" occurs only here in Josephus.

168. The above verb ἐπιτεχνάομαι is hapax in Josephus.

169. Cf. 3 Rgns 12,28 ἐποίησε(ν) δύο δαμάλ(ε)ις χρυσᾶς. Mar, Josephus, V, p. 693, n. f points out that Josephus, like 3 Rgns, refers to Jeroboam's "heifers", whereas MT talks of "male calves" (זהב עגלי). Subsequently, Josephus will use the above designation consistently when referring to Jeroboam's creations, see 8,228.230 (// 1 Kings 12,32). 248 (// 2 Chron 11,5; 2 Par reads μόσχοις). 279 (// 2 Chron 13,8; 2 Par μόσχοι). 317; 9,137 (// 2 Kings 10,29). On Josephus' version of our episode, see further E. DANIELIUS, The Sins of Jeroboam Ben-Nabat, in JQR 58 (1967-68) 95-114, 204-223, esp. pp. 99-100, 104-109.

by noting that Jeroboam "built shrines (ναΐσκους)[170] for both (calves)". The Bible does not explicitly mention such an initiative by Josephus; possibly, however, Josephus found inspiration for the notice at a later point in the source story, i.e. 1 Kings 12,31a "(Jeroboam) also made *houses* (3 Rgns οΐκους) on the high places". In any event, Josephus next mentions the sites of Jeroboam's two shrines, i.e. Bethel[171], and Dan, localizing the latter "near the sources of the Little Jordan"[172]. He draws these two place names from 1 Kings 12,29. From that same verse he derives his further notice that Jeroboam "placed the heifers in either of the shrines in the cities mentioned". Thus Josephus, in contrast to Kings, has Jeroboam first ensure that his heifers are "in place" before addressing the people concerning them.

Passing now to the royal speech itself, Josephus begins by noting that Jeroboam "having called together (συγκαλέσας) the ten tribes... harangued (ἐδημηγόρησε)[173] them in the following words (ποιησάμενος τοὺς λόγους)[174]". In 1 Kings 12,28b Jeroboam's "speech" comprises a mere half-verse: "you have gone up to Jerusalem long enough. Behold your god(s), O Israel, who brought you up out of the land of Egypt". Josephus, on the other hand, devotes two full paragraphs (8,227-228) to the royal address[175]. In the historian's version Jeroboam's word is not,

170. The double use of this term in 8,226 is its only occurrence in Josephus.

171. Lat reads Bethlehem!

172. Josephus provides a similar localization of Dan in *AJ* 5,178. Cf. also *BJ* 4,3 where he refers to "Daphne [near Dan, see THACKERAY, *Josephus*, III, p. 4, n.a], a delightful spot with springs which feed the so-called Little Jordan, beneath the temple of the golden cow (τῆς χρυσῆς βοός)...". On Josephus' various references to the sanctuary at (or near) Dan, see O. MICHEL, O. BAUERNFEIND, O. BETZ, *Der Tempel der goldenen Kuh (Bemerkungen zur Polemik im Spätjüdentum)*, in *Gott und die Götter*. FS E. Fascher, Berlin, 1958, 56-67, esp. pp. 60-61 (on *AJ* 8,225-229).

173. The verb δημηγορέω occurs 5× elsewhere in Josephus: *BJ* 2,619 (speaker: Josephus); *AJ* 9,260 (Hezekiah, here in conjunction with the participle συγκαλέσας as in 8,226); 13,406 (the Pharisees); 19,333 (Simon); *Vita* 92 (Josephus).

174. Josephus uses some variation of the above formula in introducing a "quotation" also in *AJ* 1,279.298; 2,267.310; 4,24; 5,76; 6,174; 7,26.88 (375); 8,107.231; 9,110; 10,138; 11,82.86.152.168.262.301; 12,19.44.92; 13,75.78 (*bis*).201; 14,6.12.141.143.211.221.236.249. 252; 15,126.166; 16,49; *Ap* 2,145.

175. Josephus presents the entirety of Jeroboam's speech in direct discourse. This is the first of only 10 such usages within *AJ* 8,212-420, as compared with c. 115 cases of indirect discourse, see n. 38 (in the editions of NN*Mar direct discourse is indicated by the use of quotation marks at the start and end of the material in question). The remaining 9 instances where Josephus "quotes" a character wholly in direct discourse in our segment are: 8,232 ("Jadōn" to the altar/people, // 1 Kings 13,2-3). 239b (the Bethel prophet to Jadōn, // 1 Kings 13,18).243a (the Bethel prophet to Jeroboam, no Biblical parallel). 269-272 (Ahijah to the wife of Jeroboam, // 1 Kings 14,6b-16, MT). 276-281 (Abijah to the Israelites, // 2 Chron 13,4b-12). 322b (Elijah to the Phoenician woman, // 1 Kings 17,13-14). 374b ("a certain prophet" to Ahab, // 1 Kings 20,14). 405b (Ahab to Jehoshaphat, // 1 Kings 22,18 = 2 Chron 18,17).

Several remarks are in order regarding the above list. In four instances (8,227-228.232.269-272.276-281) Josephus employs direct discourse for longer set speeches

however, simply longer; it also takes on the character of an adroit excercise in persuasive speech. This last feature is evident already in the opening words Josephus ascribes to the king. Jeroboam begins by appealing to the hearers'[176] "knowing" the truth "that every place has God (πᾶς τόπος ἔχει τὸν θεὸν)[177] in it and that there is no one spot set

(monologues), while the remaining six involve briefer words in the context of a dialogue. Josephus allots direct discourse to both his "good" (Jadōn, Elijah, Ahab's counterpart) and "bad" (Jeroboam, Bethel prophet, Ahab) characters. All but one of the 10 instances (8,243a) have a Biblical source- itself invariably in direct discourse.

Also of interest is a consideration of the above uses in light of the observations of THÉROND, *Discours*, pp. 146-151 and VILLALBA I VARNEDA, *Method*, pp. 92-111 (see his list of *AJ*'s "main quotes in direct speech", p. 110) regarding *oratio recta* in *BJ* and *AJ* overall. Such a consideration leads to the following results: Thérond (p. 146) begins his discussion by noting that in *BJ* direct discourse "c'est de loin le mode d'expression préféré de Josèphe, beaucoup plus employé que les deux autres procédés [i.e. indirect discourse, mixture of indirect and direct disourse]...". Thérond further notes (ibid.) that in *BJ* the majority of the pivotal "grands discours" are formulated throughout in direct discourse. This holds true, to some degree, also in *AJ* 8,212-420 where the segment's longest speeches are, in fact, given completely in direct discourse, see 8,227-228 (Jeroboam). 269-272 (Ahijah). 276-281 (Abijah). On the other hand, however, the equally extended speech of "Jehu" to Baasha in 8,299-300 utilizes indirect discourse *in toto*. Finally, Thérond (ibid., pp. 148-151) identifies two rather different functions for direct discourse in *BJ*: occasionally, Josephus employs this mode of reported discourse at a moment when a given character exhibits his/her peculiar psychology, whereas, more often, direct discourse is alloted, in "de-individualizing" fashion, to those personages who function as mouthpieces for Josephus' own views on the course of the action. In the direct discourse speeches of *AJ* 8,212-420 the latter of these functions is certainly less to the fore given the fact that in all but one of these instances (8,243a) Josephus is reproducing, with greater or lesser exactitude, sentiments he found ascribed, already in the Bible itself, to a given figure. In addition, while in 8,227-228 Josephus develops a (direct discourse) speech for Jeroboam on the basis of 1 Kings 12,28b's brief royal word, the former composition hardly articulates the historian's own views on the religious questions at issue. On the other hand, on occasion, Josephus' recourse to direct discourse within 8,212-420 does seem, as in *BJ*, associated with a moment of psychological disclosure. Specifically, the direct discourse words he attributes (with minimal or non-existent Biblical basis) to Jeroboam in 8,227-228 and the Bethel prophet in 8,243a, respectively, do seem to reflect the deceitful but convincing mode of operation characteristic of these two figures in his presentation. For the rest Josephus' (rare) use of direct discourse in 8,212-420 appears influenced by the urge to interject an occasional note of vividness into his account and, particularly in the three great speeches of 8,227-228.269-272.276-281, to further highlight the speakers' words. On the shift from indirect to direct discourse in 8,212-420, see n. 38.

176. In 8,227 Jeroboam addresses the assembled tribes as "fellow countrymen" (ἄνδρες ὁμόφυλοι). Josephus attributes the same form of address to Saul when speaking to the Benjaminites about David (see *AJ* 6,251, cf. 1 Sam 22,7) and to Herod when announcing his plan to rebuild the Temple (15,382 – note the similarity with the situation here in 8,227).

177. Compare *AJ* 10,250: Daniel was "believed to have the divine (spirit) (ἔχων τὸ θεῖον) in him". On the notion of "having God", see H. HANSE, ἔχω κτλ, in *TWNT* 2 (1935) 816-832, esp. pp. 822-823; idem, *"Gott Haben" in der Antike und im frühen Christentum. Eine religions- und begriffsgeschichtliche Untersuchung* (Religionsgeschichtliche Versuçhe und Vorarbeiten, 27), Berlin, 1939, pp. 89-91, 98 who cites parallel formulations in Epictetus, *Dissertationes* 1.9.7;2.8.17;4.1.145 and the quotation of Herophilus by Origen, *In Psalmos* XI.352.

apart (ἐν ἀποδεδειγμένον χωρίον)[178] for His presence (ἐν ᾧ πάρεστιν), but everywhere He hears (ἀκούει) and watches over (ἐφορᾷ) His worshippers (θρησκεύοντας)[179]". Remarkably, however, the theological principle here invoked by Jeroboam is one previously enunciated by none other than Solomon, and that precisely on the occasion of the dedication of the Temple in Jerusalem, see 8,108 "(we are persuaded) that Thou (God) art present (πάρει) and not far removed. For, as Thou seest all things (ἐφορᾶν) and hearest (ἀκούειν) all things, ... Thou art present (συμπάρει) with everyone who asks for guidance..."[180].

By thus recalling to his audience the "teaching" of Solomon, the Josephan Jeroboam, with unmistakable irony, procures for his subsequent anti-Jerusalem Temple remarks a point of departure from the most unlikely-but for that very reason- most credible of sources, the builder of the Jerusalem Temple himself. Having thus posited the theological principle of the Temple's dispensability, Jeroboam goes on to draw the appropriate "practical" conclusion: "therefore I do not think I should now urge (ἐπείγειν) you to go (πορευθέντας) so long a journey to Jerusalem (εἰς Ἱεροσόλυμα), the city of our enemies, in order to worship (προσκυνεῖν)[181]". With this formulation Jeroboam continues to evidence his persuasive capabilities. Over against the peremptory "you have gone up to Jerusalem long enough" of his Biblical counterpart (1 Kings 12,28bα), the king expresses himself with winning diffidence: rather than "forbidding", he "does not urge" his subjects. In the above characterization of Jerusalem Jeroboam likewise

178. The above expression occurs only here in Josephus. ROM Lat read ἐναποδεδειγμένον.

179. See θρησκείας, 8,225 and cf. n. 164.

180. With Josephus' affirmation of God's ubiquity in 8,227 and 8,108 above, compare the words he attributes to Antipater in *BJ* 1,630 "... From the Judge in heaven, who sees all (ἐφορᾷ πάντα), who is present everywhere (πανταχοῦ πάρεστιν)...". See further *AJ* 2,24 where Rubel refers to God's providence "present in every place" (πανταχοῦ παροῦσαν) and Josephus' comment in 6,263 on Saul's slaughter of the priests of Nob: (those of humble station prior to their elevation) "are persuaded that He (God) is present (πάρεστι) in all that happens in life and that He not only sees (ὁρᾷ) the acts that are done, but clearly knows even the thoughts whence those acts are to come".

Just as Josephus makes Jeroboam echo the word of Solomon (see above), so the latter himself in the address Josephus attributes to him in 8,108 appears to be mouthing an Homeric reminiscence, i.e. of *Iliad* 3,277 (Agamemnon's prayer to Zeus): "(thou sun) ὅς πάντ' ἐφορᾷς καὶ πάντ' ἐπακούεις". E. NORDEN, *Agnostos Theos*, Leipzig-Berlin, 1923[2], p. 19, n. 2 and following him L.H. FELDMAN, *Josephus as a Biblical Interpreter: The 'AQEDAH*, in *JQR* 75 (1985) 212-252, p. 223, n. 36 see Josephus' utilization of the Homeric verse in 8,108 as an instance of Stoic influence upon him in that the same verse is cited by the first century A.D. Stoic Heraclitus in his *Quaestiones Homericae* 23. It should, however, be noted that Heraclitus' own "Stoicism" has been called into question, see F. BUFFIÈRE, *Héraclite, Allégories d'Homère*, Paris, 1962, pp. XXXVII-XXXIX. Note too that while Heraclitus does cite the Homeric verse in question, his comments are concerned, not with the verse as such, but rather with its context.

181. Compare προσκυνῆσαι... εἰς Ἱεροσόλυμα πορευθέντι, 8,225.

contrives to insinuate additional, non-religious motives why the Israel-'
ites should cease repairing there, i.e. the long journey involved as well
as Jerusalem's status as "the city of our enemies"[182].

Having thus discounted the claims of the Jerusalem Temple, Jeroboam now (8,228) offers a rationale for his own alternative cultic
arrangements. Once again, he takes, ironically, as his starting point the
words of Solomon himself who, at the dedication of the Temple
addresses God with the words "I have built this Temple to Thy name
(κατεσκεύακα τὸν ναὸν ἐπώνυμον)...", 8,108. Jeroboam, at this juncture in his discourse, recalls these words of Solomon, in order, however,
to assert that the Temple's construction was, after all, simply a human
initiative: "for it was a man that built that temple (κατεσκεύακε[183] τὸν
ναὸν)". But if so, then with equal right another man/king- in casu
Jeroboam himself- might act to provide for the religious requirements
of his people. And, in fact, that is just what Jeroboam now claims to
have done: "I too have made two golden heifers [see 8,226] bearing the
name of God (ἐπωνύμους τῷ θεῷ)[184] and I have consecrated
(καθιέρωσα)[185] them, one in the city of Bethel and the other in Dan, in
order that those of you who live nearest either of these cities may go to
them and worship God (προσκυνῶσιν[186] τὸν θεόν, see 8,225)". In this
formulation Jeroboam's crassly idolatrous designation of the calves as
"god(s)" in 1 Kings 12,28b gets drastically reworked in the interests of
the king's monotheistic plausibility. The calves themselves are not
"gods"; rather, just like Solomon's Temple, they "bear the name of
(the one true) God" who is the one to be "worshipped" in Bethel and
Dan. Nor does Jeroboam fail, here too, to invoke more practical
considerations in support of his innovations: Jerusalem is a long way
off, whereas all his subjects are "near" to one or other of the new
shrine-cities.

In concluding Jeroboam's speech, Josephus draws on the notice of 1
Kings 12,31b (and 13,33) about the king's "making" non-Levitical
priests for the "high places". Josephus transposes this Biblical statement of what the king did into an announcement by Jeroboam of his
intentions: "I shall appoint for you priests and Levites[187] from your

182. With this designation of the Southern capital, compare the prophet (Shemaiah)'s
reference to the Israelites as "countrymen" in his address to Rehoboam and his people in
8,223.

183. Thus the reading adopted by NN*NaMar. PE read κατεσκεύασε.

184. Compare Solomon's above-cited reference to the Temple in his prayer of 8,108
σοι [sc. τῷ θεῷ]... τὸν ναὸν ἐπώνυμον. For the phrase "bearing the name of God", see
also 16,45.

185. Note Josephus' use of the participle καθιερωμένον in reference to Solomon's
Temple in 8,102.

186. So NN*Mar. MSP, followed by Na, read προσκυνήσωσιν; E has προσκυνῆτε.

187. The above collocation "priests and Levites" occurs elsewhere in Josephus in AJ
4,205.222.305 (reverse order); 9,4.12.144.147.148.155.161 (reverse order).260.262 (269).

own number (ἐξ ὑμῶν αὐτῶν)[188], in order that you may have no need of the tribe of Levi (Ληουίτιδος φυλῆς)[189] and the sons of Aaron[190], but let him among you who wishes (βουλόμενος)[191] to be a priest offer up (προσενεγκάτω)[192] to God a calf and a ram (μόσχον... καὶ κριόν)[193], as Aaron, the first priest, is said to have done".

What underlines Jeroboam's above words, I suggest, is an implicit paralleling of the questions of place of worship and ministers of that worship. Jeroboam has previously argued that Jerusalem as the sole Temple site is not a religious necessity and that he, imitating Solomon's initiative, has provided the Israelites with a legitimate and fully-equivalent substitute for it. He now states his intention of giving his people the same two categories of cultic ministers – priests and Levites[194] – that functioned at Jerusalem.

273.274 (bis); 10,62.71; 11,8 (reverse order)(62).71 (reverse order).74.81.107.108.128. 134.140 (reverse order).146.151.181.182; 13,33 (reverse order).73.

188. So NN*Mar. Na adopts the reading of M which lacks αὐτῶν.

189. The above phrase "the tribe of Levi" occurs also in AJ 3,287 (4,67.214; 7,56.320).367 (bis) (376).378 (20,126). Note the peculiar conception in which Jeroboam involves himself here, i.e. that of a "non-Levitical Levite".

190. The phrase "sons of Aaron" occurs elsewhere in AJ 5,361, cf. 4,18 "Aaron and his sons".

191. Josephus seems to have adopted this participial form from 3 Rgns 13,33 "any one who would (ὁ βουλόμενος), he (Jeroboam) filled his hand and he became a priest for the high places".

192. Josephus uses προσφέρω of a cultic "bringing" (of sacrifice) also in (BJ 2,145; 3,353); AJ 1,184; 3,231.251; 6,148; 8,91.118; 11,17.107.326; 12,251.316; 13,168; 20,49.

193. As Mar, Josephus, V, p. 695, n. d points out, the prescription Josephus attributes to Jeroboam concerning the "induction offerings" for his priests-to-be here is reminiscent of LXX Lev 16,3 which enjoins that Aaron is to sacrifice the same two animals, i.e. a μόσχον and a κριόν, on the occasion of his entry into the inner sanctuary on Yom Kippur. Possibly, Josephus understood that entry as constituting the moment of Aaron's assuming his priestly prerogatives, and so assigned the same two victims for the installation sacrifice of Jeroboam's priests. As W, Josèphe, II, p. 207, n. 6 intimates, Josephus may also have had in view here 2 Par 13,9b where Abijah of Judah levels the following charge against Jeroboam and his people: "whoever comes to consecrate himself with a young bull (2 Par μόσχον) or seven rams (2 Par κριοῖς) becomes a priest of what are no gods". (In this connection note too that Jeroboam's preceding reference in 8,228 to "priests and Levites... the sons of Aaron" echoes Abijah's word in 2 Chron 13,9a "have you (the Israelites) not driven out the priests of the Lord, the sons of Aaron, and the Levites...?"). Finally, in the account of the Aaronides' actual ordination in Leviticus 8 (see Exodus 29), there is mention of the sacrifice of a bull (LXX μόσχον) and of (two) ram(s) (LXX κρίον, vv. 18,22). Thus Josephus had a variety of Biblical inspirations for the sacrifices which he has Jeroboam prescribe for his would-be priests.

194. Josephus' distinction between (Aaronide) priests and Levites here presumes, of course, P's gradations within the Israelite clergy. 1 Kings 12,31, on the other hand, presupposes Deuteronomy's conception that all Levites are (potentially) priests, see Deut 18,1. Also elsewhere Josephus explicitly adopts P's notion that the only legitimate "priests" are descendants of Aaron, see AJ 9,65 where to 2 Kings 23,5's reference to Josiah's elimination of the "idolatrous priests" he adds the specification that these "were not of the family of Aaron".

Having thus reported Jeroboam's (speciously) plausible discourse at length, Josephus closes the section by noting its effects: "by these (words) he misled the people (ἐξηπάτησε τὸν λαὸν)[195] and caused them to abandon the worship of their fathers (τῆς πατρίου θρησκείας ἀποστάντας)[196] and transgress the laws (παραβῆναι τοὺς νόμους)[197]". This notice represents the historian's expanded parallel to 1 Kings 12,30 "and this thing (3 Rgns λόγος) became a sin". That verse is likewise the only item from the complex of notices (12,29-31) following Jeroboam's word to the people (12,28b) which Josephus utilizes at this juncture in his presentation. Of the notices in question, Josephus has already "anticipated" those concerning Jeroboam's installation of the calves at Bethel and Dan (12,29) and his institution of a new clergy (12,31b), as also perhaps 12,31a's "he also made houses on the high places" (see above). As to the remaining elements in 12,29-31, the (apparent) reference to a procession involving a calf (the calves) in 12,30b ("the people before the one calf as far as Dan [+ and before the other to Bethel, so L 3 Rgns]") could seem discordant with Josephus' earlier reference to Jeroboam's having "set" the calves in their respective locales, and so is omitted by him. In place then of the various items that precede and follow 12,30a in 12,29-31, Josephus appends the following indication, foreshadowing much later developments, to his version of the former verse: "This was the beginning of the Hebrews' misfortunes (ἀρχὴ κακῶν... τοῖς Ἑβραίοις[198]) and led to their being

In here distinguishing, as 1 Kings 12,25-31 does not, the "(non-Levitical) Levites" as a separate class of clergy appointed by Jeroboam, Josephus likely has in view 2 Chron 13,13-14 (see his version of 2 Chronicles 13 in 8,274-286 below) which speaks of Jeroboam's dispossessing also the Levites. Similarly, his reference to the "priests" as "sons of Aaron" here could reflect the double use of that qualification in reference to the priests in 2 Chron 13,9-10, see n. 193.

195. Compare BJ 4,228 (the Zealots write to the Idumeans charging that Ananus) "had imposed on the people" (ἐξαπατήσας τὸν δῆμον).

196. With the above formulation "misled the people and caused them to abandon the worship of their fathers", compare Jehu's reference (AJ 9,133) to "those who had seduced the people (ἐξαπατήσαντας τὸ πλῆθος) into abandoning (ἐγκαταλιπεῖν) the worship (θρησκείαν) of the Most High God...". Variants of the phrase "abandon the ancestral worship" occur also in AJ 12,269.364.384; 19,283.284 (the edict of Claudius). On Josephus' key word (c. 250×) πάτριος, see SCHLATTER, Gott, p. 67; idem, Theologie, p. 51. Dionysius too lays great stress on adherence to "ancestral" traditions, see his statement, RA 2.23.5 "I have greatly admired these men (the Romans) for adhering to the customs of their ancestors (πατρίοις ἔθεσιν)...", cf. 4,40.1, 41.2, 78.1, 80.2.

197. Josephus uses the above expression "transgress law(s)" elsewhere in BJ 2,174 (sg.).195 (sg.).393 (sg.); AJ (3,223); 4,309; 7,168.338; 8,191; 9,153.243.281; 10,59.60.214; 11,130 (sg.).230; 12,385; 14,167; (18,59.266).271; 20,218; Ap 1,190; 2,176 (sg.). 178.204.214.276. On the term νόμος in Josephus, see H. KLEINKNECHT and W. GUTBROD, νόμος κτλ, in TWNT 4 (1942) 1016-1084, esp. pp. 1043-1044.

198. In AJ Josephus uses the above term "Hebrews" to designate the chosen people as a whole from the split under Rehoboam down to the return when he shifts to calling them "the Jews" (see 11,173), cf. 1,146 where he states that "the Jews were originally called

defeated in war (πολέμῳ κρατηθέντας)[199] by other races (ἀλλο-φύλων)[200] and to their falling captive (αἰχμαλωσίᾳ περιπεσεῖν)[201]. But of these things we shall write in the proper place (ἀλλὰ ταῦτα μὲν κατὰ χώραν δηλώσομεν)[202]".

Summary. 1 Kings and 3 Rgns do not diverge markedly as far as content goes in 12,25-31. Josephus aligns himself (negatively) with the latter in having no parallel to MT's 12,27bβ.

The above account exemplifies various of Josephus' rewriting techniques. In his parallel to 1 Kings 12,25 he introduces a clarification designed to preclude the misunderstanding that Jeroboam built Shechem and Phanūēl "from scratch". He rearranges the components of the king's reflection (see 12,26b-27), and likewise shifts the position of

Hebrews". For the "pre-split" period he also employs the designation "Israelites" as a virtual synonymn for "Hebrews" (see 2,201-202 where both terms are used for the people under Egyptian domination). In 8,212-420 the designation "Hebrews" occurs 2 × : 8,229 (= Northerners).335 ("the people of the Hebrews" = Northerners). On Josephus' various designations for the chosen people, see W. GUTBROD, Ἰσραήλ κτλ, in *TWNT* 3 (1938) 356-394, esp. pp. 372-373, 375 and ARAZY, *Appellations* (see n. 34).

The term "Hebrews" used in the above formulation of 8,229 certainly does have the Northerners ("Israelites") in view. Perhaps, however, here, as also occasionally elsewhere in Josephus's account of the divided monarchy, the term is intended at the same time to encompass the entire chosen people, abstracting from its *de facto* divisions, for whom Jeroboam's defection was the "beginning" of the process that culminated in the catastrophe of 587. In any case, note the parallelism between Josephus' formulation in 8,229 and his earlier statement in 8,211: "Concerning these acts (i.e. Solomon's apostasy) and the misfortunes (κακῶν) which befell the *Hebrews* [i.e. the chosen people as a whole] on their account, we shall find a more convenient occasion to write fully". (Mar, *Josephus*, V, p. 685, n. f avers that the reference in 8,211 is "apparently" to "Shishak's invasion of Palestine", i.e. the territory of the southern kingdom under Rehoboam as described in 8,253ff. Note, however, that Josephus motivates that invasion as retribution for the sins, not of Solomon, but of Rehoboam himself and his people (see 8,251-254). Accordingly, I would see Josephus' announcement in 8,211 as more comprehensive in scope, anticipating the whole series of disasters that overtook both divisions of the "Hebrews" from the split down to the destruction of Jerusalem).

Elsewhere, Josephus employs the above phrase "beginning of misfortune(s)" in *BJ* 7,371; *AJ* 5,306 (sg.); 15,281; 17,60.

199. With this passive construction, compare the active form "conquer in battle" in *AJ* 1,186 (6,132); 18,261; *Ap* 1,277.

200. This term occurs 67 × in Josephus.

201. This is the only occurrence of the above phrase "fall captive" in Josephus. On the verb περιπίπτω, see SPICQ, *Lexicographie*, II, 684-686.

202. Josephus does this in 9,277-282 (// 2 Kings 17) where he relates the Assyrian annihilation of Israel. In the latter passage note especially Josephus' reflective comments in 9,281-282 which contain several verbal echoes of 8,229, i.e. παραβάντας τοὺς νόμους, κακῶν.

With the above "foreshadowing formula", compare esp. *AJ* 7,89 καὶ περὶ μὲν τούτων [i.e. Michal's children] κατὰ χώραν δηλώσομεν. For a listing of similar formulae in Josephus' works, see H. DRÜNER, *Untersuchungen über Josephus*, Marburg, 1896, pp. 85-89. Dionysius also makes use of such formulae, see, e.g., *RA* 1.56.5; 2.26.6; 7.65.1.

the Biblical references to the installation of the calves (12,29) and the institution of Jeroboam's priesthood (12,31b). He eliminates the repetitions within Jeroboam's musings in 12,26b-27 as well as the mention of the people's "procession" (12,30b) which does not seem to fully accord with what precedes (see above). He expatiates on 12,30a's summary evaluation of Jeroboam's initiatives, both in terms of the nature of the offense and its eventual consequences, preparing with his reference to the latter matters to be related at a much later point. Most notable, however, is Josephus' expansion of the king's brief word in 12,28b into a model of persuasive rhetoric that makes, e.g., ironic use of the words/doctrines of the very man, Solomon, whose creation Jeroboam is trying to undermine[203].

203. At the same time, Jeroboam's speech in Josephus' version also seems to anticipate (see nn. 193, 194) elements of Abijah's battlefield address to Jeroboam and his people, 8,276-281.

III

BETHEL CONFRONTATION
(8,230-245)

1 Kings 13,1-32 relates the experiences which befall a Judean "man of God" at Bethel. This narrative comprises two distinct sections, recounting, respectively, the man's interaction with king Jeroboam (13,1-10) and with a Bethel "prophet" (13,11-32). The narrative is "framed", in turn, by a transitional introduction (12,[32]33) and a conclusion (13,33-34). In what follows I distinguish the same four components within the Josephan version.

1. *Introduction* (8,230). The opening Biblical framework verses (12,32-33) evidence repetitions (double reference to the festival instituted by Jeroboam, vv. 32aβ, 33aβ; triple mention of the king's "ascending" the altar, vv. 32bα, 33aαβ) as well as other problematic features, see below. How then does Josephus deal with such a source text? In line with 12,32 (see 12,33a), he begins with a chronological indication associating what follows with a festival inaugurated by Jeroboam as a substitute for a Judean feast – not named as such in Scripture – but naturally to be identified with Tabernacles, an identification already previously made by Josephus, see 8,225. Oddly, however, 1 Kings 12,32a (cf. 12,33a) makes Jeroboam institute his feast on the fifthteenth day of the *eighth* month notwithstanding the fact that elsewhere in the Bible (see Lev 23,33; Nu 29,12), Tabernacles is dated to the fifthteenth of the *seventh* month. Josephus, doubtless conscious of the discrepancy, formulates his dating notice thus: "when the festival (i.e. Tabernacles, see 8,225) came round (ἐνστάσης... τῆς ἑορτῆς)[204] in the *seventh* month, Jeroboam, wishing to observe it himself in Bethel, just as the two tribes were celebrating it in Jerusalem...". The historian next enumerates a series of three preparatory measures undertaken by Jeroboam on this occasion. First, he "built (οἰκοδομεῖ)[205] an altar (θυσιαστήριον)[206] before the heifer[207]". With this notice Josephus transposes into narra-

---

204. Compare 8,225 τῆς σκηνοπηγίας ἑορτῆς ἐνίστασθαι μελλούσης.

205. Josephus' other uses of the h.p. of οἰκοδομέω are *AJ* 4,172; 18,36 (middle).

206. Josephus, following 3 Rgns, employs this term 7× in our pericope (8,230. 231.232.233.242.243.244) to designate Jeroboam's reprobate "altar". In his other 17 uses of the word, by contrast, it invariably designates a legitimate Israelite altar.

207. Josephus' specification "an altar before the heifer (sg.)" here can be seen as an implicit correction of 12,32's pl. reference to the (male) "calves" (so MT, 3 Rgns,

tive 12,33a's allusion to "the altar which he (Jeroboam) made in
Bethel" (cf. 12,32aβ "he offered sacrifices upon the altar... to the
calves") which presupposes such an initiative by Jeroboam (see too 2
Kings 23,15 "the altar in Bethel... which Jeroboam made..."). Jeroboam's next move, according to Josephus, was to "make himself high
priest (ἀρχιερεύς)". This item has, as such, no basis in the Bible. One
may, however, readily discern the reasoning behind Josephus' introduction of it here: Jeroboam must be a priest if he is to have any pretense
of legitimacy when offering the sacrifice the Bible ascribes to him, while
as king he would naturally assign himself a rank corresponding to that
of the "high priest" of the existing Jerusalem cult[208]. Thereby too,
Jeroboam furthers his goal of supplying Israel with a worship system in
every respect equivalent to the Southern one, with not only "priests and
Levites", but also a "high priest".

Josephus concludes his enumeration of Jeroboam's measures at the
Bethel festival with the statement "he went up to the altar (ἐπὶ τὸν
βωμὸν ἀναβαίνει)[209] with his own priests (ἱερεῦσι)". Both components
of this last phrase have a basis in 12,32-33. There, as mentioned,
Jeroboam's "ascent" of the altar is cited three times. Similarly, 12,32bβ
states that Jeroboam "placed in Bethel the priests (B 3 Rgns ἱερεῖς) of
the high places he had made". Josephus, who passes over (or reapplies,
see above) 12,31a's reference to Jeroboam's making "houses on the
high places", likewise avoids the designation "priests of the high
places" of 12,32, calling these figures rather "his (Jeroboam's) own
priests" (cf. the king's announcement that he intends to create a
priesthood in 8,228). To these priests Josephus also gives a more
definite function in the Bethel festival: they accompany the king onto
the altar.

2. *"Prophet" vs. King* (8,231-235). The story proper of the Bethel
episode begins in 1 Kings 13,1 with the abrupt appearance of Jero-

"heifers") based on the consideration that the Bethel-shrine housed only one of the two
images confected by Jeroboam, see 1 Kings 12,29a.

208. Throughout his presentation Josephus presupposes the (Priestly/Chronistic)
conception of an uninterrupted series of "high priests" from the time of Aaron on.
Accordingly, he introduces the term where his Biblical sources speak only of "the
priest(s)", see, e.g., 5,345 (// 1 Sam 1,9, Eli); 7,222 (// 2 Sam 17,15, Zadok and
Abiathar).346 (// 1 Kings 1,7-8, Zadok and Abiathar).

209. Compare 3 Rgns 12,32aβ, 33bβ ἀνέβη ἐπὶ τὸ θυσιαστήριον. Josephus thus uses
both terms, θυσιαστήριον and βωμός, to designate Jeroboam's illegitimate altar. Conversely, he also employs both designations for legitimate Israelite altars, the former 24× in
that connection, the latter 118×. In this his usage diverges both from, e.g., LXX
Pentateuch, 1 Maccabees and NT where θυσιαστήριον (an apparent LXX neologism)
denotes legitimate altars, βωμός (the standard word for "altar" in extra-Biblical Greek)
rather illegitimate ones. Josephus' "altar language" likewise diverges from, e.g., LXX
Kings which utilizes θυσιαστήριον exclusively and for both types of altars. On the whole
subject, see S. DANIEL, *Recherches sur le vocabulaire du culte dans la Septante* (Études et
Commentaires, 61), Paris, 1966, pp. 15-32.

boam's antagonist (v. 1a). Juxtaposed to this as a seeming afterthought is (v. 1b) the notice- repetitious of the analogous references in 12,32-33- "and Jeroboam was standing by the altar to burn incense" (so RSV, MT להקטיר, 3 Rgns ἐπιθῦσαι). Josephus, making here his first and only reference to Jeroboam's "sacrificing", reverses the order of the source verse, opening his version with the temporal clause "but as he (Jeroboam) was about to offer (ἐπιφέρειν)²¹⁰ the sacrifices and the whole burnt offerings (τὰς θυσίας καὶ τὰς ὁλοκαυτώσεις)²¹¹ in the sight of all the people (ἐν ὄψει τοῦ λαοῦ παντὸς)²¹², there came...".

Having specified the moment for his protagonist's approach, Josephus now proceeds to introduce him. His source (13,1a) reads as follows: "and behold a man of God came (3 Rgns παρεγένετο) out of Judah by the word of the Lord to Bethel". In Josephus the introduction runs rather: "there came (παραγίνεται, see 8,212) to him (Jeroboam) from Jerusalem a prophet named Jadōn ('Ιάδων) whom God had sent". The following differences between the two formulations may be noted: 1) Josephus' figure comes, not generally "from Judah", but specifically "from Jerusalem". This divergence coheres with Josephus' earlier (8,230) substitution of "the festival... the two tribes were celebrating *in Jerusalem*" for 12,32's "the feast that was in Judah". Jeroboam's measures, in Josephus, are directed against Jerusalem in particular; it is thus appropriate that the challenge to those measures should emanate precisely from the Southern capital. 2) The figure is designated, not by the title given him consistently (16 ×) throughout 1 Kings 13, i.e., "man

210. Compare the synonymn προσφέρω in 8,228. Elsewhere, Josephus uses ἐπιφέρω in a cultic sense (= "offer") also in *AJ* 1,54.228; 2,308; 3,207.228.231.233.243.250.257; 4,70.75.241.308; 8,244; 9,155.257.263; 10,53; 11,110.152.297; 14,73.

211. With the above phrase "offer sacrifices and whole burnt offerings", compare Josephus' notice on Josiah, Jeroboam's antithesis, in 10,53 τὰς... ἐπέφερε θυσίας... καὶ τὰς ὁλακαυτώσεις, see also 11,110 τὰς ὁλοκαυτώσεις ἐπιφέροντες... καὶ χαριστηρίους θυσίας ἱερουργοῦντες, cf. *AJ* 4,308 where verbal forms of the above two nouns are used in conjunction.

On Josephus' introduction of a reference to Jeroboam's offering "burnt offerings" in 8,231, see the remarks of Mar, *Josephus*, V, p. 697, n. c: "Apparently, Josephus takes Heb. *ya'al* [in 12,32-33] as a *hiph'il*... form meaning 'offered the burnt offering (*'ōlāh*),' while LXX, taking it as a *qal*... form meaning 'went up,' has ἀνέβη [note, however, that Josephus does have a reference to Jeroboam's "going up", using the LXX verb, in 8,230]. Or possibly the 'whole burnt-offerings' in Josephus' text may be an interpretation of Heb. *haqṭir* [12,33]... which implies the offering of various kinds of sacrifice including the burnt offering".

Alternatively, I would suggest that Josephus' mention of Jeroboam's double offering here is due to his combining the twofold reference to the king's sacrificing as found in 12,32bα (3 Rgns τοῦ θύειν, MT לזבח) and 33bβ (3 Rgns τοῦ ἐπιθῦσαι, MT להקטיר).

212. Compare *AJ* 17,163 ἐν ὄψει τῆς πληθύος. Josephus perhaps introduces this specification with an eye to 13,4 where the presence of a "congregation" is implied by Jeroboam's order that the Judean be "seized".

of God", but rather as "prophet" (προφήτης)[213]. 3) Josephus gives the anonymous figure of 1 Kings 13,1 a name, i.e. "Jadōn", corresponding to that cited in Rabbinic tradition, i.e. "Iddo"[214]. 4) Josephus likewise avoids, as he will throughout the episode, the *Leitwort* of 1 Kings 13, used a total of 7×, i.e. "by the word of the Lord"[215]. In place thereof, he indicates the divine origin of Jadōn's intervention with the equivalent phrase "whom God had sent" (τοῦ θεοῦ πέμψαντος)[216]. Finally, Josephus specifies that in delivering his message Jadōn "was standing in the midst of the multitude" (ἐν μέσῳ τῷ πλήθει)[217]. With this addition, he makes clear that, whereas Jadōn's subsequent word is, as such, directed to the "altar" (see 13,2), it will, as the continuation of the Biblical story itself presupposes (see 13,4.11), be audible to both king and people.

1 Kings 13,2 records the man of God's direct address to the Bethel altar with its prediction of the measures "Josiah" will one day take against it. Josephus reproduces the substance of this verse, including its use of address to the inanimate altar, while modifying the wording in several respects. Thus, he drops the indication of v. 2α that the Judean addressed the altar "by the word of the Lord" just as he substitutes an

213. Josephus makes this substitution 6 further times in his version of 1 Kings 13. Similarly, TJ substitutes "prophet of the Lord" in all 16 instances where MT has "man of God" in the chapter. Perhaps both Josephus and TJ found the Biblical designation too indeterminate, see further n. 129.

Josephus uses the term "prophet" some 290×, in all but two instances (i.e., *BJ* 6,286; *AJ* 1,240) in reference to figures of the "Biblical" period. On prophets and prophecy in Josephus, see: J. BLENKINSOPP, *Prophecy and Priesthood in Josephus*, in *JJS* 25 (1974) 239-263; D.E. AUNE, *The Use of ΠΡΟΦΗΤΗΣ in Josephus*, in *JBL* 101 (1982) 419-421; C.T. BEGG, *The "Classical Prophets" in Josephus' Antiquities*, in *LS* 13 (1988) 341-357; and L.H. FELDMAN, *Prophets and Prophecy in Josephus*, in *JTS* 41 (1990) 386-422.

214. See *Sanh.* 89; *t. Sanh.* 14,10. In giving this particular name to the "man of God" of 1 Kings 13, Josephus and Rabbinic tradition are likely both inspired by the reference in 2 Chron 9,29 to "the visions of Iddo (so MT, 2 Par Ἰωήλ) the seer *against Jeroboam*". Compare, however, DRÜNER, *Untersuchungen*, p. 44 who suggests that Josephus himself devised the name Ἰάδων in 8,231 on the basis of the reading (ἐξ)Ἰούδα in 3 Rgns 13,1. Having thus transposed the source's phrase into the proper name "Jadōn", Josephus would then, according to Drüner, have gone on to provide the prophet with a new place of origin, i.e. "from Jerusalem". Somewhat similarly, THACKERAY, *Josephus the Man*, p. 92, n. 2 asks whether the name could have arisen out of the expression καὶ ἰδοὺ ἄνθρωπος τοῦ θεοῦ of 3 Rgns 13,1.

On the post-Biblical practice of supplying names for anonymous Scriptural figures, see in general: B. HELLER, *Die Scheu vor Unbekannten in Agada und Apokryphen*, in *MGWJ* 83 (1939) 170-193.

215. On Josephus' characteristic avoidance of Biblical references to the divine "word", see nn. 90.

216. Elsewhere Josephus uses πέμπω with God as subject and persons as objects in: *AJ* 6,89 (object: Moses and Aaron).131 (Samuel); 7,321 (Gad).329 (Gad); 8,197 ("a prophet").239 (the Bethel [false] prophet).299 ("Jehu" the prophet).360 (Elijah); 9,167 ("the prophets"); 10,27 (Isaiah).39 ("prophets").

217. Compare ἐν ὄψει τοῦ λαοῦ, 8,231a.

equivalent for that phrase on its first occurrence in v. 1, see above. He has Jadōn begin his actual address, not "thus says the Lord" (so v. 2aβ), but rather "God has foretold (προλέγει)²¹⁸ that...". He qualifies those whom "Josias" (Ἰωσίαν)²¹⁹ will "sacrifice" (θύσει = 3 Rgns) on the altar as "false priests" (ψευδιερεῖς)²²⁰ (compare 13,2 "priests of the high places²²¹ who burn incense upon you [the altar]"). The "false priests" in question, Josephus further specifies, will be those "living in his [Josiah's] time", i.e. rather than the priest contemporaries of Jeroboam as the Biblical formulation might seem to suggest. More worthy of note, however, is Josephus' reference to those whose bones are to be burnt. 1 Kings 13,2 speaks, in nondescript fashion, of "the bones of men". Josephus, who has already introduced "falsehood language" with his designation "false priests", substitutes a more descriptive designation: "he will burn (καύσει = B 3 Rgns)²²² upon you [the altar]

218. Just as he does with the *Wortereignisformel* (see n. 128), Josephus consistently avoids, as here, the related prophetic *Botenformel*, replacing this with some other expression indicative of the divine origin of a given communication.
Elsewhere Josephus employs the verb προλέγω with God as subject also in *AJ* 7,72; 8,406; 9,189.195; 10,33.178; 11,96. Terms for "foretelling" permeate Josephus' version of 1 Kings 13: προλέγει (8,232), προερῶ (8,232), προεῖπεν (8,233), προειρημένων (8,235), προειρηκότος (8,244).
Another difference between 13,2aβ and 8,232 is also worthy of note. In the former the Judean refers to what *the Lord* (3 Rgns ὁ κύριος) is saying against the altar, whereas in the latter Jadōn cites what *God* (ὁ θεὸς) has foretold. Josephus' substitution of "God" for "the Lord" here is in line with his overall tendency to avoid the term κύριος as a designation for the Deity (in fact, he uses the term in this sense a total of only three times in his entire corpus, i.e. *AJ* 13,68 [a quotation of LXX Isa 19,19] and 20,19 [*bis*, in the prayer of Izates]). Throughout our segment then, as throughout the "Biblical portion" of *AJ* in general, Josephus routinely substitutes "God" (or "the Deity") where his Scriptural sources refer to "the Lord", see, e.g., 8,234 (Jadōn "entreated *God*" on the king's behalf) as compared with 1 Kings 13,6b "the man of God entreated *the Lord*" for Jeroboam.
On this feature of Josephus' Biblical rewriting and the grounds for it (e.g., the non-use of κύριος as a designation for "God" in profane Greek), see: SCHLATTER, *Gott*, pp. 9-10; idem, *Theologie*, pp. 25-26; W.W. Graf BAUDISSIN, *Kyrios als Gottesname im Judentum und seine Stelle in der Religionsgeschichte*, II (ed. O. EISSFELDT), Giessen, 1929, p. 158; G. QUELL - W. FOERSTER, κύριος κτλ, in *TWNT* 3 (1938) 1038-1097, esp. p. 1083 and n. 219.
219. Josephus further qualifies "Josias" here as "of the line of David" (ἐκ τοῦ Δαυίδου γένους, cf. 3 Rgns 13,2 τῷ οἴκῳ Δαυ(ε)ιδ. The phrase "line of David" occurs also in *AJ* 8,113 ("his [David's] line").270; 9,145.166; 10,67.147.
220. Josephus' only other use of the above term "false priest(s)" is *AJ* 9,133 where it denotes the Baal clergy exterminated by Jehu. It is not found in the LXX. Note that terms signifying "truth" and "falsity" – often with an ironic twist – run throughout our pericope: ψευδιερεῖς (8,232), ἀληθῆ (8,234.242), ψευδοπροφήτας (8,236.241.242[pl.]), ψευσαμένῳ (8,240), ψεύδει (8,241), ἀληθῶς (8,243), ἀλήθειαν (8,243).
221. Recall Josephus' substitution of "his own (i.e., Jeroboam's) priests" for this same Biblical designation in his rewriting of 12,32 in 8,230.
222. Compare MT's impersonal ישרפו. L 3 Rgns reads κατακαύσει.

the bones of these²²³ misleaders of the people (λαοπλάνων)²²⁴, these imposters (ἀπατεώνων)²²⁵ and unbelievers (ἀσεβῶν)²²⁶".

In 1 Kings 13,3 the Judean announces a "sign" involving the (immediate) collapse of the altar and the spilling of what was upon it. Seemingly unmindful of the discrepancy between this notice and the announcement of 13,2 which presupposes the survival of the same altar until Josiah's day, Josephus reproduces the former's "sign announcement" with various modifications: "... that these (people) may believe (πιστεύσωσιν) that so it will be²²⁷, I shall foretell (προερῶ)²²⁸ to them a sign (σημεῖον)²²⁹ that will be given (γενησόμενον)²³⁰. The altar shall be broken (ῥαγήσεται τὸ θυσιαστήριον)²³¹ in an instant (παρα-χρῆμα) and all the fat (πιμελὴ)²³² of the victims on it (ἱερείων) shall be spilled (χυθήσεται) upon the ground²³³".

1 Kings 13,4 recounts Jeroboam's abortive attempt to have the Judean arrested and the resultant paralysis of the king's outstretched hand. Josephus, once again, amplifies with reference to the king's emotional state as well as to the immediacy and severity of the affliction that befalls him: "*Roused to fury* (παροξυνθεὶς)²³⁴ by these words of

223. Presumably, the referent of "these" here is Jeroboam himself (note the mention of his "misleading the people" in 8,229) as well as of "his own (false) priests", see 8,230.
224. Hapax in Josephus.
225. 6 × elsewhere in Josephus: *BJ* 2,259;6,288; *AJ* 20,167; *Ap* 2,145.161.216.
226. Or rather "impious ones", see W, *ad loc.*, "impies". The adjective ἀσεβής occurs 60 × in Josephus.
227. TJ has a comparable plus in its version of 13,3 "this is the sign that you (pl.) will know that the Lord sent me".
228. Compare προλέγει (subject God), 8,232a.
229. Elsewhere, Josephus uses the above expression "foretell sign(s)" in *AJ* 8,244 (see there). He explicitly associates "signs" with "belief" as here also in *AJ* 2,274.283.
230. Compare 3 Rgns 13,3 "he (who?) will give (δώσει) in that day a sign (τέρας)". On Josephus' (synonymous) use of the terms σημεῖον and τέρας, see: SCHLATTER, *Gott*, p. 52; idem, *Theologie*, p. 69; K.H. RENGSTORF, σημεῖον, in *TWNT* 7 (1964) 199-261, esp. pp. 221-223; idem, τέρας, in *TWNT* 8 (1969) 113-117, esp. pp. 122-123; H. REMUS, *Does Terminology Distinguish Early Christian from Pagan Miracles?*, in *JBL* 101 (1982) 531-551, esp. pp. 543-544.
231. 3 Rgns 13,3ba ἰδοὺ τὸ θυσιαστήριον ῥήγνυται.
232. The above term "fat" occurs also in *AJ* 3,231.243.
233. 3 Rgns 13,3bβ καὶ ἐκχυθήσεται ἡ πιότης ἡ (+ οὖσα L) ἐπ᾽ αὐτῷ.
234. Josephus frequently uses the above participial form to designate the "exaspera-tion" which prompts characters to act as they do: *BJ* 2,305.406; *AJ* 1,55; 4,156; 5,133.295; 9,24.277; 11,192; 12,204.313; 13,91.123; 14,329.437; 16,289; 17,64; 20,72; *Vita* 45.298.383.
In several of the above instances, just as he does in 8,233 // 1 Kings 13,4, Josephus introduces mention of a personage's being "enraged" where the Biblical parallel text lacks this: *AJ* 1,56 (// Gen 4,9; "enraged" at God's questioning of him, Cain asks if he is his brother's keeper); 5,295 (cf. Judg 14,20-15,3; Samson, "enraged" at being deprived of his Philistine wife, resolves on revenge); 8,392 (// 1 Kings 20,43; "enraged" at Micaiah's words, Ahab orders his imprisonment); 9,24 (// 2 Kings 1,9; "enraged" at Elijah's

the prophet, Jeroboam stretched out his hand (ἐξέτεινε τὴν χεῖρα = 3 Rgns)²³⁵ to order his arrest (κελεύων συλλαβεῖν αὐτόν)²³⁶. *But no sooner* (εὐθέως) *was his hand stretched out than* it was paralysed (παρείθη, 3 Rgns ἐξηράνθη) and he no longer had the power to draw it back to himself (καὶ οὐκέτ᾽ ἴσχυε ταύτην²³⁷ πρὸς αὐτὸν ἀναγαγεῖν)²³⁸ *but found it hanging numb* (νεναρκηκυῖαν)²³⁹ *and lifeless*"²⁴⁰.

Following the "interlude" of 13,4, 13,5 narrates the realization of the "sign" announced in 13,3. Josephus, continuing to adhere quite closely to the content and sequence of his source, has the equivalent statement "And the altar was broken (ἐρράγη δὲ καὶ τὸ θυσιαστήριον)²⁴¹ and everything on (ἀπ᾽)²⁴² it was swept to the ground (κατηνέχθη)²⁴³, as the prophet had foretold (προεῖπεν)²⁴⁴".

1 Kings 13,6-7 relates how, at Jeroboam's request, the man of God prays – efficaciously – for the restoration of the king's hand, whereupon Jeroboam issues him an invitation. Josephus embellishes, particularly with regard to the king's inner state:

> *Then, having learned that the man* (ἄνθρωπον)²⁴⁵ *was telling the truth* (ἀληθῆ) *and possessed divine foreknowledge* (θείαν ἔχοντα πρόγνωσιν)²⁴⁶, he begged him to pray that God (παρεκάλεσεν αὐτὸν δεηθῆναι τοῦ θεοῦ²⁴⁷)²⁴⁸ to bring back life (ἀναζωπυρῆσαι)²⁴⁹ to his *right* hand (τὴν

resistance, Ahaziah sends another officer against him).277 (// 2 Kings 17,3 "enraged" at Hoshea's infidelity, Shalmaneser marches against Samaria), cf. 4,156.

235. In 13,4 one encounters an instance of a very frequent Hebrew construction, i.e. *wyhy* + *waw*-consecutive (וישלח ... ויהי, 3 Rgns καὶ ἐγένετο... καὶ ἐξέτεινε). Josephus, as here, consistently avoids this construction, substituting the participial construction "having been provoked, Jeroboam stretched out his hand...". More generally, Josephus replaces the prevailing parataxis of his Biblical sources (in both their Hebrew and Greek forms) with a hypotaxis more in conformity with secular Greek style.

236. 3 Rgns 13,4 λέγων συλλάβετε αὐτόν.

237. Thus NN*Mar. Na reads (ἴσχυεν) αὐτὴν with M; SP have ἴσχυσεν αὐτὴν.

238. B 3 Rgns 13,4 καὶ οὐκ ἐδυνήθη ἐπιστρέψαι αὐτὴν πρὸς αὐτόν (L ἑαυτόν).

239. Josephus' other uses of ναρκάω are BJ 6,395; AJ 8,244 (an allusion to 8,233).

240. In the above (and what follows), I indicate Josephan additions to the source's content by means of italics.

241. 3 Rgns 13,5aα καὶ τὸ θυσιαστήριον ἐρράγη.

242. Thus the codd followed by NN*Mar. Na conjectures ἐπ᾽.

243. 3 Rgns 13,5aβ ἐξεχύθη.

244. See προερῶ, 8,232. Compare 13,5b "according to the sign (3 Rgns τέρας) which the man of God gave by the word (3 Rgns λόγῳ) of the Lord".

245. Josephus' use of the term "man" in reference to "Jadōn" here likely stands under the influence of the recurring phrase "man (3 Rgns ἄνθρωπος) of God" of 1 Kings 13 for which, otherwise, he regularly substitutes the term "prophet", see n. 213.

246. Josephus employs a similar phrase in reference to the Essene Manaemus in AJ 15,373: πρόγνωσιν ἐκ θεοῦ... ἔχων. The term πρόγνωσις occurs further in AJ 8,418; 13,300; 17,43; 18,201; Ap 1,232. On it, see SCHLATTER, Theologie, p. 234.

247. The above genitival construction "pray (the) God" occurs also in AJ 5,201; 6,49; 9,67.214; 10,12.41.176 (here with παρακαλέω as in 8,234).198.217; 11,165.

248. Compare 3 Rgns 13,6 δεήθητι (+ δὴ τοῦ προσώπου κυρίου, L) τοῦ θεοῦ σου. In MT Jeroboam makes the following double appeal: חל־נא את פני יהוה אלהיך והתפלל בעדי.

δεξιàν)²⁵⁰. So the prophet entreated God (ἱκέτευσε τὸν θεὸν)²⁵¹ to grant (παρασχεῖν)²⁵² him this (prayer), and Jeroboam, *overjoyed when* (χαίρων ἐπ')²⁵³ his hand regained its natural use (τὸ κατὰ φύσιν ἀπολαβούσης)²⁵⁴, asked (παρεκάλει, see παρεκάλεσεν 234a) the prophet to dine with him (δειπνῆσαι παρ' αὐτῷ)²⁵⁵.   (8,234b)

In 1 Kings 13,8-9 the man of God declines Jeroboam's invitation in a circumstantial reply that, e.g., twice states that he cannot "eat or drink" in Bethel. Josephus compresses, leaving out Jadōn's opening words in v. 8 "if you give me half your house" – Jeroboam has made no such offer – as well as his second reference to the eating and drinking prohibition (see v. 9b). His version of the protagonist's words thus runs:

A. CATASTINI, *1 Re 13:1-10 e la Redazione delle Tradizioni su Geroboamo I*, in *Egitto e Vicino Oriente* 10 (1987) 109-121, p. 115 calls attention to the divergence between MT's longer and 3 Rgns' shorter formulation of Jeroboam's word in 13,6 and affirms that Josephus "non conosce la tarde lezione והתפלל בעדי" of the former. Given, however, Josephus' tendency to eliminate "duplications" in his source, Catastini's claim appears open to question.

249. Elsewhere Josephus uses the above verb ἀναζωπυρέω also in *BJ* 1,44; *AJ* 2,184; 9,183; 11,240 (never with "hand" as object as here in 8,234).

250. B 3 Rgns 13,6aβ καὶ ἐπιστρέψατο ἡ χείρ μου πρὸς μέ. With Josephus' specification that it was Jeroboam's "right" hand that needs healing here, compare Lk 22,50; Jn 18,11 vis-à-vis Mk 14,47; Mt 26,51. The former passages specify, as the latter do not, that it was the "*right* ear" of the High Priest's servant which Peter cut off.

251. 3 Rgns 13,6bα ἐδεήθη... τοῦ προσώπου κυρίου. Josephus employs the above expression "entreat (the) God" also in *AJ* 1,186.188.199.268.303; 2,334; 3,6.310; 5,159. 276.280.344.345; 6,24.42.64; 7,154.204 (321).327; 8,255; 10,11.26.64.199; 11,229.231.234; 12,300.407; 19,349.

252. Josephus uses παρέχω with God as subject some 65 × .

253. Josephus uses the above construction χαίρω ἐπὶ also in *AJ* 2,15.164; 3,32.93; 4,3.184.234; 5,97; 6,141; 12,110; 13,81. Frequently, as here, Josephus introduces mention of a character's "rejoicing" at some turn of events where the Biblical parallel lacks such, see, e.g.: *AJ* 2,15 (cf. Gen 37,11; Jacob "rejoices" at Joseph's second dream). 69 (cf. Gen 40,9-15; the chief butler "rejoices" at Joseph's interpretation of his dream). 126 (cf. Gen 44,3; the brothers "rejoice" at getting Simeon and Benjamin back). 185 (cf. Gen 47,3; Pharoah "rejoices" at Jacob's arrival); 3,93 (cf. Exod 20,19; the people "rejoice" at the things spoken by Moses).102 (cf. Exod 35,21; the people "rejoice" at what they have seen and heard from Moses); 5,158 (cf. Judg 20,26; the Benjaminites "rejoice" in their victory); 6,81 (cf. 1 Sam 11,12; the people "rejoice" at Saul's election as king). 141 (no Biblical parallel; Saul returns "rejoicing" at his triumph over Amalek).209 (cf. 1 Sam 19,14; Jonathan finds Saul "rejoicing"). 273 (cf. 1 Sam 23,6; Saul "rejoices" to learn of David's whereabouts); 9,149 (// 2 Kings 11,12; the crowd "rejoices" at Joas' coronation). Compare the parallel case of the inserted reference to Jeroboam's being "enraged" at Jadōn's word against the altar, 8,233 and see n. 234.

254. The above construction "regain natural use" occurs only here in Josephus. Compare 1 Kings 13,6bβ "and his hand returned to him and became like the first".

255. Compare 1 Kings 13,7 "And the king said to the man of God, 'Come home with me and refresh yourself (3 Rgns ἀρίστησον) *and I will give you a gift*'". Josephus' omission of the last element of Jeroboam's Biblical invitation may reflect the fact that the question of the Judean's receiving "gifts" from the king does not figure in the continuation of the story.

But Jadōn said (δ᾽ ἔφησεν)²⁵⁶ that he dare not enter his house (εἰσελθεῖν πρὸς αὐτὸν)²⁵⁷ nor taste (γεύσασθαι)²⁵⁸ bread and water (ἄρτου καὶ ὕδατος)²⁵⁹ in that city (πόλει)²⁶⁰, for God had forbidden (ἀπειρηκέναι)²⁶¹ this to him²⁶² as well as to return (ποιήσηται τὴν ἐπιστροφήν)²⁶³ by the road on which he had come (τὴν ὁδὸν ἣν ἦλθεν ὅπως μὴ δι᾽ αὐτῆς)²⁶⁴...

To the prophet's citation of the negative divine command concerning his return drawn from 13,8-9 as cited above, Josephus further appends a positive counterpart. This latter, itself inspired by the narrative notice of 13,10a ("and he [the Judean] departed by another [3 Rgns ἄλλῃ] way"), reads: "saying he must go by another (δι᾽ ἄλλης)". Having thus anticipated 13,10's notice on the Judean's departure, Josephus substitutes for it the following (Biblically unparalleled) remark on Jeroboam's mental state at the end of his encounter with Jadōn: "the king admired (ἐθαύμαζεν)²⁶⁵ him for his self-control (ἐγκρατείας)²⁶⁶ but was himself in a state of fear (ἐν φόβῳ), suspecting from what had been foretold (προειρημένων) to him a change in his fortunes (μεταβολὴν... τῶν πραγμάτων)²⁶⁷ that would not be for his good (οὐκ ἀγαθὴν)²⁶⁸". With this notice Josephus looks ahead to his addendum at the end of our

256. Thus SP followed by NaMar. NN* read δέ φησιν with RO.
257. 3 Rgns 13,8αβ οὐκ εἰσελεύσομαι μετὰ σοῦ. Josephus uses the above construction εἰσέρχομαι πρὸς also in *AJ* 10,198.203; 11,226.
258. Thus codd followed by NN*Mar; Na conjectures γεύσεσθαι.
259. This is Josephus' only use of the above expression "taste bread and water". Compare 3 Rgns 13,8b οὐδὲ μὴ φάγω ἄρτον οὐδὲ μὴ πίω ὕδωρ....
260. 3 Rgns 13,8b "in this place (τόπῳ)".
261. With God as subject ἀπεῖπον occurs also in *AJ* 6,145 (God "refused" Samson's prayer).
262. Compare 1 Kings 13,9 with its reference, once again avoided by Josephus, to the "word of the Lord": "because thus it was commanded me by the word of the Lord saying... 'you shall neither eat bread nor drink water...'".
263. 3 Rgns 13,9b μὴ ἐπιστρέψῃς. Elsewhere in Josephus the above construction (= "return" here in 8,235) has the sense "pay heed, intervene", see *AJ* 2,293; 9,237; 13,78; 18,349, cf. 8,314.
264. B 3 Rgns 13,9b (μὴ ἐπιστρέψῃς) ἐν τῇ ὁδῷ (+ ἐν L) ᾗ ἐπορεύθης ἐν αὐτῇ.
265. Josephus frequently uses θαυμάζω as here in the sense "admire, marvel at" some quality of a person or thing, see e.g.: *BJ* 1,322; 3,70; 5,324; 6,112.163.268; 7,406; *AJ* 1,167; 2,87.89.252.262; 3,65; 5,143.307.317; 6,181; 8,168; 12,90.182.207.214.218; 14,368.446; 15,25.159; 18,59.300.333; *Vita* 222; *Ap* 1,175.193; 2,225.239.269.
266. Josephus uses this key term of Hellenistic ethics (and of Philo) a total of 8 × : *BJ* 2,120 (the Essenes).138 (the Essenes); 4,373; *AJ* 6,23 (Saul); 8,235 (Jadōn); 15,237 (Mariamme); 16,218 (Alexander, son of Herod).246. On it see: W. GRUNDMANN, ἐγκράτεια, in *TWNT* 2 (1935) 338-340; SPICQ, *Lexicographie*, I, pp. 61-63.
267. Josephus employs the above phrase "change(s) of fortune(s)" also in *BJ* 2,133 (bis); *AJ* 15,264; 17,346.
268. With the whole above formulation compare the Essene Simon's elucidation of Archelaus' dream in *AJ* 17,346 "the vision portended a change in the situation (μεταβολὴν πραγμάτων) of Archelaus and one that was not for the better (ἀγαθοῖς)".

episode where Jeroboam reappears – as well as to the subsequent disasters which will befall the king and his line, see below.

3. *Prophet vs. Prophet* (8,236-242). The second component narrative within 1 Kings 13 recounts the interaction between the Judean man of God and a Northern colleague (13,11-32). The latter is introduced, minimalistically and neutrally, in 13,11aα as "an old prophet (B 3 Rgns πρεσβύτης εἷς προφήτης, L προφήτης ἄλλος πρεσβύτης) dwelling in Bethel"²⁶⁹. Josephus' presentation of him, by contrast, is both more elaborate and explicitly evaluative: "a wicked old man (πρεσβύτης πονῆρος), a false prophet (πευδοπροφήτης)²⁷⁰ whom Jeroboam held in honour (εἶχεν ἐν τιμῇ)²⁷¹, being deceived (ἀπατώμενος)²⁷² by the things he said to please (τὰ πρὸς ἡδονὴν [see 8,214] λέγοντος)²⁷³ him". From the Biblical datum concerning the prophet's advanced age, Josephus further develops an implicit response to a question suggested by the source, i.e. how is it that the prophet was not present for the affair at the altar and so has to be informed of it by his sons (see below)? The historian's response to this question is that the Bethelite

269. In Rabbinic tradition this figure, anonymous in both the Bible and Josephus, is identified sometimes with Jonathan, grandson of Moses, sometimes with Amaziah, priest of Bethel in Amos' time. See L. GINZBERG, *Legend of the Jews*, VI, Philadelphia, 1939, p. 211, n. 133 for references.

270. While the contrast in 1 Kings 13 is thus between the Judean "man of God" and the Bethel "prophet", Josephus opposes Jadōn, the "prophet" from Jerusalem to the "false prophet" of Bethel. Josephus employs the same designation for the Bethelite again in 8,241, see the pl. form in 8,242. Similarly, TJ characterizes the Bethel figure as a "lying prophet" in its rendition of 1 Kings 13,11.25.29 (*bis*), just as Lucifer designates the figure as a "pseudopropheta" in his citation of 13,20 and the VL glosses L₉₁₋₉₅ found in medieval Vulgate Bibles (on these see FERNÁNDEZ MARCOS and BUSTO SAIZ, *1-2 Reyes*, pp. xliii-xlvi) use that term in rendering 13,11. All these witnesses likely derive their designations of the Bethelite from the parenthetical remark of 1 Kings 13,18, i.e. "he lied to him (the Judean man of God)".

Josephus uses the term "false prophet" a total of 16× (*BJ* 2,261; 6,285; *AJ* 8,236.241.242.318.402.406 (*bis*).409; 9,133.134.137; 10,66.104.111) as compared with no uses in MT and 10 in LXX (all but one of these in the book of Jeremiah), see: J. REILING, *The Use of ψευδοπροφήτης in the Septuagint, Philo and Josephus*, in *NT* 13 (1971) 147-156. On the designation "false prophet" in TJ, see J. RIBERA, *El profetismo segun el Targum Jonatan y el Targum Palestinense*, in D. MUÑOZ LEÓN (ed.), *Salvación en la Palabra. Targum-Derash-Berith. Memorial A. Díez Macho*, Madrid, 1986, 489-502, esp. pp. 494-495.

271. Elsewhere Josephus employs the above construction "hold in honor" also in *AJ* 2,39; 7,387; 10,189.263; 11,287; 13,223.386.

272. Compare *AJ* 10,104 where Jeremiah urges Zedekiah not to put his faith "in the false prophets (ψευδοπροφήταις) who were deceiving (ἀπατῶσιν) him" and 124 (Jeremiah asks Zedekiah): "Where now are those who asserted that the Babylonian king would not march against us again, and so deceived (ἀπατῶντες) you?". In Josephus' presentation Israel's first king and Judah's last ruler are thus paralleled as figures who brought disaster upon themselves and their people due to their giving credence to the words of "false prophets".

273. The above expression "say to please" recurs in *BJ* 1,515.

"was bed-ridden (κλινήρης)²⁷⁴ through the infirmity of old age (διὰ τὴν ἀπὸ²⁷⁵ τοῦ γήρως ἀσθένειαν)²⁷⁶".

In line with 1 Kings 13,11αβb Josephus next relates the prophet's sons²⁷⁷ reporting to him "about the prophet who had come from Jerusalem (see 8,231)". In citing their report, Josephus has them, as the Bible does not, single out for mention the fact that the Jerusalemite "had restored to life" (ζῶσαν ἀπολάβοι, cf. τῆς χειρὸς... ἀπολαβούσης, 8,234) Jeroboam's right (see 8,234) hand. He then goes on to introduce a transitional notice on the inner affects of the sons' report on the Bethel prophet which itself alludes back to his previous insertion on the relationship between him and the king: "then the old man, fearing that (δείσας μὴ, see 8,221) the stranger (ξένος)²⁷⁸ might find more favour (παρευδοκιμήσειεν)²⁷⁹ with the king than himself and enjoy greater honour (ἀπολαύοι τιμῆς, cf. εἶχεν ἐν τιμῇ, 8,236)²⁸⁰, ordered his sons...".

In describing now the Bethelite's initiatives which his "fear" prompts him to take, Josephus suppresses the question and answer sequence of 13,12 regarding the way taken by the "man of God" – a point that would, presumably, have been covered in the sons' comprehensive report to him. Rather, he proceeds immediately to his version of 13,13-14aα: "he ordered (προσέταξε) his sons to saddle (ἐπιστρώσασι)²⁸¹ his ass (τὸν ὄνον)²⁸² at once (εὐθὺς)²⁸³ and make it ready for his departure (ἕτοιμον πρὸς ἔξοδον... παρασκευάσαι)²⁸⁴. So they made haste to do as they were ordered (τῶν... σπευσάντων ὃ προσετάγησαν)²⁸⁵, and he mounted to ride in pursuit of the prophet (13,14 'man of God')".

274. Elsewhere in Josephus this term occurs only in *BJ* 2,617.

275. So codd, followed by NN*Mar; Na conjectures ὑπό.

276. This is Josephus' only use of the above phrase "from old age" as read by NN*Mar (see previous note); the reading conjectured by Na has an equivalent in *AJ* 7,344.383; 12,196. The above expression "because of infirmity" recurs in *BJ* 1,76; *AJ* 1,273 (5,5).

277. MT 1 Kings 13,11 begins "his *son* came" but then concludes "*they* told their father". Like 3 Rgns (υἱοὶ), Josephus (παίδων) reads the pl. already in the first instance.

278. 70× in Josephus.

279. The verb παρευδοκιμέω occurs also in *AJ* 7,228; 12,179; *Ap* 1,25.

280. The above phrase "enjoy honor" occurs also in *BJ* 1,121; *AJ* 2,91; 3,266; 4,58; 5,236; 6,292; 11,32.245; 13,83; 20,198.240.

281. The above verb ἐπιστρώννυμι is hapax in Josephus.

282. Josephus' masculine form here corresponds to that found in MT (החמור) and B 1 Kings 13,13 (τὸν ὄνον) as against the feminine of L (τὴν ὄνον).

283. Cf. Josephus' having Jadōn announce that the altar will be overthrown "in an instant" (8,232) and his notice that Jeroboam's hand was paralysed "immediately" (εὐθέως), 8,233. The note of urgency interjected by Josephus here in 8,237 is prolonged in the statement of 8,238 that the sons "hastened" to do as their father ordered.

284. Compare *AJ* 7,348 where Mephibosheth cites his "ordering" (κελευσθεὶς) Siba παρασκευάσαι τὰ πρὸς τὴν ἔξοδον.

285. Compare *Vita* 184 (Philip) ἔσπευδε ποιήσων ἃ προσέταξεν (i.e. Agrippa).

In 1 Kings 13,14aβ the Bethelite discovers his quarry "sitting under an oak" (3 Rgns δρῦν). Josephus, embellishing, renders "resting under a tree that was thick with leaves (δασεῖ)[286] and gave as much shade as a huge (εὐμεγέθους)[287] oak (δρυὸς)". In 13,14b there is an initial question-answer sequence between the two prophets concerning the Judean's identity. Josephus omits this (see above on 13,12) – after the sons' full report the old prophet should be able to identify his colleague right away. In his presentation then the Bethelite "first greeted him (Jadōn) and then proceeded to blame (ἐμέμφετο)[288] him for not entering his house[289] and partaking of his hospitality (ξενίων μεταλαβόντα)[290]" (// 13,15). In 13,16-17 the Judean rebuffs the invitation made him, repeating his words to Jeroboam (13,8b-9) virtually verbatim. Avoiding such repetition, Josephus has Jadōn simply aver that "he had been forbidden by God (κεκωλῦσθαι πρὸς τοῦ θεοῦ, see κωλυθείς... ὑπὸ τοῦ θεοῦ 223) to taste (γεύσασθαι 235) (food) in the house of anyone in that city".

In 1 Kings 13,18abα the Bethel prophet counters his colleague's reluctance with a speech which Josephus modifies and amplifies. Specifically, he makes the Bethelite begin by directly responding to Jadōn's previous invocation of a divine prohibition as follows: "But not in my house, at least, did the Deity (τὸ θεῖον)[291] forbid (ἀπηγόρευκε)[292] you to have food served (παραθέσθαι τράπεζαν)[293] to you". Thereafter, Josephus takes up (while also expanding – see the italicized words below) the old prophet's statement from 13,18aα, making this serve to buttress his preceding claim: "For I too am a prophet like you (προφήτης... εἰμι κἀγώ, compare B 3 Rgns κἀγὼ προφήτης εἰμί...), sharing like you in the same worship of Him (κοινωνὸς πρὸς αὐτὸν θρησκείας)[294]". In 13,18aββα the old prophet clinches his argument by

286. Thus the reading of RO followed by NN*NaMar. MSP read βαθεῖ, Lat alta. Earlier, S.A. NABER, Observationes criticae in Flavium Josephum, in Mnemosyne 13 N.S. (1885) 352-399, p. 365, taking the MSP reading βαθεῖ καὶ σκιὰν as starting point, had proposed the emendation βαθεῖαν σκιάν.

287. Elsewhere the above adjective occurs also in BJ 7,305; AJ 6,158.

288. The above verb μέμφομαι occurs 31 × in Josephus.

289. (μὴ) παρ' αὐτὸν εἰσελθόντα; compare εἰσελθεῖν πρὸς αὐτὸν, 8,235.

290. Elsewhere Josephus uses the above expression "partake of hospitality" in AJ 1,196 where Abraham extends an invitation to the three angels.

291. On this divine designation in Josephus, see R.H.J. SCHUTT, The Concept of God in the Works of Flavius Josephus, in JJS 31 (1980) 171-189, pp. 173-179 (his list of occurrences of the designation does not mention that in 8,239).

292. Elsewhere Josephus uses ἀπαγορεύω with God/the Deity as subject also in AJ 1,203; 4,102.116. Compare τὸν θεὸν ἀπειφηκέναι in Jadōn's word to Jeroboam in 8,235.

293. Josephus uses the above expression "serve food" also in BJ 5,428; 7,264; AJ 6,338.

294. This is Josephus' only use of the above expression "share in worship". The phrase "worship towards him (God)" occurs also in AJ 4,312, cf. the genitival construction τῆς θρησκείας τῆς ἐν αὐτῷ (i.e. the Temple) τοῦ θεοῦ in 8,225.

adducing what "an angel (3 Rgns ἄγγελος) spoke to me by the word of the Lord", i.e. an injunction that he give hospitality to his colleague. Josephus simplifies this rather ponderous appeal to a divine revelation by making the Bethelite claim to have been "sent by Him (God)" (ὑπ᾽ αὐτοῦ πεμφθείς, cf. 8,231 where Jadōn himself is qualified as τοῦ θεοῦ πέμψαντος) to bring you to my house as my guest (ἑστιασόμενον)²⁹⁵". Thereby, he eliminates the mediation of both the "angel"²⁹⁶ and "the word" (see above) cited in the Biblical formulation. 1 Kings 13,18 concludes with the parenthetical remark "he lied (3 Rgns ἐψεύσατο) to him" – the first (and only) evaluative remark concerning the Bethel prophet in the Biblical account. Josephus, who has already negatively characterized the figure, naturally takes up this item, while better integrating it into the flow of the narrative: "(Jadōn) believing his lies (ψευσαμένῳ πεισθείς)²⁹⁷, returned" (// 1 Kings 13,18b-19a).

In 1 Kings 13,19b the Judean eats and drinks in his colleague's home. Josephus has the pair "eating the midday meal and conversing in a friendly manner (φιλοφρονουμένων)²⁹⁸". 1 Kings 13,20-22 constitutes the turning point in the Biblical narrative. Here, the Bethel prophet conveys to his colleague a word of judgment that he himself had received from the Lord (vv. 20-21a), consisting of an accusation, formulated first negatively (v. 21b), then positively (v. 22a), and announcement of punishment (v. 22b). Josephus' reworking of this sequence is noteworthy. First, he has the divine message come, not to the Bethelite (so 13,20), but directly to Jadōn to whom God (ὁ θεός)²⁹⁹ "appears" (ἐπιφαίνεται)³⁰⁰. Josephus' reformulation here likely reflects

---

295. The above verb ἑστιάω occurs 34× in Josephus.

296. Josephus likewise eliminates Biblical references to angels in his versions of 1 Kings 19 (see below) and 2 Kings 1. On angelology in Josephus, see SCHLATTER, *Theologie*, pp. 55-56; M. MACH, *Entwicklungsstadien des jüdischen Engelglaubens in vorrabbinischen Zeit* (Texte und Untersuchungen zum Antiken Judentum, 34), Tübingen, 1992, pp. 300-332.

297. The above construction occurs only here in Josephus.

298. Compare 8,215 where the elders advise Rehoboam to respond "in a friendly spirit" (φιλοφρόνως) to the people.

299. Compare τὸ θεῖον, 8,239. On Josephus' use of θεός with (and less frequently without) the article, see SCHUTT, *Concept*, pp. 172-173.

300. Elsewhere Josephus uses God as subject of the verb ἐπιφαίνω also in *AJ* 1,191; 8,268. Just as here in 8,240 the historian introduces reference to a divine "appearance" where the Bible alludes simply to some sort of (purely) verbal communication by God. To designate these divine self-manifestations, Josephus employs a variety of (synonymous) verbs (ἐπιφαίνω, φαίνω, ἐμφαίνω). As examples of texts where Josephus interjects mention of a divine "appearance", note the following: *AJ* 1,223 (God "appears" [ἐμφανισθείς] to Abraham, compare Gen 22,1-2 "God said to Abraham"); 7,92 (God "appeared" [φανέντος] to Nathan, compare 2 Sam 7,2 "the word of the Lord came to Nathan").147 (God "appeared" [φανείς] to Nathan in a dream, compare 2 Sam 12,1 God sends Nathan to speak to David); 8,268 (God "appeared" [ἐπιφανείς] to Ahijah, compare 1 Kings 14,5 the Lord "said" to Ahijah).333 (God may "appear" [φανέντος] to Elijah a second time, compare 1 Kings 18,12 "the spirit of the Lord will carry Elijah off); 9,20 (God "appeared" [φανείς] to Elijah, compare 2 Kings 1,3 the "angel of the Lord" speaks

his view that a "false prophet" like the Bethelite is not a fitting recipient
of a divine communication[301] (as also his consistent avoidance of the
Biblical *Wortereignisformel*, see above). In the Bible (1 Kings 13,21b-
22a) the accusation against the Judean constitutes the bulk of the
Lord's word, v. 22a re-utilizing the formulations of vv. 8b-9,16-17 *in
extenso*. Conversely, v. 22b speaks only briefly and indeterminately of
the punishment awaiting the man of God, i.e. he will be denied burial
"in the grave of his fathers", thus leaving unaddressed the prior
question regarding the circumstances of his death. Josephus reverses the
proportions in his version of the divine address. For him, the fact/
nature of Jadōn's offense is sufficiently evident so as to need no
underscoring. Consequently, he has the Deity simply state that Jadōn is
to "suffer punishment" (τιμωρίαν ὑφέξειν)[302] for "transgressing His
commands" (παραβάντα τὰς ἐντολὰς αὐτοῦ)[303]. Such compression
goes together with a corresponding amplification of the divine announcement concerning Jadōn's punishment. In particular, Josephus precedes
God's statement about the burial awaiting Jadōn (// 13,22b)[304] with

to Elijah); 10,177 (God "appeared" [φανέντα] to Jeremiah, compare Jer 42,7 "the word of
the Lord came to Jeremiah").

Josephus' introduction of "appearance language" into the Biblical narratives is likely
inspired by Greek religion's characteristic emphasis on the "seeing" of the deity (as
opposed to the OT's own stress on the "hearing" of the divine word), Philo exhibiting a
similar tendency. At the same time, it should be noted that, in line with the Biblical
reserve in describing divine appearances, Josephus, in all the above passages, contents
himself simply with noting the fact of God's "appearing" without any attempt at further
description. Note too that the divine "appearances" cited by him invariably function as
an introduction to divine speech just as do the Biblical theophanies. On the whole subject,
see: SCHLATTER, *Theologie*, pp. 55-56; E. PAX, *ΕΠΙΦΑΝΕΙΑ. Ein religionsgeschichtlicher
Beitrag zur biblischen Theologie* (MTS, 10), München, 1955; idem, *Epiphanie*, in *RAC* 5
(1962) 832-909; SPICQ, *Lexicographie*, I, pp. 284-287.

301. Contrast *Sanh.* 104b where, with reference to 1 Kings 13,20, it is averred that, due
to the hospitality he extended to the Judean, the Shekinah rested upon the Bethelite
notwithstanding the fact of his being a "prophet of Baal".

302. This construction occurs also in *BJ* 2,157; *AJ* 2,129.322; 9,100.169; 11,130;
13,108; 20,41.168; *Vita* 172.342.

303. Compare 3 Rgns 13,21bβ οὐκ ἐφύλαξας τὴν ἐντολὴν ἣν ἐνετείλατό σοι
κύριος.... Note that Josephus characteristically passes over the duplicate accusation of
13,21bα with its reference to the Judean's "disobeying the *word* of the Lord".

Josephus uses the above expression "transgress commands" elsewhere in *AJ* 6,151
(Samuel's commands); 17,342 (Caesar's commands). He employs the noun ἐντολή (sg. or
pl.) as here specifically of God's "command(s)" also in 1,43; 2,274; 4,3; 7,338.342
(8,94).120.337; 10,28. G. SCHRENK, ἐντέλλομαι-ἐντολή, in *TWNT* 2 (1935) 541-555, p.
543 points out that, in contrast to LXX, Josephus, like Philo, prefers other terms to
ἐντολή when referring to divine "law(s)", i.e. νόμος, νόμοι, τὰ νόμιμα, τὰ ἔθη, θεοῦ
δόγματα. He attributes this verbal preference to the fact that in profane Greek ἐντολή is
not commonly used of a divine "command".

304. His formulation of this announcement reads "he should be deprived (ἀμοιρήσειν,
hapax) of burial (ταφῆς) in the tombs of his fathers (ἐν τοῖς πατρῴοις μνήμασι, elsewhere
AJ 7,19, cf. 10,77)". Compare 1 Kings 13,22b "your body shall not come to the tomb of

one concerning the manner of his death: "(God) revealed (ἐδή-λου)[305]... that as he went on his way a lion would meet (συμβαλεῖν) and destroy (διαφθαρήσεσθαι)[306] him". Josephus obviously found the inspiration for this latter element in the further course of 1 Kings 13 where, in fact, the Judean is assaulted by a lion on his homeward journey, see v. 24. Josephus, in turn, was likely prompted to anticipate the content of 13,24 within the Deity's address to Jadōn by his reading of 13,26 where the Bethel prophet declares, *post festum*, that the Judean's meeting death at the hand of the lion was "according to the word of the Lord which the Lord spoke to him", this even though the divine word to the Bethel prophet as cited in 13,22b makes no mention of such a fate befalling him as such. Josephus resolves this implicit discrepancy between 13,22 and 26 by having God pronounce explicitly on the manner of Jadōn's death right from the start[307].

The Biblical narrative leaves the divine communication of 13,20-22 without editorial comment, 13,23 reading simply "and after he had eaten and drunk, he saddled the ass for the prophet...". Josephus has no parallel to this notice (which, oddly, seems to suggest that the Judean responded to the divine word of doom by simply continuing with his meal). In its place he introduces the following reflection: "this came about, I think, in accordance with the will of God (κατὰ τὴν τοῦ θεοῦ βούλησιν, see 8,218)[308], in order that Jeroboam might not give heed to the words (προσέχοι... λόγοις)[309] of Jadōn who had been convicted of lying (ἐληλεγμένῳ ψεύδει)[310]". With this comment Josephus re-introduces the figure of Jeroboam who in the Bible remains

your fathers (3 Rgns εἰς τὸν τάφον τῶν πατέρων σου)". Mar, *Josephus*, V, p. 701, n. d compares Josephus' phrase "deprive of burial" with Sophocles, *Ajax* 1326 ταφῆς ἄμοιρον.

305. Elsewhere Josephus uses δηλόω with God/the Deity as subject in *AJ* 2,235 (recipient: the Egyptians); 4,312 (Moses); 5,192 (Gideon); 8,269 (Ahijah; here, mention of God's "revealing" to the prophet is preceded by reference to his previous "appearing" just as in 8,240, see below); 10,195 (Nebuchadnezzar).242 (Belshazzar).272 (Daniel). On the term, see R. BULTMANN, δηλόω, in *TWNT* 2 (1935) 60-61.

306. The verb διαφθείρω occurs c. 300× in Josephus. W, *ad loc.* renders "tu seras dévoré" – a translation which seems inappropriate given the fact that in the sequel the lion will leave Jadōn's corpse unmolested.

307. Thereby, of course, he likewise eliminates the suspense provoked by the Biblical account as to the circumstances of the Judean's end.

308. Compare Josephus' – likewise interpolated – comment on Rehoboam's rejection of the elders' advice in 8,216 "it was God, I believe, who caused him to condemn what should have been of benefit to him".

309. Other occurrences of the above phrase "give heed to words" in Josephus are *AJ* 2,49; 7,118, cf. 13,303; 16,303; 17,87.

310. Thus the conjecture of Df, followed by N*NaMar. N conjectures ὡς ἐληλεγμένου ψευδοῦς with reference to Lat "quasi fallacis et ita defuncti". The majority of codd read ἐληλεγμένῳ ψεύδει (O ψευδῆ), cf. Ed. pr. ἐληλεγμένου ψεῦδος.
Note Josephus' ironic use of "falsehood terminology" here – the one who will end up being "convicted of lying" is Jadōn, not the "false prophet" (8,236) whose "lies" Jadōn believed (8,240).

unmentioned throughout 13,11-32. His intention in so doing is to foreshadow the subsequent, ultimate dismissal of Jadōn's words by the king who, previously, had been convinced of their validity, see 8,234-235.

Josephus now gives his parallel to 13,24 which describes the lion's killing of the homeward-bound man of God while respecting his corpse and mount: "And so, as Jadōn was journeying back to Jerusalem (see 8,231.236), a lion did meet (συμβάλλει, see 8,240, 3 Rgns εὗρεν)[311] *and pulled* (κατασπάσας)[312] *him off his beast* and killed (ἀπέκτεινε, 3 Rgns ἐθανάτωσεν)[313] him; to the ass he did no harm at all (οὐδὲν... ἔβλαψε) but lay down (παρακαθεζόμενος)[314] beside him and guarded him as well as the prophet's corpse (σῶμα = 3 Rgns)"[315].

There is some discrepancy among the textual witesses as to the continuation of the Biblical narrative at this point. L* (and VL) lack an equivalent to the 13,25a of MT B which refers to the passersby's "seeing" the roadside scene. Josephus does give a shortened version of the MT B plus here leaving aside, however, its enumeration of what the witnesses saw (13,25aβ) which recapitulates 13,24b: "until some way-farers (τινες τῶν ὁδοιπόρων, see B ἄνδρες παραπορευόμενοι)[316] saw (ἰδόντες, B εἶδον) them...". He likewise simplifies the sequence of 13,25b-26a (the passersby tell what they have seen in Bethel where the old prophet hears of it): "they came to the city to tell the false prophet (see 8,236)".

The MT sequence of 13,26b-30 gives a circumstantial account of the initiatives of the Bethel prophet regarding his slain colleague: he identifies the latter from the passersby's report (v. 26b with repetition of the wording of vv. 21b,24), has his sons saddle his ass (v. 27), finds the body (v. 28, citing vv. 24b, 25aβ), brings it back to Bethel (v. 29), and buries it there (v. 30a) to the accompaniment of fraternal mourning (v. 30b). BL* (as also VL) are shorter with no parallel to vv. 26bβ-27[317]. These Greek witnesses likewise read the end of v. 29 and the beginning of v. 30 differently from MT. The latter has "and he brought him back

311. Elsewhere Josephus employs the h.p. of συμβάλλω also in *BJ* 1,47; 3,290; *AJ* 5,45; 12,274.405.428; 13,97.137; 14,33.189 (mostly of a military encounter).

312. The verb κατασπάω occurs also in *BJ* 1,649; 2,154; 5,563; *AJ* 7,241; 10,52; 11,45; 17,152.153; 18,315.

313. W., *ad loc.* renders "mit en pièces" which does not seem appropriate given the continuation of the account, see n. 306.

314. Other uses of the verb παρακαθίζω in Josephus occur in *BJ* 1,596; 3,200; *AJ* 6,235; 16,50; 19,91.

315. Josephus' formulation here explicates the wording of I Kings 13,23b "(and his body was thrown in the road) and the ass stood beside it; the lion also stood beside the body".

316. The noun ὁδοιπόρος is hapax in Josephus.

317. The L MSS 19/(b') and 108/(b) do have the sequence.

and he came to the city of the old prophet to mourn and bury him. And he laid the body in his own grave". By contrast, B gives "and the prophet brought him back to the city to bury him in his own grave...", while L reads "the prophet brought it (the body) back to the city to bury him. And he put his body in his own grave". Josephus, for his part, reduces the whole Biblical sequence to its core content, i.e. the recovery of the body and its burial. In relating the first point, he has the Bethelite prophet act through his sons rather than going to fetch the corpse himself (contrast MT 13,27-28): "he sent his sons (τοὺς υἱοὺς)[318] and brought the body (σῶμα = 3 Rgns 13,29) into the city (εἰς τὴν πόλιν = 3 Rgns)". Here, Josephus may have had in view his earlier characterization of the Bethelite as old and bed-ridden (see 8,236); now when the matter is less urgent – Jadōn will not be going anywhere at this point – he can leave it to his sons to go after his colleague. As he does with several of his other Biblical heroes, Josephus accentuates the pomp of Jadōn's interment: he is "honoured with a costly funeral (πολυτελοῦς κηδείας ἠξίωσεν)[319]".

1 Kings 13,31-32 cites the two-part word of the Bethel prophet to his sons following the Judean's burial. In v. 31 he directs that, upon his own death, he is to be buried together with his colleague. Once again, MT and 3 Rgns differ somewhat. In the former the verse concludes simply "lay my bones besides his bones", while the latter's "by his bones lay me *so that* (ἵνα) my bones may escape with his bones" explicates what the Bethelite hopes to ensure with his prescription[320]. Thereafter, the old man's word in v. 32 intimates why such a measure is required, i.e. the certain fulfillment of the Judean's "word" against both the Bethel altar and "(all) the houses of the high places which are in the cities (> 3 Rgns) of Samaria". In other words, he hopes to secure inviolability for his own remains when the Northern cultic sites are overthrown.

Josephus' version of the above sequence begins with a "burial injunction" (// 13,31bα): "he instructed his sons (τοῖς παισὶ, 3 Rgns τοῖς υἱοῖς)[321] to bury (θάψαι, 3 Rgns θάψατε) him also, when he was dead (ἀποθανόντα, 3 Rgns ἀποθάνω) with the prophet[322]". To this

318. This is the 3 Rgns designation for them throughout the pericope; in 8,236.237 Josephus called them παῖδες.

319. See the following instances where Josephus goes beyond the Bible in underscoring the splendor of a character's burial: *AJ* 7,392 (David); 9,44 (Jehoshaphat).183 (Elisha); 10,77 (Josiah).154 (Zedekiah). A similar emphasis on the pomp attending the funerals of leading personages can be noted in Dionysius, see *RA* 2.76.5; 3.22.1; 4.8.2; 6.95.1.

320. As BHS notes, 3 Rgns' formulation in 13,31 seems to have in view 2 Kings 23,18 where, at Josiah's bidding, the bones of the two prophets are left undisturbed on the occasion of the king's overthrow of the Bethel sanctuary.

321. Compare τοὺς υἱοὺς, 8,242a.

322. Cf. 1 Kings 13,31b "in this grave in which the man of God is buried in it".

directive he then appends an affirmation comparable to that of 13,32a about the realization of the Judean's previous prediction: "... saying that everything was true (ἀληθῆ, see 8,234) which he had prophesied (προεφήτευσε)[323] against that city and the altar [13,32 against the altar in Bethel] and the priests (ἱερέων, see 8,232 ψευδιερεῖς) and the false prophets (ψευδοπροφητῶν, see 8,236.241)[324]". On the other hand, however, Josephus has no parallel to the mention of the fate awaiting the "houses" of Samaria's "high places" (13,32b). This "lacuna" is understandable given both his earlier non-utilization of 12,31a's reference to these structures (see above) and the fact that in the preceding words of the man of God in 1 Kings 13 itself there was no reference to them. Thereafter, Josephus makes the Bethelite conclude with a statement which might be seen as a further explication of the 3 Rgns reading at the end of 13,31 (see above): "... but that he himself would suffer no mutilation (ὑβρισθήσεσθαι)[325] after death if he were buried together with the prophet, as their bones (ὀστῶν = 3 Rgns) could not be told apart (γνωρισθησομένων[326])[327]".

4. *Conclusion* (8,243-245). In 1 Kings 13 the Bethelite's word of vv. 31-32 is followed – immediately and abruptly – by the notice (v. 33) "after this thing Jeroboam did not turn from his evil way...". This sequence leaves unexplained how it was that Jeroboam persisted in his evildoing as though his encounter with the power-filled man of God had never happened. Josephus, however, whose version accentuates the impression made by Jadōn upon Jeroboam (see 8,234-235) and who has already intimated that, ultimately, the king will disregard the prophet's message (see 8,241). could hardly leave that question unaddressed. To respond to it, Josephus, as W[328] and Mar[329] suggest, inserts as it were,

323. Compare 13,32 "the word which he spoke by the word of the Lord against...". See 8,218 where Josephus substitutes the same verb "prophesy" for 1 Kings 12,15 // 2 Chron 10,15 "the word which the Lord spoke by Ahijah...". See also n. 90.

324. Cf. 8,232 where Jadōn's prediction (to which the Bethelite is alluding here) cites "these misleaders of the people, these imposters and unbelievers".

325. Josephus employs the verb ὑβρίζω 75 ×.

326. Thus R followed by NN*NaMar; OMSP have γνωσθησομένων.

327. In *AJ* 10,66-67 Josephus gives a compressed version of 2 Kings 23,15-20 which relates the eventual fulfillment of the various predictions enunciated in 1 Kings 13. In particular, he narrates Josiah's burning of the bones of the false prophets (see 8,231.242) upon Jeroboam's altar in accordance with the word of the "prophet" (see 2 Kings 23,16b). Curiously, however, he makes no use of 23,17-18's reference to Josiah's sparing the common tomb of man of God and old prophet even though he "sets up" just such a notice with his citation of the latter's word in 8,242 (// 1 Kings 13,31-32). On the other hand, he does introduce the notice that Jadōn's prediction concerning Josiah's desecration of the Bethel altar was fulfilled "after three hundred and sixty-one years", 10,67.

328. *Josèphe*, II, p. 210, n. 3.

329. *Josephus*, V, p. 702, n.c.

between the "after this thing" and the "Jeroboam did not turn" of 1 Kings 13,33 the following lengthy sequence which takes the form of a dialogue between king and Bethel prophet that ends with Jeroboam convinced that he may safely disregard the Judean's warnings:

> And so, after burying the prophet and giving his sons these instructions (τοῖς υἱοῖς ἐντειλάμενος, cf. ἐντειλάμενος τοῖς παισί, 8,242), being a wicked (πονηρός, see 8,236) and impious (ἀσεβής, see ἀσεβῶν 232)[330] man, he went to Jeroboam and said, "Why, I should like to know, were you disturbed (ἐταράχθης)[331] by that foolish fellow's (ἀνοήτου)[332] words?" And when the king told him what had happened to the altar and his own hand, and spoke of (ἀποκαλῶν)[333] him as a truly divine (θεῖον)[334] and excellent (ἄριστον)[335] prophet (προφήτην)[336], the old man began to weaken this opinion (τὴν δόξαν ἀναλύειν)[337] of him with cunning (κακουργῶν)[338] and, by giving a plausible explanation of the things (πιθανοῖς... χρώμενος λόγοις) that had happened, to impair their true significance (βλάπτειν... τὴν ἀλήθειαν)[339]; for he attempted to persuade (ἐπεχείρει... πείθειν)[340] him that his hand had been numbed (ναρκήσειε, see νεναρκηκυῖαν, 8,233) by the fatigue (ὑπὸ κόπου)[341] of carrying the sacrifices (θυσίας, see 8,231) and then, after being rested, had again returned to its natural condition (εἰς τὴν... ἐπανέλθοι φύσιν)[342], and that the altar, being new and having received a great many large victims (θυσίας... μεγάλας)[343], had fallen down (ῥαγείη [8,232.233] καὶ πέσοι)[344] from the weight of the things laid upon (ἐπενηνεγμένων, cf.

330. Josephus uses the above adjectival pair "wicked and impious" also in *AJ* 8,299 (Baasha);9,1 (reverse order, Ahab); 12,252 (reverse order, apostate Jews).385 (the high priest Menelaus);13,34 (Jewish renegades).

331. Josephus uses the verb ταράσσω 92 ×.

332. Josephus uses the adjective ἀνόητος 18 ×.

333. Josephus uses the verb ἀποκαλέω 19 ×.

334. Elsewhere Josephus uses the term θεῖος in reference to human figures in *AJ* 2,323 (Moses, a boy of "divine beauty"); 3,180 (Moses as "divine man"); 18,64 (the *Testimonium Flavianum*, the "divine prophets"); 19,289 (quotation of Claudius' edict referring to the "divine Augustus"); *Ap* 1,232 (quotation from Manetho on the "divine nature" of Amenophis).279 (Moses a "divine man" in Egyptian belief). On Josephus' use of this terminology in light of its Hellenistic background, see: C.H. HOLLADAY, *Theios Aner in Hellenistic Judaism* (SBLDS, 40), Missoula, MT, 1978, esp. pp. 47-102; and B. BLACK-BURN, *Theios Aner and the Markan Miracle Traditions* (WUNT, 2/40), Tübingen, 1991, esp. pp. 69-72.

335. Josephus uses the adjective ἄριστος 88 ×.

336. This is Josephus' only use of the phrase "excellent prophet". Cf., however, *AJ* 4,104 where he calls Balaam μάντις ἄριστος τῶν τότε.

337. This is Josephus' only use of the above expression "weaken opinion".

338. Josephus uses the verb κακουργέω 31 ×. Lat lacks an equivalent to the term here in 8,243. N prints it within brackets while N* omits it entirely.

339. Only here in Josephus.

340. Elsewhere *AJ* 8,172;11,276;12,273.

341. Elsewhere *AJ* 3,25;5,314;7,48.209.

342. The above phrase occurs only here in Josephus. Compare κατὰ φύσιν ἀπολαβούσης, 8,234.

343. The above phrase "great/large sacrifices" occurs also in *AJ* 8,25.125; 9,135.

344. Cf. W, *ad loc.* "s'était rompu et écroulé".

ἐπιφέρειν, 8,231) it. He then told him of the death of the man who had given these (prophetic) signs (τοῦ τὰ σημεῖα ταῦτα³⁴⁵ προειρηκότος, compare 8,232 σημεῖον... προερῶ) and how he had lost his life (ἀπώλετο) (when attacked) by a lion (ὡς ὑπὸ λέοντος)³⁴⁶. Thus, he said, there was nothing of a prophet (οὕτως οὐδὲ ἕν... προφήτου) either in his person (οὔτ ἔχεν)³⁴⁷ or in what he had spoken (ἐφθέγξατο)³⁴⁸. By these words he convinced (πείθει)³⁴⁹ the king and, having wholly turned his thoughts away (διάνοιαν... ἀποστρέψας)³⁵⁰ from God and from holy and righteous (ὁσίων... καὶ δικαίων)³⁵¹ deeds (ἔργων)³⁵², he urged him on (παρώρμησεν)³⁵³ to impious acts (ἀσεβεῖς πράξεις)³⁵⁴.   (8,243-245a)

Several observations might be made about the above sequence. Before relating the exchange itself, Josephus takes care to elucidate the old prophet's motivations in approaching the king; it is his "wickedness" and "impiety" that prompt him to go. Once again, then, Josephus leaves readers in no doubt as to how they are to regard this figure's initiatives, compare the characterization of him as a "wicked old man" in 8,236 preceding the account of his dealings with Jadōn. Also noteworthy is the aggressive manner in which the prophet seizes the initiative, forcing Jeroboam onto the defensive with a provocative question about his (the king's) credulity in allowing himself to be affected by a "foolish fellow's" utterances. Remarkable too is Josephus' portrayal of a king who takes no umbrage at being so addressed by a subject (compare his earlier response to Jadōn's provocation), but meekly tries to provide the explanations demanded of him. True to form, Jeroboam's interrogator does not allow the king the last word. Rather, he overwhelms Jeroboam with counter-arguments, carefully

345. Thus N*NaMar. RO omit, while N brackets the word.
346. RO omit this phrase.
347. SCHRECKENBERG, *Vermutungen*, p. 69 proposes εἶδεν here.
348. The verb φθέγγομαι occurs 27 × in Josephus.
349. See 8,240 where Jadōn is said to be "persuaded" (πεισθείς) by his colleague's lie. Josephus thus underscores terminologically the parallelism between Jadōn and Jeroboam, both of whom are won over by the Bethel prophet's misrepresentations to their own detriment.
350. The above expression "turn away a mind" occurs only here in Josephus.
351. The above adjectival combination occurs elsewhere in Josephus in *AJ* 6,87 (adverbially); 8,295 (reverse order); 9,35; 15,138, cf. 19,323.
352. With the above phrase "holy and righteous deeds", compare ὁσίων καὶ δικαίων ἔργων in *RA* 4.76.3.
353. Josephus uses the verb παρορμάω 25 ×. Note especially *AJ* 8,406 (the four hundred prophets "urge" Ahab to go to war); 9,199 (God "urges" Amaziah to advance against Joas); 10,76 (Destiny "urges" Josiah to combat Neco). In all these instances, as in 8,245, a king is "urged on" to take a deleterious course of action that will end up in disaster for him.
354. Josephus uses the above phrase "impious acts" also in *AJ* 8,251 (+ ἀδίκους, of Rehoboam); 10,68 (of the Israelites of Josiah's time).

reserving until the end his "trump card", i.e. the news about Jadōn's death with the divine disavowal of his mission that implies. So much then does the Bethel prophet control the encounter that one is not surprised to see him succeeding, not only in discrediting Jadōn in the eyes of Jeroboam, but also in directing the king's thoughts to fresh impieties. Josephus thus provides an explication of Jeroboam's persistence in evil (see 1 Kings 13,33) which is, at the same time, a masterful portrayal of a king brow-beaten by a subject.

As noted above, Josephus interposes the explanatory segment 8,243-245a between the opening words of 1 Kings 13,33 ("after this thing") and the remainder of 13,33-34. Thereafter (8,245b), he comes to speak (// 13,33aβb) of the evildoing committed by Jeroboam subsequent to the Bethel incident of 13,1-32. Whereas, however, the Biblical verse focusses on the king's "resuming" his promotion of a reprobate priesthood (cf. 12,31), Josephus opts for a more general formulation: "so greatly did he outrage the Deity (ἐξύβρισεν εἰς τὸ θεῖον)[355] and transgress His laws (παρηνόμησεν)[356] that every day he sought to commit some new act more heinous (μιαρώτερον)[357] than the reckless acts (τετολμημένων)[358] he was already guilty of". Here, Josephus goes beyond the Bible in affirming that the final upshot of the Bethel episode was not simply that Jeroboam reverted to his wicked old ways. Rather, he turned worse than before following that episode, thanks to the old prophet's machinations.

1 Kings 13 closes in v. 34 with the notice that Jeroboam's misdeeds resulted in the eventual annihilation of his line. This notice constitutes an appropriate transition to the prophet Ahijah's word of doom against Jeroboam's house which follows in 1 Kings 14,1-18 (MT). Josephus has no parallel to this notice, however, since he will now break off the story of Jeroboam in order to take up that of Rehoboam, see below. In place thereof he accordingly introduces the following (provisional) concluding formula for the Northern king: "so much concerning Jeroboam it may suffice us, for the present, to have written"[359]. His account of Jeroboam's doings will resume in 8,265.

---

355. Josephus uses the verb ἐξυβρίζω 31 ×. Elsewhere he employs an expression corresponding to the above "outrage the Deity" i.e., "outrage (the) God" in *BJ* 2,230 (+ "and their laws", of the Roman soldier who destroyed a Torah scroll) and *AJ* 8,265 (Jeroboam did not cease or desist from "outraging God"), cf. *BJ* 5,394; *AJ* 8,299; 9,196; 10,39. See G. BERTRAM, ὕβρις κτλ, in *TWNT* 8 (1969) 295-307, esp. pp. 303-304.

356. Josephus uses παρανομέω 42 ×. Compare especially *AJ* 6,92 where the verb stands together with ἐξυβρίζω as in 8,245 in reference to the people in Samuel's time.

357. Josephus uses μιαρός 24 ×.

358. Josephus uses τολμάω c. 190 ×. The combination of μιαρός and τολμάω found here in 8,245 recurs in 13,316 (of Aristobulus).

359. Similar closing formulae, stating that "enough" has been said on a subject, occur also in Dionysius, see *RA* 2.71.4; 9.22.5.

Summary. Positive indications for Josephus' dependence on MT 1 Kings 12,32-13,34 are lacking. On the other hand, his version does evidence points of contact with the distinctive readings of both 3 Rgns and TJ. With the former, e.g., he makes Josiah the subject of the announced bone-burning (see 13,2), speaks from the start of the Bethel prophet's son*s* (see 13,11), lacks a parallel to 13,26b-27 (on the other hand he does have a partial equivalent to MT B 13,25a absent in L*) and has something reminiscent of its plus at the end of 13,31. Recall too the many terminological affinities between Josephus' version and that of 3 Rgns. With TJ he shares the designation of the Judean as a "prophet" rather than a "man of God", the characterization of the Bethelite as a "false prophet" and mention of a motivation for the Judean's giving of a sign (cf. 13,3). Finally, Josephus' acquaintance with the *Fortbildung* of the tradition about the Bethel happening is evidenced by the fact that, like Rabbinic tradition, he confers a name, "Jadōn", on the anonymous Biblical protagonist.

AJ 8,230-245 illustrates various of Josephus' rewriting techniques. He avoids or reduces the verbal repetitions and circumstantiality evidenced particularly in 1 Kings 12,32-33 and 13,11-32. He consistently employs alternative formulations for the chapter's *Leitwörter*, i.e. "by the word of the Lord" and "man of God". Above all, however, one notes Josephus' recurrent introduction of psychological and explanatory indications in his retelling of the source story (see, in particular, his interpolated elucidation of Jeroboam's persistence in evildoing, 8,243-245a). Thereby, the story becomes more transparent, but also "flatter" than its Biblical counterpart with all the unanswered questions the latter evokes[360].

Finally, a word might be said concerning the respective focusses of the Biblical and Josephan Bethel stories. In the former, attention centers on the man of God and the operation of the divine "word" in his existence; the two Northern characters function basically to "trigger" various workings of the word in the Judean's career. In Josephus, Jadōn, I suggest, while clearly remaining the narrative's "good" character (recall that in recognition of this status Josephus has God address him directly, rather than through his colleague, with his

---

360. Josephus, of course, does not resolve all puzzlements raised by the Biblical account. Just as little as the Bible, e.g., does he elucidate the psychology of Jadōn's yielding to his colleague's blandishments after so resolutely resisting those of the king, or address the theodicy question prompted by the severity of God's punishment of one who, after all, had acted in perfect good faith. Also noteworthy, given both Josephus' "negative accentuation" of the Bethel prophet and his affirmation at the opening of *AJ* (see 1,14) about the correlation of crime and punishment which his history will inculcate, is the fact that he has nothing to say about retribution befalling one whose malicious deceits bring disaster on both his counterparts (this last observation indicates that Josephus was willing, implicitly, to allow that events do not always, in fact, transpire according to the principle set down at the start of his work).

word of doom), recedes in importance, whereas his counterparts take on enhanced significance[361].

I would further call attention to Josephus' portrayal of Jeroboam torn between conflicting urges here as reminiscent of his earlier depiction of Jeroboam's rival Rehoboam who likewise, when faced with opposing counsels, opts for the one that spells disaster for himself. The parallelism between the two monarchs' experiences in Josephus' version extends even further, however. Just as with Rehoboam's wrong choice (see 8,216), so also with Jeroboam's (see 8,241), Josephus evokes "the will of God" as operative in the option taken by the king. Here too, then, for all his accentuation of the psychological, Josephus' ultimate interest seems rather with the theological dimension of events.

361. See, e.g., the interjected references to the pair's mental states and motivations, the interpolated characterization of the Bethel prophet and above all the addition of the appended exchange between king and prophet, 8,243-245a.

IV

REHOBOAM'S REIGN
(8,246-264)

Introduction: 1 Kings 12,25-13,34 is a segment of Northern *Sondergut*, unparalleled in the Judean-centered presentation of Chronicles, which finds its immediate continuation in another section proper to Kings, i.e. the account of the death of Jeroboam's son Abijah in 1 Kings 14,1-18 (MT). Josephus, whose reworking of 1 Kings 12,25-13,34 we have just examined, departs from Kings' sequence at this point in order first to relate the reign of Rehoboam. I reserve discussion of the intent/effect of this transposition for a later point. Here, I note that for his treatment of Rehoboam's rule, Josephus had available both the brief narrative of 1 Kings 14,21-31 and the fuller parallel text of 2 Chron 11,5-12,16. As is his wont in such cases, Josephus bases himself primarily on that source which offered the more detailed presentation. In analyzing now Josephus' reworking of the Chronistic passage, I shall consider his handling of its three main components, i.e.: 1) Rehoboam's good beginnings (11,5-23); 2) Rehoboam's defection (12,1-12, cf. 1 Kings 14,21-28); and 3) closing notices for Rehoboam (12,13-16, cf. 1 Kings 14,29-31).

1. *Rehoboam's Good Beginnings* (8,246-250). As he rather regularly does with his post-Solomonic kings, the Chronicler depicts the start of Rehoboam's reign as marked by various positive developments, in the military (11,5-12), religious (11,13-17) and familial (11,18-23) spheres. Josephus (8,246) precedes his version of these notices with a re-intro-duction of Rehoboam: "now Solomon's son Roboamos, who was, as we have said before (see 8,222), king of the two tribes...". He then turns to listing in full the 15 "strong and great cities" (πόλεις ὀχυράς τε καὶ μεγάλας)[362] which Rehoboam "built" (ᾠκοδόμησε, so 2 Par). The following chart shows the forms of the city names as cited by Josephus (according to the text of Mar) in comparison with those of MT and B 2 Chron 11,6-10a:

---

362. With this phrase compare *AJ* 8,36 where Josephus refers to the "great and strongly fortified cities" (πόλεις... μεγάλας καὶ ὀχυρωτάτας) administered by Solomon's official Gabarēs and 12,6 where in a citation from the historian Agatharchides of Cnidus Jerusalem is called πόλιν ὀχυρὰν καὶ μεγάλην.

MT	B	AJ
1) בֵּית־לֶחֶם	Βαιθσέεμ	Βηθλεέμ
2) עֵיטָם	Ἀπάν	Ἡταμέ
3) תְּקוֹעַ	θεκῶε	θεκωέ
4) בֵּית־צוּר	Βαιθσουρά	Βηθσούρ
5) שׂוֹכוֹ	Σοκχώθ	Σωχώ
6) עֲדֻלָּם	Ὀδολάμ	Ὀδολλάμ
7) גַּת	Γέθ	Εἰπάν
8) מָרֵשָׁה	Μαρεισάν	Μάρισαν
9) זִיף	Ζείβ	Ζιφά
10) אֲדוֹרַיִם	Ἀδωραί	Ἀδωραίμ
11) לָכִישׁ	Λαχείς	Λάχεις
12) עֲזֵקָה	Ἀζηκά	Ἀζηκά
13) צָרְעָה	Σαραά	Σαράμ
14) אַיָּלוֹן	Ἀλδών	Ἡλώμ
15) חֶבְרוֹן	Χεβρών	Χεβρῶνα

In the above listing it is about all the seventh city name where Josephus' form (Εἰπάν) differs most noticeably from that of both MT ("Gath") and B ("Geth"). Scholars have advanced various suppositions regarding the divergence. According to Mar, Josephus' form represents a corrupted doublet of the Ἡταμέ which stands second in his list (see above)[363]. For Schlatter the form is rather a miswriting of an original Γιττα(ν), the name of the Philistine city found in AJ 5,87 etc.[364], while Na and W view it as a scribal error for Ἰπάν (cf. Lat hippam)[365]. In any event, Josephus' full enumeration of the Chronist's 15 names[366] here might seem out of line with his general tendency to abridge or leave aside extended lists of Biblical names (for an instance of this tendency within 8,212-420, see infra on 8,395). On the other hand, in listing the above sites Josephus could reckon with the general geographical interests of his cosmopolitan readers and more particularly with the personal reminiscences of some of these readers who might have passed through one or other of the cities cited during their military service in Rome's Judean war[367].

Chronicles gives a double localization for Rehoboam's cities: "in Judah" (11,5) // "in Judah and Benjamin" (11,10b). In addition to its duplication of the notice of 11,5, the latter indication involves a further

363. Josephus, V, p. 705, n. h; the view of SCHALIT, Namenwörterbuch, p. 41, s.v. Εἰπά is similar.
364. Namen, p. 40, s.v. גת.
365. N avers that it is rather Ἰπάν which is the copyist's mistake for an original Εἰπάν.
366. For more concerning the Josephan forms of the city names in relation to their counterparts in MT and 2 Par, see the notes of Mar, Josephus, V, pp. 704-705, nn. b-o.
367. I owe these suggestions to Prof. L.H. Feldman, private conversation.

difficulty, i.e. whereas according to Biblical data elsewhere, 13 of the cities mentioned are Judean – Zorah and Aijalon belong to Dan[368] – none of them stands within the boundaries of Benjamin. Josephus obviates the difficulty, at least in part. Leaving aside the localization of 11,5, he concludes his city list with the remark, adapted from 11,10, "these, which were in the tribe and territory of Judah (ἐν τῇ ᾽Ιουδαίᾳ φυλῇ καὶ κληρουχίᾳ)[369] he (Rehoboam) built first". He then goes on to state, giving no names: "he also constructed other great cities in Benjamin". With this formulation Josephus (implicitly) "corrects" the "erroneous" indication of 2 Chron 11,10 that some of the 15 cities previously cited lay in Benjamin (even while ignoring the further problem of the Danite site of two of the cities on the above list).

Drawing on, while also embellishing 2 Chron 11,11-12a, Josephus now proceeds to recount Rehoboam's provisioning of his cities: "having walled them about, he set garrisons and captains (ἡγέμονας, 2 Par ἡγουμένους) in all of them and in each of the cities stored much grain (σῖτόν)[370], wine and oil (οἶνον καὶ ἔλαιον)[371] *and an abundance of other things needed for sustenance*, and, in addition to these, shields (θυρεοὺς = 2 Par) and barbed lances (σιρομάστας, 2 Par δόρατα)[372] amounting to many tens of thousands".

2 Chron 11,13-17 relates how Rehoboam's rule was "strengthened" (v. 17) via a double wave of clerical (vv. 13-15) and lay (v. 16) Israelites fleeing Jeroboam's cultic deviations. Josephus compresses this presentation, leaving aside its detailed references to Jeroboam's measures (vv. 14b-15) – these have already been cited by him in dependence on 1 Kings 12,25-31 in 8,225-229 – as well as the duplicate "strengthening notice" of v. 17b; and combining the double Biblical "movement" into one. His abbreviated version of 11,13-17 thus reads:

> Then there came to him (Rehoboam) at Jerusalem priests from among all
> the Israelites (2 Chron 11,13 "who were in all Israel"), and Levites[373] and

368. See W.A.E. ELMSLIE, *The Book of Chronicles* (CB), Cambridge, 1916, p. 212.

369. N prints the words καὶ κληρουχίᾳ of the above phrase within brackets; Na, followed by W, reads ἐν τῇ ᾽Ιούδα κληρουχίᾳ with MSPELat. Cf. *AJ* 6,249 "to the territory of the tribe of Judah" (εἰς τὴν κληρουχίαν τῆς ᾽Ιούδα).

370. Josephus' reference to "grain" here substitutes for the more generic Biblical mention of "food", MT מאכל, 2 Par βρωμάτων.

371. In MT and B 2 Chron 11,11 the sequence is "oil and wine"; Josephus' order above corresponds to that found in the L MSS 19/b' 108/b. The above triad "grain, wine and oil" (always in this order) recurs in *BJ* 1,299 (= *AJ* 14,408); *AJ* 8,144.

372. Also elsewhere Josephus substitutes other terms for LXX's references to δόρατα ("spears"), a word which he employs only a single time in his entire corpus, i.e. *AJ* 6,244, see further below on 8,259.

373. In B 2 Par 11,13 the Levites are mentioned before the priests; Josephus' sequence corresponds to that found in MT and L. On the collocation "priests and Levites" in Josephus, see n. 187.

any others of the people who were good and righteous (ἀγαθοὶ καὶ δίκαιοι)[374] men and had left (καταλιπόντες)[375] their own cities to worship God (θρησκεύσωσιν... τὸν θεὸν)[376] in Jerusalem[377], for they would not submit to being forced to worship (προσκυνεῖν ἀναγκαζόμενοι)[378] the heifers (δαμάλεις, see 8,226)[379] which Jeroboam had made. And they added strength to [Rehoboam's][380] kingdom (2 Chron 11,17a "the kingdom of Judah") for three years[381]. (8,248)

2 Chron 11,18-23 completes the triptych concerning Rehoboam's blessed early reign with mention of the king's flourishing family arrangements. The first part of this sequence provides data on Rehoboam's various wives and his children by them. Specifically, 11,18-20 cites by name two[382] royal wives, i.e. Mahalath (2 Par Μολλάθ etc.) and Maacah (2 Par Μααχὰ) as well as their respective (Davidic) ancestors and children, namely, Rehoboam's three sons by Mahalath and four children by Maacah. Here again, Josephus drastically shortens

374. The collocation "good and righteous" occurs also in *AJ* 1,199 (reverse order); 3,71; 4,144; 6,21.93 (reverse order).147.153; 7,369.386 (reverse order); 9,100.132.216.246; 14,106.

375. Note the verbal echo of 8,225 where Jeroboam is said to fear that his subjects "will desert" (καταλείψει) him, as they now in fact do, in reaction against the calf-cult which he inaugurated precisely to forestall such an eventuality.

376. Here again (see previous note), one is reminded of the account of Jeroboam's measures in 8,225-229. In 8,228 the king informs his people that he has erected the calves in Bethel and Dan in order that they may go there "and worship God" (προσκυνῶσιν... τὸν θεόν). Instead of doing this, however, the "good and righteous" among the Israelites, we read here in 8,248, repair to Jerusalem "to worship God".

The above phrase θρησκεύω + "(the) God" occurs also in *AJ* 3,49 (8,350); 9,260.289.290; 10,63; 12,32 (the Deity); 19,297. Cf. θρησκείας... τοῦ θεοῦ, 8,225 (i.e. in the same account of Jeroboam's measures whose (partial) frustration Josephus records in 8,248).

377. Compare 2 Chron 11,16b "they came to Jerusalem to sacrifice (2 Par θῦσαι) to the Lord the God of their fathers".

378. Josephus uses the above construction "force to worship" in *AJ* 9,98 in reference to the Judean Joram's compelling his people to reverence "strange gods", see also 12,253 (Antiochus "compelled the Jews to reverence [σέβεσθαι] the gods in whom he believed").

379. Josephus' designation here corresponds to that of L 2 Par 11,15. B has rather μόσχοις = MT לעגלים. Note the contrast between Josephus' reference – when speaking in his own name – to the heifers as actual objects of worship here and the statement he earlier attributes to Jeroboam concerning his purposes in installing them at Bethel and Dan, i.e. that his people might go to these sites and "worship (προσκυνῶσιν) *God*", 8,228.

In 2 Chron 11,15 reference is made to additional reprobate objects instituted by Jeroboam, i.e. לשעירים (MT, "satyrs", RSV)/ εἰδώλοις καὶ ... μεταίοις (2 Par). Josephus leaves these aside, perhaps because no previous mention was made of them in either his or Kings' account of Jeroboam's innovations.

380. Mar, *ad loc.*, mistakenly renders "Jeroboam's" here.

381. Josephus lacks an equivalent to the duplicate notice of 2 Chron 11,17b "for they walked for three years in the ways of David and Solomon".

382. The text of 11,18a is problematic. Some witnesses read it as speaking of a third wife, i.e. Abihail, see BHS.

and simplifies. He first alludes, without naming her, to Mahalath as the "kinswoman" (συγγενῆ)[383] whom Rehoboam married and who bore him three (unnamed) children. As for Rehoboam's second wife, Josephus mentions only her first-born son, omitting all reference to her other three children: "(later marrying) Machanē (Μαχάνην)[384] whose mother was Absalom's (Ἀψαλώμου) daughter Thamarē (θαμάρης) and who was also related to him (συγγενῆ). By her he had a son (παῖς ἐξ αὐτῆς ἄρρην αὐτῷ γίνεται)[385] whom he named Abias (Ἀβίαν)[386]".

Next, anticipating the "statistics" of 11,21b (as well as the problematic

383. 2 Chron 11,18 calls her the daughter of David's son Jerimoth, i.e. a cousin of Rehoboam.

384. In 3 Rgns 15,2; 2 Par 11,20-22; 13,2 the woman is called Μααχά (= MT). Regarding the "ν" of Josephus' form, SCHLATTER, Namen, p. 74. s.v. מַעֲכָה notes that the same letter is inserted by him in other Biblical names, see Βασάνης (8,288, 3 Rgns 15,27 βαασὰ = MT) and Ἥλανος (8,307, 3 Rgns 16,8 Ἠλὰ = MT).

385. Compare AJ 7,146 παῖς ἐξ αὐτῆς γίνεται αὐτῷ (David, of Bathsheba). Josephus uses the h.p. of γί(γ)νομαι with παῖς as subject a total of 24 ×. ERIKSSON, Präsens, p. 62 calls the construction "ein allgemeiner Klassizismus".

386. In the above notice it is especially Josephus' statement concerning "Machanē's" parentage which calls for comment. In making her the daughter of "Thamarē" and granddaughter of Absalom, Josephus diverges from the Biblical indications on the matter which, for their part, do not agree among themselves. 1 Kings 15,2 calls the father of "Maacah" "Abishalom" (3 Rgns Ἀβεσ(σ)αλώμ) and 2 Chron 11,20-21 "Absalom" (2 Par Ἀβεσ(σ)αλώμ), while 2 Chron 13,2 makes "Micaiah" (2 Par Μααχά) a daughter of Uriel of Gibeah (2 Par Γαβαών). With his notice here in 8,249 Josephus is not, however, simply at variance with the Biblical data. He likewise appears to deviate (implicitly) from his own earlier indication in AJ 7,190 – itself drawn from the plus in 2 Rgns 14,27 (MT simply speaks of Absalom's begetting Tamar) according to which it was Absalom's daughter – and not rather his granddaughter (so 8,249) who was to become the wife of Rehoboam and mother of "Abias" (note that in 7,190 Josephus, in contrast to B 2 Rgns 14,27, does not mention "Tamar" by name [L designates the figure as "Maaca", harmonizing with 1 Kings 15,2; 2 Chron 11,20-21]).

Pace Mar, Josephus, V, p. 461, n.c., I cannot see that Josephus "resolves" the tension between his statements in 7,190 and 8,249. Nothing suggests that with his reference in the former to the "very beautiful daughter" of "Absalom" who subsequently married Rehoboam and bore "Abias" Josephus has anyone other than Tamar herself in mind, whereas 8,249 explicitly designates rather Machanē, daughter of Thamarē, as Rehoboam's wife and Abias' mother. At most, Josephus' leaving unnamed the daughter of Absalom who will be the wife of Rehoboam and mother of Abias in 7,190 renders the discordance less glaring than it is in B where two different daughters of Absalom, i.e. Tamar (2 Rgns 14,27) and Maaca (3 Rgns 15,2; 2 Par 11,20-21) are explicitly ascribed that role. Here as elsewhere then Josephus sacrifices the internal coherence of his own work to the desire to make room for (divergent) Biblical data. Specifically, having (implicitly) utilized the B reference of 2 Rgns 14,27 with its reference to "Tamar" as wife of Rehoboam and mother of Abias in 7,190, Josephus is subsequently confronted with the problem that in later contexts of the Bible another daughter of Absalom, i.e. Maacah, is introduced in that same role. Faced with this state of affairs, Josephus has recourse to an ad hoc solution in 8,249, i.e. without Biblical warrant he turns "Machanē" into Absalom's "granddaughter" (the foregoing discussion suggests that Josephus was unfamiliar with the L reading "Maaca" in 2 Rgns 14,27 which would have provided him with an easy resolution of the difficulty concerning the identity of Abias' mother).

notice of 11,23bβ about Rehoboam's "seeking a multitude of wives [for whom?]"), Josephus notes that while Rehoboam "had children (τέκνα δὲ εἶχεν)[387] by many other wives, he loved (ἔστερξε, 2 Par 11,21b ἠγάπησεν)[388] Machanē best (μᾶλλον)[389] of all". He then reproduces the "marital statistics" of 11,21b: "Rehoboam had eighteen lawful wives (νόμῳ συνοικούσας αὐτῷ γυναῖκας)[390] and thirty[391] concubines (παλλακὰς = 2 Par)[392], and there were born to him twenty-eight sons and sixty daughters". Finally, Josephus rounds off his account of Rehoboam's domestic situation with the notice, inspired by 2 Chron 11,22, concerning the provisions made by him for the succession: "as his successor (διάδοχον) to the kingdom he appointed (ἀπέδειξε)[393] Abias...". Whereas, however, 2 Chron 11,23abα supplements this notice with mention of the arrangements made by Rehoboam for the benefit of his other sons, Josephus, in line with his consistent focus on ("Machanē" and) "Abias", has the king assign these additional bene-factions to the the latter as well: "(Rehoboam) entrusted to him his treasures (θησαυροὺς... ἐπίστευσεν)[394] and his strongest cities (ὀχυρω-τάτας πόλεις)[395]". Josephus does not, at this point, go on to reproduce the problematic notice of 2 Chron 11,23bβ "he (Rehoboam) sought a multitude of wives (for himself or for his sons?)". Perhaps, however, he has already made (adapted) use of it earlier on in his presentation, see above.

2. *Rehoboam's Defection* (8,251-262). 2 Chron 12,1 makes the transition from Rehoboam's early "good" to his later "bad" period with the brief remark "when the rule of Rehoboam was established... he foresook the law (2 Par commandments, ἐντολὰς) of the Lord and all Israel with him". In Josephus (8,251-253) this summary remark becomes an elab-

---

387. This is the reading of Ed.pr. followed by NaMar. The codd read τέκνα δὲ, while NN* conjecture τεκνοῖ δὲ.

388. Josephus substitutes στέργω for the preferred LXX term for "love", i.e. ἀγαπάω also in *AJ* 6,199 // 1 Sam 18,22 (Saul and the people "love" David). On the latter verb in the LXX, see: S.P. SWINN, ἀγαπᾶν *in the Septuagint*, in T. MURAOKA (ed.), *Melbourne Symposium on Septuagint Lexicography* (SBL SCS, 28), Atlanta, 1990, 49-82.

389. Josephus uses the construction στέργω μᾶλλον elsewhere in *AJ* 6,58 (Saul, Abner his cousin) and 12,195 (Joseph, his son Hyrcanus).

390. The above phrase "lawful wives" recurs (in the sg.) in *AJ* 1,208 (Sarah, Abraham's "lawful wife"), cf. 5,531.

391. Josephus' figure for Rehoboam's "concubines" here corresponds to that of B 2 Par 11,21 (and VL). MT (and most LXX MSS) read "sixty".

392. RO omits the reference to Rehoboam's concubines. Josephus uses the term παλλακή 13 ×. The above collocation "wives and concubines" occurs also in *BJ* 7,247 (Pacorus of Media); *AJ* 7,70 (David); 8,193 (Solomon).

393. The above construction "appoint (as) successor" occurs also in *AJ* 9,45; 18,224.

394. The above phrase "entrust treasures" recurs in *BJ* 4,410.

395. Cf. πόλεις ὀχυράς, 8,246; compare 2 Par 11,23 ἐν ταῖς πόλεσιν ταῖς ὀχυραῖς.

orate reflection on the underlying factors in the defection, first of king and then of people of Judah in their entirety[396]:

But often, I think, a cause (αἴτιον) of men's falling into evil ways (κακῶν) and lawlessness (παρανομίας)[397] lies in the greatness of their affairs (τὸ τῶν πραγμάτων μέγεθος)[398] and in the improvement of their position (ἡ πρὸς τὸ βέλτιον[399] αὐτῶν τροπή[400])[401]. So, for example, Roboamos, seeing how greatly his kingdom had increased in strength (τὴν... βασιλείαν αὐξανομένην, see ηὔξησαν τὴν... βασιλείαν, 8,248), was misled (ἐξετράπη)[402] into unjust (ἀδίκους) and impious (ἀσεβεῖς)[403] acts (πράξεις)[404] and showed disrespect (κατεφρόνησεν)[405] for the worship of God (τῆς τοῦ θεοῦ θρησκείας, 8,225), so that even the people under his rule began to imitate (μιμητὴν γενέσθαι)[406] his unlawful deeds (ἀνομημάτων)[407]. For the morals (ἤθη) of subjects are corrupted simultaneously (συνδιαφθείρεται)[408] with the characters (τρόποις) of their rulers, and they do not allow their own moderation (σωφροσύνην)[409] to remain

396. Compare the interpolated explanation of how it was that Jeroboam did not turn from his evil ways after his encounter with Jadōn in 8,243-245a.

397. Compare the verbal form παρανομέω used of Jeroboam in 8,245. Josephus employs the noun παρανομία 64 ×. The above collocation "evil (ways)" and "lawlessness" occurs only here in Josephus.

398. Josephus uses the construction "greatness of affairs" also in BJ 7,85 (139); AJ 1,3.126 2,12; 9,223 (here in a context similar to that of 8,251); (16,306).

399. The above phrase occurs only here in Josephus. He uses the term βελτίων 15 ×.

400. N conjectures ῥοπή, a proposal not taken over by N*.

401. The above reference to prosperity provoking a hubris which in turn calls forth divine chastisement (for which see the continuation of the text) exemplifies the operation of the well-known sequence of Greek tragedy, which, as FELDMAN, Mikra, p. 500, notes, Josephus applies up as operative in other episodes of his history, e.g., the Tower of Babel episode, AJ 1,103-119. On the subject, see further: ATTRIDGE, Interpretation, pp. 119-126 ("The Analysis of Moral Decay") and for Herodotus' use of the same schema in presenting events, J.G. GAMMIE, Herodotus on Kings and Tyrants: Objective Historiography or Conventional Portraiture?, in JNES 45 (1986) 171-195, esp. pp. 175-176.

402. Josephus uses ἐκτρέπω 14 ×. On the term, see SPICQ, Lexicographie, I, pp. 235-236.

403. Josephus uses the adjectival combination "unjust and impious" only here.

404. Josephus uses the phrase "impious acts" of Jeroboam in 8,245.

405. Josephus uses καταφρονέω 107 ×; only here in 8,251, however, does it have "worship of God" (see above in the text) as (genitival) object.

406. Josephus uses the construction μιμητὴς γινέσθαι also in AJ 1,109; 4,151.154; 9,99.173; 12,203; 17,97; Ap 2,270. With Josephus' reference to the "imitation" which a king's conduct provokes on the part of his subjects here, compare the similar remarks in Ecphantus' Treatise on Kingship (277,9-11; 278,10-11), DELATTE, Royauté, pp. 34-35.

407. Josephus uses ἀνομήμα 2 × elsewhere: AJ 8,289; 14,309.

408. Josephus' other uses of συνδιαφθείρω are: BJ 4,257; AJ 2,296; 4,140; 9,167.

409. Josephus uses this key term of Greek ethics 19 ×. On it see: G. LUCK, σώφρων κτλ, in TWNT 7 (1964) 1094-1102; SPICQ, Lexicographie, II, pp. 867-874; FELDMAN, Mikra, pp. 491-492.

(παραπέμποντες)[410] a reproach (ἔλεγχον)[411] to their rulers' intemperance (ἀσελγείας)[412] but follow their evil ways (κακίαις) as if they were virtues (ἀρετῇ)[413], since it is impossible to show approval of the acts of kings except by doing as they do. This, then, was the case with the people governed by Roboamos, who, when he acted impiously (ἀσεβοῦντος, see ἀσεβεῖς, 8,251)[414] and in violation of the laws (παρανομοῦντος, see παρανομίας, 8,251), were careful not to give offence to the king (προσκρούσωσι τῷ βασιλεῖ)[415] by wishing to be righteous (δίκαιοι).

2 Chron 12,2 records that Pharoah Shishak advanced against Jerusalem in Rehoboam's fifth year "because they had been unfaithful to the Lord"[416]. Josephus begins his version of this notice with a more direct reference to the divine impetus behind Pharoah's move: "as an avenger (τιμωρὸν)[417] of the outrage (ὕβρεων)[418] to Him, God sent (ἐπιπέμπει)[419]...". Concerning God's agent "Isōkos" (Ἴσωκον)[420], he notes, anticipating a later discussion (see 8,260-262), that Herodotus "was in error" (πλανηθεὶς) in ascribing his deeds to another king, i.e. "Sesōstris" (Σεσώστρει)[421]. Josephus then reproduces the indications of 2 Chron 12,2-3 concerning the date of Shishak's advance and the forces accompanying him: "... in the fifth year of Roboamos' reign (πέμπτῳ

410. This is the only instance in Josephus where παραπέμπω has the above meaning (W, *ad loc.*, "renoncer"). The usual meaning of its 13 other uses is "escort" (see, e.g., *AJ* 2,42).

411. 28 × in Josephus.

412. 10 × in Josephus.

413. The above terms "vice" and "virtue(s)" are juxtaposed also in *BJ* 2,156; 4,325.387; *AJ* 17,101.246; 18,14; *Ap* 2,145.

414. The verb ἀσεβέω occurs 33 × in Josephus.

415. The phrase "give offence to the king" recurs in *AJ* 10,212.217.

416. This motivation for Shishak's advance is lacking in the parallel text, 1 Kings 14,25.

417. This is the only occurrence of the substantive τιμωρός in *AJ*; it occurs 4 × in *BJ*: 1,378; 3,239; 4,264.361.

418. Josephus employs ὕβρις 111 ×. Cf. the verbal composite form used of Jeroboam in 8,245.

419. Elsewhere this h.p. form occurs in *BJ* 3,299.346; *AJ* 2,13. 224. Josephus uses ἐπιπέμπω with divine subject(s) also in *AJ* 1,118 ("the gods send winds", quotation from the Sibylline Oracles); 2,13 (the Deity "sends" Joseph a second vision); 14,28 (God "sends" a mighty and violent wind).

420. MSPE read Σούσακον here, followed by NaW. This monarch is mentioned several times previously by Josephus with a variety of forms of his name appearing in the text, i.e.: *BJ* 6,436 (Ἀσωχαῖος); *AJ* 7,105 (// the plus of 2 Rgns 8,7, Σούσακος, i.e. the variant reading in 8,253) and 8,210 (// 1 Kings 11,40, Ἴσακον).

421. Compare *AJ* 10,19 where Josephus avers that the same Herodotus (see 10,18) "was in error" (πλανᾶται) in calling Sennacherib "king of the Arabs" rather than of the Assyrians. Cf. further *Ap* 1,16 (Herodotus' mendacity is exposed "by everybody") and 73 (Manetho "convicts Herodotus of being misled through ignorance on many points of Egyptian history" – here Josephus adduces a "pagan precedent" for his own venturing to critique the inaccuracies of Herodotus). Other instances of Josephus' criticizing earlier historians for their mistakes are cited by STERLING, *Historiography*, p. 244.

ἔτει τῆς 'Ροβοάμου βασιλείας)⁴²² Isōkos marched against him (ἐπιστρατεύεται⁴²³... αὐτῷ, cf. 2 Par ἀνέβη... ἐπὶ 'Ιερουσαλήμ) with many tens of thousands⁴²⁴, and there followed him one thousand two hundred chariots, sixty thousand horsemen (ἱππέων)⁴²⁵ and four hundred thousand foot-soldiers (πεζῶν)⁴²⁶". According to 2 Chron 12,3bβ Shishak's force comprised three groups of peoples, i.e. Libyans, Sukkiim⁴²⁷ and Ethiopians. Josephus passes over the second of these groups, even while using a formulation that seems to evidence awareness of the source's mention of them: "*most of these men*... were Libyans and Ethiopians (Αἰθίοπας)⁴²⁸".

Josephus amplifies 2 Chron 12,4's mention of Shishak's capture of the Judean strongholds and subsequent advance on the capital: "invading the country (ἐμβαλὼν... εἰς τὴν χώραν)⁴²⁹ of the Hebrews ('Εβραίων)⁴³⁰, he seized (καταλαμβάνεται, compare 2 Par κατεκράτησαν)⁴³¹ the strongest cities (τὰς ὀχυρωτάτας... πόλεις, see 8,250, compare 2 Par 12,4 τῶν πόλεων τῶν ὀχυρῶν) of Roboamos's kingdom *without a battle* (ἀμαχητὶ)⁴³² and, *having secured these with garrisons*

422. Compare 2 Par 12,2 ἐν τῷ πέμπτῳ ἔτει τῆς βασιλείας 'Ροβοάμ.
423. In *AJ* 13,357 Josephus uses the equivalent active h.p. form ἐπιστρατεύει.
424. Compare 2 Chron 12,3bα "the people (2 Par πλῆθους) were without number who came with him (Shishak)", cf. n. 426.
425. Josephus' reference to Shishak's "horsemen" here corresponds to the reading of MT and L etc. in 2 Chron 12,3a. 2 Par B speaks rather of "horses" (ἵππων).
426. This last datum has nothing corresponding to it as such in the source which gives precise figures only for Shishak's chariots and horse(men), cf., however, the reference to the "countless people" accompanying Shishak in 12,3bα, and n. 424.
Also elsewhere Josephus evidences the tendency to provide "exact" figures where the Bible itself does not, see DRÜNER, *Untersuchungen*, pp. 36-42; S.J.D. COHEN, *Josephus in Galilee and Rome. His Vita and his Development as an Historian* (Columbia Studies in the Classical Tradition, 8), Leiden, 1979, p. 38 and FELDMAN, *David*, p. 144 for listings of examples (Feldman points out that Josephus' aim in introducing these "precisions" is to lend his presentation a heightened air of reliability). With 8,254 compare particularly *AJ* 6,97 where, in place of 1 Sam 13,5's reference to the Philistine infantry who advanced against Saul "like the sand on the seashore in multitude", Josephus specifies that the Philistine "foot-soldiers" (πεζῶν, so 8,254) numbered 300,000. See too *AJ* 6,129 // 1 Sam 14,47; 7,127 // 2 Sam 10,16.
427. Thus the MT reading which L transliterates. B has τρωγοδύται which the editors emend to Τρωγλοδύται.
428. This accusative form corresponds to B's nominative Αἰθίοπες. L's Χουσιειμ is a translation of MT כשים.
429. Josephus uses the above construction "invade the country" also in *BJ* 1,21.25.38; *AJ* 2,239; 6,135.271 (355); 9,8.38.170; *Ap* 1,34.
430. Here the term "Hebrews" is clearly used in the "restricted" sense of "Judeans", see also n. 198.
431. So MSPE followed by Mar. NN*Na read καταλαμβάνει τε with RO. Elsewhere (see *BJ* 2,515; 4,645; *AJ* 12,343; 14,160; 20,133) Josephus uses the active h.p. of καταλαμβάνω (i.e. the RO reading in 8,255) in reference to the "capture" of a city, etc.
432. Josephus introduces this (Biblically unparalleled) specification with a view to his subsequent utilization/critique of Herodotus' account of the conquests of "Sesōstris", see below.

(ἀσφαλισάμενος)⁴³³, at last advanced against Jerusalem (ἐπῆλθε τοῖς Ἱεροσολύμοις, cf. 2 Par ἦλθεν εἰς Ἱερουσαλήμ)⁴³⁴".

2 Chron 12,5 next speaks of the sudden appearance of a "prophet", i.e. Shemaiah (2 Par Σαμ(μ)αίας) before the king and the "princes" (2 Par ἄρχοντας) of Judah who had gathered (2 Par συναχθέντας) at Jerusalem because of Shishak...". Josephus reverses the order of these two elements: it is to Rehoboam "and the multitude (τοῦ πλήθους)"⁴³⁵ who are "shut up (ἐγκεκλεισμένου)... by the advance of Isōkos's army" that "the prophet Samaias (ὁ δὲ⁴³⁶ προφήτης Σαμαίας⁴³⁷) said...". Between the two elements of this notice he interposes the following item: "although they entreated God (τὸν θεὸν ἱκετευόντων, see 8,234) to grant (δοῦναι) them victory and deliverance (νίκην καὶ σωτηρίαν)⁴³⁸, they did not (οὐκ)⁴³⁹ prevail upon God (ἔπεισαν τὸν θεὸν)⁴⁴⁰ to side with them (ταχθῆναι μετ᾽ αὐτῶν)⁴⁴¹". Via this interjected note Josephus renders the prophet's appearance less abrupt, just as he intimates the content of the subsequent prophetic word: Shemaiah comes forward to convey God's (negative) response to the assembly's preceding appeal.

The prophet's word that now follows in 2 Chron 12,5b is a kind of talion-formula: "... you abandoned (B ἐνκατελίπετε, L ἐγκατελείψατε)

433. Josephus uses ἀσφαλίζω 15 ×.

434. With a city as object the verb ἐπέρχομαι is used by Josephus also in BJ 3,132; AJ 8,142.266.303; 14,272; Vita 193; Ap 1,264.

435. Josephus makes the "multitude" rather than the "princes of Judah" the (co-) addressees of Shemaiah's word to Rehoboam, perhaps on the reflection that the people who had shared in Rehoboam's sin (see 2 Chron 12,2 // AJ 8,251-252) should also be explicitly associated with him in its sequels.

436. N conjectures γάρ with reference to Lat "enim". N* passes over this conjecture.

437. Josephus' form of the prophet's name corresponds to the majority reading of 2 Par 12,5. B reads Σαμμαίας.

Shemaiah is the same prophet who in 1 Kings 12,21-24 // 2 Chron 11,1-4 admonishes Rehoboam not to advance against Jeroboam. Recall that in his version of that incident in 8,223 Josephus, at least according to the witness of codd, leaves the prophet nameless, see n. 130.

438. With this whole formulation compare AJ 13,168 where Josephus quotes Jonathan's letter to the Spartans from 1 Maccabees 12: "we continue to entreat (παρακαλοῦμεν) Him (God) for your well-being (σωτηρίας) and victory (νίκης)". See too 14,136 where "victory" and salvation" are also collocated.

Elsewhere Josephus uses the above expression "to grant victory" (with God as subject) also in AJ 5,159; 6,82.145; 7,109; 8,382.401; 9,14;12,316. He does not elsewhere use the phrase "to grant salvation".

439. So SP followed by NaMar. NN* read ἀλλ᾽ οὐκ with ROM.

440. This accusatival construction occurs also in AJ 4,123 (Balaam hopes to "persuade God"), cf. the equivalent datival phrase in AJ 7,122;8,4. K.O. SANDES, Paul – One of the Prophets? A Contribution to the Apostle's Self-Understanding (WUNT, 2/43), Tübingen, 1991, p. 55 points to the parallel construction in Gal 1,10 ἄρτι γὰρ ἀνθρώπους πείθω ἢ τὸν θεόν.

441. Josephus uses the above middle form of τάσσω along with the preposition μετά (= "to side with") also in BJ 4,328; AJ 8,10.

me, so I will abandon (2 Par ἐνκαταλείψω) you...". Once again
substituting indirect for direct address and reversing the Biblical
sequence, Josephus renders Shemaiah's announcement as follows:
"God threatened to abandon (ἐγκαταλείψειν, cf. L)[442] them just as
they had abandoned their worship of Him (τὴν θρησκείαν αὐτοῦ
κατέλιπον, cf. τοῦ θεοῦ θρησκείας κατεφρόνησεν, 8,251)[443]".

According to 2 Chron 12,6 Shemaiah's word evokes a self-humbling
on the part of Rehoboam and the "princes of Israel" (compare 12,5
"princes of Judah"), expressed in their confession "the Lord is righteous (2 Par δίκαιος)". Josephus amplifies significantly. Not only does
he expatiate on the hearers' confession, he also introduces a reference
to the psychological state prompting them to make it:

> when they heard this, their spirits at once fell (ταῖς ψυχαῖς... ἀνέπεσον)[444],
> and, no longer seeing any (hope of) deliverance (σωτήριον, see 8,255), they
> all hastened to acknowledge (ἐξομολογεῖσθαι)[445] that God might justly
> (δικαίως, cf. 2 Par 12,6 δίκαιος) turn away (ὑπερόψεται)[446] from them
> since they had acted impiously towards Him (γενομένους περὶ αὐτὸν
> ἀσεβεῖς)[447] and had violated His ordinances (συγχέοντας τὰ νόμιμα)[448].

2 Chron 12,7-8 records the Lord's response to the assembly's self-
humbling:

> When the Lord saw that they humbled themselves, the word of the Lord
> came to Shemaiah: "They have humbled themselves; I will not destroy
> them, but I will grant them some deliverance and my wrath shall not be
> poured out upon Jerusalem by the hand of Shishak. Nevertheless, they
> shall be servants to him, that they may know my service and the service of
> the kingdoms of the countries".

Josephus adapts: God "sees" (κατιδὼν, 2 Par ἐν τῷ ἰδεῖν)[449] them "in
this state of mind and confessing their sins" (τὰς ἁμαρτίας ἀνθομολο-
γουμένους)[450]. The *Wortereignisformel* of 12,7aβ becomes "he (God)

442. With God as subject the verb ἐγκαταλείπω recurs in *AJ* 6,334 (passive, Saul has
been "abandoned" by God); 11,169 (God "does not give up [ἐγκαταλείποντα] His
providential care of us"). On the term, see SPICQ, *Lexicographie*, I, pp. 223-226.
443. Elsewhere Josephus uses the above construction "abandon the worship of God"
also in *AJ* 8,270 (see below); 11,182; 12,384.
444. The above construction recurs in *BJ* 4,50; *AJ* 8,282 (see below), cf. *AJ* 6,24.329.
445. Elsewhere Josephus uses the verb ἐξομολογέω in *BJ* 1,625; 2,602; 5,145.443; *AJ*
8,129; 16,156.
446. Josephus uses ὑπεροράω with God/the Deity as subject also in *AJ* 6,307;12,281.
447. The above construction "be impious towards" recurs in *AJ* 5,339 (subject: Eli's
sons); 9,172 (Joas).243 (Ahaz); 12,385 (Menelaus).
448. The above construction "violate ordinances" occurs also in *AJ* 13,243 in reference
to Antiochus Epiphanes.
449. It is only here in 8,257 that Josephus uses κατεῖδον with God as subject.
450. Josephus' only other use of the verb ἀνθομολογέομαι is in the similar construction he employs in reference to Ahab in *AJ* 8,362 ἀνθομολογούμενός τε τὰ ἡμαρτημένα.

said to the prophet" (εἶπε πρὸς τὸν προφήτην)⁴⁵¹. Of the divine words in 12,7b, he retains only God's promise not to "destroy" the people⁴⁵². Conversely, Josephus reproduces the continuation of the Deity's speech from 12,8 *in extenso*: "(God) would make them subject (ποιήσειν... ὑποχειρίους, compare 2 Par ἔσονται εἰς παῖδας)⁴⁵³ to the Egyptians, in order that they might learn (μάθωσι, 2 Par γνώσονται) which was the easier task, whether to serve (δουλεύειν, 2 Par τὴν δουλείαν) man or God (θεῷ)⁴⁵⁴".

2 Chron 12,9 (// 1 Kings 14,25-26) relates Shishak's despoliation of Jerusalem, moving somewhat abruptly from the fact of his coming up against the city to his "taking" of its treasures. Josephus "fills the gap" by citing various intermediate developments: "*when Isakōs took the city without a battle* (παραλαβὼν... ἀμαχητὶ [see 8,255] τὴν πόλιν)⁴⁵⁵, *Roboamos admitting him* (δεξαμένου) *because he feared him* (διὰ τὸν φόβον), *he did not abide* (ἐνέμεινε) *by the terms of the agreement* (συνθήκαις)⁴⁵⁶ *they had made*, but sacked the temple (ἐσύλησε τὸ ἱερὸν)⁴⁵⁷". These added indications serve to prepare Josephus' subsequent "correction" of Herodotus' account of "Sesōstris", see below. They likewise foreshadow later (also interpolated) Josephan descriptions of enemy actions against Jerusalem⁴⁵⁸. Following the above expansion, Josephus continues with the content of 2 Chron 12,9bα: "he

451. This same formula occurs as well in *AJ* 8,362 (of Elijah).

452. 2 Par uses καταφθερῶ, Josephus ἀπολέσειν in this connection. Conceivably, Josephus found the further divine word in 12,7b, i.e. "I will grant them some deliverance and my wrath shall not be poured out upon Jerusalem by the hand of Shishak" incommensurate with the subsequent course of the narrative in which Jerusalem is, in fact, thoroughly despoiled by Shishak, and so omitted it.

With God's promise "not to destroy them" here in 8,257, compare *AJ* 10,60 where Huldah states that the Deity has already given his sentence ἀπολέσαι τὸν λαόν. Other Josephan uses of ἀπολλύω/μι with God as subject are *AJ* 1,99.250 (passive).

453. Elsewhere Josephus uses the above construction "make subject" with God as (implicit) subject also in *AJ* 1,181;8,373 (see below);9,266, cf. 6,183;8,161.

454. Elsewhere Josephus uses δουλεύω with God as (datival) object also in *BJ* 7,323 (the Massada defenders resolve to "serve no one but God");*AJ* 7,367 (the Levites and priests serve God), cf. "servant(s) of God", *AJ* 5,39;11,90.161. On the relative paucity of the phrase "serve God" in Josephus, see SCHLATTER, *Gott*, p. 12; idem, *Theologie*, pp. 49-50.

455. Josephus' formulation here is reminiscent of that of Herodotus in *Histories* 2,102 concerning "Sesōstris": ... ἀμαχητὶ... παρέλαβε τὰς πόλιας.... See further below.

456. συνθήκη occurs 39× in Josephus as one of his substitutes for διαθήκη, see further n. 609. A. PAUL, *Flavius Josephus' "Antiquities of the Jews": An Anti-Christian Manifesto*, in *NTS* 31 (1985) 473-480, p. 474 is thus incorrect in his statement that συνθήκη is "never employed by Josephus".

457. Elsewhere when the reference is to the "sacking" of the Temple, Josephus uses rather ναός, see *BJ* 1,32; *AJ* 10,144.145.275; 11,10.91; 12,357, see *BJ* 7,44 (τὸν νεών). In 12,358 the ἱερὸν which Antiochus plots to "sack" is that of Artemis in Persia.

458. See *AJ* 10,2-4 (Sennacherib violates his earlier agreement to withdraw from Jerusalem).96-97 (Jehoiakim "receives" Nebuchadnezzar into Jerusalem "out of fear" only to have the Babylonian renege on his pledges). 100-101 (Nebuchadnezzar disregards his promises to Jehoiachin about sparing the city).

emptied the treasuries of God and the king (τοὺς θησαυροὺς ἐξεκένωσε τοῦ θεοῦ καὶ τοὺς βασιλικούς)⁴⁵⁹". To this he appends
a further notice about Pharoah's "carrying off (βαστάσας) untold
amounts (ἀναριθμήτους)⁴⁶⁰ of gold (χρουσοῦ) and silver (ἀργύρου)⁴⁶¹". Following this interjected item, he picks up the generalizing
conclusion of 12,9ba, i.e. "leaving nothing behind".

In accordance with 2 Chron 12,9bβ Josephus next speaks of a
particular despoliation perpetrated by Shishak, namely his removing
the golden "shields" (θυρεούς = 2 Par) fabricated by Solomon. The
Chronistic notice, in turn, is itself a reminiscence of 2 Chron 9,15b (≅ 1
Kings 10,16), cited by Josephus in 8,179, which concerns Solomon's
making of these "shields" (2 Par θυρεούς)⁴⁶². Inspired now by the
Chronist's additional reference in 2 Chron 9,16a (= 1 Kings 10,17,
reproduced in 8,180) regarding the "bucklers" (2 Par ἀσπίδας)⁴⁶³ made
by Solomon, Josephus here in 8,259 goes beyond 2 Chron 12,9bβ in
mentioning Shishak's removal of these objects as well.

Up till this point, Josephus seems to draw (exclusively) on the
Chronistic version for his account of Shishak's depredations. Now,
however, in terminating his enumeration of the Egyptian's booty, he
makes use of the (Chronistically unparalleled) plus at the end of 3 Rgns
14,26 "... and the golden spears (δόρατα) which David took (ἔλαβε)
from the hand of the servants (παίδων) of Adraazar king of Souba
(Σουβὰ) and brought to Jerusalem, even all that he took...". Josephus
words the item as follows: "nor did he (Shishak) overlook the golden
quivers (φαρέτρας, 3 Rgns δόρατα)⁴⁶⁴ which David had set up as an
offering to God (ἅς ἀνέθηκε Δαυίδης τῷ θεῷ)⁴⁶⁵ after taking (λαβὼν, 3
Rgns ἔλαβε) them from the king⁴⁶⁶ of Sophēnē (Σωφηνῆς)⁴⁶⁷". This

459. Josephus uses a very similar phrase in reference to the action of Joas of Judah
when confronted with the Syrian advance against Jerusalem in *AJ* 9,170: πάντας
ἐκκενώσας τοὺς τοῦ θεοῦ θησαυροὺς καὶ τοὺς τῶν βασιλείων. Compare 2 Par 12,9
ἔλαβεν τοὺς θησαυροὺς τοὺς ἐν οἴκῳ κυρίου καὶ τοὺς θησαυροὺς τοὺς ἐν οἴκῳ τοῦ
βασιλέως.

460. Josephus' other uses of the adjective ἀναρίθμητος are in *AJ* 7,58; 17,21.

461. Compare *AJ* 9,79 (the lepers) "carried off (ἐβάστασαν)... much gold (χρυσὸν)"
from the Syrian camp. Note too Josephus' use of the verb βαστάζω in connection with
subsequent despoliations of the Temple: *AJ* 10,145 (here collocated with συλάω as in
8,256).146; 12,250; 14,105.

462. In 3 Rgns 10,16 the reference is rather to "spears" (δόρατα).

463. B 3 Rgns 10,17 has ὅπλα, "weapons"; L reads θυρεοὺς, "shields".

464. Cf. above on *AJ* 8,247 where for the δόρατα of 2 Par 11,11 Josephus substitutes
σιρομάστας.

465. Josephus employs the above phrase "set up as an offering to God" also in *BJ*
1,357; *AJ* 3,219; 5,347; 6,10.133.192.244; 7,108; 12,47; 14,488, cf. 10,154 (object: "their
own [Babylonian] gods").

466. Note that Josephus does not here take over the name of this king (i.e. "Adraazar") cited in 3 Rgns 14,26; on the reasons for this omission, see below. Elsewhere,
Josephus does reproduce the Biblical mentions of the ruler in question under the name
"Adrazaros", see *AJ* 7,99 (// 2 Sam 8,3 ["Hadadezer", MT].105b (// 2 Sam 8,8).107 (*bis* //
2 Sam 8,9-10);8,204 (// 1 Kings 11,23). Thus the name was certainly not unknown to him.

467. Compare 3 Rgns 14,26 which designates Adraazar's country as "Souba" (Σουβὰ).

concluding notice in 8,259, in turn, represents the "fufillment" of Josephus' announcement in 7,104-105 which itself reflects the expanded (see the underlined sentence below) 2 Rgns 8,7 form of 2 Sam 8,7 (// 1 Chron (Par) 18,7) concerning the booty dedicated by David and its subsequent fate, compare:

2 Rgns 8,7	*AJ 7,104-105*
And David took the golden bracelets (χλιδῶνας, MT Kings/ Chron שׁלטי הזהב, 2 Par κλοιοὺς) which were on the servants (παίδων) of Adrazaar king of Souba, and brought them to Jerusalem. *And Susakim* (Σουσακὶμ) *king of Egypt took them, when he went up to Jerusalem in the days of Roboam...*	The gold quivers (παρέτρας, see 8,259) *and the suits of armour* (πανοπλίας) which the bodyguards (σωματοφύλακες) of Adados (Ἀδάδου) wore, he dedicated to God (ἀνέθηκε τῷ θεῷ, see 8,259) in Jerusalem. These were afterwards taken by the Egyptian king Susakos (Σούσακος), who marched against David's grandson Roboamos and carried off much other wealth from Jerusalem. But these things we shall narrate when we come to their proper place.

I note the following concerning the two sets of parallel texts 2 Rgns 8,7 // *AJ* 7,104-105 and 3 Rgns 14,26 // 8,259 as cited above. Both Josephan passages speak of "quivers" seized by David and later confiscated by Shishak, whereas the two Rgns passages diverge on this score, 2 Rgns 8,7 mentioning "bracelets", 3 Rgns 14,26 rather "spears". Here then, Josephus evidences a concern with "aligning" *Vorverweis* and "fulfillment". On the other hand, in 7,104 Josephus introduces a reference to "suits of armour" also taken by David which has nothing corresponding to it in either 2 Rgns 8,7 (the source text) or his own fulfillment notice, 8,259 (see n. 469). Similarly, in 7,104 Josephus cites a different group of persons as the source of the objects dedicated by David, i.e. the "bodyguards of *Adados*" than do either 2 Rgns 8,7 (the "servants of Adrazaar king of Souba") or his own 8,259 (the [unnamed] "king of Sophēnē").

The (ultimate) inspiration for Josephus' allusion to "Adados" in 7,104 is obviously 2 Sam 8,5-6 // 1 Chron 18,5-6, i.e. verses immediately preceding 2 Sam (Rgns) 8,7 // 1 Chron 18,7, his (primary) source in

---

Apart from 8,259 Josephus cites the name "Sophēnē" also in 7,99 (// 2 Sam 8,3 [Zobah, 2 Rgns Souba]); 8,204 (// 1 Kings 11,23 [Zobah, 3 Rgns Souba]), while in 6,129 he denotes the same country as Σωβᾶς (t.e.; codd ὠβᾶς). According to Mar, *Josephus*, V, p. 411, n.f., Josephus in 7,99 etc. confuses the Biblical place name "Zobah" (so MT) with the Greek name of a district in Armenia, i.e. "Sophēnē". SCHALIT, *Namenwörterbuch*, p. 117, s.v. Σωβᾶ opines that all three occurrences of "Sophēnē" in Josephus are secondary distortions of an original Σωβᾶ, see 6,129.

7,104-105, which speak, in general terms, of David's subduing "the Syrians" (so MT, 2 Rgns "Syria") who had come to the assistance of "Hadadezer" (so MT) of Zobah. Josephus gives his parallel to these preceding Biblical notices in 7,100 where he introduces a specific, Biblically unparalleled mention of "Adados, king of Damascus and Syria" as David's antagonist. Very likely, Josephus derived the name of Syria's king here (and in 7,104) from the historian Nicolas of Damascus seeing that in 7,101-103 he introduces an extended quotation from that authority which begins precisely with the words "this king (i.e. the just-cited Adados) is also mentioned by Nicolas in the fourth book of his history...". Why though does Josephus deviate from the datum of his Biblical source(s) in making the "bodyguards of *Adados* (of Syria)" rather than "the servants of Hadadezer (of Zobah)" those from whom David takes the objects he dedicates? I suggest that he does so under the influence of the overall sequence of his account of David's conquests as compared to the Biblical one(s). In 2 Samuel 8 // 1 Chronicles 18, the sequence is as follows: David defeats Hadadezer of Zobah (2 Sam 8,3-4 // 1 Chron 18,3-4). Next, he subjugates the Syrians (8,5-6 // 18,5-6). Thereupon, the Biblical presentations suddenly revert to Hadadezer in order to mention the booty David takes from him (8,7 // 18,7). Josephus eliminates this unexpected return to the subject of David's measures against the defeated Hadadezer[468] by transferring to "Adados" that despoliation to which in 2 Sam 8,7 // 1 Chron 18,7 "(the servants of) Hadadezer" fall victim. In so doing the historian has perhaps been influenced by some such notice he read in Nicolas[469]. But then, having thus based himself on Nicolas' presentation in 7,(100-103)104-105, Josephus, when he comes to relate the fulfillment (see 8,259) of his announcement in 7,105, makes, under the influence of 3 Rgns 14,26 (and 2 Rgns 8,7) an implicit "correction" of his statement in 7,104, now referring to David's having taken the "quivers", not from Adados (of Syria), but from the "king of Sophēnē". In so proceeding, he employs his standard equivalent, i.e. "Sophēnē" for the LXX place name "Souba" (see n. 467), just as he attenuates the discrepancy between his own two texts by leaving "the king of Sophēnē" unnamed in 8,259 (compare 2 Rgns 8,7 and 3 Rgns 14,26 both of which do mention "Adraazar" by name)[470]. Finally to be noted is that in his

468. Note, however, that, drawing on 2 Sam 8,8 // 1 Chron 18,8 Josephus does re-introduce "Adrazaros" in 7,105b where he relates David's capture and plunder of that king's leading cities.

469. Conceivably too, Josephus' Biblically unparalleled reference to "suits of armour" among the booty taken by David from the Syrians in 7,104 derives from this same source.

470. A similar instance of "implicit correction" was noted above in 8,249 as compared with 7,190 in connection with the question of the name of the wife of Rehoboam who bore him Abias. In that case too the discrepancy between the earlier and latter text is attenuated due to the fact that one of them omits use of a proper name: 7,190 does not name "Tamar", just as 8,259 leaves the "king of Sophēnē" anonymous.

version of 2 Rgns 8,7 in 7,105 Josephus "sets up" Shishak's initiative still more explicitly with his appended concluding formula "but these things we shall narrate when we come to their proper place".

In 2 Chron 12,10-11 (// 1 Kings 14,27-28) the Chronicler proceeds immediately to speak of the replacement objects that Rehoboam confects in place of those seized by Shishak and the use made of these. Josephus "interrupts" this sequence of "despoliation" and "replacement" with an extended series of appended notes without Biblical parallel. This "interlude" opens with mention of Shishak's "returning to his own country"[471]. There next follows a lengthy "parenthesis" (8,260-262) devoted to a critique of some statements of Herodotus in his *Histories* 2,102ff.[472] (recall the foreshadowing of this in 8,253) which, Josephus will try to show, contain garbled reminiscences concerning the Jews that, as such, provide the extra-Biblical confirmation of his people's history he is at pains to adduce throughout his work wherever possible. The critique begins with Josephus reiterating his contention (see 8,253) that Herodotus misidentifies the Pharoah whose deeds he is recording in 2,102ff.[473]. Herodotus, according to Josephus, was also in error, however, concerning the identity of those whom the Egyptian subjugated. In formulating this last charge, he first conflates elements of *Histories* 2,102.106 as follows: "(Herodotus erred) is saying that he (Sesōstris/Isōkos) marched against many other nations (ἄλλοις τε πολλοῖς... ἔθνεσι... compare 2,102 πᾶν ἔθνος) and reduced Palestinian Syria (Παλαιστίνην Συρίαν, compare 2,106 ἐν... τῇ Παλαιστίνη Συρίη) to slavery after capturing the inhabitants without a battle (ἀμαχητὶ, so 2,102)[474]". Having thus "quoted" the relevant statements of Herodotus, Josephus proceeds to a critical commentary upon them:

---

471. Note that in some witnesses 3 Rgns 14,26 does conclude "he (Shishak) brought them (Solomon's shields) *to Egypt*".

472. For the text of Herodotus, I use *Herodotus* (tr. A.D. Godley; LCL), Cambridge, MA - London, 1920-1925.

473. As will be recalled, Josephus in 8,253 asserts that while Herodotus speaks of "Sesōstris", the correct name of Rehoboam's nemesis is rather "Isōkos". On the enigmatic figure of Herodotus' "Sesōstris" (a composite, it appears, of Pharoahs spanning many centuries), see C. OBSOMER, *Les campagnes de Sésostris dans Hérodote*, Bruxelles, 1989.

474. As is pointed out by OBSOMER, *Sésostris*, pp. 51, 176, contrary to the wording of Josephus' "citation" above, Herodotus himself nowhere affirms as such that it was specifically "Palestinian Syria" whose population Sesōstris subjugated "without a fight", compare 2,102 where the historian speaks in general terms of Sesōstris "marching over the mainland (of Asia) subduing every nation to which he came". Josephus arrives at the above (mis)understanding of Herodotus' account by way of deduction from the data of 2,102 (Sesōstris erects pillars portraying female genitalia in those "cities" whose inhabitants had made "no resistance" to him) and 2,106 (Herodotus claims to have seen pillars thus inscribed precisely in "Palestinian Syria").

Now it is evident that it is our nation (τὸ ἡμέτερον ἔθνος)[475] which he means to refer to as subdued by the Egyptians[476], for he adds that their king left behind, in the country of those who had surrendered (παραδόντων) without a battle (ἀμαχητὶ), pillars (στήλας, so 2,102.106) on which he had female sex-organs (αἰδοῖα γυναικῶν)[477] engraved (ἐγγράψας, compare 2,102 ἐνέγραφε). But it was Roboamos, our king, who surrendered the city without a battle (παρέδωκεν... ἀμαχητὶ τὴν πόλιν)[478].

Josephus, however, is still not done with Herodotus' (putative) errors. His invocation (8,262) of yet another slip by the older historian takes him rather far afield from the subject at hand, i.e. the conquests of Isōkos/Sesōstris. That he does, nonetheless, pause to call attention to it at this juncture is, however, understandable in that the "error" in question occurs within a "digression" (2,104-105) devoted to the "Colchians" which interrupts Herodotus' account of Sesōstris' doings in 2,102-103,106ff. In the context of the former segment, Herodotus comes to speak, in the second half of 2,104, of the (non-)observance of the practice of circumcision by various peoples. Josephus extracts an item from this last passage which he then critiques as follows:

Herodotus also says that the Ethiopians had learned the practice of circumcision (τὴν τῶν αἰδοίων περιτομήν)[479] from the Egyptians[480], "for

475. Josephus employs this designation for the Jewish people also in *AJ* 12,127.131; 14,304.323; 19,15; *Ap* 1,68. More frequent is the variant expression τὸ ἔθνος ἥμων, see *AJ* 10,276; 11,162.185; 12,7; 14,114.186.189.265; 20,52.184.231.254; *Vita* 224; *Ap* 1,5.161.166.168.185.194.213; 2,43.220. In general, Josephus (like Philo) utilizes ἔθνος with considerable frequency (c. 145 ×) and interchangeably with λαός (for this interchange, see e.g., 8,297) to denote the Jewish community. Thereby, he departs from the usage of LXX with its (normal) distinction between the Jewish "people" and the pagan "nation(s)". See n. 37.

476. Greek reads ὑπὸ τοῦ Αἰγυπτίου, "by the Egyptian", i.e. "Isōkos", so W, *ad loc.*

477. Compare 2,102 αἰδοῖα γυναικός, 2,106 γυναικὸς αἰδοῖα. In addition to Herodotus and Josephus, this action of "Sesōstris" during his Asian campaign is also cited by the historians Hecataeus of Abdera and Manetho; they, however, speak of male rather than female genitalia engraved by him, see STERLING, *Historiography*, pp. 127-132.

478. With the above formulation compare the reference in 8,258 to Isōkos' παραλαβὼν ἀμαχητὶ τὴν πόλιν. At this point it becomes clear why Josephus takes pains to specify, as the Bible itself does not, that both the Judean fortresses (8,255) and Jerusalem (8,258) fell to Pharoah "without a fight". That specification, it now appears, is crucial to Josephus' claim (8,260-262) that Herodotus "erred" in designating those whom "Sesōstris" subdued "without a fight" as the inhabitants of "Palestinian Syria" rather than "our (Jewish) nation". At the same time, it is also clear that in order to make his "correction" of Herodotus, Josephus must have recourse to a certain literary slight of hand, i.e. he has to introduce into his retelling of the Biblical account an element – surrender without a fight – inspired by Herodotus himself.

479. The phrase "the practice of circumcision" occurs also in *AJ* 12,241; 13,319; *Ap* 2,137. Herodotus in 2,104 uses the verbal construction περιτάμνονται... τὰ αἰδοῖα. Possibly, it was the fact of their common use of the term αἰδοῖα which inspired Josephus to juxtapose his citation of the two passages of Herodotus, i.e. 2,102 and 104 in 8,261-262,

the Phoenicians and the Syrians in Palestine admit that they learned it from the Egyptians (Φοίνικες γὰρ καὶ Σύροι οἱ ἐν τῇ Παλαιστίνῃ ὁμολογοῦσι παρ' Αἰγυπτίων μεμαθηκέναι)"⁴⁸¹. Now it is clear that no others of the Syrians in Palestine (ἐν τῇ Παλαιστίνῃ Σύρων) practice circumcision (περιτέμνονται) except ourselves (μόνοι ἡμεῖς)⁴⁸². (8,262)

Having thus delivered himself of the above, rather sharp critique of

see also these passages' use of the similar expressions "Palestinian Syria" (2,102) / "the Syrians in Palestine" (2,104).

480. In fact, Herodotus' actual statement (2,104) runs: "as to the Egyptians and the Ethiopians themselves, I cannot say which nation learned it from the other (αὐτῶν δὲ Αἰγυπτιῶν καὶ Αἰθιόπων οὐκ ἔχω εἰπεῖν ὁκότεροι παρὰ τῶν ἑτέρων ἐξέμαθον)". Note that in Ap 1,171, in the context of his more extensive citation of Herodotus 2,104 as a pagan witness to the existence of the Jews (= "the Syrians in Palestine"), Josephus correctly reproduces the above statement of the historian. On Ap 1,168-172, see A. VON GUTSCHMID, Kleine Schriften 4 (ed. F. RÜHL), Leipzig, 1893, pp. 561-565 who suggests (p. 562) that in the Ap passage Josephus is copying the text of Herodotus which he had before him, whereas in AJ 8,262 he is citing from memory.

481. Josephus here quotes Herodotus (2,104) virtually verbatim: Φοίνικες δὲ καὶ Σύροι [MSS P and R Σύριοι] οἱ ἐν τῇ Παλαιστίνῃ καὶ αὐτοὶ ὁμολογέουσι παρ' Αἰγυπτίων μεμαθηκέναι. In Ap 1,169 Josephus quotes this same passage – again almost verbatim. In 1,170 he then goes to cite the continuation of 2,104, absent in AJ 8,262: "The Syrians on the banks of the rivers Thermodan and Pathenius, and their neighbours the Macrones, say that they have adopted it (circumcision) recently from the Colchians. These are the only other circumcised peoples in the world, and it is clear they imitate the Egyptians..." (there follows the citation of Herodotus' profession of ignorance about whether the Egyptians learned circumcision from the Ethiopians or vice versa which Josephus (mis)quotes in 8,262, see preceding note).

The exactitude of Josephus' citation here in 8,262 stands in striking contrast to the freedom with which he generally treats the wording of Scripture (and e.g., LA). At the same time that exactitude cannot but underscore Josephus' glaring misrepresentation of Herodotus' statement about the priority of circumcision among the Egyptians or Ethiopians which immediately precedes it in the same paragraph.

482. Compare Josephus' remark concerning Herodotus' statement about the "Palestinian Syrians" and circumcision which he appends to the quotation of that statement in Ap 1,171: "He says that the Palestinian Syrians (Σύρους τοὺς ἐν τῇ Παλαιστίνῃ) were circumcised; but the Jews are the only (μόνοι... Ἰουδαῖοι, compare μόνοι ἡμεῖς, 8,262) inhabitants of Palestine who adopt this practice. He must therefore have known this, and his allusion is to them".

Josephus' assertions in both AJ and Ap notwithstanding, it is not so clear to modern scholars to whom, in fact, Herodotus intended to refer with his phrase "the Syrians in Palestine". E.g., T. REINACH, Textes d'auteurs grecs et romains relatifs au Judaïsme, Paris, 1895, p. 2 and Thackeray (in his note to Ap 1,169, Josephus, I, p. 231, n.c.) propose that Herodotus has in view rather the Philistines (on this understanding the further question arises as to whether Herodotus was simply incorrect in ascribing – against the testimony of the OT itself – the circumcision practice to the Philistines or whether at some point prior to his time they had actually adopted the observance). On the other hand, M. STERN (ed.), Greek and Latin Authors on Jews and Judaism, I, Jerusalem, 1974, pp. 3-4 and A.B. LLYOD, Herodotus Book II Commentary, Leiden, 1988, p. 23 opine that Herodotus' reference must indeed have the Jews in mind (so Josephus) given the Biblical statements about non-circumcision among the Philistines (Stern further points out that, already prior to Josephus, Herodotus' notice was taken as a reference to the Jews by the first century B.C. historian Diodorus of Sicily in his Bibliotheca Historica, 1.28.1-3).

Herodotus, Josephus rounds off his strictures with a formula that considerably attenuates their impact: "but concerning these matters everyone may speak as he sees fit[483]".

Before proceeding to the continuation of Josephus' account, I would suggest that he had several inter-connected objectives in this "Herodotian interlude". First of all, he wants to remind readers, once again, that "Gentile" corroboration of the events of Jewish history cited by him does exist – in the great Herodotus no less. At the same time, his citation of the relevant passage(s) of the historian gives Josephus the opportunity to enhance his own reliability in the eyes of readers; with his knowledge of Jewish history he can correct even Herodotus himself. Finally, though, Josephus is careful not to appear too triumphalistic in his criticism of the venerable "father of history", modestly leaving it to readers to adjudge his strictures for themselves.

3. *Closing Notices on Rehoboam* (8,263-264). We noted above that the Chronicler appends his notice of Rehoboam's replacements for the objects pillaged by Shishak (2 Chron 12,10-11 // 1 Kings 14,27-28) directly to his mention of the Egyptian despoliation, both items standing within his account of Rehoboam's defection and its sequels, 12,1-12. In Josephus, on the other hand, the two elements in question are, as we have seen, separated by an extended excursus on Herodotus' testimony. As a result, Josephus' parallel to 12,10(11-12) becomes less a conclusion to the account of Rehoboam's sin and punishment, and more the opening component in a complex of closing notices on Rehoboam's reign (// 2 Chron 12,13-16 and 1 Kings 14,29-31). Josephus (8,263) introduces his reference to Rehoboam's replacement measures following the long parenthesis on Herodotus with a resumptive allusion to Isōkos' withdrawal (see end of 8,259). It is after Pharoah's departure that Rehoboam "making (ποιήσας, 2 Par // 3 Rgns ἐποίησεν) in place of the golden shields (θυρεῶν, see 8,259 = 2 Par 12,10; 3 Rgns 14,27 reads ὅπλα) and bucklers (ἀσπίδων)[484] an equal number of bronze, delivered them to the guards of the palace (τοῖς τῶν

---

483. Josephus uses analogous formulae in deference to the sensibilities of his Gentile audience typically in connection with extraordinary ("miraculous") events recorded by him, see, e.g., *AJ* 1,108; 2,348; 3,81; 4,158; 10,281, cf. FELDMAN, *Mikra*, p. 506.

Similar formulae are frequently used by Dionysius in the face of divergencies among his sources, see, e.g.: *RA* 1.79.3; 2.40.3; 3.35.6; 7.66.5; 8.79.4, 80.3.

484. Josephus' reference to these items alongside the "shields" here corresponds to his despoliation notice in 8,259 where the same combination appears, there, as mentioned, under the influence of 1 Kings 10,16-17 (MT) // 2 Chron 9,15-16 which speak of the two kinds of "shields" fabricated by Solomon. Josephus' double reference to "bucklers" in his account of Shishak's plundering and Rehoboam's replacement objects has no parallel in the Biblical sources.

βασιλείων φύλαξιν)⁴⁸⁵". Josephus has no equivalent to the further circumstantial indications about the "movements" of the replacement shields as reported in 2 Chron 12,11 // 1 Kings 14,28. He likewise lacks a parallel as such to the summary notice on Rehoboam's self-humbling with the resultant lifting of God's wrath and his prospering of Judah in 2 Chron 12,12. Conceivably, however, the statement he does make at this juncture concerning Rehoboam, i.e. "instead of leading the life of (μετά... διάγειν) an illustrious commander (στρατηγίας ἐπιφανοῦς)⁴⁸⁶ and a brilliant statesman (τῆς ἐν τοῖς πράγμασι λαμπρότητος)⁴⁸⁷, he reigned in great quiet and fear (ἐν ἡσυχία πολλῇ καὶ δέει)⁴⁸⁸" does reflect this latter notice. In any case, Josephus' further characterization of Rehoboam as "being all his days an enemy of Jeroboam" does clearly derive from 2 Chron 12,15b // 1 Kings 14,30, cf. 15,6⁴⁸⁹. Thereafter, Josephus presents his version of the chronological data recorded in 2 Chron 12,13aββα // 1 Kings 14,21aββα⁴⁹⁰. Whereas, however, the Bible specifies Rehoboam's age at accession (41) and length of reign (17)⁴⁹¹, Josephus here, as consistently elsewhere, substitutes mention of the king's age at death, i.e. 57 which he obtains by combining the two Biblical figures⁴⁹².

Josephus now presents his (negative) judgment on Rehoboam in line

---

485. In 1 Kings 14,27 // 2 Chron 12,10 Rehoboam confides the shields to "the officers of the runners guarding (3 Rgns οἱ φυλάσσοντες, 2 Par τοὺς φυλάσσοντας) the gate of the house of the king (L 3 Rgns 14,27 'Lord')". (In B 14,27 the runner guards are said to be "set over him" (i.e. Rehoboam), while 2 Par 12,10 specifies that it was "Sousakim" who did this.

486. This phrase occurs only here in Josephus; he uses the noun στρατηγία 30×.

487. This phrase occurs only here in Josephus; he uses the adjective λαμπρότης 17×. With Josephus' characterization of Rehoboam here as one "who did not lead the life of a brilliant statesman", contrast his notice on Jehoshaphat as a king who "enjoyed splendid fame" (λαμπρᾶς δόξης... διῆγεν), 9,16.

488. This collocation occurs only here in Josephus. The rendition of W, ad loc. sounds rather different: "dans une complète inaction mêlée de crainte". Cf. too the appended remark of REINACH, Josèphe, II, p. 214, n.4: "cette prétendue indolence de Roboam ne trouve aucun point d'appui dans les textes; Josèphe l'a simplement conclue du silence de l'Ecriture sur les détails de son règne...".

489. The Biblical text(s) speak of a continual "war(ring)" between Rehoboam and Jeroboam. Josephus' formulation – which speaks of the former as simply a life-long "enemy" of the latter – might have in view his own earlier presentation in 8,222-223 (= 1 Kings 12,21-24 // 2 Chron 11,1-4) in which Rehoboam submits to a prophetic prohibition against undertaking hostile measures against the North.

490. He passes over the notice on Rehoboam's mother found in 2 Chron 12,13bβ // 1 Kings 14,21bβ (= 14,31ba) which he "anticipates" in 8,212.

491. In B 3 Rgns 12,24a the figures are respectively 16 and 12. In L 12,24a Rehoboam reigns 20 years, while in miniscule g of 2 Par 12,13 he accedes at age 40.

492. In fact computation of the Biblical indications (41 + 17) would suggest that Rehoboam died in his 58th year. Perhaps, Josephus wrote 57 with the Biblical datum of his 17 year reign fresh in mind.

with 2 Chron 12,14 // 1 Kings 14,22[493]. In contrast, however, to the
Chronistic verse which emphasizes Rehoboam's religious failings ("he
did evil, for he did not set his heart to seek the Lord"), Josephus
highlights rather his intellectual deficiencies and their political consequences[494]: "he was a man of boastful (ἀλαζὼν)[495] and foolish
(ἀνόητος, see 8,243) nature (τὸν τρόπον), who, by not heeding (προσέχειν)[496] his father's friends (τοῖς πατρῷοις φίλοις, see 8,215), lost his
royal power (τὴν ἀρχὴν ἀπολέσας)[497]".

As he does consistently with his kings, Josephus passes over the
"source notice" for Rehoboam found in 2 Chron 12,15a // 1 Kings
14,29[498]. He does, however, follow 2 Chron 12,16 // 1 Kings 14,31 in
making mention of Rehoboam's burial and the following succession:
"he was buried (ἐτάφη= 2 Par 12,16, 3 Rgns 14,31 θάπτεται) in
Jerusalem in the tombs of the kings (ἐν ταῖς θήκαις τῶν βασιλέων)[499]
and was succeeded on the throne (διεδέξατο... τὴν βασιλείαν, see
8,212; compare 3 Rgns 14,31 // 2 Par 12,16 ἐβασίλευσεν) by his son
Abias (Ἀβίας)[500]". To his reference to Abias' succession Josephus
appends the "synchronization" of this event with Jeroboam's 18th
regnal year which he anticipates from 1 Kings 15,1 // 2 Chron 13,1.

Summary: *AJ* 8,246-264 gives no clear evidence for Josephus' dependence on the "MT" text of (Kings and) Chronicles. On the other hand,
in 8,259 he does show himself dependent on the plus of 3 Rgns
14,26[501]. We further noted that Josephus' account of Rehoboam's

493. In 1 Kings 14,23-24 it is the people of Judah as a whole, rather than Rehoboam
personally, who are the object of censure.
494. Perhaps, Josephus is motivated in thus reformulating the judgment on Rehoboam
by a concern to avoid the seeming discrepancy between 2 Chron 12,12 (Rehoboam
humbles himself) and 14 ("he did evil").
495. Josephus' only other uses of this term are in *BJ* 6,172 (of Jonathan the Jew).395
(of the Jewish rebels). On it, see SPICQ, *Lexicographie*, I, pp. 64-66.
496. The use of this term in reference to Rehoboam sets up a parallelism between him
and Jeroboam, see 8,241 "... that he (Jeroboam) might not give heed (προσέχοι)...".
Note too that Josephus attributes both kings' "not heeding" to God's influence, see 8,216
(Rehoboam) and 241 (Jeroboam).
497. This same phrase recurs in 9,208 (Jonah's prediction of Assyria's lost of hege-
mony).
498. Presumably, Josephus considered that, since his own account follows the Bible
itself, there was no point in mentioning the (lost) pre-Biblical sources cited by Kings and
Chronicles for the various kings.
499. This phrase recurs in *AJ* 7,394 in the meaning "the coffins of the kings", cf. the
equivalent expression ἐν ταῖς βασιλικαῖς θήκαις in *AJ* 9,166.243; 14,124. In 1 Kings
14,31 // 2 Chron 12,16 the phrase used is "with his fathers in the city of David".
500. Compare the various forms of this name in the Biblical witnesses: Abijam (1
Kings 14,31), Ἀβιού (B 3 Rgns 14,31), Abijah (2 Chron 12,16), Ἀβιά (L 3 Rgns 14,31; 2
Par 12,16), Josephus' form being a declined version of the last of these.
501. In this section we likewise noted Josephus' dependence on two other LXX
plusses, i.e. 2 Rgns 14,27 in *AJ* 7,190 ("Tamar" as the future wife of Rehoboam and

reign displays affinities with distinctive readings of both B (the king's 30 concubines, 8,250) and L (the sequence "olives and wine", 8,247; the term "heifers", 8,248) 2 Par 11,5–12,16.

I would emphasize two points in particular concerning Josephus' presentation of Rehoboam's reign in comparison with the Biblical one(s). First, I observe that Josephus' "amplifications" within this sequence concern above all its central component, i.e. Rehoboam's defection and its sequels. In particular, Josephus expands the Chronicler's account in 2 Chron 12,1-12 in connection with the following points: the psychology operative in the defection of both king and people, the assembly's opening (rejected) appeal to God, their emotional response to Shemaiah's first message, the circumstances of Shishak's entry into Jerusalem, the objects carried off by him, and above all, Herodotus' testimony to the happening. These various embellishments serve to heighten the significance of the episode[502] as one which can both be corroborated from pagan sources and which evidences additional links both with what precedes (see its references to Solomon's "bucklers") and follows (i.e., the various later assaults on Jerusalem that will likewise involve violations of promises made).

My second point concerns Josephus' placing of his treatment of Rehoboam. It was noted above that, in this instance, Josephus departs from Kings' sequence in situating the passage, not subsequent to the entire "Jeroboam complex" (1 Kings 12,25-14,20, MT), but in the midst of that complex, i.e. directly following the "Bethel incident" of 1 Kings 13. What prompted Josephus to undertake this rearrangement? I suggest that he did so in the interests of furthering his comparison between the first two kings of the divided monarchy. In his presentation, both Jeroboam and Rehoboam appear initially as builders (8,225.246). Both fall away from God (recall the terminological contacts between Josephus' accounts of their respective defections in 8,243-245 and 251-253) and are confronted by a prophet for having done so. Rehoboam, however, heeds Shemaiah's admonition and repents, whereas Jeroboam (ultimately) ignores Jadōn's message and persists in his sin. Via this arrangement, then, Josephus works out, over the course of 8,225-264, a sequence exemplifying contrasting modes of responding to a prophet's warnings (and their respective consequences for king and people).

mother of Abijah) and 2 Rgns 8,7 in 7,104 (Shishak's future despoliation of the objects captured by David).

502. In thus amplifying the account of 2 Chronicles 12, Josephus is following in the footsteps of the Chronicler himself whose own narrative constitutes an expanded, more theological retelling of 1 Kings 14,25-28.

V

ABIJAH'S DEATH
(8,265-273)

Introduction: At this point in his narrative Josephus, who for the preceding sequence has based himself (primarily) on the presentation of the Chronicler (2 Chron 11,5-12,16), reverts to Kings as his source, specifically its *Sondergut* account of Ahijah's prophecy against Jeroboam's son Abijah and its fufillment, 1 Kings 14,1-18 (MT). The Biblical account may be divided into the following three components: 1) *mise en scène* (14,1-5); 2) Ahijah's word (14,6-16) and 3) conclusion (14,17-18). To be noted here at the outset is that B and L* (127/c₂ excepted) give their version of this episode, not in its MT position, but rather in the context of their lengthy plus, 3 Rgns 12,24a-z, wherein 12,24g-n relates the happening in much shorter form and with a variety of other differences[503]. However one adjudges the nature of the relationship between MT and BL* here[504], it is clear that in respect to both placing and content Josephus' version is much more closely aligned with the former than with the latter. Accordingly, my discussion will focus on a comparison of the MT and Josephan versions in their respective three-fold division.

1. *Mise en scène* (8,265-268). The opening formula, i.e. "at that time" of 1 Kings 14,1 very loosely connects the subsequent story with what precedes, i.e. the Bethel incident of 1 Kings 13. Josephus, on the contrary, makes a highly circumstantial transition to the new episode in which he first definitively disposes of Rehoboam and then re-introduces the figure of Jeroboam in language echoing that of 8,245:

> This, then, is the end of Roboamos's history. But now in what follows we have to relate the events of Jeroboam's reign and how he ended his life (κατέστρεψε τὸν βίον)[505]. For he did not cease nor desist (οὐ διέλιπεν οὐδ' ἠρέμησεν)[506] from outraging God (εἰς τὸν θεὸν ἐξυβρίζων, see

503. In the "Hexaplaric recension" represented especially by A (as also by the L MS 127/c₂) the episode does stand in its MT context with a content (more or less) equivalent to that of MT, see N. FERNÁNDEZ MARCOS, *En Torno al Texto Hexaplar de 1 Re 14,1-20*, in *Sef* 46 (1986) 177-190.

504. For a summary statement concerning the differences between them in our episode, see J. GRAY, *I and II Kings* (OTL), London, 1970², p. 310.

505. This construction recurs in *AJ* 3,273; 5,184.197; 6,306.378; 7,45; 9,27.204; 10,46.59.73.143.231; 11,302; 12,359.374; 13,119.386; 19,347.350; 20,92.242; *Ap* 1,153.

506. This is Josephus' only collocation of the verbs διαλείπω and ἠρεμέω.

ἐξύβρισεν εἰς τὸ θεῖον, 8,245), but all the time (καθ᾽ ἑκάστην ἡμέραν)⁵⁰⁷ continued to erect altars (βωμοὺς ἀνιστὰς)⁵⁰⁸ on the high mountains (ἐπὶ τῶν ὑψηλῶν ὀρῶν)⁵⁰⁹ and to appoint priests from the common people (ἱερεῖς ἐκ τοῦ πλήθους ἀποδεικνὺς)⁵¹⁰. These impieties (τὰσεβήματα)⁵¹¹, however, and the punishmént (δίκην)⁵¹² attendant on them, the Deity was at no far distant time (οὐκ εἰς μακρὰν)⁵¹³ to visit (τρέψειν)⁵¹⁴ upon both his own head (εἰς τὴν... κεφαλὴν)⁵¹⁵ and the heads of all his line (γενεᾶς)⁵¹⁶. For when, at that time (see 14,1)... (8,265-266a)

Josephus follows this lengthy introductory notice with a laconic reference (// 14,1) to the sickness (κάμνοντος) of Jeroboam's son, "Obimē" (᾽Οβίμην)⁵¹⁷. He then continues with his version of Jeroboam's initial directives to his wife⁵¹⁸, // 14,2. In particular he elaborates the king's injunction that she "disguise herself"⁵¹⁹; the queen is "to remove her robe and put on the dress of a simple woman (ἰδιωτι-

507. This reading of Mar appears to reflect Lat cotidie. NN* read καθ᾽ ἑκάστην with RO, Na καθ᾽ ἡμέραν with MSPExc (this latter expression is the one found in 8,245 in reference to Jeroboam's endeavor to commit ever new offenses).

508. For this construction, see AJ 4,(192). 305; 5,111; 9,243.

509. MExc lack the term ὀρῶν in the above phrase. Variations of the expression "high mountain(s)" occur in BJ 1,134 (sg.); 4,5 (sg.); AJ 2,265; 3,76; 9,98; 11,310. Note especially 9,98 where the reference is to Joram who forced the Judeans to "go up to the highest parts of the mountains (ἐπὶ τὰ ὑψηλότατα τῶν ὀρῶν) and worship strange gods".

510. Compare Jeroboam's word to the assembled Israelites in 8,228 ἀποδείξω... ἱερεῖς ἐξ ὑμῶν αὐτῶν. Josephus' double charge against Jeroboam here in 8,265 echoes the accusations of 1 Kings 12,31a ("he made houses on the high places [3 Rgns ὑψηλῶν]") and 12,31b; 13,33 (Jeroboam makes "priests [3 Rgns ἱερεῖς] from among all the people"). Recall that whereas Josephus has not mentioned the former point previously, he had already cited the latter item in 8,228.

511. Josephus uses the substantive ἀσέβημα 20×. Cf. his reference to Jeroboam's "impious (ἀσεβεῖς) acts" in 8,245.

512. Josephus uses δίκη 156×. On the term in his writings, see SCHLATTER, Theologie, pp. 40-42.

513. Elsewhere BJ 1,490; 2,218; 3,186.193; 4,227.362; 5,457.546; 7,84.416.451; AJ 3,35.298.299; 6,38.278; 7,228; 9,170; 17,75; 20,153; Vita 23. In this enumeration note especially BJ 5,546; 7,84; AJ 9,170 where, as in AJ 8,266, the phrase is used of the "imminence" of the "punishment(s)" (δίκη) awaiting miscreants.

514. Na conjectures στρέψειν. This is the only occurrence of the above phrase "visit punishment" in Josephus.

515. This is Josephus' only use of the phrase "visit upon the head".

516. With this formulation, compare 1 Kings 13,34 (a passage left unutilized by Josephus in his version of 1 Kings 13, see above): "and this thing became a sin to the house (3 Rgns οἴκῳ) of Jeroboam so as to cut it off and to destroy it from the face of the earth".

517. Compare MT Abijah, 3 Rgns 12,24e ᾽Αβιά. According to SCHALIT, Namenwörterbuch, p. 92, s.v. ᾽Οβίμης, the form printed by Mar goes back to a Hebrew אבים vocalized as אֲבִים. Compare SCHLATTER, Namen, p. 8, s.v. אביה: "... entstanden aus ᾽Αβια-νην, der Name hat die Akkusativendung zweimal erhalten. Das o für α wird vom Lat [which reads 'Abimem' here] noch nicht anerkannt und ist häufig Eindringling".

518. In Josephus, as in MT, she remains nameless. In 3 Rgns 12,24e.g she is called ᾽Ανὼ and represented as the sister-in-law of Pharoah Susakim.

519. The version of the episode in 3 Rgns 12,24gff. lacks this "disguise motif".

κὸν)[520]". Conversely, he leaves aside 14,2αβ's (self-evident) explanation of the purpose of this procedure by the king, i.e. "that it not be known that you are the wife of Jeroboam". In 14,2b Jeroboam further enjoins his wife to repair to Shiloh where she will find Ahijah the prophet who had predicted his rise to kingship. Not mentioning Shiloh at this point (see, however, below), Josephus has Jeroboam dispatch his wife to "the prophet Achias" whom he characterizes, not simply with 14,2bβ's allusion to his prediction in 1 Kings 11,31ff. (// AJ 8,207-208), but also as "a man with a wonderful power (θαυμαστὸν ἄνδρα)[521] of foretelling the future (περὶ τῶν μελλόντων προειπεῖν)[522]".

Josephus makes no mention of the triple gift of bread, cakes and honey which in 14,3a the king directs his wife to bring to the prophet – perhaps because in the continuation of MT nothing further will be said of these[523]. In 14,3b Jeroboam's word to his wife ends with the somewhat indeterminate statement "(Ahijah) will tell you what shall happen to the child". Anticipating 14,5 where God informs Ahijah that the queen is "coming to inquire of you concerning her son", Josephus gives Jeroboam's closing directive a more specific content: "the queen is to inquire (ἀνακρίνειν)[524], as if she were a stranger (ξένην), whether the child would survive his illness (διαφεύξεται τὴν νόσον)[525]".

1 Kings 14,4a records the queen's carrying out Jeroboam's orders.

520. This is Josephus' only use of this term in AJ; it occurs 3 × in BJ: 1,449.478.519.
521. Josephus uses the above phrase "marvelous man" of Moses in AJ 3,317 and Ap 1,279.
522. This is the only occurrence of this precise phrase in Josephus, cf., however, the comparable formulations in AJ 2,205; 6,115.255; 8,109; 10,92.267; 13,300.311; 15,373; Ap 1,204. Compare the recognition about the prophet Jadōn which Josephus attributes to Jeroboam in 8,234 "he possessed divine foreknowledge".
523. Recall that in 8,234 when reproducing Jeroboam's word to "Jadōn" from 1 Kings 13,8, Josephus passes over the latter text's promise "I will give you a gift" to which no allusion is made in Jadōn's response in 13,9 // 8,235.
The version of our episode in 3 Rgns 12,24gff., by contrast, elaborates on the gifts the queen is to bring: the cakes are intended for Ahijah's "children", and "Anō" is likewise instructed to take "grapes" for him. In 3 Rgns the gifts do – as they do not in MT – figure in the continuation of the story, see 12,241 where Ahijah asks the queen why she has brought them.
524. Josephus uses this term, as here, in reference to an "inquiry" through or by prophets also in AJ 4,105 (Balaam "inquires" of God); 8,400 (Jehoshaphat asks Ahab to "inquire about" their projected campaign against Syria); 10,216 (Nebuchadnezzar "inquires" of the Magi about his dream). The last two of these texts employ the same construction, i.e. "inquire about (περὶ)" as does 8,267.
525. This same construction recurs in AJ 9,20 and 10,27 in reference to the "illnesses" of Ahaziah and Hezekiah, respectively. Compare also 9,88: Azaelos is to "inquire (ἔρεσθαι) of the prophet (Elisha) about his (Adados') illness (νόσου) and ask whether he would escape (διαφεύξεται) the danger it threatened". Cf. Jeroboam's initial instructions to "Ano" in B 3 Rgns 12,24g "go inquire of God (ἐπερώτησον τὸν θεὸν) concerning the child, whether he shall recover from his illness (εἰ ζήσεται ἐκ τῆς ἀρρωστίας αὐτοῦ)".

Josephus' version introduces explicit mention of her "changing her dress (μετασχηματισαμένη)⁵²⁶ as her husband had ordered her". Thereby, he calls attention, once again, to the "disguise motif" which he accentuates vis-à-vis MT. Josephus must likewise add "where Achias was living" to the Bible's reference to the queen's going to Shiloh (Σιλὼ)⁵²⁷, since (contrast 14,2) he has not yet mentioned the site in this context as the prophet's dwelling place. Thereafter, Josephus relates (// 14,4aβb) the divine intervention which occurs at the moment the queen approaches the house of the old prophet "whose eyes were dim (τὰς ὄψεις ἠμαυρωμένου)⁵²⁸ from age (διὰ τὸ γῆρας)⁵²⁹". In 14,5aα the divine communication to the prophet is introduced with the simple formula "and the Lord said to Ahijah". Josephus, by contrast, has God "appear" (ἐπιφανείς) to him⁵³⁰. In Josephus, as in the Bible, God's message is a double one, i.e. identification of Ahijah's caller as the wife of Jeroboam and a directive concerning what he is to say to her whose actual content is left unspecified for the moment: "(God) told (μηνύει)⁵³¹ him both that Jeroboam's wife had come to him and how he was to answer what she had come there to ask".

2. *Ahijah's Word* (8,269-272). 1 Kings 14,5bβ-6aα makes the transition to the delivery of God's message by Ahijah with a notice on the entrance of Jeroboam's wife "pretending to be another woman"⁵³². In his formulation of this item (8,269) Josephus re-utilizes his own earlier terminology: it is when the woman "entered the house in the guise of a commoner (ἰδιώτιδος) and a stranger (ξένης)", that Ahijah "cried out"⁵³³. In line with 14,6aββα Josephus makes Ahijah address the woman as "wife of Jeroboam" and ask why she has "disguised" herself

---

526. The only other occurrence of the verb μετασχηματίζω in Josephus is *AJ* 7,257 (David "changes his appearance", i.e. puts off the tokens of his mourning for Absalom).

527. Josephus calls this city Σιλοῦς in *AJ* 5,68.70.72.79.150, while in 5,170.343.357; 8,206 (Ahijah is "from the city of Silō") it has the same name as here in 8,267. LXX denominates it Σηλώ.

528. This construction recurs in *AJ* 9,56 (Elisha prays that God will "blind the eyes" of the Syrians), cf. 1,202.

529. Elsewhere Josephus uses this construction in *AJ* 5,354 (of Eli); 8,5 (of David); 12,172 (of Onias). Cf. 8,236 where the Bethel prophet is said to be bed-ridden "through the infirmity of old age (γήρως)".

530. Compare 8,240 where, in place of the *Wortereignisformel* of 1 Kings 13,23, Josephus refers to God's "appearing" (ἐπιφαίνεται) to Jadon. See n. 300.

531. Elsewhere Josephus uses the verb μηνύω with God as subject in *AJ* 6,49 (recipient: Samuel). The h.p. of the verb recurs in *BJ* 1,585; 3,344 (passive); *AJ* 5,8 (passive).292; 6,272 (passive).277; 12,187.

532. On the text-critical problem of 14,5bβ, see BHS.

533. In 3 Rgns 12,24k Ahijah charges his "servant" to go out to "Anō" to address her with words à la those of 14,6aββ. Like MT, Josephus makes no mention of Ahijah's servant.

(τί κρύπτεις σαυτήν;)⁵³⁴. Whereas, however, in 14,6bβ Ahijah next intimates the bad news he has for his caller ("for I am charged with heavy tidings for you"), Josephus represents him rather as underscoring the futility of her efforts at disguise: "for your here coming is not unknown to God (τὸν... θεὸν οὐ λανθάνεις)⁵³⁵, who has appeared (φανεὶς)⁵³⁶ to me (τέ μοι)⁵³⁷ and revealed (ἐδήλωσε)⁵³⁸ your coming, and has instructed (προσέταξε)⁵³⁹ me in the things I am to say". Thereupon (// 14,7a) Josephus has Ahijah "commission" the woman: "return, therefore, to your husband and tell (him) that God has spoken as follows" (ἀπελθοῦσα οὖν πρὸς τὸν ἄνδρα φράζε αὐτὸν ταῦτα λέγειν)⁵⁴⁰.

The word which Abijah now proceeds to confide to his hearer in 14,7b-16 is both lengthy and complex, addressing as it does the fate, not only of Abijah himself, but also of Jeroboam's line and of Israel as a whole. The first main component within 14,7bff. that may be distinguished is 14,7b-11. This judgment speech announces punishment on Jeroboam's house (vv. 10-11) for the king's failure to respond properly (vv. 8b-9) to the Lord's benefits to him (vv. 7b-8a)⁵⁴¹. Josephus follows the sequence of the source word (compare 3 Rgns, see n. 541), retaining also its direct address throughout, while compacting it considerably. Specifically, he begins with God's invoking his deeds on behalf of Jeroboam: "just as I made you great when you were a little man (...μέγαν ἐκ μικροῦ... ἐποίησα)⁵⁴², indeed were nothing, and took away (ἀποσχίσας)⁵⁴³ the kingdom (τὴν βασιλείαν) from David's line

534. The verb κρύπτω is coupled with the reflexive pronoun (= "to disguise oneself") also in *AJ* 13,108 (Ammonius disguises himself in a woman's dress).
In 3 Rgns 12,241 Ahijah's challenging question to the woman concerns, not her self-disguise (recall that the disguise motif is lacking in the 3 Rgns version) – but rather the gifts she has brought – gifts nowhere mentioned by Josephus.
535. Variants of the above expression in which "God" stands as object of the verb λανθάνω occur in *BJ* 1,84;6,37; *AJ* 2,129;4,286; 5,33.123; 11,274; 13,316; 15,376; *Vita* 83; *Ap* 2,166.
536. NN* follow R in omitting the term. NaWMar read it with the other codd. Compare ἐπιφανεὶς in 8,268.
537. SCHRECKENBERG, *Vermutungen*, p. 69 conjectures σέ μοι.
538. With the above construction "appearing (φανεὶς) he (God) revealed (ἐδήλωσε)...", compare 8,240: "God appeared (ἐπιφαίνεται) to Jadōn ... and revealed (ἐδήλου) what the punishment would be...".
539. This is the same term used of Jeroboam's "commanding" his wife in 8,266.267.
540. The reading of Mar as cited above follows one of the two conjectures put forward by N with reference to Lat ("dic ei haec praecepisse deum"), i.e. to substitute αὐτὸν for the αὐτῷ of the codd (alternatively, N suggests adding τὸν θεὸν after λέγειν). N* retains αὐτῷ, while Na reads ἀπελθοῦσαν (so MS)... ἔφραζεν (so MSPExc) αὐτῷ... .
541. In the 3 Rgns version, announcement of Abijah's death (12,241 // MT 14,12b) precedes the prediction of the extermination of Jeroboam's line (12,24mᵃ // MT 14,10-11) which is itself followed by mention of the mourning that will be made for Abijah (12,24mᵇ // MT 14,13a). 3 Rgns has no parallel to MT's 14,7b-9.
542. Compare *AJ* 2,333 where Moses cites God's power τὰ μικρὰ ποιῆσαι μεγάλα.
543. This is Josephus' only use of the verb ἀποσχίζω.

to give it to you (σοὶ... ἔδωκα)⁵⁴⁴". From the accusation against Jeroboam of 14,8b-9, Josephus leaves aside the comparison of him with David (v. 8b) and with all who preceded him (v. 9aα). Similarly, in place of the graphic image of v. 9bβ "you have cast me (God) behind your back", he speaks of Jeroboam's being "unmindful (ἠμνημόνησας) of these things (i.e. God's benefits)"⁵⁴⁵ and having "given up worshipping me" (τὴν ἐμὴν θρησκείαν καταλιπών, see 8,256 [Rehoboam and his people] αὐτοὶ τὴν θρησκείαν αὐτοῦ κατέλιπον)⁵⁴⁶. On the other hand, he does offer an equivalent for 14,9bα where Jeroboam is charged with "making other gods and molten images (מסכות)" to whom he devoted himself: "you have made gods of molten metal (χωνευτοὺς θεοὺς)⁵⁴⁷ and have honoured (ἐτίμας)⁵⁴⁸ them".

1 Kings 14,10-11 announces the punishment for Jeroboam's crimes: his entire line faces extermination and profanation of their remains. Josephus, who has previously highlighted God's elevation of the lowly Jeroboam, takes care to supplement the source's announcement with an opening statement concerning the king's personal fate: "I will again pull you down (καθαιρήσω)⁵⁴⁹". To this prediction he appends a compressed version⁵⁵⁰ of the Biblical notice on the end awaiting Jeroboam's descendants: "(I) will utterly destroy (ἐξολέσω)⁵⁵¹ all your line and will make them the prey (βορὰν) of dogs (κυσὶ) and birds (ὄρνισι)⁵⁵²".

544. Ahijah's word here is reminiscent of his earlier announcement to Jeroboam in 8,207 (// 1 Kings 11,31): σχίσας τὴν Σολομῶνος ἀρχήν... δίδωσι σοὶ... .
545. With this charge compare that made by Samuel against the people in AJ 6,60 "they had been unmindful (ἀμνημονήσειαν) of His benefits".
546. Note that TJ too eliminates the imagery of 14,9bβ, reading "you have put my service far from opposite your eyes".
547. This is Josephus' only use of this phrase.
548. So MExc followed by Mar. NN*Na read τιμᾷς with Suid, cf. ἐτίμησας (SPE) and τιμήσας (RO). Elsewhere Josephus uses "gods" as objects of τιμάω in AJ 8,194 (Solomon); 9,93 (passive).194 (passive).256 (Ahaz);18,348 (passive), cf. 19,8 (Zeus, passive).
549. Elsewhere Josephus uses καθαιρέω with God as subject only in BJ 6,411 (object: the Jews).
550. In particular, Josephus does not reproduce the graphic phrases of 14,10: "the one pissing against the wall"; "as a man burns up dung until it is all gone". Similarly, in contrast to 14,11, he does not distinguish between the city dwellers and the countrymen among Jeroboam's descendants who, according to the Biblical verse, are to be consumed by dogs and birds, respectively (see, however, 8,289 where, in a reminiscence of Ahijah's word here, Josephus does utilize the distinction made in 14,11). Finally, he also leaves aside the (superfluous) closing phrase of 14,11 "for the Lord has spoken".
551. Thus the reading of RO followed by NN*NaMar. MSPExcSuidZon have ἐξολοθρεύσω, E ἐξολευθρεύσω. The only other occurrence of ἐξόλλυμι in Josephus is AJ 8,299 (object: Baasha's line).
552. With this formulation compare BJ 4,324 where Josephus mentions that the slain priests Ananus and Jesus were cast out "a prey (βορὰ) of dogs (κυνῶν) and wild beasts (θηρίων)". The collocation "dogs" and "birds" of 8,270 recurs in 8,289 where Josephus recounts the fulfillment of Ahijah's announcement, see there.

It is at this juncture in his reproduction of Ahijah's address that Josephus proceeds to significantly rearrange the constituents of the prophet's word. In 1 Kings 14,12-16 Ahijah first pronounces on the personal fate of the sick Abijah (vv. 12-13), in order thereafter to revert to more general matters, i.e. the emergence of a destroyer of Jeroboam's line (v. 14), and the coming exile of Israel (vv. 15-16)[553]. Josephus reverses this sequence, placing the material of 14,14-16 before that of 14,12-13. His rationale in doing this is not far to seek. Thereby, he brings together Ahijah's general words of doom in a continuous sequence, with the result that the particular word concerning Abijah now becomes, not an "interruption", as in the Bible, but the culmination of the whole, whose fulfilment, in turn, follows directly (compare 1 Kings 14 where "announcement", 14,12-13 and "fulfillment", 14,17-18, are separated by 14,14-16). His rearrangement likewise enables Josephus to connect the announcement concerning the instrument who will effect the extermination of Jeroboam's dynasty (// 14,14) with that predicting its demise (// 14,10-11), rather than having them separated by the "Abijah material", 14,12-13. With these observations in mind, we may now consider Josephus' utilization of the material of 14,12-16 itself. As just noted, he (8,271) rounds off the preceeding segment on the fate of Jeroboam's dynasty with an allusion, closely modelled on 14,14, to the (unnamed) new king whom God will "set over" (ἐξεγείρε-ται)[554] the people and whose task will be to "leave alive not one" (οὐδένα ὑπολείψει)[555] of Jeroboam's line. To this notice he then attaches a compressed rendition of the double sequence concerning the people's crime and punishment, 14,15-16. In his version of these two verses, Josephus, leaving aside, in accordance with his usual practice, the figurative language of v. 15aα (Israel the "reed" whom the Lord will "shake"), proceeds immediately to retail the clear threat of exile (+ attached motivation) set out in 14,15aβ-16:

The people too shall share this punishment (μεθέξει[556] ... τῆς τιμω-ρίας)[557] by being driven (ἐκπεσὸν)[558] from their good land (τῆς ἀγαθῆς

553. 3 Rgns 12,24g-n has no parallel to MT's 14,14-16.

554. Only here in Josephus is ἐξεγείρω used in this meaning and with God as subject. In its other three occurrences the verb has different senses, see AJ 5,39; 18,107; Vita 424.

555. So NN*Mar. Na reads rather οὐδὲν ἀπολείψει with MSPExc. With the phrase οὐδένα ὑπολείψει τοῦ Ἱεροβοάμου γένους of 8,271, compare AJ 5,90 (Joshua urges the people) τοῦ γένους τῶν Χαναναίων μηδὲν ὑπολιπεῖν and 8,313 (God caused the rival Northern kings) μηδένα τοῦ γένους ὑπολιπεῖν.

556. This is the reading of E (cf.Lat) followed by NN*NaMar. The codd + Exc have μεθέξειν.

557. This is Josephus' only use of the above phrase; compare τιμωρίαν ὑφέξειν, 8,240.

558. Only here does Josephus use ἐκπίπτω with "land" as object. Cf. the similar phrase in AJ 10,59 where Josiah refers to the danger of the Judeans' being "cast out of their own country (τῆς οἰκείας ἐκπεσόντες)".

γῆς)[559] and scattered (διασπαρὲν)[560] over the country beyond the Euphrates (Εὐφράτου)[561], because they have followed (κατηκολούθησε) the impious ways (ἀσεβήμασι, see 8,266) of the king[562] and worship the gods (προσκυνεῖ θεοὺς)[563] made by him[564], abandoning their sacrifice(s) to me (τὴν ἐμὴν θυσίαν ἐγκαταλιπόν, see 8,256)[565].

Having thus related Ahijah's word on the future of dynasty and people, Josephus now (8,272), at the climax of the entire address, has him deliver an announcement concerning Abijah's sickness, the proper object of his hearer's inquiry (// 14,12-13):

And you, woman, hasten (σπεῦδε) to your husband and tell (ἀπαγγελλοῦσα)[566] him these things[567]. But your son you will find dead, for, as

559. Elsewhere Josephus employs the expression "good land" in *AJ* 3,296 (the rebel Israelites so designate Egypt); 4,242 (+ "spacious"); 5,178 (+ "fertile"), cf. 20,25. On Josephus' (attenuated) use of the key Biblical theme of "the land", see B.H. AMARU, *Land Theology in Josephus' Jewish Antiquities*, in *JQR* 71 (1980-1981) 201-221.
Finally, note that the above formulation "being driven *from their good land*" is quite reminiscent of 1 Kings 14,15aβ "the Lord will root up Israel *out of this good land...*".
560. Similar uses of the verb διασπείρω ("scatter in exile") occur in *AJ* 11,212; 12,278; *Ap* 1,33.
561. This is the LXX form for the name of the river. As Mar, *Josephus*, V, p. 717, n. a points out, Josephus agrees with TJ in specifying "beyond *the Euphrates*" as Israel's place of exile. As so often, MT speaks simply of "the River" here. Josephus makes the same "substitution" also elsewhere, see *AJ* 4,104 (// Num 22,5); 7,127 (// 2 Sam 10,16); 8,39 (// 1 Kings 5,1).
With the above phrase "(the people shall be) scattered over the country beyond the Euphrates", compare 1 Kings 14,15bα "(the Lord) will scatter them beyond the River".
562. Compare 1 Kings 14,16 "And he (Yahweh) will give Israel up *because of the sins of Jeroboam...*". Note the similar wording in Elijah's charge against Joram of Judah in *AJ* 9,99 "he had followed (κατηκολούθησεν) the impious example (ἀσεβήμασι) of the Israelite kings".
563. Elsewhere Josephus uses προσκυνέω with "gods" as (accusatival or datival) object in *AJ* 4,137; 8,317; 9,96.98.133 (135).255.261; *Ap* 1,239.261, cf. *AJ* 8,317; 9,139 (object: "the calves").
564. With this formulation compare 1 Kings 14,15bβ "because they (the people) have made their Asherim...".
565. This is Josephus' only use of the construction "abandon sacrifice(s)". Elsewhere he employs the equivalent phrase θρησκείαν ἐγκαταλιπεῖν, see *AJ* 9,133; 12,269 (in the former text the phrase is coupled with the expression "worship strange (gods)" similar to the "worship gods" of 8,271).
566. N, followed by Na, conjectures ἀπαγγελοῦσα (Mar, *Josephus*, V, p. 716, n. 4 incorrectly cites N's conjecture as ἀπαγγελλοῦσα, i.e. the reading apparently [or is there simply a typographical error in the text printed by him?] adopted by himself). N* follows ROSP's ἀπαγγέλλουσα, while MExc have παραγγέλλουσα.
567. Ahijah's words here represent a renewal of his "commission" to the woman in 8,269 ("return, therefore, to your husband and tell him that...") necessary after the long interlude of the prophet's announcements concerning dynasty and people in 8,270-271. They likewise correspond to the "arise therefore, go to your house" of 14,12a.

you enter the city[568], his life will leave him (ἀπολείψει τὸ ζῆν αὐτόν)[569]. And, when he is buried, he shall be wept for (κλαυσθεὶς) by all the people and honoured with general mourning (κοινῷ... πένθει)[570], for of all of Jeroboam's line he alone was good (ἀγαθὸς)[571].

3. *Conclusion* (8,273). In concluding our episode, Josephus markedly expands the summary "fulfillment notices" of 14,17-18. Thus whereas in 14,17 the woman's reaction to Ahijah's word is loosely juxtaposed to the word itself via the phrase "and she arose and departed", Josephus provides a more fluid transition with his "when he had prophesied (προφητεύσαντος, see 8,242) these things, the woman rushed out...". In this formulation the emotional heightening vis-à-vis the source is already apparent, "rushing out" replacing the colorless Biblical verbs. Similarly, while 14,17a moves directly from the queen's leaving Ahijah to her arrival in Tirzah, Josephus interposes the following sequence concerning her emotional state on the homeward journey:

(the woman) rushed out (ἐκπηδήσασα), thrown into confusion (τεταραγμένη)[572] and deeply grieved (περιαλγής)[573] at the death of the son spoken of; along the way she lamented (θρηνοῦσα) and beat her breast (κοπτομένη)[574] at the thought of the child's approaching end (τὴν μέλλου-

568. Josephus nowhere mentions the name of the city from which the queen sets out and to which she returns, compare 1 Kings 14,17 which speaks of her coming "to Tirzah" (in 3 Rgns 12,24kff. "Sarira" is mentioned as the woman's starting and end point). Possibly, Josephus' non-reproduction of 14,17's mention of "Tirzah" as the residence of Jeroboam has to do with the fact that earlier (8,225), following 1 Kings 12,25, when citing Shechem and Penuel as the sites of Jeroboam's palaces he makes no mention of Tirzah as a royal residence. His own first reference to "Tirzah" will come in 8,299, see there.

569. Elsewhere the above construction "life leaves" occurs in *BJ* 1,572. Compare 1 Kings 14,12b "when your feet enter the city, the child shall die" (in 3 Rgns 12,241 Ahijah tells Anō "... it shall come to pass when thou hast entered into the city, even into Sarira, that thy maidens shall come out to thee, and shall say unto thee, 'the child is dead'...").

570. This is Josephus' only use of the phrase "common mourning". With the above combination ("wept for... mourning"), compare *AJ* 7,40 where David directs all the people "to weep and mourn for (κλαίειν καὶ πενθεῖν) Abner". Compare the wording of Ahijah's announcement in 14,13a "and all Israel shall mourn for him, and bury him" (3 Rgns 12,24m reads "... the child shall be lamented, 'Alas, Lord!'...").

571. Compare 1 Kings 14,13b "because in him there was found something good (טוב) to the Lord". Like the Bible, Josephus does not specify the nature of the "goodness" he attributes to Abijah here. In *Mo'ed Qaṭan* 28b divergent Rabbinic views on the point are recorded: R. Zera claimed that the prince gave up his position and went on pilgrimage to Jerusalem, whereas R. Henana b. Papa asserted that Abijah's merit consisted in his removing the guards Jeroboam had stationed on the frontier to keep the Israelites from going to Jerusalem. See further GINZBERG, *Legends*, VI, p. 308, n. 27.

572. With the above collocation "rush out... thrown into confusion", compare *AJ* 9,150's description of Athaliah's reaction to the revolt against her: "... thrown into great confusion (τεταραγμένη), she jumped up (ἐξεπήδησε)...".

573. The term περιαλγής occurs also in *BJ* 1,644; 7,201; *AJ* 2,54; 7,171; 10,77.

574. The above collocation "lament...beat the breast" recurs, in reverse order, in *AJ* 6,377 (Josephus' description of the mourning for Saul and his sons by the people of Jabesh-Gilead).

σαν... τελευτὴν)[575], and wretched (ἀθλία)[576] over her misfortune (τοῦ πάθους)[577] and beset by irremediable woe (ἠπείγετο κακοῖς ἀμηχάνοις)[578], she pressed on with a haste (σπουδῇ, see σπεῦδε, 8,272) that meant ill luck (ἀτυχεῖ)[579] for her son – for the more she hurried, the sooner she was destined (ἐπειχθεῖσα)[580] to see him dead – but was necessary on her husband's account.

Following this interlude, Josephus reports Abijah's "expiring" (ἐκπεπνευκότα)[581] at the moment of his mother's arrival (// 14,17b). This happened, he goes on to add, "as the prophet had said". In 1 Kings 14,18b a comparable fulfillment notice, "according to the word of the Lord" (cf. 14,13a)[582], is associated with the mention of Abijah's burial and the mourning over him in 14,18a. Josephus' "reapplication" of the fulfillment notice hangs together with the fact that his account lacks an equivalent to the two items cited in 14,18a which Josephus apparently presumes readers can supply for themselves in light of Ahijah's prediction concerning them, see 8,272[583]. In place thereof he records, with a view to what follows (see below), that in accordance with Ahijah's injunction (see 8,272), "she told (ἀπήγγειλεν) the king everything".

Summary. We noted above that both as regards placement and content Josephus' account of Abijah's death is much closer to MT 1 Kings 14,1-18 than to the version found in 3 Rgns 12,24g-n. We likewise cited several minor affinities with TJ (prosaic rendition of the metaphor of 14,9; "the Euphrates" for 14,15's "the River").

Overall it may be said that Josephus reproduces the content of the extended MT narrative 1 Kings 14,1-18 both accurately and in detail. At the same time, he does omit certain features of that narrative entirely (the gifts for Ahijah; 14,18a's notice that Abijah was indeed buried and mourned). Conversely, he essays to heighten the emotional dimension of the incident with his interjected description of the queen's

575. Josephus uses this same phrase in *AJ* 4,322 in connection with the death of Moses.

576. The only other occurrence of this term in *AJ* is 16,109 (Alexander refers to Mariamme as "our unhappy mother"). In the rest of the Josephan corpus it occurs 10 × .

577. This is Josephus' only use of the phrase "wretched over misfortune".

578. This is Josephus' only use of this construction. The adjective ἀμήχανος occurs 37 × in his corpus.

579. Elsewhere, Josephus employs the adjective ἀτυχής in *BJ* 1,556.665; *AJ* 7,2; 16,116.

580. This is Josephus' second use of a form of the verb ἐπείγω in 8,273, see ἠπείγετο above.

581. The verb ἐκπνέω occurs also in *BJ* 1,272.660; 5,517; 6,195; *AJ* 12,357.

582. Note once again Josephus' avoidance of the phrase "the word of the Lord".

583. Note that also 3 Rgns 12,24n makes no mention of Abijah's "burial"; it does, however, state "and there came forth a wailing to meet her (Anō)", corresponding to Ahijah's announcement in 12,241 "when thou hast entered the city... thy maidens shall come out to meet thee, and shall say to thee,'The child is dead'".

reaction to Ahijah's announcement of her son's death. Likewise noteworthy is Josephus' re-ordering of the sequence of Ahijah's discourse in
a way that brings together related items and makes the announcement
of Abijah's death the climax of the whole (and has "prediction" and
"fulfillment" directly juxtaposed). Finally, mention should be made of
the contrast that emerges from Josephus' placing back-to-back his
versions of 2 Chron 11,5-12,16 (// 1 Kings 14,21-31) and 1 Kings 14,1-
18. In the former the prophetic message is that God will not "destroy"
Judah and its king (see 8,257), whereas in the latter just such a
destruction is announced by Ahijah for Jeroboam's dynasty and people.
The latter "prophecy", in turn, serves to prepare both imminent (the
extermination of Jeroboam's line) and more distant events (the Israelite
exile, see Josephus' previous foreshadowing of this in 8,229).

VI

JEROBOAM VS. ABIJAH
(8,274-286)

Introduction: In MT 1 Kings 14,19-20[584], the concluding notices on Jeroboam's death and the succession of his son Nadab, are directly (and rather abruptly) juxtaposed to the narrative of 14,1-18. Josephus, who bases his account also on Chronicles, finds it necessary to depart from this sequence in order to accomodate the Chronicler's more expansive account of Abijah of Judah (2 Chronicles 13 // 1 Kings 15,1-8) since this features a conflict between him and the still-reigning Jeroboam[585]. 2 Chronicles 13 itself might be divided up approximately as follows: 1) *Mise en scène* (13,1-3); 2) Abijah's address (13,4-12); 3) the battle (13,13-19); and 4) the contrasting fates of the two kings (13,20-23 [ET 13,20-14,1]). I now turn to a consideration of Josephus' version of these four segments.

1. *Mise en scène* (8,274-275a). 2 Chron 13,1-2a (// 1 Kings 15,1-2) comprises the introductory framework notices for Abijah with the following content: synchronization of his accession with Jeroboam's 18th regnal year (13,1 // 15,1), mention that he reigned 3 years (13,2aα // 15,2a)[586], and names of Abijah's mother and her father (13,2aβ // 15,2b)[587]. Josephus, for his part, does not reproduce these items at this juncture. He has already cited the Biblical synchronism when recording Abijah's accession in 8,264. In line with his usual practice, he reserves reference to the Judean's length of reign for a later point (see 8,285). Finally, seeing that the data on Abijah's maternal lineage as recorded in 2 Chron 13,2aβ do not agree either with those of 1 Kings 15,2b (see n. 587) or with his own indications on the subject (see 8,249), it is not surprising that Josephus makes no use of them. But how then does Josephus "lead into" the following battle episode? He does so beginning with a phrase that closely links that episode with the immediately preceding account of Ahijah's word, which word, Jeroboam's wife has

584. 3 Rgns has no equivalent to these verses.
585. The *Sondergut* Chronistic story of this conflict is an elaboration of the notice of 1 Kings 15,7b (// 2 Chron 13,2b) "there was war between Abijam (Abijah) and Jeroboam".
586. B and L* (127/c$_2$ reads with MT) 3 Rgns 15,1b assign "Abiou"/"Abia" a reign of *six* years (B 3 Rgns 15,1a makes Abiou "son of Jeroboam"!).
587. On this point 2 Chron 13,2 and 1 Kings 15,2 diverge; the former makes Abijah son of "Micaiah daughter of Uriel of Gibeah" (2 Par has "Maacha daughter of Uriel of Gabaon"), the latter of "Maacah daughter of Abishalom". On the problem, see n. 386.

just been said to relate to her husband (8,273). Having cited her doing so, Josephus now notes the king's reaction: "but Jeroboam took no thought (οὐδενὸς... φροντίσας)⁵⁸⁸ of these things". In other words, Jeroboam, according to Josephus, simply ignores both his own son's death and Ahijah's words of doom for his house and people. Instead of attending to these urgent matters, Jeroboam, Josephus continues, "collecting (ἀθροίσας) a large army (στρατιὰν)⁵⁸⁹, led it out to make war on Abias (ἐπὶ... Ἀβίαν... πολεμήσων)⁵⁹⁰...". Thereby, he reverses the roles ascribed to the two kings by the Chronicler. In 2 Chron 13,3a it is Abijah who – for reasons unspecified – appears to take the initiative in commencing hostilities, "Abijah went out to battle". In Josephus, on the contrary, the aggressor is clearly Jeroboam who, moreover, is assigned a motive for attacking Abijah, i.e. "he despised him on account of his youth" (κατεφρόνει γὰρ αὐτοῦ διὰ τὴν ἡλικίαν)⁵⁹¹. This divergence, in turn, seems to hold together wth the contrasting images of the royal pair Josephus wishes to convey: Jeroboam, the heedless warmonger vs. Abijah who, in accordance with the prophet's injunction to his father (see 8,223), fights, not offensively, but only defensively against Israel.

Having described Jeroboam's hostile initiative, Josephus next recounts Abijah's response. Characteristically, he begins by noting the Judean's inner state in the face of the Israelite threat: "hearing of Jeroboam's approach (ἔφοδον), he was not dismayed (οὐ κατεπλάγη)⁵⁹², but, with a spirit rising above (γενόμενος δ' ἐπάνω... τῷ

588. Compare AJ 10,4 Sennacherib "paid no regard (οὐδὲν ἐφρόντισεν) to the agreement he had made".

589. The above construction "collecting an army" recurs in BJ 1,214; 2,654; AJ 7,232; 9,112; 14,297; 18,100.

590. This is Josephus' only use of the construction πολεμέω + ἐπὶ + accusative. More frequent in his writings are the following constructions: πολεμέω + dative (see e.g., AJ 9,1), πολεμέω + direct object (AJ 8,223), πολεμέω + πρὸς + accusative (AJ 12,130).

591. Compare Diodorus of Sicily, Bibliotheca Historica 17.7.1 who refers to Darius' "despising Alexander's youth" (καταφρονήσας τῆς Ἀλεξάνδρου νεότητος). Cf. too AJ 6,188 where Josephus describes Goliath advancing against David as "contemptuous (καταφρονῶν) and confident of slaying... an adversary of an age so youthful (παῖδα ἔτι τὴν ἡλικίαν)". In connection with Josephus' reference to Abijah's "youth" above, it might be noted that neither he nor the Bible mention this king's actual age at accession.

592. Also elsewhere in his description of battle/crisis scenes, Josephus includes a notation, using a form of the verb καταπλήσσω, that the threatened party was "not dismayed", see AJ 2,286 (Moses is "undaunted" by the success of the Egyptian priests); 4,7 (the Canaanites are "undaunted" [οὐ καταπλαγέντες] by the "onset" [ἔφοδον] of the Hebrews, see the construction in 8,274); 7,122 (David is "undismayed" by the enemy coalition); 12,355 (the inhabitants of Elymais are "not dismayed" [μὴ καταπλαγέντων] by Antiochus' "attack" [ἔφοδον], see 8,274).372 (Judas is "not terrified" by the Greek assault); 13,94 (Jonathan is "not dismayed" by the enemy ambush).357 (military reverses do "not dismay" Alexander Jannaeus); 14,370 (Herod is "not discouraged" by the threats facing him); 20,79 (Izates is "not panic-stricken" by his initial reverse).

φρονήματι)⁵⁹³ above his youth and the hopes the enemy...". So animated, Abijah "raised an army (στρατιὰν ἐπιλέξας) from among the two tribes⁵⁹⁴ and confronted Jeroboam at a place called Mount Samarōn (ὄρος Σαμαρῶν)⁵⁹⁵. Josephus "anticipates" this localization from 2 Chron 13,4a where "Mt. Zemaraim" (2 Par Σομορών) is further specified as "in the hill country of Ephraim". Near this site, Josephus continues, Abijah "encamped and prepared for battle (τὰ πρὸς τὴν μάχην εὐτρέπιζεν⁵⁹⁶)"⁵⁹⁷. Thereupon, he reverts to 13,3 in order to cite its figures for the two armies, Abijah with 400,000 and Jeroboam with double that.

2. *Abijah's Address* (8,275b-281). In 13,4 the Chronicler introduces Abijah's battlefield address rather abruptly: "and Abijah stood up on Mt. Zemaraim... and said 'hear (me), O Jeroboam and all Israel'". Josephus' transition is more fluid: it was "as the armies were drawn up against each other (ἀντιπαρετάσσετο)⁵⁹⁸, ready for action (πρὸς τὰ ἔργα)⁵⁹⁹ and the hazards of war, and were about to engage (συμβαλεῖν ἔμελλε)⁶⁰⁰", that Abijah takes his initiative. Josephus, who has already utilized the localization of 13,4, now simply represents the king as "standing on a certain elevated spot" (στὰς [2 Par 13,4 ἀνέστη] ἐφ' ὑψηλοῦ τινος... τόπου)⁶⁰¹. In place of the Chronistic Abijah's simple "hear me" (2 Par ἀκούσατε) addressed to king and people, he states that the Judean ruler "motioned with his hand (τῇ χειρὶ κατασείσας)⁶⁰² and asked the people and Jeroboam⁶⁰³ first to hear (ἀκού-

---

593. Compare *AJ* 14,355 (Herod) "letting his spirit (τὸ φρόνημα) rise above (ἐπάνω) the blow...". Cf. too *RA* 5.34.1 where a Roman maiden is praised for having a "spirit (φρόνημα) superior (ἐπάνω) to her sex and age".

594. With this phrase compare *AJ* 9,188 (Amaziah) "raising an army (στρατιὰν ἐπιλέξας) from the tribes of Judah and Benjamin...".

595. Lat mons Amororum. SCHLATTER, *Namen*, p. 95, s.v. צְמָרַיִם suggests that perhaps the above phrase should be read ὄρος Σαμαρον.

596. Na reads ηὐτρέπιζεν with MSP.

597. The above phrase "prepare for battle" occurs only here in Josephus.

598. This is the reading of V (apud Hud), followed by NN*Mar. Na reads ἀντιπαρετάττετο, cf. ἀντεπράτεττο, E. In Josephus the verb ἀντιταρατάσσω occurs 11 × in battle contexts as here.

599. The phrase πρὸς (τὰ) ἔργα (τὸ ἔργον) occurs also in *BJ* 5,76 (sg.).263; *AJ* 1,115 (sg.); 2,7; 3,101 (sg.). 301 (sg.). 309; 5,27 (sg.). 118.188.330 (sg.); 11,102 (sg.). 173; 14,94.

600. This phrase recurs in *BJ* 1,215.

601. This is the position assigned to orators also elsewhere in Josephus, see *AJ* 3,84 στὰς ἐπὶ ὑψηλοῦ τινος (Moses); *Vita* 92 στὰς ἐπὶ τριγχοῦ τινος ὑψηλοῦ (Josephus).

602. Compare *AJ* 4,323 where Moses' final words to the people are introduced τῇ χειρὶ κατασείων.

603. In 2 Chron 13,4 Abijah addresses himself first to Jeroboam and then to "all Israel". Josephus' reversal of this sequence above coheres with the fact that in his version of Abijah's speech the Israelite people assumes a higher profile than in the *Vorlage*, see below.

σαι, see 2 Par) him in quiet (μεθ' ἡσυχίας) and then beginning to speak
when silence was obtained (γενομένης... σιωπῆς)"[604]. Such embellishments serve, of course, to invest the Judean's discourse with a
greater solemnity.

Abijah's actual address in 13,5-12 focusses on both political and
cultic issues of contention between North and South. The former are
addressed particularly in vv. 5-8a, the latter in 8b-12a with the whole
being rounded off with the admonition of 12b. In Josephus' version
both components are present (as is the source's use of direct address
throughout), although arranged differently and in diverse proportions.

In 2 Chron 13,5 Abijah opens the "political" portion of his remarks
with the rhetorical question addressed to Israel as a whole: "ought you
(pl.) not to know that the Lord... gave (2 Par ἔδωκεν) the kingship (B
βασιλέα, L βασιλείαν) over Israel for ever to David and his sons by a
covenant (2 Par διαθήκη) of salt"? Josephus converts this question into
the following assertion: "That God has granted (κατένευσεν)[605] the
sovereignty (ἡγεμονίαν)[606] to David and his descendants (ἐκγόνοις)
for all time (εἰς ἅπαντα χρόνον)[607], not even you are unaware (οὐδ'
ὑμεῖς ἀγνοεῖτε)"[608]. In this formulation, Josephus makes no mention of
the "(salt) covenant" between God and the Davidids cited in 13,5. That
"omission" accords with his consistent avoidance/reformulation of
LXX's uses of the term διαθήκη as a rendering of Hebrew ברית in the
sense "covenant, treaty"[609].

604. With the above description of Abijah's endeavours at getting himself a hearing,
compare *AJ* 5,235-236 where Jotham "ascended [Mount] Garizin... and shouting so as to
be heard by the crowd if they would but listen to him quietly (ἡσυχίαν), begged them to
attend to what he had to say. Silence being established (γενομένης... σιγῆς), he told
them...".

605. Elsewhere God is subject of the verb κατανεύω in *AJ* 3,7 where the object is "this
favor", i.e. making the water potable.

606. This is Josephus' only use of the above phrase "grant sovereignty".

607. Elsewhere Josephus uses the phrase "for all time" in reference to the duration of
some prerogative in: *AJ* 4,31 (Aaron's possession of the priesthood); 13,50 (citation of
Demetrius' exemption of Judaea from the poll-tax).128 (citation of Demetrius' remission
of dues).

Abijah's allusion here, of course, is to God's word to David through Nathan in 2 Sam
7,16 which Josephus cites (7,93) as follows: "(God promised) to preserve the kingdom for
(his) children's children and transmit it to them". Cf. also 8,24 (no Biblical parallel as
such) where God promises Solomon at Gibeon "to preserve the kingdom for his
descendants (ἐκγόνοις, so 8,276) a very long time (ἐπὶ πλεῖστον... χρόνον)".

608. Elsewhere as well Josephus has speakers begin their address to the hearer(s) with
the words "you are not ignorant", see *AJ* 2,335 (Moses to God); 9,261 (Hezekiah to the
Levites); 13,198 (Simon to the Jews). Compare 8,227 where Jeroboam begins his speech to
the Israelites "I think you know (γινώσκειν) that every place has God in it...".

609. In all Josephus' 32 uses of διαθήκη (16 × in *BJ*, 16 × in *AJ*, books 13-18) the term
has its standard secular Greek sense, i.e. "testament", "will", etc., see RENGSTORF,
Concordance, s.v. A variety of factors likely influenced Josephus in avoiding LXX's
specialized and recurring use of διαθήκη: the lack of parallel to that usage in the secular
Greek of his primary audience; concern not to arouse Roman suspicions by using the

In 2 Chron 13,6 Abijah shifts his focus from what the Israelites as a whole should know (13,5) to the particular case of Jeroboam who, in violation of God's ordinance, "revolted" (2 Par ἀνέστη) against the Davidid Rehoboam. Josephus, by contrast, keeps the king's words focussed on the whole body of the Israelites: "I wonder... how (θαυμάζω... πῶς)[610] you could revolt (ἀποστάντες, see 8,221) from my father (πατρὸς) and go over (προσέθεσθε) to his servant (τῷ δούλῳ, 2 Par 13,6 ὁ παῖς)[611] Jeroboam, and have now come here with him to make war on (ἐπὶ... πολεμήσοντες)[612] those who were chosen by God (ὑπὸ τοῦ θεοῦ... κεκριμένους)[613] to reign, and to deprive them of the royal power (τὴν ἀρχὴν ἀφαιρησόμενοι)[614] which still remains to them...". Abijah's concluding words here seem formulated with 13,8 ("and now you [pl., the Israelites] think to withstand *the kingdom of the Lord in the hand of the sons of David*") in view; anticipating that statement, Josephus makes it part of the comprehensive political indictment of the entire Northern population with which he has Abijah begin his discourse. To the concluding phrase above, "deprive them (the Davidids) of the royal power which still remains to them" Josephus further appends an extended polemical aside concerning Jeroboam himself reminiscent of his own earlier statements in 8,228.245.265-266: "for the larger part of the realm Jeroboam has until now been unjustly holding (ἀδίκως ἔχει)[615]. But I do not believe he will enjoy possession

term *à la* LXX with political overtones; an indirect polemic against a nascent Christianity with its emphasis on the "new covenant" (recall that in post-LXX Jewish OT translations διαθήκη is replaced by a variety of other renditions, e.g., συνθήκη). On the whole question, see: E. RIGGENBACH, *Der Begriff der διαθήκη im Hebräerbrief*, in *Theologische Studien Theodor Zahn dargebracht*, Leipzig, 1908, 291-316, esp. pp. 295-297; A. JAUBERT, *La notion d'alliance dans le Judaïsme aux abords de l'ère chrétienne*, Paris, 1963, pp. 339-349; AMARU, *Land Theology*, pp. 205-211; PAUL, *Manifesto*, passim; L.H. FELDMAN, *Josephus' Portrait of Noah and its Parallels*, in *PAAJR* 55 (1988) 31-57, esp. pp. 56-57.

610. Also elsewhere Josephus has orators express their "wonder" at some state of affairs, see *BJ* 1,198 (Antipater).501 (Archelaus).628 (Herod);3,405 (friend of Vespasian); 4,93 (Titus).238 (the priest Jesus).

611. Elsewhere too Josephus has δοῦλος where LXX reads παῖς, see *AJ* 8,173 // 3 Rgns 10,8; 8,367 // 3 Rgns 20,6. See GIBBS-FELDMAN, *Slavery*, pp. 298-299, 305.

For the above construction προστίθημι middle + dative (= to join, to go over to someone's side), see: *BJ* 1,190.291; 2,52; *AJ* 6,252; 7,27; 10,108; 12,133.275; 13,48.149; 14,20.32.132.395; 17,266.275; 18,51,181; *Vita* 87.88.123.124.155.271.314. In *AJ* 7,27; *Vita* 87.88.123 one finds the same construction ἀφίστημι + genitive + προστίθημι (middle) + dative as here in 8,276.

612. Cf. ἐπὶ (τὸν Ἀβίαν)... πολεμήσων, 8,274.

613. Elsewhere Josephus uses κρίνω of God's "choosing" some individual for a position of leadership/preeminence in *AJ* 2,28 (Joseph); 3,190 (Aaron); 4,19 (Aaron); 11,139 (Ezra); 13,299 (Hyrcanus); 19,314 (Jonathan).

614. The above phrase "deprive of (the royal) power" recurs in *AJ* 9,151; 14,331.469; 15,32; 20,243.

615. The same phrase recurs in *AJ* 14,11(*bis*): Aristobulus "wrongly holds the royal power (ἀρχήν)".

(ἀπολαύσειν, see 8,236) of this for very long, but, when he has paid God the penalty (δοὺς... δίκην)[616]... he will end his transgressions (παρανομίας) and the insults (ὕβρεων) which he has never ceased to offer (διαλέλοιπεν... ὑβρίζων)[617] Him, persuading you to do the same[618]".

Following the above interlude – which has as such no parallel in the Bible – the Josephian Abijah redirects his attention to the North's defection from Rehoboam, the focus of 2 Chron 13,6-7 as noted above. Whereas, however, the Biblical verses are formulated in the third person and highlight Jeroboam's role in the revolt, in Josephus direct address continues and it is the culpability of the whole Israelite community in the affair which is underscored:

> As for you who were never wronged in any way (μηδὲν ἀδικηθέντες)[619] by my father, but because, following the advice (συμβουλίᾳ πεισθείς)[620] of wicked men (ἀνθρώπων πονηρῶν)[621], in a public assembly (ἐκκλησιάζων)[622] he spoke in a manner that displeased you (μὴ πρὸς ἡδονὴν... ὡμίλησεν)[623], – you deserted (ἐγκατελίπετε)[624] him as it seemed (τῷ μὲν

616. Josephus uses this phrase "pay the penalty" also in *BJ* 1,58.373.378.464.501; 2,455; 4,254.493; 5,398.537.546; *AJ* 6,81.237.307.331; 7,52.152 (+ "to God" as in 8,277).236; 9,170; 12,401; 14,317; 16,8.27.165; 20,88; *Vita* 343; *Ap* 2,143. Cf. δίκην... τρέψειν in 8,266.

617. With the above collocation, compare ἐξύβρισεν... καὶ παρηνόμησεν used of Jeroboam in 8,245. Compare too Josephus' statement in 8,265 that Jeroboam "did not cease (διέλιπεν) nor desist from outraging (ἐξυβρίζων) God...". Note finally that 8,277 is Josephus' only use of the above paronomasia "offer insults".

618. Compare 8,228 "Jeroboam misled the people and caused them to abandon the worship of their fathers and transgress the laws". Note the many echoes of Josephus' own previous judgments on Jeroboam in the words he attributes to Abijah in 8,277.

619. The above phrase "do no wrong" recurs in *BJ* 1,639; *AJ* 1,319; 3,271; 4,76.86.120; 5,(108).145; 6,212.(224).295.297.331; 7,284; 8,386; 10,2.215; 11,221.275; 12,164.291; 13,55; 14,147 (242).249.346; 16,107; 17,127.218; 19,197.

620. The above phrase "follow advice" occurs also in *AJ* 6,208; 7,214.235; 11,197.

621. Josephus' inspiration for this reference is 2 Chron 13,7a which speaks of "certain worthless scoundrels (2 Par ἄνδρες λοιμοὶ υἱοὶ παράνομοι) who gathered around him". As the commentators point out, the referent of "him" in this expression is unclear: is it Jeroboam's co-conspirators (so most scholars) or rather the young advisers who led Rehoboam astray? – see R.B. DILLARD, *2 Chronicles* (WBC, 15), Waco, TX, 1987, pp. 107-108; KNOPPERS, *Rehoboam*, pp. 437-438, n. 48. Josephus resolves the ambiguity: his "wicked men" are clearly Rehoboam's wrong-headed young counsellors.

622. Josephus' other uses of the verb ἐκκλησιάζω are: *BJ* 2,490; 7,47; *AJ* 4,302; 6,56; 10,93; 12,316; 17,161; 19,158.

623. Contrast *AJ* 7,195 where Absalom is described as πρὸς ἡδονὴν ὁμιλῶν. See also 8,214: Rehoboam rouses suspicion by not "immediately assenting to the wishes (τὰ πρὸς ἡδονὴν) of the people" and 8,236: Jeroboam is "deceived by the things the Bethel prophet said to please (τὰ πρὸς ἡδονὴν) him".

624. In 8,256 the same verb is used of God's (threatened) "abandoning" of the Judeans. Mar, *ad loc.*, does not render the phrase ὑπ' ὀργῆς with which Josephus qualifies the Israelites' "desertion" of Rehoboam in 8,277, compare W, *ad loc.*, "vous l'avez abandonné, lui *par colère*".

δοκεῖν), but in reality (ταῖς δ᾽ ἀληθείαις)⁶²⁵ you have separated your-selves from (ἀπὸ... ἀπεσπάσατε) God and His laws (νόμων)⁶²⁶. And yet it would have been fair for you to forgive (συνεγνωκέναι, see 8,220) not only (μόνον) the unpleasant (δυσκόλων, see 8,220) words of a man so young (νέῳ, see νεώτερος, 2 Par 13,7b) and inexperienced (ἀπείρῳ, see δειλὸς τῇ καρδίᾳ, 2 Par 13,7b)⁶²⁷ in governing people (δημαγωγίας)⁶²⁸, but also any further disagreeable act (δυσχερὲς)⁶²⁹ to which his youth (νεότης, see 8,220) and ignorance of public affairs (ἡ ἀμαθία τῶν πραττομένων)⁶³⁰ might have led him, for the sake of his father Solomon and the benefits (εὐεργεσίας)⁶³¹ you have received from him. For the merits of the fathers (τὰς τῶν πατέρων εὐποιίας)⁶³² should be a palliation of the sins (παραίτη-σιν... ἁμαρτίας)⁶³³ of their children (ἐκγόνων, see 8,276)⁶³⁴.

All such considerations notwithstanding, the Israelites, Abijah pro-ceeds to affirm, "took no account (οὐδὲν... ἐλογίσασθε) of these things⁶³⁵ either then or now...". At this point (8,279) Josephus rejoins the thread of the Biblical discourse after an extended segment of what is essentially his own free composition following his parallel to 2 Chron 13,5. In line with 13,8 Josephus now has Abijah challenge the Israelites' grounds for confidence, both military and religious, in attacking Judah.

625. The same construction "as it seemed... but in reality" recurs in 14,291.

626. This is Josephus' only use of the verb ἀποσπάω (+ ἀπὸ) with either "God" or νόμος as object. For 8,277's qualification of the "law(s)" as "his (God's)", see e.g.: *AJ* 11,123.124.127.130.230, cf. SCHLATTER, *Theologie,* p. 62.

627. Josephus uses the above collocation "young and inexperienced" of Solomon in *AJ* 7,336. Note that Josephus here follows the Chronicler in having Abijah insist on Rehoboam's "youth" at the beginning of his reign. Recall, however, that according to 1 Kings 14,21 // 2 Chron 12,13 Rehoboam was 41 at his accession. In Josephus' own presentation this "contradiction" is not so evident in that in his version of the Biblical chronological notes for Rehoboam (see on 8,264 above) he does not reproduce the item about Rehoboam's age at accession. In the above formulation note too the echoes of Rehoboam's dispatch of Adoram in 8,220; there the king sends his official to persuade the Israelites "to forgive (συγγνόντας)... if there had been anything in it [his previous answer to them] ... ill-tempered (δύσκολον) due to his youth (νεότητος)...".

628. This is Josephus' only use of the noun δημαγωγία.

629. This term occurs 27 × in Josephus.

630. This expression occurs only here in Josephus.

631. The term εὐεργεσία occurs 42 × in Josephus. On the term and its cognates, see SPICQ, *Lexicographie,* I, pp. 307-313.

632. This is the only occurrence of this phrase in Josephus. Cf., however, *AJ* 11,169 (Nehemiah addresses the Jews): "you know how God cherishes the memory of our fathers Abraham, Isaac and Jacob, and because of their righteousness does not give up His providential care for us". On the concept of the "merits of the fathers" alluded to here, see A. MARMORSTEIN, *The Doctrine of Merits in Old Rabbinic Literature,* New York, 1968 (rpt.), esp. pp. 147-171.

633. With this phrase compare that of *AJ* 3,246 (the sacrificial victims function) κατὰ παραίτησιν ἁμαρτιῶν.

634. This is the reading of MSP followed by NaMar. NN* read ἐγγόνων, RO ἐπομένων.

635. Compare 8,274 Jeroboam "took no thought (οὐδενὸς... φροντίσας) of these things...", i.e. Ahijah's words of doom. King and people are equally heedless.

In so doing, however, the historian both rearranges and significantly expands the Biblical formulations:

you have brought (ἧκε)[636] this great army of yours against us; and in what does it place its hope of victory (τίνι... πεπιστευκὼς περὶ τῆς νίκης)[637]? Is it (ἤ)[638], perhaps, in the golden heifers (δαμάλεσι, see 8,228.231)[639] and the altars on the mountains (τοῖς ἐπὶ τῶν ὀρῶν βωμοῖς, see 8,265 ἐπὶ τῶν ὑψηλῶν ὀρῶν βωμοὺς)[640], which are proofs of your impiety and not by any means of your devoutness (δείγματα τῆς ἀσεβείας[641]... οὐχὶ τῆς θρησκείας)[642]? Or is it your numbers, which far exceed those of our army, that make you confident (εὐέλπιδας ἀπεργάζεται)[643]? But there is no strength whatever[644] in many tens of thousands when a army fights in a unjust cause (μετ᾽ ἀδικημάτων [see ἀδικηθέντες, 8,277] πολεμοῦντος)[645]. For it is only in justice and piety towards God (τῷ δικαίῳ καὶ πρὸς τὸ θεῖον εὐσεβεῖ)[646] that the surest hope (βεβαιοτάτην ἐλπίδα)[647] of conquering one's adversaries (τοῦ κρατεῖν τῶν ἐναντίων) is bound to lie[648].

With the concluding statement of the above sequence, Josephus "reconnects", once again, with the wording of his source, specifically with Abijah's affirmation in 13,10a "... as for us the Lord is our God

636. So RO Lat followed by N*Mar. Na reads ἥκετε with MS(P), while N conjectures ἥκει.
637. This particular expression occurs only here in Josephus. Compare, however, Titus' challenging questions to the defenders of Jerusalem in BJ 6,330 .... πλήθει πεποιθότες; and 6,349 τίνι πεποιθότες;.
638. So NN*, followed by Mar, with reference to Lat an. Na reads ἤ with codd E.
639. Josephus' term here corresponds to that of L 2 Par 13,8 (B has μόσχοι), cf. MT עגלי.
640. Unlike the "calves", Jeroboam's "altars" are not cited in the source-text, 2 Chron 13,8. In combining the two items here, Josephus has Abijah echo and synthesize statements on Jeroboam's misdeeds from earlier, separate contexts, see 8,226 (the calves) and 265 (the altars).
641. Josephus uses the noun ἀσεβεία some 40 ×.
642. With this phrase compare Samuel's statement to Saul in AJ 6,148 that sacrifices of the disobedient represent δείγματα τῆς πονηρίας οὐκ εὐσέβειαν.
643. This is Josephus' only use of the above phrase "make confident". The verb ἀπεργάζομαι occurs 19 × in his writings, the adjective εὐέλπις 7 × (BJ 1,215; AJ 2,270.280; 5,346; 8,6.279; 9,55).
644. NaMar read as the opening three words of this sentence ἀλλ᾽ οὐδ᾽ ἡτισοῦν, while N prints ἀλλ᾽ οὐδ᾽ ἥτις. Compare the varying readings of the codd: οὐδ᾽ ἥτις οὖν SP; οὐ δή τις RO; οὐ δή τις οὖν M.
645. This is Josephus' only use of the above phrase "fight with injustice".
646. The collocation δίκαιος and εὐσεβής (or the reverse) occurs also in AJ 7,338.341.356.384; 8,300.394; 9,236.260; 14,315; 15,182. The above phrase "pious towards the Deity" recurs in BJ 2,128; AJ 14,257, cf. AJ 7,384; 9,236; 12,42 (obj. "God").
647. The above phrase "well-founded hope" recurs in BJ 1,(293).567; 7,165.413; AJ 5,351; 8,8; (15,153); 16,238. On the term βεβαιόω, etc., see SPICQ, Lexicographie, I, pp. 182-185.
648. Compare 12,409 (Nicanor) κρατεῖ τῶν ἐναντίων.

and we have not forsaken him" and 11bα "we keep the charge (2 Par φυλάσσομεν... τὰς φυλακὰς) of the Lord our God". Josephus' formulation of these claims runs: "and this (i.e. the just-mentioned "justice and piety" that give "hope of victory") belongs to us who have from the beginning observed the laws (τετηρηκόσιν... τὰ νόμιμα)[649] and worshipped our own God (τὸν ἴδιον θεὸν σεβομένοις)[650]". In thus linking a version of 13,10a,11bα to his rendering of 13,8, Josephus, it will be noted, leaves aside the Biblical Abijah's detailed allusions to the cultic situation in both North (13,9) and South (13,10b-11a). In connection with his reference to Judah's "own God" above, Josephus goes his own way once more, qualifying that God as one "whom no hands have formed out of perishable matter (ἐξ ὕλης φθαρτῆς)[651] and no wicked (πονηροῦ) king has cunningly (ἐπίνοια) made to deceive the populace (ἐπὶ τῇ τῶν ὄχλων ἀπάτῃ)[652], but who is His own work (ὅς ἔργον ἐστὶν αὐτοῦ)[653] and the beginning and end of all things (ἀρχὴ καὶ τέλος τῶν ἀπάντων)[654]".

In concluding Abijah's speech Josephus leaves aside the king's affirmation (2 Chron 13,12a) about the presence with the Judean army of both God and the priest-trumpeters. Conversely, he expands the appeal of 13,12b ("O sons of Israel, do not fight against the Lord ... for you cannot succeed"); his Abijah ends up: "I advise you, therefore,

---

649. The above expression "observe the laws" recurs in *AJ* 8,395; 9,222.

650. Josephus uses the verb σέβω (σέβομαι) 30 × with both the Lord (as here) and "other gods/idols" (see, e.g., 9,205) as objects. See SCHLATTER, *Theologie*, pp. 97-98.

Josephus designates the God of the Jews as "their own (God)" elsewhere in *AJ* 8,192.194.335.338; 9,20, cf. 10,212 (Nebuchadnezzar's "own god").

With Abijah's double claim for Judah ("we have observed the laws and worshipped our own God") here, compare his double charge against Israel in 8,277 ("you have separated yourselves from God and his laws").

651. Josephus uses the equivalent phrase ἐκ φθαρτῆς ὕλης in reference to the mortal human body in the context of his discourse on suicide in *BJ* 3,372.

652. Compare 8,229 (Jeroboam) ἐξηπάτησε τὸν λαόν, cf. 9,18. Josephus uses the noun ἀπάτη 35 ×.

653. On this characterization of God, see SCHLATTER, *Gott*, p. 17; idem, *Theologie*, pp. 5, 6, n. 1. With reference to the designation, J.A. MONTGOMERY, *The Religion of Flavius Josephus*, in *JQR* N.S. 11 (1920-1921) 277-305, p. 285 avers: "In one passage alone Josephus takes a step into theosophy when he makes Rehoboam (sic!) declare the doctrine...".

654. With this "confession" compare Josephus' statement concerning the Jewish God in *Ap* 2,190 ἀρχὴ καὶ μέσα καὶ τέλος οὗτος τῶν πάντων, cf. PHILO, *De Plantatione* 93; Rev 21,6;22,13. On the antecedents and analogues of this formulation in Greek religio-philosophical writings (e.g., PLATO, *Leges* 4 715 D), see: W.C. VAN UNNIK, *Het Godspredikaat "Het Begin en het Einde" bij Flavius Josephus en in de Openbaring von Johannes* (Mededelingen der Koninklijke Nederlandse Akademie van Wetenschappen, Afdl. Letterkunde, N.R. 39,1), Amsterdam, 1970, esp. pp. 7-13,72-73; and J.H. NEYREY, *"Without Beginning of Days or End of Life" (Hebrews 7:3): Topos for True Deity*, in *CBQ* 53 (1991) 440-456.

even now to repent (μεταγνῶναι)⁶⁵⁵ and adopt the better plan (ἀμείνω λογισμὸν)⁶⁵⁶ of ceasing from warfare (παύσασθαι τοῦ πολεμεῖν)⁶⁵⁷ and to respect (γνωρίσαι, see γνωρισθησομένων, 8,242) (the rights of) your country (τὰ πάτρια)⁶⁵⁸ and the power which has led you on (τὸ προαγαγὸν)⁶⁵⁹ to so great a height of prosperity (μέγεθος εὐδαιμονίας)⁶⁶⁰".

3. *The Battle* (8,282-284). Josephus has noticeably modified the Biblical Abijah's battlefield address in various respects (see further below). In coming now to describe the battle itself, he hews more closely to the source's content and sequence. Following a concluding notice for the king's discourse ("such was the speech which Abias made to the people"), he recounts Jeroboam's setting of an ambush (// 13,13): "he secretly sent some of his soldiers to surround (περικυκλωσομένους)⁶⁶¹ Abias from certains parts of the camp that were not observed". Jeroboam did this, Josephus adds, "while he (Abijah) was still speaking"; Jeroboam is thus as heedless of Abijah's warnings as he was of those his wife brought him from Ahijah (see 8,274). The historian further amplifies 13,14a's reference to the Judean army's finding itself caught between Jeroboam's forces with a typical allusion to the emotional state of the troops, just as he magnifies Abijah's own role at this critical juncture: "... when he was caught (περιληφθέντος) in the enemy's midst, his army was alarmed and their spirits sank (κατέδεισε καὶ ταῖς ψυχαῖς ἀνέπεσεν)⁶⁶², but Abias encouraged (παρεθάρρυνε)⁶⁶³

655. Josephus uses μεταγινώσκω also in *AJ* 6,42; 7,22; 14,375, cf. 8,225 (Jeroboam is apprehensive) that the people might "repent" (μετανοῆσαν).

656. The phrase "better plan" recurs in 16,392.

657. Compare 14,55 (Aristobulus begs Pompey) παύσασθαι τοῦ πολέμου, cf. 14,447.

658. Compare the rendering of W, *ad loc.* "... en vous ralliant aux institutions nationales...". Cf. 8,229 Jeroboam caused the people to abandon "the paternal (πατρίου) worship".

659. This is Josephus' only use of this substantivized participle of the verb προάγω. W, *ad loc.* renders "aux principes".

660. This expression occurs also in *AJ* 2,7.214.217; 6,130; 8,126. On the key term εὐδαιμονία of Greek ethics used here by Josephus, see the observation of S. MASON, *Flavius Josephus and the Pharisees: A Composition-Critical Study* (SPB, 39), Leiden, 1991, p. 185: "... although the word... is entirely absent from the LXX, Josephus introduces it no less than 47 times in his biblical paraphrase [in the whole of the Josephan corpus the term occurs 76 ×]". See also H.-F. WEISS, *Pharisäismus und Hellenismus. Zur Darstellung des Judentums im Geschichtswerk des jüdischen Historikers Flavius Josephus*, in *OLZ* 74 (1979) 421-433, c. 427.

661. Josephus' form here corresponds to the περιεκύκλωσε of L 2 Par 13,13, compare B ἀπέστρεψεν. The verb περικυκλόω occurs also in *AJ* 6,369; 8,413.

662. Josephus employs this same collocation in reference to Saul's emotional state prior to his final battle with the Philistines in *AJ* 6,329. He has used its second element ("their spirits fell") in 8,256 in describing the Judeans' response to Shemaiah's announcement that God was threatening to abandon them.

663. Josephus employs the verb παραθαρσύνω/παραθαρρύνω only in *AJ* where it occurs 15 × .

them and urged (παρεκάλει) them to put their hope in God (τὰς ἐλπίδας ἔχειν ἐν τῷ θεῷ)⁶⁶⁴, saying that He was not encircled by the enemy (οὐ κεκυκλῶσθαι πρὸς τῶν πολεμίων)⁶⁶⁵". Josephus next reproduces, essentially unchanged, the sequence of 13,14b-15a which recounts the Judeans' cry to God⁶⁶⁶, the priests' trumpet blowing (τῶν ἱερέων τῇ σάλπιγγι σημανάντων)⁶⁶⁷ and the army's battle shout⁶⁶⁸.

2 Chron 13,15b-19 relate Judah's victory over the Israelites. In line with 13,15b.16b Josephus first underscores the divine involvement in that victory: "Then God crushed the spirit(s) (ἔθραυσε τὰ φρονήματα)⁶⁶⁹ of the enemy and broke their strength (τὰς ἀκμὰς... ἐξέλυσεν)⁶⁷⁰, while He made (ἐποίησεν) Abias's army stronger (ὑπερτέραν)⁶⁷¹". He embellishes 2 Chron 13,17a's reference to the massacre perpetrated by the Judeans subsequent to their victory: "such a slaughter was never recorded to have been made in any war (ὅσος... οὐδέποτ' ἐμνημονεύθη φόνος ἐν πολέμῳ γεγονέναι)⁶⁷² of Greeks or barbarians (οὔθ' Ἑλλήνων οὔτε βαρβάρων)⁶⁷³ as they made... when they were permitted by God to win so wonderful and celebrated

---

664. With this formulation compare *AJ* 12,300 where Judas Maccabeus exhorts his troops "to place their hopes of victory in God" (τὰς ἐλπίδας τῆς νίκης ἔχοντας ἐν τῷ θεῷ).

665. With this phrase compare *BJ* 5,338 πολεμίοις κεκυκλωμένων. Note the word play in 8,282: Jeroboam's soldiers are sent to "surround" (περικυκλωσομένους) Abias who reminds his own troops that God is not "encircled" (κεκυκλῶσθαι) by the enemy.

666. Josephus gives an explicit content to this cry: "all of them together called upon God to be their ally (τὴν παρὰ τοῦ θεοῦ συμμαχίαν, see the related datival construction in *BJ* 7,319; *AJ* 3,45)".

667. Compare 2 Par 13,14bβ οἱ ἱερεῖς ἐσάλπισαν ταῖς σάλπιγξιν. Josephus' above construction "sound the trumpet" recurs in *AJ* 7,17; 10,213.214. Recall that Josephus does not reproduce Abijah's reference to the presence of the priest-trumpeters with the Judean army of 2 Chron 13,12a. As a result his mention of them here appears rather unexpectedly.

668. Josephus' term for this "shout", i.e. ἀλαλάξαντες corresponds to the ἠλάλαξεν of L 2 Par 13,15, compare B ἐβόησαν. Elsewhere Josephus uses ἀλαλάζω in *BJ* 7,403; *AJ* 5,225; 6,191; 12,372.427.

669. This is Josephus' only use of this idiom. His verb ἔθραυσε is the same as that of L 2 Par 13,15b (here with object "Jeroboam and Israel"), compare B ἐπάταξεν.

670. Only here in Josephus.

671. The above expression "make stronger" occurs only here in Josephus.

672. Mar, *Josephus*, V, p. 724, n. a points out that this formulation is reminiscent of Thucydides 2.47.3: οὐ μέντοι τοσοῦτός γε λοιμὸς οὐδὲ φθορὰ οὕτως ἀνθρώπων οὐδαμοῦ ἐμνημονεύετο γενέσθαι.

673. Josephus uses variations of the above formula "neither Greeks nor barbarians" in underscoring the unprecedentedness of various other events he relates, see *BJ* 6,199 (a mother's eating her own child during the siege of Jerusalem); *AJ* 4,12 (of Korah's rebellion);11,299 (of the desecration of the Temple by Joannes' murder of his brother therein). Dionysius likewise several times designates events as being unprecedented in the history of both "Greeks and barbarians", see, e.g., *RA* 2.63.2; 4.79.2; 7.3.2,12.4. On the history of the "Greek/barbarian" opposition, see J. JÜTHNER, *Hellen und Barbaren. Aus der Geschichte des Nationalbewusstseins*, Leipzig, 1923.

(θαυμαστὴν καὶ διαβόητον)[674] a victory[675]". Josephus motivates this fulsome claim utilizing items drawn from 2 Chron 13,17b (the 500,000 Israelite casualties) and 19 (the Northern cities taken by Abijah): "for they struck down (κατέβαλον)[676] five hundred thousand of their foes and plundered (διήρπασαν) their strongest cities (τὰς πόλεις... τὰς ὀχυρωτάτας, see 8,255) after taking them by storm (ἑλόντες κατὰ κράτος)[677]". Drawing on 2 Chron 13,19bβ, he then proceeds to cite two of the cities conquered by Abijah: "these were Bethel (βηθήλην, 2 Par Βαιθὴλ) and its province (τοπαρχίαν)[678] and Isana ('Ισανὰν)[679] and its province (καὶ τὴν τοπαρχίαν αὐτῆς)[680]". With this reference to just two of the cities subjugated by Abijah, Josephus leaves aside a third site mentioned in 2 Chron 13,19, i.e. "Ephrain" (so MT Ketib; Qere and 2 Par have Ephrōn)[681].

4. *Contrasting Fates of the two kings* (8,285-286). 2 Chron 13,20-23 (2 Par/RSV 13,20-14,1) rounds off the preceding episode by contrasting the subsequent fates of Jeroboam and Abijah. Following 13,20a Josephus first cites the case of the Northern ruler: "and Jeroboam, after this defeat, was never again powerful (ἴσχυσεν, see 2 Par οὐκ ἔσχεν ἰσχὺν) so long as Abias lived". 2 Chron 13,20b goes on to state concerning Jeroboam that "the Lord smote him and he died", thereby seeming to suggest that his death transpired during the reign of Abijah mentioned in 13,21ff. Josephus withholds mention of Jeroboam's demise for a later

674. Mar, *Josephus*, V, p. 724, n.b points out that the same collocation of adjectives appears in Josephus' description of Eleazar's victory over the Philistines in *AJ* 7,309. Apart from *AJ* 7,309 and 8,284 the historian's only other use of the adjective διαβόητος is in 9,182 (Elisha was "renowned" for his righteousness).

675. The phrase rendered above as "win... victory" is νίκην ... λαβεῖν. It occurs also in *AJ* 4,153; 8,295; 11,64.

676. The verb καταβάλλω occurs frequently in Josephus in reference to "killing" in battle, see, e.g., *AJ* 6,369; 7,308.310.

677. The above construction αἱρέω + κατὰ κράτος is frequent in Josephus' battle accounts, see: *BJ* 1,19.32; 6,339; 7,113; *AJ* 5,180; 6,291.356; 7,160.161; 8,151.310; 9,42.105.253.278; 10,1.271; 11,91; 13,337.357; 14,478; 20,244; *Vita* 82.374; *Ap* 1,75.88. The construction occurs as well in *RA* 3.38.2; 8.19.3,36.2,91.1; 10.21.6. The above combination "take by force" + "plunder" recurs in *AJ* 7,160.

678. See W, *ad loc.*, "et sa toparchie". Josephus' use (15× in *BJ*, 8× in *AJ*) of this term – a designation (synonymous with τόπος) for an administrative sub-division of Ptolemaic and Roman Egypt – in reference to 9th century Israel is an obvious anachronism (MT [and L's e₂] 2 Chron 13,19 speaks of Bethel's "daughters", B of its "villages", κώμας). On the word see H. KORTENBEUTEL, τόπος, in *PW* 2:12 (1937) 1723 and the literature cited there.

679. Compare the readings of 2 Par 13,19: Κανὰ (B), Ιεσσηνα (e₂), Εσσηνα (b), Ανα (AN rell). MT has עֶפְרוֹן. The site "Isana" is mentioned by Josephus also in the parallel passages *BJ* 1,334 (t.e.; codd κανά) and *AJ* 14,458.

680. This last phrase is absent in RO Lat. NN*NaMar retain it.

681. Mar, *Josephus*, V, p. 725, n.d incorrectly cites the MT name of the city in question as "Ephraim".

moment (see 8,287). His doing so is likely influenced by the chronology of MT Kings which indicates that Jeroboam reigned on into the second year of Abijah's successor Asa (see 1 Kings 14,20; 15,9.25).

Turning next to the case of Abijah, Josephus states immediately: "after a reign of three years[682] dying (τελευτᾷ, compare 3 Rgns 15,8 and L 2 Par 14,1 ἐκοιμήθη, B 2 Par 14,1 ἀπέθανεν) he was buried (θάπτεται = 3 Rgns 15,8, cf. ἔθαψαν, 2 Par 14,1)[683] in Jerusalem in the tombs of his forefathers (ἐν ταῖς προγονικαῖς θήκαις)[684]". Only thereafter does Josephus cite, in an appended note (// 2 Chron 13,21abβ), the statistics for the king's sons (22), daughters (16) and wives (14)[685]. Finally, he reproduces the information cited in 13,23b: "he was succeeded (διεδέξατο δ' αὐτοῦ τὴν βασιλείαν, compare βασιλεύει, 3 Rgns 15,8; ἐβασίλευσεν, 2 Par 14,1)[686] by his son (ὁ υἱὸς)[687] Asanos ("Ασανος)[688], this youth's mother being named Machaia (Μαχαία)[689]. During his government the land of the Israelites ('Ισραη-

682. This indication concerning the length of Abijah's reign agrees with that given in 1 Kings 15,1 (+ L's 127/c₂) and 2 Chron (Par) 13,1. Contrast B and the remaining L MSS in 3 Rgns 15,1 which assign Abijah a *six* year reign.

683. Josephus uses this h.p. also in *AJ* 1,256; 5,117.232.270; 8,211.307; 9,172.215.243; 10,46; 12,285. The above combination of h.ps. "dies and is buried" occurs also in *AJ* 1,256; 5,117.270; 12,285, cf. *AJ* 2,196; 9,215.

684. This phrase occurs only here in Josephus. Compare the Biblical notices on Abijah's place of burial: "with his fathers in the city of David" (1 Kings 15,8) // "in the city of David" (2 Chron 13,23).

685. In accordance with his consistent practice (see n. 498), Josephus passes over the "source notice" of 2 Chron 13,22 = 1 Kings 15,7a. He likewise leaves aside the notice of 2 Chron 13,21aα, "Abijah grew mighty" – understandably so since he has just made mention of Abijah's death.

686. See n. 21 on 8,212.

687. RO, followed by NN*, add αὐτοῦ.

688. MT Asa, LXX 'Ασά. Josephus (like Chronicles) lacks an equivalent to either of the divergent synchronisms for Asa's accession offered by MT and LXX 1 Kings 15,9. In the former (1 Kings 15,9) Asa accedes in Jeroboam's *20th* year, while according to B L* 3 Rgns Abijah's death (cf. 15,8) and Asa's accession (15,9) take place in the *24th* year of Jeroboam (In L's 127/c₂ Abijah dies in Jeroboam's *20th* year (so MT) and Asa accedes in his *21st* year). As we will be noting, Josephus similarly provides no synchronisms in a whole series of further cases in which MT and 3 Rgns diverge.

689. Josephus' form here corresponds to the "Maacah" of MT 1 Kings 15,10 (the parallel text 2 Chron 13,23 leaves her unnamed).13 (= 2 Chron [Par] 15,16), compare 3 Rgns 15,10.13 where Asa's mother is called rather 'Ανὰ (this most likely to distinguish her from the "Maacah" who in 1 Kings 15,2= 2 Chron 13,2 appears as mother of Abijah, and so the grandmother of Asa). In 1 Kings 15,10 "Maacah" (so MT, 3 Rgns 'Ανὰ) is further qualified (just as is the "Maacah" of MT 1 Kings 15,2, compare 2 Chron 11,20-21, see above) as daughter of "Abishalom" (so MT, 3 Rgns 'Αβεσ(σ)αλώμ; like the Chronicler Josephus simply leaves the name of "Maacah's" father unmentioned).

From the above it appears that MT 1 Kings 15,2.10 assign to both Abijah and his son Asa mothers and maternal grandfathers bearing the same names (in 3 Rgns they are the sons, respectively, of "Maacah" and "Ana", each of their fathers bearing the same name, i.e. "Abes(s)alōm"). Josephus' nomenclature for the persons involved avoids all such confusion: Abijah's mother is "Machanē", daughter of "Thamarē" and granddaughter of

λιτῶν)⁶⁹⁰ enjoyed peace (εἰρήνης ἀπέλαυεν, compare ἡσύχασεν, 2 Par 14,1)⁶⁹¹ for ten years (ἐπὶ ἔτη δέκα, compare ἔτη δέκα, B 2 Par 14,1)".

Summary. MT and LXX 2 Chronicles 13 do not evidence significant differences that would be reflected in Josephus' own presentation (It might, however, be pointed out that in this sequence Josephus evidences a whole series of verbal correspondences with L as against B 2 Par, see nn. 661, 668, 669). Several of his reworkings of the Chronistic chapter do deserve attention at the end of our discussion, however. Repeatedly, as we have seen, the historian magnifies the status of the protagonist, Abijah⁶⁹². Especially noteworthy is further his wide-going "reconstitution" of the discourse attributed to the Judean king in 2 Chron 13,4-12. As will be recalled, the Chronistic speech revolves around the political and cultic offenses of Jeroboam and his people with the latter category being singled out for somewhat greater attention. The Josephan version, on the contrary, clearly puts the emphasis on the political issue, while at the same time highlighting the role of the people as a whole

"Absalōn" (8,249), while Asa is son of "Machaia" (8,286) whose father he leaves unmentioned. Here again, one perceives the care taken by Josephus in eliminating the inconsistencies of his Biblical sources.

To be noted here is likewise W's rendering, *ad loc.* of 8,286 (διεδέξατο δ'αὐτοῦ τὴν βασιλείαν ὁ υἱὸς Ἄσανος καὶ ἡ μήτηρ τοῦ νεανίσκου Μαχαία...): "il (Abias) eut pour successeur au trône... Asa... ainsi que la mère du jeune homme,... Machéa" (compare Mar "he was succeeded.... by... Asanos, this youth's mother being named Machaia"). Concerning Josephus' formulation so understood W, *Josèphe*, II, p. 219, n.2 comments: "aucun texte ne dit qu'elle ait été associée au trône". Josephus' text need not be understood as affirming this either, however.

690. Mar, *Josephus*, V, p. 725, n. h calls attention to Josephus' "slip" here; given that Asa was king of Judah, not Israel, the reference, in accord with Josephus' normal *Sprachgebrauch*, should be to the "(land of) the two tribes" or "of Jerusalem", cf. n. 139 Compare 2 Chron 13,23 "the land" (BL* + "of Judah"). That "slip" would seem to point to the historian's dependence on the indeterminate "the land" of MT (and various LXX MSS) (which he then carelessly hastens to "specify" as "of the Israelites") since it is hardly likely that if he had before him the BL* reading of 2 Par 14,1, i.e. "land of Judah" he would have replaced this with an (incorrect) mention of the "land of the Israelites".

691. This construction, "enjoy peace", occurs also in *BJ* 1,201; *AJ* 7,305; 8,38 (11,216); 14,311.

692. In this connection it might be recalled that Kings and Chronicles differ in their estimate of Abijam/Abijah. The former (see 1 Kings 15,3) rates him among Judah's "bad" kings, whereas in Chronicles (which lacks a parallel to 1 Kings 15,3) his triumph over Jeroboam clearly intimates his righteousness. Josephus' presentation aligns itself with that of the Chronicler. The Rabbis, on the contrary, charge Abijah with a variety of (non-Biblical) offenses: inhumane mutilation of the corpses of the Israelites he had slain in battle, insulting the prophet Ahijah (i.e. with his reference to the "worthless scoundrels" around Jeroboam in 2 Chron 13,7 which itself might seem to allude to Ahijah's promise of kingship to Jeroboam in 1 Kings 11,31ff.), or failure to eliminate the golden calf following his capture of Bethel as cited in 2 Chron 13,19. See GINZBERG, *Legends*, VI, p. 307, n. 16 for references.

vis-à-vis that of Jeroboam in the "revolt" against Rehoboam. Conversely, as noted, Josephus either leaves unused or reformulates in more general terms the "cultic particulars" enumerated by Abijah in 2 Chron 13,9.10b-11. Such a procedure accords with his general tendency to curtail the sources' extensive and detailed material concerning the legitimate, and especially the illegitimate, cult, see below. That tendency, in turn, may reflect Josephus' concern not to weary Gentile readers with particulars of alien religious systems, whereas his accentuation of the "political" component in Abijah's speech is likely intended to offer his audience something more congenial[693]. In this connection it should also be noted that Josephus' reworking of this political dimension of Abijah's discourse goes together with a heightened element of "Davidid apologetic" (Rehoboam never "wronged" the Israelites who, moreover, should have kept in mind Solomon's "benefits" to them). Apparently, Josephus experienced no tension between this emphasis and his equally emphatic previous insistence on the North-South split as something divinely instigated and effected – a point left unaddressed in his version of Abijah's speech[694], just as he seems unconscious of any discrepancy between the "benefits" he has Abijah claim Solomon did the Israelites and those same Israelites' invocation of the "heavy yoke" Solomon made them bear, see 8,213[695].

Finally, a word seems in order concerning the purposes and effects of Josephus' juxtaposing his version of 2 Chronicles 13 with that of 1 Kings 14. In so doing Josephus presents us with a sequence whose components' common features mutually reinforce one another. Both segments have, first of all, as their core feature a lengthy warning discourse concerning the conduct of Jeroboam and his people. In both cases too the king shows himself heedless of the warning which he receives. Therein, in turn, one may recognize Jeroboam's accentuated moral decline: Jadōn's admonition initially affected him deeply (see 8,235), whereas he simply brushes aside those of Ahijah (see 8,274) and Abijah (see 8,282). Striking too is the contrast between Jeroboam and his people here in their reaction to Abijah's address and that assumed

693. Battlefield addresses like the one he here attributes to Abijah are, of course, standard features of Greco-Roman historiography; they abound, e.g., in *RA*.

694. An analogous "tension" is not, of course, absent from the Biblical accounts themselves.

695. Similarly, the speech Josephus ascribes to Abijah with its emphasis on all the mitigating circumstances surrounding Rehoboam's ill-conceived response to the Israelites (see 8,278) appears at variance with the sharply negative judgment the historian himself pronounces on Rehoboam as "a man of boastful and foolish nature" (8,264). A further such discrepancy involves Abijah's claim that his Judeans have "from the beginning observed the laws and worshipped our own God" (8,280) vis-à-vis Josephus' description of the defection of Rehoboam and his people in 8,251-253.

by Rehoboam and the two tribes faced with Shemaiah's word. The former's failure to "repent" as Abijah ends up urging them to do (see 8,281) ensures that God will not relent with them as he did with their Southern counterparts (see 8,257), but will rather bring upon them the full destruction narrated in Josephus' subsequent account.

VII

BAASHA'S COUP
(8,287-289)

Introduction. At this point (8,287), following his utilization of the Chronistic *Sondergut* of 2 Chronicles 13 in 8,274-286, Josephus reverts to that point in Kings with which he had left off at the end of 8,273, i.e. the closing notices for Jeroboam, 1 Kings 14,19-20 (MT, > 3 Rgns). In Kings itself those notices are followed by an extensive segment, 14,21-15,24, dealing in turn with the Southern rulers Rehoboam, Abijam (Abijah) and Asa; only thereafter in 15,25 does the account of Nadab, son of Jeroboam, whose accession is mentioned in 14,20b resume. The result of this arrangement is that Kings' story "gets ahead of itself". Specifically, 1 Kings 15,16-22, in the context of a presentation concerning Asa of Judah (15,9-24), speaks of that king's conflict with Baasha of Israel, even though the latter's seizure of power via murder of Nadab will not be related until 15,28. Josephus rearranges the material of Kings so as to obviate this difficulty. In what precedes he has already dealt with the Southern kings Rehoboam and Abijah (Abijam) whom Kings treats in 1 Kings 14,21-31 and 15,1-8, respectively. He reserves his treatment of Asa (// 1 Kings 15,9-24) until after his account of Baasha's coup against Nadab. In other words then, Josephus reverses the sequence of 1 Kings 15,9-24 (or more precisely its [remote] parallel, 2 Chronicles 14-15, see below) and 15,25-30(31-32), reproducing the "Northern material" of 14,19-20 (MT) and 15,25-32 in a continuous sequence. Accordingly, when he comes to relate the war between Asa and Baasha (see 8,303-306), the latter is already familiar to the reader.

Josephus begins his new segment devoted to the Northern succession with a notice that rounds off his treatment of the Judean Abijah: "such then is the account we have received concerning Abias (καὶ τὰ μὲν περὶ Ἀβίαν... οὕτως παρειλήφαμεν)[696]". Passing over the "source notice" of 1 Kings 14,19, Josephus reproduces the content of 14,20: "Jeroboam... died (ἐτελεύτησε)... after ruling (ἄρξας, compare βασιλεύσας, 8,264) twenty-two years. He was succeeded (διαδέχεται δ᾽ αὐτὸν,

---

696. Compare *AJ* 14,491 καὶ τοῦτο μὲν τὸ τέλος τῆς Ἀσαμωναίου γενεᾶς παρειλήφαμεν. Such formulae are frequent in Dionysius, either at the beginning or end of a given account, see, e.g., his concluding notice on the reign of Numa Pompilius, *RA* 2.76.6 καὶ τὰ μὲν περὶ πομπιλίου νόμα τοσαῦτα παρελάβομεν, cf. 2.48.1,72.6; 4.40.7.

compare βασιλεύει, 3 Rgns 15,25)[697] by his son (παῖς, so 3 Rgns 15,25) Nabados (Νάβαδος)[698]...". Thereafter, he proceeds immediately to the double chronological indication furnished by 15,25: Nadab's succession comes in the second year of the reign of Asa[699] (whose accession was mentioned just previously in 8,286), and himself rules two years[700]. To the latter item he then appends a (negative) evaluation of "Nabados" inspired by 15,26: this king "resembled (ἐμφερὴς)[701] his father in impiety (ἀσέβειαν, see 8,279) and wickedness (πονηρίαν)[702]".

The core of Kings' presentation of Nadab is the notice of 15,27 on his assassination by Baasha during the former's siege of the Philistine stronghold Gibbethon. Josephus rearranges the sequence of this notice in which it is only after mention of Nadab's murder at Gibbethon that one hears of his laying siege to the site. By contrast, Josephus first records Nabados' siege (πολιορκίᾳ λαβεῖν αὐτὴν προσέμενεν, compare περιεκάθισεν, 3 Rgns 15,27)[703] of "Gabathōn" (Γαβαθῶνα, 3 Rgns Γαβαθὼν)[704], "a city belonging to the Philistines" (πόλιν Παλαιστίνων, compare τῇ τῶν ἀλλοφύλων, 3 Rgns 15,27)[705]. Only then does he recount the king's assassination: "he was killed [there] as the victim

697. Elsewhere Josephus uses the h.p. of διαδέχομαι (= "succeed") with accusative of person as here also in *AJ* 1,85; 8,313; 9,204; 18,32; 20,33.74. The same form occurs in conjunction with an accusative of office assumed in *BJ* 1,490; 2,223; 7,252; *AJ* 9,27.172.215; 10,23.81.152; 11,302; 13,253; 18,33; 20,158. See also n. 1778.

698. S reads Νάδαβος (cf. Lat Nadab), the reading followed by NaW. The form of the name read by Mar above corresponds most closely to that found in the L MSS 19 (b') and 108 (b) of 3 Rgns 15,25, i.e. Ναβάδ. Compare Nadab (MT); Ναβαθ (B 3 Rgns 15,25); Ναδάβ (L's 127/c₂ and 93/e₂, see the S reading above); Ναδάμ (82/o).

699. The L MS 127/c₂ reads "third" in 15,25. On the peculiar "royal chronology" of 127/c₂, see SCHENKEL, *Chronology*, pp. 27-31.

700. For each of the Northern rulers from Nadab through Hosea Josephus follows Kings in mentioning the number of years they reigned (Kings does not supply figures on the age of accession of the Northern monarchs as it does for their Judean counterparts, and Josephus, in turn, does not give age at death figures for the former as he does for the latter, see p. 83). Almost always, Kings and Josephus mention a Northern ruler's length of reign in their introductory notices for that ruler. Exceptions are Jehu (see 9,160 // 2 Kings 10,36) and earlier Jeroboam I (see 8,287 // 1 Kings 14,20, MT) where the relevant indication appears rather in a concluding notice. Also to be noted is that while the reign figures in Josephus and Kings generally coincide, they do diverge in two instances: Jehu (2 Kings 10,36: 28 / 9,160: 27) and Jeroboam II (2 Kings 14,23: 23 / 9,205: 40).

701. This adjective occurs 18 × in Josephus, all in *AJ*.

702. Josephus uses the noun πονηρία 43 × . Compare the collocation of the adjectival forms corresponding to the paired nouns above in Josephus' characterization of the Bethel prophet as "a wicked and impious man" in 8,243.

703. This is Josephus' only use of the above construction. In referring to the "capturing" of cities he uses alternatively λαμβάνω and its compound καταλαμβάνω (see 8,255).

704. The above form is that read by NN*Mar; NaW follow the Γαβαθὼ of MSP.

705. On the designations for the "Philistines" in LXX and Josephus, see R. DE VAUX, *Les Philistins dans la Septante*, in J. SCHREINER (ed.), *Wort, Lied und Gottesspruch. Beiträge zur Septuaginta*. FS J. Ziegler (FzB, l), Würzburg, 1972, 185-194.

of a plot" (ἐπιβουλευθεὶς... ἐκεῖ[706] ... ἀποθνήσκει)[707]". The author of this "plot", in Josephus' formulation, was "one of his (Nabados') friends (φίλου)[708] named Basanēs (Βασάνου)[709], the son of Seidos (Σειδοῦ, compare MT "Ahijah", 3 Rgns Ἀχεία)[710]". He leaves aside the source's reference to Baasha's "house" perhaps because this is so differently denominated in MT ("Issachar") and 3 Rgns (B has "Belaan", L "Beddama of Issachar") 1 Kings 15,27. Just as he will do with its recurrence in 15,33, Josephus passes over the indication of 15,28a (MT BL*) that it was in Asa's *third* year that Baasha's takeover (τὴν βασιλείαν παραλαβὼν)[711] occurred[712]. In line with 15,29a he

706. This specification that "Nadab" met his end at Gibbethon, the city he was besieging, accords with 1 Kings 15,27. It is passed over in the translations of W and Mar, while Sc, *ad loc.* does reproduce it with his םש.

707. The above verbal construction "killed as the result of a plot" recurs in *AJ* 10,47 (Amon by his servants);13,365 (Antiochus Grupus by Heracleon), cf. *BJ* 1,47; *AJ* 19,211, as well as *RA* 4.27.2. Josephus employs the h.p. of ἀποθνήσκω as here (in reference to both natural and violent deaths) also in *BJ* 1,580; *AJ* 1,237; 4,84. 93.97; 6,292.369; 9,86; 13,365.378; 14,449. The form is also used frequently by Dionysius, see ERIKSSON, *Präsens*, p. 52.

708. Josephus' qualification of Nadabos' killer as a "friend" is without Biblical warrant as such. Also elsewhere, with the Hellenistic institution of the royal "friends" in view, Josephus speaks of kings' dying at the hand of their "friend(s)" where the Bible does not, see: *AJ* 9,171 (Joas of Judah; compare 2 Kings 12,19 // 2 Chron 24,25 where the assassins are designated as Joas' "servants").203 (Amaziah of Judah is killed by his "friends"; compare 2 Kings 14,19 // 2 Chron 25,27 where unspecified conspirators kill the king).228 (a "certain friend" murders Zechariah of Israel; in 2 Kings 15,9 only the name of the regicide, i.e. Shallum is given), cf. 234 (Pekahiah of Israel is assassinated by Pekah while at a banquet "with friends"; 2 Kings 15,25 has no parallel to this detail about the circumstances of Pekahiah's murder) and *Ap* 1,148 where Josephus quotes the notice of Berossus about the Babylonian ruler Laborosoardoch being beaten to death "by his friends", compare also *RA* 3,35.3 (King Tullius along with his children is treacherously killed by his "friend" Marcius). Josephus' introduction of such notices about regicide by "friends" serves, of course, to accentuate the pathos of these events.

709. So the reading of O, followed by NN*NaMar. R has Βασσάμου, MSP Βοασάμου. Compare 3 Rgns 15,27 Βαασά, etc. Note the nominative form Βασάνης in 8,301.302.307.

710. Thus RO followed by NN*Mar, compare Εἴδου M; Εἴλου S; Ἴλου PE Lat; Μαχείλου Ed.pr.

It is difficult to see how the above variants to RO's form constitute corruptions of "Belaan" i.e. the designation of Baasha's "house" in B 3 Rgns 15,27 (see above in the text) as Mar, *Josephus*, V, p. 727, n. d avers; rather they seem to represent by-forms of Σειδοῦ itself. Note too that W, *Josèphe*, II, p. 220, n. 1 is incorrect in citing Μαχείλου as the reading of PE Lat.

According to SCHLATTER, *Namen*, p. 12, s.v. היחא "Seidou" etc. all represent corruptions of Josephus' original reading, i.e. Μαχείλου (thus Ed. pr. and NaW), while SCHALIT, *Namenwörterbuch*, p. 21, s.v. Ἀχείας affirms that the original reading was ὄνομα Ἀχείας.

711. This construction occurs some 35 × in Josephus.

712. He does this doubtless because the datum in question does not accord with his own earlier statement (8,287), derived from 1 Kings 15,25, that "Nabados" succeeded in Asa's *second* year and himself ruled *two* years (in this connection note that the L MSS 19/b', 108/b and 127/c₂ in 1 Kings 15,28 in fact do have Baasha seizing power in Asa's *fourth* year in accordance with the indications given in 15,25).

does cite Baasha's "exterminating" (διέφθειρε, see 8,240, compare 3 Rgns ἐπάταξεν) Jeroboam's "entire (ἄπαν)[713] family". 1 Kings 15,29b notes that Baasha's exterminatory deed was "according to the word of the Lord which he spoke by... Ahijah". Here too, Josephus avoids speaking of the "word" of God; his fulfillment notice reads: "and so it came about, in accordance with the prophecy of God (κατὰ τὴν τοῦ θεοῦ προφητείαν)[714]...". Similarly, he replaces 15,30 which avers that Ahijah's word of doom (see 1 Kings 14) was evoked by Jeroboam's sinfulness with a reminiscence of that prophet's announcement as recorded in 8,270 (cf. 1 Kings 14,11): "some of Jeroboam's kin met death in the city and were torn to pieces (σπαραχθῆναι)[715] and devoured (δαπανηθῆναι)[716] by dogs[717], while others died in the fields and (were eaten) by birds[718]". He then rounds off the segment and his whole survey of the history of the first Israelite dynasty with the notice "thus did the house of Jeroboam suffer fitting punishment (ἀξίαν ὑπέσχε δίκην)[719] for his impiety (ἀσεβείας, see 8,287) and lawlessness (ἀνομημάτων, see 8,251)[720]". Josephus' version of 1 Kings 14,19-20 (MT); 15,25-32, it thus appears, lacks an equivalent to the source notice of 15,31 on Nadab as well as the stray reference to the wars of Asa and Baasha in MT 15,32 (> 3 Rgns, // 15,16).

In its brevity, the above segment manifests few striking features to its rewriting of the Biblical source (where, in turn, MT and 3 Rgns do not significantly diverge). Most noteworthy, perhaps, is Josephus' bringing together of data found in separate contexts in 1 Kings 14,19-20 (MT) and 15,25-32.

Note further that Mar's translation, *ad loc.* of 8,288's reference to Baasha's assumption of power incorrectly dates this to "after the death of *Asanos*"; the referent of the pronoun αὐτοῦ in the corresponding Greek phrase is obviously "Nabados".

713. Josephus shares this specification with MT and L (ὅλον) 1 Kings 15,29; B lacks it.

714. Josephus employs the term προφητεία 38 ×. He uses the above expression (× happened) "according to the prophecy (of God)" also in *AJ* 6,136 (Saul's victory over the Amalekites); 9,129 (the extermination of Ahab's line), cf. also his more frequent expression "according to the prophecy of ×" (= some prophetic figure)".

715. The verb σπαράσσω (σπαράττω) occurs 16 × in Josephus.

716. The verb δαπανάω occurs 33 × in Josephus.

717. The expression "devoured by dogs" recurs in *AJ* 8,361 (Naboth's corpse) and 9,124 (Jezebel's remains).

718. In the above reminiscence of 1 Kings 14,11, Josephus takes over its distinction between the city-dwellers whom the dogs consume and the countrymen whom the birds devour which he had left aside in his earlier citation of Ahijah's word, *vide supra*.

719. The above construction "suffer punishment(s)" occurs also in *BJ* 7,84.333; *AJ* 1,65.99; 4,61; 6,42; 7,50.152; 9,249.282 ("fitting punishment", as in 8,289); 13,11.107.232; 14,168; 17,129; 20,218; *Ap* 2,194. Compare the alternate expression τιμωρίαν ὑπέχειν, 8,240.

720. The above collocation "impiety" and "lawlessness(es)" occurs only here in Josephus.

VIII

ASA'S VICTORY
(8,290-297)

Introduction: The author of Kings allots a mere 15 verses to the good king Asa. The Chronicler, on the other hand, allows him three whole chapters (2 Chronicles 14-16) which are themselves built up around a double sequence comprising enemy threat, royal response, prophetic address, and Asa's reaction thereto, 14,(1-7)8-15,19; 16,1-12(13-14)[721]. Following his usual procedure, Josephus bases himself on the more expansive presentation available, i.e. that of the Chronicler, although, as we shall see, abridging this significantly. Also to be noted is Josephus' situating the "Baasha material" of 1 Kings 15,33-16,7 between Chronicles' two "Asa cycles". Accordingly, this section of our investigation will deal with the first of these cycles, 2 Chronicles 14-15, within which the following components may be distinguished: 1) initial presentation of Abijah (14,1-7, EV 14,1-8); 2) Asa's Ethiopian Victory (14,8-14, EV 14,9-15); 3) Amaziah's Admonition (15,1-7); Asa's Response (15,8-19). Each of these segments has its counterpart in 8,290-297.

1. *Initial presentation of Asa* (8,290-291). The two paragraphs Josephus devotes to his initial presentation of Asa represent a highly compressed version of 2 Chron 14,1-7. He begins with a general evaluation of the king, embellishing on 14,1's "Asa did what was good and right in the eyes of the Lord": "But Asanos, the king of Jerusalem[722], was of excellent character (τὸν τρόπον ἄριστος)[723], looking to the Deity for guidance (πρὸς τὸ θεῖον ἀφορῶν)[724] and neither doing nor thinking

---

721. On the Chronicler's Asa complex, see R.B. DILLARD, *The Reign of Asa (2 Chr 14-16): An Examination of the Chronicler's Theological Method*, in *JETS* 23 (1980) 207-218.

722. Josephus perhaps derives this equivalent for the Biblical "king of Judah" from its usage by Menander in a reference to Solomon quoted by him in 8,146 ("In his [Hiram's] reign lived Abdēmonos, a young lad who always successfully solved the problems which were submitted to him by Solomon, *the king of Jerusalem*"). The title recurs in 8,314 (+ "and the two tribes").393.411.

723. Compare the characterization of Rehoboam in 8,264 as "a man of boastful and foolish nature (τὸν τρόπον)". Cf. *AJ* 13,299 where the phrase τὸν ἄριστον τρόπον has the sense "excellently".

724. With this construction compare *Ap* 2,166 (Moses persuaded all) "to look to that one [i.e. God] (εἰς ἐκεῖνον ... ἀφορᾶν)".

(ἐννοούμενος)⁷²⁵ anything that did not show due regard for piety (πρὸς τὴν εὐσέβειαν [see 8,280] εἶχε... τὴν ἀναφοράν)⁷²⁶ and the observance of the laws (τὴν τῶν νομίμων φυλακὴν)⁷²⁷".

2 Chron 14,2-4a show Asa's "doing good and right" (14,l) exemplified in his ridding Judah of various pagan cult objects (14,2.4a) and summoning his people to seek the Lord and keep God's law (14,3)⁷²⁸. For this enumeration Josephus substitutes a more general statement: "he put his kingdom in order (κατώρθωσε... τὴν... βασιλείαν)⁷²⁹ by cutting away (ἐκκόψας)⁷³⁰ whatever evil (πονηρὸν) (growths) were found in it and cleansing (καθαρεύσας)⁷³¹ it from every impurity (κηλῖδος)⁷³²". With an eye to the following battle account, Josephus (8,291) does reproduce in detail the notice of 14,7 on Asa's Judean (300,000) and Benjaminite (250,000)⁷³³ "picked men" (ἐπιλέκτων ἀνδρῶν)⁷³⁴. He likewise cites their respective weapons, i.e. "shield(s) and barbed lance(s)" (θυρεὸν καὶ σιρομάστην)⁷³⁵ and "round shields

725. The verb ἐννοέω occurs 18 × in Josephus.

726. The above phrase "have regard for piety" recurs in some codd of *Ap* 2,171. The noun ἀναφορά occurs also in *AJ* 17,190.

727. Josephus uses this phrase elsewhere in 8,195. More frequently he employs the analogous expression φυλακὴ τῶν νομῶν (see, e.g., *AJ* 4,306). For a collocation similar to the "piety and observance of the laws" here in 8,290, see *Ap* 1,212 νομῶν φυλακὴν καὶ... εὐσεβείαν.

Note the contrast between the "impiety and lawlessness" attributed to Jeroboam at the end of 8,289 and the "due regard for piety and observance of the laws" with which Asa is credited here at the start of 8,290. Josephus juxtaposes the end of Jeroboam's house and Asa's beginning with a view, *inter alia*, to creating that contrast. The contrast further serves to arouse expectations that pious Asa will enjoy a better fate than the punishment that overtook the house of sinful Jeroboam.

728. Josephus' characterization of Asa as "looking to the Deity... and neither doing nor thinking anything that did not show due regard for... the observance of the laws" might be seen as his anticipated version of this item.

729. This is Josephus' only use of the above construction; the verb κατορθόω occurs 53 × in his writings.

730. The same verb, i.e. ἐκκόπτω, is used in 2 Par 14,3 (MT 14,2) with the "groves" (MT "Asherim") as object. Josephus employs the verb 19 × – only here with "evil" (see above in the text) as object.

731. The verb καθαρεύω occurs also in *BJ* 5,227; *AJ* 1,102; 6,235; 14,160; *Vita* 79; *Ap* 1,260. SCHRECKENBERG, *Untersuchungen*, pp. 107-108 conjectures the synonymous form καθαρίσας on the consideration that whereas Greek uses καθαρεύω only intransitively, in the above phrase, i.e. "cleansing (it, Asa's kingdom) from every impurity" it would require a transitive meaning.

732. Elsewhere in Josephus κηλίς occurs only in *BJ* 2,123; 6,48.

With Josephus' avoidance of the "cultic particulars" of 2 Chron 14,2.4a in the above formulations, compare his similar non-utilization of the cultic details cited in 2 Chron 13,9.10b-11a in his version of Abijah's speech.

733. This figure corresponds to that given by B 2 Par 14,8. MT (14,7) and L read rather 280,000.

734. The above phrase recurs in *AJ* 12,313, cf. "picked myriads" in 8,222.

735. This is the reading of NN*Mar; Na reads the dival phrase θυρεῷ καὶ σειρομάστῃ with V (apud Hud). Compare 2 Par 14,8 (MT 14,7) θυρεοὺς καὶ δόρατα. The

and bows" (ἀσπίδας... καὶ τοξοτῶν, compare πελτασταὶ καὶ τοξόται, 2 Par 14,8)[736]. Conversely, Josephus completely ignores 2 Chron 14,5-6 which concern Asa's fortification measures – perhaps because these will not figure in the subsequent account[737].

2. Asa's Ethiopian Victory (8,292-294).

Josephus becomes more expansive in relating Asa's repulse of the Ethiopian invasion led by "Zaraios" (Ζαραῖος)[738], // 2 Chron 14,8-14. In 2 Chron 14,8 this invasion is juxtaposed with what precedes without any sort of transition. Josephus provides such a transition with his notice that Zaraios' advance[739] took place "after Asa had been reigning ten years" – an indication echoing his earlier statement, itself based on 2 Chron 13,23, that under Asa Judah "enjoyed peace for ten years", *vide supra*. Further according to 2 Chron 14,8 Zerah (unlike the Bible with its "the Cushite" (MT) / "Ethiopian" (2 Par), Josephus explicitly identifies him as "king" of Ethiopia) brought with him 1,000,000 men and 300 chariots. Josephus retains the latter figure, while specifying that the Ethiopian was accompanied by 900,000 "foot-soldiers" (πεζῶν) and 100,000 "horsemen" (ἱππέων)[740]. 2 Chron 14,8 concludes with the notation that Zerah halted his advance at "Mareshah" (so MT, Bc₂ Μαρισήλ); Josephus adds that Μαρίσας[741] was "in the tribe of Judah"[742]. In parallel to 14,9 (MT) Josephus next reports the counter-advance of Asa who "drew up his army over against him (ἀντιπαρατάξας, see 8,275) in a

above collocation (in the plural) appears also in 8,247 (see there) where, just as here, the term "barbed lance(s)" replaces LXX's "spears".

736. . For the above conjunction of the terms "shield(s)" (θυρεὸν) and "round shields" (ἀσπίδας), see 8,259.263.

737. By contrast in 8,246-247 Josephus does reproduce the notices of 2 Chron 11,5-11 concerning Rehoboam's "strong cities" – which subsequently (see 8,255) do get mentioned in his account of Shishak's advance.

738. In MT the king's name is "Zerah". Josephus' Ζαραῖος is the declined form of the name as found in L, i.e. Ζαραί, compare B Ζάρε.

739. Josephus describes this advance with the phrase στρατεύει μεγάλῃ δυνάμει... ἐπ' αὐτὸν. He uses the (active and middle) h.p. of στρατεύω (+ ἐπὶ) 23×, a usage corresponding to that of other Greek historians, see ERIKSSON, *Präsens*, p. 46. With the whole above construction, compare 9,61 (Hadad) στρατεύει μετὰ μεγάλης δυνάμεως ἐπὶ τὸν Ἰώραμον, cf. 10,87; 14,33.

740. Josephus' introduction of this specification is in line with his penchant for supplying exact figures where the Bible lacks these, see n. 426 on 8,254 (where the above collocation "foot-soldiers and horsemen" also occurs).

741. Thus N*Mar, cf. Μάρισας, E. According to N, "the Greek demands" the form Μαρίσης here (see, however, N*). NaW read Μαρίσσης with P. Recall that the site has already been mentioned by Josephus in his list of Rehoboam's fortified cities in 8,246.

742. This localization agrees with that previously given by him in 8,246 where "Marisa" is cited as one of 15 "Judean" cities.

certain valley (ἔν τινι φάραγγι, compare ἐν τῇ φάραγγι, 2 Par 14,10) called Saphatha (Σαφαθὰ)⁷⁴³ not far from the city (i.e. 'Marisa')⁷⁴⁴".

2 Chron 14,10 (2 Par 14,11) records Asa's pre-battle prayer. Josephus introduces that prayer with the notation that it was occasioned by Asa's "seeing (κατεῖδε)⁷⁴⁵ the Ethiopian host". In Chronicles Asa's prayer runs: "O Lord, there is none like thee to help, between the mighty and the weak [MT, compare 2 Par: it is not impossible for thee to save by many or by few]. Help us, O Lord our God, we rely on thee, and in thy name we have come against this multitude. O Lord, thou art our God; let not man prevail against thee". Josephus, who recasts the prayer in indirect address, makes Asa begin with a more specific appeal, i.e. "for victory (νίκην)⁷⁴⁶ and the destruction (ἐλεῖν, see 8,284)⁷⁴⁷ of many myriads of the enemy". He then has him continue with the following motivation for this appeal: "for, he said, in nothing else than His help (Βοηθείᾳ)⁷⁴⁸, which can make the few (ὀλίγους, compare 2 Par 14,11 ἐν ὀλίγοις) triumph (ἀπεργάσαθαι, see 8,279) over the many (κρείττους)⁷⁴⁹ and the weak over the strong (see 14,10aβ)⁷⁵⁰, would he

---

743. This is the form found in M Lat and read by SCHLATTER, *Namen*, p. 96, s.v. צְפָתָה and Mar. RO has Σαβαθὰ which NN* adopt, while NaW follow the Σαφθὰ of SP. Josephus' proper name here aligns itself with the צְפָתָה of MT as against the rendering of 2 Par 14,10, i.e. κατὰ βορρᾶν which itself seems to reflect a Hebrew צפון, see Mar, *Josephus*, V, p. 729, n.f. (compare SCHALIT, *Namenwörterbuch*, p. 108, s.v. Σαφαθά who proposes that the [Greek] Bible used by Josephus for 8,293 read ἐν τῇ φάραγγι Σαφαθὰ Μαρίσης).

744. This last precision has no counterpart in the Biblical text; compare Josephus' previously added specification (8,292) that "Marisa" lay "in the tribe of Judah".

745. In 8,257 the same verb is used of God's "seeing" the repentance of Rehoboam's people.

746. Compare 8,257 where Rehoboam and his people (unavailingly) entreat God that he might give them "victory (νίκην) and salvation".

747. SCHRECKENBERG, *Untersuchungen*, p. 108 conjectures ἀναιρεῖν with reference to 8,294 where the noun ἀναιρέσεως is used in a mention of the fulfillment of Asa's prayer of 8,293 and 8,414 (*vide infra*) where, in a context similar to 8,293, the manuscript tradition diverges between ἐλεῖν (so RO) and ἀνελεῖν (the reading adopted by modern editors).

748. Josephus employs βοήθεια specifically of divine "help" also in *BJ* 2,394; 6,40.286; *AJ* 1,157; 5,65 (God rebuked the Israelites under Joshua for "craving aught beyond His *aid*").206.216; 6,181; 7,245; 8,116 (here Solomon prays for "this *help* from [παρὰ] thee [God]", compare 8,293 Asa sets his hopes only in "help from [παρ'] him (God)").117; 9,14; 11,227; 13,65; *Vita* 290.

According to Mar, *Josephus*, V, p. 729, n. g the above formulation ("in nothing else than his help...") "seems to be a misunderstanding" of the Hebrew of 2 Chron 14,10 which reads "it is nothing for thee (God) to help".

749. With the above construction "triumph over the many", compare κρείττονα... ἀπεργάσασθαι (12,77) used of king Ptolemy's plan to fabricate a table for the shewbread which would be "far superior" to the existing one.

750. Note how in the above formulation Josephus' Asa seems to conflate the differing contrasts found in the 2 Par (few/many) and MT (strong/weak) versions of the royal prayer.

put his trust (θαρσήσας)⁷⁵¹ when going to meet Zaraios in battle (see 14,10ba)".

In 2 Chron 14,11 the narrator moves directly (and abruptly) from Asa's prayer (14,10) to the Lord's overthrow of the Ethiopians (14,11a, cf. v. 12ba) whereupon the Judeans "pursue" (v. 12aa) their "fleeing" (v. 11b) enemies who "fall until none remained alive" (v. 12aβ). Josephus (8,294) incorporates elements of this sequence into a formulation which effects a smoother transition between Asa's prayer and its result: "while Asanos spoke these words, God gave a sign (ἐσήμαινεν)⁷⁵² that he would be victorious (νίκην, see Asa's prayer for "victory" (νίκην) in 8,293), and so, with joy (χαρᾶς) at what had been foretold (προδεδηλωμένων)⁷⁵³ by God, he encountered (συμβαλὼν) (the foe) and slew (ἀποκτείνει, see ἐπάταξεν, 2 Par 14,12, here with the Lord, rather than Asa as subject)⁷⁵⁴ many (πολλοὺς)⁷⁵⁵... and those who turned to flee (τραπέντας εἰς φυγὴν) he pursued (ἐδίωξεν, compare κατεδίωξεν, 2 Par 14,13)...⁷⁵⁶". In accordance with 14,12(13)aa, he specifies that the Judean pursuit of Zerah's forces extended "as far as the territory of Gerar (ἄχρι τῆς Γεραρίτιδος χώρας)⁷⁵⁷". Thereafter, Josephus relates (// 14,12(13)bβ) that the Judeans "left off slaughtering (ἀφέμενοι... τῆς ἀναιρέσεως)⁷⁵⁸ and proceeded to plunder (ἐπὶ τὴν διαρπαγὴν, compare ἐσκύλευσαν, 2 Par 14,13, 14) the cities (τῶν πόλεων, compare πάσας τὰς πόλεις αὐτοῦ, 2 Par 14,14)⁷⁵⁹ and the camp (παρεμβολῆς)⁷⁶⁰ of the enemy (αὐτῶν)⁷⁶¹". Within the above formula-

751. Thus NN*Mar. Na reads θαρρήσας with SP. On the term θαρρέω, see SPICQ, *Lexicographie*, I, pp. 367-371.
752. Elsewhere Josephus makes God the subject of the verb σημαίνω ("reveal") in *AJ* 2,276; 6,50.92.271; 8,405.409; 10,180.238.
753. Elsewhere Josephus uses "the Deity" as subject of the verb προδηλόω in *AJ* 4,4.
754. Josephus uses the above h.p. of ἀποκτείνω also in *BJ* 1,204.664; 4,114.488; *AJ* 6,7.113.260; 8,311.376; 9,134; 10,180; 12,304; 13,235.301.356; 18,45. For occurrences of the construction in Dionysius, see ERIKSSON, *Präsens*, p. 52.
755. Variants of the above expression "engaging, he (they) kill(s) (killed) many" occur also in *AJ* 6,79.213; 8,376 (*vide infra*); 12,222.287; 13,141; 14,336 (20,79).122.
756. The above construction "kill(ed) many... pursued" occurs also in *BJ* 1,192; *AJ* 8,376; 12,344.
757. Josephus' mention of "Gerar" here corresponds to the MT and L reading in 14,12(13)aa. B has ἕως Γεδώρ.
758. This is Josephus' only use of the above phrase "leave off slaughtering"; the noun ἀναίρεσις occurs 45 × in his writings.
759. The above reading is that found in all codd except M (τῶν πολεμίων) and followed by NN*Mar. Na and W ("de la ville") adopt the conjecture of Bk, i.e. τῆς πόλεως.
760. This mention of the enemy "camp" seems to represent Josephus' version of the phrase "tents of cattle" in 2 Chron 14,14 (in 2 Par 14,15 this expression is expanded with the name of a group of people, the "A(li)mazone(i)eis", on which see ALLEN, *Chronicles*, I, pp. 167-168).
761. N holds that the whole sequence ἐπὶ τὴν διαρπαγὴν... αὐτῶν above is corrupt; he does so with reference to Lat's "ad directionem civitatis gerarenae quam caeperant eorumque castrorum protinus accesserunt".

tion's mention of the "cities" and "the camp" he inserts a Biblically unparalleled notice, i.e. "Gerar (ἡ Γεράρων)[762] was already taken". Finally, Josephus amplifies the list of booty given in 14,14aβ adding to its "sheep[763] and camels" both "a great deal of (λείαν τε πολλὴν)[764] gold and silver"[765] and "beasts of burden" (ὑποζύγια)[766].

3. *Azariah's Admonition* (8,295-297a). In Chronicles the notice of 14,14(15)bβ "then they returned to Jerusalem" serves to round off the preceding battle account; a new unit begins abruptly in 15,1-2aα with the descent of the Spirit upon "Azariah" and his resultant approach to Asa. Josephus' narrative is more fluid: Asa's return and the intervention of "Azarias" (Ἀζαρίας, so 2 Par) are combined into a single extended period: "and so, when Asanos and the army with him had received from God this great victory (... παρὰ τοῦ θεοῦ νίκην λαβόντες)[767] and gain (ὠφέλειαν)[768], they turned back (ἀνέστρεφον, 2 Par ἐπέστρεψαν) to Jerusalem. As they were approaching it, there met them on the road a prophet (προφήτης) named Azarias". In this formulation, it will be noted, Josephus passes over 2 Chron 15,1's

762. Cf. Γέραρα, *AJ* 1,207 and Γεράρων, 1,259.
763. 2 Par designates these with the term πρόβατα; Josephus calls them βοσκημάτων ἀγέλας, a phrase which occurs also in *AJ* 6,41.
764. Cf. *AJ* 5,96 where this phrase is collocated with "gold and silver" as here.
765. Compare 8,258 where Josephus introduces a similar reference to the precious metals seized in describing Shishak's despoliation of Jerusalem. Rabbinic tradition as well embellishes on the booty Asa took from the Ethiopians. According to, e.g., *Pesaḥim* 119a Asa recouped from Zerah the precious metals which the latter had taken from Shishak who, in turn, had acquired them from Rehoboam. See further *Seder 'olam* 16; *Esth. Rab.* 1.12, and cf. GINZBERG, *Legends*, VI, p. 309, n. 19.
766. Also elsewhere Josephus accentuates the wealth the Jews acquire from their defeated enemies, see, e.g. *AJ* 5,229 where he develops Judg 8,21's reference to the "crescents" which Gideon took from the necks of the camels of the vanquished Midianites into the following enumeration of the Israelites' booty several of whose items correspond to those cited in 8,294: "gold, silver, woven stuff, camels and beasts of burden". See too 7,77, where Josephus inserts a Biblically unparalleled notice about the "great wealth" David took from the Philistine camp. FELDMAN, *David*, pp. 138-139 suggests that this emphasis aims to counteract contemporary anti-Semitic portrayals of the Jews as a nation of "beggars". Finally, with the enumeration of Asa's spoils in 8,294 compare *RA* 8.30.2 where Marcius speaks of the items he might have appropriated following his victory: "much gold and silver, as well as slaves, beasts of burden (ὑποζύγια) and cattle (βοσκήματα)...".
767. With this construction compare the notice on Asa's prayer in 8,293, νίκην ᾔτει παρὰ τοῦ θεοῦ, see also 8,284: "Abias' army is permitted by God (παρὰ τοῦ θεοῦ) to win (λαβεῖν) so wonderful... a victory (νίκην)". The correspondence in wording between 8,295 and 284 accentuates the parallelism between the triumphs of Abijah and Asa, both over vastly superior forces.
768. The collocation "victory and gain" occurs only here in Josephus. With the above "theological notation" compare 2 Chron 14,11a.12bα.13aβ.

reference to the activity of the "spirit"[769], upon Azariah as well as the name of his father, i.e. Oded. Conversely, however, he goes beyond the Bible in explicitly designating Azariah as a "prophet"[770], thereby making clear, in his own way, the supernatural origins of that figure's subsequent discourse.

Azariah's actual word to the returning army in 2 Chron 15,2aβ-7 comprises four elements: 1) a summons to hear (v. 2aβ); 2) the enunciation, in both positive and negative terms, of the talion principle governing the relation between God and people (v. 2b); 3) a problematic middle section in which it is unclear whether the references to the people's experiences of affliction and repentance have to do with the past (so most commentators) or the future (vv. 3-6)[771]; and 4) a motivated exhortation (v. 7). Josephus' version of the discourse corresponds only rather loosely to its Biblical prototype[772]. He has Azariah

769. His doing this is in accordance with Josephus' overall tendency to omit or reformulate Biblical references to the "spirit" – whether of man or God, see E. BEST, *The Use and Non-use of Pneuma by Josephus*, in *NovT* 3 (1959) 218-223, esp. pp. 223-225. See next note.

770. Cf., however, the text-critically problematic 2 Chron 15,8 (MT) where the term "the prophet" is used of Oded, Amaziah's father. SANDES, *Paul*, p. 2, n.4 points out that, just as here in 8,295, Josephus substitutes the designation "prophet" where the Bible speaks rather of an operation of the "spirit" upon some individual also in *AJ* 5,285 (// Judg 13,25, Samson) and 9,10 (// 2 Chron 20,14, Jahaziel). He sees Josephus' procedure in these instances as exemplifying a wider tendency in post-biblical Judaism to accentuate the connection between the "spirit" and prophecy.

771. The question arises due to the fact that the MT of vv. 3.5 and 6b lacks verbs. LXX has future tense verbs in vv. 4 and 6a, cf. the present in 5a. The Targum, by contrast, makes the entire unit concern the past of the "Northern Kingdom", this likely under the inspiration of the mention of "Israel" in v. 3. On the whole question see the commentaries.

772. According to AMARU, *Land Theology*, p. 223 Josephus' version of the discourse has the events of 70-73 A.D. in view.

Josephus' version of Azariah's speech evidences a noteworthy movement from indirect (8,295-296a) to direct (8,296b-297a) and back to indirect (8,297b) discourse. Other instances of the shift from indirect to direct discourse within a single address in 8,212-420 are: 8,352 (God to Elijah, // 1 Kings 19,15-18).367 (the Syrian envoys to Ahab, // 1 Kings 20,5b-6).368-369 (Ahab to the Israelites).402b (Jehoshaphat to Ahab, // 1 Kings 22,7b = 2 Chron 18,6b).407-408 (Zedekiah to Ahab, cf. 1 Kings 22,24b = 2 Chron 18,23b). In each of these instances the shift occurs within a word of some length, whether of a good (God, Azariah, Jehoshaphat) or bad (Ahab, Zedekiah) character.

THÉROND, *Discours*, p. 142 notes that the shift in question occurs "assez souvent" in *BJ* (he lists no occurrences of the "double shift" noted above in *AJ* 8,295-297a). Just as with the integral use of direct discourse (see n. 175), the shift from one form of discourse to another is much less in evidence in our segment of *AJ*. Thérond, *ibid.*, pp. 143-146 further identifies various "functions" of the shift: counteracting the monotony of prolonged indirect discourse; "authentication" of the words in direct discourse as truly coming from the speaker; "valorisation" of the speaker who, at a given point, is allowed to speak for himself. All these factors, in varying degrees, seem operative also in Josephus' use of the "shift" in 8,212-420. In particular, it might be noted that in several of the instances cited above (8,367.368-369.407-408), the shift occurs in speeches which evidence expansion vis-à-vis the Biblical parallels. The conjoined effect of such expansion and the noteworthy –

begin by directing Asa's army to "halt their journey". He then expatiates on the principle enunciated positively in 15,2bα ("the Lord is with you, while you are with him. If you seek him he will be found by you"), applying it to the case of both their recent triumph and the nation's future: "... they had obtained this victory from God (ταύτης... τῆς νίκης παρὰ τοῦ θεοῦ τετυχηκότες)⁷⁷³ because they had shown themselves righteous (δικαίους) and pure (ὁσίους)⁷⁷⁴ and had always acted in accordance with the will of God (κατὰ βούλησιν θεοῦ)⁷⁷⁵. If, then, he said, they so continued (ἐπιμένουσι)⁷⁷⁶, God would grant them always to overcome their foes (κρατεῖν... τῶν ἐχθρῶν)⁷⁷⁷ and live happily (τὸ ζῆν μετ᾽ εὐδαιμονίας)⁷⁷⁸". He then has Azariah take up the negative side of the principle set out in 15,2bβ ("but if you foresake [2 Par καταλίπητε] him, he will foresake you"): "but if they abandoned His worship (ἀπολιποῦσι... τὴν θρησκείαν)⁷⁷⁹, everything would turn out to the contrary (ἅπαντα τούτων ἐναντία συμβήσεσθαι)⁷⁸⁰". Azariah next continues "and the time would come when no true prophet (ἀληθὴς... προφήτης)⁷⁸¹ will be found (εὑρεθήσεται)⁷⁸² among your (i.e. Asa's) people (ὄχλῳ)⁷⁸³ nor any priest to give righteous judgement (τὰ δίκαια χρηματίζων)⁷⁸⁴, but (your) cities shall be laid waste (αἱ

because rather rare – shift to direct discourse does serve to accentuate the status of the speaker. See further VILLALBA I VARNEDA, *Method*, pp. 115-117 and nn. 39, 175.

Finally, M. KRENKEL, *Josephus und Lukas*, Leipzig, 1894, pp. 329-331 points out that among NT writers it is above all Luke (see, e.g., Luke 5,14; Acts 1,4-5; 7,6-7; 17,2-3; 23,22; 24,4-5) whose "quotations" evidence a comparable shift from indirect to direct discourse. He sees this communality as reflective of Josephus' "Einfluss auf Lucas' Sprache".

773. For the above phrase "obtain victory", see *AJ* 4,129. Compare also 8,295a παρὰ τοῦ θεοῦ νίκην λαβόντες.

774. This adjectival collocation occurs in reverse order in 8,245.

775. On this phrase in Josephus, see n. 88.

776. With reference to Lat "quos in eius mandatis permanentes", N opines "vid. aliquid excidisse" at this point.

777. The expression "overcome enemies" occurs also in *BJ* 5,39; *AJ* 1,327; 3,46; 7,209.217; 8,352; 9,36; 13,214.

778. The above phrase "live happily" occurs also in *AJ* 2,168. Cf. also 8,281 where Abijah urges the Israelites to "respect the power which has led you on to so great a height of prosperity (εὐδαιμονίας)".

779. This is the only use of this construction in Josephus, cf. the phrase attributed to Shemaiah in 8,256 τὴν θρησκείαν αὐτοῦ κατέλιπον.

780. This is the only occurrence of this phrase in Josephus.

781. Josephus uses this same designation for Elisha in 9,23, cf. 8,234 where Jeroboam is said to recognize that Jadon ἀληθῆ τὸν ἄνθρωπον.

782. This same form occurs in 2 Par 15,2.4.

783. Compare 2 Chron (Par) 15,3 "Israel".

784. This is the only occurrence of this phrase in Josephus. In having Azariah refer to the threatened lack of the services of a "priest", Josephus aligns himself with the MT and L formulation in 2 Chron 15,3 which does refer to (the loss of) a "teaching priest" as against B which does not.

πόλεις ἀνάστατοι)[785] and the nation (τὸ ἔθνος)[786] scattered (σπαρήσεται) over all the earth to lead the life of aliens (ἔπηλυν)[787] and
wanderers (ἀλήτην)[788]" (// 15,3-6). Several comments are in order
concerning the relationship between the above formulation and its
Biblical source. First of all, in Josephus' rendition, Azariah speaks of
future eventualities (cf. 2 Par) rather than of the past events MT (most
likely) has in view. Of the three items which according to MT and L 2
Chron 15,3 Israel lacked/ will lack, i.e. God, teaching priest (> B) and
law, Josephus seems to amalgamate the second and third in his phrase
"any priest to give righteous judgment", whereas he substitutes "true
(ἀληθὴς) prophet" for the Biblical "true (2 Par ἀληθινῷ) God"[789]. For
Azariah's following threat, i.e. "your cities (πόλεις) shall be laid
waste", Josephus may have been inspired by 2 Chron 15,6a which
alludes to the (past) "breaking in pieces" (so MT) or the (future)
"warring" (so 2 Par) of "(nation against nation), city (2 Par πόλις)
against city". Without Biblical parallel as such is then the culminating
announcement of exile for Asa's people[790] attributed to Azariah by
Josephus: "the nation shall be scattered over all the earth", although
conceivably, as Mar suggests[791] he formulates this item under the
(distant) influence of 2 Chron 15,5 (MT) which reads "in those days no
people to the one going out or the one coming in, for great disturbances
upon all the inhabitants of the lands". In any event, note finally that
Josephus makes no use of 15,4 which speaks of the people's (effica-
cious) "returning to the Lord" in their distress.

Josephus closes Azariah's speech with a warning/admonition which
flows directly out of the omnious prospect the prophet has just presented: "he therefore advised (συνεβούλευεν)[792] them to be virtuous

---

785. The phrase "wasted cities" occurs also in *BJ* 1,269; *AJ* 1,137; 10,89.

786. Cf. the expression ἔθνος πρὸς ἔθνος (referring to the "nations" in general) in 2
Par 15,6. Note the equivalency between the word ἔθνος (= the Jews) here in 8,297 and the
ὄχλῳ used just previously by Azariah in 8,296. Cf. too Josephus' use of ἔθνος to designate
the Jews in 8,261 and n. 475.

787. Elsewhere: *BJ* 3,493.500.532; *AJ* 1,159; 8,127; 12,392; 17,293; *Ap* 1,314.

788. Josephus' only other use of the term ἀλήτης is in *AJ* 3,87.

789. He may have done this because he found the notion of Israel's "lacking the true
God" – be it even in the Exile – excessive and unacceptable given its definitive status as
the Lord's chosen people. Conversely, Josephus might readily have come to the idea of
associating "prophet" and "priest" here in view of the frequent Biblical collocation of the
two groups, see, e.g., 2 Kings 23,2, cf. too his earlier (non-Biblical) designation of Azariah
as "prophet" in 8,295.

790. With this compare the anticipations of the Israelite dispersion in 8,229.271. In the
latter text the verb used of Israel's "scattering" is διασπαρὲν, compare σπαρήσεται in
8,297.

791. *Josephus*, V, p. 731, n.c.

792. Compare the conclusion to Abijah's appeal to the Israelites in 8,281 "I advise
(συμβουλεύω) you...".

(ἀγαθοῖς) while they still had time, and not ungraciously refuse (φθο-νῆσαι) the benevolence (εὐμενείας)⁷⁹³ of God" (contrast the loose connection of Azariah's closing exhortation to strength and courage in 15,7 with what precedes in 15,2-6).

4. *Asa's Response* (8,279b). 2 Chron 15,8-19 relates in considerable detail a whole series of measures taken by Asa in response to Azariah's appeal, e.g., destruction of idolatrous objects (see vv. 8bα, 16), repair and embellishment of the sanctuary (vv. 8bβ,18), sacrifices (v. 11), and covenant-making (vv. 12-15). In contrast to this lengthy, particularizing presentation, Josephus treats the sequels to Azariah's word in a half-paragraph. He opens this sequence with a transitional formula "when the king and the people (ὁ λαὸς)⁷⁹⁴ heard (ἀκούσας) these (words)..." reminiscent of 2 Chron 15,8aα "when he (Asa) heard these words (2 Par ἐν τῷ ἀκοῦσαι τοὺς λόγους τούτους)". He then proceeds: "they rejoiced (ἐχάρησαν)⁷⁹⁵, and all together and each privately (κοινῇ... καὶ κατ' ἰδίαν)⁷⁹⁶ took thought (πρόνοιαν ἐποιοῦντο)⁷⁹⁷ for what was right (τοῦ δικαίου)⁷⁹⁸. The king also sent men throughout the country to watch over the enforcement (ἐπιμελησομένους)⁷⁹⁹ of the laws (νομίμων)⁸⁰⁰". The first of these notices vaguely recalls elements of the covenant-making scene described in 2 Chron 15,12-15: "they entered into a covenant to seek the Lord... whoever would not seek the Lord, should be put to death, whether young or old, man or woman... and Judah rejoiced (2 Par 15,15 ηὐφράνθησαν) over the oath...". As for Asa's dispatch of the "law enforcers", this could represent a retrojection by Josephus of a similar initiative related of Asa's son Jehoshaphat in 2 Chron 17,7-9 (// 8,395, *vide infra*) intended to accentuate the parallelism – already discernible in Chronicles itself – between these two

---

793. Josephus uses the term εὐμένεια to denote the divine "benevolence" elsewhere in *AJ* 1,111;2,299.341;3,46;5,213;8,119;15,198, cf. also 16,104. Only here does he use the above expression "refuse benevolence".

794. With this designation, compare ὄχλῳ (8,296) and τὸ ἔθνος (8,297a). One finds a similar oscillation between the terms ἔθνος and λαὸς in reference to the "chosen people" also in *AJ* 6,35-36 and 11,229.

795. Cf. the phrase μετὰ χαρᾶς used of Asa's advance against the Ethiopians in 8,294.

796. Josephus uses this construction also in *AJ* 3,219; 4,310; 5,92; 14,253, cf. *BJ* 1,201.537; 2,199; 4,226; 7,260; *AJ* 13,166; 14,151.309; 16,39; *Ap* 2,259.

797. This expression "take thought" occurs also in *BJ* 4,317; 7,304; *AJ* 1,283; 2,189; 4,239; 5,173; 7,44.95.259; 8,335; 10,157; 11,48.93; 12,153; 19,287; *Vita* 62.74.77.160.184; *Ap* 1,9.

798. Compare δικαίους (8,295) and τὰ δίκαια (8,297a).

799. On the term ἐπιμελέμαι etc., see Spicq, *Lexicographie*, I, pp. 67-71, 270-276.

800. This is the only occurrence of the above construction "watch over (the enforcement of) the laws" in Josephus (for the noun νόμιμα, see 8,280). Compare 8,290 where Josephus refers to Asa's concern for τὴν τῶν νομίμων φυλακήν.

"good" kings[801]. Another possible source of inspiration for the latter item could be the notice of 2 Chron 14,4 "Asa commanded Judah to keep the law". In any case, Josephus' depiction of Asa and his people's positive response to Azariah's word serves to further the contrast he has been developing throughout our segment between the Southern kings (and their people) who do pay heed to admonitions sent them by God (see 8,256, Rehoboam) and the Northern rulers who do not (see 8,245.274.282, Jeroboam). The pattern will surface once again in his presentation of the Israelite ruler Baasha (8,298-306), see below.

Summary. Josephus' textual affinities in the above pericope are quite varied. He agrees with B (against MT and L) on the number of Asa's Benjaminite soldiers (see 2 Chron 14,7). His "futuristic version" of 15,3-6 parallels that of 2 Par, although contentually it is quite different from both 2 Par and MT. Josephus aligns himself with MT L contra B in designating "Gerar" as the Ethiopians' place of refuge (see 14,12), just as in his reference to the "priest" in his version of 15,3. Finally, like MT but in contrast to 2 Par, he gives a proper name to the "valley" where Asa encamps (see 14,9), and lacks a reference to the "Alimazons" in his enumeration of the booty taken by Asa (see 14,14).

The most striking feature to Josephus' rewriting of 2 Chronicles 14-15 is his abridgement of the material, particular its opening and closing sections, i.e. 14,1-7 and 15,8-19. How is this state of affairs to be explained? Several lines of explanation – none of them, admittedly, fully convincing – suggest themselves. We have, first of all, already noted in connection with Josephus' version of Abijah's speech the historian's tendency to avoid the sort of cultic details – of which there are many in 2 Chronicles 14–15 – that his readers would not have found congenial[802]. In addition, Josephus' omissions of/generalizing substitutions for the Chronicler's cultic specifics could represent his way of dealing with the apparent discrepancy between Abijah's assertion of Judah's unbroken fidelity to the Lord and his laws (see 8,280, cf. 2 Chron 13,10-11, see also the similar affirmation of Azariah concerning Judah in 8,295) and the indications in 2 Chronicles 14-15 that the same Abijah's successor faced a nation in which all kinds of idolatrous practices flourished – and that both before and after Asa's campaign against Zerah. Vague references to Asa's elimination of "evil growths"

---

801. Note Josephus' interjected comment in 8,395 concerning the people's enthusiastic acceptance of the law in Jehoshaphat's time ("and so much were all the people pleased with this [the teaching mission dispatched by Jehoshaphat] that there was nothing for which they were so ambitious or so loved as the observance of the laws [νόμιμα]") which may be compared with his notice here in 8,297 that Asa and his people "all together and each privately took thought for what was right".

802. Note conversely that Josephus reproduces the battle account of 2 Chron 14,9-15 *in extenso*, this being an item more readily accessible to Gentile readers.

and "every impurity" (8,290) as well as to his dispatch of "law enforcers" (8,297) serve to render the discrepancy less glaring[803].

Also worthy of note is Josephus' unambiguously "futuristic" version of Azariah's words in 2 Chron 15,3-6 with their prospect of exile for Judah[804]. Josephus has already oriented readers towards the North's demise by citing the relevant prediction of Ahijah (see 1 Kings 14,15-16) in 8,271 (see also 8,229). Here, he has another prophet, Azariah, speak words that foreshadow a like fate for Judah[805].

803. Josephus' procedure here further allows him to attenuate the discordance within 2 Chronicles 14-15 between 14,2.4a (Asa institutes a thorough-going cultic "cleanup") and 15,8 ("abominable idols" are still extant in "all the land of Judah and Benjamin"). Similarly, Josephus non-reproduction of the notice of 2 Chron 15,8 about Asa's removing the idols also "from the cities which he had taken in the hill country of Ephraim" avoids the seeming confusion in Chronicles as to whether it was Abijah (so 2 Chron 13,19) or Asa (so 2 Chron 15,8;17,2) who captured the Ephraimite sites. Josephus, who reproduces 2 Chron 13,19 in 8,284 will change the "Asa" of 2 Chron 17,2 to "Abijah" in 8,394, *vide infra*, thereby generating a presentation which is internally self-consistent.

804. Also in *Lev.Rab.* 19,9 the words of Azariah of 2 Chron 15,3 are understood as referring to the future, wherein God's justice, the High Priesthood and the Sanhedrin will all cease to function.

805. Similarly, in his account of Shishak's despoliation of Jerusalem (see 8,258-259) Josephus introduces features that look ahead to subsequent enemy aggressions against the city.

IX

BAASHA VS. ASA
(8,298-306)

Introduction: In the preceding section (8,290-297) Josephus gives his version of the Chronicler's account of Asa's first (good) period, 2 Chronicles 14-15. In Chronicles itself there follows immediately the narrative of the king's latter years (2 Chronicles 16) during which things go awry with and for him. This second sequence within the Chronicler's presentation of Asa begins with the king, under attack by Baasha of Israel, turning to Ben-hadad of Syria for aid, 2 Chron 16,1-6. The latter passage, in turn, is taken over by the Chronicler largely verbatim from 1 Kings 15,16-22 which constitutes part of an account concerning Asa, 15,9-24. In Kings itself, however, Josephus found, in another context, i.e., 1 Kings 15,33–16,4 further material concerning Asa's antagonist Baasha. Wishing to utilize this material as well, Josephus places his rendition of it prior to his reproduction of 1 Kings 15,16-22 // 2 Chron 16,1-6 as an introduction to the latter. Thereby, he brings together in a continuous segment materials on Baasha's reign that stand in two distinct contexts in Kings[806].

Here at the outset a word should be said about the delimitation of the above pericope of *AJ*. In fact, it is difficult to know where to conclude the segment which opens with 8,298. In any case, it must be conceded that there is no radical break after 8,306. Indeed, Baasha's death occurs only at the start of 8,307, and thereafter the narrative flows smoothly on with his successors. In order, however, not to end up with an excessively lengthy unit for analysis, I have opted to take paragraphs 8,298 and 306 as the boundaries of a segment in which Baasha plays a leading, active role throughout. In carrying out my analysis of the unit so delimited, I further distinguish two main sections, i.e. 8,298-302 (Baasha's depravity, // 1 Kings 15,33 – 16,4) and 8,303-306 (the Baasha/Asa/Ben-hadad triangle, // 1 Kings 15,16-22 // 2 Chron 16,1-6).

1. *Baasha's Depravity* (8,298-302). Josephus begins (8,298) his new unit with an elaborate transition (compare 8,265) comprising a (provisional) closing formula for Asa and the resumptive re-introduction of Baasha

---

806. Recall his similar treatment of the material on Jeroboam and his line of 1 Kings 14,19-20 (MT) and 15,25-32 in 8,287-289 ("Baasha's coup").

from 8,288-289: "Such was the state of things under Asanos, the king of the two tribes. I shall now return (ἐπάνειμι)[807] to the people of Israel and their king Basanēs[808] who killed Jeroboam's son Nabados and seized the royal power (κατασχόντα τὴν ἀρχήν)[809]". He next reproduces the data of 1 Kings 15,33: Baasha "reigned" (ἐβασίλευσεν, compare 3 Rgns βασιλεύει) at "Tharsē" (Θαρσῇ)[810] for twenty-four years[811]. In 15,34 there follows a stereotyped judgment formula on Baasha (see 15,26) as one who continued Jeroboam's misdeeds. Josephus accentuates this Biblical condemnation: "being more wicked and impious (πονηρὸς... καὶ ἀσεβὴς)[812] than Jeroboam *and his son*[813], he brought many evils (πολλὰ... κακὰ διέθηκε) upon the people[814] and gravely outraged (ἐξύβρισεν, see 8,245.246, of Jeroboam) God".

807. Josephus uses this term in resumptive formulae also in *BJ* 7,274; *AJ* 6,350; 8,393; 16,178; 18,80.

808. (... τὸ πλῆθος τῶν Ἰσραηλιτῶν καὶ τὸν βασιλέα αὐτῶν Βασάνην). Thus NN*Mar. Na reads τὸν τοῦ πλήθους τῶν Ἰσραηλιτῶν Βασιλέα Βασάνην with MSP Lat, cf. the translation of W, *ad loc.* "... au roi du peuple d'Israël, Basa...".

809. The above phrase (= "hold, seize power") occurs also in *BJ* 1,218; *AJ* 5,197.254.359; 8,3.316; 9,177.234; 10,143.231; 11,31; 14,11.270.290; 18,100; 20,29. Compare the alternative expression τὴν βασιλείαν παραλαβὼν in Josephus' earlier description of Baasha's coup in 8,288.

With the above transition compare 8,287 where, as here, Josephus is shifting back to the Northern kingdom after a "Southern interlude": "Such then is the account we have received concerning Abias. Now Jeroboam...".

810. Thus the emendation of Hud, adopted by Na SCHLATTER, *Namen*, p. 114, s.v. תִּרְצָה, Mar and SCHALIT, *Namenwörterbuch*, p. 53, s.v. θάρση. The codd have θαρσάλη (cf. Lat Tersalin), a reading followed by N, II, p. 241 and W, *ad loc.* Compare MT "Tirzah" and 3 Rgns θερσά.

Recall that this is Josephus' first reference to "Tirzah", 1 Kings 14,17's reference to it as Jeroboam's residence being passed over by him. Accordingly, he appends to the city's name a notice, unparalleled in 1 Kings 15,33, about Baasha's "having made it his residence" (οἰκητήριον πεποιημένος [thus MSP followed by NaMar; N reads πεποιηκὼς with RO]).

811. Josephus omits the synchronic notice of 15,33 that Baasha's usurpation occured in Asa's "third" (the L MSS 19/b' 108/b and 82/e₂: fifth) year, just as he leaves aside the equivalent notice of 15,28 in 8,288, see p. 115 and n. 712.

812. Josephus uses this same collocation of the Bethel prophet in 8,243.

813. The Biblical parallel text, 1 Kings 15,34, lacks this reference to "Nadab". Given, however, Josephus' previous statement (// 1 Kings 15,26) that Nabados "resembled" his father "in impiety and wickedness" (8,287, note the substantival equivalents of the adjectival pair used of Baasha in 8,298), it is natural that when referring to Baasha's "being wicked and impious", he would compare him with Jeroboam's son as well.

814. The phrase "bring (many) evils upon" occurs also in *BJ* 1,304; *AJ* (2,242); 6,68.132; 8,304 (10,91); 11,161; 20,5. With this (Biblically unparalleled) reference to the harm done "the people" by Baasha Josephus may have in view his subsequent account of Baasha's invasion of the South and the economic losses for Judah that involved, see 8,304 where the same construction is used in reference to Baasha's invasion. On this understanding the specific referent of the term "people" here in 8,299 would be the Southerners (and not rather Baasha's own subjects as one might initially suppose).

In both Kings and Josephus Baasha's conduct calls forth a divine message of condemnation[815]. 1 Kings 16,1 introduces this word with a *Wortereignisformel* which designates "Jehu son of Hanani" as recipient. Here again, Josephus avoids reference to the Lord's "word"; according to him, God "sent" (πέμψας, compare 8,231 where the prophet Jadōn is qualified as "sent [πέμψαντος] by God") the prophet (προφήτην)[816] Jēūs ('Iηοῦν)[817] to him (αὐτῷ)[818].

Jehu's discourse in 16,2-4 is a composite of Deuteronomistic formulae, reminiscent of Abijah's word against Jeroboam in 14,7-11, with v. 2 constituting the accusation, vv. 3-4 the announcement of punishment for Baasha's line. Reversing Kings' order, Josephus commences Jehu's speech – which he formulates throughout in indirect discourse – with a general prediction of doom for Baasha's house: "(Jēūs) warned (προεῖπε)[819] him that He would destroy all his line (διαφθερεῖν αὐτοῦ πᾶν τὸ γένος)[820] and would utterly crush (ἐξολέσειν, see 8,270) them under the same calamities (κακοῖς) as He had brought (περιέβαλεν) upon the house (οἶκον)[821] of Jeroboam" (cf. 16,3b "... I will make your house [3 Rgns οἶκον] like the house of Jeroboam..."). Josephus leaves aside the reapplication of the language of 1 Kings 14,11 in 16,4 (the corpses of Baasha's descendants will be consumed by dogs and birds just as were those of Jeroboam's heirs). The historian's abridgement of the source's announcement of punishment (16,3-4) is offset by his amplification of its accusation (16,2). Like 16,2 Josephus begins the accusation with a reference to Baasha's elevation by God: "having been made king (βασιλεὺς... γενόμενος, compare 3 Rgns ἔδωκά σε ἡγούμενον)[822] by him...". In 16,2 this allusion is juxtaposed to mention of Baasha's subsequent misdeeds. Josephus (8,300) expatiates on Baasha's reprobate response: "... he had not requited (ἡμείψατο) His kindness

---

815. In MT the word is said to be "concerning/ against (על) Baasha", whereas in 3 Rgns it is directed "to (πρὸς)" him.

816. This designation for "Jehu" is lacking in 1 Kings 16,1 although it does occur in 16,7. Compare Josephus' (non-Biblical) designation of Azariah as "prophet" in 8,295.

817. This is the emendation of SCHOTANUS, followed by modern editors. Compare 'Iησοῦν RO; 'Ioῦν MSP; Γιμοῦ E; Gimun Lat. MT 1 Kings 16,1 has Jehu, B 'Eἰoυ, L 'Ioύ.
As with Azariah (see 8,295), Josephus leaves unmentioned the name of Jehu's father, i.e. Hanani.

818. In representing "Jēūs" as delivering the message to Baasha, Josephus aligns himself with 3 Rgns 16,1 as against MT where the prophet's word is said simply to be "concerning" Baasha, see n. 815.

819. Cf. Jadōn's opening word in 8,231 ὁ θεὸς προλέγει.

820. Compare 8,288 (Baasha) ἅπαν τὸ Ἰεροβοάμου γένος διέφθειρε.

821. Compare AJ 2,276 where Moses is said to hope that God was able τοὺς Αἰγυπτίους κακοῖς περιβαλεῖν.

822. Compare Ahijah's word to Jeroboam in 8,270 "I (God) made you great...".

(εὐεργεσίαν, see 8,278)[823] by justly and piously (δικαίως... καὶ εὐσε-βῶς, see 8,280)[824] governing the people (τῷ... προστῆναι τοῦ πλήθους)[825] – a course which would, in the first place, be of benefit (ἀγαθά) to those who followed it, and then pleasing to God (τῷ θεῷ φίλα)[826] as well – but had imitated (ἐμιμήσατο)[827] Jeroboam, the vilest of men (κάκιστον)[828], and, although Jeroboam himself was dead (τῆς ψυχῆς ἀπολομένης)[829], had revealed his wickedness (πονηρίαν ἐνεδείξατο)[830] as still living". Having thus emphasized the affinity in conduct between the two kings, Josephus rounds off Jehu's speech with a reiteration of its opening word of doom: "therefore... Basanēs should justly (εἰκότως)[831] experience a same ill fate (πεῖραν... ἕξειν... συμφο-ρᾶς)[832] since he had acted in a like manner".

In Kings nothing is said as such of Baasha's reaction to Jehu's word "concerning" (so MT) or "to" (so 3 Rgns) him. Josephus who has previously referred to God's "sending" Jēūs to the king, likewise introduces a lengthy, rather bombastic, description of the (non-)affect of the prophetic message upon him:

> But Basanēs, although he heard beforehand (προακηκοὼς)[833] what evils (κακὰ)[834] were destined to befall (συμβήσεσθαι)[835] him together with his whole family because of his reckless conduct (τοῖς τετολμημένοις, see 8,245), did not restrain himself (ἡσύχασεν)[836] thereafter in order to avoid being thought still more wicked (πονηρὸς, see 8,299) and so meeting death, nor seek, by repenting (μετανοήσας, see 8,225, cf. 8,281) thence-

823. Josephus uses the above phrase "requite kindness(es)" also in *AJ* 6,341; 8,326; 12,54; 15,233; 17,327; 19,184.

824. Compare the characterization of Baasha as "wicked and impious" in 8,299.

825. The whole above phrase "justly and piously governing" has a close parallel in *AJ* 7,356 where David instructs Solomon ἵνα εὐσεβῶς καὶ δικαίως προστῇ.

826. The above expression "pleasing to God" occurs also in (*BJ* 7,327); *AJ* 4,109; 5,123; 6,294.

827. The verb μιμέομαι occurs 41 × in Josephus.

828. This superlative adjectival form is used elsewhere by Josephus in reference to persons in *AJ* 2,128 (Joseph's brothers).136 (Joseph's brothers); 4,167 (the two and a half tribes); 7,50 (Ishbosheth's murderers);11,257 (Haman).265 (Haman); 16,209 (Phero-ras).212 (Pheroras).

829. This precise construction occurs only here in Josephus, cf. *AJ* 6,317 τὴν ψυχὴν... ἀπολλυμένην.

830. This is Josephus' only use of the phrase "reveal wickedness".

831. This adverb is employed 25 × by Josephus.

832. This is Josephus' only use of the above expression, "experience ill-fate".

833. Josephus' only other use of the verb προακούω is in *BJ* 1,262, cf. *AJ* 15,67 where it is conjectured by Na.

834. Note the recurrence of forms of the κακ- root throughout our pericope: κακοῖς (8,299), κάκιστον (8,300), κακά (8,301), κακοῖς, κακίας (8,302), κακώσωσι (8,303), κακά (8,304), cf. κακίαν in 3 Rgns 16,7.

835. This phrase "evils befall" recurs in *Ap* 1,259.

836. For the verb ἡσυχάζω in the above meaning "(not) restrain oneself", see *AJ* 7,277; 10,117.

forth at least of his past misdeeds (περὶ τῶν παρῳχημένων)[837], to obtain pardon (συγγνώμης... τύχῃ)[838] from God (παρὰ τοῦ θεοῦ)[839]; on the contrary, like those who have a prize held out before (προκειμένων... ἄθλων)[840] them and, in their earnest effort to obtain it (περί τι σπουδάσωσιν), do not leave off striving towards it (περὶ τοῦτο ἐνεργοῦντες)[841], so too Basanēs, after the prophet had foretold (προειρηκότος, see προεῖπε, 8,299) what was to come (τὰ μέλλοντα)[842], acted as if these greatest of misfortunes (μεγίστοις κακοῖς)[843], the death of his family (ὀλέθρῳ γένους)[844] and the destruction of his house (οἰκίας ἀπωλείᾳ)[845], were blessings instead (ὡς ἐπ' ἀγαθοῖς)[846], and became still worse (χείρων ἐγένετο)[847]; every day (καθ' ἑκάστην ἡμέραν)[848], like a champion of wickedness (ἀθλητὴς κακίας)[849], he increased his labours (πόνοις προσετίθει)[850] on its behalf. (8,301-302)[851]

837. The above construction "repent of past misdeeds" occurs also in *BJ* 7,378 and *AJ* 7,153 (of David).

838. The above expression "obtain pardon" occurs also in *BJ* 1,506; *AJ* 1,190.311; 11,226; 19,334; *Vita* 227.

839. This phrase is lacking in RO which N follows. NaWMar and Sc all read it.

840. The above phrase "prize(s) held out" recurs in *AJ* 8,208; 16,313; 18,173; 19,131.

841. F. KREBS, Recension of NIESE, *Flavii Josephi Opera II*, in *Wochenschrift für klassische Philologie* 3 (1886) 1094-1098, c. 1096 proposes to eliminate the preposition περί in the above phrase on the grounds that authors of the Hellenistic period, e.g., Polybius and Diodorus, favor construing ἐνεργεῖν with the simple accusative. He is followed by C. RAAB, *De Flavii Josephi Elocutione Quaestiones Criticae et Observationes Grammaticae*, Erlangen, 1890, p. 20 who adds in support of this proposal that the term in question could be due to dittography with the περὶ in the preceding phrase περί τι σπουδάσωσιν (see above in the text) and that elsewhere Josephus construes ἐνεργεῖν either intransitively or with the accusative.

842. With the above expression "...the prophet had foretold what was to come", compare 8,267 where Jeroboam speaks of Ahijah as "a man with a wonderful power of foretelling the future (περὶ τῶν μελλόντων προειπεῖν)".

843. Lat lacks an equivalent to the term κακοῖς; N, followed by Na, qualifies it as "fort. spurium". N*Mar retain the word without comment. The phrase "the greatest (of) evil(s)" occurs also in *BJ* 4,371.397; 7,270.342; *AJ* 3,274; 5,149; 14,370; 20,5.

844. Compare 9,108 ἐπ' ὀλέθρῳ τοῦ γένους τοῦ Ἀχάβου.

845. This is the only occurrence of the phrase "destruction of one's house" in Josephus. Elsewhere the nouns ὄλεθρος and ἀπώλεια are collocated also in *AJ* 2,301.

846. With the above formula "the greatest of misfortunes... (were) blessings instead", compare *BJ* 7,270 (the Zealots) τὰ μέγιστα τῶν κακῶν ἀγαθὰ νομίζοντες.

847. The above phrase "become worse" recurs in *BJ* 5,414; *AJ* 4,142; 9,121; 16,205.

848. Compare 8,245 Jeroboam, disregarding Jadōn's warning, "every day (καθ' ἡμέραν) sought to commit some act more heinous than the reckless acts he was already guilty of".

849. Compare Philo's designation of Jacob as τὸν ἀθλητὴν τῶν καλῶν ἐπιτηδευμάτων in *De Somniis* 1.20.126.

850. This construction occurs only here in Josephus.

851. The above passage constitutes, as it were, Josephus' replacement for the continuation of 1 Kings 16,2-4 in 16,5-7. Of the elements making up the latter passage, Josephus leaves aside 16,5 (source notice) and 7 (supplementary reference to Jehu's prophecy) entirely. He presents the data of 16,6 (Baasha's death and burial, succession of Elah) at a latter point, i.e. 8,307 (see below).

With the above description, Josephus accentuates Baasha's similarity to Jeroboam who reacted with a like heedlessness to the warnings of Jadōn, Ahijah and Abijah[852]. Conversely, the above presentation sets Baasha in sharp contrast with his Southern counterpart Asa who, in the immediately preceding episode (see 8,297), responds positively to a prophetic admonition, see above.

2. *Baasha/Asa/Ben-hadad triangle* (8,303-306). In Kings (1 Kings 15,16-22) and Chronicles (2 Chron 16,1-6) the triangular incident involving Israel, Judah and Syria stands within their respective accounts of Asa. Josephus, on the contrary, incorporates the happening within his presentation of Baasha. Specifically, he represents Baasha's act of aggression against Judah as the culmination to that king's career of evil-doing as described in 8,301-302[853]: "*and finally*, he took his army (τὴν στρατιὰν παραλαβὼν)[854] and again attacked (πάλιν ἐπῆλθε)[855]...". From 1 Kings 15,17b // 2 Chron 16,1b he derives (with modification) the name of Baasha's objective, i.e. "Aramathōn" (Ἀρα-μαθῶνι)[856], compare Biblical "Rama(h)". Josephus introduces a double qualification of the site: it was "a city of no little importance" (τῶν οὐκ ἀφανῶν)[857] and located "forty stades from Jerusalem" (στα-δίους ἀπεχούσῃ Ἱεροσολύμων τεσσαράκοντα)[858]. In contrast to the

852. Thus both reject the invitation to "repent", see 8,281 (Jeroboam) and 8,301 (Baasha). Both too are only made worse by the prophets' exhortations, see 8,245 (Jeroboam) and 301 (Baasha).

853. Recall that Jeroboam's disregard of Ahijah's warning finds expression in his invading Judah as well, see 8,274.

854. The conjecture of N for the above participle, i.e. ἀναλαβὼν, is abandoned by N*. The phrase "taking the army" above occurs also in *BJ* 2,201; 7,163.

855. This introduction to Baasha's aggression contrasts with the transition to the episode in both Kings ("and there was war between Asa and Baasha... all their days", 1 Kings 15,16) and Chronicles ("in the thirty-sixth [B 2 Par 38th] year of the reign of Asa", 2 Chron 16,1). Josephus' above reference to Baasha's "again" attacking the Judean city in question could be a reminiscence of the Kings verse, with its allusion to the continuous hostilities between the two kings, however.

856. So S, followed by NaWMar and Sc; N reads Ἀρμαθῶνι, cf. R ἀρμα-θῶνι. Elsewhere Josephus mentions a city he calls Ἀρμαθά (see *AJ* 5,342; 6,35.47.67.155.220.290, cf. N's reading in 8,303). According to Mar, *Josephus*, V, p. 735 this would be the same city as that cited here in 8,303 as "Aramathōn". SCHLATTER, *Namen*, pp. 103-104, s.v. רָמָה and SCHALIT, *Namenwörterbuch*, p. 15, s.v. Ἀραμαθών and p. 16, s.v. Ἀρμαθά, on the contrary, distinguish, within the references in question, between the (Ephramite) birthplace of Samuel cited by Josephus in 5,342 etc. and the Judean city mentioned in 8,303ff.

857. Josephus employs the above phrase "not insignificant" also in *BJ* 7,411 (cf. *AJ* 18,69). The notation supplies an implicit rationale for Baasha's choice precisely of "Ramah" as his target.

858. For similar distance indications introduced by Josephus, see DRÜNER, *Unter-suchungen*, pp. 42-43. KREBS, Recension of NIESE (see n. 841) , c. 1095, evoking "die Rücksicht auf den Hiatus" and comparing *AJ* 8,346 μέχρι τῆς Ἰεζαρήλας πόλεως, proposes inserting the article before "Jerusalem" also in the above phrase.

Bible Josephus has Baasha "fortify" (ὠχύρου) rather than "build" the already existing city of "Aramathōn/Ramah"[859] following his "taking" (καταλαβόμενος)[860] of it – a point not mentioned in Scripture as such. In place, finally, of the somewhat obscure Biblical formulation concerning the purpose of Baasha's initiative ("that he might permit no one to go out or come in to Asa..."), Josephus provides the following clear statement: "for he had previously determined (προδιεγνωκὼς)[861] to leave a force in it, in order that they might use it as a base from which to set out and attack (κακώσωσι)[862] the kingdom of Asanos".

1 Kings 15,18 // 2 Chron 16,2 relates Asa's response to Baasha's initiative: he dispatches the precious metals of temple[863] and palace to Ben-hadad (LXX υἱὸν Ἀδέρ)[864], the king of Syria (Aram) resident in Damascus. Josephus (8,304) prefaces this item with a reference to Asa's motivation in acting as he does – itself inspired by his previous notice on Baasha's aims: "but Asanos, who feared (φοβηθεὶς)[865] the enemy's attack (ἐπιχείρησιν)[866] and thought that (λογισάμενος ὡς, see 8,225) the army left in Aramathōn might inflict great damage (πολλὰ διαθήσει κακὰ, see 8,299) upon the entire country ruled by him...". At the same time, he omits mention both of the "source" of the "gold and silver" (χρυσὸν καὶ ἄργυρον)[867] sent by Asa[868] as well as the name of their

859. Compare his analogous treatment of the "building references" of 1 Kings 12,25 in 8,225. In 8,306 Josephus will, however, use the term "build" in reference to Baasha's activity at the site.

860. Cf. 8,255. Elsewhere Josephus uses the above participle of the "taking" of cities etc. in *AJ* 7,282; 12,244.389; 15,180, cf. the synonymous active participle in 14,284.410.457.

861. Josephus' only other use of the verb προδιαγινώσκω is *AJ* 17,94.

862. The verb κακάω occurs 88 × in Josephus.

863. B and the L MS 82/o 3 Rgns 15,18 lacks mention of Asa's taking treasures from the Temple. In, e.g., *Pesaḥim* 119a it is affirmed that the treasures in question were those Asa had himself earlier taken from Zerah (see 2 Chron 14:14-15). Cf. GINZBERG, *Legends*, VI, p. 309, n. 20 and n. 765.

864. 1 Kings 15,18 cites the names of the Syrian's father (Tabrimmon, MT) and grandfather (Hezion, MT) as well.

865. Compare Josephus' – also interjected – notice on Rehoboam's surrendering to Shishak: διὰ τὸν φόβον (8,258).

866. The above noun occurs 41 × in Josephus.

867. Josephus' sequence in the above phrase corresponds to that of 2 Par 16,2 whereas MT Kings and Chronicles as well as 3 Rgns 15,18 have "silver and gold".

Conceivably in passing over the Biblical indication that Asa obtained the treasures with which he will bribe Ben-hadad from the Temple and palace, Josephus has in view the fact that according to his earlier notice (8,258) Shishak had "entered the treasuries of God and the king, and carried off untold amounts of gold and silver, *leaving not a single thing behind*" in Rehoboam's reign, with the result that Asa could not draw on these sources (at the same time, however, he does make implicit reference to the replenishment of Judah's coffers under Asa in his account of that king's despoiling the Ethiopians in 8,294, cf. n. 765).

868. In Josephus he does so via "envoys" (πρέσβεις). In 1 Kings 15,18 they are designated as "servants" (3 Rgns παίδων), while 2 Chron 16,2 does not specify by whom Asa "sent" his tribute.

recipient whom he calls simply "the king of Damascus" (Δαμασ-κηνῶν)"⁸⁶⁹.

1 Kings 15,19a // 2 Chron 16,3a formulate Asa's appeal to Ben-hadad, doing so obscurely in both MT and LXX. The Hebrew utilizes a nominal phrase "a covenant (ברית) between me and between you, (and) between my father and your father", whereas 3 Rgns 15,19 (B) reads "arrange (διάθου, L 'let there be') a covenant (διαθήκην) between me (+ 'and you', L and 2 Par 16,3) and (+ 'between', L and 2 Par 16,3) my father and your father". True to his consistent *Sprachgebrauch*, Josephus avoids LXX's use of διαθήκη (= "treaty"); his Asa asks the Syrian to "become his ally" (συμμαχεῖν)⁸⁷⁰, "recalling (ὑπομιμ-νήσκων)⁸⁷¹ that there had been friendship (φιλία) between them since their fathers' time (πατρῷα)⁸⁷²". He likewise omits the entire second half of Asa's message in which the Judean calls attention to the "gift" he has sent and requests Ben-hadad to "break your covenant (3 Rgns 15,19b διαθήκην) with Baasha"⁸⁷³. The first of these items appears both superfluous and crass – Ben-hadad can very well see Asa's "gift" for himself –; the latter will be incorporated into Josephus' subsequent narrative.

1 Kings 15,20aα // 2 Chron 16,4aα touches only briefly on Ben-hadad's immediate, affirmative reaction to Asa's appeal: he "hearkens" to him. Josephus elaborates on the response of the Syrian (whom he continues to leave unnamed): he "gladly accepted" (ἀσμένως ἐδέξατο)⁸⁷⁴ Asa's "large sum of money" (τῶν χρημάτων τὸ πλῆ-θος)⁸⁷⁵ and, as requested, "made an alliance" (συμμαχίαν

---

869. See *AJ* 9,244 where Josephus calls Hazael ("Arasēs") "king of Syria and Damascus". Conceivably, Josephus' leaving aside the Biblical name of the Syrian king, Ben-hadad, in our pericope has to do with the fact that he has previously stated (see *AJ* 7,103) that "Adados" (i.e. Ben-hadad III) was active under Ahab, a later king of Israel, see further below.

870. Thus the conjecture of N followed by NaMar for the συμμαχίαν of codd (to which N* reverts).

871. The verb ὑπομιμνήσκω occurs 21 × in Josephus.

872. The above phrase πατρῷα φιλία recurs in *BJ* 1,274.281.293; *AJ* 4,102; 14,398, cf. τοῖς πατρῴοις φίλοις in 8,264. Compare *AJ* 9,30 where Josephus introduces the following motivation as to why Joram of Israel requests Jehoshaphat's cooperation in his projected campaign against Moab: "since he had from the first been his father's friend" (φίλος... τῷ πατρί). On Greek "political friendship", see G. STÄHLIN, φίλος κτλ, in *TWNT* 9 (1973) 144-169, p. 148.

873. In 2 Par 16,3 Asa's request runs rather "... turn away Baasha from me...".

874. With various objects this construction occurs also in *AJ* 4,131; 7,230; 12,188.382; 18,101; 20,23.

875. Variants of this phrase recur in *BJ* 1,519; 2,592; *AJ* 2,173.202; 4,97.224; 10,83; 13,273.

ἐποιήσατο)⁸⁷⁶ with the Judean, this after "breaking off friendly relations" (διαλύσας... φιλίαν)⁸⁷⁷ with Baasha.

1 Kings 15,20aβ // 2 Chron 16,4aβ relate Ben-hadad's further initiatives: he dispatches his commmanders against the Israelite cities. Josephus' amplified version of this notice reads: "he sent (πέμψας, LXX ἀπέστειλεν) the commanders (ἡγεμόνας, LXX ἄρχοντας) of his own force (δυνάμεως, so LXX) to the cities ruled by him (i.e. Baasha, compare Bible "the cities of Israel") with orders to ravage (κακοῦν) them⁸⁷⁸". In 1 Kings 15,20b // 2 Chron 16,4b there follows an enumeration of four specific locales which Ben-hadad "smote" (LXX ἐπάταξεν). The names of the various sites vary considerably among the various Biblical textual witnesses and between all of them and Josephus' own enumeration: "so they (the Syrian forces) set out and burnt (ἐνεπίμπρασαν) some of the cities and sacked (διήρπασαν)⁸⁷⁹ others, including Aiōn (Αἰῶνα)⁸⁸⁰... Dan (Δάνα)⁸⁸¹, Abellanē (Ἀβελλάνην)⁸⁸² and many others⁸⁸³".

876. The above phrase "make an alliance" recurs in *AJ* 13,227.335. The substantive συμμαχία, one of Josephus' replacements for LXX διαθήκη, occurs c. 87× in his writings. (Recall that the same term is read by the codd in 8,304, see n. 870).

877. This is the only occurrence of the above phrase "dissolve friendship" in Josephus. The terms συμμαχία and φιλία juxtaposed by Josephus in 8,305 occur frequently in Hellenistic treaty texts, often in conjunction, see the Greek word index in H. BENGSTRON (ed.), *Die Staatsverträge des Altertums* II, München, 1975², and III, ed. H.H. Schmitt, 1969. See also Thucydides, *History* 6.34.1; Polybius, *History* 31.l.1.3; Diodorus, *Bibliotheca historica* 17.49.3; Dionysius, *RA* 2.11.1; 4.49.1, as well as their collocation in *AJ* 4,102; 7,66.107 12,419; 13,32.45.110.152.170.223.250.261.264.334; 14,185.197.257.267.

878. Note the operation of the talion principle which Josephus' terminology underscores here: whereas Baasha's forces were to "ravage" (κακώσωσι) Asa's kingdom (8,303), the Syrian troops end up "ravaging" (κακοῦν) his own territory (8,305).

879. Josephus collocates the above verbs, ἐμπίμπρημι and διαρπάζω, also in *BJ* 2,504; 4,340; 6,353; *AJ* 6,192; 13,116; 20,121.125.172.185.187.

880. This is the emendation proposed by Hud and followed by NaMar (cf. the variant reading Αἰών in 2 Par 16,4). NN* read Ἰωάνου with M, cf. ROSP's Ἰωάννου on which W bases himself for his form "Yoannès". SCHLATTER, *Namen*, p. 85, s.v. עִיּוֹן and SCHALIT, *Namenwörterbuch*, p. 67, s.v. Ἰώνη opt for the form Ἰωνη(ν). Compare 1 Kings 15,20/ 2 Chron 16,4 (עִיּוֹן), 3 Rgns 15,20 (Ἀϊν), B 2 Par 16,4 (Ἰώ).

881. Hebrew reads "Dan" as does 3 Rgns 15,20, compare Δανὼ in B 2 Par 16,4.

882. Thus the reading of MSP followed by NaWMar. NN* read Ἀβελάνην as does SCHALIT, *Namenwörterbuch*, p. 1, s.v. Ἀβελάνη. According to SCHLATTER, *Namen*, p. 9, s.v. אָבֵל, Josephus' original form was Ἀβελ-μαχα-ια. Compare 1 Kings 15,20 (בֵּית-אָבֵל מַעֲכָה), B 3 Rgns 15,20 (Ἀδελμάθ, L Ἀβελμαά), 2 Chron 16,4 (אָבֵל מָיִם), B 2 Par 16,4 (Ἀβελμὰν, v.l. Ἀβελμαίν).

Note that in *AJ* 7,288 Josephus renders 2 Sam 20,14 "Abel-maacah", cf. the MT form in 1 Kings 15,20, by Ἀβελωχέα (v.l. Ἀβελμαχέα). According to SCHALIT, *Namenwörterbuch*, p.1, s.v. Ἀβελμαχέα (who adopts the variant reading in 7,288 as the original one) "handelt es sich um ein und dieselbe Stadt", i.e. in both 7,288 and 8,305.

883. Compare 1 Kings (3 Rgns) 15,20 "and all Chinneroth with all the land of Naphtali", 2 Chron 16,4 "and all the store cities of Naphtali", 2 Par 16,4 "and all the country round about Nephthali". Josephus' vague reference to "and many other (cities)" here may represent his way of resolving the discrepancy among the Biblical sources concerning the identity of the final locale ravished by Ben-hadad.

1 Kings 15,21 and 2 Chron 16,5 differ somewhat regarding Baasha's response to the Syrian invasion. In both the Israelite "hears" and stops "building" Ramah. In the former, however, he then "dwelt (וַיֵּשֶׁב, compare 3 Rgns 15,21 ἀνέστρεψεν= וַיָּשָׁב) in [3 Rgns εἰς] Tirzah", while in the latter verse Baasha "let his work cease". Josephus' version supplies a motive for Baasha's actions[884]: "when the king of Israel heard (ἀκούσας, see 3 Rgns ἤκουσεν) of this, he left off building (οἰκοδομεῖν) and fortifying (ὀχυροῦν, see ὀχυρόυ, 8,303)[885] Aramathōn, and returned (ἀνέστρεψεν, so LXX, contrast MT)[886] *in haste to bring help to his injured* (κακουμένοις, see κακοῦν, 8,305) *subjects*".

Our incident concludes in 1 Kings 15,22 // 2 Chron 16,6 with Asa utilizing the materials Baasha had assembled at Ramah to build "Geba" (of Benjamin) and "Mizpah"[887]. Josephus renders this closing notice thus: "Then Asanos (took)[888] the materials (ὕλης, Bible: "stones and timber") prepared by Basanēs for building (πρὸς οἰκοδομίαν, 3 Rgns [B] / 2 Par ἃ ᾠκοδόμησεν) and with them erected (ἀνήγειρεν, 3 Rgns/ 2 Par ᾠκοδόμησεν) *two strong cities* (πόλεις... καρτεράς)[889] *in the same region*[890], one of which was called Gabaa (Γαβαὰ)[891] and the other Maspha (Μασφά)[892]".

In both Josephus' Biblical sources the above account is followed by the conclusion to Asa's reign, 1 Kings 15,23-24 // 2 Chron 16,11-14, in the latter with the *Sondergut* episode of the king's confrontation with the seer Hanani concerning his overture to Ben-hadad supervening in 16,7-10. Josephus entirely passes over this last happening, while reserving his own closing notice on Asa for a subsequent moment, see 8,314-

884. Compare his earlier motivation for Baasha's fortifying of "Aramathōn" in 8,303, likewise interjected by him.

885. On Josephus' collocation of these two verbs here, see n. 859 on 8,303.

886. Note that unlike 3 Rgns 15,21 (cf. also MT) Josephus does not specify that it was to "Tirzah" that Baasha "returned"; his subsequent statement (see 8,307) that Baasha died "in the city of Tharsē" (see below) seems, however, to presuppose his familiarity with that specification.

887. The above proper place names are those of MT Kings and Chronicles, see also 2 Par 16,6 Γαβαὰ (B Γάβαε) and Μασφά. 3 Rgns 15,22 renders with common nouns, i.e. "(every) hill (βουνὸν) of Benjamin" and "(the) lookout" (σκοπιάν), respectively.

888. In the Bible there is a preliminary reference to Asa's assembling "all Judah" to which Josephus has no equivalent.

889. This phrase recurs in *BJ* 1,321;2,503 (3,290).464;4,432.

890. With this geographical specification, compare the indications Josephus introduces concerning the localization of "Marisa" (8,292) and "the valley of Saphatha" (8,293).

891. Thus the reading of NN*Mar, cf. Lat gabaa. NaW and SCHLATTER, *Namen*, p. 33, s.v. גֶּבַע follow the Γαβὰ of MSP, see the reading(s) of 2 Par 16,6 cited in n. 887. In any case, Josephus leaves aside the specification of 1 Kings 15,22 (> 2 Chron 16,6) that the first city built by Asa was "in Benjamin".

892. So NaMar following Hud, cf. Lat masphas. W reproduces the Μεσταφάς of MSP; N reads Μασταφάς with RO, while SCHALIT, *Namenwörterbuch*, p. 84, s.v. *Μασφαθή* opts for Μασφαθή. Compare the 2 Par 16,6 reading cited in n. 887. The site is likewise mentioned by Josephus in *AJ* 6,22.60;10,158.159.168.172.173.

315. Conversely, he follows the foregoing story of Baasha's incursion with further material concerning the Northern Kingdom drawn from 1 Kings 16,5-28, *vide infra*.

Summary: The above sequence offers few positive indications as to the text-form(s) of Kings and Chronicles available to Josephus in composing it. In speaking of Baasha's "returning" in the face of the Syrian invasion, Josephus aligns himself with 3 Rgns 15,21 against 1 Kings 15,21 (as well as MT and LXX 2 Chron 16,5 – recall, however, that the difference here is only a matter of divergent vocalizations, see above). With B 3 Rgns 15,18 he shares a negative communality, i.e. his non-mention of the Temple as source for Asa's "gift" to Ben-hadad (in fact, however, Josephus says nothing about whence Asa derived his offerings, whereas B does agree with the other Biblical text-witnesses in mentioning their coming from the palace treasury).

Noteworthy in 8,298-306 is Josephus' compiling of materials drawn from different contexts in Kings into a presentation focussed on Baasha. This figure receives a further (negative) accentuation via Josephus' insertions within the unit which underscore the parallelism between him and Jeroboam – see especially the lengthy reflection on Baasha's heedless response to Jehu's warnings (8,301-302) which then expresses itself in his attack on Judah. Recall as well Josephus' characteristic avoidance of the term "covenant" (διαθήκη) employed several times in the two Biblical source passages.

X

NORTH/SOUTH CONTRAST
(8,307-315)

In 8,307-315 Josephus develops a contrast between the disorders that characterize the North's history in the period from the death of Baasha to the accession of Ahab (8,307-313) and the South's stability under the long-reigned Asa (8,314-315). For the former he draws on 1 Kings 16,5-28, for the latter on 1 Kings 15,24 (cf. 2 Chron 16,7-17,1).

The present unit begins (8,307) with a statement linking it with what precedes, i.e. "after this (i.e. the Ramah fiasco) Basanēs had no further opportunity (καιρὸν... ἔσχεν)[893] to march against Asanos"[894]. This "inability" is explicated (see 1 Kings 16,6a) in terms of Baasha's speedy demise[895]. The deceased is then "buried (θάπτεται, so 3 Rgns 16,6)[896] in Tharsē" (θαρσῇ, MT "Tirzah")[897], whereupon his son Elanos (Ἤλανος, MT "Elah", 3 Rgns Ἐλά) "took over his kingdom" (παρα-λαμβάνει... τὴν ἀρχὴν, compare B 3 Rgns 16,6b βασιλεύει, L* ἐβα-σίλευσεν)[898].

From 1 Kings 16,8bβ Josephus extracts the information that Elah's reign lasted two years (he leaves aside, as something self-evident, that

893. The above construction "have (an) opportunity" recurs in *BJ* 1,375; *AJ* 6,284; 11,321; 20,200.

894. Compare 8,285 where Josephus appends a similar notice to his account of Jeroboam's defeat by Abijah: "and Jeroboam, after this defeat, was never again powerful so long as Abias lived". The parallelism underscored by Josephus between Jeroboam and Baasha thus extends to the military impotence in which they both end up.

895. For Kings' idiom "he slept with his fathers", Josephus substitutes another circumlocution, i.e. "he was overtaken by fate" (ἐφθάσθη... ὑπὸ τοῦ χρεών) which occurs only here in his writings.

896. On Josephus' use of this h.p. form, see n. 683.

897. This emendation, proposed by Hud with reference to Lat "Thersa" (cf. 3 Rgns θερσά), has been generally accepted. Compare RO Ἀρσῇ; MSP Ἀρσάνῃ. Josephus has previously cited this city as Baasha's "residence" in 8,299, see n. 686.

898. The above construction recurs in *AJ* 5,271 (h.p. as in 8,307); 7,345.348; 9,93.95.177,227; 10,84 (h.p.).103.231 (h.p.); 12,46; 14,330; 16,96.294 (h.p.); 17,27; 18,105.108; 20,63.151.153.249; *Ap* 1,94. Compare the equivalent expression τὴν βασι-λείαν παραλαβὼν in 8,288.

In contrast to the Bible Josephus provides no "synchronism" of Elah's accession with the regnal year of his Southern counterpart, Asa. His failure to do so may be related to the fact that MT and 3 Rgns diverge both in their placing of this synchronism and the actual figure given: according to the former's 16,8 Elah started to rule in Asa's 26th year, while the latter's 16,6 makes it rather the 20th year (127/c₂ 29th).

Finally, note that according to his usual procedure Josephus leaves aside the "source notice" for Baasha found in 16,7.

Elah governed from his father's residence, i.e. "Tirzah"). According to 1 Kings 16,9a Elah ended up the victim of a plot instigated by his officer (in MT L designated as "commander of half his chariots", in B "commander [ἄρχον] of half his horses") named Zimri (3 Rgns Ζαμβρ(ε)ὶ). In Josephus Elanos "died" (τελευτᾶ, see 8,285)... "being treacherously slain (φονεύσαντος... ἐξ ἐπιβουλῆς)⁸⁹⁹ by Zambrias (Ζαμβρίου)⁹⁰⁰, the commander (ἱππάρχου)⁹⁰¹ of half of his body of horsemen". According to 1 Kings 16,9b-10a Zimri (Zambrei) himself murders Elah in the house of the royal official Arza (BL* Ὡσὰ, 19/b' and 82/o Ἀσὰ) in Tirzah where the king was "drinking himself drunk". Josephus modifies this presentation in several respects. The assassination occurs while Elanos is being "entertained at table" (κατευωχηθέντα)⁹⁰² by "Ōsa" (Ὡσᾶ)⁹⁰³, the king's "steward" (οἰκονόμῳ, so 3 Rgns). Similarly, instead of attributing Elah's murder to Zimri himself acting (apparently) without confederates, Josephus offers this more plausible scenario: "Zambrias persuaded some of the horsemen under his command to rush upon (ἐπιδραμεῖν)⁹⁰⁴ him (Elanos), and had him killed (ἀπέκτεινε, compare 3 Rgns 16,10 ἐθανάτωσεν)⁹⁰⁵". Josephus further provides an explanation why, as the Bible seems to suggest, Elah suffered assassination without any resistance being made on his behalf. This could happen, he notes, because the king "was quite alone (μεμονωμένον)⁹⁰⁶, without his soldiers and commanders, who were all occupied in the siege of Gabathōn in the Philistine country (τῆς Γαβαθώνης... τῆς Παλαιστίνων)⁹⁰⁷". He obtains this last indication by anticipation from 1 Kings 16,15 (see below)⁹⁰⁸.

899. With the above construction compare 20,239 (the High Priest Jonathan) τελευτήσαντος... ἐξ ἐπιβουλῆς.

900. Thus NMar and SCHALIT, Namenwörterbuch, p. 49, s.v. Ζαμβρίας. NaW and SCHLATTER, Namen, p. 49, s.v. זִמְרִי read Ζαμαρίου (Ζαμάρις) with MSPE.

901. Elsewhere BJ 1,527; 2,310.531; AJ 8,309; 14,210.

902. The verb κατευωχέομαι occurs 12 × in Josephus, all in AJ.

903. So NMar (= BL* 3 Rgns 16,9). NaW read Ὀλσᾶ with SPE. Hud conjectures Ὀρσᾶ, while SCHLATTER, Namen, p. 22, s.v. אַרְצָה and SCHALIT, Namenwörterbuch, p. 93, s.v. Ὀρσάς propose Ὀρσά (from a Hebrew אַרְצָה).

904. Elsewhere Josephus uses ἐπιτρέχω (with various meanings) in BJ 1,18; 7,199.362; AJ 9,225; 11,305; 12,28; 14,442; Vita 158; Ap 1,183.

905. Compare, however, 8,310 where Josephus does speak of Zambrias himself killing Elanos.

906. Josephus uses the verb μονόω (passive) elsewhere in AJ 5,277.280; 7,298; 8,331; 9,200; 13,363; 14,19; Vita 95.

907. Compare 8,288 Γαβαθῶνα πόλιν Παλαιστίνων.

908. Once again (see n. 898), Josephus refrains from "synchronizing" an event for which the Biblical sources offer divergent figures. In MT 16,10.15 Zimri's coup takes place in Asa's 27th year. B lacks an equivalent indication in its rendering of both verses. L 3 Rgns 16,10 likewise lacks a synchronization, while in 16,15 its witnesses diverge both from MT and from each other, MSS 19/b'108/b and 93/e₂ dating the happening to Asa's 22nd, 127/c₂ to his 21st year. Note further that MT's chronology in 1 Kings 16,8-15 appears

1 Kings 16,10b-13(14) relate Zimri's annihilation of Baasha's line. 3 Rgns has no equivalent to MT's vv. 11b-12a in which v. 11a's mention of the overthrow of Baasha's house is further elaborated prior to the fulfillment notice of vv. 12b-13[909]. Josephus' version stands closer to the more expansive MT whose components it reproduces in the following sequence, vv. 10b.12b.13,11b thus: "after slaying (φονεύσας, cf. φονεύσαντος, 8,307) Elanos[910], Zambrias (Ζαμβρίας)[911]... made himself king (βασιλεύει, compare 3 Rgns 16,10b ἐβασίλευσεν)[912] and destroyed the entire family of Basanēs (πᾶσαν τὴν Βασάνου γενεὰν... διαφθείρει)[913] in accordance with the prophecy (προφητείαν) of Jēus ('Ιηοῦ)[914]". Drawing on 1 Kings 16,11-12a (MT), Josephus proceeds to elaborate on the end of Baasha's house as follows: "for it came about that, because of his impiety (ἀσέβειαν), his house (οἶκον, so 3 Rgns 16,11b) perished root and branch (πρόρριζον ἀπολέσθαι)[915] *in the same way as the house of Jeroboam was destroyed* (διαφθαρέντα, cf. διαφθείρει, 8,309a) *as we have narrated* (i.e. in 8,289)[916]". In the above formulation, note Josephus' characteristic substitution of "in accordance with prophecy" for 1 Kings 16,12b's "according to the word of the Lord" and his explicit paralleling of the fates of Baasha's and Jeroboam's houses[917]. As is his practice, Josephus leaves aside the appended source notice of 16,14 for Elah.

The transitional verse 1 Kings 16,15 synchronizes Zimri's accession with the corresponding regnal year of Asa (so MT L)[918], specifies that

internally inconsistent: Elah succeeds in Asa's 26th year (16,8), rules two years (16,8) and then is assassinated in the Judean's 27th year (16,10.15).

909. BHS suggests that 3 Rgns' shorter text is the result of homoioteleuton – see "Baasha" at the end of v. 11a and the beginning of v. 12b.

910. Contrast 8,308 where Zambrias has his men kill Elanos.

911. Thus NMar. Na reads Ζάμαρης with E, W Ζαμάριος with MSP. See n. 900 for the divergent readings of the first occurrence of the name of Elah's overthrower in 8,307.

912. Josephus leaves aside the resumptive phrase, duplicating 1 Kings 16,10b, of 16,11a "it came to pass when he reigned when he sat upon the throne...".

913. Compare 8,289 ("Basanēs") ἅπαν τὸ 'Ιεροβοάμου γένος διέφθειρε. Josephus uses the above h.p. of διαφθείρω (active or passive) also in *BJ* 1,102.226.316.324.334; 2,13; 4,343.451.642; *AJ* 4,97; 5,183; 6,135; 9,23; 12,374; 13,269; 14,124; 20,2, cf. *RA* 4.48.2; 5.31.1.

914. Thus the emendation of Hud ·followed by N*NaWMar, compare the corresponding accusative form 'Ιηοῦν widely conjectured in 8,299, see n. 817. RO has 'Ιηοῦς, the form printed by N and adopted by SCHLATTER, *Namen*, p. 53, s.v. יהו, MSP 'Ιοῦς.

With the above fulfillment notice, compare 8,289 (Basanēs eliminates Jeroboam's line) "in accordance with the prophecy (προφητείαν) of God", see also n. 714.

915. This expression recurs in 8,314 (see there) and 11,213.

916. Compare Josephus' version of Jehu's prophecy against Baasha in 8,300 "... Basanēs should justly experience a like ill fate (i.e. as Jeroboam) since he had acted in a like manner".

917. Recall his previous accentuation of the (reprobate) affinities between the two rulers themselves.

918. See further n. 908.

the former reigned seven days (thus MT L, B years), and mentions the continuing Philistine siege of Gibbethon. Like B 3 Rgns 16,15 Josephus has no equivalent to the first of these items (just as, à la 3 Rgns 16,10 he passes over 1 Kings 16,10's earlier synchronization for Zimri's seizure of power). He reserves mention of Zimri's length of reign for his concluding notice on the usurper (vide infra), while he has already "anticipated" the third datum of 16,15 in describing Elah's demise, see 8,308. Accordingly, he now (8,310) immediately presents his version of 1 Kings 16,16-17: "now when the army (ἡ στρατιὰ) besieging Gabathōn (πολιορκοῦσα τὴν Γαβαθώνην, see τὴν πολιορκίαν τῆς Γαβαθώνης, 8,308) learned what had befallen the king and that Zambrias had killed him (ἀποκτείνας αὐτὸν, B 3 Rgns 16,16 ἔπαισεν τὸν βασιλέα)[919] and was ruling the kingdom (ἔχει τὴν βασιλείαν)[920], they (αὐτὴ = ἡ στρατιὰ), in turn, chose their commander (τὸν ἡγούμενον, so B 3 Rgns 16,16, cf. L* τὸν ἡγεμόνα) Amarinos (Ἀμαρῖνον)[921] as king (ἀπέδειξε βασιλέα, compare ἐβασίλευσαν, B 3 Rgns 16,16b)[922]". Next, basing himself on 1 Kings 16,17, Josephus relates the initiatives undertaken by "Amarinos" against "Zambrias": "he withdrew his army from Gabathōn, and came (παραγίνεται, see 8,212) to Tharsē (see 8,299.307), the royal city (τὸ βασίλειον)[923], attacked (προσβαλὼν, L 3 Rgns 16,17b περιεκάθισεν) it, and took it by storm (κατὰ κράτος αἱρεῖ)[924]", anticipating this last item from 1 Kings 16,18aα ("when Zimri saw that the city was taken...").

---

919. Compare 8,308 where Zambrias incites others to "kill" (ἀπέκτεινε) Elanos.

920. The above construction occurs also in AJ 8,21; (15,18).177.262; 16,141; 19,296.

921. This is Josephus' form of the name which appears differently in 1 Kings 16,16 MT (Omri), B (Ζαμβρεί, i.e. the same name given Elah's assassin in 3 Rgns 16,9ff., compare MT Zimri) and L (Ἀμβρεί/Ἀμβρί). According to Schlatter, Namen, p. 87, s.v. עָמְרִי "J. las עָמְרִי". Schalit, Namenwörterbuch, p. 9, s.v. Ἀμαρῖνος avers "Der griechische Text des J. ging, wie es scheint, auf eine Lesart עֲמָרִי zurück, also griechisch: Ἀμαρι".

922. Note that according to MT 1 Kings 16,16b "all Israel" makes "Omri" king. Josephus' reference (corresponding to 3 Rgns' "the people in the camp") to the "army" besieging Gibbethon as the subject of this action makes better sense in that a portion of "all Israel" is actually supporting "Zimri" at the moment.

923. On the various meanings of the term βασίλειον (sg. and pl.) in Josephus, see Rengstorf, Concordance, s.v.

1 Kings (3 Rgns) 16,17 speaks of "all Israel" accompanying Omri from Gibbethon to Tirzah. Here again, Josephus, with his singular reference to Amarinos, avoids the problematic Biblical indication that "Omri" enjoyed the backing of Israel in its entirety.

924. See ἑλόντες κατὰ κράτος (8,284, Abijah of the Israelite cities). With the entire above construction προσβαλὼν τῇ πόλει κατὰ κράτος αἱρεῖ, compare the description of Herod's assault on Jerusalem in 14,478 προσβαλὼν κατὰ κράτος εἷλε τὴν πόλιν, cf. Vita 99. Josephus uses the above h.p. of αἱρέω elsewhere some 29 × ; the form is likewise frequent in other classical and post-classical Greek historians, see Eriksson, Präsens, p. 49.

Drawing now on 1 Kings 16,18abα, Josephus proceeds to recount Zambrias' reaction to Amarinos' assault: "Zambrias, seeing (ἰδὼν, B 3 Rgns εἶδεν) the city's (τὴν πόλιν, 3 Rgns ἡ πόλις) fall (ἠρημένην)[925], fled (συνέφυγεν, 1 Kings 16,18 "goes") into the inmost part of the palace (εἰς τὸ μυχαίτατον[926] τῶν βασιλείων)[927] and, setting it (αὐτὰ)[928] on fire (ὑποπρήσας)[929], allowed himself to be consumed with it (συγκατέκαυσεν)[930]". To this description of Zambrias' end Josephus then appends the chronological notice he has held over from 1 Kings 16,15a, i.e. "after a reign (βασιλεύσας, 3 Rgns ἐβασίλευσεν) of (only) seven days"[931].

1 Kings 16,19 attributes Zimri's demise to his indulgence in Jeroboam's sin. Doubtless conscious of the implausibility of this affirmation given the length and circumstances of Zimri's reign, Josephus leaves it aside, just as he does the "source notice" of 16,20. He thus passes directly from Zimri's death (16,18) to the development cited in 16,21, i.e. the split between the adherents of Tibni (B θαμνεὶ, L θαβεννεί) and Omri (B Ζαμβρεί, L Ἀμβρεί/Ἀμβρί). Josephus' version of this item reads: "immediately thereafter the people of Israel (ὁ τῶν Ἰσραηλιτῶν λαός, 3 Rgns ὁ λαὸς Ἰσραήλ) were divided into two parties (διέστη, 3 Rgns μερίζεται)[932], some wishing Thamanaios (θαμαναῖον)[933] to be their king, others, Amarinos". In 16,22 which relates the triumph of Omri's partisans, 3 Rgns exhibits a double plus: following "and Tibni (Thamnei, B) died" (v. 22bα), it reads "and his (Tibni's) brother at that time', just as after 'and Omri (Zambrei, B) ruled" (v. 22bβ) it continues "after Thamnei (B)". Josephus' narration of the happening clearly aligns itself more closely with MT's shorter formulation: "And, as

---

925. Thus the conjecture of Bk (cf. Lat detentam) adopted by WMar. N prints the majority reading of the codd, i.e. ἠρημωμένην (RO have ἐρημωμένην). Na hesitantly conjectures ἠλλοτριωμένην. Compare B 3 Rgns 16,18 προκατείλημπται.

926. Elsewhere, Josephus uses this nominalized superlative form in BJ 2,612; 3,27; 5,427 (pl.); AJ 7,229.

927. Compare MT "into the citadel (ארמון) of the king's house"; 3 Rgns εἰς ἄντρον τοῦ οἴκου τοῦ βασιλέως. Josephus' reading here aligns itself with that of TJ: "into the inner chamber (לאדרון) of the house of the king".

928. Thus the conjecture of NN* adopted by NaMar for the αὐτὸ of codd.

929. This is the only occurrence of ὑποπίμπρημι in AJ; in BJ it appears 16×. Compare 3 Rgns ἐνεπύρισεν.

930. Josephus' only other use of συγκατακαίω is in AJ 3,242.

931. This datum corresponds to that found in MT and L as against B "seven years", see above in the text.

932. With the above phrase "the people (λαός) were divided", compare AJ 12,228 and 18,53 where διίστημι is used with τὸ πλῆθος as subject.

933. This is the form read by NN*Mar and SCHALIT, Namenwörterbuch, p. 53, s.v. θαμαναῖος. NaW follow OP's θαμαναῖον. Cf. B θαμνεί. Josephus omits the name of "Tibni's" father, i.e. Ginath (MT)/ Γωνώθ (B)/Γωνώθ (L).

those who wanted Amarinos to rule were victorious (νικήσαντες)⁹³⁴, they killed (ἀποκτείνουσι) Thamanaios"⁹³⁵.

1 Kings (3 Rgns) 16,23 consists of various chronological indications: Omri becomes king (definitively) in Asa's *31st* year, and reigns 12 years, six of these in Tirzah (3 Rgns θερσά). Josephus (8,312) introduces several variations/expansions in his reproduction of these notices: "... Amarinos became king (βασιλεύει, so 3 Rgns 16,23a, cf. on 8,309) of all the people (παντὸς... τοῦ ὄχλου)⁹³⁶ in the *thirtieth year*⁹³⁷ of the reign of Asanos and he reigned (ἦρξεν, 3 Rgns βασιλεύει)⁹³⁸ twelve years (ἔτη δώδεκα, 3 Rgns δώδεκα ἔτη), six of them in the city of Tharsē (ἐν Θάρσῳ)⁹³⁹ and the rest in a city called Sōmareōn ([ἐν] Σωμαρεῶνι)⁹⁴⁰, known to the Greeks⁹⁴¹ as Samaria (Σαμαρείᾳ)⁹⁴²". With this mention of "Samaria" Josephus anticipates 1 Kings 16,24 which describes Omri's purchasing from a "Shemer" (B Σέμηρ, L Σέμμηρ) a hilltop site which he fortifies and names "Shomeron" (B Σεμερών, L Σομορών) after its former owner. Josephus words the data of 16,24 as follows: "So (οὕτως) it was called by Amarinos (Ἀμαρῖ-

934. Compare 1 Kings 16,22a "the people who followed Omri overcame (ויחזק, see L ὑπερεκράτησε, B lacks an equivalent to this verb) the people who followed Tibni...".

935. 1 Kings (3 Rgns) 16,22αβ simply states that "Tibni died" (3 Rgns ἀπέθανεν), leaving it unspecified whether his death was a natural or violent one and if the latter who "killed" him. Josephus' reference to the "victory" of Amarinos' partisans naturally suggests the idea of their "killing" Thamanaios, the leader of the other party.

936. This specification (compare Biblical "over Israel") reflects the fact that already previously "Omri" was recognized as "king" by some portion of the Israelites, see 8,310 // 1 Kings 16,16. Recall that Josephus avoids the source's previous references (see 1 Kings 16,16 [MT].17) to "all Israel" supporting Omri, see nn. 922, 923.

937. Josephus' synchronization is thus "off" by one year from the Biblical notice that Omri's accession occurred in Asa's *31st* year. It may, on the other hand, be noted that his figure here does accord with his own previous chronological indications in 8,287ff.: Nadab accedes in Asa's 2nd year and rules for 2 years, i.e. into Asa's 4th year (8,287). Assassinating Nadab in the 2nd year of his reign (i.e. Asa's 4th year), Baasha rules 24 years (8,298), i.e. into Asa's 28th year. Elah succeeds his father Baasha in Asa's 28th year and rules two years (8,307), i.e. into Asa's 30th year during which Zimri's rule of seven days (8,307) and the accession of Omri also occur (8,312). By contrast, neither MT (Zimri accedes in Asa's 27th year, rules 7 days and is succeeded by Omri in Asa's 31st year) nor L's 19/b'108/b 93/e₂ (Zambrei seizes power in Asa's 22th year, reigns 7 days and is followed by "Ambr(e)i" in Asa's 31st year) are internally coherent. (Recall that B and the L MS 82/o lack a synchronization for the accession of Zimri to whom the former ascribes a reign of 7 *years*).

938. Note Josephus' variation for 3 Rgns 16,23's double βασιλεύει.

939. Thus NN*Mar. Na reads θαρσῇ with E. See n. 897 on the form of the city's name in 8,308.

940. Thus NMar following Hud. Na reads Σεμαρεῶνι, SCHLATTER, *Namen*, p. 112, s.v. שמרון Σωμαρωνι. Compare (ἐν) Μαρεώνη (ROSP), Μαρεώνι (M), Μερεώνη (EZon), in... mareon (Lat).

941. Similar formulae as to how "the Greeks call" assorted objects, persons and places occur elsewhere in *AJ* 1,123.124.126; 3,186.217; 10,248; 11(148).184; 13,188.

942. Josephus likely anticipates this form from 3 Rgns 16,28.

νος)⁹⁴³ after Sōmaros (Σωμάρου)⁹⁴⁴, the man who had sold him the mountain (ὄρος, so 3 Rgns)⁹⁴⁵ on which he built (κατεσκεύασε) the city⁹⁴⁶".

1 Kings 16,25-26 constitutes the judgment notice on Omri who is accused of doing "more evil than all who were before him" (v. 25b). Echoing this judgment, Josephus (8,313) avers that Omri "was in no way different (διέφερε... οὐδὲν) from those who had reigned before him except in being worse (τῷ χείρων... εἶναι, see 8,302 (Basanēs) χείρων ἐγένετο) than they". To this mention of the earlier Israelite kings, Josephus, with his subsequent reflection in view (see 8,314), adds: "for they all sought to turn the people away from God (ἀποστήσωσιν ἀπὸ τοῦ θεοῦ τὸν λαὸν)⁹⁴⁷ by daily impieties (τοῖς καθ' ἡμέραν ἀσεβήμασι)⁹⁴⁸, and therefore God caused them to destroy (ἐλθεῖν) one another and leave no one of their family (γένους) alive (ὑπολιπεῖν)⁹⁴⁹".

Passing over the source notice for Omri (16,27), Josephus now gives his equivalent to 1 Kings 16,28: "(Amarinos) also died (ἐτελεύτησε, Kings "slept with his fathers") in Samaria (Σαμαρείᾳ, so 3 Rgns) and was succeeded (διαδέχεται... αὐτὸν, B 3 Rgns 16,28b βασιλεύει)⁹⁵⁰ by his son (παῖς, 3 Rgns υἱὸς) Achab (Ἄχαβος, 3 Rgns Ἀχαάβ)".

943. The words οὕτως Ἀμαρῖνος above represent Mar's conjecture which is adopted by SCHALIT, Namenwörterbuch, p. 9, s.v. Ἀμαρῖνος and which itself goes back to the remark of N, I, p. 244, n. 9 "regem Amarinum intellegendum esse puto" (in his text N prints the reading of RO, i.e. αὐτὸς Σωμαραῖος). Na adopts the emendation of Hud, i.e. αὐτὸς Σεμαρεῶνα (cf. αὐτὸς Σαμάραιον MSP), while SCHLATTER, Namen, p. 112, s.v. שֶׁמְרוֹן advocates Σωμαρωνα. Finally, F. HAUPTVOGEL, Welche Handschriften sind für eine Ausgabe der lateinischen Übersetzung der ἀρχαιλογία des Josephus besonders wertvoll?, in Programm des k.k. Deutschen Stadtsgymnasiums der Kleinseite in Prag 1913-1914, Prag, 1914, 1-9, p. 9 advocates the reading of the Latin MS Prager Codex XIV A 14 (designated by him as P), i.e. "(in civitate qua) samareon (appellatur)".

944. Thus NWMar as well as SCHLATTER, Namen, p. 112, s.v. שֶׁמֶר and SCHALIT, Namenwörterbuch, p. 117, s.v. Σώμαρος. Na reads Σεμάρου, while HAUPTVOGEL, Handschriften, p. 9 suggests samaro in accord with P's "samareon" (see previous note), cf. ME Σαμάρου.

945. Josephus leaves aside the Biblical purchase price, i.e. "two talents of silver".

946. Josephus' reference to Omri's "building the city" seems more logical than 1 Kings 16,24's reference to his "building (3 Rgns ᾠκοδόμησεν) the mountain". See the similar case in 8,225.

947. Elsewhere Josephus uses the above phrase "turn away the people" in AJ 7,256; 8,198. Only here, however, does he add the specification "from God".

948. With this general reference to the "daily impieties" of the Israelite rulers, compare Josephus' previous notices on Jeroboam ("every day he sought to commit some new act more heinous...", 8,245) and Baasha ("every day... he increased his labours on its [wickedness'] behalf", 8,302).

949. Compare Ahijah's prediction (8,271) that the usurper whom God is to raise up "will not leave alive (ὑπολείψει) one of Jeroboam's line (γένους)".

950. Josephus uses the same two verbs "die" and "succeed" in 8,287 (Jeroboam-Nadab).

Josephus' reference to Omri's "dying in Samaria" represents a kind of conflation of the double notice of 1 Kings 16,28a: "Omri slept with his fathers, and was buried in Samaria". Given his death in Samaria, Omri's burial there can be presupposed.

At this juncture in MT Kings the narration of Ahab's reign (1 Kings 16,29-22,40) picks up immediately[951]. Josephus, on the contrary, opts first to round off his survey of Northern history from Elah to Ahab with a reflection (8,314) wherein he incorporates the notice of Asa's death which in Kings stands at the conclusion of its "Asa sequence" (1 Kings 15,9-24) in 15,24. This reflection reads:

> From these events one may learn (μαθεῖν) how close a watch the Deity keeps (ἐπιστροφὴν ἔχει)[952] over human affairs (τῶν ἀνθρωπίνων πραγμάτων)[953] and how He loves (ἀγαπᾷ)[954] good men (ἀγαθούς) but hates (μισεῖ)[955] the wicked (πονηρούς)[956], whom He destroys root and branch (προρρίζους ἀπόλλυσιν, see 8,310). For many of the kings of Israel, because of their lawlessness (παρανομίαν, see 8,251) and iniquity (ἀδικίας)[957], one after the other in a short space of time were marked (ἐγνώσθησαν)[958] for destruction (διαφθαρέντες, see 8,309.310) together with their families (γένος)[959], while Asanos, the king of Jerusalem and the two tribes[960], because of his piety (εὐσέβειαν, see 8,290) and righteousness (δικαιοσύνην)[961] was brought by God (ὑπὸ τοῦ θεοῦ προήχθη)[962] to a long and blessed old age (μακρὸν καὶ εὔδαιμον... γῆρας)[963] and, after a

951. 3 Rgns has a long plus following 1 Kings 16,28 (16,28a-h) which largely parallels MT 1 Kings 22,41-50's framework notices on Jehoshaphat. Josephus has nothing equivalent to the former sequence.

952. This is the only occurrence of this precise expression in Josephus. Elsewhere he uses an equivalent formulation involving the verb ποιεῖσθαι, see *AJ* 2,293 (8,235, see n. 263); 9,237; 13,78; 18,349.

953. Elsewhere the above expression "human affairs" recurs in *AJ* 13,171.

954. Elsewhere in Josephus God appears as subject of the verb ἀγαπάω in *AJ* 1,75 (object: Noah).99 (Noah).223 (= "to be well-content", Joseph's brothers); 8,173 (the Israelites). On the term in Josephus, see SCHLATTER, *Theologie*, p. 38 and n. 3 who points out that Josephus does not use the noun ἀγάπη.

955. Elsewhere in Josephus God appears as subject of the verb μισέω in *BJ* 3,376 (object: suicide); *AJ* 6,138 (the Amalekites); 8,129 (the unfaithful Hebrews); 20,166 (the impiety of the rebels).

956. Na reads μοχθηρούς with MSP.

957. Josephus uses ἀδικία 34 ×. Only here is it collocated with παρανομία.

958. So RO followed by NN*Mar. Na reads ἡρέθησαν following Hud. Sc, *ad loc.* adopts the εὑρέθησαν of MSP.

959. Note the echo of Josephus' statement in 8,313 "... God caused them (the Israelite kings) to destroy (ἐλθεῖν) one another and leave no one of their family (γένους) alive" here.

960. Note Asa's composite title here; elsewhere in our segment Josephus designates the southern rulers either as "king of Jerusalem" (8,290) or as "king of the two tribes" (8,246, cf. 274).

961. Josephus uses the above collocation "piety and righteousness" elsewhere in *AJ* 6,160.265; 8,124; 9,16; 10,50; 12,56; 14,283; 15,375; 18,117. On the term δικαιοσύνη in Josephus, see G. QUELL - G. SCHRENK, δίκη κτλ, in *TWNT* 2 (1935) 176-229, esp. pp. 195-196; M.J. FIEDLER, *Δικαιοσύνη in der diaspora-jüdischen und intertestamentarischen Literatur*, in *JSJ* 1 (1970) 120-143, esp. pp. 129-134; FELDMAN, *Mikra*, pp. 492-493.

962. With this construction compare *AJ* 13,80 (Alexander Balas) "had been restored to the throne by the providence of God (διὰ τὴν τοῦ θεοῦ πρόνοιαν... προαχθέντι)".

963. Josephus uses the expression "long old age" elsewhere in *AJ* 1,98. He employs the adjective εὐδαίμων 55 ×, cf. the cognate noun in 8,281.296.

reign of forty-one years, died (ἀπέθανε, compare ἐκοιμήθη, 3 Rgns 15,24, ἐκοιμήθη... καὶ ἐτελεύτησεν, 2 Par 16,13) in a happy state (εὐμοίρως)⁹⁶⁴.

Josephus derives the basic data for the above mention of Asa's length of reign and death from 1 Kings 15,10a.24aα (// 2 Chron 16,13). Having thus illustrated the "retributive principle" in both its negative and positive aspects, Josephus rounds off the unit with a series of further notes regarding Asa. Omitting mention of the king's burial (1 Kings 15,24aβ, cf. the amplification of this in 2 Chron 16,14)⁹⁶⁵, he proceeds immediately to the accession of Jehoshaphat: "upon his death he was succeeded in the kingship (διεδέξατο τὴν ἡγεμονίαν, compare B 3 Rgns 15,24 βασιλεύει [L and 2 Par 17,1 ἐβασίλευσεν]... ἀντ' αὐτοῦ)⁹⁶⁶ by Josaphat ('Ιωσαφάτης, B 3 Rgns 15,24 'Ιωσαφάθ, L 'Ιωσαφάτ) his son (υἱός, so 3 Rgns 15,24 // 2 Par 17,1) by a wife named Abida (Ἀβιδᾶς)⁹⁶⁷". To this mention of Jehoshaphat he adds the following notices which look ahead to his subsequent treatment of the king: "[That this one (τοῦτον) imitated (μιμητὴν, see 8,251) his ancestor (προπάππου)] David⁹⁶⁸ in courage (ἀνδρείαν)⁹⁶⁹ and piety (εὐσέβειαν,

964. This term is hapax in Josephus. With the above reflection compare the moral of his entire work as formulated by Josephus in *AJ* 1,14 "... the main lesson to be learnt (μάθοι) from this history... is that men who conform to the will of God, and do not venture to transgress laws that have been excellently laid down, prosper in all things beyond belief, and for their reward are offered by God felicity (εὐδαιμονία); whereas, in proportion as they depart from the strict observance of these laws, things (else) practicable become impracticable, and whatever imaginary good thing they strive to do ends in irretrievable disasters". Compare too the reflections Josephus appends to his account of Ahab's death in 8,418-420, *vide infra*.

965. Earlier, Josephus passes over 1 Kings 16,28's reference to Omri's burial, see above. His failure to cite Asa's burial is all the more remarkable given his penchant elsewhere for accentuating the pomp surrounding the interment of Biblical heroes, see above on 8,242 (Jadōn).

966. Neither here or elsewhere does Josephus synchronize Jehoshaphat's accession with the regnal year of his Northern counterpart. Compare the divergent indications on the point in MT 1 Kings 22,41 ("the fourth year of Ahab") // BL* 3 Rgns 16,28a ("the 11th [127/c₂ 12th] year of Omri").

967. Josephus derives the queen's name from 1 Kings 22,42b where she is called "Azubah"; compare L3 Rgns 16,28a Γαζουβά; 2 Par 20, 31 Ἀζουβά. SCHLATTER, *Namen*, p. 84, s.v. עֲזוּבָה qualifies the Josephan form of the queen's name as "rätselhaft". SCHALIT, *Namenwörterbuch*, p. 2, s.v. Ἀβιδᾶ comments that Josephus' form "... ist wohl Metathese von Ἀδιβᾶ = עֲזִיבָה עֲדִיבָה... letztere Form ist durch Verschreibung des ו in י entstanden".
Josephus omits the name of "Abida's" father given in 1 Kings 22,42 // 2 Chron 20,31 as "Shilhi" and in 3 Rgns 16,28a as Σελεεί (2 Par 20,31 Σαλι).

968. The above rendition in which Josephus is understood to be referring to Jehoshaphat ("this one"), great-great-great grandson of David follows the translations of W and Sc, *ad loc*. Mar, by contrast, supposes the passage to be speaking rather of Asa, see his rendering "that *Asanos* imitated his *great-grandfather* (*sic*; in fact David was Asa's great-great grandfather) David...". Mar's understanding seems to misconstrue the sense of the τοῦτον with which the sentence begins, i.e. it refers back to the just- mentioned Jehoshaphat (see W, *ad loc* "ce dernier") rather than to his father Asa whose name occurs at an earlier point in the passage. W's rendition also seems to make better sense in the

see 8,314)[970], all men have recognized from his deeds. But there is no great necessity (κατεπείγει)[971] to speak of this king just now[972]".

Summary. In the above passage, Josephus' "agreements", now with LXX, now with MT, are basically "negative" ones. Like the former he has no equivalent to the MT synchronisms in 16,8 (but see 3 Rgns 16,6).10 and 15. In line with MT he lacks the 3 Rgns pluses both in 16,22 and the lengthy one following 16,28. His reference to Zimri's retiring into "the inmost part" of the palace echoes the wording of TJ in 1 Kings 16,18.

Like several of those discussed earlier, also this pericope attests to Josephus' penchant for combining and rearranging materials which in Kings stand in different contexts, *in casu* 1 Kings 15,24 and 16,6-28. The most noteworthy feature, however, to Josephus' "rewriting" in the above unit is his interjection of the concluding reflections of 8,314. These reflections do provide an explicit general moral, lacking in the Bible, to the many particular events related in what precedes. At the same time it cannot be denied that in them Josephus, in the interests of developing a clearcut contrast between Asa and his Northern counterparts, in fact distorts the Biblical evidence regarding the former's end. In particular, he says nothing of the foot disease which, according to 1 Kings 15,23b, befell the Judean in his old age. Still less does Josephus give readers any inkling of the fact that, in Chronicles, this item figures within a full-blown critique of the aged Asa who, when denounced by the seer Hanani (2 Chron 16,7-9) for having had recourse to Syrian aid (2 Chron 16,1-6 // 8,303-306), reacts with repressive measures against both Hanani himself and other persons (16,10) and whose subsequent foot malady elicits no repentance. In other words then Josephus with his unqualifiedly positive summation concerning Asa's lifelong rectitude

context; in saying that he need not speak of "this king just now" (see above in the text), Josephus is pointing forward to his eventual return to the figure of Jehoshaphat, whereas he has already definitively finished with Asa.

With the above construction "imitator of his ancestor", compare *AJ* 12,203 where Hyrcanus is urged to be an "imitator of his sire" (μιμητὴν... τοῦ γεγεννηκότος), cf. 17,97 where Herod charges Antipater with being an "imitator" (μιμητῇ) of his reprobate brothers.

969. On the Greek cardinal virtue of "courage" in the writings of Josephus, see FELDMAN, *Mikra*, pp. 490-491.

970. The above collocation "courage and piety" is used (in reverse order and with the term "justice" intervening) in (an implicit) reference to David (with whom Jehoshaphat is being compared here in 8,315) in God's word to Samuel concerning the son of Jesse he is to anoint king in *AJ* 6,160.

971. Josephus uses the above verb κατεπείγω 10×; only here, however, does it function within a closing formula.

972. Josephus returns to Jehoshaphat only in 8,393. The entire intervening segment, 8,316-392, is devoted to Ahab.

which God rewards with "a blessed old age" and a "happy death" simply ignores the conflicting data of his sources[973]. In this instance at least Josephus subordinates fidelity to the Biblical record to the exigencies of inculcating a moral involving sharp contrasts[974].

Finally, it might be noted that Josephus' non-utilization of the "negative" data of 2 Chron 16,7-12 regarding Asa[975] corresponds to his earlier dispensing with much of the material of 2 Chronicles 14-15 concerning Asa's "good period" (see above). The result of this twofold abridgement is that Josephus' portrait of Asa lacks much of the detail as well as the nuances of the Chronistic *Asabild*.

973. Josephus' procedure here is not likely explanable in terms of his use of a divergent Biblical text since both MT and LXX (Kings and Chronicles) do give the material in question.

974. Of course, Josephus' "distortion" is not a simple "perversion" of the Biblical data. For both Kings and Chronicles, after all, Asa is basically a good king, certainly better than any of his Northern contemporaries. Similarly, his 41-year reign does contrast markedly with the instability that plagued the Northern kingdom of his time. With Josephus' "white-washing" of Asa, compare the Rabbinic tendency to accentuate his wrong-doing. See e.g., *Soṭa* 10a where, with reference to 1 Kings 15,22 (Asa's impressing "all Judah" to build Geba and Mizpah), it is affirmed that the king failed to show due deference to the sages by requiring them to labor as well and so was punished with the foot disease spoken of in 15,23. For more details, see GINZBERG, *Legends*, IV, pp. 184-185.

975. Josephus' omission of the confrontation between Hanani and Asa (2 Chron 16,7-9) is all the more remarkable given the many comparable scenes which he does take over from the Bible. Note in particular his use of 2 Chron 19,1-3 in *AJ* 9,1 where the Chronicler relates a prophetic denunciation of another "good" king, i.e. Jehoshaphat for his collusion with reprobate Israel, i.e. a misdeed analogous to that for which Hanani censures Asa in 2 Chron 16,7-9.

XI

AHAB INTRODUCED
(8,316-318)

After the reflective interlude of 8,314 (315), Josephus (8,316) resumes his retelling of Kings' survey of Northern history with Ahab whose accession he has mentioned at the end of 8,313. *AJ* 8,316-318 is then the Josephan parallel to Kings' initial presentation (1 Kings 16,29-34) of this monarch who will predominate throughout 8,316-420 (// 1 Kings 16,29-22,40).

Josephus' source account opens in 16,29 with chronological indications: acceding in Asa's 38th year (so MT, 3 Rgns 16,29 "the second year of Jehoshaphat"), Ahab reigned 22 years. Josephus leaves aside the first of these items[976], while wording the second as follows: "Now Achab... dwelt in Samaria and exercised the royal power (τὴν... ἀρχὴν κατέσχεν, see 8,298, compare 3 Rgns 16,29 ἐβασίλευσεν) for twenty-two years". With 16,30 begins Kings' (negative) evaluation of Ahab who, in terms reminiscent of those used for Omri in 16,26, is said to have "done evil more than all that were before him" (see the reiteration of this charge in 16,33b). Josephus amplifies this judgement in a phraseology recalling his comment on Omri in 8,313: "in no way did he (Achab) make a new departure (καινίσας)[977] from the kings before him except, indeed, to invent (ἐπενόησεν) even worse courses (πρὸς τὸ χεῖρον, see 8,302.313)[978] in his surpassing wickedness (καθ᾽ ὑπερβολὴν πονηρίας)[979], while closely imitating (ἐκμιμησάμενος, see μιμητὴν, 8,315)[980] all their misdeeds (κακουργήματα)[981] and their outrageous behaviour to God (τὴν πρὸς τὸ θεῖον ὕβριν, see 8,253.277)[982]". Josephus follows this general accusation with a more particular one, inspired by 1 Kings 16,31a with its reference to Ahab's "walking in the

---

976. His doing so corresponds to his tendency, observed already earlier, to omit Biblical "accession synchronisms" precisely where, as here, MT and LXX diverge, see on *AJ* 8,286 (Asa).298 (Baasha).307 (Elah).311 (Zimri).315 (Jehoshaphat).

977. Elsewhere in Josephus καινίζω occurs in *AJ* 1,155; 4,292; 12,126; 13,41.

978. In the text printed by Mar this phrase is preceded by the particle γε. RO lacks the word which N (but not N*) prints within brackets.

979. Although Josephus employs many analogous constructions, this is his only use of this precise expression.

980. Josephus uses the verb ἐκμιμέομαι also in *BJ* 7,269.428; *AJ* 15,271.

981. Elsewhere *BJ* 1,637; 2,587; *AJ* 2,141.148; 5,43; 15,348; *Vita* 356.

982. Compare *AJ* 6,61 where the people's demand for king is qualified as ἡ πρὸς τὸν θεὸν ὕβρις.

sins of Jeroboam": Ahab's depravity, he affirms, consisted above all in his "emulating (ζηλώσας)[983] the lawlessness (παρανομίαν, see 8,245.314) of Jeroboam". To this last charge Josephus adds, *à la* 16,31a ("as if it had been a light thing to walk in the sins of Jeroboam..."), "for he too worshipped (προσεκύνησε) the heifers (δαμάλεις, see 8,226)[984] which Jeroboam had made (κατασκευασθείσας, see 8,228.280) and, in addition, constructed (προσεμηχανήσατο)[985] other unheard of objects of worship (παράδοξα)[986]". With the latter notice Josephus apparently has in mind 16,32-33a where Ahab is charged with making both an altar and temple for Baal in Samaria as well as an "Asherah", see further below.

Josephus now comes (// 1 Kings 16,31bα) to speak of Ahab's marrying (ἔγημε... γυναῖκα, 3 Rgns ἔλαβεν γυναῖκα) "Jezabelē" (Ἰεζαβέλην, 3 Rgns Ἰεζάβελ) whose father "Ithōbalos" (Ἰθωβάλου, MT Ethbaal, 3 Rgns Ἰεθ(ε)βάαλ)[987] he makes king, not only of Sidon (so 1 Kings), but also of Tyre (see below on 8,324). 1 Kings 16,31b is the only mention of Jezebel in the Biblical source pericope which thereafter reverts to Ahab and his misdeeds. Josephus, on the contrary, accentuates the personage of Jezebel. Thus whereas in 16,31bβ it might appear that Ahab took up the cult of Baal on his own volition, Josephus explicitly states that it was "from her that he learned (ἀφ' ἧς... ἔμαθεν)[988] to worship (προσκυνεῖν, cf. προσεκύνησεν 3 Rgns 16,31bβ) her native gods (ἰδίους... θεοὺς)[989]". Josephus further introduces a Biblically unparalleled characterization of Jezebel, calling her

983. Josephus uses the verb ζηλόω 4x elsewhere in *AJ*: 6,343; 14,116.154; 20,41 (the two uses in *AJ* 14 are quotations from Greek sources). This relative paucity of usage likely has to do with the term's being a cognate of the noun ζηλωτής (itself used only 3 × in *AJ* [10,49 (t.e.); 12,271; 20,47] as opposed to 57× in *BJ*), the self-designation of the anti-Roman rebels of whose activities Josephus so vehemently disapproved, see further n. 1209 below.

984. With this formulation contrast 8,228 where Jeroboam tells the people that he has installed the heifers "... in order that... you may go [i.e. to Bethel and Dan] and worship (προσκυνῶσιν) God". Cf. however *AJ* 9,139 where one reads the same formulation as in 8,317: "Jehu permitted the Israelites to bow down to (προσκυνεῖν) the golden heifers (δαμάλεις)".

985. The verb προσμηχανάομαι is hapax in Josephus.

986. Other uses of this nominalized pl. form in Josephus are *BJ* 4,238; 6,63; *AJ* 15,379.

987. Josephus likely draws his form of the name of Ahab's father-in-law from the historian Menander whose mention of "Ithōbalos" he cites in 8,324 (*vide infra*) and *Ap* 1,124 (SCHLATTER, *Namen*, p. 22, s.v. אֶתְבַּעַל opines that Josephus found his form of the name rather in another Hellenistic historian cited by him, i.e. Dius, see *Ap* 1,112-120).

988. SCHLATTER, *Matthäus*, p. 386 compares this construction with Mt 11,29 (καὶ μάθετε ἀπ' ἐμοῦ). He further points out that the more usual construction in Josephus (see, e.g., *AJ* 18,314), as also in Philo, is μαθεῖν παρά τινος.

989. This expression (= "false gods") occurs elsewhere in *AJ* 4,138; 8,338; 9,288 (sg.); 10,154.212 (sg.). See n. 650 for uses of the expression (in the sg.) to designate Israel's own God.

"a creature (γύναιον)⁹⁹⁰ both forceful (δραστήριον)⁹⁹¹ and bold (τολ-μηρόν)⁹⁹²". To Jezebel he likewise ascribes, as illustrative of the "lengths of licentiousness (ἀσέλγειαν⁹⁹³, see 8,252) and madness (μανίαν)⁹⁹⁴" to which she went, the initiatives which 1 Kings 16,32-33a assign rather to Ahab, i.e. the founding of a temple (ναὸν... ᾠκο-δόμησε, 3 Rgns ἐν οἴκῳ... ὃν ᾠκοδόμησεν)⁹⁹⁵ for "Belias" (Βε-λίαν)⁹⁹⁶ and the planting (κατεφύτευσε, 3 Rgns ἐποίησεν)⁹⁹⁷ of a "grove (ἄλσος)⁹⁹⁸ of all sorts of trees (παντοίων δένδρων)⁹⁹⁹". Nor is

990. This term occurs 36 × in Josephus. SCHLATTER, *Theologie*, p. 148 comments "Das häufige 'Weiblein', γύναιον... spricht nicht von Hochschätzung für die Frau".

991. Josephus uses this adjective, sometimes substantivized (see, e.g., *BJ* 1,283), 23 ×. On occasion it is employed with positive connotations, see, e.g., *AJ* 5,182 where Keniaz is called "vigorous (δραστήριος) and noble-hearted". Other unambiguously negative uses of the term are *BJ* 2,590 (of John of Gischala); 4,312 (John); *AJ* 9,27 (the wicked Joram of Israel is called "a man of bold action").

992. Josephus' usage of this term (30 ×) is comparable to that of the preceding adjective. Persons of whom it is used *in malam partem* are: Diophantus (*BJ* 1,529), Glaphyra (2,116), two Zealots (4,343); Nimrod (*AJ* 1,113); the false accuser of a virgin (*AJ* 4,248); David (*AJ* 6,178, in Eliab's reproach to him); Naboth's accusers (*AJ* 8,358); the Jewish law-breaker (*AJ* 11,130); and Antipater (*AJ* 17,32).

993. ExcSuid read ἀσέβειαν here.

994. Josephus uses the substantive μανία 26 ×. Only here does he collocate it with ἀσέλγεια.

995. Elsewhere Josephus uses the above expression "build a temple" also in *BJ* 7,427 (the Leontopolis Temple); *AJ* 3,129; 5,68; 7,334.342 (*bis*).371 (all of the Jerusalem Temple). With the above expression, compare Josephus' (derogatory) references to Jeroboam's shrines at Bethel and Dan in 8,226 οἰκοδομήσας ναΐσκους.

996. Thus NN*Mar. NaW read Βῆλον. SCHLATTER, *Namen*, p. 29, s.v. בַּעַל suggests Βελεων or Βηλεων, while SCHALIT, *Namenwörterbuch*, p. 22, s.v. would read Βάαλ, the 3 Rgns form. Compare M Βέλ (in marg Βελεί), P Βῆλαν, S Βήλα, EZon Βῆλ, Lat Bahel. Elsewhere in Josephus where this deity is mentioned on finds the (MT/LXX) form "Baal", see *AJ* 9,135.136.138 (*bis*).154.

Josephus further specifies "Belias" here in 8,318 as "the Tyrian god" (ExcSuid add "and of the Sidonians") cf. his earlier designation of Ithōbalos as king also of "Tyre". The same specification recurs in 9,138.

Josephus does not explicitly mention the "altar" which according to 1 Kings 16,32a Ahab built in the Baal temple in Samaria, presuming this to be included in Jezebel's construction of a temple complex (in further contrast to 16,32 Josephus likewise does not specify as such where the Baal temple was built).

997. Josephus uses the verb καταφευτέω also in *AJ* 1,37.140; 10,226; *Ap* 1,141.

998. Like LXX Josephus employs this term in rendering MT references to (an/the) "Asherah". See also 8,336; where for 1 Kings 18,19 "prophets of Asherah" he reads with 3 Rgns "prophets of the groves" (here in 8,318 Josephus' "a grove" [ἄλσος] corresponds to B 3 Rgns 16,33a as against L's "*the* [τὸ] grove"). On the whole subject of the versions' (and Josephus') rendering of MT's references to "Asherah", see W.L. REED, *The Asherah in the Old Testament*, Fort Worth, TX, 1949, pp. 6-9; and J. BARR, *Seeing the Wood for the Trees? An Enigmatic Ancient Translation*, in *JSS* 13 (1968) 11-20, esp. p. 15.

999. With the above phrase "planted a grove of all sorts of trees", compare *AJ* 10,226 = *Ap* 1,141 where Josephus refers to Nebuchadnezzar "planting trees of all kinds" (καταφυτεύσας... δένδρεσι παντοδαποῖς), cf. *Ap* 1,199 where Josephus cites (Pseudo-)

Josephus content to simply transfer to Jezebel the above offenses which Kings ascribes to her husband. With a view to later references to the functionaries of the Baal cult in Samaria (see 1 Kings 18,19; 2 Kings 10,19), he makes the queen already here "appoint (κατέστησε) priests and false prophets (ψευδοπροφήτας)[1000] to this god"[1001]. Only after this extended sequence focussed on Jezebel does Josephus return, at the very end of the pericope, to Ahab himself, stating of him: "he had many such men (i.e. Jezebel's priests and false prophets of Baal) about him, and in folly (ἀνοίᾳ)[1002] and wickedness (πονηρίᾳ)[1003] he surpassed (ὑπερβεβληκὼς, compare καθ᾽ ὑπερβολὴν πονηρίας, 8,316) all the kings before him", cf. 1 Kings 16,33b. Josephus thus lacks a parallel to the appended notice in MT and B 1 Kings 16,34 according to which under Ahab a certain Hiel of Bethel rebuilt Jericho, sacrificing two of his sons in the process thereby fulfilling the curse pronounced by Joshua in Jos 6,26. This omission is all the more remarkable in that in his version of the latter text in *AJ* 5,31, Josephus, going beyond the Bible itself, explicitly mentions, obviously with the content of 1 Kings 16,34 in view, that he will subsequently relate the realization of the curse. Mar in his comment on this phenomenon[1004], noting that also L lacks a parallel to MT and B's 1 Kings 16,34, suggests that Josephus who in 8,318 would be following a text-form *à la* L, simply "forgot" his earlier promise in 5,31[1005]. Alternatively, however, I would propose that here in 8,318 Josephus "thought better" of his previous announcement, i.e. he ultimately decides not to relate the content of 1 Kings 16,34 whose (seeming) reference to human sacrifice might prove offensive to Gentile readers[1006]. In other words, what perhaps Josephus "forgot" to do was to go back and delete his earlier announcement

Hecataeus' description of the Jerusalem Temple-complex wherein there was "no trace of a plant, in the form of a sacred grove (ἄλσῶδες) or the like".

1000. On Josephus' use of the term "false prophet", see n. 270.

1001. With the above formulations which attribute the reprobate cultic measures in question to Jezebel, compare *AJ* 9,138 where Josephus states: "Baal was the god of the Tyrians, to whom *Achab*, wishing to please his father-in-law Ithōbalos... had built a temple (ναόν, so 8,318) in Samaria and had appointed prophets...".

1002. This term occurs 20 × in Josephus.

1003. This is Josephus' only use of the above collocation "folly and wickedness".

1004. *Josephus*, V, p. 16, n. a, cf. p. 743, n. e.

1005. A comparable instance of "forgetfulness" on Josephus' part can be noted in connection with *AJ* 7,89. Here Josephus states that he will treat "in its proper place" the children Michal bore to her second husband. As Mar, *Josephus*, V, p. 407, n.d, points out, however, in fact he makes no further mention of Michal.

W, *Josèphe*, I, p. 299, n. 2 alludes to another possible explanation for the omission of 1 Kings 16,34 in *AJ* 8,318, i.e. something has fallen out of our text of Josephus at this point.

1006. In this connection it might be noted that Josephus does pass over entirely certain problematic items of the Biblical record, e.g., Reuben's intercourse with his father's concubine (Gen 35,22) and the golden calf episode (Exodus 32). Compare too his *Verharmlosung* of the Genesis 22 incident in *AJ* 1,222-236, on which see FELDMAN, *'AQEDAH*.

about the fulfillment of Joshua's curse of 5,31 – as could easily have happened given the extensive period it took him to complete *AJ*[1007].

Summary: The above pericope offers few definite indications concerning the Biblical text(s) available to Josephus in composing it. His lack of parallel to 1 Kings 16,34 (MT and B) constitutes a "negative agreement" with L which, however, need not preclude his knowledge of the content of that verse, see above. His reference to a "grove" where MT 16,33a speaks of an "Asherah" parallels LXX usage.

Josephus' reworking of 1 Kings 16,29-34 is notable above all for his accentuation of the figure of Jezebel vis-à-vis her husband. By thus highlighting the queen at the start, Josephus better prepares readers for Jezebel's dominant role in what follows.

1007. FELDMAN, *'AQEDAH*, p. 252 points out that Josephus spent "at least a dozen years" (79/81-93/94) writing this work.

XII

ELIJAH'S INITIAL MINISTRY
(8,319-327)

With 1 Kings 17,1 the author of Kings introduces Elijah who will figure prominently throughout much of 1 Kings 17-2 Kings 2. Kings' "Elijah complex" itself commences in chap. 17 with a series of three miracle stories, i.e. Elijah's providential nourishment at the stream (17,1-7), his multiplication of food (17,8-16) and the resuscitation effected by him (17,17-24). In discussing Josephus' version of the passage, I distinguish the same three divisions within it.

1. *Elijah at the stream* (8,319). In a single, short paragraph Josephus gives a condensed version of the circumstantial account of Elijah's initial movements as related in 1 Kings 17,1-7. The (minimalistic) personal data provided on Elijah in 17,1a differ somewhat in MT and 3 Rgns: the former speaks of "Elijah the Tishbite, of the settlers (מִתּשָׁבֵי) of Gilead", while the latter reads "Eliou (B)/ Elias (L) the prophet (> L) the Tishbite from Thes(se)bōn (= מִתּשָׁבֵי?) of Galaad". Josephus' own introduction of the figure, while somewhat closer to 3 Rgns here, goes its own way in several respects. Thus, he does not mention Elijah by name as this point[1008], calling him "a certain prophet (προφήτης... τις, see B 3 Rgns 17,1 ὁ προφήτης) of the most high God (τοῦ μεγίστου[1009] θεοῦ)[1010]". He likewise leaves aside the epithet "the Tishbite" found in both MT and 3 Rgns, while, like the latter, associating the prophet with a city, i.e. "Thesbōnē" (Θεσβώνης)[1011] in

---

1008. He cites the name for the first time in 8,329. W, *Josèphe*, II, p. 227, n. 2 asks whether the name might have fallen out of the text of 8,319. Recall that in his version of 1 Kings 12,22 // 2 Chron 11,2 in 8,223 Josephus leaves the prophet Shemaiah unnamed.

1009. Thus NaMar following MSPE; N reads μεγάλου with RO.

1010. Josephus has Jonah call himself by the same designation "prophet of the most high God" in 9,211 (note that whereas MT 1 Kings 17 never uses the term "prophet" for Elijah, Josephus employs the term 7× of him in his parallel, 8,319-327).

The above phrase "most high God" is used by Josephus elsewhere in *AJ* 6,86; 7,353; 8,343; 9,133.211.288.289; 10,68; 11,3.90; 12,257; 13,64.65; 15,385. On it see SCHLATTER, *Gott*, pp. 18-19; ID., *Theologie*, pp. 247-248. Possibly, Josephus found his inspiration for the expression here in 8,319 in the oath formula of 1 Kings 17,1bα where Elijah invokes "the Lord the God of Israel" (so MT, compare B 3 Rgns "the Lord the God of hosts [τῶν δυνάμεων], the God of Israel", L* "the Lord" (127/c₂ + the God of hosts).

1011. Thus NaMar with MSPE (compare B 3 Rgns 17,1 θεσβὼν). N and SCHLATTER, *Namen*, p.114, s.v. תּשָׁבֵי read θεσσεβώνης with RO (compare L 3 Rgns 17,1 θεσσεβών), while SCHALIT, *Namenwörterbuch*, p. 54, s.v. θεσεβώνη adopts θεσεβῶνης, cf. Lat Thesebon.

"Galaditis" (Γαλαδίτιδος)[1012]. In parallel with 17,1b Josephus has Elijah inform Ahab of an imminent drought. In the Bible Elijah's announcement is prefaced by an oath formula ("[Elijah] said to Ahab, /'As the Lord... lives...'"). Josephus, although he will subsequently refer to Elijah's "having *sworn* these things", does not, in accord with his usual practice, reproduce this oath formula as such. Rather, he has Elijah "approach" (προσελθὼν) Ahab and say that "God had foretold (προλέγειν... τὸν θεὸν)[1013] to him that...". Similarly, while in 1 Kings 17,1bβ Elijah affirms that there will be "no dew or rain these years except at my word", Josephus again avoiding the term "word", has the prophet state: "He (God) would not give rain (ὕσειν, cf. 3 Rgns ὑετός)[1014] in those years (ἐν ἐκείνοις τοῖς ἔτεσι, 3 Rgns τὰ ἔτη ταῦτα) nor send down (καταπέμψειν) dew (δρόσον, 3 Rgns δρόσος)[1015] upon the land[1016] until he himself should appear (εἰ μὴ φανέντος[1017] αὐτοῦ)". With this last indication Josephus likely has in view 1 Kings 18,1 where God addresses Elijah "go, *show yourself* to Ahab, and I will send rain upon the earth" (see too Josephus' own later formulation in 8,334 where he has Elijah swear to Obadiah that he would "positively appear (φανήσεται) before Achab that very day").

In 1 Kings 17,2-5 Elijah receives a divine "word" directing him to betake himself to a stream and giving him assurances about his nourishment there, which word the prophet proceeds to carry out. Josephus, who eliminates the reference to Elijah's own "word" in his version of 1 Kings 17,1bβ, has no equivalent to this sequence as such. Rather, he comes immediately to recount Elijah's actual move to and stay by a stream: "having sworn (ἐπομόσας, see 17,1bα)[1018] to these things, he withdrew... and made his home (ποιούμενος... τὴν διατρι- βήν, compare 3 Rgns 17,5 ἐκάθισεν)[1019] beside a stream (χειμάρρῳ, so

---

1012. Thus Mar, cf. Lat Galaditidis. NNa read Γαλααδίτιδος with codd. Compare LXX Γαλαάδ.

1013. Compare Jadōn's opening word to Jeroboam's altar in 8,232 ὁ θεὸς... προλέγει.

1014. Elsewhere in Josephus God appears as subject of the verb ὕω in *AJ* 1,89; 2,189; 7,297; 8,322.343; 9,37; 14,22.391, cf. 18,285.

1015. This is the only occurrence of the above expression "send down dew" in Josephus, cf., however, *AJ* 3,26.27. Note that with his above sequence "(give) rain" – "(send down) dew" Josephus reverses the order of 1 Kings 17,1, "dew and rain".

1016. Note how Josephus' formulation above makes more explicit the divine control over the sources of water (compare 17,1bβ "there shall be neither dew nor rain these years..."). Possibly, he found his inspiration for the above wording in 1 Kings 17,14 where Elijah refers to "the day when *the Lord sends rain* upon the earth".

1017. W, *Josèphe*, II, p. 227, n. 4 proposes reading φήσαντος here, thus giving the rendering "until he himself should say so", compare 1 Kings 17,1bβ "except at my word". RO read φάναντος.

1018. The verb ἐπόμνυμι occurs 12 × in Josephus.

1019. The above phrase "make one's home" recurs in *AJ* 18,123; 20,121; *Vita* 270.

3 Rgns)[1020], which also gave him water to drink (τὸ ποτὸν εἶχε)", see 1 Kings 17,5b.6b. As a result, Elijah's move becomes a matter of his own initiative, rather than of obedience to God's command as it is in Kings. Again, whereas in 1 Kings 17,3 Elijah is enjoined to proceed "eastward" (3 Rgns κατὰ ἀνατολάς), Josephus has him withdraw "into the south country" (εἰς τὰ πρὸς νότον μέρη)[1021]. Josephus does not hesitate to follow 1 Kings 17,6a in recounting Elijah's miraculous feeding[1022]: "as for his food (τροφὴν)[1023] the ravens (κόρακες, so 3 Rgns)[1024] brought (προσέφερον, 3 Rgns ἔφερον) it to him every day"[1025].

2. *Elijah's Multiplication Miracle* (8,320-324). In 1 Kings 17,7 the notice on the drying up of the brook (3 Rgns χειμάρρους) due to the lack of rain rounds off the chapter's first section. Josephus, on the contrary (8,320), makes this item the introduction to the following episode: "when the river (ποταμοῦ, compare χειμάρρῳ, 8,319)[1026] dried up (ἀναξηρανθέντος, 3 Rgns ἐξηράνθη)[1027] for want of rain (ἀνομβρίαν, compare 17,7b "because there was no rain [3 Rgns ὑετὸς] upon the earth")[1028], he came (παραγίνεται, see 8,212.231, 3 Rgns 17,10 ἐπορεύθη)...". In accordance with 1 Kings 17,10aα he identifies Elijah's

---

1020. With Josephus' highly indeterminate "a (certain) stream" above, compare the much more specific Biblical reference to "the brook Cerith (3 Rgns "Corrath") that is before Jordan". His leaving the stream unnamed likely hangs together with his shifting Elijah's place of refuge from the "east" to the "south" of the land, see next note.

1021. Conceivably, Josephus makes Elijah go "south" (i.e. to Judah) rather than "east" on the consideration that the territory east of the Jordan would still be under the authority of Ahab whom the prophet has just antagonized and so would not afford him a secure refuge (recall that in 1 Kings 19 Elijah eludes Jezebel's wrath by going south to Judean Beersheba).

1022. Compare *Gen.Rab.* 33.5 where the "rationalistic" opinion of R. Judah is cited that the term הָעֹרְבִים of MT 17,6 refers, not to "ravens" as the conveyers of Elijah's sustenance, but rather to the inhabitants of the town of "Oreb" who provided him with food. See further GINZBERG, *Legends*, VI, p. 317, n. 6.

1023. Josephus employs the above combination ποτόν and τροφήν (or its reverse) also in *BJ* 2,133; 7,278; *AJ* 6,360.377; 7,159.274; 11,232.

1024. Josephus' one remaining use of this term is *AJ* 1,91 (the raven dispatched by Noah).

1025. On the other hand, he has no parallel to 1 Kings 17,3 where God promises Elijah that ravens will bring him food; thus in his version, the birds appear to act on their own volition in provisioning the prophet. Note too that the Biblical notice on Elijah's feeding in 17,6a is more specific than the Josephan one in several respects: "the ravens brought him bread (3 Rgns ἄρτους) *in the morning* and meat (3 Rgns κρέα) *in the evening*".

1026. Note the same variation in Josephus' version of 2 Kings 3: τῷ χειμάρρῳ (9,35)/ τὸν ποταμὸν (9,36).

1027. The verb ἀναξηραίνω is hapax in Josephus.

1028. Josephus' other uses of ἀνομβρία are *AJ* 8,324 (*bis*).328;14,22 (*bis*).

destination as "Sarephtha" (Σαρεφθὰ)[1029], while amplifying the Bible's localization ("which belongs to Sidon", 17,9) of this site with his "not far from Sidon (Σιδῶνος)[1030] and Tyre[1031] – it lies between them". Only then are we informed that the prophet did this "at the command of God" (τοῦ... θεοῦ κελευσάντος)[1032] (compare the *Wortereignisformel* of 17,8) who had assured him (see 17,9b) that a "widow" (γυναῖκα χήραν, compare γυναικὶ χήρᾳ, 3 Rgns 17,9b) would "provide him with food" (παρέξει τροφάς, cf. διατρέφειν σε, 3 Rgns 17,9b)[1033]. To the notice of 1 Kings 17,10aββa about the woman[1034] gathering sticks[1035] at the city gate, he adds mention of God's "revealing" (τοῦ... θεοῦ δηλώσαντος, see 8,240.269) at this moment that this is indeed the one who will "give him food" (διατρέφειν, so 3 Rgns 17,9). With this addition Josephus gives a "theological response" to the question as to how Elijah recognized "the right woman" in Zarephath[1036].

In 1 Kings 17,10bβ Elijah "calls to" (3 Rgns ἐβόησεν ὀπίσω) the woman, directing her to bring him water. The Josephan prophet is more polite, first "approaching" (προσελθὼν, see 8,319) and "greeting" her, just as he "asks" (παρεκάλεσεν) rather than "commands" (compare 3 Rgns 17,10bβ λάβε δὴ) her to bring him the water[1037]. As in 1 Kings 17,11 Josephus then has Elijah call her back to ask also for bread[1038]. In 17,12 the woman responds to this further request with an oath formula invoking "the Lord your (Elijah's) God" wherein she affirms that she and her son (so MT, 3 Rgns has the plural τέκνοις; the

1029. Thus MSP Lat followed by NaWMar and Schalit, *Namenwörterbuch*, p. 107, s.v. Σαρεφθά. N and Schlatter, *Namen*, p. 97, s.v. צְרְמָה read Σαριφθὰν with R. Compare 3 Rgns 17,9.10 Σάρεπτα.

1030. Josephus' form here corresponds to that found in the L MSS (b'/19 93/e₂ excepted) in 3 Rgns 17,9 (cf. MT צִידֹן, compare B Σειδωνίας).

1031. Cf. the previous designation of Ithōbalos as "king *of Tyre* and Sidon" in 8,317 where, as here, the mention of Tyre has no Biblical parallel.

1032. The above formula "at the command of God" occurs also in *AJ* 1,110.154 (184).187.259.279.294.323.337; 4,46.55.112.165; 5,65.230; 6,139; 7,92. Josephus likewise employs many other variant expressions with God as subject of the verb κελεύω.

1033. The above phrase "provide food" recurs in *AJ* 14,48; 15,309. Compare the expression τροφὴν... προσέφερον used of the ravens provisioning Elijah in 8,319.

1034. Josephus specifies that she is a "labouring woman" (γυναῖκα χερνῆτιν), the same phrase he uses of the "witch of Endor" in *AJ* 6,339.

1035. Josephus uses the participle ξυλιζομένην in reference to this action, compare 3 Rgns 17,10 συνέλεγεν ξύλα.

1036. With this accentuation of the theological element of the narrative, contrast Josephus' non-mention of the divine word that prompts Elijah's initial movements in 1 Kings 17,2-5.

1037. Perhaps Josephus' concern here is that the Jewish prophet not appear overbearing in his dealings with a Gentile in the eyes of his pagan readers, cf., however, what follows where Josephus does represent Elijah "commanding" the woman.

1038. This time Josephus makes Elijah "command" (ἐκέλευσε, compare B 3 Rgns 17,11b εἶπεν λήμψε δή). Like MT and B 1 Kings 17,11 Josephus lacks an equivalent to the attached indication καὶ φάγομαι found in L etc.

same divergence occurs also in vv. 13,15) are on the verge of starvation with only a minute quality of meal and oil remaining. As with 17,1 (see above), Josephus avoids citing the wording of the Biblical oath formula. In his version the (presumably pagan) woman simply "swears" (ὀμοσάσης, compare ἐπομόσας, 8,319) – by whom is not said. Her actual declaration refers to her one "child" (τέκνῳ, see MT) and accentuates their desperate predicament: "(she swore) that she had nothing in the house except a handful of meal (ἀλεύρου δράκα, 3 Rgns δρὰξ ἀλεύρου) and a little oil (ὀλίγον ἔλαιον = 3 Rgns), and said that she was setting out for home, after gathering (συνειλοχυῖαν, 3 Rgns συλλέγω) the wood (τὰ ξύλα, 3 Rgns δύο ξυλάρια) to knead the meal and make (ποιήσῃ, 3 Rgns ποιήσω) bread (ἄρτον, 3 Rgns αὐτὸ) for herself and her child; after this was eaten (δαπανηθέντα[1039], 3 Rgns φαγόμεθα) they must perish consumed by hunger (ἀπολεῖσθαι λιμῷ, 3 Rgns ἀποθανούμεθα)[1040], for there was no longer anything left".

1 Kings 17,13-14 recounts Elijah's response to the widow, comprising a new directive (v. 13) with a motivating assurance (v. 14). Josephus, retaining the direct discourse of the source, amplifies the assurance with which he has Elijah commence his reply: "(he said) be of good courage (θαρσοῦσα, 3 Rgns θάρσει) and go your way (ἄπιθι, 3 Rgns εἴσελθε) in hope of better things (τὰ κρείττω προσδοκῶσα)[1041]". In accordance with 17,13bα he then has Elijah enjoin the woman: "first (πρῶτον, 3 Rgns ἐν πρώτοις) prepare (ποιήσασα, 3 Rgns ποίησον) a little [food] (βραχὺ; 1 Kings 17,13 specifies "a little cake" [B ἐνκρυφίαν μικρὸν]) and bring it to me (ἐμοὶ... κόμισον, 3 Rgns ἐξοίσεις μοι)". In place of the *Botenformel* of 17,14aα ("for thus says the Lord..."), Josephus substitutes "for I prophesy (προλέγω) to you...[1042]". Following this introduction the historian gives his version of 17,14aβ: "neither the bowl of meal (ἀλεύρων... τὸ ἄγγος, 3 Rgns ἡ ὑδρία τοῦ ἀλεύρου) nor the jar of oil (ἐλαίου τὸ κεράμιον, B ὁ καψάκης τοῦ ἐλαίου) shall be empty (ἐπιλείψειν, 3 Rgns uses two different words for the "depletion" of the bowl and jar respectively, i.e. ἐκλείψει... ἐλαττονήσει) until God sends rain (μέχρις οὗ ἄν ὕσῃ ὁ θεός, cf. 8,319 ὕσειν αὐτὸν [God])[1043]".

1039. RO δαπανηθέντας.

1040. The above construction "perish of hunger" occurs only here in Josephus.

1041. Compare 1 Kings 17,13aβ where Elijah instructs the woman: "do according to your word (3 Rgns ῥῆμα)". Note, once again, Josephus' avoidance of the term "word". With the above formulation "be of good courage... in hope of better things", compare *AJ* 11,241 where Artaxerxes "encourages" (παρεθάρρυνεν) Esther to "hope for the best" (τὰ κρείττω προσδοκᾶν).

1042. Compare 8,319 where for the oath formula introducing Elijah's announcement to Ahab of 1 Kings 17,1 Josephus has the prophet speak of what "God has foretold (προλέγειν)...".

1043. Compare 1 Kings 17,14bβ "until the day the Lord gives rain (3 Rgns τοῦ δοῦναι... [+ τὸν, B] ὑετὸν) upon the earth".

1 Kings 17,15-16 concludes the pericope by noting the realization both of Elijah's directive (v. 15a) and his assurance (vv. 15b-16) to the woman. Josephus (8,323) prefaces his notice on the woman's following of Elijah's instructions (// 17,15a) with the transition "when the prophet had said these things...". He then continues: "she went to her home (17,15 'she went') and she did (ἐποίησε, so 3 Rgns) as he had told her (τὰ εἰρημένα, cf. MT [+ 127/c₂] 'according to the word of Elijah', > BL*); and she had enough food for herself and her child (τῷ τέκνῳ, so MT, 3 Rgns τὰ τέκνα, see above) and the prophet". Thereafter, he leaves aside the verbal repetition of 17,14 in the "fulfillment notice" of 17,16a, as well as the conjoined reference to the "word of the Lord" in 16b. In place thereof he substitutes the statement "nor did they lack anything to eat until the drought (αὐχμὸς)[1044] ended (compare 8,322 'until God sends rain')".

At this juncture (8,324) Josephus pauses to insert a non-Biblical reference, i.e. Menander's account concerning Ithōbalos of Tyre, father-in-law of Ahab, the king to whose reign the Bible ascribes the great drought narrated in 1 Kings 17-18:

> This rainless time (ἀνομβρίας, see 8,320) is also mentioned by Menander in his account of the acts of Ithōbalos ('Ιθωβάλου, see 8,317), the king of Tyre (τοῦ Τυρίων... βασιλέως)[1045], in these words: "there was a drought (ἀβροχία) in his reign, which lasted from the month of Hyberberetaios[1046] until the month of Hyberberetaios in the following year. But he made supplication (ἱκετείαν)[1047] (to the gods), whereupon a heavy thunderstorm broke out. He it was who founded the city of Botrys in Phoenicia, and Auza in Libya." This, then, is what Menander wrote, referring to the drought (ἀνομβρίαν) which came in Achab's reign, for it was in his time that Ithōbalos was king of Tyre[1048].

1044. The term αὐχμὸς recurs in *BJ* 4,457; *AJ* 7,297; 12,259; 14,22; 15,300; 18,285.

1045. Cf. Josephus' previous designation of Ithōbalos as τοῦ Τυρίων... βασιλέως in 8,317. As will be recalled, in designating Ithōbalos as "king of Tyre (and Sidon)" there Josephus goes beyond 1 Kings 16,31's reference to him simply as "king of Sidon". It now becomes apparent why he does this, i.e. to set up the subsequent identification between the Biblical monarch and the one spoken of by Menander. Josephus' procedure here is reminiscent of his introducing references to Rehoboam's surrendering Jerusalem "without a battle" into his versionof the Biblical account(s) of Shishak's despoliation of the city (8,258) with a view to his later association of that happening with Herodotus' reference to Pharoah's subjugating various peoples "without a battle" (8,261), see above.

1046. This Greek month name is equivalent to late October, see SCHALIT, *Namenwörterbuch*, p. 121, s.v. Other uses of the name by Josephus are *BJ* 2,528; 4,63.83; *AJ* 3,239 ("in the seventh month which the Macedonians call Hyperberetaeus"); 12,143.

1047. N suggests a lacuna in the text before this term.

1048. Josephus previously cites Menander for his testimony – itself purportedly a translation from the Phoenician records – concerning Hiram and Solomon in *AJ* 8,144-146. He gives a longer extract from that same passage of Menander in *Ap* 1,116-125 in a context dealing with "Phoenician" references to Judaism. This latter extract contains (1,123) another reference to king "Ithōbalos" whom it calls "priest of Astarte"; to him it attributes the murder of his predecessor Phelles as well as a lifespan of 48 years and a

3. *Elijah's Resuscitation* (8,325-327)[1049]. Following the "interlude" of 8,324, Josephus rejoins the source for its account of Elijah's reviving the woman's son[1050], 1 Kings 17,17-24. In 17,17 the narrative relates that "after these things" (i.e. the multiplication miracle of 17,8-16) the boy became so ill that he was left without breath. In view of the "interruption" of 8,324, Josephus commences with an elaborate resumptive transition, "now the woman of whom we spoke above, who gave food to the prophet – her son (παιδός, 3 Rgns υἱός)[1051]...". Josephus next cites the boy's sickness, somewhat amplifying 17,17's presentation of this: "he fell so seriously ill (καταπεσόντος εἰς νόσον, 3 Rgns ἡ ἀρρωστία αὐτοῦ κραταιὰ σφόδρα)[1052] that he ceased to breathe (τὴν ψυχὴν ἀφεῖναι)[1053] *and seemed to be dead* (νεκρόν)[1054]". In 17,18 the woman's address to Elijah follows directly on the mention of her son's illness. Josephus prefaces her speech with reference to a preceding emotional outburst by her: "whereupon she wept bitterly (ἀνακλαιομένη)[1055], injuring herself with her hands (ταῖς τε χερσὶν αὐτὴν αἰκιζομένη)[1056] and uttering such cries as her grief prompted (ὑπηγόρευε τὸ πάθος)[1057]...[1058]". Josephus transposes the obscure opening words of the woman in 17,18 ("what to me and to you, O man

reign of 32. Josephus likewise cites Menander's account of the Assyrian campaign against Tyre during the reign of its king Elulaios in *AJ* 9,283-287. Finally, Josephus is likely once again citing Menander in his (unattributed) quotation concerning the series of Tyrian leaders in the period between Nebuchadnezzar and Cyrus in *Ap* 1,155-158. On Menander (called "of Ephesus" in *Ap* 1,116) and Josephus' use of him, see: H.J. KATZENSTEIN, *The History of Tyre*, Jerusalem, 1973, pp. 78-80; G. GARBINI, *Gli "Annali di Tiro" e la storiografia fenica*, in R.Y. EBIED and M.J.L. YOUNG (eds.), *Oriental Studies Presented to Benedikt S.J. Iserlin*, Leiden, 1980, 114-127; and J. VAN SETERS, *In Search of History*, New Haven-London, 1983, pp. 195-199.

1049. On this text, see in general L.P. HOGAN, *Healing in the Second Temple Period* (NTOA, 21), Freiburg-Göttingen, 1992, pp. 216-217.

1050. In Josephus as in the Bible, the son is nameless. E.g., in *y Sukk.* 5.55a and *Gen. Rab.* 98.11 he is identified with the future prophet Jonah, cf. GINZBERG, *Legends*, VI, p. 318, n. 9.

1051. In 8,322.323 Josephus designates the son with the term τέκνον.

1052. The above expression "fall seriously ill" occurs also in *BJ* 1,582; *AJ* 7,383; 9,87; 12,279.357; 13,304.398.

1053. The above construction "cease to breathe" recurs in *AJ* 5,147; 7,325; 9,119; 11,52; 12,430; 14,369; 17,178; 19,107. Compare B 3 Rgns 17,17 οὐχ ὑπελείφθη ἐν αὐτῷ πνεῦμα [L πνοὴ ζωῆς, see MT נשמה]. Also elsewhere Josephus frequently avoids LXX's uses of πνεῦμα in reference to either the divine or human "spirit", see n. 769.

1054. Josephus' inspiration for this "embellishment" of the Biblical notice on the boy's illness is likely the woman's statement in 1 Kings 17,18: "... you have come to "cause the death (3 Rgns θανατῶσαι) of my son".

1055. Josephus' other uses of the verb ἀνακλαίω are *AJ* 7,42; 17,13, cf. the variant reading in 7,252.

1056. This is Josephus' only use of the above expression.

1057. Josephus employs the construction "grief prompts" also in *BJ* 1,277 (Herod).544 (Tiro).

1058. Compare the description of the grief of Abijah's mother which Josephus introduces into his version of 1 Kings 14 in 8,273.

of God?'') into the clear statement "she reproached (κατητιᾶτο) the prophet (τὸν προφήτην)"[1059]. Thereupon, the historian cites the woman's "reproach" in terms reminiscent of 17,18b: "(Elijah's coming was to) convict her of sin (ἐλέγξαντα τὰς ἁμαρτίας αὐτῆς, 3 Rgns τοῦ ἀναμνῆσαι [L + τὰς] ἀδικίας μου)[1060] and on that account causing the death of her son (τοῦ παιδὸς τετελευτηκότος, 3 Rgns θανατῶσαι τὸν υἱόν μου)[1061]". 1 Kings 17,19a records Elijah's lapidary response to the woman's complaint: "give me your son". Josephus amplifies considerably: "but he urged her to take heart (θαρρεῖν, see 8,322) and give her son over to him (παραδοῦναι τὸν υἱὸν αὐτῷ, 3 Rgns δός μοι τὸν υἱόν σου), for he would restore him to life (ζῶντα... ἀποδώσειν)[1062]". In line with 17,19b Josephus now proceeds to narrate Elijah's initiatives with the boy's body: "so she gave him over (παραδούσης, see Elijah's directive παραδοῦναι above; compare 17,19 "he took him from her bosom"), and he carried (βαστάσας, 3 Rgns ἀνήνεγκεν) him into the chamber (τὸ δωμάτιον, 3 Rgns τὸ ὑπερῷον) in which he himself lived (ἐν ᾧ διέτριβεν, 3 Rgns ἐν ᾧ... ἐκάθητο) and placed (καταθείς, 3 Rgns ἐκοίμισεν) him on the bed (ἐπὶ τῆς κλίνης = B 3 Rgns 17,19 [L has ἐπὶ τὴν κλίνην])".

1 Kings 17,20-21 comprises three elements: Elijah addresses God with an accusatory question (v. 20), twice stretches himself (3 Rgns "breathed upon" [ἐνεφύσησεν]) over the body (v. 21a), and then once more prays, asking the Lord to restore the boy's "breath" (3 Rgns ψυχή, v. 21b). Josephus leaves aside the middle item above which disrupts the flow of Elijah's speech to the Deity, formulating this as follows: "he cried aloud (ἀνεβόησε, so 3 Rgns) to God (τὸν θεὸν)[1063], saying that He would ill requite (οὐ καλῶς ἀμείψεσθαι)[1064] the woman if he took her son from her (τὸν υἱὸν αὐτῆς ἀφαιρησόμενον, 3 Rgns τοῦ θανατῶσαι τὸν υἱὸν αὐτῆς)[1065]". He then has the prophet continue "and he prayed God to send the breath into the child again (τὴν ψυχὴν

1059. Compare TJ 1 Kings 17,18 "What is there to me and to you, prophet of the Lord?". See n. 129 on Josephus' (and TJ's) overall tendency to avoid the Biblical designation "man of God".

1060. This is the only occurrence of the precise phrase "convict of sin" above in Josephus; analogous expressions appear in BJ 7,447 and Vita 339.

1061. Note that with his interjected phrase "and on that account" above Josephus makes explicit what is only implicit in the Biblical version of the woman's complaint, i.e. that Elijah's "killing" her son was in punishment for her sins.

1062. This is Josephus' only use of the above expression "restore to life".

1063. This is Josephus' only use of the above expression "cry aloud to God".

1064. Thus the conjecture of N followed by NaMar. The codd read ἀμείψασθαι which reading is reflected in W's rendering: "(lui reprochant) d'avoir mal recompensé celle qui...". This is the only occurrence of the above phrase "ill requite" in Josephus. In 1 Kings 17,20 Elijah's initial word to God has the form of a question: "hast thou (God) brought calamity (B κεκάκωκας)...?".

1065. Like the Bible Josephus has Elijah use somewhat accusatory language towards God. Compare TJ's softening of this language in its version of 17,20 "Let there be no evil to her, and let her son not die".

[8,325] εἰσπέμψαι... τῷ παιδί, Β ἐπιστραφήτω δὴ ἡ ψυχὴ τοῦ παιδα-
ρίου τούτου εἰς αὐτόν)[1066] *and give him life* (παρασχεῖν... τὸν
βίον)[1067]".

In describing the divine response to Elijah's appeal, the various
witnesses to 1 Kings 17,22 vary among themselves. Shortest is B "and it
happened thus and the child cried out". MT (+ L's 127/c₂) reads
rather "The Lord hearkened to the voice of Elijah and the soul of the
child came into him again, and he revived", while L* gives "and it
happened thus and the soul (ψυχὴ) of the child returned into him. And
the child cried out". Josephus (8,327) aligns himself with the more
expansive formulations of MT and L*, even while accentuating the
miraculousness of the happening and elucidating the motives behind
God's intervention: "Thereupon God, because He took pity (τοῦ...
θεοῦ κατοικτείραντος)[1068] on the mother and also because He wished
graciously to spare (χαρίσασθαι) the prophet from seeming to have
come to her for the purpose of harming her (ἐπὶ κακῷ)[1069], beyond all
expectation (παρὰ πᾶσαν προσδοκίαν)[1070] brought (the child) back to
life (ἀνεβίωσεν)[1071]". Josephus passes over as something self-evident
the notice of 1 Kings 17,23 about Elijah's restoring the cured boy to his
mother. In recounting the woman's reaction to the cure, Josephus
prefaces her statement of recognition (// 17,24) with the notice that she
"thanked (εὐχαρίστει)[1072] the prophet[1073]". According to Kings 17,24
the woman's recognition is a double one: Elijah is a "man of God" (see
17,18) and the Lord's "word" in his mouth is "true" (3 Rgns ἀληθι-
νόν). Avoiding, once again, the Biblical phrases "man of God" and
"word (of the Lord)", Josephus has the woman voice her realization
that "the Deity spoke (διαλέγεται)[1074] to him (Elijah)".

Summary: Like 3 Rgns Josephus has a place name ("Thesbōnē") for

1066. The above phrase "send the breath" occurs only here in Josephus.

1067. For the above phrase "confer life" with God as subject, see *AJ* 4,122. Compare
Josephus' amplification of 1 Kings 17,17 in 8,325 with the phrase "he seemed to be dead".

1068. Josephus uses the verb κατοικτείρω elsewhere in *BJ* 2,497; *AJ* 7,184.193;9,43.
This is the only occurrence with God as subject.

1069. The above formulation "(seeming) to have come to her for purposes of harming
her" (πρὸς αὐτὴν ἐπὶ κακῷ παρεῖναι) echoes the woman's own accusation against Elijah
in 8,325 "(she reproached the prophet) for having come to her (τῆς παρ' αὐτῇ παρουσίας)
to convict her of sin".

The above phrase ἐπὶ κακῷ occurs also in *BJ* 1,503; 2,469; *AJ* 2,113 (pl.); 6,300; 7,253
(pl.); 17,36 (pl.). Only here is it associated with the verb παρεῖναι.

1070. The above phrase "beyond (all) expectation" recurs in *BJ* 4,102; *AJ* 5,358;
13,106. It echoes the word προσδοκῶσα used in Elijah's address to the woman in 8,322.

1071. Josephus' other uses of the verb ἀναβιόω are *AJ* 11,9 (the "reviving" of ancient
worship) and 18,14 (the "new life" of the righteous).

1072. Josephus employs the above h.p. of εὐχαριστέω also in *BJ* 1,457; 2,2; *AJ* 8,387;
11,66; 12,165.

1073. Compare TJ 1 Kings 17,24 "I know that you are a *prophet* of the Lord".

1074. Only once elsewhere does Josephus use διαλέγομαι with God (the Deity) as
subject, i.e. *AJ* 3,89 (God "speaks to" the Mosaic generation).

MT's "settlers" (recall, however, that the difference here between MT and 3 Rgns is simply a matter of a divergent vocalization of the same consonantal text), while like B (and against MT and L) he employs the designation "prophet" for his protagonist at the opening of the pericope, see 1 Kings 17,1. On the other hand, he goes together with MT against 3 Rgns in citing only one "child" for the widow throughout his version of 1 Kings 17,8-24.

Several points concerning Josephus' reworking of 1 Kings 17 may be highlighted here. As elsewhere, he deletes items that might appear self-evident or repetitious (e.g., the sequence of the Lord's directive to Elijah and the latter's execution of this in 17,2-5 or the restoration of the boy to his mother, 17,23). Conversely, he does introduce new material of his own – see the citation of Menander (8,324), which, in turn, he sets up with the interpolated reference to Ithōbalos as "king of Tyre" in 8,317, as well as the references to the woman's grief (8,325), Elijah's self-confident assurances (8,325) and God's motives (8,327). On the terminological level, Josephus' consistent avoidance of the chapter's *Leitwort*, i.e. "word of the Lord" (17,2.5.8.16.24) as well as its double "man of God" (17,18.24)[1075] is worthy of note. In place of the latter designation he introduces the title "prophet", entirely absent in MT 1 Kings 17, no less than 7×. Likewise remarkable is the fact that nowhere in the pericope does Josephus employ the proper name "Elijah".

Finally, in view of the controverted question of Josephus' stance towards the Biblical miracles[1076], it is of interest to note that, in this instance at any rate, Josephus shows no hestitation in reproducing the three extraordinary happenings related in 1 Kings 17, i.e. the provisioning of Elijah by ravens, the multiplication of the widow's supplies, and the cure of her son. In fact, one notes a certain embellishment of the last of these happenings by Josephus (cf. Elijah's self-confident claim about being able to restore the boy to life and the reference to God's motivation in responding to the prophet's appeal).

1075. On this point see the remarks of O. BETZ, *Miracles in the Writings of Flavius Josephus*, in L.H. FELDMAN and G. HATA (eds.), *Josephus, Judaism and Christianity*, Detroit, 1987, 212-235, p. 220: "This negative attitude of Josephus towards the designation 'Man of God' does not support the argument Josephus knew of the 'Theios Aner'... . If this were true, Josephus would have used this title for Elijah, especially in rendering the passages I Kings 17:18 and 24. In my opinion such a type of 'Theios Aner', a wise man and miracle worker, never existed in Hellenism during the NT age; it is a product of the *Religionsgeschichtliche Schule*".

1076. On the question, see e.g.: G. DELLLING, *Josephus und das Wunderbare*, in *NT* 2 (1958) 291-309; G. MACRAE, *Miracle in the Antiquities of Josephus*, in C.F.D. MOULE (ed.), *Miracles. Cambridge Studies in their Theology and History*, London, 1965, 127-147; H.R. MOEHRING, *Rationalization of Miracles in the Writings of Flavius Josephus*, in E.A. LIVINGSTONE (ed.), *Studia Evangelica* 6 (TU, 112), 1973, 376-383; O. BETZ, *Das Problem des Wunders bei Flavius Josephus im Vergleich zum Wunderproblem bei den Rabbinnen und im Johannesevangelium*, in O. BETZ - K. HAACKER - M. HENGEL (eds.), *Josephus-Studien*. FS O. Michel, Göttingen, 1974, pp. 23-44; idem, *Miracles* (see preceding note).

XIII

ELIJAH ON CARMEL
(8,328-346)

Continuing to follow the sequence of 1 Kings, Josephus now comes to relate the events of its chapter 18. This lengthy chapter may be approximately subdivided as follows: 18,1-16 (coming together of Elijah and Ahab); 2) 18,17-40 (Elijah's triumph on Carmel); and 3) 18,41-46 (sequel: the rainstorm). I turn now to a consideration of Josephus' handling of these three segments.

1. *Elijah and Ahab Brought Together* (8,328-334). 1 Kings 18,1 makes the transition to the following episode with a double chronological notice: "after many days... in the third year" (cf. "these [two] years", 17,1). Josephus, by contrast, dates the subsequent happening "after a little time had passed (χρόνου δ' ὀλίγου διελθόντος)[1077]". Perhaps, his divergent indication stands under the influence of Menander's notice, quoted by Josephus in 8,324 (see above), that the drought in Ahab's time lasted precisely one year; after the various incidents of 1 Kings 17, that "year" would now be just about up[1078]. In any case, Josephus likewise modifies the sequence and wording of 18,1aβb-2a. For the latter's "the word of the Lord came to Elijah... 'Go, show yourself to Ahab and I will send rain upon the earth'. So Elijah went to show himself to Ahab", he reads: "(the prophet) in accordance with the will of God (κατὰ βούλησιν τοῦ θεοῦ, see 8,218) went (παραγίνεται, see 8,231.320, compare 3 Rgns ἐπορεύθη)[1079] to King Achab to inform (δηλώσων) him that rain (ὑετόν) was coming".

In 18,2b there is a parenthetical remark about the severity of the famine "in Samaria". Josephus generalizes this notice: "Now at that time a famine (λιμός, so 3 Rgns) held the whole country in its power (κατεῖχε τὴν χώραν ἅπασαν)[1080]". He expatiates on this indication with a reference (partially) inspired by and designed to prepare Ahab's directive as cited in 1 Kings 18,5: "and there was a lack of necessary

---

1077. This chronological indication occurs also in *AJ* 7,96.303; 9,27; 10,17; 12,199; 19,300. See VILLALBA I VARNEDA, *Method*, p. 119, n. 276.

1078. Recall how in 8,255.258 Josephus "tailors" his presentation of Shishak's invasion of Judah with an eye to the quotation of Herodotus he will give in 8,260-261.

1079. With the above formulation "(Elijah) went in accordance with the will of God", compare 8,320 παραγίνεται τοῦ θεοῦ κελεύσαντος.

1080. The above construction "hold the whole country in power" recurs in *AJ* 9,280; 13,353; 14,314. Only here in 8,328, however, is it used with "famine" as subject.

provisions (τῶν ἀναγκαίων ἀπορία)[1081] so that not only did men have a scarcity of bread (ἄρτων[1082] σπανίζειν)[1083] but, because of the drought (ἀνομβρίαν, see 8,320), the earth did not yield (τὴν γῆν... ἀναδιδόναι)[1084] the grass necessary for the pasturing of horses (ἵπποις, see ἵππους, 3 Rgns 18,5) and other beasts (κτήνεσι, cf. 3 Rgns 18,5 ἡμιόνους)". Josephus follows his expanded version of 18,2b with his parallel to 18,3a, the king's summoning of his official "Obadiah": "So the king called (καλέσας, 3 Rgns ἐκάλεσεν) Obedias ('Ωβεδίαν, BL* Ἀβδειού, 19/b' 108/b 93/e₂ Ἀβδιού)[1085] who was in charge of his estate (τὸν... ἐπιμελόμενον αὐτοῦ τῶν κτημάτων)[1086]". Whereas, however, in 18,3b-4 an extended parenthesis (see RSV) concerning Obadiah's Yahwistic zeal supervenes between Ahab's summons of (18,3a) and his charge to (18,5) Obadiah, Josephus keeps these last items together, "delaying" reference to the official's piety to a later point. He renders, employing indirect discourse, Ahab's word to Obadiah from 18,5 with "(Ahab told him) that he wished him to go out (ἀπιέναι)[1087] to the springs of water and winter streams (ἐπὶ τὰς πηγὰς τῶν ὑδάτων καὶ τοὺς χειμάρρους, compare 3 Rgns 18,5 ἐπὶ [τὰς >B] πηγὰς τῶν ὑδάτων καὶ ἐπὶ [τοὺς >B] χειμάρρους) in order to cut (ἀμησάμενοι)[1088] any grass that they might find (εὑρεθείη, 3 Rgns εὕρωμεν) near them and give it to the beasts (κτήνεσιν, see 8,328) for fodder". To the Biblical Ahab's word Josephus attaches a further one, intended, like his earlier remark about the effects of the famine, to prepare a later development in the story, i.e. Obadiah's informing Elijah of Ahab's world-wide pursuit of him, 18,10. Drawing on the wording of that subsequent Biblical verse, Josephus at this juncture has Ahab continue "he also said (καὶ)[1089] that he had sent (περιπέμψαντα, B 3 Rgns 18,10 ἀπέστειλεν) men throughout the entire earth (κατὰ πᾶσαν τὴν οἰκου-

---

1081. This same construction occurs also in *AJ* 12,378.

1082. So ROM, followed by NaWMar. N reads αὐτῶν with SP, see I, p. xli (Na, II, p. xxv remarks that N's comments there "minime persuasit").

1083. This is Josephus' only use of the expression "have a scarcity of bread".

1084. The above construction "earth yields" occurs also in *BJ* 5,213; *AJ* 1,49, cf. 3,281; 4,205.

1085. On Josephus' form of the name, see SCHALIT, *Namenwörterbuch*, p. 127, s.v.: "Ist 'Ωβεδίας sekundär? Dann wäre Αβδιας der LXX die Form des Archetypus".

1086. Josephus' formulation here seems to reflect the title given Obadiah in MT 1 Kings 18,3, i.e. אשר על־הבית, compare 3 Rgns τὸν οἰκονόμον (cf. 8,308 where Josephus' designation of "Osa" as Elah's οἰκονόμος does correspond to the term used by 3 Rgns 16,9, MT reading the same expression as in its 18,3). Josephus' one other use of the above expression "looking after possessions" is *AJ* 10,16.

1087. Thus the conjecture of Hud followed by NNaMar for the ἀπεῖναι of codd.

1088. Josephus' pl. participle here likely stands under the influence of the double use of verbs in the first person pl. in 3 Rgns 18,5 – neither of which have a parallel in MT.

1089. N opines that something has fallen out before this word.

μένην)¹⁰⁹⁰ to look for (ζητήσοντας, 3 Rgns 18,10 ζητεῖν)¹⁰⁹¹ the prophet Elijah (Ἠλίαν)¹⁰⁹², but they had not found (οὐχ εὑρηκέναι, B 3 Rgns 18,10 οὐχ εὕρηκεν) him". Josephus then closes Ahab's discourse with the words "(Ahab) commanded Obedias to accompany (συνέπεσθαι, compare the 3 Rgns plus at the start of the king's speech in 18,5 καὶ διέλθωμεν) him".

Next, in parallel to 18,6, Josephus relates that king and minister "divide up" (μερισάμενοι, 3 Rgns B ἐμέρισαν) "the roads" (τὰς ὁδοὺς, 3 Rgns τὴν ὁδόν, contrast MT את הארץ), each going his separate way. To this notice he then attaches his version of 18,4 which he had earlier passed over: "Now it had happened at the time when Queen Jezabelē killed (ἀπέκτεινε, 3 Rgns 18,4 τύπτειν)¹⁰⁹³ the prophets (18,4 specifies these as "prophets of the Lord") that Obedias hid (κρύψαι, B ἔκρυψεν) a hundred prophets in underground (ὑπογείοις)¹⁰⁹⁴ caves (σπηλαίοις)¹⁰⁹⁵ and fed (τρέφειν, LXX διέτρεφεν) them, though giving them *only* (μόνον) bread and water¹⁰⁹⁶". Josephus thus utilizes the datum of 18,4 to "fill in" the interlude between Obadiah's parting from Ahab (18,6) and his encountering Elijah (18,7); thereby, the item becomes less disruptive than in its Biblical placing. Thereupon, Josephus resumes his narration with the notice, derived from 18,7a, "as Obedias, therefore, was separated from the king and was alone (μόνωθέντι, compare the 3 Rgns plus in 18,7aα explicitly referring to Obadiah's being "alone" [μόνος]), the prophet Elijah met (συνήντησεν) him (compare 18,7aβ "and behold [> B] Elijah came [B, > MT and L] to meet [εἰς συνάντησιν] him").

1090. In 1 Kings 18,10 the reference is to "no nation or kingdom". Josephus uses the above phrase "throughout the earth" also in *BJ* 2,364; 5,161; 7,43 (+ "entire" as in 8,329); *AJ* 11,196; 12,48; 13,77; 14,110.

1091. With the entire above phrase "sending throughout the whole earth to look for", compare *AJ* 11,196 where Artaxerxes is advised ζητῆσαι δὲ περιπέμψαντα καθ' ὅλην τὴν οἰκουμένην (i.e. beautiful virgins to replace his wife Vashti).

1092. Josephus' form of the prophet's name, here and elsewhere, corresponds to that found in L, compare B Ἠλειού. Recall that this is Josephus' first mention of Elijah by name.

1093. Note that the verb used by Josephus here of Jezebel's "killing" of the prophets does occur in 3 Rgns 18,12 when Obadiah invokes his deed in speaking to Elijah.

1094. On this emendation, adopted by NaWMar, see Mar, *Josephus*, V, pp. 750-751, n.a; SCHALIT, *Namenwörterbuch*, p. 33, s.v. Γάρις. NN* print the reading of RO, i.e. ὑπὸ Γάρις. Lat has no equivalent to the phrase.

1095. Josephus' plural here corresponds to the ἐν δύο σπηλαίοις of L 3 Rgns 18,4; compare B ἐν σπηλαίῳ corresponding to the singular "cave" of MT. Josephus passes over the further Biblical specification that Obadiah hid the prophets "by fifties".

1096. In thus highlighting the paucity of the prophets' fare, Josephus goes beyond the Bible itself. In so doing he perhaps has in view his earlier statement (8,328) about the severity of the famine which would not have allowed Obadiah to provide his *protegés* with anything more. Note too that in *AJ* 8,410 (= 1 Kings 22,27) Ahab prescribes a diet of "nothing but bread and water" for another prophet, i.e. Micaiah, see below.

MT 1 Kings 18,7b-8a recounts the initial exchange between Elijah and Obadiah as follows: "... he (Obadiah) recognized him (ויכרהו, 3 Rgns 'he hastened', ἔσπευσεν), and fell on his face, and said, 'Is it you, my lord Elijah?' And he said to him [to Abdeiou, L] , '(it is) I (> L)'." Josephus reformulates in a more logical sequence with Obadiah first ascertaining the prophet's identity before paying homage to him: "Obedias inquired (πυθόμενος) of him who he was (cf v. 7bβ), and when he found out (cf. v. 8a), did obeisance (προσεκύνησεν, 3 Rgns ἔπεσεν ἐπὶ πρόσωπον αὐτοῦ) to him¹⁰⁹⁷". He then rounds off this opening exchange by having Elijah direct Obadiah to go report his coming to Ahab, // 18,8b.

1 Kings 18,9-14 reports at length Obadiah's vehement objection to Elijah's directive. Josephus too devotes considerable space (8,332-334a) to Obadiah's answer, though avoiding some of the repetitions found in the Biblical version. As in 18,9 Josephus makes Obadiah begin with an indignant question concerning the assignment just given him by Elijah: "the other (Obadiah) then asked what harm (κακὸν) he himself had done (πεπονθότα)¹⁰⁹⁸ him (Elijah) that..." (compare 18,9a "wherein have I sinned [3 Rgns ἡμάρτηκα] that...?"). Josephus likewise varies the characterization of Ahab in Obadiah's opening word. In 18,9b Obadiah speaks of Ahab as one who will kill *him* should he do as Elijah has just enjoined. According to Josephus, however, here anticipating Obadiah's subsequent statement in 18,10a¹⁰⁹⁹, it is Elijah himself who would be the object of the king's hostile initiative: "(he was sending him to) one who was seeking (ζητοῦντα, 3 Rgns 18,10 ζητεῖν σε) to kill (ἀποκτεῖναι, see 8,330 and 3 Rgns 18,12) [the prophet] and had searched (ἐρευνήσαντα) every land (πᾶσαν... γῆν) for him (Elijah)". Josephus further reworks Obadiah's word in 18,10, eliminating the "oath formula" of v. 10aα and explicating Ahab's hostile intentions: "did he (Elijah) perhaps not know that the king had not overlooked a single place where he might send (ἀπέστειλε= B) to lead (Elijah) to death (ἀνάξοντας... ἐπὶ θανάτῳ)¹¹⁰⁰ if they caught him?". Josephus passes over 18,10b with its mention of Ahab's "adjuring" (so MT, והשביע, compare 3 Rgns "burned", ἐνέπρησεν) the nations that they were not hiding Elijah from him¹¹⁰¹, as well as Obadiah's "citation" of Elijah's directive to him (v.8b) in v. 11. In other words, Josephus so

1097. The remark of W, *Josèphe*, II, p. 229, n. 5, i.e. that Obadiah's question about Elijah's identity is a "détail... ajouté par Josèphe" is not correct, see 1 Kings 18,7bβ.

1098. The above construction "do harm" recurs in *BJ* 7,392; *AJ* 3,21; 9,90; 11,155; 12,376.401; 13,43.108; 20,161; *Vita* 207.

1099. Recall Josephus' previous anticipation of 18,10a in 8,329 "(Ahab) also said that he had sent men throughout the entire earth to look for Elijah...".

1100. This is Josephus' only use of the above construction "lead to death".

1101. Josephus has anticipated this last item in 8,329 "(the men dispatched by Ahab) had not found Elijah", cf. also the continuation of Obadiah's word.

reworks the first part of Obadiah's response (18,9-11) that reference to the danger facing Obadiah himself at Ahab's hands disappears; all attention goes to the threat the king poses for the prophet.

It is only then in the second part of his speech that Obadiah comes, in Josephus' presentation, to speak of the threat which Elijah's sending him to Ahab entails for himself. On this point, Josephus conveys the general sense of 1 Kings 18,12a where Obadiah voices his fear that Elijah will not "stay put" with the result that when Ahab is unable to find him, he (Obadiah) will be executed for bringing the king false information about the prophet's whereabouts. Josephus words this item thus: "Indeed, he said, he was afraid that (εὐλαβεῖσθαι... μὴ)[1102] if God appeared (τοῦ θεοῦ φανέντος)[1103] to Elijah a second time (πάλιν)[1104], (the prophet) might go away to another place (εἰς ἄλλον... τόπον, compare 3 Rgns 18,12 "to a land [3 Rgns εἰς (τὴν, L) γῆν] which I do not know"), and then, when the king sent for him, he would not be able (μὴ δυνάμενος)[1105] to find him in whatever part of the world he might be, and so he himself would be put to death (ἀποθάνη, 3 Rgns καὶ ἀποκτενεῖ με)[1106]". In this formulation note Josephus' substitution, in line with his tendency to avoid mention of God's "spirit", of an allusion to the Deity's "appearing" to Elijah for the Biblical mention of the "spirit of the Lord" (3 Rgns πνεῦμα κυρίου) carrying Elijah off[1107]. Josephus likewise leaves aside Obadiah's concluding affirmation in 18,12 about his being a life-long "God-fearer", just as he omitted the earlier anticipation of this claim in 18,3b.

1102. The same construction occurs also in *AJ* 6,157 where Samuel states that he is "fearful lest...".

1103. The precise phrase above occurs also in *AJ* 7,92 of God's "appearing" to Nathan.

1104. Josephus has not previously mentioned a divine "appearance" to Elijah as such, and so it is not immediately clear why he should speak of God's manifesting himself "again" to the prophet here. Perhaps, the reference is to God's "revealing" to Elijah that the woman whom he meets at the city gate is the one he has designated to feed him, 8,321.

1105. So NN*NaMar. Compare MSP καὶ μὴ δυναμένου.

1106. The Greek of the apodosis of Obadiah's statement in 8,333 as printed by Mar reads: εἶτα διαμαρτὼν αὐτοῦ, [note that Mar's comma here is absent in the text as printed by NN*Na] πέμψαντος τοῦ βασιλέως, μὴ δυνάμενος εὑρεῖν ὅπου ποτ᾽ εἴη γῆς ἀποθάνη. With Mar's rendition of this sequence above, compare that of W, *ad loc.*: "... et qu'alors le roi m'envoyant te chercher et n'ayant pu te trouver nulle part, je paie de ma mort sa déconvenue".

1107. BEST, *Use*, pp. 224-225 cites 1 Kings 18,12 as one of those Biblical references to the activity of God's spirit that "were so embarassing that they dropped without leaving a trace" from Josephus' presentation. Other such instances would be the passages recounting the operation of the divine spirit upon Samson, i.e. Judg 14,6 (// *AJ* 5,287).19 (// 5,294). It should be pointed out, however, that the notion of a supernatural impetus to Elijah's movements does not simply "fall out" in Josephus' version of 1 Kings 18,12. Recall too that also elsewhere Josephus substitutes an operation by God himself for Biblical references to some divine agency, the "word" in particular, acting upon an individual.

In place thereof he has Obadiah warn the prophet "to look out for his safety" (προνοεῖν... τῆς σωτηρίας)[1108], cf. his previous accentuation of the danger facing, not Obadiah, but Elijah himself. Next, he draws on 18,13 (itself a recapitulation of 18,4, earlier left aside by Josephus, see above) in relating Obadiah's invocation of his endeavors on behalf of the threatened prophets: "(he told him) of his zeal on behalf of (περὶ [τοὺς ὁμοτέχνους]... σπουδὴν)[1109] Elijah's fellows in the prophetic art (ὁμοτέχνους)[1110], for he had saved (σώσειεν) a hundred prophets after Jezebelē had destroyed (ἀνῃρηκυίας, B ἀποκτείνειν) all the others, and had kept them hidden and fed them". Just as in the case of 18,11, Josephus omits Obadiah's second citation of Elijah's word to him (18,8) in 18,14. Instead, he immediately proceeds to an amplification of Elijah's response in 18,15. In so doing he turns Elijah's reply into an explicit directive, re-utilizing the wording of his earlier injunction in 8,331: "But Elijah bade him go without any fear to the king, first giving him sworn assurances (δοὺς... πίστεις ἐνόρκους)[1111] that he would positively appear (φανήσεται, 3 Rgns 18,15b ὀφθήσομαι αὐτῷ)[1112] before Achab that very day".

2. *Elijah's Triumph on Carmel* (8,335-343a). In 1 Kings 18, v. 16 (Obadiah informs Ahab who then goes to meet Elijah) constitutes the conclusion of the chapter's opening segment, vv. 1-16. Josephus (8,335) makes the notice rather the introduction to what follows, i.e. the king's challenging query to the prophet, 18,17: "When Obedias informed (μηνύσαντος, 3 Rgns 18,16a ἀπήγγειλεν) the king of Elijah's (approach), Achab went to meet (ὑπήντησεν, 3 Rgns ἐπορεύθη εἰς συνάντησιν) and asked him *in anger* (μετ' ὀργῆς)[1113]...". In 1 Kings 18,17b Ahab directs a short (seemingly superfluous) query to the prophet (cf. Obadiah's question to Elijah in 18,7): "Is it you, you troubler of Israel?" Josephus amplifies: "(Ahab asks) whether it was he who had brought evil (κακώσας, see 8,303.305) upon the Hebrew

---

1108. The above construction "look out for one's safety" occurs also in *AJ* 6,10; 9,153; 11,231; *Vita* 301.

1109. Josephus' reference here to Obadiah's "zeal" could be inspired by the mention in 18,12 (and 18,3) of his "fearing the Lord". The above construction σπουδή περὶ + acc. occurs some 36 × in Josephus.

1110. The term is hapax in Josephus.

1111. Compare the oath formula of 18,15a "as the Lord of hosts lives..." which Josephus, here as generally elsewhere, avoids. The above phrase "(give) sworn assurance(s)" occurs also in *AJ* 2,253; 6,291; 9,145; 10,2. On the term πίστις, see SPICQ, *Lexicographie*, II, pp. 697-703.

1112. Cf. 8,319 where Elijah announces that there will be no rain "until he himself should appear (φανέντος)".

1113. This reference to Ahab's emotional state is without Biblical basis as such.

people (τὸν Ἑβραίων λαὸν)[1114] and had caused the barrenness of the soil (ἀκαρπίας)[1115]". In introducing Elijah's response (// 18,18), Josephus comments that Elijah spoke to Ahab "without flattering him in the least (ὁ δ᾽ οὐδὲν ὑποθωπεύσας αὐτὸν εἶπεν)[1116]". In 18,18 Elijah makes a double counter-charge against the king and his house: "you have forsaken the commandments of (> 3 Rgns) the Lord (+ your God, 3 Rgns) and followed the Baals". For his part, Josephus has the prophet affirm that "it was Achab himself and his family (τὸ γένος αὐτοῦ, 3 Rgns ὁ οἶκος τοῦ πατρός σου) who had brought on all these misfortunes (τὰ δεινὰ) by introducing (ἐπεισενηνοχότας)[1117] foreign gods (ξενικοὺς... θεοὺς)[1118] into the country and worshipping (σέβοντας)[1119] them, while their own (God) (τὸν... ἴδιον αὐτῶν, compare 8,280 τὸν ἴδιον θεὸν), who was the only (μόνος) (true) one God (θεός)[1120], they had abandoned (ἀπολελοιπότας)[1121] and no longer gave Him any thought (πρόνοιαν... ποιουμένους, see 8,297)[1122]".

In 1 Kings 18,19 Elijah directs Ahab to assemble the Israelites along with the 450 prophets of Baal (so MT, 3 Rgns "of shame" [τῆς αἰσχύνης]) and 400 prophets of Asherah (so MT, 3 Rgns "of the groves" [τῶν ἀλσῶν]) maintained by Jezebel to Mt. Carmel. Josephus' version of the prophetic directive (8,336) runs thus: "(he bade him) go off (ἀπελθόντα)[1123] and gather (ἀθροῖσαι, 3 Rgns συνάθροισον) all

1114. Compare 18,17 "troubler of Israel" (3 Rgns ὁ διαστρέφων τὸν Ἰσραήλ). On the lips of Ahab the term "Hebrews" in the above phrase designates the Israelites in first place, although a more encompassing meaning, i.e. the chosen people as a whole, is not excluded given the extent of the drought, see n. 198 and further below on 8,341.

1115. Josephus' other uses of ἀκαρπία are AJ 2,85.92; 8,115; Ap 1,305.306.

1116. This is Josephus' only use of the verb ὑποθωπεύω. S. Εκ, Herodotismen in der jüdischen Archäologie des Josephus und ihre textkritische Bedeutung (Kungl. Humanistika Vetenskapssamfundet i Lund, Årberåtellelse 1945-1946), Lund, 1946, pp. 21-62, 213, p. 21 identifies Josephus' phrase here as a Herodotian reminiscence, compare Histories 1.30.3 Σόλων δὲ οὐδὲν ὑποθωπεύσας λέγει... (Ek likewise notes the same phase occurs several times in the extant fragments of Nicolas of Damascus).

1117. This is the conjecture adopted by NN*NaMar. Compare ἐνηνοχότας RO; ἐπεισενηνοχότα S²P; εἰσενηνοχότα Ε. Josephus' only other use of the verb ἐπεισφέρω is Vita 74.

1118. Josephus uses the above expression "foreign gods" also in AJ 5,101.107; 8,127 (337).338.350; (9,27).96 (133); 10,52.65.66. Note that here it constitutes a generalizing substitution for the "Baals" of 1 Kings 18,18; Josephus will make similar substitutions elsewhere in our pericope, see below.

1119. SP² reads σέβοντα here. The above expression "worship gods" recurs in AJ 4,137; 8,192; 9,27 ("foreign gods").193.255.288; 12,126.

1120. Note this interjected monotheistic affirmation which will be re-echoed later in Josephus' account.

1121. Compare 8,296 ἀπολιποῦσι... τὴν θρησκείαν (i.e. of God). The expression "abandon God" of 8,335 occurs only here in Josephus.

1122. With Elijah's accusation here ξενικοὺς... θεοὺς... σέβοντας... τὸν δ᾽ ἴδιον... μηδεμίαν ἔτι πρόνοιαν αὐτοῦ ποιουμένους, compare Josephus' notice on Solomon in AJ 8,192 τοὺς ἐκείνων [i.e. his foreign wives] σέβονται θεοὺς παρέντες τιμᾶν τὸν ἴδιον.

1123. So SP followed by Mar. NN*NaW read ἀνελθόντα with R.

the people (πάντα τὸν λαὸν, 1 Kings 18,19 'all Israel')[1124] to him (πρὸς αὐτὸν, see πρὸς μὲ in the direct discourse of 3 Rgns 18,19) on Mount Carmel (εἰς τὸ Καρμήλιον ὄρος, compare B εἰς [L + τὸ] ὄρος τὸ Καρμήλιον) as well as *his* prophets and those of his wife[1125] – telling him how many there were [compare 1 Kings 18,19 450 prophets of Baal, 3 Rgns "of shame"] – and also the prophets of the groves (τοὺς τῶν ἀλσῶν προφήτας, 3 Rgns τοὺς προφήτας τῶν ἀλσῶν), some four hundred (πετρακοσίους, so 3 Rgns) in number[1126]".

Josephus next (8,337) gives his parallel to 18,20, the convoking of the assembly by Ahab: "and, when at Achab's summons (Ἀχάβου δια-πέμψαντος, 3 Rgns ἀπέστειλεν Ἀχαὰβ) they had all (18,20 specifies 'all *the prophets*') gathered together (συνέδραμον, B ἐπισυνήγαγεν, L συνήγαγε) on the afore-mentioned mountain (18,20 'on Mount Car-mel')...". This notice, in turn, introduces his version of the opening of 18,21 where he has Elijah "standing in their midst (σταθεὶς αὐτῶν... μεταξύ, compare 18,21 'Elijah drew near to all (the people, > B)'[1127]...". In formulating the prophet's actual address to the assembly, Josephus elucidates the figurative obscurity of Elijah's open-ing question ("how long will you hobble on two crutches?") with a clear, prosaic question: "how long would they go on living in that way, divided in thought and opinion (τῇ διανοίᾳ καὶ ταῖς δόξαις)[1128]". He likewise amplifies (and generalizes) the alternative with which the Biblical Elijah confronts his hearers, i.e. "if the Lord is God, follow him, but if Baal, then follow him". In Josephus' rendition this becomes: "if they believed the native God (τὸν ἐγχώριον θεὸν)[1129] to be the only true God (ἀληθῆ καὶ μόνον [see 8,335])[1130], he urged them to follow Him (ἔπεσθαι τούτῳ, 3 Rgns πορεύεσθε ὀπίσω αὐτοῦ)[1131] *and His commandments* (ἐντολαῖς)[1132], but if they thought nothing of Him

1124. Cf. 8,335 where Josephus substitutes "the Hebrew people (λαὸν)" for 18,18's "Israel".

1125. With this formulation compare 8,318 which cites Jezebel's appointment of "prophets" for "Belias" and then goes to note that Ahab had "many such men around him".

1126. Josephus leaves aside the Biblical specification that the prophets "ate at Jezebel's table".

1127. Compare Josephus' reference to Jadōn "standing (σταθεὶς) in the midst of the multitude..." in 8,231.

1128. This is Josephus' only use of this collocation.

1129. The only other occurrence of this expression in Josephus is *AJ* 18,198 (pl.). The related expression ἐπιχώριος θεός occurs in *AJ* 9,99. See SCHLATTER, *Gott*, p. 20; idem, *Theologie*, p. 46.

1130. Elsewhere Josephus applies this collocation to God in *AJ* 8,343; 10,263, cf. *BJ* 7,323; *AJ* 6,148. On the phrase "the only God" in Greek religio-philosophical writings, see G. DELLING, *ΜΟΝΟΣ ΘΕΟΣ*, in *TLZ* 77 (1952) 469-476, esp. c. 474.

1131. Josephus' other uses of the above expression "follow God" (ἔπομαι + dative) are *AJ* 1,20; 7,212.

1132. This element has nothing equivalent in 18,21 itself, cf. however, MT 1 Kings 18,18 (Elijah accuses Ahab and his family) of abandoning "the commandments (מצות) of

(μηδὲν δὲ τοῦτον ἡγουμένους)¹¹³³ that and, instead, considered that they ought to serve (θρησκεύειν, see 8,227.248) the foreign (τῶν ξενικῶν) (gods)¹¹³⁴, he advised them to go with these (αὐτοῖς κατακολουθεῖν, see 8,271; compare 3 Rgns 18,21bα πορεύεσθε ὀπίσω αὐτοῦ, i. e. Baal)¹¹³⁵". In line with 18,21bβ Josephus then (8,338) notes the crowd's failure to respond to Elijah's challenge, making this a transition to what follows: "then, as the people (τοῦ... πλήθους, 3 Rgns ὁ λαὸς) made no answer to these words...".

1 Kings 18,22-24 relate Elijah's proposal that the opposing deities, the Lord and Baal, manifest their capacities by igniting a sacrifice prepared by their respective adherents. Josephus begins the sequence with the prophet clarifying, already at the outset, what he has in mind: "Elijah asked that a test (διάπειραν)¹¹³⁶ be made of the respective powers (ἰσχυός) of the foreign gods (τῶν ξενικῶν θεῶν, see 8,335.337) and his own (τοῦ ἰδίου, compare τὸν... ἴδιον αὐτῶν, 8,335)..." (see 18,24bα "the God who answers by fire, he is God"). Thereafter, his Elijah (// 18,22) contrasts himself as the Lord's "sole" (μόνος, 3 Rgns μονώτατος)¹¹³⁷ prophet with his numerous opponents. In referring to the latter, he has Elijah state "their (gods) had four hundred". This allusion seems inspired by the 3 Rgns plus at the end of 18,22 where Elijah refers, not only to the 450 prophets of Baal (so MT)¹¹³⁸, but also to "the four hundred prophets of the groves" (for these see 8,336 // 3 Rgns 18,19). In 1 Kings 18,23-24abα Elijah details the procedure he is proposing for both parties. Josephus makes him first enumerate the various steps both are to take: "(he asked that he be allowed) to take an ox (βοῦν) and after slaughtering (θύσας, 3 Rgns μελισάτωσαν) it (ταύτην)¹¹³⁹, place (ἐπιθεῖναι, 3 Rgns ἐπιθέτωσαν) it on a pile of wood

(> 3 Rgns) the Lord". Josephus does not elsewhere use the above phrase "follow commandment(s)".

1133. Compare the similar phrase used in Elijah's accusation against Ahab and his line in 8,335 ... μηδεμίαν ἔτι πρόνοιαν αὐτοῦ ποιουμένους.

1134. Compare 1 Kings 18,21αβ where the reference is to "Baal" as Yahweh's rival. Note that, here again, Josephus introduces a generalizing reference to "foreign (gods)" for the Bible's mention of Baal, see 8,335 (where the construction is "worship [σέβοντας] foreign gods"). Josephus uses the above expression "serve (foreign) gods" also in AJ 8,127.192.

1135. Compare TJ 1 Kings 18,21 which, in contrast to both Bible and Josephus, does not represent Elijah as offering the audience a "choice" between two deities: "How long are you to be divided into two divisions? Is not the Lord God? Serve before him alone. And why are you going astray after Baal in whom there is no profit?"

1136. Josephus' other uses of διάπειρα are in AJ 1,223; 2,125; 4,96; 6,199.230; 9,126.

1137. Josephus' self-designation for Elijah here echoes his reference to God as μόνος in 8,335.337.

1138. At this juncture in his narrative Josephus makes no reference to this category of "prophets" although he did allude to them previously in 8,336 (// 1 Kings 18,19).

1139. W, ad loc. renders βοῦν by "génisse" (Mar "ox") here given this feminine form of the demonstrative adjective referring to it. Compare 1 Kings 18,23, MT (הפר), 3 Rgns (τὸν Βοῦν).

(ξύλοις, 3 Rgns ἐπὶ [τῶν > L] ξύλων) without kindling a fire (πυρὸς οὐχ ὑφαφθέντος, 3 Rgns πῦρ μὴ ἐπιθέτωσαν), and that they do the same[1140]". He then continues: "then they should call upon (ἐπικαλέσασθαι)[1141] their gods (τοὺς ἰδίους θεούς, see 8,335.338, 3 Rgns ἐν ὀνόματι θεῶν ὑμῶν) and he upon his *to set the wood on fire*[1142], for if this happened, they (αὐτούς)[1143] would learn (μαθήσεσθαι)[1144] the true nature of God (τὴν ἀληθῆ φύσιν τοῦ θεοῦ)[1145]".

With 18,24bβ the historian notes the people's acceptance of Elijah's suggestion, again (compare 8,338 // 1 Kings 18,21b) formulating this as a transition to what follows: "when this proposal was accepted (ἀρεσάσης... τῆς γνώμης)[1146]...". He then reproduces Elijah's directives to his opponents from 18,25 in shortened form: "Elijah bade the prophets (προφήτας, MT "prophets of Baal", 3 Rgns "prophets of shame") select (ἐκλεξαμένους, 3 Rgns ἐκλέξασθε) an ox (βοῦν)[1147] and sacrifice first (πρώτους... θῦσαι [see θύσας, 8,338], 3 Rgns ποιήσατε πρῶ-

---

1140. In 1 Kings 18,23 Elijah first makes his proposal concerning what the pagan prophets are to do (v. 23aβ) and then what he what he himself will do (v. 23b). Josephus in 8,338 reverses this sequence, at the same time intimating a reason why he does so: "he... being His (God's) only prophet while their gods had four hundred, be allowed to take an ox... and that they do the same". (Note, however, that in what follows Josephus will observe the Biblical order in which the prophets do in fact prepare their offering prior to Elijah).

1141. In 3 Rgns 18,24aα the verb used for the "crying out" which Elijah enjoins upon the prophets is βοᾶτε; note, however, that in v. 24aβ when Elijah refers to his own action the verb used is ἐπικαλέσομαι. Thus, Josephus' form above represents an anticipation and re-application to the prophets of the verb used in 3 Rgns of the appeal that Elijah undertakes to make.

1142. This specification as to what the prophets are to ask their gods to do lacks a parallel as such in 18,24, cf., however, the phrase "the God who answers by fire, he is God" in v. 24bα.

1143. Thus RO followed by NMar. NaN* adopt the τότε of MSP.

1144. NN* conjecture μαθήσεσθ᾽ about which Na, II, p. xxv comments "Ns coniecturam... non intelligo".

1145. Elsewhere Josephus employs the above phrase "the nature of God" in *AJ* 1,15.19; 2,146; 4,269; 10,42; *Ap* 1,224; 2,168 (*bis*).180.248.250, cf. *AJ* 8,107; *Ap* 1,232 ("the divine nature"). On the concept of "nature" in Josephus, see SCHLATTER, *Gott*, p. 20; idem, *Theologie*, p. 6; H. KÖSTER, φύσις κτλ, in *TWNT* 9 (1973) 246-271, esp. pp. 263-264.

With the abstract "lesson" that the contest between Elijah and the prophets is designed to teach according to Josephus here, compare the more concrete formulation in 1 Kings 18,24bα: "the God who answers by fire, he is God". Such generalization/abstraction is characteristic of Josephus' version of the episode in comparison with the Biblical one.

1146. Related constructions to the above occur in *AJ* 7,216; 9,84; 12,381; *Vita* 369. Compare 1 Kings 18,24bβ "all the people answered and said 'the word (B ῥῆμα, L λόγος) which you have said is good'." Once again, Josephus avoids reproducing a Biblical use of the term "word".

1147. Cf. βοῦν... ταύτην, 8,338. With Josephus' reference to "an ox" here in 8,339, compare "the ox" of MT (הפר) and L (τὸν βοῦν) 18,25 (B reads τὸν μόσχον, this in contrast to its τὸν βοῦν in 18,23).

τοὺς)¹¹⁴⁸ and call upon (ἐπικαλέσασθαι, see 8,338, 3 Rgns ἐπικαλεῖσθε) their own gods (τοὺς αὐτῶν¹¹⁴⁹ θεοὺς, compare 8,338 τοὺς
ἰδίους θεοὺς)¹¹⁵⁰".

Josephus likewise drastically shortens the description of the prophets'
(unavailing) initiatives found in 18,26, reducing this to the transitional
phrase "since nothing came (οὐδὲν ἀπήντα)¹¹⁵¹ of the prophets'
prayers (εὐχῆς)¹¹⁵² and appeals (ἐπικλήσεως)¹¹⁵³ after they had sacri-
ficed (θύσασι, see 8,338.339)¹¹⁵⁴...". Josephus now proceeds to cite the
prophet's words to his rivals (// 18,27): "... Elijah¹¹⁵⁵ mocked
(σκώπτων, 3 Rgns ἐμυκτήρισεν)¹¹⁵⁶ and told them to call (καλεῖν, 3
Rgns ἐπικαλεῖσθε – recall Josephus' previous use of this compound
form in 8,338.339) the(ir) gods (τοὺς θεούς)¹¹⁵⁷ in a loud voice
(μεγάλῃ βοῇ, 3 Rgns ἐν φωνῇ μεγάλῃ)". As in 18,27b Josephus has
Elijah continue his mocking word to the prophets with an enumeration
of the reasons why they must call loudly upon their god(s). In so doing
he seems, however, to align himself more with MT than 3 Rgns, even
while going his own way vis-à-vis both formulations. In MT's 18,27b
Elijah lists no less than four reasons why Baal must be loudly invoked:
"either he is musing (שִׂיחַ) or he has gone aside (שִׂיג לוֹ) or he is on a
journey (דֶרֶךְ לוֹ) or perhaps he is asleep (יָשֵׁן)". Of these four reasons, 3
Rgns appears to retain only three, passing over the allusion to Baal's
"being on a journey", thus: "...he is meditating (ἀδολεσχία [+ τις, L]
αὐτῷ ἐστιν), or else perhaps he is engaged in business (χρηματίζει) or

1148. Note that Josephus leaves aside the motivation which in 18,25aβ Elijah appends
to his preceding directive to the prophets, i.e. "for you are many" (recall that in 8,338
Josephus invokes the fact of his being the "only" prophet of the Lord as opposed to the
400 prophets of the gods as the reason why *he* should be allowed to proceed first, see
n. 1140). Josephus likewise has nothing corresponding to Elijah's final directive to the
prophets in 18,25aβ, i.e. "set no fire" – this demand having been enunciated just
previously in 8,338 // 18,24.

1149. Thus the conjecture of NN* followed by NaMar. Codd E read αὐτῶν.

1150. Josephus' plural form "gods" in 8,339 corresponds to the L reading in 3 Rgns
18,25bα "call upon the name of your gods (θεῶν)". B in the same phrase reads the sg.
θεοῦ, while MT's אלהיכם might be understood as either sg. or pl.

1151. Also *BJ* 5,356; *AJ* 3,10; 15,181.

1152. In MSPE the word αὐτοῖς follows εὐχῆς; Na adopts this plus.

1153. This is Josephus' only use of the above collocation "prayer and appeal".

1154. In the above formulation Josephus omits the chronological indications found in
18,26 ("from morning until noon") and 27aα ("and at noon"). He will, however, utilize
these indications at a later point, see below. He likewise leaves unused the notice of
18,26bβ "(the prophets) limped about the altar which they had made", perhaps because
there was no mention of an "altar" in what precedes.

1155. Josephus, like MT, lacks the qualification of Elijah as "the Tishbite" of 3 Rgns
18,27.

1156. Josephus' other uses of σκώπτω are *BJ* 2,299; 5,120.375; *Ap* 2,49.

1157. Compare Elijah's aside in 18,27aβ "(cry aloud) for he (Baal) is a god". Once
again, Josephus generalizes a Biblical reference to the particular deity, Baal.

perhaps he is asleep (καθεύδει)...". Josephus, for his part, does utilize the MT's "journey reference", coupling this with mention of a divine "sleep" which in both MT and 3 Rgns figures as the last of Elijah's "reasons": "... for either they (note the plural here referring to the 'gods' whom Elijah has just urged the prophets to invoke in a loud voice) were on a journey (ἀποδημεῖν) or were asleep (καθεύδειν, see 3 Rgns)¹¹⁵⁸".

1 Kings 18,28 relates the prophets' reaction to Elijah's exhortation: "they cried aloud, and cut themselves according to their custom (> B) with swords and lances, until the blood gushed out upon them". Josephus prefaces his reproduction of this notice with a chronological indication derived from 18,26 (MT B; L lacks an equivalent) and previously passed over by him: "(so they did this, i.e. the 'crying aloud' previously enjoined by Elijah) 'from dawn to midday' (ἀπ᾽ ὄρθρου... μέχρι μέσης ἡμέρας, cf. B 3 Rgns 18,26 ἐκ πρωΐθεν ἕως μεσημβρίας)". He then continues: "(they) cut (πεμνόντων, 3 Rgns κατετέμνοντο) themselves with swords (μαχαίραις)¹¹⁵⁹ and barbed lances (σιρομάσταις, 3 Rgns [+ ἐν, L] σειρομάσταις)¹¹⁶⁰ after the custom of their country (κατὰ τὸ πάτριον ἔθος)¹¹⁶¹".

In 18,29 both MT and 3 Rgns begin with a reference to a further activity by the prophets, i.e. their "prophesying". Josephus has no equivalent to this item, perhaps finding reference to such an activity, so intimately associated with the Lord's envoys, objectional when attributed to these pagan figures¹¹⁶². Thereafter, the two witnesses diverge; according to MT (the prophets prophesied) "until the time of the offering of the oblation, but there was no voice, no one answered, no one heeded" (see 18,26). By contrast, 3 Rgns reads: "and it came to pass as it was the time of the offering of the sacrifice that Elijah... spoke to the prophets... 'Stand by for the present, and I will offer my sacrifice'. And they stood by and departed". In this instance Josephus

1158. On Josephus' omission of the first two items in MT's (and 3 Rgns') list as cited above in the text, see Mar, *Josephus*, V, pp. 754-755, n. b who suggests that he may have interpreted these *à la* TJ as referring to the god's "relieving himself" and "so omitted the unseemly detail". On the meaning of the Hebrew collocation in question, see further G.A. RENDSBURG, *The Mock of Baal in 1 Kings 18:27*, in *CBQ* 50 (1988) 414-417.

1159. Josephus' plural form here corresponds to that of MT and L (ἐν μαχαίραις) as against the singular of B (ἐν μαχαίρᾳ).

1160. Josephus leaves aside the graphic Biblical detail about the prophets' cutting themselves "until the blood gushed out upon them".

1161. This phrase corresponds to the plus of 1 Kings 18,28 MT and L (κατὰ τὸν ἐθίσμον αὐτῶν), lacking in B. The above phrase "ancestral custom(s)" occurs elsewhere in Josephus in *BJ* 2,195; 4,102.136; 7,424; *AJ* 5,90.101; 9,95.137; 11,339; 12,255.271.280; 13,397; 14,194.213.216.233.258(the same construction as in 8,340).263; 15,267; 16,1.35.171 (= 8,340); 19,290; 20,100; *Ap* 1,317; 2,10.

1162. Note that TJ's rendition of the opening of 1 Kings 18,29, i.e. "they (the prophets) danced" (וריסתטשׁ) likewise eliminates mention of their "prophesying".

clearly aligns himself with the variant 3 Rgns text which, however, he reproduces in shortened form: "(the prophets cut themselves) until, when about to offer his sacrifice (μέλλων... ἐπιτελεῖν τὴν θυσίαν[1163], compare 3 Rgns ὁ καιρὸς τοῦ ἀναβῆναι τὴν θυσίαν)...[1164]". Before proceeding with his "sacrifice", however, Elijah, in Josephus' presentation, first issues a double directive: "he bade them (the prophets) retire (ἀναχωρῆσαι)[1165] and the others (i.e. the assembled people) draw near" (ἐγγὺς προσελθόντας; with this second directive Josephus anticipates 18,30aα where Elijah enjoins the people "come near to me" [3 Rgns προσαγάγετε πρός μέ]. To the latter injunction he appends a "motivation" peculiar to himself, i.e. "to watch that he should not secretly apply fire to the wood"[1166]. With 18,30aβ he then notes the crowd's compliance with Elijah's summons, at the same time making this the transition to what follows: "then, when the crowd had come near..." (τοῦ... ὄχλου προσελθόντος, 3 Rgns ... προσήγαγεν πᾶς ὁ λαὸς πρὸς αὐτόν).

Following the above preliminaries, Josephus now relates the series of measures undertaken by Elijah. Once again, comparison between Josephus and "the Bible" is complicated by divergencies between MT and 3 Rgns. According to MT (1 Kings 18,30b) Elijah's first action is to "repair the ruined altar of the Lord". 3 Rgns reserves this item until a later point, i.e. following the opening words of 18,32. Josephus deviates from both witnesses, making no reference, either here or subsequently, to an "altar" repaired by Elijah, perhaps because its existence (and destruction) have not been previously mentioned in the Bible[1167].

1163. The words τὴν θυσίαν in the above phrase are not found in RO; NN*Sc omit them, whereas NaMar read them with MSPE Lat.

1164. Josephus uses the above phrase "offer sacrifice(es)" elsewhere in BJ 1,153; 4,168; 7,72; AJ 1,58.341; 3,228.235.238.269; 4,31.123.241; 5,114.266; 6,101.151; 7,329.332; 8,25.169; 9,135.271.273; 10,24.43.72.275; 11,9.110; 12,253; 14,260.477; 18,19 (bis).234; 19,71; Ap 1,282; 2,48. With the above expression "when about to offer his sacrifice", compare μέλλοντος ἐπιφέρειν τὰς θυσίας... in 8,231 (Jeroboam).

1165. Compare 3 Rgns 18,29 as cited above where the prophets are first enjoined by Elijah to "stand by (μετάστητε) for now" and then are said to have, in fact, "stood by and departed (ἀπῆλθον)". Josephus' above formulation conflates Elijah's command and its "execution" by the prophets, while also avoiding the seeming discrepancy between the prophets' both "standing by" and "going away" in the latter.

1166. This insertion seems designed to preclude any suspicions readers might have as to the credibility of the following happening. In Rabbinic tradition, the above Betrugs-motif is associated rather with the Baal-prophets, specifically their leader Hiel (the rebuilder of Jericho, see 1 Kings 16,34) who is said to have hidden himself under the prophets' altar with a view to setting fire to their sacrifice, but was slain by a snake sent by God. See GINZBERG, Legends, IV, p. 198 and VI, p. 319, n. 15.

1167. In leaving the altar of MT 1 Kings 18,30b unmentioned, Josephus likewise avoids the problem posed by the MT sequence of 18,30.32 which seems to speak of two different altars even though subsequently only one altar will be cited. Rabbinic tradition makes the ruined altar spoken of in MT 1 Kings 18,30b one built by Saul and subsequently torn down by the people of Samaria, see GINZBERG, Legends, VI, p. 319, n. 13.

Instead, he moves directly to the prophet's initiatives with the twelve stones as related in 18,31a (MT and 3 Rgns): "... he took (λαβὼν, 3 Rgns ἔλαβεν) twelve stones (δώδεκα λίθους, so 3 Rgns) one for (each) tribe of the Hebrew people (κατὰ[1168] φυλὴν τοῦ λαοῦ τῶν Ἑβραίων)[1169]". Leaving aside the (extraneous) citation of Gen 35,10 in 18,31b (which itself picks up on the mention of "Jacob" [MT] // "Israel" [3 Rgns] in v. 31a), "... to whom the word of the Lord came, saying, 'Israel shall be your name'", Josephus proceeds immediately to Elijah's further measures (//18,32): "... and with them (the stones) he erected (ἀνέστησεν, 3 Rgns ᾠκοδόμησεν) an altar (θυσιαστήριον)[1170], around which he dug (ὤρυξε, 3 Rgns ἐποίησεν) a very deep trench (δεξαμενὴν ... βαθυτάτην)[1171]". In parallel with 18,33a Josephus now recounts Elijah's preparing of the altar: "next he placed the faggots" (συνθεὶς τὰς σχίζας)[1172] on the altar (ἐπὶ τοῦ βωμοῦ, 3 Rgns ἐπὶ τὸ θυσιαστήριον)[1173] and upon them (κατ' αὐτῶν, i.e. the "faggots") laid

1168. N (but not N*) suggests inserting the word ἕνα prior to κατὰ here.

1169. Compare MT ("according to the number of the sons of *Jacob*") and 3 Rgns ("according to the number of [+ the twelve, L] tribes of *Israel*") 18,31a. With Josephus' above reference to "the Hebrew people", compare 8,335 where Elijah accuses Ahab of bringing evil "upon the Hebrew people" (τὸν Ἑβραίων λαὸν). Here in 8,341 the phrase clearly designates, not the "Northerners" (its primary referent in 8,335, see above), but the entire twelve-tribe chosen people.

1170. This is Josephus' only use of the above phrase "erect an altar"; compare οἰκοδομεῖ... θυσιαστήριον used of Jeroboam in 8,230, cf. also βωμοὺς ἀνιστὰς in 8,265. Josephus' word for "altar" here in 8,341 is the same found in 3 Rgns 18,32αβ where, however, the reference is to Elijah's restoring the ruined "altar" (= MT 1 Kings 18,30b), not the "building" of a new "altar" with the twelve stones as cited in MT 18,32αα (3 Rgns' version of this notice reads simply "he built the stones"). Thus with his specification that Elijah used the stones to erect "an [new] altar", Josephus aligns himself with MT's wording in 18,32αα as against that of 3 Rgns (note that with L* [19/b' 108/b excepted] Josephus has no equivalent to the [self-evident] indication of MT B 18,32αα that Elijah "built [the altar] *in the name of the Lord*").

1171. Josephus' adjective "very deep" above replaces the specification "as great as could contain two measures of seed" used in reference to Elijah's "trench" in 18,32b. Elsewhere Josephus uses the noun δεξαμενή in *BJ* 5,157.181 ("deep canals"); 7,176; *AJ* 2,259. The term is his equivalent for MT's תְּעָלָה which in L is transliterated as θααλὰ/θαλαά and translated by B with θάλασσαν.

1172. 3 Rgns 18,33 contains a double mention of this operation, i.e. in v. 33αα (ἐστοίβασεν [so B, L ἐπέθηκε] τὰς σχίδακας (= MT) and v. 33ba (ἐπέθηκεν τὰς σχίδακας, no MT parallel). Like MT 18,33 Josephus mentions Elijah's operation with the faggots only once.

Josephus uses σχίζα elsewhere in *AJ* 1,228 (Abraham lays "cleft wood" on the altar [ὁ βωμὸς, see 8,341] which had been prepared for the sacrifice of Isaac); 3,227 ("the altar [τὸν βωμὸν, see 8,341]... already laden with wood").

1173. Compare θυσιαστήριον in 8,341a where Josephus speaks of the erecting of this altar (the same variation in terms for "altar" occurs also in 8,230, see above). 3 Rgns employs one and the same term, i.e. θυσιαστήριον in its references to Elijah's altar throughout 18,32-38.

In his above specification that Elijah placed the wood "on the altar" Josephus goes together with 3 Rgns against MT 1 Kings 18,33 which lacks that specification.

(ἐπιθείς, 3 Rgns 18,33bα ἐπέθηκεν) the victims (τὰ ἱερεῖα)[1174]". In thus confining himself to two actions by the prophet (arranging the wood, placing the parts of the victim upon the wood), Josephus leaves aside the (self-evident) intervening action cited in 1 Kings 18,33αβ, i.e. "(Elijah) cut the bull (so MT, 3 Rgns τὸ ὁλοκαύτωμα) in pieces".

Josephus next presents his parallel to 1 Kings 18,34a, the (initial) "wetting down" of the sacrifice: "he ordered (προσέταξε) (the people to take) four jars (τέσσαρας... ὑδρίας, so B 3 Rgns 18,34 [= MT]; L 'two') filled with water (πληρωθείσας[1175] ὕδατος, compare MT מים ...מלאו, B "take [λάβετε] for me four jars of water") *from the fountain* (ἀπὸ τῆς κρήνης)[1176] and pour (κατασκεδάσαι, B ἐπιχέετε)[1177] over the altar (τοῦ θυσιαστηρίου)[1178]".

In 1 Kings 18,34b Elijah causes the "watering process" to be repeated twice more. Josephus omits this repetitive item, proceeding immediately (// 18,35) to the effects of that process: "so that the water (αὐτὸ) overflowed (ὑπερβαλεῖν) and the *whole*[1179] trench (δεξαμενὴν, MT התעלה [cf. L τὴν θαλαά], B τὴν θάλασσαν)[1180] was filled (γεμισθῆναι, B ἔπλησαν)[1181] [with water] (ὕδατος = 3 Rgns)[1182] *as though from a welling spring* (ὡς πηγῆς[1183] ἀναδοθείσης)[1184]".

In 1 Kings 18,36-37, Elijah, the preparations enumerated in 18,34-35 completed, turns to invocation of God. Josephus (8,343) reproduces the wording of the prophet's rather extended prayer[1185] in much shortened

---

1174. This is Josephus' only use of the above phrase "lay victims".

1175. The sequence ὑδρίας προσέταξε πληρωθείσας read by NaMar in 8,341b follows MSPE Lat. NN* read the RO variant ἐκέλευσεν ὑδρίας.

1176. This item has no equivalent in 1 Kings 18,34, although cf. the mention of the "brook (3 Rgns χειμάρρουν) Kishon" in 18,40. With the insertion of the item here Josephus anticipates a possible reader query, i.e. where did Elijah's hearers obtain the water he directs them to bring, especially given the prevailing drought?

1177. The verb κατασκεδάννυμι is hapax in Josephus.

1178. Note the shift back here to the term originally employed to designate Elijah's "altar" in 8,341 after the βωμοῦ in what immediately precedes. Josephus' indication that the water is to be poured "on the altar" is a compression of the notice of 18,34αβ where Elijah directs that it be poured "(L + "on the altar") on the burnt offering and on the wood". Note further that, like MT and L, Josephus has no equivalent to the B plus at the end of 18,34αβ, i.e. "and they did so".

1179. This specification is peculiar to Josephus.

1180. See n. 1171.

1181. Josephus uses γεμίζω also in *AJ* 2,303; 6,113; 8,118.

1182. Josephus' formulation above is a compression of the wording of 18,35 "and the water ran round about the altar, and filled the trench also with water".

1183. Thus the conjecture of NN*, followed by WMarSc. Na adopts the simple πηγῆς of codd.

1184. Compare *BJ* 7,278 πηγὴν ἀναδιδόντος. Like the previous reference to "the spring" (τῆς κρήνης) this item has, as such, no equivalent in the Biblical text of which it represents a simple (and rather obvious) *Ausmalung*.

1185. 3 Rgns 18,36-37 exhibits a number of plusses, see BHS.

form: "having done these things[1186], he began to pray to God (εὔχεσθαι τῷ θεῷ)[1187] and entreat Him (καὶ παρακαλεῖν αὐτὸν)[1188] to
manifest (ποιεῖν... φανερὰν)[1189] His power (δύναμιν)[1190] to the
people (λαῷ) which had now for so long a time been in error (πεπλανημένῳ, see 8,253.260)[1191]".

1 Kings 18,38 narrates the divine response to Elijah's appeal. Once
again, MT and LXX diverge – at least as far as the order of events is
concerned. The former reads "the fire... consumed the burned offering,
and the wood, and the stones, and the dust, and licked up the water
that was in the trench", whereas 3 Rgns' sequence runs "the fire...
consumed the burnt offering and the wood and the water in the trench
and the stones, and the fire licked up the dust". Josephus, here again,

1186. This transitional phrase is Josephus' (vague) parallel to the opening chronological indication in MT 18,36 (> 3 Rgns) "and at the time of the offering of the
oblation". Recall that this same chronological notice stands prior to the narration of
Elijah's measures (18,30-35) in 18,29 (// 8,340). Supposing he knew the MT plus in 18,36,
Josephus may have reflected that Elijah's previous measures would put us now at a
moment long after that specified in 18,29 and so modified the wording of the former
passage as he does.

1187. Compare the opening reference to Elijah's "prayer" in MT ("... Elijah... came
near and said, 'O Lord, God...'") and 3 Rgns ("Elijah cried out to heaven and said, 'O
Lord, God...'").

With Josephus' verbal form εὔχεσθαι here, compare the nominal form εὐχῆς used of
the prophets' "prayer" in 8,339. Josephus' other uses of the above phrase "pray
to (the) God" are *AJ* 1,245 (6,184); 7,203 (290.357); 8,124; (9,8).57; 10,18.255;
11,17.31.119(12,285).314; 13,13; 14,22.28, cf. 18,211 ("the gods").

1188. The text here is problematic. Na follows the codd in reading καλεῖν αὐτὸν καὶ.
N proposes παρακαλεῖν αὐτὸν and then, with reference to Lat "(clamare) ut faceret",
either to omit the following καὶ of the codd or to suppose that something has fallen out of
the Greek text. N*, prints the codd's καλεῖν, preceded by an * indicating a lacuna.

1189. The above construction "make manifest" occurs also in *BJ* 2,300; *AJ* 1,65;
2,41.160.238; 3,73; 4,48.216; 5,213; 6,91.268; 7,222.294.307; 8,155.170.174.415; 9,53;
10,56.203; 11,203.207.253; 12,109.189.204.379.403; 13,283.347; 15,145; *Vita* 290; *Ap*
1,1.5.58.

1190. Compare 8,338 where Elijah asks "that a test be made of the respective powers
(ἰσχύος) of the foreign gods and his own". Cf. also *AJ* 9,55 (// 2 Kings 6,17a) where
Elisha appeals to God "to reveal (ἐμφανίσαι) His power (δύναμιν) and presence
(παρουσίαν)" to the Syrian army.

1191. With the above summation of the content of Elijah's prayer compare the
prophet's words as cited in 18,37 (MT): "Answer me, O Lord,... that this people (3 Rgns
λαός) may know that thou, O Lord art God, and thou hast turned (הסבת, B ἔστρεψας)
their heart back (3 Rgns 'the heart of this people after you')". Conceivably, Josephus'
allusion to the people's "having been in error" above is a reminiscence of the concluding
mention in 18,37 (MT) of "God's having turned the people's hearts back" understood *in
malam partem* (on this understanding of the Biblical phrase, see J.A. MONTGOMERY and
H.S. GEHMAN, *Kings* (ICC), Edinburgh, 1951, p. 305. Note too TJ's rendering of 1 Kings
18,37 "Receive my prayer, Lord, with the fire; receive my prayer, Lord with rain; and
may this people know by your doing for them the signs that you, Lord, are God, and by
your loving them you are asking from them by your Memra to bring them back to fear of
you. *And they gave you a divided heart*". See also the Rabbinic interpretations of 1 Kings
18,37b cited in GINZBERG, *Legends*, VI, p. 320, n. 18.

goes his own way with respect to both of these formulations: "And, *as he said this*[1192], suddenly, in the sight of the multitude (τοῦ πλήθους ὁρῶντος)[1193], fire fell from heaven (πῦρ ἐξ οὐρανοῦ... ἔπεσε)[1194] [on the altar] (ἐπὶ τὸν βωμόν, compare ἐπὶ τοῦ βωμοῦ, 8,341)[1195] and consumed (ἐδαπάνησεν, 3 Rgns κατέφαγεν) the sacrifice (θυσίαν [see 8,340], B 3 Rgns τὰ ὁλοκαυτώματα)[1196], so that even the water went up in steam (ἀνακαῆναι)[1197], and the ground (τὸν τόπον)[1198] became completely dry (ψαφαρόν)[1199]".

1 Kings 18,39 depicts the people's response to God's intervention: they see (> 3 Rgns), fall on their faces, and twice confess that the Lord is (3 Rgns + "truly") God. Josephus (8,343a), in contrast to his procedure with 18,38, expatiates on this notice: "when the Israelites (18,39 'all the people'; compare 8,335.341, 'the people of the Hebrews') saw (ἰδόντες)[1200] (this), they fell (ἔπεσον, 3 Rgns ἔπεσεν) upon the

1192. This transitional phrase, insisting on the immediacy of God's response, is peculiar to Josephus.

1193. Josephus anticipates this item from the MT plus at the start of 1 Kings 18,39 "when all the people *saw it*...".

1194. Compare MT "and fire of the Lord fell" and 3 Rgns καὶ ἔπεσεν πῦρ παρὰ κυρίου ἐκ τοῦ οὐρανοῦ. Josephus' formulation has in common with the 3 Rgns plus in 18,38 its reference to "heaven" as the source of the fire; in contrast to both MT and 3 Rgns, it does not explicitly mention "the Lord" as the one sending the fire.

With the above phrase "fire from heaven" compare *BJ* 4,484 where Josephus designates the conflagration which destroyed the cities of the plain as τοῦ θείου πυρός.

1195. Note Josephus' continued alternation between the two words for altar, θυσιαστήριον and βωμός. 1 Kings (3 Rgns) 18,38 does not mention the "altar" as such.

1196. With the above rendering ("fire fell from heaven on the altar and consumed the sacrifice"), compare those of Mar and W from both of which something seems to have fallen out. The former renders "fire fell from heaven and consumed the altar", leaving out of account the phrase τὴν θυσίαν, while the latter's "une flamme s'abattit du ciel... et dévora la victime" makes no reference to the "altar" on which the fire falls.

The above phrase "consume sacrifice(s)" recurs in *AJ* 4,75. With the whole above formulation ("... suddenly, in the sight of the multitude, fire fell from heaven on the altar and consumed the sacrifice"), compare *AJ* 3,207 (// Lev 9,24) "when the victims were laid upon the altar, of a sudden (αἰφνίδιον) a fire (πῦρ) blazed up therefrom spontaneously and, like a flash of lightening before their eyes (ὁρώμενον), consumed (ἐδαπάνα) everything on the altar (ἐπὶ τοῦ βωμοῦ)" and 8,118 (// 2 Chron 7,1) "... a fire (πῦρ) darted out of the air and, in the sight of all the people (πάντων ὁρώντων), leaped upon the altar (ἐπὶ τὸν βωμόν), and seizing on the sacrifice (θυσίαν), consumed it all (κατεδαίσατο)". Thus, God's "consumption" of Elijah's sacrifice as described here in 8,342 puts one in mind of his earlier responses to those of Moses and Solomon.

1197. In 1 Kings 18,38 the reference is to the fire's "consuming (3 Rgns κατέφαγεν) the water". Josephus' wording is more specific.

1198. In 1 Kings 18,38 the fire consumes "the dust" (3 Rgns τὸν χοῦν).

1199. Elsewhere Josephus uses this adjective in *AJ* 3,1.9. In the above enumeration of the objects engulfed by the heavenly fire, Josephus passes over two items cited explicitly by both MT and 3 Rgns 18,38, i.e. "the wood" and "the stones", substituting for these the more comprehensive term "altar".

1200. This reference to the people's "seeing" corresponds to the MT plus at the start of 18,39 (recall that Josephus has already anticipated this item in relating the coming

earth (ἐπὶ τὴν γῆν)[1201] and worshipped (προσεκύνουν)[1202] (the) one God (ἕνα θεὸν)[1203], whom they acknowledged (ἀποκαλοῦντες) as the Almighty (μέγιστον, see 8,319) and only true (ἀληθῆ [compare the 3 Rgns plus ἀληθῶς in 18,39) μόνον [see 8,335.336]) (God)[1204], while the others (ἄλλους) were mere names invented (ὀνόματα... πεποιημένα)[1205] by unworthy (φαύλης)[1206] and senseless (ἀνοήτου, see 8,264)[1207] opinion (δόξης, see δόξαις, 8,337)[1208]".

1 Kings 18,40 rounds off the episode by relating the end of Elijah's opponents: at his command (v. 40a) the people seize the prophets of Baal (v. 40bα) whereupon *Elijah* brings them down to the brook Kishon and butchers them there (v.40bβ) . Josephus compresses command and execution into a single sequence: "then they seized (συλλαβόντες, 3 Rgns συνέλαβον) their (i.e. the 'other gods', 18,40 'the prophets of Baal') prophets and killed (ἀπέκτειναν, 3 Rgns ἔσφαξεν)[1209] them at Elijah's behest (τοῦτο[1210] παραινέσαντος)".

down of the fire; Josephus thus goes beyond the Bible in his emphasis on the public character of the divine response to Elijah's sacrifice and prayer).

1201. Thus MSPEZon followed by N*NaMar. RO has ἐπὶ τῆς γῆς. Elsewhere Josephus uses the above phrase "fall upon the earth" in *AJ* 3,310; 6,334; 7,381. In 1 Kings (3 Rgns) 18,39 the people "fall on their faces".

1202. Elsewhere Josephus collocates the phrases "fall on the ground" and "worship" in *AJ* 6,334 (Saul before Samuel) and 7,381 (the people before God). Cf. too the people's response to the divine "consumption" of Solomon's sacrifices (8,118, see n. 1196) in 8,119 προσεκύνει πεσὼν ἐπὶ τοὔδαφος.

1203. Compare 8,335.336 with their (non-Biblical) emphasis on the unicity of God.

1204. With the above construction, compare *AJ* 7,380 (David) "addressing (ἀποκαλῶν) Him (God) as father and source of the universe...".

1205. Thus the reading of MSP followed by NaMar. NN* read ὀνόματι... πεποιημένους with RO.

1206. This adjective occurs 29 × in Josephus.

1207. This is Josephus' only collocation of the above adjectives.

1208. With the above concluding addition to the wording of 18,39 Josephus balances the people's previous "positive" confession with a "negative" one directed against the other gods, just as throughout the pericope he plays off the "one true (nature of) God" against the foreign other gods.

1209. In contrast to 1 Kings (3 Rgns) 18,40 Josephus here makes the people rather than Elijah himself the one to butcher the prophets. According to BETZ, *Problem*, p. 33, cf. *Miracles*, pp. 219-220, the fact that Josephus does not attribute the massacre to Elijah himself is indicative of an anti-Zealot posture, evidenced also elsewhere in his rewriting of the material on Elijah, the Zealot hero (compare *AJ* 6,155 where, in contrast to 1 Sam 15,33 ["Samuel hewed Agag in pieces before the Lord"], Josephus refers to the prophet's "ordering Agag to be instantly put to death"). It should, however, be kept in mind that subsequently in 8,347 Josephus will cite Jezebel's hearing that "*Elijah had killed* the prophets" (// 1 Kings 19,1) while in 8,350 (no Biblical parallel) Elijah himself informs God that "*he had killed* the prophets of the strange gods". It is not clear then that Josephus is in fact animated by an "anti-Zealot" *Tendenz* in his rewriting of 1 Kings 18,40 (which itself can, of course, be understood in a causative sense, i.e. Elijah made the people kill the prophets). In this connection note too that in *AJ* 4,152-154 Josephus does follow Num 25,6-14 in its laudatory account of the execution of the renegade Zimri and his paramour

3) *Sequel: The Rain* (8,343b-346). 1 Kings 18,41-46 narrates the sequel to Elijah's Carmel triumph, i.e. the coming of the rain which the prophet had been 'sent by God to announce (18,1 // 8,328). This new sequence opens in 18,41 with Elijah telling Ahab "go up (3 Rgns ἀνάβηθι), eat and drink, for there is the sound of the rushing (3 Rgns feet) of the rain (3 Rgns ὑετοῦ)". Josephus modifies the Biblical directive in several respects: "he also told the king to go (πορεύεσθαι) to his midday meal (ἄριστον)[1211] *without further care* (μηδὲν ἔτι φροντίσαντα, cf. 8,274 [Jeroboam] οὐδενὸς τούτων φροντίσας), for *in a little while*[1212] he should see the rain sent by God (τὸν θεὸν ὕοντα, compare μέχρις οὗ ἂν ὕσῃ ὁ θεός, 8,322)[1213]". In 18,42 king and prophet separate: Ahab "goes up (where?) to eat and drink", while Elijah ascends "the summit (ראש > 3 Rgns) of Carmel" where he "bows down" upon the ground with his face between his knees. Josephus (8,344) varies somewhat: "And so Achab departed, while Elijah went up (ἀναβὰς, 3 Rgns ἀνέβη) to the summit (ἀκρωτήριον, see MT)[1214] of Mount Carmel (Καρμηλίου[1215], 3 Rgns Κάρμηλον) and, sitting (καθίσας, 3 Rgns ἔκυψεν) on the ground (ἐπὶ τῆς γῆς, 3 Rgns ἐπὶ τὴν γῆν), leaned (προσηρείσατο[1216], 3 Rgns ἔθηκεν) his head (18,42 'face') upon his knees (τοῖς γόνασι, B ἀνὰ μέσον τῶν γονάτων ἑαυτοῦ)".

Elijah now (18,43a) directs his servant to "go up" and "look out to sea". Josephus renders: "he ordered his servant (θεράποντα, 3 Rgns παιδαρίῳ)[1217] to go up (ἀνελθόντα, 3 Rgns ἀνάβηθι) *to a certain look-*

Cozbi by Phineas, another Zealot hero (although admittedly he does not take over the "Zealot/jealousy" terminology employed of Phineas in Num 25,11.13). On Josephus' version of Numbers 25, see W.C. van Unnik, *Josephus' Account of the Story of Israel's Sin with Alien Women in the Country of Moab (Num. 25:1ff.)*, in M.S. Herma van Voss *et al.* (eds.), *Travels in the World of the Old Testament.* FS M.A. Beek, Assen, 1975, 241-261.

1210. Thus NaMar. NN* omit.

1211. Compare Biblical "go up, eat...". Josephus' formulation eliminates the Bible's reference to an "ascent" by Ahab whose end-point is left unspecified. Mar's rendering of ἄριστον (which can also mean "breakfast", see LSJ, s.v.; W, *ad loc.*, "son repas") by "midday meal" here has in view the previous chronological notice of 8,339 (the prophets cry out "from dawn to midday"). In the Bible it would appear that it is already evening by this point, see 1 Kings 18,29.36.

1212. This temporal specification as to when Ahab may expect the rain has no Biblical equivalent.

1213. Note the explicit reference, unparalleled in 1 Kings 18,41, to the divine source of the coming rain.

1214. Josephus' only other use of this term is in *AJ* 9,124 where it denotes the "extremities" of Jezebel's body.

1215. Thus NN*NaMar. OMSPE read Καρμήλου.

1216. The verb προσερείδω is hapax in Josephus.

1217. On Josephus' use of the term θεράπων, see Gibbs-Feldman, *Vocabulary*, pp. 293-294.

out (ἐπί τινα σκοπὴν)¹²¹⁸ and gaze (ἀποβλέπειν, 3 Rgns ἐπίβλεψον) at the sea (εἰς τὴν θάλασσαν, 3 Rgns ὁδὸν [τῆς] θαλάσσης)". To this rendition of 18,43a he adds a rationale for the prophet's injunction inspired by what follows: "and if he (the servant) saw a cloud rising in any direction (cf. 18,44 [MT] 'a cloud... rising out of the sea') to tell him of it, for until now the sky had been clear (καθαρῷ... τῷ ἀέρι)¹²¹⁹". Next, 1 Kings 18,43b reports the sequel to Elijah's initial directive: "and he (3 Rgns the lad) went up (> 3 Rgns) and looked. And he said, 'There is nothing.' And he (3 Rgns Elijah) said (+ and you, B) 'go again (+ and look, L) seven times (+ and return seven times, B).' (+ and the lad returned seven times, 3 Rgns)". In this instance, Josephus follows the more expansive 3 Rgns version, even while compressing it: "so (the servant) went up (ἀναβάντος) and several times (πολλάκις, L 3 Rgns ἑπτάκις) informed him that he saw nothing". In 1 Kings 18,44a the servant on his seventh look reports "a little cloud, like a man's palm (or footprint, MT כף, 3 Rgns ἴχνος, TJ 'palm of the hand' [כפסת יד]) rising out (L 3 Rgns bringing water from) of the sea". Josephus' version of this item runs: "but after the seventh time (ἕβδομον ἤδη, 3 Rgns ἐν τῷ ἑβδόμῳ) he came and told him that he had seen a spot of blackness (μελαινόμενον) in the sky (τοῦ ἀέρος) no larger (οὐ πλέον, 3 Rgns μικρὰ ὡς) than a man's footprint (ἴχνους ἀνθρωπίνου, 3 Rgns ἴχνος ἀνδρὸς)". In 18,44b Elijah tells the servant to "go up" (where?, see the references to Ahab's "going up" in 18,41-42) and tell Ahab to "make ready" (+ "your chariot", 3 Rgns) and "descend" (whither?). Josephus elaborates: "when Elijah heard this, he sent (πέμπει, whom?)¹²²⁰ to Achab (where is he?), bidding (κελεύων)¹²²¹ him go back (ἀπέρχεσθαι, 3 Rgns κατάβηθι) *to the city*¹²²² before the rain should pour down in torrents (πρὶν ἢ καταρραγῆναι τὸν ὄμβρον, 3 Rgns μὴ καταλάβῃ σε ὁ ὑετός)"¹²²³. 1 Kings 18,45 relates first the start of the rain and then that Ahab rode (וירכב, 3 Rgns "he wept", ἔκλαιεν)¹²²⁴ and went to Jezreel (L* Ἰεζραήλ, B Ἰσραήλ).

1218. With this addition, Josephus specifies where it is that the servant is to "go up". The expression "a certain look-out" occurs also in *AJ* 3,22, cf. 3,36 (and the variant in 19,329).

1219. The above expression "clear air (sky)" occurs also in *AJ* 3,83;6,229. With this addition, Josephus underscores the prophet's foreknowledge; compare 8,326 where he has Elijah affirm – as the Bible does not- that he would restore the woman's son to her alive.

1220. Josephus uses the h.p. of πέμπω as here over 130× (6× in 8,212-420: 8,345.347.358.360.367.375).

1221. With Elijah as subject κελεύω is a *Leitwort* of Josephus' version of the Carmel episode and its sequel, see 8,331.334.336.339 (*bis*).340.345. By means of the term Josephus underscores Elijah's authoritative status.

1222. Josephus introduces this specification concerning Ahab's appointed destination with the references to "Jezreel" in 18,45b-46 in view.

1223. This is Josephus' only usage of the above phrase "pour down rain".

1224. On the 3 Rgns reading here, see D.W. GOODING, *Ahab according to the Septuagint*, in *ZAW* 76 (1964) 269-289, p. 272.

Josephus reverses this sequence: "So the king went (παραγίνεται) to the city of Jezarēla ('Ιεζάρηλαν)[1225], and not long after (μετ' οὐ πολύ, 3 Rgns καὶ ἐγένετο ἕως ὧδε καὶ ὧδε) the sky (τοῦ ἀέρος, 3 Rgns ὁ οὐρανὸς) was darkened (ἀχλύσαντος, 3 Rgns συνεσκότασεν)[1226] and overcast (καλυφθέντος) with clouds (νέφεσι, 3 Rgns [ἐν] νεφέλαις)[1227], a violent (λάβρον) wind (πνεῦμα, 3 Rgns πνεύματι)[1228] (came up) and a heavy rain (πολὺς ὄμβρος [see 8,345], 3 Rgns [ὁ] ὑετὸς μέγας)[1229] fell (ἐπιγίνεται, 3 Rgns ἐγένετο)[1230]". In line with 18,46 he concludes the episode with mention of Elijah's accompanying Ahab to Jezreel: "and the prophet, who was filled with spirit of God (ἔνθεος γενόμενος, 18,46 "hand of the Lord")[1231], ran (συνέδραμε, 3 Rgns ἔτρεχεν)[1232] beside the chariot (τῷ... ἅρματι) of the king[1233] as far as (μέχρι, B εἰς, L ἕως) as the city of Jezarēla ('Ιεζαρήλας)[1234]".

Summary: MT 1 Kings and 3 Rgns 18 evidence numerous differences. In instances of such divergence Josephus' version aligns itself, now with one witness, now the other. With 3 Rgns (and against MT) he has in common, e.g., his reference to Ahab's house abandoning the Lord

1225. Thus the conjecture of Mar (compare L* 'Ιεζραήλ) who refers to 8,355 where this form of the city's name (in the genitive) occurs. N reads 'Ιερέζηλα with RO (N* prints rather 'Ιεζάρηλα) a form which SCHLATTER, *Namen*, p. 61, s.v. זְרְעֶאל (similarly SCHALIT, *Namenwörterbuch*, p. 58, s.v. 'Ιεζάρηλα) regards as a corruption of the original 'Ιεζέρελα as found in 8,407 etc. Finally Na follows Hud in reading 'Ιεσράηλαν, while W opts for the 'Ιεσράηλ of MSP.

1226. Josephus' only other use of the verb ἀχλύω is 3,203 ("darkness descended" over the tabernacle).

1227. The above expression "overcast with clouds" occurs only here in Josephus.

1228. This is Josephus' only use of the phrase "violent wind".

1229. The above phrase "much rain" recurs in *AJ* 13,237.

1230. Josephus uses the above expression "rain falls" also in *AJ* 5,205.

1231. Josephus uses the term ἔνθε(ε)ος 6× elsewhere: *BJ* 3,353 (of Josephus himself); 4,33 (Vespasian).388 ("an ancient saying of inspired men"); *AJ* 6,56 (// 1 Sam 10,6 "the spirit of the Lord is to come upon" Saul).76 (// 1 Sam 11,6 "the spirit of God came upon Saul); 9,35 (// 2 Kings 3,15 'the hand of the Lord comes upon' Elisha; here Josephus makes the same substitution as in his rewriting of 1 Kings 18,46 in 8,346). In all these instances, *BJ* 4,388 excepted, one finds the same construction as in 8,346, i.e. ἔνθεος + γίνομαι. The term ἔνθεος does not occur in LXX, but is used in profane Greek, see the phrase ἔνθεος γίνομαι in, e.g., Plato, *Ion* 534 B; *RA*, 2.48.1. On Josephus' use of the term "inspired", see SCHLATTER, *Theologie*, p. 60; HOLLADAY, *Theios Aner*, p. 65. Finally, note that also TJ replaces MT (and 3 Rgns)'s reference to "the hand of the Lord" in 18,46, i.e. with the phrase "a spirit of power from before the Lord".

1232. Josephus omits 18,46bα's reference to Elijah's "girding his loins".

1233. In 1 Kings 18,46bβ Elijah runs "before (3 Rgns ἔμπροσθεν) Ahab". Presumably, Josephus derives his reference to the king's "chariot" from the 3 Rgns plus in 18,44 ("[make ready] your chariot"), see above.

1234. Once again the name of the city raises text-critical difficulties. MSP give the double form 'Ισραήλας Άζάρου. Editors generally omit the latter element while reading the first in line with the form adopted by them for the initial mention of the city in 8,346, thus: N ('Ιερέζηλας), N*Mar ('Ιεζαρήλας), Na ('Ιεσαραήλας), W (Yesraēl).

himself (8,335, see 18,18), Elijah's allusion to the 400 "prophets of the groves" in his word to the people (8,338, see 18,22), mention of Elijah's injunction to the false prophets to withdraw (8,340, see 18,29), and his speaking of a single altar (re-)built by Elijah (8,341, see 18,30-32). On the other hand, he goes together with MT (against 3 Rgns) for the taunt about the rival deity "being on a journey" (8,339, see 18,27), the people's "seeing" the heavenly fire (8,342, see 18,39) and Elijah's ascending "the summit" of Carmel (8,344, see 18,42). On still other occasions, he follows a reading shared by L and MT against B, e.g.: Obadiah's reference to Ahab's not being able to "find" Elijah (8,334, see 18,12); the designation of the prophets' victim as an "ox" rather than a "(male) calf" (8,339, see 18,25); the prophets' use of "swords" (8,340, see 18,28) to wound themselves "according to custom" (8,340, see 18,28). In addition, his account evidences affinities with distinctive L readings: the name Ἠλίας and the reference to the "caves" in which Obadiah conceals the prophets (8,330, see 1 Kings 18,4.13). Finally, there exist several (negative) points of contact between Josephus and TJ for this chapter: both, e.g., avoid MT and 3 Rgns's statement that Elijah's opponents "prophesied" (see 18,30), just as both employ a substitution for the reference in 18,46 (MT and 3 Rgns) to the operation of the "hand of the Lord" upon Elijah.

Josephus' rewriting of 1 Kings 18 evidences a multitude of more or less minor omissions (see e.g., the second and third pourings of water on the altar, 18,34b), additions (e.g., the interjected references to the effects of the famine which prepare Ahab's directives to Obadiah in 8,328), as well as rearrangements (e.g., mention of Obadiah's good deeds only subsequent to Ahab's injunctions to him, 8,330, compare 18,3b-4). His consistent avoidance of the source's proper name "Baal" (cited by him earlier on in 8,318) in favor, e.g., of "foreign gods" is noteworthy. Thereby, the Carmel contest takes on a more general character wherein the people come to the realization that there is only "one true God", the others being "mere names invented by unworthy and senseless opinion" (8,343). In other words, in Josephus' version the story assumes an explicitly universalistic and monotheistic dimension lacking in the narrative of 1 Kings 18 itself[1235].

1235. A similar phenomenon is observable in Josephus' reworking of the story of Israel's sin with the alien women of Numbers 25 in AJ 4,126-155. As noted by VAN UNNIK, Account, p. 26, Josephus' version omits mention of "Baal of Peor" as the deity with which Israel "yoked" itself (see Num 25,3.5), speaking rather of the people "accepting the belief in the plurality of gods (θεούς... πλείονας)", 4,139. Thereby, as van Unnik (ibid.) remarks: "he (Josephus) took away a certain 'dating' of the story and gave it a more general character". The two stories further have in common the fact that both end with the idolatrous opponents being "killed" (ἀποκτείν), see 4,153 and 8,343.

Also to be noted is that Josephus makes no attempt to eliminate or
play down the miraculous fire from heaven of 18,38 (see 8,342). Here
again (see the previous section), it becomes clear that one canot speak
of a consistent "rationalizing" tendency in the historian's approach to
Biblical miracles[1236].

1236. On the other hand, Josephus does not embellish the Biblical episode with all
manner of additional "miracles" as does Rabbinic tradition, on which see GINZBERG,
Legends, IV, pp. 197-199 and VI, pp. 319-321, nn. 14-21.

XIV

ELIJAH AT SINAI
(8,347-354)

The story of 1 Kings 19 revolves around Elijah's encounter with the Lord at Horeb. It may be divided into the following three segments: 1) 19,1-8 (journey to Horeb); 2) 19,9-18 (Horeb revelation); and 3) 19,19-21 (sequel: the call of Elisha). I shall use these same three divisions for my analysis of Josephus' version.

1. *Elijah's Journey* (8,347-349). In 1 Kings 19,1 Ahab sets matters in motion by informing Jezebel of "all that Elijah had done and how he had slain all (> 3 Rgns) the prophets" (see 18,40). In Josephus (8,347) Jezebel[1237] simply "learns" of the "signs given (σημεῖα ... γενόμενα, see 8,232) by Elijah and that he had killed (ἀπέκτεινεν)[1238] their (Ahab's and Jezebel's, compare 8,336 "his (Ahab's) prophets and those of his wife") prophets" – from whom is not stated. 1 Kings 19,2 recounts Jezebel's reaction to what she is told. Josephus modifies this notice in several respects, eliminating, e.g., the queen's opening "oath formula" (["if you are Elijah and I am Jezebel, > MT] so may the gods [B God] do to me, and more also..."), while introducing a reference to her emotional state: *she was filled with anger* (ὀργισθεῖσα)[1239] and sent (πέμπει [see the same h.p. in 8,345], 3 Rgns ἀπέστειλεν) messengers (ἀγγέλους)[1240] to him, threatening (ἀπειλοῦσα) to kill (ἀποκτείνειν, see ἀπέκτεινεν, 8,347a) him by their hands (δι' αὐτῶν)[1241] just as he had destroyed (ἀπολέσειε)[1242] her[1243] own prophets".

1237. Like B, but against MT and L, he qualifies her here as "wife" (γυνὴ) of Ahab.

1238. Compare 8,343 where it is the people who "kill" (ἀπέκτειναν) the prophets at Elijah's behest. On this "discrepancy" between 8,347 and 343, see n. 1209. (Note, however, that here in 8,347 RO do read the plural "they killed" in line with 8,343).

1239. Compare Josephus' qualification of Ahab's emotional state when confronting Elijah in 8,335: μετ' ὀργῆς.

1240. 1 Kings 19,2 reads "a messenger"; 3 Rgns lacks an equivalent.

1241. Mar, *Josephus*, V, pp. 758-759, n. d points out that the above specification that Jezebel's "messengers" would themselves kill Elijah lacks an explicit Biblical warrant. As he also notes, however, the above phrase might also be rendered "threatening *through them* to kill him". So understood it would correspond to the Biblical formulation.

1242. Note that here again (see n. 1238) Elijah is said to have put the prophets to death personally.

1243. Compare 8,347a where the prophets are designated as "their", i.e. those of Ahab and Jezebel.

1 Kings 19,3-4aα relates Elijah's initial response to Jezebel's threat: in his fear (so 3 Rgns καὶ ἐφοβήθη = Hebrew וַיִּרָא; MT vocalizes וַיַּרְא, "he saw") the prophet betakes himself to Beersheba "of Judah" where he leaves his servant, himself pushing on into the wilderness. Josephus' formulation expatiates on the source's geographical indications: in fear of this (φοβηθεὶς, see 3 Rgns) Elijah fled (φεύγει, 3 Rgns ἔρχεται)[1244] to the city called Bersūbee (Βερσουβεὲ)[1245] – *it is the furthest city in that part of the territory of the tribe* of Judah (τῆς χώρας... τῆς Ἰούδα φυλῆς, Β γῆν Ἰούδα) *which borders on the country of the Idumaeans*[1246] – and after leaving (καταλιπὼν, 3 Rgns ἀφῆκεν) his servant (θεράποντα, 3 Rgns παιδάριον)[1247] there, he withdrew (ἀνεχώρησεν, 3 Rgns ἐπορεύθη) into the desert (εἰς τὴν ἔρημον, 3 Rgns ἐν τῇ ἐρήμῳ)[1248]". In parallel to 19,4b he next recounts Elijah's prayer for death, embellishing the Biblical prophet's statement about being "no better than" his forbears: "he prayed (εὐξάμενος, see εὔχεσθαι, 8,342) that he might die (ἀποθανεῖν, so 3 Rgns)[1249], saying that he was no better than his fathers (οὐ γὰρ δὴ κρείττων εἶναι τῶν πατέρων, Β ὅτι οὐ κρείσσων ἐγώ εἰμι ὑπὲρ τοὺς πατέρας μου) *that he should long for life* (ζῆν γλίχηται)[1250] *when they were gone*". Thereafter, in accordance with 19,5a, he has Elijah lay down to sleep (κατεκοιμήθη[1251], 3 Rgns ἐκοιμήθη) under a certain tree (πρός τινι δένδρῳ)[1252]".

At this point in the Biblical account, there occurs (19,5b-8a, MT and B) a sequence in which Elijah twice receives (angelic) instructions to eat and drink what is offered him and does as directed. Josephus, in line with the L MSS 82/o93/c₂127/e₂ which lack vv. 6bβ-8aα, compresses this double sequence into a single one: "But he was wakened (18,5b

1244. Josephus uses the above h.p. of φεύγω a total of 30 ×. The full construction of 8,348, "flees to (a) city" recurs in *AJ* 5,246, cf. 7,126 (with the imperfect).

1245. Josephus mentions this southern site also in *AJ* 1,212; 6,32; 9,157. See SCHLATTER, *Namen*, p. 23, s.v. בְּאֵר שֶׁבַע and SCHALIT, *Namenwörterbuch*, p. 29, s.v. Βηρσουβαί for a list of the numerous variant readings found in the codd.

1246. Only here does Josephus associate "Beersheba" with "Idumea" (= Hebrew "Edom"), see *AJ* 2,3.

1247. The same difference in their respective terms for "servant" occurs also in *AJ* 8,344 and 3 Rgns 18,43, see above.

1248. Josephus leaves aside 19,4's specification that Elijah advanced "a day's journey" into the desert.

1249. In 19,4b Elijah's prayer for death is cited twice: first (4bα) in indirect and then (4bβ) in direct discourse. Josephus has an equivalent only to the former.

1250. This phrase occurs only here in Josephus.

1251. Thus MSP followed by NaMar. NN* reads κατακοιμηθεὶς δὲ with RO.

1252. In 1 Kings (3 Rgns) 19 Elijah's positioning himself under a tree is mentioned twice, i.e. in vv. 4aβ and 5a. In both instances MT specifies that the "tree" in question was a "broom tree" (רֹתֶם). In its 4aβ 3 Rgns transliterates ῥαθμέν (B)/ ῥαθαμείν (L), while in 5a it renders (ὑπὸ [τὸ] φυτόν). Josephus avoids the repetition, mentioning Elijah's "tree" only once and designating it indeterminately ("a certain tree") – perhaps because he was unfamiliar with the Biblical name for it.

"touched") by someone (τινος, 3 Rgns 19,5b τις)[1253] and, when he arose (ἀναστὰς, 3 Rgns ἀνέστη), found (εὑρίσκει, 3 Rgns 19,6a ἐπέβλεψεν... καὶ ἰδοὺ) food and water set before him[1254]. So he ate it and, after gathering strength from the food (συλλεξάμενος ἐκ τῆς τροφῆς ἐκείνης τὴν δύναμιν)[1255]...". Leaving aside the specification of 19,8b that Elijah's subsequent journey to "Horeb" took forty days and forty nights, Josephus continues: "he went (παραγίνεται [see 8,346], 3 Rgns ἐπορεύθη) to the mountain (εἰς... τὸ ὄρος, 3 Rgns ἕως ὄρους)[1256] called Sinai (Σιναῖον)[1257] where Moses is said to have received (λαβεῖν) the laws (νόμους) from God (παρὰ τοῦ θεοῦ)[1258]".

2. *Horeb Revelation* (8,350-352). Josephus now gives his version of 18,9a, Elijah's "settlement" on the mountain: "And he found in it a certain (τι) hollow (κοῖλον)[1259] cave (σπήλαιόν [see 8,330], so 3 Rgns)[1260] which he entered (εἴσεισι, 3 Rgns εἰσῆλθεν), and there made his abode (ποιούμενος... μονήν, 3 Rgns κατέλυσεν)[1261] for some time". In 1 Kings 19,9b Elijah is interrogated by a "word of the Lord" as to why he has come to the spot. Following his usual practice, Josephus avoids reference to the divine "word", writing rather: "but a voice (φωνῆς)[1262] (which came) from someone (τινος)[1263], he knew

1253. Here Josephus shares with 3 Rgns 19,5b its vague designation for Elijah's waker as compared with the "angel" (מלאך) of MT. Note, however, that in 18,7 B does reproduce MT's reference to "an angel of the Lord" (L* lacks an equivalent to 18,7, see above). On Josephus' elimination of Biblical references to angels, see n. 296.

1254. The wording of 19,6a is more specific: "there was at his head a cake baked on hot stones and a jar of water".

1255. Compare 3 Rgns 19,8aβ ἐν τῇ ἰσχύι τῆς βρώσεως ἐκείνης. The above phrase "gather strength" occurs also in *BJ* 1,161; *AJ* 13,370; 18,113.

1256. Like B and L* (127/c₂ excepted) Josephus lacks the specification "mountain *of God*" of MT 19,8b.

1257. This is Josephus' substitution for the Biblical designation "Horeb", a name never used by the historian. Conversely, he employs the phrase "(Mount) Sinai" elsewhere in *AJ* 2,283.284.291.323.349; 3,1.62.75.76.95.100.212.222.286.295; 4,43; 8,104; *Ap* 2,25.

1258. The phrase "receive laws from God" in the above expansion concerning the mountain to which Elijah repairs occurs only here in Josephus. Cf., however, *AJ* 3,286;8,104 where, when mentioning "Sinai", Josephus appends a comparable reference to its being the site of divine law-giving. With Josephus' specification concerning the "mountain" here compare TJ "the mountain upon which the glory of the Lord had been revealed...". Cf. also *Meg.* 19b which introduces an explicit connection between the divine revelations to Moses and Elijah with its indication that the two figures stood in the same "cave" (see Exod 33,17ff. and 1 Kings 19,13) for their respective revelations.

1259. The Bible lacks this specification.

1260. Note that both MT and 3 Rgns 19,9a speak of "*the* cave" in contrast to Josephus' indeterminate "a certain cave". Note further that in *BJ* 3,341 Josephus takes refuge in "a cave" (σπήλαιον) whence he emerges to surrender to the Romans. On other parallels between Elijah's and Josephus' own "cave experiences", see below.

1261. The above construction "make one's abode" recurs in *AJ* 13,41, this being the only other use of the term μονή in Josephus.

1262. This is the term used for Elijah's interrogator subsequently in the Biblical account, see 19,13b. Other references to God's "voice" in Josephus are *BJ* 4,626 ("voice

not whom[1264], asked him why *he had left the city*[1265] to come to that spot (τί παρείη... ἐκεῖσε, 3 Rgns τί σὺ ἐνταῦθα)". Josephus likewise significantly reworks the prophet's reply as cited in 19,10. Specifically, he omits the middle section of that reply (v. 10aβbα) in which Elijah enumerates the misdeeds of the Israelites[1266] and designates himself as the only "prophet" left[1267]. Conversely, he transposes Elijah's opening reference to his "zeal" (3 Rgns 19,10aα ζηλῶν ἐζήλωκα)[1268] into a reminiscence of the previous episode: "whereupon he said that it was because he had killed (κτεῖναι)[1269] the prophets of the strange gods (τοὺς προφήτας τῶν ξενικῶν θεῶν)[1270] and had convinced the people (λαὸν) that the only true God (μόνος... θεὸς, see 8,335.337) was the Eternal (ὁ ὤν)[1271], whom they had worshipped from the beginning (ἀπ' ἀρχῆς ἐθρήσκευσαν)[1272]; it was for this reason that he was being sought (ζητεῖσθαι, 3 Rgns ζητοῦσι) for punishment (πρὸς τιμωρίαν) *by the wife of the king*[1273]".

of God", to Josephus [note this additional terminological parallel between the historian's account of Elijah at the mountain and his own self-depiction]); *AJ* 1,185 (Abraham); 2,283 ("voices", Moses); 3,88 ("immortal voice", Moses).90 ("a voice which came from on high", the people at Sinai; 4,43 ("thy [God's] voice", Moses). On these uses, see SCHLATTER, *Theologie*, p. 55; O. BETZ, φωνή κτλ, in *TWNT* 9 (1973) 272-302, esp. p. 284.

1263. Compare 8,349 "(Elijah) was wakened by someone (τινος)".

1264. This is Mar's rendering of the phrase ἐξ ἀδήλου. Compare W, *ad loc.* "mystérieuse", Sc, *ad loc.* שבא ממקום. The phrase appears also in *BJ* 5,46.

1265. Presumably, the referent in this expansion of the Biblical formulation is "Jezaréla", see 8,346.

1266. This enumeration might seem out of line with their "conversion" as described just before in 1 Kings 18,39.

1267. This reference appears to ignore the hundred (Yahwistic) prophets preserved by Obadiah (see 18,4 // 8,330).

1268. BETZ, *Problem*, p. 33; ID., *Miracles*, p. 219 explains Josephus' non-utilization of Elijah's invocation of his "zeal" for the Lord in terms of his own anti-Zealotism, see n. 1209. On the concept of "zeal" in Biblical and post-Biblical Judaism, see M. HENGEL, *Die Zeloten* (AGSU, 1), Leiden, 1961, pp. 150-234.

1269. Elijah's designating himself as the one to have "killed" the prophets here accords with Josephus' formulations in 8,347, but contrasts with that in 8,343, see n. 1238.

1270. Compare Josephus' previous designations for these figures: "false prophets to this god (Baal)" (8,318); "his (Ahab's) prophets and those of his wife" (8,336); "prophets of the groves" (8,336); "their (the other gods') prophets" (8,343); "their (Ahab's and Jezebel's) prophets" (8,347); "her (Jezebel's) own prophets" (8,347).

1271. This phrase is absent in MSPE Lat and has no equivalent in the translation of W, *ad loc*. With the phrase compare LXX Exod 3,14 ἐγώ εἰμι ὁ ὤν (in his paraphrase of this passage in *AJ* 2,276 Josephus states that he "is forbidden to speak" of the name God revealed to Moses; conceivably, the omission of the phrase in the above-cited codd at 8,350 is inspired by this statement). Only here does Josephus employ the designation ὁ ὤν for God. On it, see M. MACNAMARA, *The New Testament and the Palestinian Targum to the Pentateuch* (AnBib, 27), Rome, 1966, p. 103 and F. BÜCHSEL, εἰμί, ὁ ὤν, in *TWNT* 2 (1935) 396-398.

1272. Compare Abijah's reference to his people ἀπ' ἀρχῆς... τὸν ἴδιον θεὸν σεβομένοις, 8,280.

1273. With this last specification, inspired by the notice on Jezebel's initiative of 19,2 (// 8,347), compare 19,10bβ's indeterminate "*they seek* my life to take it away".

1 Kings 19,11a introduces the response to Elijah's reply (19,10) with "and he (God) said". Josephus, who just previously had mentioned a (divine) "voice" addressing Elijah, makes this "and again he heard (ἀκούσας) (a voice telling him)¹²⁷⁴...". In 19,11aβ the prophet is told "go forth and stand on the mountain (3 Rgns + "tomorrow", αὔριον) before the Lord...". Josephus's version of this directive incorporates the chronological plus of 3 Rgns: "(Elijah is told) to come out (προελθεῖν)¹²⁷⁵ into the open air (εἰς τὸ ὕπαιθρον, compare 19,11 'on the mountain before the Lord')¹²⁷⁶ on the morrow (τῇ ἐπιούσῃ)". The historian has no equivalent to MT v. 11aβ's (anthropomorphic) reference to the Lord's "passing by" Elijah at this point (in 3 Rgns this "passage" is something announced for the next day, "the Lord will pass by (παρελεύσεται)", whereas in MT it transpires immediately, "and behold the Lord passed by (עֹבֵר)")¹²⁷⁷. Instead, he provides a motivation for the previous divine command that Elijah come out, i.e. "for so he should learn what he must do", thereby preparing the subsequent directives Elijah will receive (see 19,15-16).

At this juncture, prior to relating the phenomena described in 19,11b-12, Josephus, anticipating 19,13a, introduces the notice that Elijah, as directed, did "come out (προῆλθεν) of the cave the next day". In so doing, he disposes of the anomaly of the Biblical presentation in which the phenomena of vv. 11b-12 seem to transpire without Elijah's being present for this in that it is only subsequently, in v. 13a, that the prophet is said to exit the cave. Thereupon, he presents a very condensed version of the well-known sequence of 19,11b-12 where, after the mighty wind, earthquake, and fire in which Yahweh is each time said "not to be", there follows "a still small voice" (so RSV)¹²⁷⁸. Josephus reduces this four-fold climatic sequence to the following indications: "he heard (ἐπακούει, compare 19,13 "when Elijah heard [3 Rgns ἤκουσεν]) (the earth) rumble (σεισμοῦ, B 3 Rgns συσσεισμός) (see v. 11b) and saw (ὁρᾷ) a brilliant fiery light (λαμπρὰν πυρὸς αὐγὴν, 3 Rgns 19,12a πῦρ)¹²⁷⁹. And when all became quiet (cf. v. 12b)¹²⁸⁰...".

1274. Perhaps, Josephus anticipates this transitional reference to Elijah's "hearing" from 19,13aα "it came to pass when Elijah heard (3 Rgns ἤκουσεν)....".

1275. So NN*NaMar. ROMSE read προσελθεῖν.

1276. With the above construction "come out into the open air", compare *AJ* 6,229 where Jonathan ἐξαγαγὼν αὐτὸν (David) εἰς ὕπαιθρον... ἀέρα.

1277. On the differences between 3 Rgns and MT in 19,11, see J.W. WEVERS, *Exegetical Principles Underlying the Septuagint Text of 1 Kings ii 12-xxi 43*, in *OTS* 8 (1951) 300-322, p. 305.

1278. For an alternative understanding of the Hebrew expression קול דממה דקה, see J. LUST, *A Gentle Breeze or a Roaring Thunderous Sound?*, in *VT* 25 (1975) 110-115. To be noted in any case is that Josephus' rendition does accord with the RSV's understanding of the phrase in question, see below.

1279. With Josephus' sequence here "... rumble... brilliant fiery light", compare *AJ* 9,225 which describes God's smiting Uzziah with leprosy: "a great tremor (σεισμός) smote the earth... and a brilliant (λαμπρὸν) shaft of sunlight gleamed...".

He then picks up the thread of the Biblical narrative with 19,13b where a "voice" (3 Rgns φωνή) addresses Elijah[1281]. In Josephus a "divine voice" (φωνὴ θεία)[1282] speaks to the prophet. Unlike its counterpart in 19,13bβ, that voice does not, however, repeat the question of 19,9b about the reason for Elijah's being there, just as there is no repetition of Elijah's answer to that question, such as one finds in 19,14. Rather, the voice begins with a Biblically unparalleled "exhortation" that Elijah "not be alarmed (ταράττεσθαι, see 8,243.273) by what was happening[1283], for none of his enemies[1284] should have him in their power (κρατήσειν, see 8,229.280.286.296)". Thereafter, Josephus gives his version of the charge to Elijah in 19,15-16[1285]. Reversing the Biblical order in that charge, however, he first has the voice tell Elijah to "appoint (ἀποδεῖξαι)[1286] Jehu ('Ιηοῦν, B Εἰοῦ, L 'Ιοὺ), the son of Nemesaios (Νεμεσαίου, MT Nimsi, B Ναμεσθεὶ, L Ναμεσσεὶ)[1287] to be king of the people (πλήθους, 19,16 'king over Israel')". Only in second place is Elijah then told to designate "Azaēlos" (Ἀζάηλον, MT Hazael, 3 Rgns Ἀζαήλ) as "(king) of Damascus (Δαμασκοῦ)[1288] in Syria (τῶν Σύρων, B τῆς Συρίας)". In accordance with this shift, Elijah is previously instructed to "return to his own land" (ὑποστρέψαντα εἰς

1280. See the comment of W, *Josèphe*, II, p. 232, n. 7 on Josephus' rewriting here: "remarquer avec quelle platitude Josèphe écourte ici le magnifique récit de la Bible".

1281. In proceeding directly from 19,12b to v. 13b, Josephus passes over the reference in 19,13a to Elijah's coming out of the cave which he anticipated earlier. In 19,13aβ Elijah is said to "wrap his face in his mantle" before going out of the cave. In his earlier mention of Elijah's leaving the cave, Josephus omits this item since it would militate against the subsequent "seeing" of the fiery light which he will attribute to the prophet.

1282. Josephus likely found inspiration for his qualification of the "voice" which addresses Elijah as "divine" in 19,15 where "the Lord" responds to Elijah's answer (v. 14) to the question of the "voice" to him (v. 13).
Josephus uses the above phrase "divine voice" in his retelling of Gen 15,13 in *AJ* 1,185, cf. 2,283 where Moses is said to have heard τὰς τοῦ θεοῦ φωνὰς. See also n. 1262.

1283. Conceivably, the reference to Elijah's "alarm" here is inspired by the notice in 19,13aβ (not used as such by Josephus) to Elijah's "wrapping his face in his mantle" understood as expressive of his fear in the face of the phenomena cited in vv. 11b-12, see n. 1282.

1284. In what precedes (see 8,347.351) Josephus has cited only Jezebel as threatening Elijah's life. His reference to the prophet's "enemies" here could, however, be inspired by Elijah's word in 19,10 "*they seek* my life".

1285. Josephus has no parallel to the new introduction of the speaker, i.e. "and the Lord said to him" of 19,15aα. Thereby, he avoids the problem as to the relation between the "voice" who addresses Elijah in 19,13 and "the Lord" who speaks to him in 19,15.

1286. In the Bible Elijah is instructed to "anoint" all three figures mentioned. Josephus chooses a more general term in recognition of the fact that none of the three were in fact "anointed" by Elijah and only Jehu was anointed at all.

1287. In *AJ* 9,105 where ROSPE have Ἀμασῆ as the name of Jehu's father N conjectures Νεμεσαίου as here in 8,352.

1288. This is the conjecture of NN* followed by Mar and Sc for the ἐκ Δαμασκοῦ of codd which NaW adopt. Josephus' reference to "Damascus" here is likely inspired by 1 Kings 19,15aβ where Elijah is instructed to "go to the wilderness *of Damascus*".

τὴν οἰκείαν)¹²⁸⁹, rather than to "the wilderness (+ of the way, 3 Rgns) of Damascus" (so 19,15αβ). As in 19,16b Josephus has the voice's final instruction concern Elijah's successor: "… he should make Elisha ('Ελισσαῖον, 3 Rgns 'Ελισ(σ)αῖε)¹²⁹⁰, of the city of Abela (Ἀβέλας)¹²⁹¹ prophet in his place (ἀντ' αὐτοῦ… προφήτην, 3 Rgns χρίσεις εἰς προφήτην ἀντὶ σοῦ)". In parallel to 19,17 Josephus further has the voice announce that Hazael and Jehu will perpetrate killings. At the same time, however, he introduces a clarification concerning the identity of the kings' victims and a motivation for their actions: ("But," said the voice), "of the impious (ἀσεβοῦς) people (ὄχλου) Azaēlos shall destroy (διαφθερεῖ, 3 Rgns θανατώσει) some, and Jehu others". Conversely, he omits the indication of 19,17b that Elisha too will be involved in the coming blood-letting¹²⁹². Thereafter, he passes over God's statement in 19,18 that he (so MT and L, in B the subject is "you", i.e. Elijah himself) is preserving a remnant of 7,000 who have not abandoned themselves to the worship of Baal, a notice which could seem to conflict with the preceding episode (1 Kings 18,39) where, it appears, the entire people has rejected the worship of Baal.

3. *Elisha's Call* (8,353-354). Josephus makes the transition to the segment's final episode with an elaborated version of the indeterminate notice "so he departed from there" of 19,19aα, i.e. "when Elijah heard these words he returned (ὑποστρέφει [see ὑποστρέψαντα, 8,352], 3 Rgns ἀπῆλθεν)¹²⁹³ to the country of the Hebrews (εἰς τὴν Ἑβραίων χώραν [see 8,255] compare 8,352 εἰς τὴν οἰκείαν)¹²⁹⁴". Following 19,19abα, Josephus next recounts Elijah's approach to Elisha: "he came upon (καταλαβὼν, 3 Rgns εὑρίσκει) Elisha, the son (παῖδα, 3 Rgns υἱὸν) of Saphatēs (Σαφάτου, MT Shaphat, B Σαφάθ, L Σαφάτ)¹²⁹⁵, as

---

1289. The above construction "return to one's own land" recurs in *AJ* 6,80; 8,175; 12,312; 13,31.394; *Vita* 144.310 and with slight variations in *Vita* 16.63; *Ap* 2,289.

1290. At this point Josephus leaves aside the name of Elisha's father given in 19,16b, i.e. Shaphat. He will, however, cite the name subsequently in 8,353.

1291. MT Abel-meḥolah, B 'Εβαλμαουλὰ, L Ἀβελμεοὺλ. The statement of W, *Josèphe*, II, p. 233 that LXX, A excepted, lacks mention of Elijah's hometown in 19,16 is incorrect.

1292. Here too BETZ, *Problem*, p. 34 sees Josephus' modification of the Biblical text reflecting his anti-Zealot posture, see n. 1209.

1293. The only other occurrence of the h.p. of ὑποστρέφω in Josephus is *AJ* 16,270.

1294. In the Bible there is a seeming discrepancy between 19,15 (Elijah directed to go "to the wilderness of Damascus") and 19,19 (he encounters Elisha, presumably in the latter's hometown of Abel-meḥolah (19,16), west of the Jordan). Josephus avoids the difficulty: Elijah is told to return "to his own land" (i.e. Israel) and accordingly, does return to "the country of the Hebrews (= Israelites)".

1295. Recall that Josephus passes over 1 Kings 19,16's mention of Elisha's father in the context of the divine word to Elijah; thereby, he avoids the Bible's two-fold citation of the name in close proximity, i.e. in 19,16 and 19.

he was ploughing (ἀροῦντα, L ἦν ἀροτριῶν)¹²⁹⁶, and some others with him, who were driving twelve yoke (ζεύγη δώδεκα, 3 Rgns has the same phrase in reverse order)¹²⁹⁷, and going up (προσελθών, Β ἐπῆλθεν ἐπ' αὐτόν) to him, he threw (ἐπέρριψεν, so Β, L ἔρριψεν)¹²⁹⁸ his own mantle (ἱμάτιον, 3 Rgns μηλωτὴν) over him (αὐτῷ, 3 Rgns ἐπ' αὐτόν)". In response to this gesture, Elisha, Josephus reports, "immediately began to prophesy" (προφητεύειν ἤρξατο). This item has no equivalent in the account of 1 Kings 19,19-21. On the other hand, however, one notes that also in *AJ* 6,166 Josephus interjects a reference to David's "beginning to prophesy" at the moment of his receiving the Spirit when anointed by Samuel where the Biblical parallel, 1 Sam 16,13, lacks such¹²⁹⁹. To the preceding insertion Josephus appends the notice, derived from 19,20aα, that Elisha "leaving (καταλιπών, 3 Rgns κατέλιπεν) his oxen (τοὺς βόας = L*; Β 82/ο τὰς βόας, MT הבקר), followed (ἠκολούθησεν, Β 3 Rgns κατέδραμεν ὀπίσω)¹³⁰⁰ Elijah". In so doing, Elisha (// 19,20aβ) "asked to be allowed (δεηθείς... συγχωρῆσαι)¹³⁰¹ to take leave (ἀσπάσασθαι, 19,20aβ "kiss")¹³⁰² of his parents (γονεῖς)¹³⁰³". In 19,20bβ (MT L) Elijah answers Elisha's request with the obscure words "Go back again for (> L) what have I done to you?" (compare Β "... because I have done to you"). Clarifying

1296. Like MT 19,19 Josephus lacks a parallel to the 3 Rgns specification that Elisha was ploughing "with oxen". He will, however, make reference to Elisha's oxen in what follows.

1297. Josephus' phrase "and some others... twelve yoke" is his equivalent to 19,19bα "with twelve yoke [+ of oxen, 3 Rgns] before him and he was with the twelfth".

1298. Josephus' only other use of the verb ἐπιρρίπτω is *BJ* 4,332.

1299. Cf. 6,222 where Josephus' mention of Saul's envoys "beginning to prophesy" does have a basis in the source text, i.e. 1 Sam 18,19. Josephus' insertion of references to "prophesying" in 6,166 and 8,354 is illustrative of his more general tendency to accentuate the "prophetic element" in his retelling of Israel's Biblical history; on this point see BEGG, *Classical Prophets*, esp. p. 342, n. 7.

1300. Josephus' verb here is likely derived from 3 Rgns 19,21aβ where Elisha declares to Elijah καὶ *ἀκολουθήσω* ὀπίσω σου, a declaration omitted by Josephus, see below.

G. KITTEL, ἀκολουθέω κτλ, in *TWNT* 2 (1935) 210-216, p. 211 points out that Josephus, in line with profane usage, avoids the LXX and NT (see, e.g., Matt 10,38) "Semiticizing" phrase "follow after" in favor of ἀκολουθέω + dative (as here in 8,354 ἠκολούθησεν Ἠλίᾳ). Kittel further avers (pp. 212-213): "Bei Josephus spielt... überhaupt kein präganter Gebrauch von ἀκολουθεῖν eine nennenswerte Rolle"; *AJ* 8,354 would be the only Josephan text where the verb denotes a *"Jüngernachfolge"* (see, however, 20,188 which speaks of those who "followed (ἀκολουθήσαντες) a certain imposter" into the desert during the administration of Festus.

1301. Variants of the above expression "asked to be allowed" occur also in *AJ* 2,277; 7,191.196; 13,67 (*Vita* 173).

1302. Only here in 8,354 does Josephus (twice, see below) use ἀποτάσσω (middle) in the sense "bid farewell". In other senses the verb occurs also in *BJ* 3,69; *AJ* 11,232.344; 16,330; 19,377.

1303. With this plural form, Josephus aligns himself with MT (and L*) where Elisha refers to both his father and mother as against Β 93/e₂ which speak only of the former.

matters, Josephus simply states that Elijah told Elisha to do as he had requested and that the latter did indeed "part" (ἀποταξάμενος) from his parents – a point not mentioned in the Bible as such. Conversely, he omits 19,21aβ's account of Elisha's slaughtering the oxen and distributing their flesh to his people, perhaps because no such action is envisaged in Elisha's previous request to Elijah[1304]. He does, however, draw on 19,21b ("he went after Elijah and ministered to him") for his notice "he went with (εἴπετο, 3 Rgns ἐπορεύθη ὀπίσω)[1305] (the prophet); *and as long as Elijah was alive*[1306] he was his disciple (μαθητής)[1307] and attendant (διάκονος)[1308]". He rounds off the entire sequence with the (Biblically unparalleled) formula "such, then, is the history of this prophet".

Summary: Josephus' version of 1 Kings 19 evidences occasional contacts with the peculiar readings of both 3 Rgns and MT. With the former he shares, e.g., his reference to Elijah's "fearing" Jezebel (8,348, cf. 3 Rgns 19,3), as well his designation of the one who nourishes the prophet on his journey as "somebody" (8,349, see 3 Rgns 19,5, cf., however, 19,7, MT and 3 Rgns) and the specification that it was "on the morrow" that Elijah came out of the cave (8,351, see 3 Rgns 19,11). Conversely, he has in common with MT a "negative agreement", i.e. his lack of parallel to the additional words 3 Rgns attributes to Jezebel

1304. BETZ, *Problem*, p. 34 sees in this "omission" yet another instance of Josephus' endeavor to eliminate "Zealot features" from his version of Biblical history.

1305. See ἔπεσθαι in 8,337 where, just as here in 8,354, it replaces the πορεύω ὀπίσω construction of LXX (3 Rgns 18,21).

1306. The Bible lacks this specification about the duration of Elisha's service to Elijah.

1307. This key NT term appears only 3 × in LXX, i.e. the A reading in Jer 13,21; 20,1; 26,9. Josephus employs it a total of 14× : *AJ* 1,200 (Lot, disciple of Abraham); 6,84 (Joshua, disciple of Moses); 8,354; 9,28.33 (Elisha, disciple of Elijah).68.106 (disciple(s) of Elisha); 10,158.178 (Baruch, disciple of Jeremiah); 13,289 (Hyrcanus, disciple of the Pharisees); 15,3 (Samaias, disciple of the Pharisee Pollion);17,334 (pseudo-Alexander, disciple of an unnamed Jew); *Ap* 1,14 (earliest Greek philosophers, disciples of Egyptians and Chaldeans).176 (Clearchus, disciple of Aristotle); and 2,295 (Jews ready to be disciples of any who observed the divine precepts prior to themselves). On Josephus' use of the term, see K.H. RENGSTORF, μαθητής, in *TWNT* 4 (1942) 392-466, esp. p. 442; and M.J. WILKINS, *The Concept of Disciple in Matthew's Gospel* (NovTSup, 59), Leiden, 1988, 111-116.

1308. Like μαθητής this term occurs 14 × in Josephus. Contrast his designation for Elijah's (earlier) "servant", i.e. θεράπων (8,344.348) (Note that in 9,54-55 the terms διάκονος and θεράπων are used interchangeably in reference to the "servant" of Elisha).

W. BEYER, διακονέω κτλ, in *TWNT* 2 (1935) 81-93, p. 91 with reference to Josephus' use of διάκονος in 8,354 affirms that here Elisha is being depicted as "der Rabbinerschüler seines Meisters". He likewise calls attention to two passages in *BJ* where Josephus designates himself respectively as "thy (God's) minister" (διάκονος, 3,354) and "minister (διάκονον) of the voice of God" (4,626; here the designation is put on the lips of Vespasian). On Josephus' overall use of διακον- words against the background of Biblical and extra-Biblical Greek usage, see J.N. COLLINS, *Diakonia. Reinterpreting the Ancient Sources*, Oxford-New York, 1990, esp. pp. 111-115,120-121,129-130,141-144,164.

in 19,2, i.e. "if you are Elijah, I am Jezebel"[1309]. In making Elisha ask to take leave of his parents (8,354) he aligns himself with MT L* 19,20 against B. With L* too he shares a negative agreement, i.e. his non-utilization of the MT and B sequence 1 Kings 19,6bβ-8aα.

Josephus' version of 1 Kings 19 is remarkable chiefly for its consistent abridgement of the source, particularly the latter's repetitious elements, i.e. 19,5b-8a[1310].9-10.11b-12.13bβ-14, see also 17b-18, 21a. In comparison with the source he seems intent on getting through the narrative as quckly as possible[1311]. In the same line he rearranges the sequence of 19,11b-12 and 13 in the interests of a more logical narrative sequence. Similarly, he rewords problematic items in the Biblical account: Elijah is to "appoint" rather than "anoint" the three figures designated by God (8,352, compare 1 Kings 19,15-16).

1309. It should, however, be recalled that Josephus has no equivalent to Jezebel's entire opening oath formula in 19,2, including that portion of it shared by both MT and 3 Rgns.

1310. Note, however, that L* too lacks an equivalent to MT B 19,6bβ-8aα; conceivably, then, Josephus' "abridgement" in this instance reflects rather his dependence on a text à la that of L.

1311. His doing so may reflect an apprehension that enlightened readers might find the supernaturalistic features (angelic "touches", God's "passing by", the divine "voice" that addresses Elijah) that permeate 1 Kings 19 off-putting. In this connection, note his aside in the context of his narration of the Sinai theophany – with which he brings our episode into explicit connection (see 8,349 "the mountain called Sinai, where Moses is said to have received the laws from God") – in AJ 3,81 "Of these happenings each of my readers may think as he will; for my part, I am constrained to relate them as they are recorded in the sacred books".

XV

NABOTH'S MURDER
(8,355-362)

Introduction[1312]: As is well-known, the placing of the story of Naboth's vineyard varies in MT and 3 Rgns; in the former it constitutes 1 Kings 21, whereas in the latter the episode (= 3 Rgs 20) stands directly after 1 Kings 19. It is controverted which of these sequences is the more original[1313]. In any event, however, Josephus' placing of the pericope corresponds to that in 3 Rgns. Accordingly, I shall treat his version of the passage at this point, citing the Biblical source text by its familiar MT chapter number, however. For purposes of analysis, 1 Kings 21 may be divided into the following units: 1) Ahab vs. Naboth (21:1-4); Jezebel's intervention (21:5-16); and 3) God's word against Ahab (21,17-29).

1. *Ahab vs. Naboth* (8,355-356a). Josephus loosely attaches the Naboth story to what precedes with the formula: "now a certain Naboth (Νάβωθος)[1314] from the city of Jezarēl (᾿Ιεζαρήλου)...[1315]. 1 Kings 21,1 states that the Jezreelite Naboth "had a vineyard in Jezreel (> 3 Rgns) beside the palace (היכל, οἴκῳ L; compare B ἅλῳ) of Ahab...". In Josephus' formulation this becomes: "Naboth was the king's country

---

1312. On Josephus' treatment of this Biblical episode, see the summary remarks of A. BAUMANN, *Naboths Fasttag und Josephus*, in *Theokratia* 2 (1970-1972, FS K.H. Rengstorf), Leiden, 1973, 26-44, esp. p. 38 who notes parallels between Naboth's trial as narrated in *AJ* and Josephus' account of his own trial at Tiberias in *Vita* 290-303.

1313. On the question, see H.-J. STIPP, *Elisha-Propheten-Gottesmänner. Die Redaktionsgeschichte des Elishazyklus und verwandter Texte, rekonstruiert auf der Basis von Text- und Literarkritik zu 1 Kön 20.22 und 2 Kön 2-7* (ATSAT, 24), St. Ottilien, 1987, pp. 418-430.

On other differences between 1 Kings 21 and 3 Rgns 20, see GOODING, *Ahab*, pp. 272-277 and P.-M. BOGAERT, *Le repentir d'Achab d'après la Bible hébraïque (1 R 21) et d'après la Septante (3 Règnes 20)*, in G.F. WILLEMS (ed.), *Élie le Prophète. Bible, Tradition, Iconographie* (Publications de l'Institutum Iudaicum), Leuven, n.d., pp. 39-58.

1314. Thus N* followed by Mar. N prints RO's Ναβώθης, while Na adopts the Νάβουθος of MSPExc, likewise favored by SCHLATTER, *Namen*, p. 78, s.v. נָבוֹת. Compare 3 Rgns Ναβουθαί.

1315. So NN*Mar, SCHLATTER, *Namen*, p. 61, s.v. יִזְרְעֶאל, SCHALIT, *Namenwörterbuch*, p. 58, s.v. ᾿Ιεζάρηλα. NaW read rather ᾿Ιζάρου with SPExcSuid. Compare B ᾿Ισραηλείτη, L ᾿Ιεζραηλίτη etc.

With Josephus' opening phrase above compare B 3 Rgns 20,1 "and there was a vineyard to Nabouthai..."; MT (as also L 3 Rgns 20,l) has an opening chronological plus, i.e. *"and it came to pass after these things*, (there was a vineyard...)".

neighbor (ἀγρογείτων)¹³¹⁶". Josephus next rearranges and reworks Ahab's proposition to Naboth as cited in 21,2. The Biblical Ahab says "give (3 Rgns δός) me your vineyard that I may have it for a vegetable garden, because it is near my house; and I will give you a better vineyard for it; or if it seems good to you, I will give you its value in money (+ and it will be my vegetable garden, 3 Rgns)". In Josephus the king first asks Naboth to "sell (ἀποδόσθαι) his field (ἀγρόν) next (πλησίον, 3 Rgns ἐγγίων) to his own lands at any price (τιμῆς ὅσης βούλεται)". Ahab desires Naboth's plot, as Josephus has the king then state, "in order that he might join (it to them) and make one property¹³¹⁷". Thereupon, Ahab concludes his request as follows: "or, if he did not wish to take money for it, he would permit him to select any one of his own fields"¹³¹⁸. In Josephus' portrayal Ahab thus seems to offer Naboth still more generous terms than does his Biblical counterpart: any price, any one of the royal fields.

In 21,3 Naboth rebuffs Ahab, employing an oath formula: "the Lord (B 3 Rgns 20,3 my God, L the Lord my God) forbid that I should give you the inheritance of my fathers". Josephus reformulates Naboth's response to eliminate its invocation of God and to provide a more explicit motivation for his refusal: "But the other (Naboth) refused to do this, saying that he would himself enjoy the fruits (καρπώσεσ-θαι)¹³¹⁹ of his own land (γῆν)¹³²⁰ which he had inherited from his father (ἣν ἐκληρονόμησε τοῦ πατρός, 3 Rgns τὴν κληρονομίαν πατέρων μου)". 1 Kings 21,4 describes Ahab's reaction to Naboth's refusal: the king's dejection, his taking to his bed, turning away (3 Rgns hiding) his face, and refusing nourishment¹³²¹. Josephus begins his version of this sequence by noting that the king was "aggrieved (λυπηθείς, MT סַר וְזָעֵף, L συγκεχυμένος καὶ ἐκλελυμένος, B τὸ πνεῦμα ... τεταραγμένον), as if at an insult (ὡς ἐφ᾽ ὕβρει), at not getting the

1316. This term is hapax in Josephus, who, subsequently, will utilize the term "vineyard" of 21,1.

1317. This rationale – which draws on 1 Kings 21,2's reference to Naboth's property being "near" Ahab's house – appears to make more sense than the one which the Bible attributes to the king, i.e. his desire to make a vegetable garden out of Naboth's vineyard. Ahab, one might suppose, could lay out a vegetable garden anywhere on his own properties and so would not have needed Naboth's plot for that particular purpose.

1318. Compare 21,2 where Ahab first offers Naboth another vineyard and only then invokes a second possibility, i.e. a money settlement. Josephus reverses the Biblical sequence in his version of the king's word.

1319. Thus ExcSuid followed by NN*NaMar. The codd read καρπώσασθαι.

1320. The above idiom "enjoy the fruits of the land" recurs in AJ (2,192) 4,242.

1321. B 3 Rgns 20,4aα differs markedly from MT (and L); for the latter's opening words "and Ahab went to his house vexed and sullen" it reads simply "and the spirit of Achab was troubled", just as it has no equivalent to the sequence "because of what Naboth... had said to him; for he said, 'I will not give you the inheritance of my fathers (L + and the spirit of Ahab was troubled = B 20,4aα)'" of MT 21,4aβ.

other's property[1322]". He then enumerates two actions indicative of the king's state of mind of which only the second has a Biblical equivalent, i.e. "he would neither bathe nor take food" (οὔτε λουτρὸν προσηνέγκατο οὔτε τροφήν)[1323], leaving aside 21,4bα's reference to Ahab's "taking to his bed"[1324].

2. *Jezebel's intervention* (8,356b-360a). A new segment commences in 1 Kings 21,5 with the queen's appearing to inquire about Ahab's behavior. Josephus expands her question in wording that echoes his preceding description of Ahab's reaction: "... (Jezebel) inquired why he grieved (λυπεῖται, see λυπηθείς, 8,356a) and would neither bathe (λούεται, see λουτρὸν, 8,356a) nor have his midday meal (ἄριστον) or supper (δεῖπνον)[1325] served (παρατίθεται) to him". In 21,6 Ahab responds with an "objective" account of the exchange between himself and Naboth, citing their respective words (see vv. 2-3) partly verbatim. In Josephus, by contrast, the king's answer is both more emotionally charged and less repetitious of previous formulations: "he told her of Naboth's contrariness (σκαιότητα)[1326] and how, in spite of his having used mild words (χρησάμενος ἐπιεικέσι... λόγοις)[1327] towards him, hardly in keeping with (ὑποδεεστέροις)[1328] the royal authority (βασιλικῆς ἐξουσίας)[1329], he had been insulted (ὑβρισθείη, see ὡς ἐφ᾽ ὕβρει, 8,356a) by being refused what he had asked for". The couple's conversation concludes in 21,7 with Jezebel getting the last word: "do you now govern Israel? Arise, and eat bread, and let your heart be cheerful; I will give you the vineyard of Naboth the Jezreelite". Eliminating the queen's opening (contemptuous?) question and specifying its closing assurance, Josephus formulates her response as follows: "she, however, urged him not to be dispirited (μικροψυχεῖν)[1330]

1322. With this specification about the grounds for Ahab's feeling "aggrieved" compare the MT (and L) plus in 1 Kings 21,4aβ cited in the previous note.

1323. This collocation occurs only here in Josephus.

1324. Subsequently, however, he will make use of this source item, see 8,359.

1325. The terms "midday meal" and "supper" are collocated (in reverse order) also in *BJ* 3,86.

1326. The term is hapax in Josephus.

1327. The above phrase "use mild words" occurs only here in Josephus. The above adjective ἐπιεικής appears 29 × in the Josephian corpus, cf. the substantive ἐπιείκεια in 8,214.

1328. The adjective ὑποδεής occurs also in *AJ* 4,23; 8,138; 11,273.

1329. The above phrase "royal authority" occurs only here in Josephus. With Ahab's description of his dealings with Naboth here, compare 8,215 where the elders advise Rehoboam "to speak in a friendly spirit and in a more popular style than was usual for the royal dignity". Ahab thus implicitly represents himself here as acting, as Rehoboam himself did not, on that advice (ironically, however, while Rehoboam's disregard of the advice provokes resistance on the part of his subjects, Ahab's following of it does not make his subject, Naboth, any more amenable to the king's wishes – contrary to the affirmation of the elders in 8,215).

1330. The term is hapax in Josephus.

over these things, but to cease grieving (παυσάμενον... τῆς λύπης)[1331] and turn (τρέπεσθαι)[1332] to caring for his body as usual (ἐπὶ τὴν συνήθη... τοῦ σώματος πρόνοιαν)[1333], for she would attend (μελήσειν)[1334] to (περὶ) Naboth's punishment (τιμωρίας)[1335]".

Josephus next proceeds to relate (// 21(20),8b) Jezebel's subsequent initiative: "and she at once (παραχρῆμα)[1336] sent (πέμπει, see the same h.p. in 8,345; 3 Rgns ἀπέστειλεν) letters (γράμματα)[1337] in Achab's name (ἐκ τοῦ Ἀχάβου ὀνόματος, 3 Rgns ἐπὶ τῷ ὀνόματι Ἀχαὰβ)[1338] to the chief men (ὑπερέχοντας[1339], 3 Rgns τοὺς πρεσβυτέρους καὶ... τοὺς ἐλευθέρους) among the Jezarēlites (Ἰεζαρηλιτῶν)[1340]". 1 Kings 21,9-10 records the content of Jezebel's directives. Josephus has her enjoining the leaders "to keep a fast (νηστεῦσαί, 3 Rgns νηστεύσατε νηστείαν) and hold an assembly (ποιησαμένους ἐκκλησίαν, see 8,222)[1341] over which Naboth, *since he came of an illustrious family* (γένους ἐπιφανοῦς)[1342], was to preside (προκαθίσαι, 3 Rgns καθίσατε τὸν Ναβουθαὶ ἐν ἀρχῇ τοῦ λαοῦ)[1343]". Her instructions then continue: "and, after they should have brought (παρασκευασαμένους, B 3 Rgns

1331. With this construction compare *AJ* 7,256 where Joab exhorts David παυσάμενος... τῆς ἀδίκου λύπης.

1332. Thus NN*Mar. Na reads τραπέσθαι with (M)SPExcSuid.

1333. The above phrase "care of the body" occurs only here in Josephus, just as does the expression "wonted care".

1334. The verb μέλω occurs 16× in Josephus.

1335. This is Josephus' only use of the expression "attend to punishment". With the phrase compare 8,351 where Elijah states that he is "being sought (ζητεῖσθαι) for punishment (πρὸς τιμωρίαν) by the wife of the king". As this terminological affinity suggests, Josephus in 8,347-362 juxtaposes two stories of attempted "punishment" by Jezebel of those who stand up to her husband, the first (involving Elijah) unsuccessful, the second (Naboth) "successful".

1336. Josephus' introduction of this term underscores the queen's resoluteness.

1337. Josephus' pl. form here corresponds to MT's ספרים as against the sg. of 3 Rgns 20,8 ([τὸ] βιβλίον) and TJ (note, however, that in 21(20),9 both B (L continues to read the sg.) and TJ refer to Jezebel's "letters").

1338. Josephus leaves aside as self-evident the notice of 21(20),8a on Jezebel's "writing" and "sealing" the letter(s).

1339. In 8,293 this participle has the meaning "the strong".

1340. Thus NN*Mar and SCHALIT, *Namenwörterbuch*, p. 58, s.v. Ἰεζαρηλῖται following Hud. NaW read Ἰεσραηλιτῶν with codd. Compare 21,8b "who dwelt with Naboth in his city".

1341. With the above collocation "keep a fast and hold an assembly", compare *AJ* 10,93 νηστεύοντος τοῦ δήμου καὶ ἐκκλησιάζοντος.

1342. This is the only occurrence of this precise phrase in Josephus. L.H. FELDMAN points out that Josephus, in line with Hellenistic practice, frequently introduces references to the "good birth" of his (Biblical) personages, see *Josephus' Portrait of Saul*, in *HUCA* 53 (1982) 45-99, pp. 59-62, esp. p. 60, n. 37; idem, *Josephus' Version of Samson*, in *JSJ* 19 (1988) 171-214, esp. p. 173, n.8. Josephus' (non-Biblical) adscription of noble birth to Naboth here does have a Rabbinic parallel, see *Sanh.* 48b; *t. Sanh.* 4.6.

1343. This is the only occurrence of the verb προκαθίζω in *AJ*; it recurs in *BJ* 1,538 and 2,27.

20,10 ἐγκαθίσατε) three[1344] unscrupulous (τολμηρούς)[1345] men to bear witness against him (καταμαρτυρήσοντας αὐτοῦ, L [B has no equivalent to MT L 21(20),10αββ] καταμαρτυρησάτωσαν αὐτοῦ) to the effect that he had blasphemed both God (τὸν θεόν... βλασφημήσας)[1346] and the king (τὸν βασιλέα)[1347], they were to stone him to death (καταλεῦσαι, L λιθοβολήσατε)[1348] and so make an end of him (διαχρήσασθαι, L καὶ ἀποθανέτω)[1349]".

1 Kings 21,11-13 (MT, L) relates in detail and largely verbatim the execution of Jezebel's various orders. Josephus, in the line of B which has no parallel to 21,10αββ-13αα, limits himself to noting the fulfillment of the two key measures enjoined by the queen: "Thus, as a result of the queen's letter (ὡς ἔγραψεν)[1350], Naboth was accused of having blasphemed both God and Achab (καταμαρτυρηθεὶς βλασφημῆσαι τὸν θεόν τε καὶ Ἄχαβον, 3 Rgns 20,13αβ καὶ κατεμαρτύρησαν αὐτοῦ... εὐλόγηκας θεὸν καὶ βασιλέα) and was stoned to death *by the people* (βαλλόμενος ὑπὸ τοῦ πλήθους ἀπέθανεν, 20,13bβ καὶ ἐλιθοβόλησαν αὐτὸν [ἐν] λίθοις, καὶ ἀπέθανεν)[1351]". He passes over as self-evident the fact of the notables' report to Jezebel concerning the execution of her orders, 21,14. Instead, he moves directly to his (shortened) version of 21,15, the queen's reaction to their report: "When Jezabelē heard (ἀκούσασα, 3 Rgns ἤκουσεν) of this, *she went in to the king*[1352] and

---

1344. In 21(20),10 Jezebel specifies the number of Naboth's accusers as two. Josephus' divergent figure is in line with his version of the "law of witness", Deut 19,15 ("... only on the evidence of *two* witnesses or of *three* witnesses shall a charge be sustained") in *AJ* 4,219: "... let there be *three* [witnesses] or at least two, whose evidence shall be accredited by their past lives". GINZBERG, *Legends*, VI, p. 312, n. 39 affirms that here in 8,358 Josephus is dependent on "the old Halakah" which would have required three witnesses in capital cases instead of the later norm of (only) two. FELDMAN, *Mikra*, p. 516 argues that this supposition is not compelling. On Josephus' use of Deut 19,15 in his writings overall, see further H. VAN VLIET, *No Single Testimony. A Study of the Adoption of the Law of Deut. 19:15 Par. into the New Testament*, Utrecht, 1958, 26-30.

1345. In 8,318 this same term is used of Jezebel herself. Compare 3 Rgns 20,10 υἱοὺς παρανόμων.

1346. Elsewhere Josephus employs the above phrase "blaspheme god(s)" also in *AJ* 4,202.207; 6,187; 8,359.392 (with εἰς); 10,233 (with εἰς).242; *Ap* 2,237.

1347. The above phrase "blaspheme the king" recurs in *BJ* 2,406 (with εἰς); *Vita* 407. In MT and L (B has nothing equivalent) 21(20),10 the expression used is the euphemistic "(Naboth) blessed (L εὐλόγηκε) God and king". Josephus' transposition of this formulation into a reference to "blasphemy" is paralleled in TJ (וגדיפת), as also in VL 20,10 (maledixisti).

1348. Josephus uses the verb καταλεύω a total of 13 ×. His employment of it here echoes his version of the law of Lev 24,16 in *AJ* 4,202 ὁ δὲ βλασφημήσας θεὸν καταλευσθείς.

1349. Josephus employs the verb διαχράομαι 30 ×.

1350. Cf. ἔγραψεν... βιβλίον, 3 Rgns 20,8αα (recall that in his version of 21[20],8 Josephus does not explicitly mention Jezebel's "writing" her "letters").

1351. Note Josephus' specification, unparalleled in 20,13 ("they stoned"), as to the identity of those "stoning" Naboth.

1352. 1 Kings 21,15 does not mention this initial action of Jezebel's as such.

bade (ἐκέλευσεν, cf. κελεύουσα, 8,358; 3 Rgns εἶπεν) him take possession of Naboth's vineyard (κληρονομεῖν[1353] τὸν Ναβώθου ἀμπελῶνα[1354], 3 Rgns κληρονόμει τὸν ἀμπελῶνα Ναβουθαὶ) without
paying for it (προῖκα)[1355]". With the last indication Josephus underscores the advantage that has accrued to Ahab: he could not get
Naboth's field even "at any price" (8,355); now, through Jezebel's
offices, he will have it "for free".

Josephus prefaces his version of 21,16 concerning Ahab's response to
his wife's word with a reference to the emotional impact of her
statements upon the king: "he was pleased (ἥσθη, see 8,218 where the
same term is used of Rehoboam's reaction to the advice of the younger
men) at what had happened"[1356]. Similarly, whereas 21,16b has him
simply "arising", Josephus presents a more dramatic picture: "Achab
leaped (ἀναπηδήσας) from his bed (κλίνης)[1357] and went (ἦκε, 3 Rgns
κατέβη = MT) to see (ὀψόμενος, 3 Rgns κληρονομῆσαι, see 21(20),15)
the vineyard of Naboth".

3. *God's Word to Ahab* (8,360b-362). In introducing the divine communication to Elijah which sets in motion the remainder of the episode,
Josephus interjects a reference to God's "being angry" (ἀγανακτήσας)[1358] at what had transpired. In place of the *Wortereignisformel*
of 21,17 (so MT, 3 Rgns "the Lord said to Elijah…"), he states "God
sent (πέμπει)[1359] the prophet[1360] Elijah". From the lengthy divine
commissioning of Elijah in 21,18 Josephus extracts two core items:

1353. Note the contrast in meaning between κληρονομέω as used here in 8,359 (=
"seize unjustly") and 8,355 where it refers to Naboth's legitimately "inheriting" property
from his father.
1354. This is Josephus' first use of this term to designate Naboth's property. Previously, he employed the (non-Biblical) terms ἀγρόν (8,355) and γῆν (8,355).
1355. Elsewhere in Josephus this term occurs in *BJ* 1,483.553; *AJ* 7,332; 10,241;
13,385; 17,11; *Ap* 2,200. Compare 21(20),15bα "which he did not give you for money".
Josephus leaves aside the (self-evident) motivation for Jezebel's injunction as cited in
21(20),15bβ "for Naboth is not alive but dead".
1356. Compare the 3 Rgns plus at the end of 20,16 which offers a quite different slant
regarding Ahab's reaction to Jezebel's announcement: "Ahab rent his garments and
donned sackcloth [cf. 20,27] and it came to pass after these things…". On 3 Rgns plus
here, see C.F. BURNEY, *Notes on the Hebrew Text of the Book of Kings*, London, 1903 (rpt.
New York, 1970), pp. 248-249; WEVERS, *Principles*, p. 313.
1357. 21,16b ("Ahab arose") lacks mention of Ahab's "bed"; recall that earlier
Josephus passed over 21,4's reference to the king's "taking to his bed (3 Rgns κλίνης)".
His mention of the royal "bed" here does suggest that he was familiar with the reference
to it in 21,4.
1358. Josephus uses ἀγανακτέω with God as subject also in *AJ* 1,202 (object: the
Sodomites).
1359. Compare 8,231.299 where Josephus likewise replaces a Biblical *Wortereignisformel* with reference to God's "sending" a prophet.
1360. This specification takes the place of "the Tishbite" of 1 Kings 21,17.

(Elijah is sent) "to Naboth's field (χωρίον) to meet Achab ('Αχάβῳ συμβαλοῦντα, B εἰς ἀπαντὴν 'Αχαὰβ)[1361]". Conversely, he expands on the laconic question (so MT 21,19aβ; in 3 Rgns the words are formulated as a statement): "have you killed and also taken possession?" In Josephus God instructs the prophet: "to ask him (Ahab) about what he had done and why, after killing (κτείνας, 3 Rgns ἐφόνευσας) the real owner (τὸν ἀληθῆ δεσπότην) of the field (χωρίου), he had himself unjustly (ἀδίκως) taken possession of it (κληρονομήσειεν, 3 Rgns ἐκληρονόμησας)". After pausing to note – as the Bible itself does not – that Elijah did in fact appear before the king ("and when he came to him..."), Josephus continues immediately with Ahab's response to Elijah's word, cf. 21,20a. In so doing Josephus reverses the Biblical sequence in which the royal response comes only after the prophet's announcement of punishment for Ahab in 21,19b. In addition, however, Josephus drastically modifies the tenor of the king's response itself. In 21,20a Ahab reacts to the preceding judgment speech of 21,19b with what appears to be a sarcastic question: "have you found (3 Rgns εὕρηκας) me, O my enemy?". The Josephan Ahab responds in a quite different tone: "the king said (the prophet) might do to him as he wished, for he had acted shamefully (αἰσχρὸν... ὄντα) and had been taken by him in sin (ἐπὶ ἁμαρτήματι ληφθῆναι ὑπ᾽ αὐτοῦ)[1362]". Conceivably, Josephus came to this formulation by construing Ahab's question of 21,20aβ ("have you found me...?") as a statement/admission, i.e. you have found (caught) me (in the act). In any case, the confession he attributes to Ahab here all the more redounds to the king's credit in that, as noted above, in Josephus it precedes the words of doom which in the Bible stand prior (21,19b) to Ahab's response in 21,20a[1363].

In 1 Kings 21,19b the word of doom Elijah is charged to convey to Ahab runs as follows: "... in the place where dogs licked up the blood of Naboth shall dogs lick your own blood". Josephus incorporates his version of this announcement – which he situates after Ahab's words of penitence, see above – into his (drastically condensed) rendition of Elijah's following judgment speech, 1 Kings 21,20b-24(25-26): "whereupon the other said that in that very place where (κατ᾽ ἐκεῖνον... τὸν

1361. In having God instruct Elijah to meet Ahab at Naboth's field here, Josephus skirts the problematic double indication concerning Ahab's whereabouts found in 1 Kings 21(20),17 "(go down to meet) Ahab... who is in Samaria... behold he is in the vineyard of Naboth (which, according to MT 1 Kings 21,1, was situated 'in Jezreel')".

1362. With the above translation by Mar of Ahab's "confession", compare the (more accurate) one of W, ad loc.: "... il avait honte d'être surpris par lui en faute". Only here in 8,361 does Josephus employ the above construction "taken in sin".

1363. Josephus' portrayal of a repentant Ahab here in contrast to the mocking king of 1 Kings 21,20a has a parallel in the 3 Rgns plusses in 20,16 (see n. 1356) and 27 (see below) which likewise accentuate Ahab's sorrow for his offense.

τόπον ἐν ᾧ, cf. L 20,19ba ἐν τῷ τόπῳ ᾧ) where Naboth's body (νεκρὸν) had been devoured by dogs (ὑπὸ κυνῶν δαπανηθῆναι)[1364] his own blood (αἷμα, so 3 Rgns) and his wife's[1365] should be shed (χυθήσεσθαι)[1366], and all his family (γένος) should perish (ἀπολεῖσθαι)[1367]". Having thus reproduced, in markedly abbreviated form, the doom announcements of 1 Kings 21,19b.21-22a.23-24, Josephus now proceeds to cite the motivating accusations of 21,20b.22b somewhat more expansively (and in more specific terms): "because he had unscrupulously (τετολμηκότος, see τολμηρούς, 8,358) committed these so impious deeds (ἀσεβῆσαι, see 8,253), and in violation of his country's laws (παρὰ τοὺς πατρίους νόμους [> RO])[1368], had unjustly (ἀδίκως, see 8,360) slain (ἀνῃρηκότος, see 8,334) a citizen (πολίτην)[1369]".

Josephus passes over the additional, third person charge concerning Ahab's idolatry found in 1 Kings 21,25-26. Instead, he moves directly

1364. Josephus' wording here echoes that used of the destruction of Jeroboam's line by Baasha in 8,289 ὑπὸ κυνῶν σπαραχθῆναι καὶ δαπανηθῆναι, see also 9,124 where the same phrase "devoured by dogs" is used in reference to Jezebel's corpse. Conversely, Josephus' formulation of Elijah's threat diverges from that of 1 Kings 21,19b itself where the prophet refers to dogs "licking the blood of Naboth" rather than "devouring his corpse" (note, however, that in 8,407 Josephus will draw on 21,19's reference to the "licking" of Naboth's blood by dogs in a word he attributes to the prophet Zedekiah, see below. It appears then that Josephus did know the wording of our 21,19b, but modified it here in 8,361 in line with his own expression in 8,289).

Note finally that Josephus lacks an equivalent to the double plus of 3 Rgs 20,19b: not only dogs, but also pigs, licked Naboth's blood, while "harlots" are going to "wash" in the blood of Ahab. Of these two amplifications, the latter prepares the notice of 1 Kings 22,38ba (MT and 3 Rgns) that such a use of Ahab's blood by harlots did in fact occur, while the former has in view the corresponding plus in 3 Rgns 22,38aβ that pigs joined the dogs in licking Ahab's blood (Josephus has an equivalent to the first of these items in 22,38, but not to the second, see below on 8,417).

1365. With this reference to Jezebel's fate, Josephus combines the announcement of 21,19b concerning Ahab with that of 21,23 ("And of Jezebel the Lord also said, 'The dogs shall eat Jezebel within the bounds of Jezreel'"). The historian's "conflation" of the two distinct Biblical announcements was a natural one in that both speak of what "dogs" will do with the remains of a dead person.

1366. Josephus' only other use of the above phrase "shed blood" is BJ 4,72. Here again, Josephus' wording diverges from that of 21,19b where Elijah announces rather that Ahab's blood will be "licked" by dogs. His formulation, i.e. "Ahab's and Jezebel's blood will be shed" might be seen as Josephus' generalizing substitute for the two somewhat divergent expressions of 21,19b (Ahab's blood will be *licked* by dogs) and 23 (dogs will *devour* Jezebel). As mentioned in note 1364, however, subsequently Josephus will make use of the language of 21,19b when he has Zedekiah "cite" Elijah's announcement about dogs "licking" Ahab's blood.

1367. This announcement concerning Ahab's family represents Josephus' condensation of the lengthy prediction on the subject attributed to Elijah in 1 Kings 21,21b-22.24. Its wording echoes the notice of 8,309 on the end of Baasha's dynasty: "his house (οἶκον) perished (ἀπολέσθαι) root and branch...".

1368. Elsewhere Josephus employs the above phrase "against the ancestral laws" in BJ 1,649. The expression "ancestral law(s)" is quite frequent in his works, occurring some 48 ×.

1369. On this term and its cognates, see SPICQ, Lexicographie, II, pp. 710-720.

to a description of Ahab's response to Elijah's words of doom. This description both parallels and expands on MT 21,27 – somewhat in the line of the 3 Rgns plusses in the verse[1370]. Josephus starts off here by noting "then Achab began to feel grief (λύπη, see 8,356.357) and remorse (μετάμελος)[1371]..." (compare 3 Rgns' opening plus in 20,27 "and because of the word Ahab was pierced with sorrow (B κατενύγη) before the Lord and went about weeping (κλαίων))". Common to both MT and B 21(20),27 is the enumeration of four distinct actions undertaken by Ahab in response to Elijah's word: he rends his clothes, dons sackcloth[1372], fasts and "goes about dejectedly (אט)" (so MT; B has simply "he went", while L lacks the item entirely). Josephus passes over the first of these indications and re-arranges the sequence of the remaining three: "putting on sackcloth (σακκίον ἐνδυσάμενος, 3 Rgns ἐζώσατο σάκκον ἐπὶ τὸ σῶμα αὐτου)[1373], he went with bare feet (γυμνοῖς τοῖς ποσὶ διῆγεν)[1374], and touched no food (οὐχ ἁπτόμενος τροφῆς, 3 Rgns ἐνήστευσεν)[1375]". To these indications, drawn from the Bible, Josephus adds a further item of his own: "and confessed his sins (ἀνθομολογούμενός [ROM ἀνομολογούμενός] τε τὰ ἡμαρτημένα)[1376], seeking in this way to propitiate God (καὶ[1377] τὸν θεὸν οὕτως ἐξευμενίζων)[1378]".

1370. On these, see BURNEY, Kings, pp. 248-249 and GOODING, Ahab, pp. 273-277.

1371. Josephus' other uses of this term are AJ 2,108; 18,299; 19,260.

1372. In fact, both witnesses make double reference to Ahab's wearing of sackloth: MT 1 Kings 21,27 reads "... he put sackcloth upon his flesh... and lay in sackcloth...", while in 3 Rgns 20,27 the second reference constitutes an allusion to the plus of 20,16 (see n. 1356): "he also put on sackcloth in the day that he smote Nabuthai the Jezraelite (L + and his son, cf. 2 Kings 9,26 where Jehu refers to a divine oracle against Ahab which speaks of the Lord's seeing 'the blood of Naboth *and the blood of his sons*')".

1373. The above construction "put on sackcloth" occurs only here in Josephus. The verb ἐνδύω is construed with σάκ(κ)ος in AJ 7,40.327;8,385;11,221.256. Recall that unlike his Biblical source verse (MT and 3 Rgns), Josephus makes only a single reference to Ahab's wearing of sackcloth.

1374. This is Josephus' equivalent to the concluding indication in MT 1 Kings 21,27 "he went about dejectedly" (compare B "he went"). As THACKERAY, Josephus, the Man, p. 82, points out, Josephus' phrase corresponds to that of TJ in 1 Kings 21,27 which likewise speaks of the king's going about "barefoot" (יחיף). (The same indication appears also in y. Sanh. 28b, 51-52 where Rabbi Yehoshua ben-Levi affirms that the word אט in 1 Kings 21,27 means "barefoot"). With the above reference to Ahab's going "with bare feet", compare AJ 7,202 where David ascends the Mount of Olives "with bare feet" (= 2 Sam 15,30) in his flight from Absalom.

1375. The above construction "touch no food" recurs in BJ 2,139; AJ 10,260.

1376. The only other occurrence of the verb ἀνθομογέομαι in Josephus is in the very similar construction of 8,257 (the Judeans in the face of Shishak's invasion) τὰς ἁμαρτίας ἀνθομογουμένους.

Compare the earlier "confession" which Josephus, modifying the Biblical formulation, attributes to Ahab in 8,361 "... the king said the prophet might do with him as he wished, for he had acted shamefully and had been taken by him in sin (ἁμαρτήματι)".

1377. Thus NN*WMar; Na conjectures ὡς.

1378. Josephus' two others uses of the above phrase "propitiate God" are AJ 11,115 (the Jews under Ezra);12,113 (the poet Theodectes).

In 21,28 a *Wortereignisformel* (expanded in 3 Rgns with "and the Lord said") introduces the divine response to Ahab's penitential initiatives. Josephus' introductory formula parallels the 3 Rgns plus: "(God) said (εἶπεν= 3 Rgns)[1379] to the prophet". The MT form of the divine word itself, 21,29, opens with a double reference to Ahab's self-humbling: "have you (Elijah) seen how Ahab has humbled himself before me? Because he has humbled himself before me...". 3 Rgns lacks a parallel to the second of these references, whereas Josephus, for his part, has a equivalent to this item, but not to the question with which the verse commences in both MT and 3 Rgns: "... while Achab lived (Kings: in his days), He would put off punishing (ὑπερβαλεῖσθαι τὴν... τιμωρίαν, 3 Rgns οὐκ ἐπάξω τὴν κακίαν)[1380] his family (γένους)[1381], since he repented of his violent deeds (ἐπεὶ ἐπὶ[1382] τοῖς τετολμημένοις [see τετολμηκότος, 8,361] μετανοεῖ)[1383], but He would carry out His threat (τελέσειν... τὴν ἀπειλὴν, 3 Rgns ἐπάξω τὴν κακίαν)[1384] on Achab's son (Kings: in the days of his son)[1385]". Josephus rounds off

1379. The term is lacking at this juncture in RO and omitted by NN* (see n. 1382). It is read by NaMar following MSPE ExcSuid.

1380. This is the only occurrence of the above construction "put off punishment" in Josephus.

1381. Josephus' specification here that it is the punishment of Ahab's *family* that God will postpone during the king's lifetime represents an implicit "correction" of the Biblical formulation of 21,29bα "I will not bring the evil in his (Ahab's) days" which might suggest, contrary to the actual course of events (see 1 Kings 22), that Ahab himself will escape all personal retribution. Josephus likely found his inspiration for the specification in the phrase with which MT 21,29 ends "(in the days of his son I will bring the evil) *upon his* (Ahab's son) *house* (> 3 Rgns)".

1382. Thus the conjecture of Mar. Na reads ἐπεὶ alone with SPEExc, while NN* follow the wording of RO, i.e. εἶπεν ἐφ᾽ οἷς ἐπὶ, see n. 1379.

1383. The above construction μετανοέω ἐπὶ + dative occurs also in *BJ* 4,350; *AJ* 2,320; 5,240; 6,143; 7,264; 10,123; 11,317. Compare the μετανοέω + περὶ + genitive construction of 8,301.

1384. This is the only occurrence of the above expression "carry out (a) threat" in Josephus.

1385. With the sequence of 8,362 (Ahab's repentance, God's positive response thereto), compare Josephus' version of the conclusion of the David-Nathan exchange (2 Samuel 12) in *AJ* 7,153: "At these (Nathan's) words the king was dismayed and greatly troubled, and with tears of grief (λύπης, see λύπη, 8,362) admitted his impiety... whereupon God took pity on him and was reconciled to him. And He promised to preserve both his life and his kingdom, for He said, now that he repented (μετανοοῦτι, see μετανοεῖ, 8,362) of his deeds, He was no longer displeased with him". This "paralleling" of Ahab and David coheres with the positive touches which Josephus elsewhere introduces in his portrayal of the former. With 8,362's coupling of "confession" and God's modification of previously announced punishment, compare also 8,257 "...they (Rehoboam's subjects) all hastened to acknowledge that God might justly turn away from them since they had acted impiously toward Him and had violated His ordinances. But when God saw them... confessing their sins (see 8,362), he said to the prophet (εἶπε πρὸς τὸν προφήτην, see πρὸς τὸν προφήτην εἶπεν, 8,362) that he would not destroy them but would, nevertheless, make them subject to the Egyptians...".

the whole incident with the addition: "and so the prophet revealed (ἐδήλωσε, see 8,240) these things to the king"[1386].

Summary: MT and 3 Rgns exhibit a number of differences in 1 Kings 21(20), some rather substantive. Josephus agrees with the latter, first of all, in his placing of the chapter immediately after Elijah's "Horeb (Sinai) experience", 1 Kings 19. In addition, his parallel to vv. 27-28 contains several reminiscences of the 3 Rgns plusses in these verses, see above. His lack of a chronological indication at the beginning of the episode and of the extended description of the carrying out of Jezebel's directives corresponds to B's shorter version of the affair as against the more expansive MT and L readings in vv 1 and 11-12 (on the other hand, he does follow MT and L 21(20),10aββ in the citation, absent in B, of Jezebel's injunction concerning the accusation to be made against Naboth and the manner of his execution). Conversely, in "negative" agreement with MT against 3 Rgns, he lacks a parallel to the latter's plusses in 21(20),16 (Ahab's acts of penitence upon hearing Jezebel's report) and 19b (pigs licked Naboth's blood, harlots to wash in Ahab's), see too his equivalent to the motivating statement concerning Ahab's repentance in 8,362 corresponding to the MT plus in 21,29. We likewise noted two striking affinities between Josephus and TJ in this episode: both have Naboth charged with "blaspheming" rather than "blessing" (so MT 3 Rgns) God (8,358-359, compare 21,10.13) and both allude to Ahab's going "barefoot" as a sign of penitence (8,362, compare 21,27). Finally, in his adscription of "noble birth" to Naboth (8,358), Josephus agrees with Rabbinic tradition.

Josephus markedly abridges the rather repetitious narrative of 1 Kings 21 (see his similar treatment of 1 Kings 19), even in those portions where MT and 3 Rgns agree, above all in the case of its extended judgment speech of 21,19b, 20b-24(25-26). His reversal of the sequence of 21,19b and 20 is likewise noteworthy. Josephus goes beyond the Bible in citing the emotional states of the characters: Ahab is "pleased" at Naboth's death, God "angered" at the same. He further introduces various corrective modifications of problematic Biblical items, e.g., the site of Elijah's encounter with Ahab (compare 21,17-18) and God's last word concerning his intentions with Ahab (compare 21,29).

Already in this passage, it may lastly be noted, Josephus' Ahab emerges as an ambiguous figure who is generous in his initial dealings with Naboth, but then incensed at being "insulted" by . him and

---

1386. Compare his similar addition in 8,273 where he notes that the queen "told" Ahijah's words to Jeroboam. Cf. also his interjected notice in 8,361 that Elijah did in fact approach Ahab as directed by God.

"pleased" at his demise. Similarly, he twice represents the king as
assuming a penitential posture, once before and once after Elijah's
word of doom – in the former instance without Biblical precedent
(although see 3 Rgns 21,16). As such, the Josephan figure stands
intermediary between the maximally reprobate Ahab of MT (although
see 21,27-29) and the 3 Rgns king whose penitence is highlighted in the
plusses of 20,16.27[1387].

1387. On the MT and 3 Rgns portrayals of Ahab, see the article of Gooding cited in
n. 1224. On Josephus' overall treatment of Ahab, see too L.H. FELDMAN, *Josephus'*
Portrait of Ahab, in *ETL* 67 (1992) 57-78.

XVI

AHAB'S SYRIAN WARS
(8,363-392)

The extended narrative of 1 Kings 20,1-43 relates Ahab's double triumph over Syria and his subsequent denunciation by a prophet. In Josephus, as in 3 Rgns, this narrative follows, rather than precedes (so MT), the Naboth incident. To facilitate discussion of Josephus' version, I subdivide the text of 1 Kings 20 into the following units: 1) Ahab's initial victory (20,1-21); 2) his definitive triumph (20,22-30a); and 3) sequels (20,30b-43).

1. *Ahab's Initial Victory* (8,363-378a). Within the unit 1 Kings 20,1-21, one may distinguish an introductory segment concerning the abortive negotiations between Ahab and Ben-hadad of Syria, 20,1-9. This segment begins quite abruptly in both MT and 3 Rgns with mention of the Syrian king's collecting his forces. Josephus takes care to provide a more flowing transition between this new episode and the preceding one: "at the same time (κατὰ τὸν αὐτὸν καιρὸν)[1388] that this state of affairs existed for Achab...". Initially, he designates Israel's antagonist as "the son of Adados" (ὁ τοῦ Ἀδάδου υἱὸς, compare MT Ben-hadad, 3 Rgns υἱὸς Ἀδέρ); subsequently, he will speak simply of "Adados"[1389]. Whereas MT calls Ahab's opponent "king of Aram" (= L

1388. This phrase occurs also in *BJ* 4,585; *AJ* 6,325; 8,176; 9,7; 10,15 (with ὑπὸ); 12,265. More frequent is the equivalent expression κατὰ τοῦτον τὸν καιρὸν (*BJ* 1,218; 2,309, etc.).

1389. RAHLFS, *Septuaginta-Studien*, III, p. 109 points out that also in his list of Solomon's governors in *AJ* 8,35-37 (// 1 Kings 4,8-11) Josephus omits the "son of" element from various of the names cited.

Following W and Mar, B.Z. WACHOLDER, *Josephus and Nicolaus of Damascus*, in L.H. FELDMAN and G. HATA (eds.), *Josephus, the Bible and History*, Leiden, 1989, 147-172, p. 151 suggests that Josephus' form "Adados" – which differs markedly from the υἱὸς Ἀδέρ of 3 Rgns – for Ahab's antagonist may derive from Nicolaus of Damascus. Wachholder's suggestion is prompted by the observation that Josephus "sets up" the episode of "Adados'" attack on Samaria here in 8,363 in an appendix (7, 101-103a) to his account, 7,100 (= 1 Sam 8,5-6 // 1 Chron 18,5-6) concerning David's victory over the Syrians (in 7,100, undoubtedly drawing on Nicolaus, Josephus cites, as the Biblical sources do not, the name of the Syrian king vanquished by David, i.e. (an earlier) "Adados"), precisely by quoting "the fourth book" of Nicolaus' *History*. The relevant section (7,103a) of this citation reads as follows: "The most powerful of all these kings [i.e. the ten successors of 'Adados', David's contemporary, and all bearing of the same name] was the third who, in his desire to make good his grandfather's defeat, marched against the Jews and sacked the country now called Samaritis" (WACHOLDER, *Josephus*, p. 151 calls attention to the chronological difficulty involved in Nicolaus' (and Josephus')

king of Syria; B lacks the title), Josephus makes him "king of Syria and of Damascus"[1390]. This figure, Josephus proceeds to relate (// 20,1aα), "collected an army (δύναμιν... συναγαγὼν, 3 Rgns συνήθροισεν... πᾶσαν τὴν δύναμιν αὐτοῦ)[1391] *from all parts of his country*". Expanding on 20,1aβ's reference to the thirty-two "kings" who accompany Ben-hadad on his campaign, Josephus provides further background concerning these figures: the Syrian *made allies* of the thirty-two kings *beyond the Euphrates*[1392]". His forces thus gathered, Adados "marched against (ἐστράτευσεν ἐπὶ) Achab" (// 20,1b; compare Josephus' quotation of Nicolas in 7,103a [Adados III] "... marched against [στρατεύσας ἐπὶ] *the Jews*")[1393].

Already in 1 Kings 20,1b Ben-hadad is "besieging" and "fighting against" Samaria. Prior to reproducing this reference, Josephus introduces an extended circumstantial notice responding to a possible reader question, i.e. why was it that Ahab allowed the Syrians to penetrate as far as his capital without offering resistance? Josephus' "response" to this question runs: "(Ahab), not having an army equal to his, did not draw up for battle (πρὸς μάχην... οὐ παρετάξατο)[1394], but shut up (ἐγκλείσας, see 8,255) all (the wealth) of the country in the most strongly fortified cities, while he himself remained in Samaria, for this city was surrounded (περιεβέβλητο) by exceedingly strong walls (τείχη)[1395] and seemed in all ways difficult to take (δυσάλωτος)[1396]".

making "Adados" (III) the grandson of a contemporary of David who died c. 90 years before the start of Ahab's reign). To this quotation Josephus then appends (7,103b) a *Vorverweis* to his presentation in 8,363ff.: "And in so writing he has not departed from the truth, for this is the Adados who invaded Samaria when Ahab reigned over the Israelites. About this we shall speak in the proper place" (recall that in the same context, i.e. 7,105, Josephus sets up another later incident of his history, i.e. Shishak's despoliation of Jerusalem under Rehoboam, see pp. 77-79).

On Nicolaus, see further B.Z. WACHOLDER, *Nicolaus of Damascus*, Berkeley - Los Angeles, 1962.

1390. This same title (with its two components reversed) is employed of "Adados'" liked-named ancestor in *AJ* 7,100. Compare 8,304 (the anonymous "king of Damascus").352 (Azaēlos king of Damascus of the Syrians, t.e., see n. 1288).

1391. The above phrase "assembly a force" occurs also in *BJ* 1,28.290; 3,8; 7,252; *AJ* 12,289; 13,46.58.148.174.186.196.

1392. WACHOLDER, *Josephus*, p. 151 and n. 40 suggests that Josephus may have derived this non-Biblical specification (as well as other of his "embellishments" of 1 Kings 20) from Nicolaus, see n. 1389.

While Josephus does thus expatiate on Adados' "allies", he passes over the reference at the end of 20,1aβ to the king's "horses and chariots".

1393. Compare Josephus' own wording of Nicolaus' notice in 7,103b, "this is the Adados who invaded Samaria (ὁ στρατευσάμενος ἐπὶ Σαμάρειαν) when Achab reigned...".

3 Rgns 21(20),1 twice mentions the Syrian advance against Samaria, once in 1bα (so MT), the other in its plus at the end of 1aα. Like MT, Josephus mentions the advance only once and that at the same point as MT, i.e. in his version of 20,1bα.

1394. The above construction "draw up for battle" occurs also in *AJ* 7,11; 12,426.

1395. The above construction "surrounded by a wall" occurs elsewhere in *BJ* 2,218.606; 7,173.276; *AJ* 8,154; 11,89; 13,16.26.393; 15,297; *Ap* 1,87. The reference to

Thereafter, he gives his parallel to the notice of 20,1bβ on Ben-hadad's "besieging" Samaria: "The Syrian with his force (ἀναλαβὼν τὴν δύναμιν)[1397] came to Samaria, placed his army around it and besieged it (περικαθίσας [3 Rgns περιεκάθισαν]... ἐπολιόρκει)[1398]".

In 1 Kings 20,2-3 Ben-hadad dispatches "messengers" (B and L's 82/ o 93/e₂ lack the specification) to lay claim to both Ahab's material and human (wives and children) possessions. Josephus (8,365) makes the Syrian demand a more courtly and circumstantial affair. The messengers come with their demands only after Ahab has agreed to receive them. Ahab, in turn, does this in response to the "herald" (κήρυκα) whom Adados "sent" (πέμψας)[1399] to request that the Israelite receive his "envoys" (πρεσβευτάς, L* 3 Rgns 21,2 ἀγγέλους) "that through them he might inform (δηλώσει) him of his wishes". Again expatiating on the Biblical account, Josephus further notes that Ahab did in fact consent to receive the envoys. As in 21,3, the Syrian messengers thereupon begin by stating their master's demands: "at their king's command (κατ᾽ ἐντολὴν τοῦ βασιλέως, 21,3a 'thus says Ben-hadad'), the envoys said that Achab's wealth (πλοῦτον, 21,3b 'your silver and your gold') and his children (τέκνα, so 3 Rgns)[1400] and wives (γυναῖκας, 3 Rgns γυναῖκες)[1401] belonged (τυγχάνειν) to Adados (21,3b 'are mine')". In Josephus the Syrians do not, however, confine themselves to announcing Adados's demand; they also make a (conditional) promise on his behalf: "if Achab came to terms (ὁμολογήσῃ) and allowed him (αὐτὸν [MSPE αὐτῷ, cf. on 8,385] συγχωρήσῃ) to take of these what he pleased, he would withdraw his army (τὴν στρατιὰν ἀπάξει)[1402] and raise the siege (παύσεται πολιορκῶν)[1403]". Given such a promise, one

Samaria's "strong walls" which Josephus introduces here will recur later in the episode, see 8,371.

1396. Josephus uses this adjective elsewhere in reference to fortifications, etc., in *BJ* 1,411; 3,26.61.157.248.290; 5,142; 7,176.370; *AJ* 9,237; 12,367; 13,223; *Ap* 1,152.

With the above "explanatory interpolation" compare the similar interjected notice in Josephus' version of the siege of Samaria by Ben-hadad under Joram: "Joram... not thinking himself a match for the Syrians, shut himself up in Samaria, relying on the strength of the walls" (9,61, compare 2 Kings 7,24 which speaks only of Ben-hadad's commencing his siege of Samaria).

1397. Elsewhere the above construction "taking a force" occurs in *BJ* 1,333; 3,29 (pl.).145.459; *AJ* 8,411 (pl.); 10,110 (+ "he came" as in 8,364); 12,272.287.315. 343.350.367; (13,9).37.123 (+ "he came").337; 14,38.

1398. Josephus uses the above construction "placing round.. he (they) besieged" also in *BJ* 2,44; *AJ* 12,328.367; 13,324.

1399. The same phrase "sending a herald" recurs in *AJ* 10,75 which relates Neco's overture to Josiah.

1400. Like B 3 Rgns 21,3 Josephus lacks the specification found in both MT and L (τὰ κάλλιστα) that it was Ahab's "fairest" children Ben-hadad was demanding.

1401. In 20(21),3 the order is the reverse: "wives and children".

1402. Elsewhere *BJ* 4,9; *AJ* 7,290.393; 10,19; 13,334; 14,453.

1403. Compare the similar construction παύω πολιορκία in *BJ* 5,371; *AJ* 7,290 (+ "withdraw the army" as in 8,365); 13,324.

better understands Ahab's alacrity in assenting to the Syrian demands as reported in 20,4 of which Josephus' indirect discourse version reads: "Thereupon Achab bade the envoys go and tell their king that both he and all those belonging to him were the possessions (κτήματα) of Adados".

In 20,5 the citation of Ahab's reply is followed, rather abruptly, by the statement "the messengers came again and said...". Josephus, for his part, fills in the "missing links" of the Biblical sequence: It is "when they reported these words to him" that Adados "sent" (πέμπει) his envoys once again. According to 20,5b-6 Ben-hadad's second communication begins with a reiteration, in equivalent terms, of his previous claim, see 20,2b-3. It then goes on to enunciate a new, additional demand, i.e. on the morrow Syrian officials are to search the dwellings of Ahab *and his servants* and appropriate whatever their (so 3 Rgns, MT your, i.e. Ahab's) eyes fancy. Josephus formulates the new Syrian overture thus: "(Adados demands that) since he admitted (ἀνωμολογη-κότα)[1404] that all his belongings were Adados's [see Ahab's words to this effect in 8,366], that he receive the servants (δούλους, 3 Rgns παῖδας) who were to be sent (πεμφθησομένους, B 3 Rgns ἀποστελῶ) to him the next day (εἰς τὴν ἐπιοῦσαν, 3 Rgns ταύτην τὴν ὥραν αὔριον) to search (ἐρευνήσασι [see 8,332], B ἐρευνήσουσιν) the palace(s) (τά τε βασίλεια, L τοὺς οἴκους [B τὸν οἶκον] σου) and the houses (οἴκους, so 3 Rgns) of his friends and relatives (φίλων καὶ συγγενῶν, 3 Rgns παίδων)[1405] and give them (21,6 they will take) whatever they may find there that was most desirable (κάλλιστον), (adding), '*what doesn't please them* (ἀπαρέσαντα)[1406] they will leave for you (σοὶ καταλεί-ψουσιν)'[1407]".

In relating Ahab's (second) response (see 20,7-9) Josephus begins with an interjected reference to the king's emotional state: "but Achab was indignant (ἀγασθεὶς)[1408] at the second message of the Syrian

1404. Elsewhere Josephus uses the verb ἀνομολογέομαι in *BJ* 7,82.255; *AJ* 14,166; 15,84; 19,207.

1405. Elsewhere Josephus employs the above collocation "friends and relatives" in *BJ* 1,460 (reverse order).538 (reverse order).556 (reverse order).571.620 (reverse order) (2,82); 3,436 (reverse order); 4,223; *AJ* 4,257 (reverse order); 6,59.317; 7,43 (sg., reverse order).164 (sg., reverse order) (7,270); 16,156 (reverse order).380.381 (reverse order); 17,93; 18,23 (reverse order).99 (reverse order); 19,175 (reverse order). Here in 8,367, as in many of the other usages cited, it is unclear if, with the term συγγενής, Josephus has in view (a king's) actual blood relative(s), or rather the well-known Hellenistic court title, see n. 54.

1406. The term ἀπαρέσκω is hapax in Josephus.

1407. Note the shift to direct discourse here at the conclusion of the envoys' words. The above addition to the wording of 21,6 represents another accentuation of the courtliness of the royal exchange by Josephus: Adados will not, his envoys promise, leave Ahab destitute.

1408. It is only here that Josephus uses the verb ἄγαμαι in the above meaning. Elsewhere (see *BJ* 6,187; *AJ* 10,200; 12,219.281.307; 15,25; 19,136) it has the sense "admire".

king...". He then (// 20,7a) has the king summon an assembly (συναγαγὼν εἰς ἐκκλησίαν τὸ πλῆθος, L* 3 Rgns ἐκάλεσεν... πάντας τοὺς
πρεσβυτέρους Ἰσραὴλ)[1409]. At this juncture (but see below), Josephus
passes over the words with which Ahab commences his actual address
in 20,7αβ, "mark now, and see how this man is seeking trouble".
Instead, he has Ahab begin by citing Adados's demand, // 20,7b. Here
again, MT and 3 Rgns diverge. In the former Ahab states that he
refused Ben-hadad neither the persons nor the things demanded by
him. In 3 Rgns, by contrast, Ahab avers that when asked to give up his
family members, he signified his readiness to hand over (rather) his gold
and silver. In both instances, it remains unclear in what the difference
between the two Syrian demands consists, and why Ahab accedes to the
first with alacrity but is unwilling to submit to the second. Josephus
clarifies the point[1410]. He does so basing himself on a feature, present
as such in the Biblical versions of Ben-hadad's successive demands, but
left unmentioned in Ahab's word to the assembly, i.e. the claim of 20,3
speaks only of Ahab's own possessions, whereas that of 20,6 explicitly
extends also to those of his "servants". Josephus makes the distinction
in question the basis for the expansive word he now attributes to Ahab,
initially in indirect and then in direct discourse:

he himself was ready in the interests of their (αὐτοῦ)[1411] peace and safety
(σωτηρίας... καὶ εἰρήνης)[1412] to give up *his own* (τὰς ἰδίας) wives and
children (τέκνα)[1413] to the enemy [cf. 20,7b] and yield all *his* possessions
(πάσης παραχωρῆσαι κτήσεως)[1414], *for* this was what the Syrian had
demanded when he sent his envoys the first time. "But now he insists on
sending his servants (δούλους πέμψαι, cf. 8,367 τοὺς πεμφθησομένους...
δούλους) to search (ἐρευνῆσαι, see 8,367) *all* houses and leave (καταλιπεῖν, see καταλείψουσιν, 8,367) none of the most desirable (καλλίστων,
see κάλλιστον, 8,367) possessions (κτημάτων, see κτήματα, 8,366) in
them, for he wishes to find a pretext for making war (πρόφασιν...

1409. Josephus' substitution of "the people" as a whole here for the Bible's more
restrictive "all the elders of the land" (so MT, L* 3 Rgns "of Israel", see above) has in view
20,8 where, not only the elders, but "all the people" (3 Rgns λαός) respond to the king's
address.
    The above phrase "bring the people together for an assembly" recurs in *BJ* 1,372; *AJ*
4,63; *Vita* 280; *Ap* 1,224. The expression "call together for assembly" occurs as well in *BJ*
1,606; *AJ* 1,142.309; 5,72.93; 9,8; 11,228; 13,114.
    1410. Rabbinic tradition does the same in its own way. In *Sanh.* 102b the reference in
1 Kings 20,6 to "whatever pleases you (Ahab, so MT)" in Ben-hadad's second demand is
interpreted as an allusion to the scroll of the Law which Ahab is unwilling to hand over to
the Syrian.
    1411. Thus NN*Mar following the codd (subj: τὸ πλῆθος); Na reads αὐτῶν with
Ed.pr., cf. Lat cunctorum.
    1412. This is the only occurrence of this collocation in Josephus.
    1413. Josephus' form here corresponds to the τῶν τέκνων of L 3 Rgns 21,7b. Compare
B's υἱῶν (+ καὶ... θυγατέρων).
    1414. The above expression "yield (all) possessions" occurs only here in Josephus.

πολέμου λαβεῖν, cf. 3 Rgns 20,7αβ κακίαν... ζητεῖ)¹⁴¹⁵, and though he knows that on your account I would not spare what belongs to me, he is trying hard to make this disagreeable treatment (ἀηδοῦς [RO αἰδοῦς] of *you* an occasion for war (ἀφορμὴν... εἰς τὸ πολεμεῖν)¹⁴¹⁶. Nevertheless, I shall do what you think best.   (8,368-369)

After the foregoing, greatly expanded version of the king's speech which in the Bible comprises a mere half-verse, Josephus proceeds to cite the assembly's advice to Ahab. In so doing, he both expands and specifies the indeterminately concise "do not heed or consent" of 20,8 with his "then the people (τὸ... πλῆθος, compare 3 Rgns οἱ πρεσβύτεροι καὶ πᾶς ὁ λαός, see τὸ πλῆθος, 8,368) said that he ought not to listen (μὴ... ἀκούειν, 3 Rgns μὴ ἀκούσῃς) to Adados's terms but should treat him scornfully (καταφρονεῖν, see 8,251.274) and prepare for war". Josephus likewise elaborates on Ahab's reply to the Syrian (20,9a "all that you first demanded... I will do, but this thing I cannot do"¹⁴¹⁷): "... he told them to go back and say that *for the sake of the citizens' safety* (τῆς τῶν πολιτῶν ἀσφαλείας)¹⁴¹⁸ he still agreed to the demands *first* made by Adados, but would not submit (ὑπακούει) to the second demand". Vis-à-vis 20,9b which states that "the messengers departed and brought him (Ben-hadad) word again", Josephus highlights the active role of Ahab: "he then dismissed them".

1 Kings 20,10-18 constitutes an extended transition between the breakdown of negotiations in 20,1-9 and the actual battle report in 20,19-21. Josephus' parallel is 8,371-378a. He opens the new segment with a transitional phrase, "when Adados heard these words, he was greatly vexed (δυσχεράνας)¹⁴¹⁹". In line with 20,10 he goes on to report Adados' new, threatening message to Ahab. From that message he omits, as is his custom, the opening oath formula "the gods (3 Rgns ὁ θεὸς) do so to me and more also". He likewise provides an interpretative rendition¹⁴²⁰ of the obscure wording of the Syrian's threat itself. In

---

1415. With the above expression "pretext for making war", compare *BJ* 7,239 τὴν τοῦ πολέμου πρόφασιν.

1416. With the above expression "occasion for war", compare *BJ* 2,324 τὴν ἀφορμὴν τοῦ πολέμου and 5,397 ἀφορμαῖς πρὸς τὸν πόλεμον. On the specific nuances of the terms πρόφασις and ἀφορμή juxtaposed by Josephus in 8,369, see VILLALBA I VARNEDA, *Method*, pp. 8-11 who points out (p. 11) that the same juxtaposition occurs in *AJ* 20,82 "the Parthian king was swayed by their words to seek a war, but having no honest pretext (προφάσεως δικαίας μηδεμίαν ἀφορμὴν ἔχων)...".

1417. On this formulation in relation to what precedes, see C.T. BEGG, *"This Thing I Cannot Do" (1 Kgs 20,9)*, in *SJOT* 2 (1989) 23-27.

1418. The above phrase "the safety of the citizens" recurs in *AJ* 12,161.

1419. The verb δυσχεραίνω occurs 26 × in Josephus. Compare the (also interpolated) reference to Ahab's "becoming indignant" in 8,368.

1420. Compare Mar, *Josephus*, V, p. 770, n. b "Josephus seems to have *misunderstood* [my italics] the Heb. (and Luc.) text of 1 Kings xx.10...".

MT and L this reads literally "if the dust of Samaria will suffice for handfuls (לִשְׁעָלִים/ ταῖς δραξὶ, compare B ταῖς ἀλώπεξιν = לְשֻׁעָלִים, 'for foxes') for the people who are at my feet". In Josephus Adados's threat runs: "his army would take each man a handful of earth (κατὰ δράκα [see L δραξὶ] γῆς) and erect earthworks (χῶμα ἐπεγείρειν)[1421] higher than the walls in which he had such sublime confidence (τῶν τειχῶν οἷς καταφρονεῖ)[1422]". Josephus elucidates as well the Syrian's intention in making his threat: "in this way displaying to him the great number of his force (ἐμφανίζων... δυνάμεως)[1423] and seeking to strike terror (καταπληττόμενος, see 8,274)[1424]".

In 20,11 Ahab responds to Ben-hadad's threat with a proverb: "let not him that girds on (his armor) boast as he that puts (it) off" (so MT, 3 Rgns "let not the crooked man boast like the erect man"). Just as he does with Adados's word in 20,10 Josephus substitutes an elucidatory paraphrase: "... the time to boast (καυχᾶσθαι, 3 Rgns καυχάσθω) was not when arming oneself (καθωπλισμένον)[1425] but after coming off victorious in battle (τῇ μάχῃ κρείττω γενόμενον)[1426]".

1 Kings 20,12a narrates Ben-hadad's "hearing" Ahab's reply while "drinking (3 Rgns πίνων) with the kings (see 20,l) in booths". In Josephus the messengers find Adados "dining" (δειπνοῦντα) with the allied (see 8,363) kings[1427] and make their report. According to

---

1421. J.L. LIEZENBERG, *Studia Flaviana. Observationes criticae in Flavii Josephi Antiquitates Judaicas*, Schiedam, 1899, p. 88 conjectures ἐπεγερεῖν (note that this is the only occurrence of the above phrase χῶμα... ἐπεγείρειν in Josephus, whereas the equivalent phrase χῶμα ἐγείρεω occurs several times, see *AJ* 10,131; 12,363; 13,156; 14,61).

1422. The above phrase with its καταφρονέω + dative construction (= "to have confidence in") is highly reminiscent of that used by Josephus in describing the Jebusite response to David's siege of Jerusalem in *AJ* 7,61 καταφρονοῦντες τῇ τῶν τειχῶν ὀχυρότητι, see Mar, *Josephus*, V, pp. 390-391, n. b.

Josephus' above reference to Ahab's "confidence" in the walls of his capital here in 8,371 picks up on his earlier (likewise interjected) notice that Ahab "remained in Samaria for this city was surrounded by exceedingly strong *walls* and seemed in all ways difficult to take" (8,364). See also *AJ* 9,61 where Josephus introduces the remark (compare 2 Kings 7,24) that, in the face of the Syrian invasion, Joram "shut himself up in Samaria, relying (θαρρῶν) on the strength of its walls" (see further n. 1395).

1423. For the above phrase "display... force", see 8,109 (subject: God) and 10,9 (Hezekiah).

1424. With this formulation Josephus continues to "echo" his previous description of David's siege of Jebusite Jerusalem (see n. 1422), see 7,62: "David presses the siege in order to show (ἐμφανίσων, t.e.) his strength (ἰσχὺν)... and to strike terror (καταπληξόμενος) into any others who might treat him... as the Jebusites had done...".

1425. Other occurrences of καθοπλίζω in Josephus are *BJ* 2,434; 4,167.421; 6,161; *AJ* 2,341; 5,244; 8,186; 9,148; 20,122.

1426. This is the only occurrence of this construction in Josephus. As Mar, *Josephus*, V, p. 771, n.a points out, Josephus' version of the Biblical proverb cited by Ahab is somewhat reminiscent of that of TJ, "let not he who girds himself and goes down into battle boast like a warrior who wins and goes up from it".

1427. Josephus leaves aside the Biblical specification that the Syrian revels were taking place "in tents".

20,12bα Ahab's response provokes Ben-hadad to order measures against Samaria. For this item Josephus seems to align himself with 3 Rgns which in place of MT's indeterminate "take your positions" (so RSV, Heb. שׂימוּ) has Ben-hadad order the "building of siege walls" (οἰκοδομήσατε χάρακα)". Once again, however, he formulates more expansively: "(Adados) at once gave orders (ὁ δ᾽ εὐθέως τοῦτο προσέταξε)[1428] to build a stockade around the city (περιχαρακοῦν τὴν πόλιν)[1429] and throw up earthworks (χώματα βάλλεσθαι)[1430] and not leave any way of besieging it untried".

In Kings, the execution of Ben-hadad's directive (see v. 12bβ) is followed immediately (and abruptly) by the approach of an unnamed "prophet" with a promise of victory for Ahab (20,13). Between these two items Josephus interposes a notice concerning the impact of the Syrian initiatives on the besieged Israelites: "while these things were being done (// v. 12bβ), Achab was in a terrible state of anxiety (ἐν ἀγωνίᾳ δεινῇ)[1431] together with all his people (λαῷ)[1432]". Thereafter, Josephus, continuing his amplification of 20,13, notes that Ahab "took heart (θαρρεῖ) and was relieved of his fears (τῶν φόβων ἀπολύεται)[1433] thanks to the message brought him by a "certain prophet" (προφήτου τινὸς)[1434]. Having thus elaborated on the "occasion" for the prophet's appearance, Josephus reduces his actual message to its essential content: "God promised (ὑπισχνεῖσθαι, 20,13bα "thus says the Lord...")[1435] to deliver these many myriads of the enemy (τῶν πολεμίων μυριάδας, see 8,293) into his hand (ποιήσειν... ὑποχειρίους, see

---

1428. NN* suggest that something has fallen out after the word τοῦτο in the above sequence, a suggestion seconded by Mar.

1429. This is the only occurrence of this construction in Josephus.

1430. This construction occurs also in *BJ* 5,496. Compare χῶμα ἐπεγείρειν in 8,371.

1431. Josephus uses this same expression of Saul etc. in *AJ* 6,107 and of Sennacherib in 10,22.

1432. Such a reference to the "terror" experienced by the Israelites in the face of an overwhelming enemy threat is a standard element of Josephus' battle accounts, see, e.g., *AJ* 5,204 "the Israelites and Barak were dismayed at the multitude of the enemy" (in what follows the prophetess Deborah allays their fears with a promise of divine support, cf. the reassuring intervention of the "prophet" in 8,373a); 5,64 "this host of enemies dismayed both Joshua himself and the Israelites" (subsequently, God responds with a promise of victory).

1433. The above construction "be relieved of fears" occurs only here in Josephus.

1434. Cf. his designation of Elijah as προφήτης τις in 8,319. According to GRAY, *Kings*, p. 424 and GINZBERG, *Legends*, VI, p. 371, n. 36 Josephus identifies this prophet with the Micaiah of 1 Kings 22. Note, however, that here in 8,373 Josephus leaves the prophet of 20,13 unnamed. It is only subsequently in his version of 20,35 that Josephus introduces the name "Micaiah". It is, however, not so clear that 20,13 and 20,35 are referring to one and the same prophet- or that Josephus understood them as doing so, see further below.

1435. Elsewhere Josephus uses ὑπισχνέομαι with God as subject in *AJ* 1,103; 2,170.175.331; 3,7.306.314; 4,5.168; 5,65.93; 6,21; 8,197.

8,257 where this phrase is used of God's intented subjection of Judah to the Egyptians)". In so doing, he passes over both the prophet's rhetorical question in 20,13bα "have you seen this great multitude (B τὸν ὄχλον τὸν μέγαν τοῦτον)?"[1436] and 13bβ's indication concerning the purpose of God's announced intervention, i.e. "and you (sg., Ahab) shall know that I am the Lord".

In 20,14a Ahab asks through whom God will effect the promised victory and is told that it will be "by the young men of the governors of the provinces". Then in 20,14b the king inquires who is to initiate battle, the answer being that he is to do so. Josephus reduces this double question-answer sequence to a single one, while adding an explanation as to why God is entrusting the military initiative to Ahab: "and when he asked through whom (διὰ τίνων, 3 Rgns ἐν τίνι) the victory would be won, (the prophet) said, 'Through the sons of the governors (διὰ τῶν παίδων... τῶν ἡγεμόνων, 3 Rgns ἐν τοῖς παιδαρίοις τῶν ἀρχόντων τῶν χορῶν [so B; L χωρῶν]) with you to lead them (ἡγουμένου σοῦ) because of their inexperience (διὰ τὴν ἀπειρίαν ἐκείνων)'[1437]".

Following the exchange of 20,13-14 Ahab (20,15) "musters" the 232 (so MT L, B 230) "young men..." and then the 7,000 (so MT, B 60, L 60,000) "people of Israel". Josephus leaves aside the second grouping, perhaps because the prophet's announcement said nothing of a role for them (Josephus will, however, subsequently refer to the presence of an Israelite backup force, see below). In his presentation, Ahab summons "the sons of the governors" (τοὺς τῶν ἡγεμόνων υἱούς [compare 8,373 τῶν παίδων τῶν ἡγεμόνων]) who, as in MT and L 20,15, number 232. In 20,16-17a (see also 20,19) there is a (double) narration of the noontime (v. 16a) Israelite sally[1438] against the riotous Syrian camp. Josephus compacts these notices into a single indication: "when Achab learned that the Syrian was giving himself up to feasting and taking his ease (πρὸς εὐωχίαν καὶ ἄνεσιν πετραμμένον)[1439] [see v. 16b], he

1436. This phrase does, however, provide the likely inspiration for the Josephan prophet's reference to "these many myriads of the enemy" whom God promises to subject, see above in the text.

1437. W, Josèphe, II, p. 237 renders the last part of the above sentence "vu l'impéritie de tes adversaires", i.e. the Syrians. It seems, however, that the referent of the ἐκείνων here is rather to the "sons of the governors" mentioned immediately before (so Mar) who would be less militarily "experienced" than Ben-hadad's troops. Note too that W's footnote 1, ibid. is misplaced; it appears to refer to the word "adversaires" of his translation whereas it actually concerns the preceding phrase "les fils de tes capitaines".

1438. In MT 20,16 "they" (apparently the 272 and the 7,000 of 20,15) "go out"; in B "he (Ahab) goes out", while in L the king "goes out with them".

1439. Josephus uses virtually the same phrase in reference to the Shechemites in AJ 1,340. In addition, he employs the first component of the above construction, i.e. "turn to feasting" also in AJ 9,16.156; 12,98; 17,205 (with κατ') while the phrase "turn to enjoyment" occurs also in AJ 3,219 (t.e.).

opened the gates and sent the youths out (ἐξέπεμψε τοὺς παῖδας, B ἐξῆλθον παιδάρια ἀρχόντων τῶν χορῶν) [see v. 17a]". In 20,17b-18 Ben-hadad is informed of the Israelite advance, and directs that those approaching be apprehended – whether they come for peace or for war. In relating the Syrian's injunctions – given in response to the report of his "lookouts" (τῶν σκοπῶν)[1440] – Josephus has him allude first to the more likely intention of the advancing Israelites: "... he sent out some of his men to meet them, with instructions that, if the others came out to battle (εἰς μάχην, 3 Rgns εἰς πόλεμον), they should bind (δήσαντες, B συλλαβεῖν) them and bring them to him; and even if the enemy came out peacefully (εἰρηνικῶς, 3 Rgns εἰς εἰρήνην)[1441], they should do the same thing". At this point Josephus introduces a parenthetical notice, seemingly inspired by the reference – previously passed over by him, see above – in 20,15b to Ahab's 7,000 (so MT) additional troops: "but Achab had still another army waiting within the walls". His reference to this force's (initially) being held in reserve inside the city accords with the prophet's statement (see 20,12) that victory over the Syrians is to be won, in first place, by the 272, while diverging from 20,19 where, in a resumption of 20,16a, both forces mentioned in 20,15 sally out prior to the start of hostilities. In the same line Josephus now (8,376b) specifies that it was the "sons of the nobles" (οἱ... τῶν ἀρχόντων [compare 8,374 ἡγεμόνων] παῖδες) who "engaged the guards and killed many of them, while the rest they persued as far as their camp" (συμβαλόντες τοῖς φύλαξι πολλοὺς αὐτῶν ἀποκτείνουσι καὶ τοὺς ἄλλους ἄχρι τοῦ στρατοπέδου διώκουσιν)[1442] – compare 20,20a where these initiatives are attributed to "Israel". Only at this point, following the initial, decisive success of the 272, does Josephus relate that Ahab, seeing their victory, "released (ἐξαφίησι) all of his second army (στρα-τιὰν)[1443] as well". To Ahab's reserves "who suddenly fell" (αἰφνιδίως ἐπιπεσοῦσα)[1444] on them, Josephus then attributes the rout of the main body of the Syrian army which "fled from the camp, leaving all their armour behind" (τὰς πανοπλίας... καταλιπεῖν)[1445]. Josephus

1440. In 20,17b the identity of those "reporting" to Ben-hadad is not specified.

1441. Josephus uses the term εἰρηνικῶς 18 ×. B 3 Rgs 21,18 reads "for peace they are *not* coming out"; like MT, L lacks the negation.

1442. With the above description, compare the wording of Josephus' account of Asa's victory over the Ethiopians in 8,294 συμβαλὼν... πολλοὺς ἀποκτείνει τῶν Αἰθιόπων καὶ τραπέντας εἰς φυγὴν ἐδίωξεν ἄχρι τῆς Γεραρίτιδος χώρας.

For the h.p. of ἀποκτείνω used in 8,376, see n. 754; the h.p. of διώκω used in the same formulation recurs in *BJ* 1,336; *AJ* 6,116.119; 7,77; 10,110; 12,429.

1443. The above construction "release an army" occurs only here in Josephus, cf. 9,84 (Joram) τὸ πλῆθος ἐξαφῆκεν.

1444. This construction occurs also in *AJ* 6,79.362; 7,73; 9,82; (18,319).

1445. This is Josephus' only use of this precise phrase. In other "battle contexts" he does, however, refer to a routed army's "throwing off (down) its armour", see *AJ* 6,113; 12,410; 13,141.

precedes this notice with an explanation as to how the (numerically inferior) Israelites achieved their victory: "for these (the Syrians) had not expected (προσεδόκων)¹⁴⁴⁶ them to come out against them, and for that reason were unarmed (γυμνοῖς) and drunk (μεθύουσι)¹⁴⁴⁷ when they were attacked¹⁴⁴⁸...". It is in this context that he also incorporates the notice of 20,20b on Ben-hadad's horseback flight: "the king barely saved himself (διασωθῆναι¹⁴⁴⁹ μόλις)¹⁴⁵⁰ by making his escape on horseback (ἐφ' ἵππου, B ἐφ' ἵππου [L ἵππῳ] ἱππέως)¹⁴⁵¹". 1 Kings 20,21 rounds off the foregoing battle account by citing the personal initiatives of Ahab who goes out (cf. 20,16a where his egress is already mentioned), captures (so 3 Rgns ἔλαβεν; MT "smote", ויך) horses and chariots and kills many Syrians. Here again, Josephus both rearranges (it would seem more logical for Ahab to dispose of the Syrians before looting their military supplies) and expands on the Biblical data: "Achab went a long way (πολλὴν ὁδὸν... ἤνυσεν)¹⁴⁵² in pursuit of the Syrians, and slew (ἀναιρῶν, 3 Rgns ἐπάταξεν) them. Then after plundering (διαρπάσας, see 8,204.284.305) their camp, in which there was no little sum of wealth and also a large quantity of gold and silver¹⁴⁵³, and taking (λαβών, see 3 Rgns ἔλαβεν) the chariots and horses (in 20,21b the order is "horses and chariots") of Adados, he returned (ἀνέστρεψεν) to the city¹⁴⁵⁴".

1446. With the phrase αἰφνιδίως ἐπιπεσοῦσα τοῖς Σύριος...οὐ γὰρ προσεδόκων αὐτους of 8,377, compare Josephus' description of Saul's attack on Nahash ("Naas") in AJ 6,79 ἐπιπίπτει... αἰφνιδίως οὐ προσδοκῶσι τοῖς ἐχθροῖς....

1447. This mention of the Syrians' being "drunk" does have a basis in the Biblical record, cf. 20,16 which speaks of Ben-hadad "drinking himself drunk" (B πίνων μεθύων) along with the allied kings.

1448. Josephus' above description with its reference to the Israelites "falling suddenly" on the "unexpecting, unarmed and drunken" Syrians is reminiscent of his account of David's victory over the Amalekites in AJ 6,362: David comes upon the "already drunken" (μεθύοντας) Amalekites and "falling suddenly (ἐπιπεσὼν αἰφνιδίως) upon them, he made a great slaughter of them, for being unarmed (γυμνοὶ) and expecting (προσδοκῶντες) no such thing...". See also 1,177 where, in his parallel to Gen 14,15, Josephus speaks of the "Assyrians" routed by Abraham as being "incapable of fighting through drunkenness (ὑπὸ μέθης)". FELDMAN, David, p. 167 suggests that in these instances Josephus' language may be inspired by Herodotus' account (Histories 1.211) of a victory won by Cyrus the Persian.

1449. Thus MSP followed by NaMar. NN* read σωθῆναι (cf. σώζεται, 3 Rgns 21,20b) with ROE.

1450. Josephus uses the above construction "barely save (oneself)" also in BJ 1,280; AJ 13,375; 14,377.

1451. Compare MT "upon a horse and horsemen".

1452. The above expression "go a long way" recurs in AJ 2,323; 5,52; 14,16. Ahab would indeed have had to track the Syrians "a long way", as Josephus interjects here, in order to kill them seeing that they are already said to have "fled", 8,377.

1453. Compare Josephus' likewise interjected reference to the precious metals taken by Asa in his plundering of the Ethiopian camp in 8,294, and see n. 766.

1454. Compare 8,295 where, following their defeat and despoliation of the Ethiopians, the Judeans under Asa "turned back (ἀνέστρεφον) to Jerusalem".

222 AJ 8,363-392

2. *Ahab's Definitive Victory* (8,378b-384a). The account of Ahab's second, definitive victory over Ben-hadad, 20,22-30a, opens with a transitional sequence, 20,22-25, concerning Israelite (v. 22) and Syrian (vv. 23-25) preparations for renewed hostilities. In parallel to 20,22 Josephus has "*the* prophet" (i.e. the one previously cited in 8,373 // 20,13) warn the victorious Ahab to "prepare himself (παρασκευάζεσθαι) and hold his force in readiness (compare 20,22a, 'come [> 3 Rgns] and strengthen yourself [3 Rgns κραταοῦ] and know and see what you will do')". Ahab should do this seeing that "next year (τῷ ἐπιόντι... ἔτει, 3 Rgns ἐπιστρέφοντος τοῦ ἐνιαυτοῦ) the Syrian would again attack him (στρατεύσοντος ἐπ᾽ αὐτόν, 3 Rgns ἀναβαίνει ἐπὶ σέ)". Thereafter, Josephus adds the notice that, in fact, Ahab "attended to these things".

1 Kings 20,23 portrays Ben-hadad's "servants" (3 Rgns παῖδες) rather unceremoniously taking the initiative in proffering him their advice. Josephus (8,379), by contrast, is careful to represent the Syrian king as the one to initiate matters, just as introduces an expansive link with what precedes: "Now Adados, after escaping from the scene of the battle (διασωθεὶς [see 8,377] ἐκ τῆς μάχης)[1455] with as much of his force as he could save, took counsel (συνεβουλεύσατο) with his friends (φίλοις)[1456] concerning how he should again take the field (πῶς ἐπιστρατεύσηται)[1457] against the Israelites". The Syrian's counselors begin (20,23abα) with advice concerning the optimal site for the projected new battle. Josephus words as follows: "they were of the opinion (ἐδίδοσαν γνώμην)[1458] that he should not engage them in the hills (ὄρεσιν) on the ground that their god (τὸν ... θεὸν αὐτῶν) had most power (δύνασθαι) in such places[1459], and for that reason they had recently been defeated (νενικῆσθαι)[1460]". In line with 20,23bβ he then has the "friends" express confidence that "they would conquer (κρατήσειν, B κραταιώσομεν) them if they fought the battle (ποιησαμένους τὴν μάχην, 3 Rgns πολεμήσομεν) in the plain (ἐν πεδίῳ, B κατ᾽ εὐθύ)". In vv. 24-25a Ben-hadad is given additional advice, this time about the reconstitution of his forces. Specifically, he is first urged to dismiss the "kings" (v. 24aβ, cf. 20,l). Josephus expatiates: "(they also advised him) to send back to their homes (ἀπολῦσαι πρὸς τὰ οἰκεῖα, 3 Rgns

1455. Josephus uses the above phrase "escape from battle" also in *BJ* 1,47.368; *AJ* 7,1.

1456. Josephus' substitution of this Hellenistic court term for the "servants" of 20,23 is in accord with his procedure elsewhere, see n. 54. Elsewhere as well Josephus refers to a giving or taking of "counsel" by/from (royal) "friends", see *AJ* 1,209; 11,195; 12,263; 20,117; *Vita* 99.

1457. Thus the conjecture of Na followed by Mar. N* reads πῶς ἄν ἐπιστρατεύσηται with the codd, while N prints πῶς ἄν ἐπιστρατεύσαιτο.

1458. This construction occurs also in *AJ* 11,253.

1459. Compare the wording of 20,23aβ: MT "their god(s) (are) god(s) of the mountains" and 3 Rgns θεὸς ὀρέων θεὸς Ἰσραήλ, καὶ οὐ θεὸς κοιλάδος [L κοιλάδων].

1460. Compare 20,23aγ "and so they were stronger (B ἐκραταίωσεν) than we".

ἀπόστησον... εἰς τὸν τόπον [MT ממקרם] αὐτῶν [so B, L αὐτοῦ])¹⁴⁶¹ the kings *whom he had brought along as allies* (συμμάχους, see 8,363.372)".

In 20,24b Ben-hadad is urged to substitute "commanders" for the kings. This raises the question what troops those commanders would have under them since, presumably, the dismissed kings would take their forces with them. Josephus, with an eye to the difficulty, has the friends advise Adados to "retain their (the kings') armies" (στρατιὰν... κατασχεῖν)¹⁴⁶², while "appointing satraps in their place" (ἀντ᾽ ἐκείνων σατράπας¹⁴⁶³ καταστήσαντα, B θοῦ [L θὲς] ἀντ᾽ αὐτῶν σατράπας [MT פחות]). In 20,25a Ben-hadad's advisers call on him to raise a new force equal in men, horses and chariots to the one that had been lost. Josephus, who has previously made the friends urge the retention of the "foreign" troops, adapts this counsel as follows: "... to fill the ranks of those who had been killed (20,25 'like the fallen army'), he should levy a force (στρατολογῆσαι δύναμιν, B ἀλλάξομέν [L ἄλλοξόν = MT] σοι δύναμιν)¹⁴⁶⁴ *from their own country* (ἐκ τῆς χώρας τῆς αὐτῶν)¹⁴⁶⁵, as well as horses and chariots (ἵππους καὶ ἅρματα, 3 Rgns ἵππον... καὶ ἅρματα)". He passes over the reiteration of the advisers' affirmation that fighting in the plain will surely lead to Syrian victory (v. 25bα = 23b). In its place, he rounds off the whole segment with the notice (// v. 25bβ), "thereupon he (Adados) approved of these words as well spoken, and arranged his force (διεκόσμησε τὴν δύναμιν)¹⁴⁶⁶ accordingly".

1 Kings 20,26-30a constitutes the chapter's second battle account. This opens with a notice (v. 26) on Ben-hadad's advance to the Israelite site Aphek (3 Rgns Ἀφέκα) at the "return of the year" (see v. 22). Josephus' equivalent notice (8,381) runs: "At the beginning of spring (ἀρξαμένου... ἔαρος, B ἐπιστρέψαντος τοῦ ἐνιαυτοῦ)¹⁴⁶⁷ Adados, gathering his army (ἀναλαβὼν τὴν στρατιὰν)¹⁴⁶⁸, marched against the

1461. The above construction "send back to their homes" occurs also in *AJ* 5,74; 6,94 (with ἐπὶ); (9,249).251; 10,41; 20,33 (οἰκείαν).

1462. The above construction "retain an army" recurs in *AJ* 7,76.

1463. Josephus uses the term "satrap" 36 × . With the above phrase "appoint satraps" compare *AJ* 10,249.

1464. This is Josephus' only use of the above phrase "levy a force". The verb στρατολογέω occurs also in *BJ* 1,550; 4,263; 5,380.395; *AJ* 5,144; 18,84.

1465. Compare Josephus' description of Adados's first advance in 8,363 "he collected a force (δύναμιν) from all parts of his country (ἐξ ἁπάσης τῆς χώρας)" in which the specification concerning the source of Adados's force is likewise introduced by Josephus.

1466. The above construction "arrange one's force" occurs only here in Josephus. Other uses of the verb διακοσμέω are *AJ* 1,31; 3,71.114.219; 6,31; 7,85; 15,331.

1467. With the above reference to Adados's launching his campaign "at the beginning of spring", compare 12,293 where Antiochus prepares to invade Judaea περὶ τὴν ἀρχὴν τοῦ ἔαρος.

1468. Compare the equivalent phrase of 8,364 in the description of Adados's first campaign: ἀναλαβὼν τὴν δύναμιν.

Hebrews (see 8,255.353, compare 20,26 'to fight against *Israel*') and, after coming to a certain city which is called Apheka (Ἀφεκὰ = 3 Rgns), encamped (στρατοπεδεύεται)[1469] *in a great plain* (ἐν μεγάλῳ... πεδίῳ)[1470]". V. 27 narrates Ahab's counter-move, describing his force with the image of "two little flocks of goats" facing the Syrians who "fill the country". As usual, Josephus turns image into prosaic elucidation: "and Achab met him (ἀπαντήσας αὐτῷ, B 20,27αβ παρεγένοντο εἰς ἀπαντὴν αὐτῷ) with his force and encamped over against him (ἀντεστρατοπεδεύσατο)[1471], although his army (στράτευμα) was very small in comparison (ἀντιπαραβαλλόμενον)[1472] with the enemy". At this point (20,28) "a (so MT L; B 'the') man of God" approaches Ahab to announce that because the Syrians had asserted his dominion to be limited to the hill-country (see v. 23), God intends to give them into Israel's power in order that "you (MT pl., 3 Rgns sg.) shall know that I am the Lord". In Josephus this divine envoy becomes "the prophet"[1473], who "approaches" (προσελθόντος, 3 Rgns προσῆλθεν) Ahab "again"[1474]. To this prophet Josephus attributes the following message: "God would give him victory (νίκην... τὸν θεὸν ... διδόναι [> ROM], 20,28bα 'I will give [3 Rgns δώσω] this great army into your hand')[1475] in order that He might show His power (τὴν ἰδίαν ἰσχὺν ἐπιδείξηται)[1476] to exist not only in the hills (ὄρεσιν) but also in the plains (πεδίοις) [see the advisers' words in 8,379 "they should not engage them in the hills... they would conquer them if they fought... in the plain"], which was what the Syrians did not believe".

Following 20,29a Josephus next notes the seven-day (ἑπτὰ... ἡμέρας)[1477] interlude during which "both armies remained quiet (ἡσύχαζον) in their camps facing each other (ἀντεστρατοπεδευκότες, see

1469. Josephus uses the h.p. of στρατοπεδεύω (active and middle) 28 ×. The same usage occurs in Dionysius, see ERIKSSON, *Präsens*, p. 46.

1470. This specification as to where the Syrians "camp" lay has no equivalent in the Bible as such (although cf. 20,27bβ "and Syria filled the land [3 Rgns γῆν]"). It does, however, pick up the words of the royal advisers as cited in 8,380 (// 20,23b.25b) "they would conquer them if they fought the battle in the plain (ἐν πεδίῳ)".

1471. Josephus' only other use of this verb is in 8,382, see below.

1472. Josephus' other uses of ἀντιπαραβάλλω are in *Ap* 2,163.226.

1473. Compare TJ 'the prophet of the Lord".

1474. Both his designation of the figure as "*the* prophet" and the mention of his approaching Ahab "again" unscore that for Josephus this personage is to be identified with the one who had addressed the king earlier in the episode, see 8,373 (// 20,13) and 378 (// 20,22). This identification is in line with B 20,28's "*the* man of God" as against MT and L's "a man of God", see above in the text.

1475. Elsewhere in Josephus God stands as subject of the above phrase "to give victory" also in *AJ* 5,159; 6,82.145; 7,109; 8,401; 9,14; 12,316. Compare 8,295 παρὰ τοῦ θεοῦ νίκην λαβόντες... τῆς νίκης παρὰ τοῦ θεοῦ τετυχηκότες.

1476. Elsewhere Josephus uses the above expression "show power" also in *BJ* 1,215 (of Herod); *AJ* 2,332 (God); 14,184 (God).

1477. Thus the conjecture of NN* followed by NaMar corresponding to 3 Rgns 20,29a. Codd read ἡμέραις.

8,381; compare 3 Rgns παρεμβαλ(λ)οῦσιν οὗτοι ἀπέναντι τούτων)".
20,29b gives only the briefest account of the battle itself that is finally joined on the seventh day; essentially, all we are told is that the Israelites killed 100,000 (so MT and B; L 120,000) Syrian infantry. Josephus reserves this Biblical datum for a later point, while adducing various particulars concerning the preliminaries to the conflict and that conflict itself: "but, when on the last day (20,29aβ 'on the seventh day') *the enemy came out of their camp at dawn* (ὑπὸ τὸν ὄρθρον)[1478] *and drew themselves up for battle* (παραταξαμένων εἰς μάχην)[1479], *Achab also led his force out against them* (ἀντεπεξῆγε... τὴν οἰκείαν [> NN*] δύναμιν [RO ἰδίαν γνώμην])[1480]. *Then, after engaging (them)* (συμβαλών, B 20,29aβ καὶ προσήγαγεν ὁ πόλεμος) *in a battle that was stubbornly fought* (καρτερᾶς τῆς μάχης γενομένης)[1481], *he put the enemy to flight* (τρέπεται τοὺς πολεμίους εἰς φυγὴν)[1482] *and followed hard in pursuit* (διώκων ἐπέκειτο)[1483]. *And they were killed* (ἀπώλοντο) *by their own chariots and by one another*[1484]". He ends this extended account by utilizing (in reverse order) the notices of 20,29bβ (the Syrian battlefield casualties) and 30a (their flight to Aphek and death under its collapsing walls): "although a few of them succeeded in escaping to their city Apheka (διαφυγεῖν εἰς τὴν Ἀφεκὰ πόλιν αὐτῶν, 3 Rgns ἔφυγον... εἰς Ἀφέκα εἰς τὴν πόλιν). But these too perished (ἀπέθανον

1478. Josephus uses this phrase also elsewhere in reference to the moment at which military operations commence, see *AJ* 5,45; 10,137, cf. 12,307 ("near [περὶ] dawn"). In addition, Josephus employs other, equivalent expressions in noting that military initiatives begin around "dawn", see *BJ* 1,139.332 (2,552); 3,253; 5,51.538; 6,24; *AJ* 5,60; 8,414; 9 (12).54.

1479. This construction occurs also in *BJ* 1,381; *AJ* 6,26 (in this account of Samuel's victory over the Philistines one finds a sequence quite similar to that of 8,382, προελθόντων ἐκ τοῦ στρατοπέδου τῶν πολεμίων καὶ παραταξαμένων εἰς μάχην, i.e. προῆλθεν ἐκ τοῦ στρατοπέδου ἡ τῶν πολεμίων δύναμις καὶ παρατάσσεται εἰς μάχην).174; 9,12. Cf. also the equivalent phrase used of Ahab πρὸς μάχην... (οὐ) παρετάξατο in 8,364.

1480. With the above phrase compare *AJ* 6,170 (Saul's victory over the Philistines) ἀντεπεξάγει... τὴν στρατιὰν (6,170 and 8,383 are Josephus' only two uses of the verb ἀντεπεξάγω).

1481. Josephus uses this same genitival expression in *BJ* 1,101; *AJ* 1,175; 6,368; 7,13; 12,409; 15,151; *Vita* 327. Cf. also the related expressions "stubborn battle" (*BJ* 2,47.302; 6,47; *AJ* 17,258) and "the battle was (γίνεται) stubborn" (*AJ* 5,66; 15,111).

1482. Josephus uses the above h.p. of τρέπω (active, passive, middle) some 30× in battle contexts in his writings, see, e.g., *AJ* 6,135;13,59. The same usage is frequent in Dionysius, see ERIKSSON, *Präsens*, p. 47.

1483. Thus the conjecture of NN* followed by Mar. Na reads διώκων ἐνέκειτο κτείνων; in this reading the second term is his own conjecture, while the third stands in MSPEZon.

1484. Compare *AJ* 5,206 where Josephus describes the route of the Canaanites by the Israelites under Barak and Deborah: "... discomforted by their own cavalry, the enemy fell, many being crushed to death beneath *the chariots*" (this last detail is not as such present in the source text Judg 4,15 which speaks simply of the Lord's routing "Sisera and all his chariots").

δὲ καὶ αὐτοί)¹⁴⁸⁵ when the walls fell upon them (τῶν τειχῶν αὐτοῖς ἐπιπεσόντων, 3 Rgns καὶ ἔπεσεν τὸ τεῖχος ἐπὶ...) – twenty-seven thousand of them (δισμύριοι ἑπτακισχίλιοι, 3 Rgns εἴκοσι καὶ ἑπτὰ χιλιάδας). And in that battle another hundred thousand (μυριάδες δέκα [E δώδεκα])¹⁴⁸⁶ were slain (διεφθάρησαν, 3 Rgns ἐπάταξεν)".

3. *Sequels* (8,384b-392). In 1 Kings 20,30b-43 the account of Ahab's second triumph over Syria (20,22-30a) is followed by a sequel, itself consisting of two parts: l) Ahab's sparing of Ben-hadad (vv. 30b-34) and 2) a prophetic announcement of punishment for his doing so (vv. 35-43). The former segment begins (v. 30b) with mention of the Syrian king's flight "to the city, (into) a chamber in a chamber" (so MT, 3 Rgns εἰς τὸν οἶκον [τοῦ] κοιτῶνος εἰς τὸ ταμεῖον). With an eye to what follows (see 20,31), Josephus' version introduces a reference to the "servants" who accompany the fugitive Adados: "Adados.. fled (φεύγων, 3 Rgns ἔφυγεν) *with some of his most faithful servants* (πιστο-τάτων οἰκετῶν)¹⁴⁸⁷ and hid (ἐκρύβη, 3 Rgns εἰσῆλθεν) in an underground (ὑπόγειον) chamber (οἶκον, so 3 Rgns)¹⁴⁸⁸".

In line with MT 20,31 Josephus next has Adados's servants address their master with a proposal (in 3 Rgns Ben-hadad himself makes the proposal to his servants)¹⁴⁸⁹. The servants (or Ben-hadad himself, so 3 Rgns) begin, by invoking the benignity of the Israelite kings (MT מלכי חסד, 3 Rgns βασιλεῖς ἐλέους). Similarly, Josephus has the servants characterize Israel's monarchs as "humane" (φιλανθρώπους, see 8,214) and "merciful" (ἐλεήμονας, see 3 Rgns)¹⁴⁹⁰. The historian's underscoring of this feature of his source is understandable given contemporary Gentile claims that Jews lacked concern for other peoples¹⁴⁹¹. In 20,31b the servants (so MT; in 3 Rgns it is Ben-hadad

1485. LIEZENBERG, *Studia*, p. 88 conjectures οὗτοι for αὐτοί here with reference to the scribal confusion between the two forms observable e.g., in *AJ* 6,231 where for the οὗτος of codd Na reads αὐτός.

1486. Josephus' figure here agrees with that of MT and B (ἑκατὸν χιλιάδας) as against the 120,000 of L.

1487. The above expression "most faithful servants" occurs also in *AJ* 2,252; 6,205; 9,88. On the term οἰκεύς in Josephus, see GIBBS-FELDMAN, *Slavery*, pp. 294-295. Recall that in 8,379 the reference is to Adados's "friends" (φίλοις).

1488. Like 3 Rgns, Josephus lacks an equivalent to MT's reference to Ahab's initial entry "into the city".

1489. On this difference, see WEVERS, *Principles*, p. 316; S.J. DE VRIES, *1 Kings* (WBC, 12), Waco, TX, 1985, p. 244.

1490. Josephus' only other use of this adjective is in *AJ* 10,41 (where it is likewise collocated with φιλάνθρωπος) in Manasseh's prayer that God make the Babylonian enemy "humane and merciful".

1491. On this point see FELDMAN, *Mikra*, pp. 494-496. As illustrative of Josephus' interest in accentuating Jewish good-will towards Gentiles, see *AJ* 8,117 where at the conclusion of his prayer at the dedication of the Temple Solomon requests God to answer the petitions also of Gentile pilgrims (8,116) "for so would all men know... that we are

himself who talks of what "we" might do, see above) go on to cite two particular gestures of supplication by which they hope to secure Benhadad's life (sackcloths on loins, ropes on the head). The Josephian version of their proposal is worded more generally: "by using the customary form (τῷ συνήθει τρόπῳ)[1492] of supplication (ἱκετείας, see 8,324) they could obtain his (αὐτῷ)[1493] life (τὴν σωτηρίαν... λαβεῖν)[1494] from Achab". Unlike Kings, Josephus takes care to note explicitly that Adados's assent to his servants' proposal was both asked for and given: "(when they told him they could obtain his life) if he would allow them (συγχωρήσειν αὐτοῖς)[1495] to go to him, he let them go (ἀφῆκεν)[1496]".

In 20,32aα the Syrians go forth decked in their sackcloth and ropes. Josephus, in relating their departure, now does cite these particulars, adding an explanatory note concerning them: "so they dressed in sackcloth (σάκκους ἐνδυσάμενοι, B περιεζώσαντο σάκκους περὶ τὰς ὀσφύας αὐτῶν)[1497] and put ropes around their necks (σχοινία ταῖς κεφαλαῖς περιθέμενοι, B ἔθεσαν σχοινία ἐπὶ τὰς κεφαλὰς αὐτῶν, L ἔδησαν σχοινίοις τὰς κεφαλὰς αὐτῶν)[1498] – this was the manner in which the ancient Syrians appeared as suppliants (ἱκέτευον, see ἱκετείας, 8,385)". Acording to 20,32bα (MT) the Syrians "came to" (> 3 Rgns) Ahab from whom they ask, in their master's name, the life of "your servant Ben-hadad". Josephus expands: "going (παρεγένοντο, see MT) to Achab, they told him that Adados begged (δεῖσθαι) him to spare his life (σώσειν αὐτὸν)[1499] and would always be his servant (εἰς ... δοῦλον αὐτοῦ, 3 Rgns δοῦλός σου) in return for his kindness (τῆς χάριτος)[1500]". At the end of 20,32 Ahab responds to the Syrians' words

not inhumane (ἀπάνθρωποι) nor unfriendly (ἀλλοτρίως) to those who are not of our country..." (in 1 Kings 8,43 the motivation as to why God should answer the prayers of Gentiles is a different, "proselytizing" one: "... in order that all the peoples of the earth may know thy name and fear thee, as do thy people Israel, and that they may know that this house which I have built is called by thy name"). See further 9,43 (// 2 Kings 3,27): in the face of the Moabite's king's sacrifice of his son, Jehoram and Jehoshaphat (as also the allied king of Edom) "felt pity for him... and being moved by a feeling of humanity (ἀνθρώπινον) and compassion (ἐλεεινὸν, see ἐλεήμονας, 8,385), they raised the siege...".

1492. This phrase recurs in BJ 2,74; AJ 5,113; 12,95; 14,226 (pl.).

1493. Thus RO followed by NN*NaMar. MSP read αὐτῶν.

1494. This construction occurs only here in Josephus.

1495. Compare the accusative construction in 8,365 αὐτὸν... συγχωρήσῃ.

1496. > RO; Lat reads "dimisit eos hoc agere". N, ad loc., comments "fort. aliud scripsit Iosephus".

1497. The above construction occurs also in AJ 7,40.327; 11,221.256, compare σακκίον ἐνδυσάμενος, 8,362.

1498. It is not clear why Mar, ad loc. renders κεφαλαῖς in the above phrase "(ropes around their) necks", compare W, ad loc. "... la tête entourée de cordes" and Sc, ad loc. חבלים סביב לראשם.

1499. Cf. σωτηρίαν αὐτῷ, 8,385b. Josephus' formulation here is closer to that of MT (תחי־נא נפש = L) than to B's ζησάτω δὴ ἡ ψυχή ἡμῶν.

1500. Regarding the above phrase δοῦλον αὐτοῦ τῆς χάριτος, SCHRECKENBERG, Untersuchungen, p. 109 comments: "... scheint eine Sinnstörung vorzuliegen; denn was

with a question/declaration concerning Ben-hadad: "Does he still live
(3 Rgns ζῇ)? He (is) my brother (3 Rgns ἀδελφός)". Josephus notably
expands Ahab's statement, highlighting his magnanimity towards the
hapless foe: "(and the king), after saying that *he rejoiced at* his survival
(συνήδεσθαι[1501] φήσας αὐτῷ περιόντι)[1502], *and not having suffered
any harm* (μηδὲν... πεπονθότι)[1503] *in the battle, promised* (κατεπηγγείλατο)[1504] *that he would show him the same honour and goodwill*
(τιμὴν καὶ εὔνοιαν)[1505] one would accord a brother (ἀδελφῷ)". 1
Kings 20,33aα describes, rather obscurely, the Syrians' reaction
to Ahab's preceding words. RSV renders MT "Now the men were
watching for an omen (יְנַחֲשׁוּ, cf. 3 Rgns οἰωνίσαντο), and they quickly
took it up from him and said, 'Yes, your brother Ben-hadad'"[1506].
Josephus' presentation at this point, however he may have come to it, is
shorter and clearer: the Syrians "received his oath (λαβόντες... ὅρκους
παρ' αὐτοῦ)[1507] *not to do Adados any wrong* (ἀδικήσειν, see 8,277)
when he appeared[1508]...". In 1 Kings 20,33b Ben-hadad "comes forth"
to Ahab who takes him into his chariot. Once again, Josephus markedly embellishes: "... *they departed and brought him (Adados) forth*
(προάγουσι)[1509] *from the chamber in which he had hidden* (ἐκ τοῦ οἴκου
ἐν ᾧ ἐκέκρυπτο[1510], see 8,384 εἰς ὑπόγειον οἶκον ἐκρύβη) and brought

---

soll 'Knecht seiner Gnade bedeuten'?". Accordingly, he conjectures ἀντὶ τῆς χάριτος with
reference to Josephus' use of ἀντὶ (= "in return for") in, e.g., *AJ* 6,338.

1501. This is Josephus' only use of συνήδομαι in *AJ*; the verb occurs 6× in *BJ* and
once in *Vita*.

1502. Εκ, *Herodotismen*, p. 20 identifies the above phrase as an "Herodotian reminiscence", comparing it to Herotodus' notice (3.36.6) on Cambyses' word to Croseus
συνήδεσθαι ἔφη περιέοντι.

1503. The phrase (τὸ) μηδὲν πάσχειν occurs also in *BJ* 1,341.359; 2,324; 3,322;
5,316.409; *AJ* 2,106; 3,102; 7,388; 8,20.210; 9,83; 10,100.259; 11,134; 13,156; 14,170.463;
15,135.197.

1504. The verb κατεπαγγέλλομαι occurs also in *AJ* 6,78; 7,93; 8,6.

1505. The above combination "honour and good will" recurs in *AJ* 6,257 (reverse
order); 7,51 (reverse order); (16,22); 20,205 (reverse order). On εὔνοια and its cognates,
see SPICQ, *Lexicographie, Supplément*, 316-321, esp. p. 317 (uses of the above collocation
outside Josephus).

1506. On 1 Kings 20,33a, see BURNEY, *Kings*, pp. 239-240.

1507. The above phrase "receive oath(s)" recurs in *BJ* 4,523; 6,387; *AJ* 5,299 (+ παρ'
αὐτοῦ, as in 8,386); 7,24; 9,143; 10,100.102 (+ παρ' αὐτοῦ); 11,47; 12,8.376.382.396;
13,156; 14,108 (+ παρ' αὐτοῦ); 19,247; *Vita* 78.

Mar, *Josephus*, V, pp. 778-779, n.b noting that "Scripture says nothing of an oath
given by Ahab", suggests that Josephus may have understood Ahab's declaration in 1
Kings 20,32bβ "he is my brother" as an oath.

1508. Josephus' specification of the content of Ahab's "oath" here takes the place of
the directive issued by him to the Syrians in 20,33aβ "Then he said, 'Go and bring him'".

1509. Other occurrences of the h.p. of προάγω in Josephus are *AJ* 3,89; 6,13.

1510. So MSP followed by NaMar. NN* read κέκρυπτο with RO.

him (προσάγουσι)[1511] to Achab, *who was seated in a chariot*[1512]. *He then did obeisance to him* (προσεκύνησεν αὐτόν)[1513], *but Achab gave him his right hand* (... δὲ διδοὺς[1514]... τὴν δεξιὰν)[1515] and let him come up into the chariot (ἀναβιβάζει[1516] ἐπὶ τὸ ἅρμα, Β ἀναβιβάζουσιν αὐτὸν πρὸς αὐτὸν [> MT] ἐπὶ τὸ ἅρμα) *and, after embracing* (or: kissing) *him* (καταφιλήσας)[1517], *bade* (ἐκέλευε)[1518] *him take heart* (θαρρεῖν, see 8,322) *and not be apprehensive of any outrage* (μηδὲν τῶν ἀτόπων προσδοκᾶν)[1519]...".

1 Kings 20,34a records Ben-hadad's pledge to Ahab that he will return the previously captured Israelite cities and open up Damascus to Israelite trade. Josephus precedes his version of these specific promises with a more general statement by Adados: *"he thanked* (εὐχαρίστει)[1520] *him and promised* (ὡμολόγει, see 8,262.365) *to show himself mindful* (ἀπομνημονεύσειν)[1521] *of his beneficence* (εὐεργεσίας, see 8,287.300) *all the days of his life*[1522]". He then has Adados continue (// 20,34a): "and he offered to give back the cities (τὰς πόλεις... ἀποδώσειν, 3 Rgns τὰς πόλεις... ἀποδώσω σοι) *of the Israelites* which the king*s* before him (20,34a 'my father') had taken away (ἀπήνεγκαν, 3 Rgns

1511. Josephus' other uses of the h.p. of προσάγω are *BJ* 5,317; *AJ* 12,131 (middle); 14,272 (middle).417 (middle).

1512. With this allusion Josephus prepares 20,33bβ where Ahab invites Ben-hadad to mount his "chariot" which, in the Bible, has not previously been mentioned.

1513. Thus the reading of RO followed by NN*NaMar as well as by G. SCHMIDT, *De Flavii Josephi Elocutione Observationes Criticae*, in *Jahrbücher für classische Philologie. Supplementband* 20 (1894) 345–550, p. 384 who points out that Josephus regularly construes προσκυνέω with the accusative (see in our segment *AJ* 8,225.248.271.317 [*bis*].331.343). Compare MSP προσεκύνησεν αὐτῷ.

1514. Thus the conjecture of N, followed by NaMar. The codd (and N*) read δ' ἐπιδούς, while E has δὲ δούς.

1515. The above phrase "give the right hand" recurs in *BJ* 2,451; 3,334; 5,325; 6,318.345.356.378; *AJ* 18,326.328.329.

1516. Thus RO followed by NN*Mar; Na reads ἀνεβίβασαν with MSP. The difference between the readings of the Josephan codd here corresponds to that between MT and LXX regarding the subject of the verb in 1 Kings 20,33bβ; the former reads וַיַּעֲלֵהוּ (Ahab made Ben-hadad ascend), while the latter has ἀναβιβάζουσιν αὐτὸν (Ben-hadad's servants make him ascend).

1517. Josephus' only other uses of the verb καταφιλέω are *AJ* 7,284 (subject Joab, object Amasa) and 11,59 (subject Darius, object Zerubbabel). In both these instances Mar translates "kiss".

1518. Thus RO followed by NN*Mar; Na reads ἐκέλευσε with MSP.

1519. The phrase οὐδὲν (μηδὲν) ἄτοπον occurs further in *AJ* 6,44.88.234.355; 11,134; 16,326.331.

With Josephus' description here compare that of Tullus' dealings with the Roman suppliant Marcus Cariolanus in *RA* 8.2.1 "Tullus gave him his hand (ἐμβαλὼν δεξιὰν) and, raising him from the hearth, bade him be assured (θαρρεῖν... ἐκελέυσεν) that he should not be treated in any way unworthy of his valour...".

1520. Thus codd followed by NN*Mar; Na reads ηὐχαρίστει with E.

1521. Other uses of ἀπομνημονεύω by Josephus are *BJ* 1,223; 7,431; *AJ* 14,212.315; 15,34.376.

1522. Compare 8,385 where the Syrians promise on Adados's behalf: "he would always be his servant in return for his kindness".

ἔλαβεν), and to throw Damascus open (ἀνήσειν) (to them) so that they might travel there (ἐξελαύνειν εἰς αὐτήν)[1523], just as his fathers had been able to go to Samaria[1524]".

1 Kings 20,34b is problematic in both MT and LXX. The verse-half speaks of a covenant-making and a dismissal, but leaves unclear which king is the subject and which the object of these actions. The most probable understanding is that reflected in RSV "[And Ahab said] 'I will let you go on these terms (בברית, 3 Rgns διαθήκη)'. So he [Ahab] made a covenant (ברית, 3 Rgns διαθήκην) with him [Ben-hadad] and let him go". Josephus clarifies matters, once again avoiding the term διαθήκη (= "covenant")[1525] while conversely accentuating Ahab's chivalry: "Then, after they had made sworn covenants (ὅρκων καὶ συνθηκῶν)[1526], Achab presented him with many gifts (δωρησάμενος) and sent him away (ἀπέπεμψεν[1527], 3 Rgns ἐξαπέστειλεν) to his own kingdom[1528]". He then rounds off the whole episode with the added notice "so ended the expedition (στρατείας [ROM στρατιᾶς]) of Adados... against (ἐπὶ) Achab and the Israelites[1529]".

As noted above, Ahab's (apparent) good deed in 20,30b-34 evokes a divine word of condemnation in 20,35-43. The latter item is itself given an elaborate *mise en scène* which occupies the greater part of vv. 35-43. Specifically, we have first the preparatory incident of the "wounding" of a prophetic figure, vv. 35-37. This opening event, in turn, begins in v. 35 with a "certain man from the sons[1530] of the prophets"[1531] asking "his fellow" to strike him "by the word of the Lord". Josephus replaces the Biblical circumlocution for the former figure with the simple "a certain prophet" (προφήτης... τις)[1532]. More notably, he gives the

1523. RENGSTORF, *Concordance*, s.v. ἐξελαύνω likewise gives the verb the meaning "travel" here; compare W, *ad loc.* "s'y installer".

1524. Compare 1 Kings 20,34aβ "you may establish bazaars (חוצות, B ἐξόδους, L ἔξοδον) for yourself in Damascus, as my father did in Samaria". Note Josephus' double generalization of the wording of 20,34a: it was the *kings* before Adados (rather than "his father" alone) who had taken the Israelite cities, just as it was his *fathers* (as opposed to merely "his father") who enjoyed business concessions in Samaria.

1525. See n. 609.

1526. Josephus employs the above hendiadys also in *BJ* 2,453 (reverse order); *AJ* 6,253; 7,111 (reverse order).

1527. So NN*NaMar. M reads ἀποπέμπει, SP ἀπέπεμπεν and E ἔπεμψεν.

1528. The above expression "giving gifts he sent away" occurs also in *BJ* 1,238 in reference to Herod's dismissal of the Tyrians.

1529. Compare Josephus' notice on the commencement of Adados's second campaign in 8,381 "... gathering his army (τὴν στρατιάν) Adados marched against (ἐπὶ) the Hebrews...".

1530. TJ reads "from the students" (מתלמידי).

1531. Note that 20,38 will designate this same figure simply as "the prophet".

1532. This is the same designation used by Josephus of the figure who conveys a message of reassurance to Ahab in 8,373 (see also 8,319, of Elijah); subsequently, that figure is called "the prophet" (8,378.382). The fact that Josephus employs this indefinite

figure a name, i.e. "Michaias" (Μιχαίας), in this aligning himself with Rabbinic tradition[1533]. This identification may readily be accounted for in that the prophetic figure of 20,35-43 pronounces judgment on Ahab (20,42), thereby putting one in mind of the king's characterization of "Micaiah" in 1 Kings 22,8 as one who "never prophesies good concerning me, but evil". Josephus likewise specifies "Micaiah's" counterpart (20,35 "his fellow", 3 Rgns πλησίον) as an "Israelite", and has the prophet "bid" that he be "struck" (πλῆξαι [RO πλήξειν], 3 Rgns πάταξον) precisely "on the head" (εἰς τὴν κεφαλὴν)[1534]. Once more avoiding a Biblical reference to God's "word", Josephus substitutes a characteristic phrase, i.e. "for it was in accordance with the will of God (κατὰ βούλησιν τοῦ θεοῦ)[1535] that he should do so".

Drawing on 20,35b-36 Josephus now relates the sequels to the prophet's request of his fellow Israelite: "when he refused, (the prophet) warned him (προεῖπεν αὐτῷ) that for disobeying (παρακούσαντι)[1536] the commands of God (τῶν τοῦ θεοῦ προσταγμάτων[1537], compare 20,36a 'because you did not listen to the voice of God' [3 Rgns τῆς φωνῆς Κυρίου]) he should meet a lion (λέοντι περιτυχόντα) and be killed (διαφθαρήσεσθαι, 3 Rgns πατάξει σε [ὁ] λέων)[1538]. This was what happened to the man[1539]".

According to 20,37 the blow, requested but denied in v.35, is given by "another man" who, at the prophet's urging, "smites and wounds him". Just as with v. 35, Josephus introduces specifications and variations in his retelling of v. 37: "So the prophet went to another (ἑτέρῳ, 20,37aα "he found another [3 Rgns ἄλλον] man") and gave him the same order (προστάσσων, see προσταγμάτων, 8,389a)[1540] and, when

expression here now in 8,389 suggests that he has view a distinct figure from the one who speaks to Ahab in 8,373-382, see n. 1434.

1533. See *Seder 'Olam* 20 (note that here this name is given explicitly also to the nameless "prophet" of 1 Kings 20,13.22.28); *Sanh.* 89b; *t. Sanh.* 14.15b. On Josephus' tendency to name anonymous Biblical figures, see n. 214.

1534. Josephus likely finds the inspiration for this specification in 20,38 where the wounded prophet appears with a bandage "over his eyes".

1535. On this phrase see n. 88.

1536. Thus MSP followed by NaMar; NN* read παρακούσαντα with RO.

1537. This is Josephus' only use of the above formula "disobey the commands of God". Elsewhere the above expression "command(s) of God" occurs in *BJ* 3,361; *AJ* 2,291; 5,192; 6,136.165; 11,106.

1538. Josephus' formulation of "Micaiah's" announcement to the Israelite here recalls the wording of 8,240 where he recounts God's announcement to the disobedient Jadōn: "he should suffer punishment for transgressing his (God's) commands (παραβάντα τὰς ἐντολὰς αὐτοῦ)... a lion would meet him and destroy him (λέοντα... συμβαλεῖν... ὑφ' οὗ διαφθαρήσεσθαι)".

1539. Josephus's wording here represents a condensation of 20,36b with its repetition of the language of 20,36aβ: "and as soon as he had departed from him, a lion met him and killed him".

1540. Once again, Josephus compresses the Biblical wording with its repetition of language previously employed, compare 20,37aβ "he said, 'strike me, I pray' (= 20,35aβ)".

the man struck (πλήξαντος, see πλῆξαι, 8,389) and crushed his skull (θραύσαντος... τὸ κρανίον)[1541]...".

In 20,38-43 the duly wounded prophet encounters Ahab. Vv. 38-39 introduce this encounter as follows: "So the prophet departed, and waited for the king by the way, disguising himself (ויתחפש; 3 Rgns 'he bound', κατεδήσατο) with a bandage (so 3 Rgns τελαμῶνι, MT 'with dust', באפר). And as the king passed, he cried to the king...". Josephus rearranges and simplifies this sequence, eliminating its references to the prophet's departing and waiting as well as to the king's "passage": "he bound up (καταδησάμενος, 3 Rgns κατεδήσατο)[1542] his head (κεφαλήν, see 8,389) and, going to the king, told him ...". He then proceeds to present his version of the prophet's address, 20,39aβb-40a: "he had served in his army (συνεστρατεῦσθαι)[1543], and had had one of the prisoners (αἰχμαλώτων)[1544] turned over to him for guarding (παραλαβεῖν ἐπὶ φυλακῇ [MSP¹ φυλακήν])[1545] by his officer (ταξιάρχου)[1546], but (the prisoner) had escaped (φυγόντος)[1547], *and he was in danger of being put to death* (κινδυνεύειν... ἀποθανεῖν)[1548] *by (the officer) who had turned (the man) over to him* and had threatened to kill (ἀπειλῆσαι... ἀποκτείνειν, see 8,347) (him) if the prisoner escaped (διαφύγοι)[1549]".

In relating next the further exchange between king and prophet (// 20,40b-41), Josephus closely follows the Biblical sequence: confirmation of sentence by king, prophet's uncovering himself, king's recognition of prophet. His version (8,391) of these developments runs: "Achab then said the (punishment of) death was a just one (δίκαιον)[1550], whereupon he unbound his head (λύσας τὴν κεφαλὴν [cf.

1541. Compare the more general wording of 20,37bβ "and the man struck him, smiting and wounding him". Josephus' specification has in view 20,38's reference to the prophet's having a bandage "over his eyes" (cf. his previous request to be struck "on the head", 8,389).

1542. Josephus' other uses of καταδέω are *AJ* 5,309;17,160.

1543. The verb συστρατεύω occurs a total of 20× in Josephus. Compare 20,39aβ "your servant went out in the midst (B ἐπὶ τὴν στρατείαν) of the battle".

1544. On Josephus' use of the term αἰχμάλωτος, see GIBBS-FELDMAN, *Slavery*, p. 287.

1545. The above construction "turn over for guarding" occurs only here in Josephus.

1546. The term ταξίαρχος occurs a total of 20× in Josephus. With the above description compare the more indefinite wording of 20,39 "and behold a man (3 Rgns ἀνήρ) turned [> 3 Rgns] and brought to me a man (3 Rgns ἄνδρα), and said, 'Keep this man...'".

1547. Cf. 20,40aβ "he was gone" (B οὗτος οὐκ ἦν). Josephus leaves aside the preceding words of the prophet in 20,40aα "and as your servant was busy here and there".

1548. The above idiom "be in danger of being put to death" recurs in *AJ* 4,188; 6,358; 7,216; 10,203; 14,356; *Vita* 252.416.

1549. With these concluding words of "Micaiah", Josephus explicates the "man's" (fictive) warning as "quoted" by the prophet in 20,39bβ "if by any means he be missing (3 Rgns ἐκπηδήσῃ), your life shall be for his life". At the same time he leaves aside the "alternative punishment" of 20,39bγ "or else you shall pay a talent of silver" since this has no function in the continuation of the narrative.

1550. Compare MT 20,40b "the king of Israel said to him, 'so shall your judgment

8,389.390])[1551] and was recognized (ἐπιγινώσκεται, 3 Rgns ἐπέγνω) by him as the prophet Michaias (20,41b *fine* 'as one of the prophets')[1552]". Josephus further prefaces Michaias's concluding judgment speech (see 20,42) with an introductory explication of the prophet's previous action: "he had employed this trick (σοφίσματι)[1553]... as a way of introducing what he was going to say, which was that (ὡς)[1554]...". In citing (8,392) the words of 20,42 themselves, Josephus modifies and rearranges[1555]: "God (ὁ θεὸς)[1556] would punish (μετελεύσεται)[1557] him for having allowed Adados who had blasphemed Him (βλασφη-μήσαντα εἰς αὐτὸν)[1558] to escape punishment (διαδράναι τὴν τιμω-ρίαν)[1559], and would cause him to die at Adados's hands and Achab's people (λαὸν, 3 Rgns λαός) at the hands of his army (στρατιᾶς)[1560]".

In 20,43 (MT) the episode ends with Ahab returning "resentful and sullen to his house (> 3 Rgns) in Samaria" without respondng to the prophet's previous statements. Josephus proceeds the Biblical notice with a *Vorspiel* of 1 Kings 22,26-27 where Ahab commands the imprisonment of Micaiah: "incensed (παροξυνθεὶς, see 8,233 where the

---

(משפט) be; you yourself have decided (חרצת) it' ". The Greek witnesses diverge. B reads "... behold you have murdered (ἐφόνευσας = Heb. הרצת) snares (ἔνεδρα) from me", while L has "behold righteously (δικαστὴς, cf. δίκαιον, 8,391) you have murdered (ἐφόνευσας) from me...".

1551. Compare 20,41a "then he made haste to take the bandage (so 3 Rgns, MT 'dust') from his eyes".

1552. Josephus' specification accords with his earlier naming of "Michaias" as the prophet-hero of the episode in 8,389. Cf. also 1 Kings 22,8 where Ahab seems to know all about Micaiah.

1553. Josephus' other uses of σόφισμα are in *AJ* 6,218; 8,143.167; *Vita* 130.380.

1554. RO lacks this particle. N brackets it, while N* omits it entirely.

1555. W, *ad loc.* renders the prophet's words in 8,392 in direct discourse, whereas the Greek, followed by Mar, uses indirect discourse.

1556. NN* conjecture ὅτι θεὸς, see previous note.

1557. Elsewhere Josephus uses μετέρχομαι with God/the Deity as subject in *BJ* 1,584.631; *AJ* 2,304; 3,299; 4,47.

1558. The reference here is to the claims about the limitations of the Lord's power by the Syrians cited in 8,379.382. Compare the direct object construction "blaspheme (the) God" in 8,358.359.

1559. This is Josephus' only use of the phrase "escape punishment". With the above "accusation", compare that of 20,42aβ "because you have let go out of your hand the man whom I have devoted to destruction (MT חרמי, 3 Rgns ἄνδρα ὀλέθριον)" (RSV). The phrase rendered "devoted to destruction" might also be understood actively, i.e. "trying to destroy me (God)", cf. Josephus' characterization of Adados above as "the one blaspheming God". On the question, see P.D. STERN, *The ḥerem in 1 Kgs 20,42 as an Exegetical Problem*, in *Bib* 71 (1990) 43-47.

1560. Compare 20,42b "therefore your life shall go for his life and your people for his people". Josephus' inclusion of the Biblical word of doom also for Ahab's people involves him in an apparent inconsistency in that subsequently (see 8,405) he goes beyond the Bible in having Micaiah explicitly state that none of Ahab's subjects will fall with him in the upcoming battle with the Syrians, see below.

same participle is used of Jeroboam's 'indignation' at Jadōn) at the
prophet, Achab ordered him to be locked up (ἐγκλεισθέντα) and kept
under guard (φυλάττεσθαι)...''. Thereupon, he concludes, Achab
"greatly troubled (συγκεχυμένος)[1561] by Michaias's words[1562], returned
to his house (εἰς τὴν οἰκίαν)[1563]".

Summary: Here again, Josephus' account evidences affinities now with
one textual witness, now with another. He agrees with MT against both
B and L on a number of points: Ben-hadad's servants, not the king
himself, are the first to speak following the catastrophe of Aphek
(8,384, see 20,31); those servants ask to "go to Ahab" to request their
king's (rather than "our") life (8,385, see 20,31); Ahab (rather than the
Syrian retainers) causes Ben-hadad to ascend the former's chariot
(8,387 [note, however, the variant reading here], see 20,33); it is
specified that Ahab went "to his house" (8,392, see 20,43). Conversely,
he aligns himself with 3 Rgns against MT, e.g., in making the Syrian
king expressly command the erection of "earthworks" (8,372, see 20,12)
as well as in his reporting that Ahab "took" the Syrian horses and
chariots (8,378, see 20,21; compare MT "he smote"). With MT and L
20,10 he has Ben-hadad speak of "handfuls (of dust)" – contrast B's
"foxes", while he follows MT and B *contra* L in citing 100,000 (rather
than 120,000) Syrian casualties on the Aphek battlefield (8,384, see
20,29). Josephus' version of Ahab's proverb in 20,11 is more reminiscent of TJ's formulation than those of either MT or 3 Rgns. He agrees
with TJ too in designating the "man of God" of 20,28 (MT and 3
Rgns) as "the prophet". Finally, with Rabbinic tradition he gives the
name "Micaiah" to the (Biblically anonymous) prophetic figure of
20,35-43.

Perhaps the most remarkable feature to Josephus' handling of 1
Kings 20 is the fact that, contrary to his treatment of 1 Kings 19 and 21
(MT) in what precedes, he reproduces the chapter's extended content
with little abridgement[1564]. How is this state of affairs to be explained?
I suggest, first of all, that given the unit's focus on political and military

---

1561. This term corresponds to the first of the two participles used by B in 21,43 to
describe Ahab's inner state; Josephus has nothing equivalent to its second term, i.e.
ἐκλελυμένος (L reads συνεχόμενος καὶ κλαίων).

1562. This specification concerning the grounds for Ahab's distress has no Biblical
equivalent as such.

1563. Thus Mar with codd Lat; BkNN*Na conjecture rather οἰκείαν. Josephus'
reference to Ahab's returning "home" corresponds to the MT plus in 20,43a (see above).
Conversely, however, he has no equivalent to the reference in MT and 3 Rgns 20,43b to
the king's coming "to Samaria".

1564. He does, however, eliminate "functionless" (see e.g., the alternative penalty
prescribed for the loss of the prisoner, 20,39) or superfluous (see the reference to Ahab's
going both "to his house" and "to Samaria" in MT 20,43) source items.

matters, Josephus would have felt no qualms about rehearsing the story for Gentile readers *in extenso*. In addition, the source story gave Josephus the opportunity to counteract anti-Jewish prejudices concerning, e.g., the Jews' lack of military capability[1565] and particularism with its portrait of Ahab the successful general who is a model of chivalry in his dealing with a hapless foreign foe (just as he evidences exemplary solicitude for the welfare of his own subjects, see the largely Josephan address attributed to Ahab in 8,368-369).

The last remark suggests another point. Ahab, all his political virtues notwithstanding, ends up, in Josephus as in the Bible, condemned by God for his indulgence towards a "blasphemer" (8,392). Such a presentation underscores the priority of the religious dimension for Josephus; it is God's honor above all which has to be maintained – not only against the pagan Syrian but also against the Israelite Ahab – however admirable the latter might otherwise appear[1566].

1565. On this point, see FELDMAN, *Mikra*, p. 490.

1566. In this connection note that, in contrast to his dealings with Elijah after the Naboth affair, Ahab this time evidences no repentance, but rather takes aggressive action against "Micaiah" who confronts him.

XVII

JEHOSHAPHAT'S EARLY REIGN
(8,393-397)

Introduction: At this point, following a long segment devoted to Ahab and drawn exclusively from Kings (8,316-392 // 1 Kings 16,29-21,29), Josephus reverts to the figure of Jehoshaphat whose accession he had recorded in 8,315. In so doing he likewise turns, once again, to the Chronicler (2 Chronicles 17) as the source for his account of the felicitous beginnings of that king's reign. Josephus' rationale for introducing the material of 2 Chronicles 17 precisely at this point in his account, notwithstanding its disruption of the sequence of Kings' "Ahab narrative", is readily apparent. Thereby, following the movement of 2 Chronicles 17-18 itself, he provides background concerning the figure of Jehoshaphat who plays a leading role in the subsequent story of Ahab's demise (1 Kings 22 // 2 Chronicles 18).

2 Chronicles 17 may be divided up as as follows: 1) Jehoshaphat's piety and prosperity (vv. 1-6); 2) his educational initiative (vv. 7-9); and 3) tribute and military organization (vv. 10-19).

1. *Jehoshaphat's Piety and Prosperity* (8,393-394). Josephus begins his new unit with a double transitional notice called for after the lengthy preceding section devoted exclusively to Ahab: "such, then, was the condition of Achab. But I shall now return to (ἐπάνειμι... ἐπὶ, see 8,298) to Josaphat, the king of Jerusalem[1567]...". Of Jehoshaphat, Josephus next relates (// 17,1b-2) "he increased his kingdom (αὐξήσας τὴν βασιλείαν)[1568] and stationed forces (δυνάμεις... καταστήσας)[1569] in the cities (πόλεσι) of the country inhabited by his subjects[1570]; no less did he establish garrisons (φρουρὰς [RO φυλάς] ἐγκαθίδρυσεν)[1571]

1567. The same designation "king of Jerusalem" is used of Asa in 8,290.

1568. Compare 2 Chron 17,1b "he strengthened himself against Israel". Josephus' alternative wording may be intended to avoid the seeming discrepancy between this notice and 2 Chronicles 18 // 1 Kings 22 where Jehoshaphat and Ahab appear as allies. Note further that Josephus leaves aside the reference in 17,1a to Jehoshaphat's accession which he has already recounted in 8,315.

1569. Josephus employs the above construction "station forces" also in *AJ* 13,6.

1570. The above notice represents Josephus' "conflation" of the two-fold statement of 2 Chron 17,2abα (Jehoshaphat) "placed forces (2 Par ἔδωκεν δύναμιν) in all the fortified cities (2 Par πόλεσιν) of Judah and he set garrisons (2 Par κατέστησεν ἡγουμένους) in the land of Judah (2 Par in all the cities of Judah)...".

1571. This is the only occurrence of the verb ἐγκαθιδρύω in *AJ*; it appears 4× in *BJ*: 2,185.197.266; 6,47.

in those (cities) of the territory of Ephraim (τῆς 'Εφραῖμου)[1572] which had been taken (καταληφθείσαις)[1573] by his grandfather (πάππου, see 8,218)[1574] Abias[1575] when Jeroboam reigned over the ten tribes[1576]". Thereafter, he presents a compressed version of 2 Chron 17,3-6 which (twice) cites the Lord's favor towards righteous Jehoshaphat. Specifically, he leaves aside 17,3bα's reference to the king's "walking in the earlier ways of his father (David)"[1577] as well as the notices on his "not seeking the Baals" (v. 3bβ) and "removing the high places and Asherim" (v. 6b)[1578]. Rather, Josephus confines himself to generalities: "moreover he had the favour and assistance (εὐμενές... καὶ συνεργὸν)[1579] of the Deity[1580] since he was upright and pious (δίκαιος... καὶ εὐσεβὴς, see 8,280.300)[1581] and daily sought (καθ᾽ ἑκάστην ἡμέραν... ζητῶν)[1582] to do something pleasing and acceptable to God

1572. So NaMar following SP. NN* read τῆς 'Εφράμου. Compare 2 Par 'Εφράιμ, the reading of M.

1573. So NaMar following P. RO have καταληφθείσης, MS καταλειφθείσαις, while NN* read καταληφθείσης.

1574. N, ad loc.: "post πάππου adde ὅς vel simile". This proposal is not taken over in N*.

1575. The Greek rendered by "which... by Abias" above, i.e. ταῖς ὑπὸ 'Αβία, is Mar's conjecture (cf. ὑπὸ 'Αβία, MSP). NN* read simply 'Αβία (so RO), while Na proposes ταῖς ἐπὶ 'Αβία.

1576. Compare 2 Chron 17,2bβ "and in the cities of Ephraim which Asa his father had taken (2 Par προκατελάβετο)". Josephus' designation of Abijah (Abias) as the one who conquered the Ephraimite cities here stands in contradiction with both 2 Chron 17,2 and 15,8 (not reproduced by Josephus, see above) which assign that conquest rather to Asa. Josephus' adscription here in 8,393, on the other hand, is in harmony both with his own 8,284 and with the latter's source text, i.e. 2 Chron 13,19. In other words, whereas the Chronicler attributes the subjugation of the Ephraimite cites to both Abijah and Asa, Josephus consistently ascribes that deed to Abijah alone, see Mar, Josephus, V, p. 783, n. c. Compare Sc, n. 497, ad loc. who suggests that Josephus' form 'Αβία here in 8,393 could be due to a misreading of the אביו of MT 2 Chron 17,2 and W, Josèphe, II, p. 226, n. 4 who raises the possibility that Josephus had "un autre [i.e. than our 2 Chron 17,2] texte sous les yeux".

1577. "David" is missing in a few Hebrew MSS and B 2 Par 17,2 which read simply "...in the earlier ways of his father" (i.e. Asa).

1578. Josephus' non-mention of these latter items could have in view the fact that he has portrayed the reign of Asa, Jehoshaphat's predecessor, as characterized by consistent royal "piety and righteousness" (8,314) which would seem to preclude the existence of such abuses in Judah at the moment Jehoshaphat begins his reign. See above on the comparable case of Josephus' non-utilization of the Chronicler's notices on various cultic deviations removed by Asa himself.

1579. This is the only occurrence of this particular collocation in Josephus. He does, however, use the term εὐμενής of God (often in combination with other related terms) some 40 × ; on it see SCHLATTER, Gott, p. 62; Theologie, p. 30. He uses the term συνεργὸν in reference to God also in AJ 1,268 (object: Esau) and 7,91 (object: David), cf. further BJ 2,201; 6,38 (39); AJ 8,130 where God appears as subject of the verb συνεργέω.

1580. Compare 2 Chron 17,3a "The Lord was with Jehoshaphat" and 5a "therefore the Lord established the kingdom in his hand".

1581. Compare the "piety and righteous" Josephus attributes to Asa in 8,314.

1582. Compare 8,245 where Josephus states of Jeroboam "every day he sought (καθ᾽

(ἡδύ... καὶ προσηνὲς τῷ θεῷ)¹⁵⁸³". On the other hand, he does make use of 17,5b's mention of the presents given Jehoshaphat: "and those around him honoured (ἐτίμων) him with kingly (βασιλικαῖς)¹⁵⁸⁴ gifts (δωρεαῖς)¹⁵⁸⁵, so that he amassed very considerable wealth (πλοῦτόν... βαθύτατον)¹⁵⁸⁶ and acquired the greatest glory (δόξαν ἄρασθαι μεγίστην)¹⁵⁸⁷".

2. *Jehoshaphat's Educational Initiative* (8,395).

2 Chron 17,7-9 relates how, in his third year, Jehoshaphat dispatched a group of both lay ("princes") and clerical (Levites, priests) officials to "teach" in the Judean cities. Josephus' account of this initiative leaves unmentioned both the role of the Levites (cited before the priests in 2 Chron 17,8) and the whole series of proper names of the figures involved (MT has 16, 2 Par 14, see BHS)¹⁵⁸⁸ found in the source. His condensed version reads thus: "Now in the third year of his reign (τρίτῳ δ' ἔτει τῆς βασιλείας, 2 Par ἐν τῷ τρίτῳ ἔτει τῆς βασιλείας αὐτοῦ) he summoned (συγκαλέσας, see 8,215.226) the governors of the country (τοὺς ἡγεμόνας τῆς χώρας, 2 Par τοὺς ἡγουμένους αὐτοῦ) and the priests (ἱερεῖς = 2 Par), and ordered them to go throughout the country (τὴν γῆν [SP χώραν] περιελθόντας)¹⁵⁸⁹ and teach (διδάξαι, 2 Par διδάσκειν) all the people therein (ἐπ' αὐτῆς)¹⁵⁹⁰, city by city (κατὰ πόλιν, 2 Par ἐν

ἡμέραν ζητεῖν) to commit some new act more heinous than the reckless acts he was already guilty of".

1583. This is the only use of the above adjectival collocation in Josephus. He employs the phrase ἡδὺς τῷ θεῷ also in *AJ* 3,189; 12,47; for προσηνής see 8,215.

1584. So NN*Mar following RO; NaW read βασιλεῖς with MSPE Lat, the latter rendering the Greek οἱ πέριξ Βασιλεῖς as "les rois d'alentour".

1585. The above construction "honour with gifts" recurs in *BJ* 1,646; *AJ* 19,165. Compare 2 Chron 17,5bα "and all Judah gave gifts (2 Par ἔδωκεν... δῶρα) to Jehoshaphat" (Josephus' indefinite "those around him" for Chronicles' "all Judah" may have in view 2 Chron 17,11 which speaks of the neighboring peoples' paying tribute to Jehoshaphat).

1586. Cf. ὁ πλοῦτος ὁ βαθὺς, *BJ* 6,442.

1587. This is Josephus' only use of the above construction "acquire glory". The phrase "great glory" recurs in *BJ* 6,442 (here in combination with the expression "ample wealth" as in 8,394); *AJ* 12,49; 17,345. For the above combination "wealth and glory", see *AJ* 8,129 (reverse order).166 (reverse order, of Solomon); 10,272. Josephus' wording here clearly echoes that of 17,5bβ "there was to him much wealth (2 Par πλοῦτος) and glory (2 Par δόξα)". His inclusion of this particular item from the sequence 17,3-6 reflects his concern to counteract contemporary claims about the Jews as an undistinguished and impecunious people, see n. 766.

1588. In his note on *AJ* 1,129 where Josephus affirms that he has Hellenized Hebrew names "with a view to euphony and my readers' pleasure", THACKERAY, *Josephus*, IV, p. 63, n. g points out that the same concern leads Josephus to "omit lists of strange names as unnecessary". Examples of such omissions cited by him are *AJ* 7,369; 11,68.152; 12,57 to which the case of 8,395 (// 2 Chron 17,7-8) might be added. Thackeray further notes that pagan Greek writers like Strabo followed a similar procedure in their use of sources.

1589. Compare the phrase used in Josephus' description of Jehoshaphat's later teaching mission in 9,2 (// 2 Chron 19,4) τὴν χώραν... περιερχόμενος.

1590. Thus N*Mar, cf. R ἐπ' αὐτῇ. N conjectures ἐν αὐτῇ, while Na follows the ὑπ' αὐτὸν of SPE Lat.

πόλεσιν Ἰούδα), the laws of Moses (τοὺς Μωυσέος νόμους)[1591], both to keep (φυλάσσειν)[1592] them and to be diligent (σπουδάζειν, see 8,253.302) in worshipping God (περὶ τὴν θρησκείαν τοῦ θεοῦ, see 8,225.251.256)[1593]". The Chronicler says nothing explicitly about the impact of Jehoshaphat's initiative. Josephus remedies this lacuna with his addition "and so much were all the people (πλῆθος) pleased (ἥσθη, see 8,218.360) with this that there was nothing for which they were so ambitious (φιλοτιμεῖσθαι)[1594] or so much loved (ἀγαπᾶν) as the observance of the laws (τηρεῖν τὰ νόμιμα, see 8,291)[1595]".

3. *Tribute and Military Organization* (8,396-398). In 17,10-19 the Chronicler treats in more detail various matters touched on in the general introduction of 17,1-6, i.e. the tribute received by Jehoshaphat (see 17,5b) and the military initiatives undertaken by him (see 17,2). This

---

1591. NN* read Μωσείους here, a reading about which SCHLATTER, *Theologie*, p. 62, n. 1 comments: "bleibt ganz vereinzelt und ist nicht glaublich. Wenn der Schreiber ein Adjectiv beabsichtigt hat, 'die mosaischen Gesetze', gehört der Formel zu den christlichen Eintragungen in den Text des Josephus".

Elsewhere Josephus employs the above phrase "the Mosaic laws" in *AJ* 4,243; 8,191; 9,153.187; 10,59.62.63.72; 11,17.76.108.121.154; 13,74.79.279; 18,81; 20,44 (sg.).115; *Vita* 134.

2 Chron 17,9b does not specify as such what it was that the delegation "taught" the Judeans (in TC they are said to teach "the fear of the Lord"). It does, however, allude to Jehoshaphat's envoys' "having the book of the law (2 Par νόμου) of the Lord with them". Josephus' statement that the commission taught "the laws (νόμους) of Moses" seems inspired by this allusion.

1592. Elsewhere Josephus employs the above construction "keep the law(s)" in *BJ* 2,202 (sg.); *AJ* (3,223); 4,159 (191.210).318; 7,130.338.374; 10,63; 13,54; 19,290; *Vita* 160; *Ap* 1,160; 2,184 (sg.).194.278, cf. *AJ* 16,49; *Ap* 1,317.

1593. The above construction "be diligent in worshipping God" recurs in *AJ* 1,222 (Isaac);4,61 (Korah).306 (the people). Elsewhere too Josephus associates keeping the (Mosaic) law(s) and worship of God, see *AJ* 4,306; 8,120; 9,2 (Jehoshaphat's second teaching mission, // 2 Chron 19,4) τὸν λαὸν ἐκδιδάσκειν τά τε νόμιμα τὰ διὰ Μωυσέος ὑπὸ τοῦ θεοῦ δοθέντα καὶ τὴν εὐσέβειαν τὴν πρὸς αὐτόν and 10,63 where Josiah compels the people θρησκεύσειν τὸν θεὸν καὶ φυλάξειν τοὺς Μωυσέος νόμους.

1594. The verb φιλοτιμέομαι occurs 30 × in Josephus.

1595. With the above reference to the people's "ambition and love to keep the laws" SCHLATTER, *Theologie*, p. 154 compares *AJ* 16,158 "the Jewish nation is... accustomed to admire (ἠγαπηκέναι) righteousness rather than glory" and 15,375 where the Essene Manaēmus addresses Herod "the best attitude... would be to love (ἀγαπήσειας) justice and piety towards God and mildness towards your citizens". As other exemplifications of this Josephan emphasis, see also 8,297 "when the king (Asa) and the people heard these words (of the prophet Azariah) they rejoiced, and all together and each privately took thought for what was right" and 10,63 (the outcome of Josiah's effort to "compel the people to worship God and keep the laws of Moses", see n. 1593) "and they eagerly assented and undertook to do what the king (Josiah) urged upon them...".

With reference to *AJ* 8,395 and 3,222-223.317-322, S. SCHWARTZ, *Josephus and Judean Politics* (Columbia Studies in the Classical Tradition, 18), Leiden, 1990, pp. 195-198 speaks of a "sub-theme" in *AJ*, i.e. "the Hebrews, and later the Jews, were so devoted to the observance of Jewish law they they would rather die (and/or fight) than transgress it".

supplementary segment opens in 17,10 with the statement that "fear of the Lord" restrained the surrounding kingdoms from attacking Jehoshaphat. Josephus leaves aside this "theological note", merely stating (8,396) "the neighboring peoples (οἵ... προσχώριοι, cf. 8,394 οἱ πέριξ) also continued to cherish (στέργοντες, see 8,249) Josaphat and remained at peace (εἰρήνην ἄγοντες)[1596] with him".

2 Chron 17,11 singles out the tribute brought Jehoshaphat by the Philistines (monetary) and the Arabs (in kind), with the Biblical witnesses differing concerning the latter (MT and L 7,700 rams and 7,700 he-goats, B 7,700 rams). Here again, Josephus goes his own way in various respects: "and the Philistines (οἱ... Παλαιστῖνοι, 2 Par [ἀπὸ] τῶν ἀλλοφύλων)[1597] paid him the appointed tribute (τακτοὺς[1598] ἐτέλουν... φόρους)[1599], while (the) Arabs (Ἄραβες, 2 Par οἱ Ἄραβες) supplied (ἐχορήγουν, 2 Par ἔφερον) him *every year*[1600] with three hundred and sixty lambs (ἄρνας, B κριοὺς προβάτων) and as many kids (ἐρίφους, L τράγους = MT אלפים)[1601]". In this instance, the discrepancy between Josephus' figure and the Biblical one(s) is especially marked. It likely reflects the historian's use of a source text divergent from both MT and 2 Par in that elsewhere Josephus does take over "inflated" Biblical numbers (see e.g., AJ 9,29 where he reproduces 2 Kings 3,4's figure of 200,000 bovines for Mesha's tribute to Joram of Israel), just as he is also intent, as has been noted, on underscoring the wealth amassed by Jews in their dealings with foreigners[1602].

In 17,12-19 the Chronicler enumerates Jehoshaphat's military arrangements. He begins (17,12-13) by citing the king's construction of fortresses and store-cities as well as his distribution of men and supplies. Josephus' version of these notices is shorter, leaving out such items as 17,12a's general reference to Jehoshaphat's "growing greater" and the various localizations given in vv. 12b-13: "he also fortified large cities, among which were strongholds[1603], and prepared a force of

1596. This construction occurs also in *BJ* 2,345.

1597. See n. 705.

1598. This is Josephus' only use of the adjective τακτός, although see *BJ* 2,469 where it is proposed as an emendation by Reinach.

1599. Compare 2 Chron 17,11a (the Philistines) "brought (2 Par ἔφερον) Jehoshaphat gifts and silver (and) presents".

1600. This specification is introduced by Josephus.

1601. W, *ad loc.* renders ἐρίφους by "béliers", a meaning not cited in LSJ. Josephus uses the above collocation "lambs and kids" also in *AJ* 3,222.231; 9,268; 10,70 (reverse order); 11,137.

1602. See the comment on the figures given by Josephus for the Arabs' tribute in 8,396 by W, *Josèphe*, II, p. 241, n. 2: "Les chiffres de Josèphe sont si modérés qu'on peut se demander s'il les a changés lui-même ou s'il les lisait déjà sur son modèle".

1603. (πόλεις τε ᾠχύρωσε μεγάλας ἄλλας τε καὶ βάρεις). Text-critically problematic in this reading as proposed by NaMar is above all its final term, βάρεις. This noun form does stand in SP (as also in L 2 Par 17,12, compare Β οἰκήσεις). NN* on, the other hand, prefer the adjectival form βαρεῖς found in ROM, as does W, see his rendering, *ad loc.* "villes grandes et imposantes".

soldiers (δύναμιν στρατιωτικὴν)[1604] and weapons against his enemies (καὶ ὅπλα πρὸς τοὺς πολεμίους)[1605]".

2 Chron 17,14-18(19) breaks down the forces available to Jehoshaphat by tribe and commander. Josephus gives what appears to be a conflated version of these data: "From the tribe of Judah there was an army of three hundred thousand heavy-armed soliders (ὁπλιτῶν, see 8,308; 2 Par 17,14b υἱοὶ δυνατοὶ δυνάμεως), of which Ednaios ('Εδναῖος)[1606] had command (τὴν ἡγεμονίαν εἶχεν, 2 Par [Ednaas, etc.] ὁ ἄρχων)[1607], and two hundred thousand under Joannes ('Ιωάννης)[1608], who was at the same time (κὰκ τῆς) commander (ἡγεμὼν, 2 Par ἡγούμενος) of two hundred thousand archers (τοξοτῶν, 2 Par τοξόται) on foot (πεζῶν)[1609] from the tribe of Benjamin[1610]. Another commander (ἄλλος δ' ἡγεμὼν)[1611] named Ochobatos ('Οχόβατος)[1612] put at the king's disposal a host (πλῆθος) of one hundred and eighty thousand (so 17,18) heavy-armed soldiers (ὁπλιτῶν, 2 Par δυνατοὶ πολέμου)". Following these figures the historian concludes (// 17,19) "These did not include (πάρεξ ὧν, 2 Par ἐκτὸς ὧν) the men whom the king had sent (διέπεμψε, 2 Par ἔδωκεν) to the several best fortified cities (εἰς τὰς ὀχυρωτάτας... πόλεις, 2 Par ἐν ταῖς πόλεσιν ταῖς ὀχυραῖς)".

1604. This phrase appears also in 13,225. Compare 17,13b "he had soldiers, mighty men of valor...".

1605. Thus MSP Lat followed by NaMarWSc. NN* adopt the shorter reading of RO, i.e. simply πρὸς πολέμους. Josephus' mention of "weapons" in the reading of Mar *et al.* might be seen as his (specifying) equivalent to the "stores" (2 Par ἔργα) which Jehoshaphat accumulates according to 2 Chron 17,13a.

The reference to the "enemies" of Jehoshaphat in the above reading comes as something of a surprise given Josephus' immediately preceding reference to the king's being "cherished" by the "neighboring peoples", 8,396. (On the other hand, it does intimate a rationale for the king's defensive measures as cited here in 8,397).

1606. Compare MT עַזְרָה‎, B 'Εδναάς, L Αἰδηάς.

1607. The above construction "have command" occurs also in *AJ* 11,184; 18,88; 19,17.

1608. Compare MT יְהוֹחָנָן‎, 2 Par 'Ιω(α)νάν.

1609. Elsewhere Josephus speaks of "foot archers" in *BJ* 3,68, cf. 2,500.

1610. Contrast 2 Chron 17,15 where Jehohanan's command is limited to *280,000 Judeans*, whereas, according to 17,17, *Eliada* is general of the 200,000 *Benjaminite* bowmen (who are likewise said to "carry shields" – a point not mentioned by Josephus). Note further that Josephus leaves completely unmentioned Amasiah (2 Par Massaias etc.) to whom 17,16 assigns 200,000 Judean troops.

1611. By haplography RO omits the entire sequence κὰκ τῆς.... ἄλλος δ' ἡγεμὼν in 8,397.

1612. SoNaWMar, following MSP. N conjectures Ωδάβαθος, N* rather Ωχάβαθος (cf. RO ᾧ χάβαθος), while SCHLATTER, *Namen*, p. 56, s.v. יְהוֹזָבָד‎ suggests 'Ιωζαβαδος, as does SCHALIT, *Namenwörterbuch*, p. 95, s.v. 'Οχόβατος (he also mentions the possibility of an original 'Ιοζάβατος). Compare MT יְהוֹזָבָד‎, 2 Par 'Ιωζαβάδ.

Summary: In content, MT and LXX largely cohere in 2 Chronicles 17. Where they do differ, e.g., in the (non-)mention of David as the "father" of Jehoshaphat in 17,3 (so B vs. MT L) or the number of proper names cited in 17,7-8, Josephus goes his own way with respect to both. In one instance, i.e. the number of beasts supplied to Jehoshaphat by the Arabs (8,396 // 2 Chron 17,11b), it appears likely that Josephus is utilizing a text differing from both MT and 2 Par.

In comparison with the preceding segment (// 1 Kings 20), Josephus, in his rewriting of 2 Chronicles 17, reverts to his more usual practice of eliminating many of the source's particulars, e.g., the cultically prohibited items of 17,3.6 as well as the proper names of 17,9-10 and 14-18 (in part). His only major expansion is the notice on the effects of Jehoshaphat's teaching mission (8,395). Finally, he "corrects" the name "Asa" in 17,2 to "Abijah" in order to bring the reference into line with his presentation elsewhere.

XVIII

AHAB'S DEATH
(8,398-420)

The final section of *AJ* 8,212-420 to be examined in this study is the account of Ahab's death at the hands of the Syrians[1613]. The Bible gives a double version of the episode, i.e. 1 Kings 22,1-40[1614] and 2 Chron 18,1-34. Whereas the respective openings and conclusions of the two versions vary, their core narratives are verbally parallel to a large extent. The Biblical account(s) may be divided up as follows: 1) the initial royal encounter (1 Kings 22,1-4 // 2 Chron 18,1-3); 2) the double prophetic consultation (1 Kings 22,5-28 // 2 Chron 18,4-27); the battle, ending with Ahab's death (1 Kings 22,29-35 // 2 Chron 18,28-34); 4) closing notices for Ahab (1 Kings 22,36-40, no parallel in Chronicles)[1615]. Each of these four divisions has its pendant in 8,398-420.

1. *Initial Royal Encounter* (8,398-399). Although they will, as noted above, subsequently run largely parallel to each other, Kings and Chronicles do differ – at least at the outset – in their respective introductions to our episode, i.e. the meeting between Jehoshaphat and Ahab. Josephus, who has just reproduced the *Sondergut* section concerning Jehoshaphat's early reign, 2 Chronicles 17, bases his own introduction on the more expansive Chronistic one, i.e. 2 Chron 18,1-2, as opposed to that of 1 Kings 22,1-2, even while contriving to utilize elements of the latter as well, see below. More specifically, passing over the notice of 18,1 on Jehoshaphat's wealth and glory – a duplicate of 17,5bβ cited by him in 8,394b – Josephus moves immediately to the matter of the Judean's "marriage alliance" with Ahab as mentioned in 18,1b which provides the proximate occasion for Jehoshaphat's visit to Samaria related in what follows. His parallel to 18,1b reads thus: "Now

---

1613. This section represents a reworked version of my article *The Death of King Ahab According to Josephus*, in *Anton* 64 (1989) 225-245.

1614. With 3 Rgns 22, the B text becomes, once again, a witness to the "kaige recension" after its extended "non-kaige" ("old Greek") section, 3 Rgns 2,12–21,29. SCHENKEL, *Chronology*, pp. 62-63 affirms that the "kaige reworking" in 22,1-40 (i.e. the section of the chapter that concerns us here) has been only a superficial one.

1615. In Chronicles mention of Ahab's death (2 Chron 18,34 // 1 Kings 22,35) is followed immediately by the account of Jehoshaphat's return to Jerusalem, 2 Chron 19,1-3. Josephus gives his version of the latter passage in *AJ* 9,1-6, following his parallel to 1 Kings 22,36-40.

Joshaphat married (ἠγάγετο, 2 Par ἐπεγαμβρεύσατο) his son *Joram* (Ἰωράμῳ) to the daughter of Achab... *her name being Othlia* (Ὀθλίαν)¹⁶¹⁶". Like 2 Chron 18,2aα ("after some years")¹⁶¹⁷ Josephus gives only a vague indication concerning the interval between the conclusion of the marriage and Jehoshaphat's visit to Samaria: "after some time (χρόνον)". He does, on the other hand, considerably embellish 18,2aβ's reference to the "meats" offered the Judean and his entourage by Ahab: "Ahab gave him a friendly welcome (φιλοφρόνως... ὑπεδέξατο)¹⁶¹⁸ and, after splendidly entertaining (ἐξένισε λαμπρῶς)¹⁶¹⁹ the army (στρατὸν) which had accompanied him, with an abundance of grain and wine and meat¹⁶²⁰...".

2 Chron 18,2b reports the proposal subsequently made to Jehoshaphat by Ahab: "he induced him (MT ויסיתהו, B ἠγάπα [a likely corruption of ἠπάτα], L ἔπεισε) to go up (2 Par + 'with him') to Ramoth-gilead". There follows a reiteration of the same proposal in 18,3a (// 1 Kings 22,4a): "Ahab said to Jehoshaphat 'Will you go up with me to Ramoth-gilead?'". Josephus combines the double mention of Ahab's proposition in 2 Chron 18,2b-3a into a single (amplified) sequence. To denote the Israelite's request for Jehoshaphat's assistance, he employs a "neutral" term, i.e. "he invited (παρεκάλεσε, cf. L 2 Par 18,2b "he persuaded") him to become his ally (συμμαχῆσαι)¹⁶²¹ in a

1616. Thus NN*Mar SCHALIT, *Namenwörterbuch*, p. 92, s.v. Ὀθλία. Na reads Γοθολίαν with SP Lat. Cf. the remark of SCHLATTER, *Namen*, p. 89 s.v. עֲתַלְיָה: "Γοθολια ist zu entfernen, weil es aus der Sept. kam. R gilt Ὀθλια; es sieht wie halbe Angleichung an die Sept. aus."
Josephus derives the names of the couple, not mentioned in 2 Chron 18,1 itself, from the subsequent Biblical accounts, i.e. Joram from 2 Kings 8,16 (// 2 Chron 21,6) and "Othaliah" from 2 Kings 8,25 (// 2 Chron 22,2).
1617. Compare the definite time indication concerning Jehoshaphat's visit in 1 Kings 22,2 "in the third year", i.e. of the peace between Israel and the Syrians, 1 Kings 22,1.
1618. Elsewhere *AJ* 6,321; 7,30; 8,201; 13,170.289; 14,51.
1619. Also elsewhere Josephus accentuates, in a wording similar to that of 8,398, the "hospitality" practiced by various Biblical personages, see e.g., *AJ* 7,30 (// 2 Sam 3,20) "David received (Abner) in friendly fashion (δεξαμένου δ' αὐτὸν φιλοφρόνως) and entertained (ξενίσαντος) him with splendid (λαμπρᾷ) and lavish feasts..."; 9,31 (compare the source story 2 Kings 3 where there is no mention of such hospitality) "Joram was splendidly entertained" (ξενισθεὶς λαμπρῶς – 8,398 and 9,31 are the only uses of this phrase in Josephus); 9,59 (cf. 2 Kings 6,23) "Joram entertained (ἐστιάσας) the Syrians very splendidly (λαμπρῶς) and lavishly (φιλοτίμως)". Josephus' emphasis on the hospitality of his characters seems designed to win the sympathy of a Gentile audience for whom hospitality was a key cultural value, see FELDMAN, *David*, pp. 154-155.
1620. The above triad occurs only here in Josephus; elsewhere he collocates "grain, wine and olive (oil)", sometimes adding "cattle" as well, see *BJ* 1,299; *AJ* 14,408.
With the above description of Ahab's reception of Jehoshaphat and his forces, compare 2 Chron 18,2β "Ahab killed an abundance of sheep and oxen for him and for the people (2 Par λαῷ) who were with him".
1621. With the above construction "invite to become an ally", compare παρακαλῶν συμμαχεῖν (t.e.) in 8,304, see n. 870,

war against the king of Syria *in order to recover* (ἀφέληται) the city of Aramatha in Galadēnē (τῇ Γαλαδηνῇ... Ἀραμαθὰν)[1622], for it had first belonged to his father but had been taken away (ἀφηρῆσθαι)[1623] *from him by the Syrian's father*". With the above formulation Josephus, one notes, goes beyond the data of 2 Chron 18,2b-3a (// 1 Kings 22,4a). It may, however, be that he has been influenced in so doing by 1 Kings 22,3 "and the king of Israel said to his servants, 'Do you know that Ramoth-gilead (belongs) to us and we keep quiet and do not take it out of the hand of the king of Syria?' ". Note here especially Ahab's claim that Ramoth-gilead, though belonging to Israel, is currently under Syrian control. Inspired, as it seems, by this item, Josephus has Ahab speak above of "recovering" the city while likewise providing an explanation of Ramoth-gilead's present status, i.e. it had been seized by the previous king of Syria. For this last affirmation Josephus, in turn, could have based himself on yet another Biblical datum, i.e. the reference by Ben-hadad to "the cities which my father took from your father" in 1 Kings 20,34 (cf. 8,387 where the Syrian promises to return the "Israelite cities which the kings before him had taken away")[1624].

In 2 Chron 18,3b Jehoshaphat gives a double affirmative answer to Ahab's proposition, the first (// 1 Kings 22,4b) in indirect, the second (> 1 Kings/3 Rgns 22,4b) in more direct terms: "I (am) as you are, my people (2 Par λαός) as your people (Kings/Rgns + my horses as your horses). (We will be) with you in the war". Josephus begins with a version of the Judean's second statement according to Chronicles: "Thereupon Josaphat willingly offered his aid (τὴν βοήθειαν ἐπαγγειλα-μένου)[1625]". To this he appends a "literalistic" rendition of Jehoshaphat's previous word about his "people" being "as" Ahab's, i.e. "he too had a force (δύναμιν) not smaller than Achab's".

Having thus made Jehoshaphat refer to the troops available to him, Josephus next interjects a notice on his "sending for his force (μεταπεμ-ψαμένου τὴν δύναμιν)[1626] (to come) from Jerusalem to Samaria". Conceivably, Josephus makes this addition on the consideration that Jehoshaphat would hardly have brought an army "equal to" that of Ahab along with him on a courtesy call to Samaria (curiously, however, he neglects to mention the actual arrival of Jehoshaphat's troops in

1622. Elsewhere in Josephus other forms are also used to designate this site: "Ariman of Galadēnē" (*AJ* 4,173) and "Aramathē of Galaditis" (8,411.417; 9,105.106.112), see SCHLATTER, *Namen*, pp. 103-104, s.v. רָמָה; SCHALIT, *Namenwörterbuch*, p. 15, s.v. Ἀραμαθά.

1623. Note the word play between the various forms of the verb ἀφαιρέω in Ahab's speech to Jehoshaphat here in 8,399.

1624. This last item further provides an implicit "legitimation" for Ahab's proposed undertaking, i.e. Ben-hadad's failure to carry through, in the case of Ramoth-gilead, on his promise in 8,387.

1625. Cf. *AJ* 6,25 (Samuel speaks) βοηθήσειν... τὸν θεὸν ἐπαγγέλλεται.

1626. This construction recurs in *Vita* 161.

what follows). In any case, Jehoshaphat's "summons" opens up a narrative interlude before the campaign against Ramoth-gilead can commence which it is necessary for Josephus to fill. He does this by "anticipating" an item which occurs at a later point in the source(s), i.e. the description of the royal "session" in 1 Kings 22,10a // 2 Chron 18,9a: (Ahab and Jehoshaphat) "were sitting on their thrones, arrayed *in their robes* (> 3 Rgns 22,10), at the threshing floor at the entrance of the gate of Samaria¹⁶²⁷". Josephus' condenses the item, omitting mention of the monarchs' vesture and leaving the localization of their "session" more indeterminate: "... the two kings *went out of the city* (cf. the mention of Jehoshaphat's 'coming to Samaria' in 8,398), each sitting upon his throne (καὶ¹⁶²⁸ καθίσαντες ἐπὶ τοῦ ἰδίου θρόνου ἑκάτερος, compare 2 Par 18,9 καθήμενοι ἕκαστος ἐπὶ θρόνου αὐτοῦ)". According to the Biblical sequence (see 1 Kings 22,10b // 2 Chron 18,9b), Ahab and Jehoshaphat look on from their thrones while the four hundred prophets previously presented in 1 Kings 22,6 // 2 Chron 18,5 continue their prophesying. At this point, Josephus has not yet introduced the 400. Accordingly, he devises a different activity to occupy the two enthroned monarchs, i.e. "they distributed pay (τὸ στρατιωτικὸν διένεμον)¹⁶²⁹ to their respective armies (οἰκείοις [RO ἰδίοις] στρατιώταις)¹⁶³⁰.

Such an initiative might readily have suggested itself to Josephus, the military man conscious of the urgency of securing the loyalty of one's troops in this way prior to a campaign.

2. *Double Prophetic Consultation* (8,400-410). Following his "anticipation" of the Biblical royal session, Josephus now reverts to an earlier point in the source story, i.e. the beginning of the prophetic consultation. In 1 Kings 22,5 // 2 Chron 18,4 Jehoshapahat says to Ahab: "Inquire first for the word (> B 3 Rgns and 2 Par) of the Lord". Josephus both specifies and expatiates on the content of the Judean's request: "*And Josaphat bade him call the prophets, if there were any*

1627. So MT Kings and Chronicles. In B 3 Rgns 22,10 the session takes place rather "in the gates of Samaria" while L locates it "in the way of the gate of Samaria". Finally, 2 Par 18,9 gives "in the open space (ἐν τῷ εὐρυχώρῳ) at the entrance of the gate of Samaria".

1628. Thus MSPE Lat followed by NaMar; NN* omit with RO.

1629. The above construction occurs also in *AJ* 12,294, cf. also *BJ* 5,349 "the appointed day having arrived for the distribution of the soldiers' pay (διαδοῦναι τοῖς στρατιώταις τροφάς), Titus ordered his officers to parade the forces and count out the money to each man in full view of the enemy". Cf. further *RA* 5.28.2 where the king's secretary "sat upon the tribunal while numbering the soldiers and making a record of the pay due them".

1630. Likewise the Targum goes its own way in rendering 2 Chron 18,9a: "le roi d'Israël et Josaphat... revêtus des habits royaux étaient assis en rond (formant) comme la moitié d'une gîte, l'un consultant les prophètes de mensonge, l'autre cherchant l'enseignement de devant yhwh et priant à l'entrée de Samarie ...".

there[1631], *and inquire of them concerning* (ἀνακρῖναι περὶ, see 8,267) *the expedition against the Syrian, whether they advised them* (αὐτῷ)[1632] *to take the field* (ποιήσασθαι τὴν στρατείαν, see 8,223) *at that time*". He likewise adduces a motive for Jehoshaphat's concern for securing prophetic guidance regarding the advisability of the proposed campaign. In so doing he utilizes, while further amplifying with a *Rückverweis* to the events of 1 Kings 20 (see especially 20,34), the opening chronological notice, previously passed over by him in favor of the Chronistic introduction to our episode, of 1 Kings 22,1: "*For* there was, indeed, peace and friendship (εἰρήνη... καὶ φιλία)[1633] between Ahab and the Syrian, which had lasted three years, *from the time when Achab had taken him captive and released him until that very day*".

In 1 Kings 22,6a // 2 Chron 18,5a Ahab assembles "*the* prophets", four hundred in number, to whom he poses a question involving an alternative: "shall I go to battle against Ramoth-gilead or shall I forbear?" Josephus (8,401) designates the four hundred as "his" (Achab's) prophets, cf. 1 Kings 22,23 // 2 Chron 18,22 where Micaiah refers to "your (Ahab's) prophets"; thereby, he already intimates the suspect nature of their testimony. Josephus likewise has Ahab confine himself, in posing his question, to that alternative favored by himself with no mention of the other. On the other hand, he gives a more expansive formulation to the one question Ahab does ask: "So Achab called (καλέσας) *his* prophets... and bade (ἐκέλευσεν) them to inquire of God (ἔρεσθαι τὸν θεόν)[1634] whether, if he marched against Adados ("Αδαδον)[1635], He would grant him victory (δίδωσιν αὐτῷ... νίκην, see 8,382) and the overthrow of the city (καθαίρεσιν[1636] τῆς πόλεως)[1637]

1631. This parenthetical aside is a kind of anticipation of Jehoshaphat's request for a "second opinion" in 1 Kings 22,7 // 2 Chron 18,6 "is there not here another prophet...?" One might see an ironic undertone to the formulation Josephus attributes here to Jehoshaphat as well: the Judean "wonders outloud" whether true prophets are to be found in the reprobate Northern Kingdom.

1632. Thus NN*Mar. MSP¹ read αὐτῶν, while P², followed by Na, has ἐπ' αὐτὸν.

1633. This collocation occurs also in *AJ* 12,394 (reverse order) and 18,375.

1634. Thus NaMar following MP. This reading is likewise endorsed by SCHMIDT, *Observationes*, p. 378 who points out that elsewhere in Josephus (see *AJ* 4,87; 7,7.76) ἔρεσθαι, when used with an "object", always takes the accusative (Schmidt further avers that here in 8,401 P's ἐρέσθαι represents the better reading). By contrast, NN* read τοῦ θεοῦ with ROS.

1635. Thus N*NaMar, cf. E τὸν ῎Αδαδον. N reads ἐπὶ ῎Αδερα (cf. R ἀδερὰ), qualifying the phrase as "spurium vid". Note that 1 Kings 22 // 2 Chronicles 18 nowhere mention "Ben-hadad" by name. Josephus derives the king's name from 1 Kings 20 (in his version of which the Syrian is likewise called "Adados", see above).

1636. Elsewhere in Josephus the noun καθαίρεσις occurs in *BJ* 5,348; 6,311; *AJ* 14,437; 16,78; 17,136.206; 20,222.

1637. SCHRECKENBERG, *Untersuchungen*, p. 109, noting that the above construction occurs nowhere else in Josephus, suggests that its opening word is a corruption of an original αἵρεσις which elsewhere in Josephus is construed with the terms "city", "fortress", etc, cf. also Lat's "captationem civitatis" in 8,415.

on which he was about to wage war (δι᾽ ἥν ἐκφέρειν.. τὸν πόλεμον)¹⁶³⁸". According to 1 Kings 22,6b // 2 Chron 18,5b the prophets
direct Ahab "to go up", promising that the Lord (so Kings, "God",
Chronicles) will give Ramoth-gilead into his hand. Josephus eliminates
any mention of the deity from the prophets' answer, which, conversely,
he elaborates with yet another allusion back to 1 Kings 20: "the
prophets advised him to take the field (ἐκστρατεῦσαι, see 8,274), saying
that he would defeat (κρατήσειν) the Syrian and have him in his power
(λήψεσθαι ὑποχείριον)¹⁶³⁹ as before¹⁶⁴⁰".

In the Bible Jehoshaphat next (1 Kings 22,7 // 2 Chron 18,6), asks,
rather abruptly, "Is there not another (> 3 Rgns) prophet of the Lord
of whom we may inquire?". Josephus prefaces the king's question with
an indication as to its motivation, just as he appends an elucidation of
what the proposed second consultation is meant to ascertain: "...
Josaphat who saw (συνεὶς) by their words that they were false prophets
(ψευδοπροφῆται, see 8,242)¹⁶⁴¹, asked Achab whether there was some
other (ἕτερος, 2 Par 18,6 ἔτι) prophet of God (προφήτης τοῦ θεοῦ, 3
Rgns // 2 Par προφήτης τοῦ κυρίου)¹⁶⁴², 'in order that we may know
[note the shift to direct discourse here] more clearly (ἀκριβέστερον
μάθωμεν)¹⁶⁴³ what is going to happen¹⁶⁴⁴'". Ahab's reply to Jehoshaphat's second query runs as follows (1 Kings 22,8a // 2 Chron 18,7a):
"there is yet [> 3 Rgns] one man... but I hate him for he never

1638. Elsewhere Josephus uses the above phrase "wage war" also in *BJ* 6,329; 7,77;
AJ 5,151.186.338; 6,141; 7,101; 9,30.275; 12,228.327; 13,144.369; 14,4; 18,115.124; 20,69;
Vita 306; *Ap* 1.261. (In these other instances, however, Josephus construes the phrase
either with ἐπὶ (e.g., *AJ* 9,30) or πρὸς (e.g., *AJ* 9,275) rather than with διά as here in
8,401.
    The entire formulation of Ahab's query above is reminiscent of Saul's "consultation"
of the "high priest" Achitob in *AJ* 6,122 "... the king summoned (καλέσας) Achitob...
and bade (κέλευει) him ascertain (γνῶναι) if God would grant them (δίδωσιν αὐτοῖς)...
to proceed to the camp of the foe and destroy such as were found therein".
    1639. The above construction "to get into one's power" recurs in *BJ* 3,143; *AJ* 5,298;
12,278.386.403; *Vita* 82.271.292.416; *Ap* 1,99.
    1640. The reference of this chronological indication is of course to the scene of Ben-
hadad's submission to Ahab, following his defeat by the Israelite in 1 Kings 20,33-34 (//
8,387).
    1641. Compare TJ on 1 Kings 22,6 which renders MT's "the prophets" as "the
prophets of falsehood".
    1642. For the above phrase "prophet of God", see *AJ* 8,319 ("of the most high God",
Elijah).338 ("his [God's] prophet", Elijah); 9,33 (Elisha).211 ("of the most high God",
Jonah); 10,92 (pl., Jeremiah's predecessors).
    1643. The above phrase "learn clearly" recurs in *AJ* 18,79; 20,71.
    1644. With the above "motivation", compare that which Josephus attributes to
Jehoshaphat in his similar request for a prophetic consultation in the context of the
Moabite campaign in 9,33 "in order that through him (the prophet) we may learn
(μάθωμεν) from God what we must do" (the source text, 2 Kings 3,11a, lacks a
corresponding motivation for Jehoshaphat's suggestion – just as does Josephus' *Vor-
lage(n)* here in 8,402).

prophesies good concerning me, but evil, Micaiah the son of Imlah" (so MT). Josephus begins Ahab's answer in close parallelism to the Biblical formulation: "there was one, but he hated (μισεῖν, 2 Par ἐμίσησα, 3 Rgns μεμίσηκα) him because he had prophesied evil (κακὰ προφητεύσαντα, 2 Par προφητεύων [3 Rgns λαλεῖ] ... εἰς κακά)...". Like the source(s) too, he reserves the name of the prophet in question, i.e. "Michaias (Μιχαίαν, 3 Rgns // 2 Par Μειχαίας, MT מִיכָיְהוּ), son of Jemblaios" ('Ιεμβλαίου)¹⁶⁴⁵, for the very end of Ahab's reply. Between these elements taken over from the source, he interjects another *Rückverweis* to his own earlier version of the encounter between Ahab and "Micaiah", i.e. "and he had foretold (προειπόντα) that he should be conquered (νικηθεὶς) by the Syrian king and meet his death (τεθνήξεται), for which reason he was now keeping him in prison (ἐν φυλακῇ... ἔχειν)¹⁶⁴⁶...".

In 1 Kings 22,8b // 2 Chron 18,7b Jehoshaphat reacts to Ahab's statement concerning Micaiah with a soothing interjection "let not the king say so". Josephus gives a more assertive Judean, who, aware of Ahab's feelings towards the prophet, nevertheless, "asked (κελεύσαντος, W 'insisted')¹⁶⁴⁷ that he be produced". Thereupon, in line with 1 Kings 22,9 // 2 Chron 18,8, he relates Ahab's dispatching of an envoy to summon Micaiah¹⁶⁴⁸.

In the Bible (see 1 Kings 22,10-12 // 2 Chron 18,9-11), a rather extended interlude supervenes before one hears anything more of the official whom Ahab had dispatched to "quickly" bring Micaiah (1 Kings 22,9 // 2 Chron 18,8). This interlude is given over to a description of the "performance" of the four hundred prophets, Zedekiah in particular, before the enthroned kings. Josephus eliminates this "gap"; his version of 1 Kings 22,9 // 2 Chron 18,8 is followed directly by his parallel to 1 Kings 22,13-14 // 2 Chron 18,12-13 which relates the dialogue between official and prophet as they make their way towards the kings. Josephus (8,404) both specifies and shortens the words attributed to Micaiah's summoner: "on the way the eunuch (ὁ

1645. Thus P² followed by NaMar. NN* read 'Ομβλαίου with R, SCHLATTER, *Namen*, p. 62, s.v. יִמְלָה advocates 'Ιαμβλεου, while SCHALIT, *Namenwörterbuch*, p. 59, s.v. proposes 'Ιεμβλαῖος (or conceivably 'Ιομβλαῖος). Compare 'Ιεμιάς (B 3 Rgns); Ναμαλεί (L 3 Rgns/ 2 Par); 'Ιεμαάς (B 2 Par).

1646. Compare Josephus' wording in the referent-text, 8,392 (Micaiah informs Ahab) "that God would cause him to die (ἀποθανεῖν) at Adados's hands... Achab ordered him to be locked up and kept under guard".
The witnesses and editions differ for what concerns the final words of Ahab's reply here in 8,403: NaMar follow MSP Lat ... τοῦ Σύρων Βασιλέως καὶ διὰ ταῦτα ἐν φυλακῇ νῦν αὐτὸν ἔχειν, whereas N opts for RO's ... τοῦ Σύρου, ἐν φρουρᾷ δὲ νῦν αὐτὸν ἔχειν.

1647. In fact, the term is the same used in Jehoshaphat's initial call for a prophetic consultation in 8,400 "he bade (ἐκέλευσεν) him (Ahab) call the prophets...".

1648. Like 3 Rgns // 2 Par Josephus designates the envoy as an "eunuch" (εὐνοῦχον); MT's סָרִיס may have this meaning, but is also used in the broader sense of "official".

εὐνοῦχος)¹⁶⁴⁹ informed (ἐδήλωσεν) him that all the *other* prophets (πάντας τοὺς ἄλλους¹⁶⁵⁰ προφήτας) had foretold victory (νίκην... προειρηκέναι, cf. προειπόντα... νικηθείς, 8,403) ...¹⁶⁵¹". Josephus' envoy stops there, leaving Micaiah to draw his own conclusions, compare 1 Kings 22,13bβ // 2 Chron 18,12bβ where the messenger enjoins the prophet: "let your word be like the word of one of them, and speak favorably". Conversely, Josephus expands on the terse retort attributed to Micaiah in 1 Kings 22,14 // 2 Chron 18,13 ("as the Lord (God, Chronicles) says to me, that I will speak"): "thereupon the prophet said that *it was not possible for him* (ὁ δὲ οὐκ ἐξὸν αὐτῷ)¹⁶⁵² *to tell falsehoods in God's name* (καταψεύσασθαι τοῦ θεοῦ)¹⁶⁵³, but (ἀλλ’)¹⁶⁵⁴ he must speak (ἐρεῖν) whatever He might tell him (ὅ τι ἂν αὐτῷ... εἴπη, compare 3 Rgns ἃ ἂν εἴπη... πρός με...) about the king".

Following 1 Kings 22,15aα // 2 Chron 18,14aα, Josephus next notes Micaiah's arrival before Ahab. Thereafter, however, he passes over the initial exchange between king and prophet recorded in 1 Kings 22,15aββ // 2 Chron 18,14aββb in which Micaiah responds to Ahab's question whether he should advance against Ramoth-gilead with a word that (ironically) mimics that of the prophets in 1 Kings 22,12 // 2 Chron 18,11. Instead, Josephus directly links mention of Micaiah's arrival with the king's "adjuration" of him which in the Bible (1 Kings 22,16 // 2 Chron 18,15) comes as Ahab's exasperated response to the prophet's opening "favorable" word to him: "and when he came to

1649. Josephus employs the same designation for this figure as in his initial reference to him in 8,403. By contrast both Kings and Chronicles (MT and LXX) shift to another term in their second mention of him: in 3 Rgns 22,9 // 2 Par 18,8 he is called an "eunuch" (see previous note), while in 22,13 // 18,12 the term used is rather "the messenger" (LXX ὁ ἄγγελος). Josephus' use of the same term on both occasions eliminates any uncertainty as to the identity of the figure in the second instance.

1650. With this term, absent in the source text(s), Josephus has the eunuch insist on Micaiah's link with his colleagues. Compare the scepticism concerning the existence of (true) prophets in Ahab's kingdom voiced by Jehoshaphat in 8,400 "he bade him call the prophets *if there were any there*".

1651. Compare the vaguer Biblical formulations of the messenger's words to Micaiah which refer to the prophets' speaking "good" about the king "with one mouth".

1652. Josephus elsewhere uses the verb ἔξεστιν in reference to what is (not) divinely/ legally "possible" also in, e.g., *BJ* 6,426; *AJ* 13,252.373; 15,419; 20,268.

With reference to *AJ* 16,24, LIEZENBERG, *Studia*, p. 89 proposes emending the above phrase to ὁ δὲ ὡς οὐκ ἐξὸν (καταψεύσασθαι τοῦ θεοῦ φήσας, ἀλλ’ ἐρεῖν...).

1653. So NN*Mar; Na reads καταψεύδεσθαι with MSP. The same construction read by Mar above recurs in *BJ* 6,288 (subject: the false prophets at the time of the siege of Jerusalem) and *AJ* 10,178 (the survivors of Jerusalem's destruction suspect Jeremiah of "belying God").

In the above formulation note Josephus' characteristic elimination of the Biblical "oath formula" as well as the condemnation of the 400 prophets implicit in his having Micaiah affirm that *he* cannot "tell falsehoods in God's name" (cf. the designation of the 400 as "false prophets" in 8,402).

1654. N "fort. spurium" (N* prints the word without this indication).

Achab and the king adjured him to speak the truth to him (λέγειν αὐτῷ τἀληθὲς... ἐνωρκίσατο[1655], 3 Rgns ἐξορκίζω [2 Par ὁρκίζω] σε ὅπως [2 Par ἵνα μὴ] λαλήσῃς πρός με [2 Par + πλὴν τὴν] ἀλήθειαν)[1656)...". The reason for Josephus' "omission" of the first, Biblical exchange between king and prophet is patent: in the Bible Micaiah's first word to Ahab is a materially false prediction since God will not, in fact, hand over Ramoth-gilead to the king. Josephus, who has just represented Micaiah as claiming that "it is not possible for him to tell falsehoods in God's name" resolves the problem posed by the Biblical sequence by simply ignoring it.

Like 1 Kings 22,17a // 2 Chron 18,16a Josephus has Micaiah respond to Ahab's "adjuration" by relating his vision of the Israelite army scattered on the mountains like shepherdless sheep. At the same time, he also underscores the divine source of the prophet's vision and provides elucidation of the imagery it employs: "he said that God had shown (δεῖξαι, 3 Rgns ἑώρακα, 2 Par εἶδον)[1657] him the Israelites [Bible: (all) Israel] in flight, being pursued (διωκομένους) by the Syrians and dispersed (διασκορπιζομένους, 3 Rgns // 2 Par διεσπαρμένους)[1658] by them on the mountains (εἰς τὰ ὄρη, 3 Rgns // 2 Par ἐν τοῖς ὄρεσιν) like flocks of sheep (ποίμνια, 3 Rgns ποίμνιον, 2 Par πρόβατα) that are left without their shepherds (ποιμένων ἠρημωμένα, 3 Rgns ᾧ [2 Par οἷς] οὐκ ἔστιν ποιμήν)". The attached divine comment, as cited by Micaiah in 1 Kings 22,17b // 2 Chron 18,16b, runs "and the Lord said, 'These have have no master(s)[1659], let each return to his home in peace'". Josephus, reversing the sequence of the two components in this word, elucidates its reference to Israel's having "no master(s)": "he also said that (God) had revealed (σημαίνειν, see 8,294)[1660] that his men should return to their homes in peace (μετ' εἰρήνης ἀναστρέψειν εἰς τὰ ἴδια, B 3 Rgns ἕκαστος εἰς τὸν οἶκον

1655. The verb ἐνορκίζομαι is hapax in Josephus.

1656. In Kings and Chronicles Ahab adjures Micaiah to speak the truth "in the name of the Lord". Josephus, in line with his practice of not reproducing the wording of "oaths" with their mention of the divine name, leaves aside this specification.

1657. Elsewhere Josephus uses δείκνυμι with God as subject in BJ 2,259; AJ 10,205.277; 13,322.

1658. The verb διασκορπίζω is hapax in Josephus. On διασκορπισθήσονται (Zech 13,7) in Mark 14,27 and John 16,32 (σκορπισθῆτε εἰς τὰ ἴδια κἀμὲ μόνον ἀφῆτε), cf. F. Neirynck, in Evangelica (BETL, 60), Leuven, 1982, pp. 461-462, 478-479: "Le passage de Flavius Josèphe (Ant. 8,404-405) mérite, semble-t-il, d'être signalé dans les commentaires sur Jn 16,32" (p. 462).

1659. Thus MT Kings and Chronicles as well as 2 Par. Compare B 3 Rgns "the Lord (is) no God to them"; L "if like a lord (κυρίως) they (are) to God".

1660. Compare W, ad loc. "cela signifiait...".

αὐτοῦ ἐν εἰρήνῃ ἀναστρεφέτω), but that he alone (μόνον)¹⁶⁶¹ should fall in battle (πεσεῖσθαι... ἐν τῇ μάχῃ)¹⁶⁶²".

In accordance with 1 Kings 22,18 // 2 Chron 18,17 Josephus makes Ahab respond to Micaiah's announcement by reminding Jehoshaphat that he had anticipated just such a word from the prophet: "When Michaias had spoken these words, Achab said (φησί)¹⁶⁶³ to Josaphat, 'Did I not tell you (ἐδήλωσά σοι, 3 Rgns [οὐκ] εἶπα πρὸς σέ [2 Par σοι]) a little while ago how this fellow (τἀνθρώπου) feels towards me (πρός με διάθεσιν)¹⁶⁶⁴ and that he has prophesied evil things (τὰ χείρω προεφήτευσε¹⁶⁶⁵, 3 Rgns // 2 Par προφητεύει... κακά)¹⁶⁶⁶ for me?'".

Also following the Bible, Josephus places the answer to Ahab's denigrating comment on the lips, not of its addressee, i.e. Jehoshaphat, but of Micaiah himself. Micaiah's speech of self-defense is, however, very different in its Biblical and Josephan versions. In the former (see 1 Kings 22,19-23 // 2 Chron 18,18-22), Micaiah invokes his vision of the heavenly court's deliberations which culminates (22,23 // 18,22) in God's commissioning a "lying spirit" to "inspire" Ahab's prophets. By contrast, Josephus' Micaiah delivers a speech (8,406a) which, to a large extent, simply echoes his earlier statements to the royal messenger (8,404) and to Ahab himself (8,405): "But Michaias answered that it was his duty (προσῆκεν αὐτῷ)¹⁶⁶⁷ to listen to all things uttered by God (πάντων ἀκροᾶσθαι τῶν ὑπὸ τοῦ θεοῦ προλεγομένων)¹⁶⁶⁸, and that

1661. In introducing this term into his formulation, Josephus involves himself in an implicit contradiction with his own version of Micaiah's earlier word of doom for Ahab, 8,392 (// 1 Kings 20,42) where the prophet announces that also Ahab's people will by killed by the Syrians, see n. 1560. At the same time, it should be noted that Josephus' reference here to Ahab "alone" being slain does accord with the tradition preserved in *y. Sanh.* 11,30c. The latter text addresses the problem of the disparity between the announcement of 1 Kings 20,42 and the affirmation which, like Josephus, goes beyond the Bible in making it, i.e. that Ahab was the only Israelite to fall in battle before Ramoth-gilead. The Talmudic text resolves the difficulty with the assertion that the blood shed by an unnamed "righteous man" (Jehoshaphat?, Micaiah?) in the course of the Ramoth-gilead battle effected propitiation for the people of Israel (who thus escaped the doom earlier pronounced over them by Micaiah), see G.A. WEVERS (tr.), *Sanhedrin Gerichtshof. Übersetzung des Talmud Yerushalmi* IV/4 (ed. M. HENGEL *et al.*), Tübingen, 1981, p. 315, n. 87. – See also above n. 1658 (on John 16,32).

1662. The above construction "fall in battle" occurs also in *AJ* 5,14; 7,113; 13,100 (14,434); 15,158 (17,265); *Ap* 2,212.

1663. Thus NaMar following V (apud Hud); NN* omit with the remaining codd.

1664. With this construction compare *AJ* 6,239 (Jonathan to David) δηλώσων δὲ τῷ φίλῳ τὴν τοῦ πατρὸς διάθεσιν.

1665. Compare *AJ* 10,268 τῶν προφητῶν τὰ χείρω προλεγόντων.

1666. With the above Biblical wording, compare Ahab's word to Jehoshaphat concerning Micaiah in 8,403: κακὰ προφητεύσαντα.

1667. The above construction, "it is a duty for, befits one" employing a infinitive or finite form of προσήκω + dative recurs in *BJ* 2,7.443.447; 3,210; 4,348; *AJ* 4,143.262; 6,342; 7,246.314.

1668. Elsewhere Josephus uses ἀκρόαομαι of a "hearing" of God's words also in *AJ*

they were false prophets (ψευδοπροφῆται, see 8,402) who had led him on (παρορμήσειαν)[1669] to make war in the hope of victory (ἐλπίδι νίκης)[1670], and that he (alone) must fall in battle (πεσεῖν... μαχό-μενον)[1671]". What prompts Josephus to so drastically modify his source(s) here? For one thing, he may have felt uncomfortable with its representation of a human "seeing" God[1672], and of intermediate beings ("angels") around him[1673]. Above all, however, Josephus would have found unacceptable the Bible's tracing back the prophets' "lying speech" to a divine initiative – he disallows any imputation of false-hood to Micaiah (see above) – how much more must he do the same in the case of God himself[1674]. At the same time, it may be noted that the second half of Micaiah's above word with its reference to the "false prophets" (ψευδοπροφῆται) does seem to reflect the prophet's conclud-ing statement in 1 Kings 22,23 // 2 Chron 18,22, i.e. "the Lord has put a *lying* (3 Rgns // 2 Par ψευδὲς) spirit in the mouth of all your prophets (3 Rgns/ 2 Par προφητῶν)".

Next, Josephus goes beyond the Bible in noting that Micaiah's words did have some impact on the king: "so Achab had cause for thought (ἦν ἐπ' ἐννοίᾳ)[1675]". Thereafter, he rejoins Scripture's sequence (see 1 Kings 22,24 // 2 Chron 18,23) in relating the prophet Zedekiah's

3,93 (the people); 4,329 (Moses). For προλέγω with God as subject, see 8,232. With the whole above formulation compare Micaiah's word to the eunuch in 8,404 "... he must speak whatever God might tell him about the king".

1669. Josephus uses the same verb παρορμάω in reference to the Bethel "false prophet's" leading Jeroboam astray in 8,245.

1670. Elsewhere Josephus uses the above phrase "hope(s) of victory" in *BJ* 6,4; 7,369; *AJ* 12,300; 13,92.

1671. The above phrase "fall fighting" occurs also in *AJ* 6,345; 7,238; 13,371. Compare Micaiah's earlier announcement (8,405) that Ahab πεσεῖσθαι... ἐν τῇ μάχῃ.

1672. Note that while Josephus does refer to Isaiah in *AJ* 9-10, he makes no use of the account of the prophet's call, Isaiah 6, with its reminiscences of the heavenly court scene of 1 Kings 22 // 2 Chron 18. In the Targums to 1 Kings 22,19 and 2 Chron 18,18 one observes as well a certain tendency to attenuate Micaiah's unqualified claim to have seen Yahweh himself; TJ has him see "the glory (יקרא) of Yahweh", while in TC he beholds "the glory of the Shekinah (איקר שכנתיה) of Yahweh".

1673. See the remark of SCHLATTER, *Theologie*, p. 9 "... die Engel hat er (Josephus) nie neben Gott gestellt".

1674. By contrast both the Targums and *Sanh.* 89a,102b; *Šabb.* 149b amplify the "heavenly court scene" with further particulars, noting that "the spirit" who volunteers to mislead Ahab is that of Naboth who emerges from the chamber of the righteous to do so. In accepting the offer by Naboth's spirit, the Lord at the same time stipulates, however, that it will not be allowed to return to its place among the righteous once it has accomplished its mission. In *Šabb.* 149b alternative explanations are offered for this divine stipulation: God's reprobation either of lying or of bringing evil upon others – both misdeeds of which Naboth's spirit has volunteered to make itself guilty. In any event, one notes that also these texts, in their own way, attempt to disassociate God and the operation of the "lying spirit" – something which Josephus effects by simply passing over the offending passage.

1675. This phrase is hapax in Josephus.

response to Micaiah's preceding speech of self-defense. As will be recalled, Josephus had passed over 1 Kings 22,11 // 2 Chron 18,10's reference to Zedekiah in the context of the royal "session" (see on 8,399). Accordingly, at this point, he must "introduce" Zedekiah to the reader. He does so with the phrase "a certain Sedekias (Σεδεκίας, thus 3 Rgns // 2 Par), one of the false prophets (ψευδοπροφητῶν)[1676]".

At this juncture, 1 Kings 22,24 // 2 Chron 18,23 recounts Zedekiah's slapping Micaiah and asking, (MT Kings) "how did the Spirit of the Lord go from me to speak to you?"[1677] – a query whose import is not immediately obvious. Josephus, for his part, greatly expands Zedekiah's reaction to Micaiah's speech. He has the former address himself in the first place, not to Micaiah, but to Ahab, who, as he had noted just previously, was affected by Michaiah's words, thus making rebuttal by Zedekiah imperative. In Josephus' presentation Zedekiah begins by "urging" (παρῄνει) Ahab "not to pay any attention (μὴ προσέχειν)[1678] to Michaias, for he did not speak a word of truth (λέγειν... αὐτὸν οὐδὲν ἀληθές)[1679]". He goes on to have Zedekiah buttress this appeal by invoking the discrepancy between Micaiah's prediction about Ahab's end and Elijah's earlier announcement on the subject:

> And as proof of this [Micaiah's lack of credibility] he instanced (τεκμηρίῳ... ἐχρήσατο)[1680] the prophecies of Elijah, who was better able than Michaias to foresee the future (τὰ μέλλοντα συνιδεῖν)[1681], for, he said, when Elijah had prophesied in the city of Jezarēla ('Ιεζαρήλᾳ)[1682] in Naboth's field (ἀγρῷ, see 8,355), he had foretold (προειπεῖν) that the dogs

1676. The Targum on 2 Chron 18,10 likewise designates Zedekiah as a "false prophet". In his introduction of Zedekiah, Josephus omits the name of his father, i.e. Chenaanah (LXX Χανάαν etc.).

1677. Compare 2 Chron/Par "which way did the Spirit of the Lord go from me to speak to you?"; 3 Rgns B "what sort of a spirit of the Lord is that which has spoken in you?"; 3 Rgns L "what sort of spirit of the Lord went from me to speak in you?"; TJ and TC "at what moment did the spirit of prophecy from before Yahweh leave me to speak to you?".

1678. Compare 8,241 (Jadōn is killed by the God-sent lion) "that Jeroboam might not give heed (μὴ προσέχοι) to the words of Jadōn". As will be pointed out, Josephus introduces a variety of other verbal links between his stories of Jeroboam and Ahab in their dealings with "true" and "false" prophets.

1679. Cf. Ahab's adjuration of Micaiah in 8,404 λέγειν αὐτῷ τἀληθές. See also 8,244 where the Bethel prophet states concerning Jadōn whom he is trying to discredit in the eyes of Jeroboam: "there was nothing of a prophet either in his person or in what he had spoken". Note further RA 3.71.2: Tarquinus attempts to show up the augurer Neirus as a charlatan "who did not speak a word of truth" (μηθὲν ἀληθὲς λέγοντος).

1680. The above construction "instance in proof(s)" recurs in BJ 1,633; AJ 4,246.311; Ap 1,69 (2,125).

1681. With this construction compare AJ 7,391 where David is said to have been "most apt in perceiving (νοῆσαι) and understanding (συνιδεῖν) the course of future events (περὶ τῶν μελλόντων)".

1682. Thus Mar. NaW read 'Ιζάρᾳ with SP, while NN* and SCHLATTER, Namen, p. 61, s.v. יִזְרְעֶאל propose 'Ιεζερήλα.

would lick up (ἀναλιχμήσεσθαι)[1683] Achab's blood[1684] just as (they had licked up the blood) of Naboth[1685] who had been stoned to death by the crowd (καταλευσθέντος ὑπὸ τοῦ ὄχλου)[1686] at his bidding (δι᾽ αὐτὸν)[1687]. "It is clear (δῆλον), then, said Sedekias, that this man is lying (ψεύδεται)[1688], since he contradicts (τἀναντία λέγων)[1689] a greater prophet (τῷ κρείττονι προφήτῃ)[1690] in saying that within three days you shall meet death (τεθνήξεσθαι)[1691].

Here then Josephus establishes a connection between the present episode and yet another earlier happening, i.e. the Naboth incident[1692]. Josephus now contrives to give the Biblical mention of Zedekiah's striking Micaiah (1 Kings 22,24a // 2 Chron 18,23a) a function within his lengthy refutation of the latter's veracity. He does this by having Zedekiah first recall an earlier episode where an individual raised his hand against another to his own harm, i.e. the paralysis which afflicted Jeroboam's hand when he stretched it out to order Jadōn's arrest (see *AJ* 8,233 // 1 Kings 13,4). That happening at Bethel suggests to Zedekiah the following "test": "But you shall know (γνώσεσθε δ᾽)[1693]

1683. Josephus' only other use of this verb is in 8,417.

1684. Compare the rendering of the above words by W, *ad loc.* "(Elijah had said that) "les chiens lécheraient le sang d'Achab dans la ville d'Izara, dans le champs de Naboth".

1685. Note that Zedekiah's "citation" of Elijah here is closer in wording to 1 Kings 21,19 than is Josephus' own previous "quotation" of Elijah's word in *AJ* 8,361 "in that very place where Naboth's *body had been devoured* by the dogs, his own blood *would be shed...*".

1686. Compare 8,359 (Naboth) βαλλόμενος ὑπὸ τοῦ πλήθους.

1687. Compare 8,358 where it is rather Jezebel who "orders" (κελεύουσα) the execution of Naboth (cf. 8,359 "as a result of the *queen's* letter, Naboth... was stoned to death by the people"). Zedekiah's formulation here in 8,407 is, on the other hand, in accordance with Elijah's accusation against Ahab as cited in 8,361, i.e. "he had unjustly slain a citizen".

1688. Compare 8,240 where Josephus refers to Jadōn's "believing his (the Bethel prophet's) lies" (ψευσαμένῳ πεισθεὶς).

1689. This construction occurs also in *AJ* 6,233; 13,308; *Ap* 1,15. 226.

1690. RO read κρίνειν τὸν προφήτην. With Zedekiah's appeal to the disagreement among prophets as grounds for not believing Micaiah, compare *AJ* 10,106 where Josephus introduces the remark that king Zedekiah's failure to credit the prophecies of Jeremiah and Ezekiel was due to the seeming discrepancy between them as to whether or not he would "see" Babylon. See further on 8,417.

1691. Zedekiah's statement here that Micaiah had announced Ahab's death "within three days" is puzzling since neither Josephus nor the Bible records such an announcement on Micaiah's part. See GINZBERG, *Legends*, VI, p. 312, n. 42 who takes the phrase as asserting that "Ahab would be slain in a place three days journey distant from there [Jezreel]" (cf. W, *ad loc.* "le roi mourra d'ici trois jours").

1692. The Talmud and the Targumim make that same connection in their own way by identifying the "volunteer spirit" in the heavenly court scene as that of Naboth, see n. 1674.

1693. > RO; SP γνώσεσθαι δ'. It is not immediately clear who is the intended subject of the above pl. verb (Ahab and Jehoshaphat?) since in what precedes Zedekiah has been addressing himself specifically to Ahab.

whether he is really a true (ἀληθὴς) (prophet)[1694] and has the power of the divine spirit (τοῦ θείου πνεύματος ἔχει τὴν δύναμιν)[1695]; let him right now (εὐθὺς)[1696], when I strike (ῥαπισθεὶς)[1697] him, disable (βλαψάτω)[1698] my hand, as Jadaos ('Ιάδαος)[1699] caused the right hand (δεξιάν, so 8,234) of King Jeroboam to wither (ἀπεξήρανε, compare παρείθη, 8,233) when he wished to arrest (συλλαβεῖν, see 8,233) him. For I suppose you must have heard (ἀκήκοας)[1700] that this thing happened".

Following the foregoing statement Josephus finally comes to relate the Biblical datum of Zedekiah's striking Micaiah. In so doing he omits the accompanying question of 1 Kings 22,24b // 2 Chron 18,23b (see above), having incorporated its reference to the "spirit" into Zedekiah's preceding word to Ahab. Rather, he goes on to note the sequels of the blow, first for Zedekiah, then for Ahab: "accordingly, when he struck (πλήξαντος, 3 Rgns // 2 Par ἐπάταξεν, cf. ῥαπισθεὶς, 8,408) Michaias[1701] and suffered no harm as a result (μηδὲν συνέβη παθεῖν)[1702], Achab took courage (θαρρήσας)[1703] and was eager (πρόθυμος)[1704] to lead his army against (ἄγειν τὴν στρατιὰν... ἐπὶ, see 8,381) the Syrian[1705]". To this notice concerning Ahab's resolve he further appends a reflective remark about the power operative in the king's decision: "it was Fate (τὸ χρεὼν)[1706], I suppose, that prevailed (ἐνίκα)

1694. Compare AJ 9,23 where Elijah invokes "fire from heaven" in order "to prove whether he was a true prophet (προφήτης ἀληθὴς)...".

1695. Zedekiah's reference to the "divine spirit" here is likely inspired by the mention of the "spirit of the Lord" in Zedekiah's question to Micaiah in 1 Kings 22,24b // 2 Chron 18,23b. BEST, Use, p. 222 notes that Josephus regularly substitutes the phrase "divine (θεῖον) spirit" for the Bible's "spirit of God/the Lord". Josephus' other uses of the above expression "divine spirit" are AJ 4,108 (Balaam); 6,166.222 (David); 10,239 (Daniel) in the last three of these texts one finds the same construction, i.e. "have the divine spirit" as in 8,408).

1696. Compare 8,233 where Jeroboam's hand is paralyzed "immediately" (εὐθέως) upon his extending it against Jadōn.

1697. Josephus' only other use of the verb ῥαπίζω is in AJ 11,54.

1698. The verb βλάπτω occurs twice in Josephus' story of Jadōn, see 8,241.243.

1699. So N*Mar. SPE have Ἴαδος (Lat Iadon). Note that throughout 8,230-245 the form used is Ἰάδων which form is read by NaW and SCHALIT, Namenwörterbuch, p. 56, s.v. also here in 8,408.

1700. Note the shift to the sg. here after the preceding pl. γνώσεσθε.

1701. Josephus leaves aside the Biblical specification that Zedekiah smote Micaiah "on the cheek". Note the verbal echo of 8,390 where "Micaiah" is "struck" (πλήξαντος) at his own request.

1702. The above construction "suffer no harm as a result" recurs in AJ 5,175; 10,276; 12,252.

1703. See 8,293.322.326.373.387.

1704. This adjective occurs a total of 110× in Josephus.

1705. Compare the earlier reference (8,406) to Ahab's "having cause for thought" in light of Micaiah's words.

1706. On Josephus' use of this term, see n. 1800.

and made (ἐποίει) the false prophet (τοὺς ψευδοπροφήτας)[1707] seem more convincing (πιθανωτέρους)[1708] than the true one (ἀληθοῦς, see ἀληθής, 8,408), in order to hasten Achab's end (ἵνα λάβη τὴν ἀφορμὴν[1709] τοῦ τέλους)[1710]".

Having related Zedekiah's success in convincing Ahab, Josephus is still not done with that prophet. Rather, he "clinches" Zedekiah's triumph by having him now perform the "sign" with the iron horns with its attached promise of victory over Syria which he had passed over at the earlier point in our episode where the Bible (see 1 Kings 22,11 // 2 Chron 18,10) relates it. Josephus words this "delayed" item as follows: "Then Sedekias made horns of iron (σιδήρεα ποιήσας κέρατα, 3 Rgns // 2 Par ἐποίησεν... κέρατα σιδηρᾶ) and told (λέγει)[1711] Achab that God (θεὸν)[1712] had revealed (σημαίνειν, see 8,294.405) to him that with these he should subdue (καταστρέψεσθαι, see 8,200.265)[1713] the whole of Syria[1714]". As a result, in Josephus' presentation, it is, in the first place, to that "sign" – rather than to Zedekiah's blow and question (so the Bible) – that Micaiah's response, drawn by Josephus from 1 Kings 22,25 // 2 Chron 18,24, is directed. In formulating the prophet's reply, Josephus once again evidences his penchant for "spelling things out": "But Michaias said that within a few days [Bible: "you will see it on that (which?) day"][1715] Sedekias would change his hiding-place (κρυβόμενον)[1716] from one secret chamber to another (ταμιεῖον ἐκ ταμιείου)[1717] *in seeking to escape punish-*

1707. W, *ad loc.* renders the Greek pl. more precisely as "aux faux prophètes".

1708. Josephus employs the term πιθάνος in reference to the Bethel false prophet in 8,243 πιθανοῖς... χρώμενοις λόγοις. The above construction "make convincing" occurs also in 14,113.

1709. Josephus employs the above phrase "take an occasion" elsewhere in *BJ* 1,502; *AJ* 2,237 (10,256); 13,411; 16,71; *Vita* 375.

1710. With this "aside" compare 8,241 where, following God's announcement of Jadōn's punishment, Josephus states "this came about, I think, in accordance with the will of God (note that what is here attributed to God's will is ascribed to 'Fate' in 8,409), in order that Jeroboam might not give heed to the words of Jadōn...". Cf. the similar editorial comments in 9,199; 10,76; 16,397.

1711. Josephus uses the above h.p. of λέγω a total of 10 ×. In three instances it serves to introduce indirect discourse (*AJ* 2,272; 6,206 and here in 8,409), in six others direct discourse (*AJ* 1,228; 4,176; 6,66.172.179 [t.e.].251; 10,244), while in 9,78 it does not introduce a "quote".

1712. So NN*Mar. Na conjectures θεὸς, a reading rejected by SCHMIDT, *Observationes*, p. 429.

1713. Thus NN*NaMar following Lat. RO has καταστρέψασθαι, MSP καταστρέψαι.

1714. N designates the entire above sentence as "suspecta"; N*, however, prints it without brackets.

1715. Cf. Zedekiah's reference in 8,408 to Micaiah's (purported) prediction that Ahab is to die "within three days", see n. 1691.

1716. So NN*Mar. Na reads κρυβησόμενον with MSP.

1717. Thus the conjecture of Df followed by NN*NaMar. The codd have ταμεῖον ἐκ ταμιείου, as do EZon. With the above phrase compare B 3 Rgns 22,25 εἰσέλθης ταμεῖον

ment (φυγεῖν... τὴν δίκην)[1718] *for his lying words* (τῆς ψευδολο-γίας)[1719]". He then concludes his account of the prophetic consultation by citing, in abridged form, Ahab's directive concerning Micaiah's incarceration (1 Kings 22,26-27 // 2 Chron 18,25-26): "Thereupon the king ordered him to be led away to (ἀπαχθέντα... πρὸς, 3 Rgns ἀποσστρέψατε αὐτὸν πρὸς) Achamōn (Ἀχάμωνα)[1720], the governor of the city (τὸν τῆς πόλεως ἄρχοντα)[1721], for imprisonment (φυλάττεσ-θαι)[1722] and that he should be supplied (χορηγεῖσθαι) with nothing but bread and water[1723]". In so formulating Ahab's word, Josephus leaves aside the king's bravado concluding reference, "until I return in peace". He likewise then dispenses with Micaiah's corresponding response (1 Kings 22,28 // 2 Chron 18,27): "And Micaiah said, 'If you return in peace, the Lord has not spoken by me'. And he said, 'Hear, all you peoples'"[1724].

3. *The Battle* (8,411-415). Both the Biblical and Josephan accounts of the battle in which Ahab loses his life are preceded by a series of notices concerning the preparations for this conflict. In a first such notice, Josephus, drawing on 1 Kings 22,29 // 2 Chron 18,28, cites the advance of the two allied kings towards Ramoth-gilead: "And so Achab and

τοῦ ταμείου τοῦ κρυφίου/ B 2 Par 18,24 εἰσελεύσεται ταμεῖον ἐκ ταμείου τοῦ κατακρυ-βῆναι.

1718. This construction occurs also in *AJ* 6,305 (of Nabal).

1719. Other uses of this term in Josephus are *BJ* 7,444.449; *AJ* 3,308; 17,105.334; *Vita* 261; *Ap* 1,3.105.293.

Note the recurrence of (truth and) falsehood terminology which permeates this segment.

1720. MT Kings and Chronicles have אָמוֹן; 3 Rgns Σεμὴρ etc.; 2 Par Ἐμὴρ etc. On the form of the name in 8,410 SCHLATTER, *Namen*, p. 19, s.v. אָמוֹן comments: "Das führt nicht auf eine hebräische Variante חכמון neben אמון, sondern wird ein Gemenge sein; der Schreiber schrieb zuerst irrtümlich den beständig vorkommenden Namen des Königs Ἀχαβον und korrigierte sich dann. Der Folgende verband den Fehler mit der Korrektur". Compare SCHALIT, *Namenwörterbuch*, p. 21, s.v. Ἀχάμων: "Möglicherweise ist die Form... als korrumpiertes ἄρχων (3 Reg 22,26) + Αμων anzusehen".

1721. This is the same title used of "Emer" in 2 Par 18,25 (elsewhere in Josephus it occurs in *AJ* 6,8.343; 13,165; 19,291, all 4× in the pl.); compare 3 Rgns 22,26 where "Semer" is called βασιλέα τῆς πόλεως.

Josephus makes no mention of the second captor for Michaiah cited by Ahab in Kings and Chronicles, i.e. Joas, " the king's son" (in 2 Par this title is preceded by "governor"). This omission conceivably relates to the fact that in the subsequent Biblical accounts concerning the sons and successors of Ahab (i.e. Ahaziah and Jehoram) this figure nowhere appears.

1722. This same form is used by Ahab in his earlier directive about Micaiah's imprisonment in 8,392. Compare 3 Rgns 22,27 θέσθαι τοῦτον ἐν φυλακῇ.

1723. Bible: "feed him with the bread of affliction (3 Rgns/2 Par θλίψεως) and the water of affliction". Josephus' formulation here in 8,410 recalls his reference to Obadiah's "giving" (χορηγοῦντα) the hundred prophets "only bread and water" in 8,330.

1724. 3 Rgns 22,28 lacks the second half of the prophet's above statement which itself corresponds to Mic 1,2aα.

Josaphat... marched *with their forces* (ἀναλαβόντες τὰς δυνάμεις ἤλα-σαν) to the city of Aramathē in Galaditis (Ἀραμάθην[1725]... τῆς Γαλαδίτιδος)[1726]". To this notice he adds mention of the Syrian counter-advance, thereby explaining why it did not come to an actual siege of the city: "When the Syrian king heard of their march (στρα-τείαν)[1727], he, in turn, led his army against (ἀντεπήγαγεν[1728]... στρα-τιὰν) them and encamped (στρατοτεδεύεται) not far from the city of Aramathē (Ἀραμάθης)[1729]".

The historian next follows the Biblical record in relating a pre-battle "settlement" dealing with the combat dress to be worn by the two allied kings. For this item he aligns himself with LXX as opposed to MT. In 1 Kings 22,30a // 2 Chron 18,29a the latter has Ahab instruct Jehosha-phat that while he will "disguise himself", the Judean is to wear his own royal robes; the former makes the Israelite king tell Jehoshaphat to don Ahab's robes. While following, as mentioned, LXX on this point, Josephus goes his own way by speaking of an "agreement" between the two kings rather than of Ahab's "dictating" to Jehoshaphat (so both MT and LXX): "Now Achab and Josaphat had agreed (συνέθεντο) that Achab should take off (ἀποθέσθαι) his royal garments (τὸ βασιλι-κὸν σχῆμα)[1730] and that the king of Jerusalem should *take his place in the line of battle* (στῆναι ἐν τῇ παρατάξει)[1731] with the other's robe on (τὴν αὐτοῦ στολὴν ἔχοντα, 3 Rgns // 2 Par καὶ σὺ ἔνδυσαι τὸν ἱματισμόν μου)". Passing over the notice of 1 Kings 22,30b // 2 Chron 18,29b that Ahab did, in fact, "disguise himself" whereupon the two kings advance into battle, Josephus proceeds to append a comment of his own about the royal "agreement": "by this trick they thought (κατασοφιζόμενοι)[1732] to escape (the fate) foretold (προειρημένα) by Michaias. But Fate (τὸ χρεών, see 8,409) found him even though he was without his garment(s) (σχήματος)[1733]". He motivates the latter

1725. Thus MSP followed by N*Mar. N prints Ῥαμάθην, Να Ἀραμαθὰν.

1726. Compare 8,399 τῇ Γαλαδηνῇ... Ἀραμαθὰν.

1727. So NaMar for the στρατιὰν of codd followed by NN*.

1728. This is Josephus' only use of the verb ἀντεπάγω.

1729. With the above description of the movements of the opposing forces compare Josephus' portrayal of Adados's advance to Aphek and Ahab's counter advance in 8,381.

1730. In Kings and Chronicles the reference is to Ahab's "disguising himself". The above construction "take off garments" recurs in *AJ* 11,223. Only here in 8,412 does Josephus employ the phrase "royal garment(s)".

1731. This item has no parallel as such in the Biblical sources. It might, however, reflect the phrase used by Ahab of himself in 1 Kings 22,30aβ // 2 Chron 18,29aβ: "I will enter into battle".

1732. This pl. form is conjectured by N whom NaMar follow. The codd have the sg. (subject Ahab), whether in the nominative (so ROE) or the accusative (MSP [Lat]), see W, *ad loc.* "croyant".

Josephus' other uses of the verb κατασοφίζομαι are *AJ* 6,219 (Michal "tricks" Saul); 7,15 (Abner tries to "dissuade" Asael from pursuing him).

1733. Compare the words (8,269) which Josephus has the prophet Ahijah address to

statement, in turn, with a notice whose content he draws from 1 Kings
22,31 // 2 Chron 18,30: "*For* Adados (see 8,401)... had given orders
(παρήγγειλε, 3 Rgns // 2 Par ἐνετείλατο) *to his army* (τῇ στρατιᾷ)
[through the chiefs (διὰ τῶν ἡγεμόνων)]¹⁷³⁴ that they should slay
(ἀναιρεῖν) no one else but only (μόνον, see 8,405) the king of the
Israelites¹⁷³⁵".

Josephus begins his battle account proper with an expanded version
of 1 Kings 22,32-33 // 2 Chron 18,31-32: "So when the battle was
joined (τῆς συμβολῆς γενομένης)¹⁷³⁶ and the Syrians saw (ἰδόντες, 3
Rgns/ 2 Par εἶδον)¹⁷³⁷ Josaphat *standing before the lines* (ἐστῶτα πρὸ
τῆς τάξεως, see στῆναι ἐν τῇ παρατάξει, 8,412), they thought (εἰκάσαντες, 2 Par εἶπαν, 3 Rgns εἶπον)¹⁷³⁸ that he was Achab (Bible: the
King of Israel), and rushed upon him, but, on surrounding him
(ὥρμησαν 8,256.303] ... περικυκλωσάμενοι [see 8,282], 3 Rgns ἐκύκλω-
σαν αὐτὸν πολεμῆσαι) and coming close, they saw (ἔγνωσαν, 3 Rgns/
2 Par εἶδον) that it was not he, and all of them turned back (ἀνεχώρησαν ὀπίσω, 3 Rgns/2 Par ἀπέστρεψαν ἀπ' αὐτοῦ)". In the above
sequence Josephus passes over several items present in 1 Kings 22,32
and/or 2 Chron 18,31. Specifically, he makes no mention of Jehoshaphat's "cry" cited by both Biblical texts, perhaps finding it "unkingly"
(and in violation of the Judean's previous agreement to present himself
as Ahab). He likewise has nothing equivalent to the double *Sondergut*
notice in 2 Chron 18,31 concerning the divine response to Jehoshaphat's cry: "... the Lord helped him. God drew them away from him".
Thus in Josephus, the Syrian withdrawal from Jehoshaphat is motivated simply by their seeing him at close quarters and thereby recognizing
that he is not Ahab.

Josephus next proceeds to "anticipate" the notices of 1 Kings 22,35 //
2 Chron 18,34 concerning the duration and intensity of the battle:

the wife of Jeroboam: "Why do you disguise yourself? For your coming is not unknown
to God...".

1734. Mar has nothing equivalent to this item in his translation, compare W, *ad loc.*
"(à la armée) par la voix des chefs". Compare 2 Par τοῖς ἄρχουσιν τῶν ἁρμάτων τοῖς μετ'
[> B 3 Rgns] αὐτοῦ.

Like Chronicles (MT LXX) Josephus lacks the specification found in 1 Kings 22,31
that the Syrian's commanders numbered thirty-two (this figure is derived from 1 Kings
20,1.17 which speak of Ben-hadad's thirty-two ally kings in his earlier campaign against
Ahab).

1735. Compare 1 Kings 22,31 // 2 Chron 18,30 "Fight with neither the small nor the
great, but only (2 Par μόνον, 3 Rgns μονώτατον) the king of Israel".

1736. This genitive absolute construction occurs also in *BJ* 1,120. 172.250.369
(2,232).263 (290); 4,547; (6,159.251); *AJ* 4,161; 5,336; 7,73.236; 10,86; 12,351.

1737. In the Bible it is "the commanders of the chariots" who "see".

1738. The verb εἰκάζω occurs 37 × in Josephus.

"from early dawn[1739] until late afternoon (ἄχρι δείλης ὀψίας)[1740] they fought (μαχόμενοι, see μαχόμενον, 8,406)..."[1741]. To this notice, in turn, he appends the non-Biblical (and rather implausible) statement "and the victorious (νικῶντες, see νικηθείς, 8,403) (Syrians), in accordance with the king's command (κατὰ τὴν τοῦ βασιλέως ἐντολήν, see κατ᾽ ἐντολὴν τοῦ βασιλέως, 8,365)[1742], killed no one (ἀπέκτειναν οὐδένα, see μηδένα... ἀναιρεῖν, 8,413), seeking to slay (ἀνελεῖν [RO ἑλεῖν]) only (μόνον, see 8,405.413) Achab and not being able to find him".

Rejoining now the Biblical account, Josephus relates the eventual wounding of the Israelite king by an arrow. In MT 1 Kings 22,34 // 2 Chron 18,33 (as also L 3 Rgns) Ahab's wounder shoots him "accidentally" (לתמו, L ἀφελῶς), whereas in B 3 Rgns and 2 Par he does so "with a good aim" (εὐστόχως). Josephus' formulation seems somewhat more reminiscent of MT's reference to an accidental wounding: Ahab's assailant "wounded" (τιτρώσκει, 3 Rgns // 2 Par ἐπάταξεν) him while "shooting arrows (τοξεύσας, 2 Par ἔτεινεν τόξον) at the enemy". More noteworthy is the fact that, in contrast to the vague designation of Ahab's shooter as "a certain man" (2 Par ἀνὴρ), Josephus qualifies him much more precisely as "one of the king's pages (παῖς... βασιλικός)[1743], named Amanos (Ἀμανὸς)". In giving this name to the bowman, Josephus is likely identifying him with the Syrian officer "Naaman" whose leprosy is cured in 2 Kings 5[1744]. Finally, in de-

1739. Mar reads with E (similarly MSP) the following sequence here: πάντες, ἀρχομένης δ᾽. Compare NN* ἀπό τε ἀρχομένης (thus RO Lat), Να πάντες. ἀπ᾽ ἀρχομένης δ᾽.

1740. The word ὀψίας is absent in RO Lat and omitted by N*. The above construction "late afternoon" occurs also in AJ 3,3; 6,120; 7,130. With the whole phrase above, compare 13,97 ἀπὸ πρωῒ μέχρι δείλης ὀψίας. Josephus' formula here seems to reflect the expanded wording of 3 Rgns 22,35aβ (MT "until evening"), i.e. ἀπὸ πρωῒ ἕως ἑσπέρας.

1741. By means of the above "interlude", Josephus avoids the abrupt juxtaposition of the Syrian "withdrawal" from Jehoshaphat and the immediately following wounding of Ahab present in the Biblical sequence(s).

1742. The reference here is to 8,413 (Adados) "commanded (παρήγγειλε) his army...".

1743. This is the only occurrence of this phrase in Josephus.

1744. Thus, e.g., RAPPAPORT, Agada, p. xxiv; GINZBERG, Legends, VI, p. 313, n. 43; Mar, Josephus, V, p. 795, n.b. These authors point out that elsewhere in Jewish tradition Ahab's slayer is indeed identified with the Syrian army commander Naaman of 2 Kings 5, see Targum on 2 Chron 18,33, Midr. Tehillim 78, 350 (ad Ps 78,11) and Midr. Sam. 11,80. At the same time it should be noted that the extant text of Josephus lacks a parallel to the whole segment 2 Kings 4,6-6,8 so that one cannot be sure that Josephus did in fact identify the "royal page Amanos" of 8,414 with the general of 2 Kings 5. Note further the remarks of SCHLATTER, Namen, p. 42, s.v. בֶּן־הֲדַד: "... wird Αναμος ονομα zu streichen sein. Der Text gibt keinen Namen für den Schützen, der Ahab tötlich traf, und die Einwerkung eine anderen Quelle ist in der Erzählung gar nicht sichtbar, die lediglich den Bibeltext wiedergibt. Αμανος war ursprünglich entstelles Αδαδος und wurde dann zum Namen des Schützen gemacht". Compare SCHALIT, Namenwörterbuch, p. 89, s.v. Ναμάνος: "Es ist in A 8,414 Ναμανός statt Ἀμανός zu lesen. Schlatters Ausführungen...

scribing Ahab's wound, Josephus aligns himself with LXX as opposed to MT 1 Kings 22,34 // 2 Chron 18,33. For the latter's "between the scale armour and the breastplate" (so RSV, MT בין הדבקים ובין השׁרין) and the former's "between the lung and the breast (plate)" (ἀνὰ μέσον τοῦ πνεύμονος καὶ ἀνὰ μέσον τοῦ θώρακος), he reads "through the breastplate in the lung (διὰ τοῦ θώρακος κατὰ τοῦ πνεύμονος)[1745]".

In next recounting the wounded Ahab's withdrawal (see 1 Kings 22,34b // 2 Chron 18,33b), Josephus (8,415) provides an additional motive for the king's response to his misfortune: "*Achab, however, decided not to let his army* (στρατεύματι, see 8,275.381) *see what had happened lest they should be put to flight* (τραπείησαν [SP Lat τραπῆ δεῖσαν]), and ordered his driver (ἡνίοχον, 3 Rgns // 2 Par ἡνιόχῳ)[1746] to turn the chariot (ἐκτρέψαντα[1747] τὸ ἅρμα)[1748] and carry him off the field of battle (ἐξάγειν[1749] τῆς μάχης, 3 Rgns // 2 Par ἐξάγαγέ με ἐκ τοῦ πολέμου)[1750], for he had been *gravely* (χαλεπῶς) *and even mortally* (καιρίως)[1751] wounded (βεβλῆσθαι, 3 Rgns τέτρωμαι, 2 Par ἐπόνεσα)". By means of the above expansion, he makes Ahab withdraw not, as might appear from Scripture, simply out of concern with his own condition, but in a desire to keep up the army's morale. In the same line, Josephus amplifies his version of 1 Kings 22,35 // 2 Chron 18.34[1752]: "But though he was in great pain (ὀδυνώμενος)[1753], he remained upright in his chariot (ἔστη ἐπὶ τοῦ ἅρματος, 3 Rgns // 2 Par ἦν ἑστηκὼς ἐπὶ τοῦ ἅρματος)[1754] until the setting of the sun (δύνοντος ἡλίου, 2 Par δύναντος τοῦ ἡλίου, 3 Rgns ἕως ἑσπέρας) and then, with

sind falsch. Der Josephustext ist bis auf das fehlendes N intakt und ist gegen Schlatter zu halten".

1745. This is Josephus' only use of the term πνεύμων.

1746. Josephus' other uses of ἡνίοχος are in *AJ* 10,278; 18,168; 19,257.

1747. Thus NN*Mar. Na reads ἐκστρέψαντα, cf. MSP (Lat?) ἐπιστρέψαι.

1748. In the Bible Ahab directs the driver to "turn his hand(s)".

1749. MSP ἐξαγαγεῖν.

1750. This is Josephus' only use of the above phrase "carry off from (the field of) battle".

1751. This is the only occurrence of the above collocation "grave(ly) and mortal(ly)" in Josephus. Cf. *AJ* 9,105 where he refers to Joram's τοξευθείς... οὐ καιρίως.

1752. The Chronicler's parallel text, i.e. 18,34 lacks the notice on the flow of Ahab's blood into his chariot found in 1 Kings 22,35bβ (MT; in B this notice appears twice, i.e. at the end of the verse [so MT], but also after v. 35a, while in L it precedes mention of Ahab's death in v. 35b). The absence of this item in Chronicles is understandable in that this source, unlike Kings, will not tell of the sequels to Ahab's death, i.e. the washing out of the royal chariot and the profanation of Ahab's blood on that occasion (see 22,38) which it is designed to prepare.

1753. Elsewhere Josephus uses passive forms of the verb ὀδυνάω in *BJ* 1,459.467.559; 5,546; 6,183; *AJ* 6,155; 7,46.

1754. Like MT 1 Kings 22,35aβ // 2 Chron 18,34aβ Josephus lacks the specification found in the LXX of these two verses that Ahab's "stand" lasted "from early (morning) (> 2 Par) until evening" (recall, however, that he has an "anticipation" of this item, conjoined with his version of the notice 22,35aα about "the battle growing hot that day" in 8,414 *"from early dawn until late afternoon they fought"*). Note further that Josephus

the blood drained out of him (λιφαιμήσας)[1755], expired (ἀπέθανε = 3 Rgns // 2 Par ἀπέθανεν)"[1756].

4. *Closing Notices for Ahab* (8,416-420). In 1 Kings 22 mention of Ahab's death in v. 35bα (MT B [in L this item stands in v. 35bβ]; recall that the Chronicler's account terminates with this item, 2 Chron 18,34b) is followed by formulations which differ somewhat in MT and 3 Rgns. MT 22,36-37aα reads "and about sunset a (the) cry (הָרִנָּה)[1757] went through (וַיַּעֲבֹר) the army, 'every man to his city and every man to his country'. So the king died". 3 Rgns renders rather "and at the going down of the sun the herald of the army (στρατοκήρυξ)[1758] stood (ἔστη) saying (λέγων), 'every man to his city and to his own land (γῆν, B; L κληρονομίαν), for (ὅτι) the king is dead (τέθνηκεν)'"[1759]. Josephus, for his part, words the notice on Israel's retreat in line with 3 Rgns even while introducing certain amplifications/adaptations: "and so, as night had now fallen (νυκτὸς... γενομένης), *the Syrian army retired to its camp*[1760] and, when the herald (στρατοκήρυκος)[1761] announced (δηλώσαντος) that (ὅτι, see 3 Rgns) Achab was dead

likewise fails to reproduce the specification about Ahab's standing "facing the Syrians" of 22,35aβ // 18,34aβ.

1755. Thus the conjecture of N followed by NaMar. Compare λειφαιμήσας (RO); λιποθυμήσας (MSP); λειποθυμήσας (E); factus exsanguis (Lat). The verb λιφαιμέω is hapax in Josephus.

Compare 1 Kings 22,35bβ (MT B) "and the blood of the wound flowed (B ἐξεπορεύτο) into the bottom of the chariot".

1756. It might be pointed out here that, subsequently, Josephus, following the lead of the Bible itself, will narrate the death of king Josiah (*AJ* 10,74-77, see 2 Kings 23,29b-30 // 2 Chron 35,30-35) in a way that recalls that of Ahab here in 8,414-415. Both monarchs are wounded by an arrow in the course of battle which they had eagerly initiated, this leading to their withdrawal and eventual death. Note too that Josephus explicitly attributes the two kings' advancing to their respective dooms, notwithstanding warnings not to do so (these are placed on the lips of, respectively, the prophet Micaiah and Pharoah Neco), to the influence of some impersonal power, i.e. "Fate" (τὸ χρεών, 8,409.412) for Ahab and "Destiny" (τῆς πεπρομένης, 10,76) for Josiah. See C.T. BEGG, *The Death of Josiah: Josephus and the Bible*, in *ETL* 64 (1988) 157-163.

1757. In *Sanh.* 39b this "cry" is interpreted as a song of rejoicing over the overthrow of the wicked Ahab.

1758. As BHS points out, LXX's term here could simply presuppose a different vocalization of MT's consonantal form, i.e. הָרֹנָה instead of הָרִנָּה. Note that TJ likewise speaks of a "herald" in its version of 1 Kings 22,36.

1759. Note that in both MT and 3 Rgns there is a double mention of Ahab's death, i.e. 22,35bα and 37aα.

1760. Compare Josephus' likewise interpolated notice that, in the face of the allied advance, Adados "led his army against them and encamped not far from the city of Aramathē", 8,411.

1761. The term στρατοκήρυξ here is the same as that used in 3 Rgns 22,36. It is hapax in Josephus (just as the only occurrence in LXX is in the Rgns verse). Josephus employs the simple κήρυξ in *BJ* 2,624; *AJ* 8,365 (see above); 10,75.

(τέθνηκεν= 3 Rgns), *they returned to their own country* (ἀνέζευξαν εἰς τὰ ἴδια)[1762]...".

Josephus now comes to relate his parallel to the complex of notices in 1 Kings 22,37aβ-38 concerning the coming of Ahab's body to Samaria, its burial there, the washing out of the chariot at "the pool of Samaria", and the shameful treatment of the king's blood by dogs and harlots in accordance with a – not further specified – "word of the Lord". In rendering this sequence Josephus begins: "carrying (κομίσαντες) the body (νεκρὸν) of Achab to Samaria and burying (θάπτουσι)[1763] it there ...[1764]". He then goes on to cite the Israelites' "washing (ἀποπλύναντες)[1765] the chariot[1766] which was stained (καθημαγμένον)[1767] with the king's blood (φόνῳ)[1768]".

In 1 Kings 22,38aα the "washing" takes place "at the pool (fountain) (B ἐπὶ τὴν κρήνην, L ἐν τῇ κρήνῃ) *of Samaria*", i.e. the same city in which Ahab has just been buried. Josephus, on the contrary, situates the washing rather "in the spring (ἐν τῇ κρήνῃ, see L) *of Jezarel* ('Ιεζαρήλα)[1769]". Josephus' shifting of sites here is motivated by the consideration that 1 Kings 22,38 – which nowhere mentions "Jezreel" as such – leaves the impression that the subsequent profanation of Ahab's blood took place also at Samaria – in contradiction to the prediction of Elijah (see 1 Kings 21,19) that the king's blood would be licked up in the place where Naboth had encountered this fate, i.e. Jezreel. Anticipating, while further specifying the fulfillment notice of 22,38bβ "according to the word of the Lord which he spoke (+ through Elijah, so a few Hebrew and Greek MSS)", Josephus next states that, following the cleansing of the chariot, the Israelites "acknowledged (ἐπέγνωσαν) the truth (ἀληθῆ, see 8,404.407.408) of Eli-

1762. This notice represents a transposition into narrative of the herald's directive to the Israelite army in 3 Rgns 22,36b. With its wording (which occurs only here in Josephus) compare that of Micaiah's description of his vision to Ahab in 8,405 (God had revealed that his men) ἀναστρέφειν εἰς τὰ ἴδια.

1763. Josephus uses this h.p. form also in *AJ* 1,237; 4,78; 5,124.317; 6,293.377; 14,123.

1764. Compare 22,37aβb "he (3 Rgns they) came to Samaria and they buried (3 Rgns ἔθαψαν) the king (+ Ahab, L) in Samaria".

1765. Elsewhere Josephus uses ἀποπλύνω in *AJ* 3,114 and 6,120 (here too of a "washing away" of blood).

1766. Josephus' refering to the washing of Ahab's *chariot* here agrees with MT 22,38aα against B which speaks rather of the "washing" (ἀπένιψαν) of Ahab's "blood" (L "they washed the blood from the chariot").

1767. Josephus' only other use of the verb καθαιμβάσσω is in *BJ* 4,201 (the blood of the wounded Zealots "stains" the Temple).

1768. With the above idiom "stained with blood" compare the alternate expression φόνῳ μιαίνω used in *AJ* 7,92 and 371 (both times of David).

Josephus derives his reference to the blood "staining" Ahab's chariot from 1 Kings 22,35bβ "and the blood of the wound flowed into the bottom of the chariot" (cf. his previous utilization of this item in 8,415 "with the blood drained out of him").

1769. Thus Mar. NN* 'Ιεζερήλα, Na 'Ιζαρα (so SP).

jah's prophecy (προφητείαν, see 8,289.309)[1770]". They did this, he goes on to affirm (// 22,38αβbα), "for the dogs licked up (ἀνελιχμή-σαντο[1771] [see 8,407], B ἐξέλιξαν, L ἔλειξαν)[1772]; and thereafter the harlots (αἱ ἑταιριζόμεναι, 3 Rgns αἱ πόρναι)[1773] used to bathe (λουόμε-ναι... διετέλουν, 3 Rgns ἐλούσαντο)[1774] in the pool in this (blood) (ἐν τῇ κρήνῃ... τούτῳ)[1775]".

Having thus noted that Elijah's prediction was fulfilled in what transpired with Ahab's blood at the pool of Jezreel, Josephus rounds off his narrative of the king's end by adding the reminder "but he died (ἀπέθανε, see 8,415) in Aramathē (Ἀραμάθη)[1776], as Michaias had foretold (προειρηκότος)[1777]". Thereby, he prepares the reflections which he will append to the Biblical story, see below.

1770. Note the characteristic substitution of "prophecy" for "word of the Lord" here. The above construction "know the truth of prophecy" occurs only here in Josephus, cf. ἐπιγνῷ τὴν ἀλήθειαν, 20,128.

1771. This is the conjecture of Hud followed by NN*NaMar; the codd have ἀνελικ-μήσαντο.

1772. Like MT and L Josephus lacks the further mention, found in B 3 Rgns 22,38αβ of "pigs" consuming Ahab's blood along with the dogs. (Recall that in his version of Elijah's announcement of Ahab's doom in 8,361 Josephus, like 1 Kings 21,19, has no equivalent to 3 Rgns 20,19's reference to "pigs" which serves to set up the B plus of 22,38).

1773. Josephus' only other use of the verb ἑταιρίζω is in AJ 5,306 where he employs the sg. participle in reference to Delilah.

F. HAUCK - S. SCHULZ, πόρνη κτλ, in TWNT 6 (1959), 579-595, pp. 588-589 point out that, also elsewhere, Josephus avoids the terms πόρνη and πορνεύω where LXX uses these in reference to Jewish figures and comment: "Ganz unverkennbar wirkt sich in dem allen das Bestreben des Jos aus, die Sittlichkeit seines Volkes als vorbildlich hinzustellen".

1774. Note the shift here from the one-time action denoted by 3 Rgns' aorist to the ongoing practice signified by Josephus' construction.

1775. Compare W, ad loc. "à cette fontaine", a rendering in which τούτῳ is taken to modify the feminine noun κρήνῃ. With the above phrase "in the pool in this (blood)" Josephus provides a double specification on where(in) the harlots washed themselves. In this he further extends 3 Rgns' expansion of MT 22,38bα, the former reading "the harlots washed themselves in the blood (+ of him, L)" for the latter's simple "the harlots washed themselves". In Josephus it is in the water of the pool as previously impregnated with the king's blood that the harlots wash.

In contrast to the Josephus who does take over the (MT/3 Rgns) reference to harlots washing themselves (in Ahab's blood), stand the formulations of the TJ and Vulgate versions of 1 Kings 22,38bα, both of which speak rather of a washing of "weapons" (זינה, habenas). With these versions' "softening" of the Biblical presentation, compare as well the Rabbinic traditions (e.g., Meg. 3a; Mo'ed Qatan 28b; Targum Zech. 12.11) which accentuate the honorableness of Ahab's burial, likening this to that of Josiah, see GINZBERG, Legends, VI, p. 313, n. 44.

1776. Thus NN*Mar; NaW follow MSP's ῥαμαθῶνι.

1777. Thus MSPE followed by NaMar. NN* read προειπόντος with RO. Note that in his previous "citations" of Micaiah's announcements concerning Ahab's doom (see 8,392.403.405.406.408) Josephus does not explicitly have him predict the king's death "at Aramathē" (compare 8,408 where Zedekiah "quotes" Micaiah as stating that Ahab is to die "within three days" even though the latter's previously cited predictions do not contain this specification about the "when" (or where) of Ahab's demise, see n. 1690.

In Josephus' source there now follows Kings' standard concluding framework notices concerning Ahab, 1 Kings 22,39-40. Of this material Josephus (8,420, *fine*) makes use only of 22,40b for his notice on Ahab's "being succeeded" (τοῦτον... διεδέξατο)[1778] by his son "Ochozias" ('Οχοζίας, MT Ahaziah, 3 Rgns 'Οχοζείας)[1779]. Conversely, he follows his standard practice in omitting the "source notice" of 22,39. He likewise passes over the formula "so Ahab slept with his fathers" of 22,40a which both duplicates 22,35bα/38aα and, in its seeming suggestion that Ahab died a peaceful death[1780], conflicts with the account given in 22,35-38 (and taken over by Josephus). In place of the omitted source material of 22,39-40a, Josephus precedes the "succession notice" of 22,40b with the following lengthy reflection of his own composition:

> Now, since there befell (συμβάντων) Achab (the fate) spoken of by the two prophets[1781], we ought to acknowledge (ἡγεῖσθαι) the greatness of the Deity (μέγα... τὸ θεῖον)[1782] and everywhere honour (σέβειν) and reverence (τιμᾶν)[1783] Him, nor should we think the things (which are said) to flatter us or please us (τὰ πρὸς ἡδονὴν καὶ βούλησιν)[1784] more worthy of

1778. In 8,287.313 Josephus uses the h.p. of the same construction, see n. 697. For the aorist construction used here in 8,420b, see *AJ* 19,316; 20,237.240; *Ap* 1,124.

1779. In MT B 1 Kings 22,39-40 are themselves followed by a summary account of Jehoshaphat's reign (22,41-50) and the opening notices on Ahaziah of Israel (22,51-53). At this juncture in his presentation Josephus omits the material of 22,41-53, appending directly to the death of Ahab (8,398-420) his version (9,1-17) of the Chronistic *Sondergut* sequence (2 Chronicles 19-20) concerning the fortunes of Jehoshaphat subsequent to the death of his Northern counterpart. Thereafter, he gives his parallel to 1 Kings 22,51-53 in 9,18.

1780. This is the regular meaning of the above phrase throughout the OT, see M.A. O'BRIEN, *The Deuteronomistic History Hypothesis: A Reassessment* (OBO, 92), Freiburg-Göttingen, 1989, p. 245 and nn. 64-66.

1781. Likewise the Targum on 2 Chron 18,33 and *Sanh.* 39b speak explicitly of Ahab's end as fulfilling the prophecies of both Micaiah and Elijah (both texts further understand the term לתמו of 2 Chron 18,33 as pointing to this double fulfillment, see TC's rendering of it by לאשלמא). Note also the analogous case of 10,141 where Josephus, in recounting the punishment of king Zedekiah, points out that the two apparently discrepant prophecies of Jeremiah and Ezekiel concerning that king's fate both came to realization, see n. 1690.

1782. With this formulation compare the moral drawn by Josephus from fate of Haman (11,268) "wherefore I am moved to marvel at the Deity (τὸ θεῖον) and to recognize His wisdom and justice...". Cf. also the expression "acknowledge (ἄγω) God" in *BJ* 7,410; *AJ* 1,72 (8,337; 20,85.90).

1783. Josephus uses the above verbal collocation "honour and reverence" with God/ the Deity as object also in *AJ* 4,318 where the dying Moses reminds the people that "it behoves you to revere and honour Him...". Here, after his lengthy account of Ahab who singularly failed to heed this lesson, Josephus pauses to reiterate it.

1784. With this collocation, compare *AJ* 5,179 καθ' ἡδονὴν καὶ βούλησιν ἰδίαν (of the Israelites' mode of life following their settlement in the land). See also 8,236 (Jeroboam is deceived) by the things the Bethel prophet said "to please (πρὸς ἡδονὴν) him", and recall the many other verbal contacts between the "Jadōn episode" and Josephus' account of Ahab's death as cited above.

belief (πιθανώτερα)[1785] than the truth (ἀληθείας), but should realize (ὑπολαμβάνειν) that nothing is more beneficial (συμφορώτερον)[1786] than prophecy (προφητείας, see 8,417) and the foreknowledge which it gives (τῆς διὰ τῶν τοιούτων προγνώσεως [see 8,234])[1787], for in this way God enables us (παρέχοντος... τοῦ θεοῦ)[1788] (to know) what to guard against (φυλάξασθαι). And further, with the king's history before our eyes (στοχαζομένους)[1789], it behoves us to reflect on (λογίζεσθαι... προσῆκε [see 8,406])[1790] the power of Fate (τὴν τοῦ χρεὼν [see 8,409.413] ἰσχύν), and see that not even with foreknowledge is it possible to escape it (μηδὲ προγινωσκόμενον αὐτὸ διαφυγεῖν)[1791], for it secretly enters the souls of men (ἀνθρωπίνας ψυχὰς)[1792] and flatters them with fair hopes (ἐλπίσι κολακεῦον χρησταῖς)[1793], and by means of these it leads them on (περιάγει) to the point where it can overcome (κρατήσει) them. It appears, then, that by this (power, i.e. Fate) Achab's mind was deceived (τὴν διάνοιαν ἀπατηθείς)[1794] so that while he disbelieved (ἀπιστῆσαι)[1795] those who foretold his defeat (τοῖς προλέγουσι τὴν ἧτταν)[1796], he believed (πεισθεὶς) those who prophesied (προφητεύσασι) things that pleased him (πρὸς χάριν)[1797], and so lost his life (ἀποθανεῖν, see 8,415.417).   (8,418-420a)[1798]

1785. See Josephus' remark in 8,409 "it was Fate... that made the false prophet(s) seem more convincing (πιθανωτέρους)...".

1786. Josephus' other uses of σύμφορος are in BJ 4,177; 5,73; AJ 5,286; 6,60; 7,281; 8,23; 9,260; Ap 2,274.294.

1787. The above Greek phrase is better rendered with W, ad loc. "et la prescience de l'avenir obtenue grâce aux prophètes", who takes προφητῶν from earlier on in 8,418 as the referent of τῶν τοιούτων in the above phrase.

1788. Josephus employs this same genitive absolute construction in AJ 6,366 "God enabled" David's men to avenge themselves on their enemies. For God as subject of παρέχω, see also 8,234.296.

1789. Josephus' other uses of στοχάζομαι are in BJ 4,103.374; 7,327.455; AJ 7,74; 8,132; 10,32; 12,212; 14,3; 15,330 (bis); 16,210. In 8,132; 10,32; 12,212 the verb is construed with the preposition ἐκ as here in 8,419.

1790. The above phrase "it behoves to reflect" occurs only here in Josephus.

1791. Compare BJ 6,314 ... οὐ δυνατὸν ἀνθρώποις τὸ χρεὼν διαφυγεῖν οὐδὲ προορωμένοις.

1792. The above phrase "souls of men" occurs only here in Josephus.

1793. This is Josephus' only use of the above phrase "flatter with fair hopes". The verb κολακεύω occurs also in BJ 1,542.566; 2,152.213.276; AJ 2,80; 11,54; 14,51; 16,158.254; Vita 367. For the phrase "fair hopes", see AJ 6,275; 7,234; 13,421; 15,302; 18,294.

1794. The above construction "deceive the mind" recurs in AJ 11,39 where wine is said to do this. Compare 8,236 Jeroboam was "deceived" (ἀπατώμενος) by the things the Bethel prophet "said to please him".

1795. The verb ἀπιστέω occurs 41 × in the Josephan corpus.

1796. Josephus uses the above phrase "foretell defeat" also in AJ 9,198; 12,342.

1797. The above phrase πρὸς χάριν occurs also in 12,398 (+ πρὸς ἡδονὴν, see 8,418); 16,399; Vita 149; Ap 1,25.

1798. The series of notices which Josephus appends to his description of king Zedekiah's punishment in AJ 10,141-142 comprise a sequence comparable to that of 8,417-420 on Ahab's demise: in both mention of the fulfillment of two seemingly divergent prophecies concerning a king's end (see n. 1690) is followed by a reflection about the lessons to be drawn from this. It thus appears that Josephus intends the death

The above reflection, it will be noted, echoes Josephus' earlier emphasis on "fates" role in Ahab's demise. As such the reflection likewise serves- just as does his non-inclusion of the Biblical heavenly court scene- to play down God's complicity in falsehood; it is fate which sets in motion the process of man's deception, not God[1799]. In thus furthering his apologetic purposes Josephus does, on the other hand, introduce, it must be recognized, a kind of dualism which, in turn, raises questions concerning divine omnipotence- Josephus appears to allow here that, in some cases, God's intention of diverting humans from their harmful courses is frustrated by the machinations of fate. However Josephus may have resolved this problem in his own mind, his reflection does, finally, leave us with a practical principle of conduct, i.e. one must be particularly wary of the flattering and pleasing words of others which are likely to represent the lures of malevolent fate[1800].

Summary: With regard to Josephus' Biblical text(s) for our pericope, this is little positive evidence for his use of "MT" Kings and/or Chronicles (although see his reference to the washing out of Ahab's "chariot" *à la* MT 1 Kings 22,38 as against B(L)). Conversely, he aligns himself with the distinctive readings of 3 Rgns // 2 Par in a whole series of instances: Jehoshaphat's wearing his own rather than Ahab's robes in battle (8,412, see 1 Kings 22,30 // 2 Chron 18,29); the nature of Ahab's wound (8,414, see 1 Kings 22,34 // 2 Chron 18,33) and the announcement of the king's death and Israel's resultant withdrawal (8,416, see 1 Kings 22,37-38aα). On the other hand, like MT and L 1 Kings 22,38aβ, he has no parallel (see 8,417) to the B plus about pigs too eating Ahab's blood. Josephus' version further manifests noteworthy affinities here and there with elements proper to the Targums on Kings and Chronicles. Thus in line with TJ on 1 Kings 22,6 he designates (8,402) the 400 as "false prophets", while in parallel to TC on 2 Chron 18,10 he labels (8,406) Zedekiah "one of the false prophets". With TC on 2 Chron 18,33 he further shares his (apparent) identification (8,414) of Ahab's slayer with "Naaman", as well the explicit affirmation that the circumstances of Ahab's death brought to fulfillment the words of both Elijah and Micaiah (see 8,418) – a point also made in Rabbinic tradition, *vide supra*.

---

of Ahab to foreshadow what happens with Judah's last king. On the Josephan portrayal of Zedekiah, see C.T. BEGG, *Josephus' Zedekiah*, in *ETL* 65 (1989) 96-104.

1799. Josephus' invocation of fate throughout our pericope also, of course, helps accomodate the Biblical story to the understanding of a Gentile audience.

1800. On "fate" and its relation to God, etc. in Josephus, see e.g.: SCHLATTER, *Theologie*, p. 43; G. STÄHLIN, *Das Schicksal im NT und bei Josephus*, in O. BETZ, K. HAACKER, M. HENGEL (eds.), *Josephus-Studien*. FS O. Michel, Göttingen, 1974, 319-343, pp. 331-343; SCHUTT, *God*, pp. 183-186; VILLALBA I VARNEDA, *Method*, pp. 58-62.

Josephus' version of Ahab's death offers some particularly striking examples of his various modes of dealing with the Biblical source and its (perceived) problems. He, e.g., deletes the two segments in which a deceptive word is attributed either to a ("true") prophet (see 1 Kings 22,15 // 2 Chron 18,14) or to God himself (see 1 Kings 22,19-23 // 2 Chron 18,18-22), in the latter instance substituting a brief restatement of Micaiah's earlier (veracious) announcements, see 8,406. In place of 1 Kings 22,38's reference to the pool "of Samaria", he speaks (8,417) of the Jezreel pool (spring), thereby eliminating the seeming discrepancy between Elijah's announcement (1 Kings 21,19) and its "fulfillment" (22,38) in the Bible. At the same time he also rearranges items in the Biblical sequence, e.g., he "anticipates" the royal "session" of 1 Kings 22,10 // 2 Chron 18,9, while "delaying" Zedekiah's word and sign (1 Kings 22,11 // 2 Chron 18,10). Josephus' most noteworthy additions to the source account(s) are the "demonstration" of Micaiah's unbeliev-ability which he places on the lips of Zedekiah in 8,407-408 with its echoes of the narratives of 1 Kings 13 and 21 as earlier retold by him and the reflections with which he rounds off his narration in 8,418-420. Finally to be noted is Josephus' integration (8,398-400) of the divergent data presented him by the respective introductory sections of 1 Kings 22 (vv. 1-4) and 2 Chronicles 18 (vv. 1-3).

What now are the distinctive features of the Josephan story of Ahab's death which result from the historian's application of the above procedures? Vis-à-vis the Bible, Josephus accentuates the equality and harmony of the Ahab-Jehoshaphat relationship, just as he gives us a more magnanimous, reflective Israelite ruler[1801]. He somewhat down-plays the role of Micaiah, while (negatively) enhancing that of Zede-kiah[1802]. In "explaining" Ahab's end, he invokes "the power of fate" (8,419) rather than tracing it back to God himself as does Scripture. Overall, it may be said that Josephus presents us with a narrative that is more "transparent", tightly integrated with what precedes and follows, and overtly didactic (see especially the concluding reflections of 8,418-420a)[1803]. On the other hand, one can only admit that the Josephian version is a far "flatter" one, stripped as it largely is of the ambiguities, ironies, and puzzlements which give the Scriptural story its hold upon the reader.

1801. Recall that likewise in his version of the narratives of 1 Kings 20 and 21, Josephus incorporates positive touches into his depiction of Ahab.

1802. Compare his similar treatment of the two prophetic figures of 1 Kings 13 in 8,230-245. There too, as noted above, Josephus' interest seems to go more to the person of the "false prophet" of Bethel than to his "true" counterpart, Jadōn.

1803. At the same time Josephus' presentation is not, of course, without conceptual difficulties of its own, see, e.g., the unresolved (and even unaddressed) problem of the relationship between God's power and the influence of fate.

CONCLUSIONS

The preceding chapters have presented a mass of detailed observations which will not be repeated here. Rather, I shall now attempt, in light of those observations, to formulate some synthetic remarks concerning Josephus' account in 8,212-420. I group my remarks around the following headings: A) Josephus' integration of his Biblical sources; B) Josephus' text(s) of the Biblical sources; C) Josephus' rewriting techniques; and D) final comparison and evaluation of Josephus' version vis-à-vis the Bible[1804].

A. Integration of Biblical Sources

In composing his account of the early divided monarchy (*AJ* 8,212-420), Josephus had available two rather distinct sources, i.e. 1 Kings 12-22 and 2 Chronicles 10-18. In fact, it is only in their respective openings (1 Kings 12,1-24 // 2 Chron 10,1-11,4, the split) and closings (1 Kings 22,1-40 // 2 Chron 18,1-34, death of Ahab) that these two sources evidence any sustained correspondence (cf. also 1 Kings 15,16-22 // 2 Chron 16,1-6, the Asa-Baasha conflict). For the rest, the two Biblical narratives largely go their own ways. Kings gives a presentation which concentrates on Northern rulers (see its *Sondergut* segments on Jeroboam, 1 Kings 12,25-14,20 [MT] and Ahab, 1 Kings 16,29-21,29), whereas the Chronicler focusses, even more exclusively, on the succession of Southern monarchs, Rehoboam, Abijah, Asa and Jehoshaphat who in Kings receive relatively short shrift.

How then does Josephus deal with the above state of affairs? It is, first of all, clear that the historian did not opt to follow one source to the exclusion of the other. Rather, he aims to give both sources their due via a maximal utilization of their peculiar materials in his own account. Specifically, taking Kings' more extensive and Northern-oriented sequence as a basis, Josephus integrates therein the Chronicler's detailed treatment of the Judean rulers[1805]. Thus, in 8,246-264 he inserts (see 8,274-286) within the "Jeroboam bloc" (1 Kings 12,25-14,20, MT) both the extensive material of 2 Chron 11,5-12,16 on Rehoboam's reign (cf. the much shorter "parallel" account of 1 Kings 14,21-31) and the

---

1804. The provisional character of these "conclusions" should be emphasized at the outset. They are based on my reading of one half of one book of the 20-book *AJ*. As such, they are obviously in need of testing and refinement in light of *AJ* as a whole, its "Biblical section" in particular.

1805. Consult chart, p. 6.

Sondergut narrative of Abijah's victory over Jeroboam (2 Chronicles 13). Thereafter, he works into a sequence focussed on Jeroboam's successors (8,287-289.298-315) and drawn from 1 Kings 14,19-20; 15,23-16,28, an (abridged, see below) version (8,290-297) of the Chronicler's fuller account of Asa's good beginnings, 2 Chronicles 14-15 (compare 1 Kings 15,9-23). Similarly, in 8,393-397 he interrupts the flow of the "Ahab sequence" (8,316-392.398-420 // 1 Kings 16,29-22,40) with a segment inspired by 2 Chronicles 17 on Jehoshaphat's felicitous early reign (compare Kings' summary treatment of this ruler's entire reign in 1 Kings 22,41-50, MT).

Josephus' interest in making the fullest possible use of the data of both his sources also comes to expression in those instances where the sources do evidence extended parallelism, see above. His account of Ahab's death (8,398-420 [+ 9,1]) furnishes the clearest illustration in this regard. As will be recalled, whereas the core story of the two Biblical narrations of this episode (1 Kings 22,5-35 // 2 Chron 18,4-34) manifests a wide-going verbal identity, their respective openings (1 Kings 22,1-4 / 2 Chron 18,1-3) and sequels (1 Kings 22,36-51/ 2 Chron 19,1-3) notably diverge. In both cases, as we saw above, Josephus contrives to utilize the distinctive data of each account (for the former, see 8,398-400, for the latter, 8,416-9,1). In 1 Kings 12,1-24 // 2 Chron 10,1-11,4 (the split) the two Biblical narratives cohere even more closely than do 1 Kings 22 // 2 Chronicles 18, so that here (see 8,212-224) there was relatively little need for Josephus to concern himself with incorporating the peculiarities of one or other source (1 Kings 15,16-22 // 2 Chron 16,1-6 is another such case on a smaller scale). Note, however, that in 8,221 Josephus does offer an adaptation of the notice on the assumption of kingship by Jeroboam and Rehoboam respectively found in 1 Kings 12,20 but absent in 2 Chronicles 10.

The above observations make clear that fidelity to both his sources in their contentual peculiarities is a key feature of Josephus' account in 8,212-420. In accordance with that fidelity he makes room for virtually all the special material of Kings and Chronicles dealing with the period under discussion here.

B. TEXT(S) OF BIBLICAL SOURCES

In my introduction I spoke of the uncertainty surrounding the question concerning the text(s) of Kings and Chronicles employed by Josephus. At this point, following my detailed comparison of 8,212-420 with its Biblical source material, that uncertainty remains to a large extent. It does so given a variety of considerations. First of all, for large portions of the material in question, MT and LXX (BL) simply coincide (this is particularly the case in Chronicles, less so, e.g., in 1 Kings // 3 Rgns 17-22). In such instances, taken for themselves, one has, obviously, no basis for deciding whether Josephus was working with one witness rather than other. An analogous quandry is posed by those cases in which, e.g., MT goes together with L against B[1806]. How in such cases is one to decide that Josephus is dependent on Hebrew "MT" as opposed to Greek "L" (or vice versa)?

But also where MT and LXX (BL) evidence divergent readings obscurities remain. Thus, e.g., Josephus' agreements with a distinctive reading of MT or LXX are frequently "negative" in character, i.e. he shares with one witness its lack of some item found in the other. The probative value of such negative agreements for the question of Josephus' dependence on that witness with which he shares the "agreement" is clearly limited, however, given the fact that he does not hesitate to leave aside numerous source items, common to both MT and LXX, which he found unsuitable for some reason, see below. In other words, it is, in many cases, quite conceivable that Josephus did, in fact, have a given item – the lack of which he shares with MT or LXX – before him in his Biblical text, but suppressed this on his own initiative apart from the "precedent" of the other witness(es)[1807].

This brings us to the case of the "positive agreements" between Josephus and the distinctive readings of MT or LXX. These, of course, have a greater weight in that it is certainly easier to imagine that, where such agreements exist, they are due to Josephus' dependence on what he found in his source than that he spontaneously formulated an item not found in his actual source(s), but which just happens to correspond to the reading of a text-form not available to him. Still, even here, caution is in order. For one thing, several of Josephus' "positive" agreements with LXX against MT are cases where the difference between LXX and MT is a matter of the former's reading the Hebrew consonantal text with a vocalization other than MT's. E.g., in 8,347 Josephus agrees with 3 Rgns 19,3 in noting that Elijah "feared" (Hebrew וַיִּרָא) Jezebel, whereas MT's vocalized text reads וַיַּרְא, "he saw". Is Josephus' agreement here with LXX necessarily to be ascribed to his dependence on it – rather than a proto (unvocalized) MT? Is it not rather equally conceivable that Josephus had before him the unvocalized Hebrew form וירא and, on his own, understood it as a reference to Elijah's "fear" – all the more when such a reference seems more appropriate in the context than an allusion to the prophet's "seeing"?

1806. See, e.g., 2 Chron 15,3 where MT and L have a reference to a "priest" lacking in B.

1807. See, e.g., my discussion, p. 21 of Josephus' lack of parallel, shared by him with 3 Rgns 12,17, to the notice on Rehoboam's reigning over the "people of Israel who dwelt in the cities of Judah" found in both 1 Kings 12,17 and MT/LXX 2 Chron 10,17.

Again, among the more obvious positive agreements between Josephus and LXX against MT (and vice versa) are those involving proper names. As L.H. Feldman points out, however[1808], agreements of this sort are to be treated with circumspection since there would have been a natural tendency on the part of copyists to assimilate Josephus' name forms to those of their own (LXX) Bible(s)[1809]. And finally, after all, one does need to reckon with the possibility that Josephus, faced with the (apparent) problems posed by a MT-like text, could, independently, have modified such a text in the line of the LXX. All the more is such a possibility to be entertained given not only that the "solutions" to difficulties of "MT" common to LXX and Josephus are often rather obvious ones, but also that, even in cases of positive agreement with LXX against MT, Josephus so often gives that "agreement" his own twist.

Given the above cautionary notes, what now can be said concerning the text(s) of Kings and Chronicles utilized by Josephus in 8,212-420? First of all, our segment does evidence a least a few positive indications of the historian's dependence on a MT-like text in this portion of his work. The most noteworthy example in this regard is the story of the death of Jeroboam's son Abijah related by Josephus in 8,265-273. As was noted, the placing and content of this episode differ markedly in MT and 3 Rgns. In the former, the account (1 Kings 14,1-18(19-20)) constitutes the finale of the "Jeroboam complex" (1 Kings 12,25-14,20), while in the latter it stands within the long plus (3 Rgns 12,24a-z)[1810] which supervenes between MT 1 Kings 12,24 and 25. Similarly, the MT and 3 Rgns forms of the story diverge strikingly in the details of their respective content. Specifically, MT is considerably longer than its Greek counterpart, offering a number of particulars absent in the latter (e.g., the disguise motif, 14,2.6; Ahijah's prediction of a new king for Israel and of Israel's eventual exile, 14,14-16). Conversely, the shorter 3 Rgns version exhibits various details (e.g., Anō as the name of Jeroboam's wife) lacking in MT. In light of all these divergences between MT and 3 Rgns, it is of considerable interest to note that Josephus' version unambiguously, and in all respects, aligns itself with the former against the latter. Thus, he situates the incident at a point, i.e. following his version of 1 Kings 13, comparable to its position in MT[1811]. In

1808. FELDMAN, *Mikra*, p. 456.

1809. Here one should also keep in mind the numerous variants, precisely in the case of forms of the proper names evidenced by the MSS tradition both of LXX and of Josephus.

1810. Recall that Josephus has no equivalent to this plus (just as he lacks a parallel to the complex of notices concerning Jehoshaphat which follows MT's 1 Kings 16,28 in 3 Rgns).

1811. Recall that Josephus does reverse the sequence of 1 Kings 14,1-18 (19-20) and 14,21-31 (// 2 Chron 11,5-12,16) in 8,246-273.

addition, Josephus' account exhibits several of the features proper to MT's narration (e.g., the queen's disguising herself), but none of those peculiar to 3 Rgns (e.g., the name "Anō"). The conclusion seems incontrovertible then that, at least in this instance, Josephus did make use of a text of Kings *à la* that of MT. Also elsewhere in 8,212-420, however, one finds other positive affinities between Josephus and MT, albeit of a rather minor nature. Thus in 8,293 Josephus gives a proper name ("Saphatha") to the "valley" near Maresah where Asa assembles his forces against the Ethiopians reminiscent of MT 2 Chron 14,10 "Zephathah", whereas 2 Par speaks of a valley "*north of* Maresa".

The just-cited examples of positive affinities between Josephus and MT Kings and Chronicles against LXX are especially worthy of note given the contemporary tendency to virtually exclude a use by Josephus of a Semitic-language source for the Books of Samuel[1812]. The above examples suggest that, whatever may be the case in Samuel, Josephus did utilize a Semitic (Hebrew, "proto-MT") text of Kings (and Chronicles) as Rahlfs maintained long ago[1813]. On the other hand, my analysis of 8,212-420 has made clear that in this segment Josephus does depend, and in first place, on a LXX-like text of Kings and Chronicles. Thus, with regard to the sequence of Josephus' presentation, recall that he narrates the episodes of MT 1 Kings 20 and 21 in reverse order just as does LXX. The points of contentual contact between the historian's account and LXX where the latter differs from MT are too numerous to rehearse here, see, however, the summaries to the treatments of 8,328-346 (// 1 Kings 18, Elijah on Carmel). 363-392 (// 1 Kings 20 [LXX 21], Ahab's Syrian wars) and 398-420 (// 1 Kings 22/ 2 Chronicles 18, Ahab's death).

Josephus' use of a Greek text of Kings and Chronicles in 8,212-420 is clear. Less clear is the precise character of that Greek text. This last question arises particularly in view of the widely-held position that in the later Historical Books from Samuel on Josephus depends specifically on a L-like text, i.e. as opposed to that represented by B (see Introduction). The results of my investigation are not particularly supportive of such a view for what concerns 3 Rgns and 2 Par at least. On the one hand, we noted several instances where Josephus' readings go together with those of B against MT and L, i.e. the numbers of Rehoboam's concubines (8,250, cf. 2 Chron 11,21) and Asa's Benjaminite troops (8,291, see 2 Chron 14,7)[1814]. On the other hand, where the historian agrees with L against B, L itself frequently will be found to go

---

1812. As proponents of this tendency might be mentioned: ULRICH, *Biblical Text*, p. 93 and SPOTTORNO, *Remarks*, p. 283.

1813. See n. 5.

1814. See also 8,355.359 where Josephus aligns himself with the shorter B text of 3 Rgns 20 (21),l.11-12 against the more expansive L (and MT) one.

together with MT[1815], see, e.g., the reference to the lack of a "priest", common to MT and L 2 Chron 15,3 and 8,296, but absent in B, with the resultant uncertainty as to which text (MT?, L?) Josephus is, in fact, utilizing, see above. Similarly, one of the most noteworthy correspondences between Josephus and L, against both MT and B, i.e. their non-mention of the rebuilding of Jericho under Omri (see 1 Kings 16,34) is a "negative agreement" which can be explained otherwise than in terms of Josephus' dependence on a L(-like) text lacking the item, *vide supra*[1816]. In sum, while it is clear that Josephus' positive affinities are more with "LXX" than with "MT" where these witnesses differ, evidence seems lacking for the additional conclusion that – in 8,212-420 at any rate – his Greek text is closer to L than to B (or vice versa)[1817].

Finally, in the course of my analysis I noted a fair number of instances in which Josephus evidences notable affinities with distinctive readings of TJ and/or TC. Some of these affinities are terminological in nature (e.g., both TJ and Josephus substitute "prophet" for MT/LXX "man of God", just as both – as MT/LXX do not – explicitly designate the Judean's Bethelite antagonist as a "false prophet"). Others of them involve matters of content (e.g., TJ and Josephus have in common the motivation they provide for the "sign" announced by the Judean in 1 Kings 13,3 as well as their reference to Ahab's going "barefoot" following Elijah's word of doom, contrast MT and LXX 1 Kings 21[20],27). Recall too that TC and Josephus (8,314) give a (the same?) name to Ahab's anonymous slayer of 1 Kings 22,34 // 2 Chron 18,33. How though are such affinities to be accounted for? In my view, one does better not to think in terms of a direct utilization by Josephus of Aramaic Biblical versions *à la* our TJ and TC. For one thing, the date of the literary fixation of these Targums remains unresolved (and likely unresolvable)[1818]. Moreover, the terminological commonalties between

---

1815. In this connection recall Allen's finding that in Chronicles the L family of MSS is the one which has undergone the most extensive assimilation to MT, see n. 11.

1816. In the same line recall the negative correspondence between L 3 Rgns 18,32aα and 8,341: both lack the specification that it was "in the name of the Lord" (so MT B) that Elijah "built" (the altar). Similarly, like L's 3 Rgns 19, Josephus (see 8,349) lacks a parallel to the MT B sequence 19,6bβ-8a.

Positive, though minor, agreements between Josephus and L against MT and B in our segment include: the forms of the proper names Ζαραῖ(ος) (8,292, see L 2 Par 14,9); Ἠλίας (8,331, see L 3 Rgns 17,1ff.); Ἰεζαρήλ(ας) (8,343 [t.e.], see L 3 Rgns 18,45); the sequence "wine-oil" (as opposed to "oil-wine") (8,247, see L 2 Par 11,11b); and the reference to "caves" as the refuge of the prophets concealed by Obadiah (8,330, see L 3 Rgns 18,4).

1817. In this connection it should be recalled that virtually B's entire text for the passage of Kings utilized by Josephus in our segment, i.e. 3 Rgns 12-21, is "non-kaige" and as such less divergent from L than it is in the "kaige" portions of Samuel and Kings, see n. 11.

1818. On the date of TJ, see HARRINGTON-SALDARINI, *Targum Jonathan*, pp. 13-14, on that of TC, LE DÉAUT-ROBERT, *Chroniques*, I, pp. 24-27.

Josephus and the Targums might very well represent cases of comparable, but independent, "linguistic preference" or equally independent extrapolation from elements present in the source Biblical text(s)[1819]. As to the contentual parallels between Josephus and the Targums cited above, I would suggest that these were derived by both from a common tradition – whether written or oral – of Biblical interpretation/elaboration. From that same tradition, I further suggest, Josephus drew as well various particulars of his account in 8,212-420 which, while unparalleled in MT, LXX and Targum, do have their pendants in our Talmuds and Midrashim[1820] (for which, of course, the same questions as to stratification/dating arise as with the Targums).

In conclusion, the evidence of 8,212-420 suggests that for this segment of *AJ*, Josephus had as his primary source a text of Kings and Chronicles like that of "LXX", but also utilized on a occasion a proto-MT Hebrew text. In addition, he had access to traditions now incorporated in the extant Targums, Talmuds and Midrashim.

C. JOSEPHUS' REWRITING TECHNIQUES

To facilitate my discussion of Josephus' manner of treating his Scriptural sources, I distinguish the following procedures identifiable throughout 8,212-420: 1) omissions, 2) rearrangements, 3) modifications, and 4) additions. At the outset it should be emphasized that the boundaries between these procedures are rather fluid (e.g., "rearrangement" is itself a kind of "modification") and that frequently they are used in conjunction (e.g., Josephus often interjects something of his own in place of a Biblical item omitted by him).

1. *Omissions*

Josephus leaves aside a considerable number of small-to-medium size items of the Biblical sources from his own presentation[1821]. As I suggested in the course of my analysis, Josephus' omissions are dictated by a variety of (sometimes overlapping) concerns which may be identified with greater or lesser assurance in particular instances. The historian, e.g., tends to abridge the *Vorlage* when this evidences "repetition" of the same or similar happenings[1822] and or excessive circum-

---

1819. See n. 270 where I suggest that Josephus' and TJ's common designation of the Bethelite as a "false prophet" represents such a parallel "extrapolation" from the notice of 1 Kings 13,18 (MT/LXX) on that figure's "lying" to his Judean colleague.

1820. See, e.g., Josephus' naming of the Judean man of God of 1 Kings 13 as "Jadōn" (8,231) or his reference to Naboth's "noble birth" (8,358).

1821. Under this heading I am concerned with items found in MT and LXX and which, accordingly, I suppose to have been available to Josephus in his Biblical text(s), but deliberately left unused by him.

1822. See, e.g., his "reductions" of the triple pouring of water on Elijah's altar (1 Kings 18,33-34) in 8,341 or of Elijah's double "feeding" (1 Kings 19,5-8) in 8,349.

stantiality[1823]. Josephus is likewise wont to dispense with elements of the Biblical account(s) that appear self-evident or might readily be supplied mentally by the reader[1824]. Again, he passes over, on various occasions, items not likely to be of interest to uninitiated Gentile readers, e.g. lists of Hebrew names[1825] or matters of cultic detail[1826]. Especially noteworthy are further Josephus' omissions of "problem passages" of his Biblical material. Of these, Josephus' narrative of Ahab's death (8,398-420, see 1 Kings 22 // 2 Chronicles 18) furnishes two striking examples. In that segment, as noted above, Josephus simply drops the initial exchange between Micaiah and Ahab (1 Kings 22,15 // 2 Chron 18,14), just as he eliminates the prophet's account of his heavenly court vision (1 Kings 22,19-23 // 2 Chron 18,18-22) given the deception these appear to attribute to prophet and Deity, respectively. Closely related to the foregoing category is Josephus' non-utilization of Biblical materials which do not accord with a point he is trying to convey. The most dramatic illustration of this class of omissions is provided by the historian's "ignoring" the Biblical data on Asa's less than felicitous end (see 1 Kings 15,24a // 2 Chron 16,7-12) in the interests of the North-South contrast he develops in 8,307-315. Finally to be recalled under this heading is Josephus' consistent omission of the Biblical "source notices" for the kings of Judah and Israel – a natural procedure considering that he is basing himself directly on the "Bible", not those earlier sources.

Josephus thus omits, on various grounds, quite a few elements which he (apparently) had before him in his sources[1827]. He is, however, by no means consistent in his omissions. While, e.g., it might have been expected that Josephus would spare readers the names of the 15 cities fortified by Rehoboam according to 2 Chron 11,5-12, he does in fact reproduce the entire list (see 8,246). Again, he does not invariably leave aside Biblical mentions of the obvious. Indeed, on occasion, he goes beyond the Bible in explicitly relating items it takes for granted, e.g.,

1823. See, e.g., his "compression" of the elaborate narrative of the Bethelite's measures vis-à-vis the corpse of his colleague (1 Kings 13,26-30) in 8,242 or of Elijah's going to the brook (1 Kings 17,2-5) in 8,319.

1824. See, e.g., his omission of the notice about the Judean setting out for home (1 Kings 13,10) or the reference in 1 Kings 22,10 // 2 Chron 18,9 to the two monarchs' being "clothed (with their robes)".

1825. E.g., he leaves aside the names of those dispatched by Jehoshaphat to teach the people cited in 2 Chron 17,7-8, see 8,395.

1826. E.g., in his version of Abijah's speech to the Israelites in 8,276-281 he does not reproduce the Judean's enumeration of all the components of "true worship" possessed by his people found in 2 Chron 13,11-12. He likewise passes over the "cultic specifics" of 2 Chronicles 14-15 in his account of Asa's beginnings, 8,290-297.

1827. Of course, plausible explanations for these omissions are not forthcoming in every instance. Why, e.g., does he omit the name "Elijah" in his version of that figure's activities throughout 8,319-327 (// 1 Kings 17)?

the fact of Jeroboam's wife's delivery of Ahijah's word of doom (8,273) or of Ben-hadad's advance in response to that of Ahab and Jehoshaphat (8,411). As we shall see, such "inconsistency" is characteristic for Josephus' application of all the procedures under discussion here.

2. *Rearrangements*

For the most part, Josephus simply follows his sources in their arrangement of material, i.e., both within individual episodes and for the sequence of episodes[1828]. He does, however, allow himself occasional liberties in both respects. I noted above in discussing Josephus' integration of the material of his two Biblical sources that he basically adopts the order of Kings, inserting material from Chronicles at appropriate junctures. Occasionally, however, one finds Josephus reordering and re-combining the sequence of happenings proper to Kings itself. In Kings, e.g., it is only after Jeroboam has disappeared from the scene (14,20, MT) that the reign of Rehoboam is dealt with (14,21-31). Josephus, on the contrary, interposes his account of Rehoboam (8,246-264) within the source's "Jeroboam bloc" (1 Kings 12,25-14,20, MT), i.e., prior to the death of Jeroboam's son Abijah (8,265-273 // 1 Kings 14,1-18, MT). Again, whereas Kings' notices on Jeroboam's death and its immediate sequels (14,19-20 [MT]; 15,25-32) are separated by a lengthy segment devoted to the first three Southern rulers, 1 Kings 14,21-15,24, Josephus brings the former notices together in a continuous segment, 8,287-300. Similarly, Kings treats the Judean Asa (see 1 Kings 15,9-24) and his Northern contemporaries Baasha through Omri (see 15,33-16,28) separately. Josephus, on the other hand, interweaves his account of the two sets of rulers, incorporating items from Kings' Asa narrative in the middle (see 8,303-306 // 1 Kings 15,16-22 = 2 Chron 16,1-6, the Asa-Baasha conflict) and end (8,314-315 // 1 Kings 15,24, cf. 2 Chron 16,7-17,1, Asa's death and the succession of Jehoshaphat) of a lengthy section (8,298-315) featuring the doings of the Northern monarchs.

Also within a given unit Josephus will sometimes rearrange the Biblical disposition of the material. He does so both in discourse and narrative contexts. The former case may be illustrated by his "reconstitution" of the components of Ahijah's word to the wife of Jeroboam (1 Kings 14,7-16) in 8,270-272 wherein he brings together related topics and makes announcement of Abijah's death the climax of the whole (see also his reordering of the elements of Abijah the Judean's battlefield speech, 2 Chron 13,4-12 in 8,276-281). Josephus' version of Ahab's death (8,398-420 // 1 Kings 22 = 2 Chronicles 18) exemplifies

---

1828. See, e.g., 8,316-392 where he reproduces the (LXX) sequence of 1 Kings 16,29-21,29.

his rearrangement of a narrative sequence: he anticipates the royal "session" (8,399 // 1 Kings 22,10 // 2 Chron 18,9) in order to fill up the interlude during which Jehoshaphat's army is being summoned from Jerusalem, just as he delays Zedekiah's sign with the horns (8,409 // 1 Kings 22,11 // 2 Chron 18,10), associating this with his other references to the activity of that "prophet".

3. Modifications

Josephus' modifications of the sources' presentations may roughly be divided into three categories: terminological, stylistic and contentual. I shall treat each of these in turn.

a) *Terminological modifications*: As we have seen, Josephus rather consistently substitutes his own equivalents for a whole series of characteristic Biblical terms and formulae. These include: man of God, word of the Lord, (angel)/spirit/hand of the Lord, the *Botenformel*, διαθήκη (= "covenant") and the actual wording of "oaths". In some cases, e.g., the Biblical designation "man of God", Josephus' procedure is paralleled in the Targum; both regularly replace that designation with the more definite term "prophet". Josephus' avoidance of "δια-θήκη/covenant", for its part, seems to be prompted by the fact that the term was not used with this meaning in extra-LXX Greek. As for the other expressions cited, a concern with upholding absolute monotheism (over against various sorts of divine hypostases, e.g., "spirit of the Lord") and guarding the divine name against profanation (as could happen when this is used in an oath formula) may be operative.

b) *Stylistic modifications*: Josephus introduces a wide range of stylistic modifications in his reworking of the sources. He replaces the monotonous parataxis of MT and LXX with multiple subordinate clauses in an effort to give his account a more elegant and flowing character. He likewise tends to substitute indirect for direct discourse. He transposes the Bible's vivid metaphors into their prosaic equivalents, another tendency he shares with the Targum[1829]. More generally, he constantly elucidates and makes more specific Scriptural formulations whose import is not immediately clear. In 1 Kings 22,4 // 2 Chron 18,3, e.g., Jehoshaphat requests Ahab to "inquire first of (the word of the) Lord". Josephus spells out just what the Judean is asking of his counterpart: "... Josaphat bade him call the prophets... and inquire of them concerning the expedition against the Syrian..." (8,400). Obviously, Josephus' aim in such instances is to facilitate readers' comprehension of events.

1829. See, e.g., his "translation" of 1 Kings 14,9 "you (Jeroboam) have cast me (the Lord) behind your back" in 8,270 "you have given up worshipping me"; compare TJ "you put my service far from opposite your eyes".

c) *Contentual modifications*: Josephus also modifies items of content found in the sources. Generally, these modifications would seem to be dictated by the historian's consciousness of the problematic character of a given item within its proximate or wider Biblical context. Two examples of such "corrective modifications" may be recalled here. In 1 Kings 21,29 (MT) the Lord announces that he will "not bring evil in Ahab's own days". This formulation could suggest that Ahab himself will die in peace, contrary to what, in fact, befalls him in 1 Kings 22. Accordingly, Josephus reformulates this announcement: "while Achab lived he (God) would put off punishing *his family...*" (8,362). Again, 1 Kings 22,38 has the washing of Ahab's chariot and, it would seem, the subsequent profanation of his blood transpire "by the pool of Samaria", thereby generating an apparent discrepancy with Elijah's prediction (1 Kings 21,19) that the latter event would take place in Jezreel, the site of Naboth's vineyard (1 Kings 21,1). Josephus rewords the notice of 1 Kings 22,38 so as to obviate the difficulty: the royal chariot is washed out "in the spring of Jezarēl" (8,417)[1830].

4. *Additions*

Josephus not only modifies the existing wording of his source text(s); he also makes additions thereto. These additions vary widely in length and character. The following (often overlapping) categories may be distinguished:

a) *Stylistic additions*: Josephus frequently inserts items which serve to improve the style of the original. Under this heading mention may be made of his recurrent interpolation – both within and between units – of closing and/or transitional formulae designed to smooth over the Bible's often abrupt movement from one topic to another. Among instances of this phenomenon, I would recall the following: In 8,224 subsequent to his account of the split (// 1 Kings 12,1-24 // 2 Chron 10,1-11,4) and prior to commencing his narrative of Jeroboam's initiatives (8,225-229 // 1 Kings 12,25-31), Josephus interposes a note concerning the procedure he intends to observe in treating the reigns of the divided monarchy's first two rulers: "I shall now relate first the acts of Jeroboam... and then in what follows we shall tell what happened in the reign of Roboamos... For in this way an orderly arrangement can be preserved throughout the history". See too 8,282 where Josephus "rounds off" Abijah's battlefield address to the Israelites (8,276-281 // 2

1830. Recall too Josephus' transfer of Jeroboam's "festival" (i.e. Tabernacles) from the eighth (so 1 Kings 12,32-33) to the seventh month (8,230) in accordance with Biblical indications elsewhere concerning the date of Tabernacles.

Chron 13,4-12) with the formula "such was the speech which Abias made to the people" before recounting Jeroboam's response [1831].

b) *Naming additions*: In a whole series of contexts, Josephus supplies names for figures the Bible (MT and LXX) leave anonymous: "Jadōn" for the "man of God" of 1 Kings 13; "Michaias" for the "prophet" of 1 Kings 20,35ff.; "Amanos" (Naaman?) for Ahab's slayer in 1 Kings 22,34 // 2 Chron 18,33. In all these instances, as we have seen, the names given by Josephus correspond to those found in the Targum and/or Rabbinic tradition. In his version of Ahab's death (8,398-420), on the other hand, Josephus, seemingly on his own, provides a name for the Biblically anonymous king of Syria, i.e. "Adados" (see 8,401.412), which name he draws from the account of the earlier conflict between Ahab and the Syrians, 1 Kings 20 (MT). At the same time, it should be recalled that Josephus is not consistent in his "naming names" where the Bible does not. Twice, in fact, he leaves anonymous figures to whom the Bible itself does give a name, i.e. Shemaiah who forbids Rehoboam to march against Israel (1 Kings 12,21-24 // 2 Chron 11,1-4, compare 8,223 "the prophet") and Elijah at the outset of his ministry (see 1 Kings 17,1, compare 8,319 "a certain prophet").

c) *Elucidatory additions*: A number of Josephus' additions provide supplementary indications concerning phenomena cited in the Biblical record with which Gentile readers would likely be unfamiliar. Several of these "elucidations" concern Palestinian locales. Of Dan, e.g., he notes that it is "near the sources of the Little Jordan" (8,226), while he expands the Biblical localization of Beersheba (1 Kings 19,3) as follows: (Bersūbee) is the "furthest city in that part of the territory of the tribe of Judah which borders on the country of the Idumaeans" (8,348). In the same line he couples mention of "Sōmareōn" (t.e.) with the notation that this city "is known to the Greeks as Samaria" (8,312). In addition to such "geographical" elucidations, Josephus provides comparable parenthetical indications concerning the defeated Syrians' donning of sackcloth and ropes in approaching Ahab, i.e. "this was the manner in which the ancient Syrians appeared as suppliants" (8,385). Finally, he occasionally incorporates into his version of some metaphorical Biblical formulation wording designed to elucidate that formulation, see, e.g., 8,404 where in citing Micaiah's (initial) vision of Israel scattered on the mountains like sheep without a shepherd (1 Kings 22,17a // 2 Chron 18,16a), he works in a clarifying reference to the Israelites "in flight, being pursued by the Syrians and dispersed by them...".

1831. Cf. the similar formulae in 8,245 (*fine*).298 (*fine*).315 (*fine*).324 (*fine*).393.

d) *Additions from Gentile authors*: Josephus likewise endeavors to make his telling of Biblical history more accessible (and credible) to his Gentile audience by incorporating excerpts from non-Jewish authors where these (purportedly) provide confirmation and/or supplementary information concerning events narrated in the Bible. In 8,212-420 he cites two such pagan authorities, i.e. Herodotus (8,253 *fine*.260-262) and Menander (8,324), the former in connection with Shishak's campaign against Palestine, the latter for his mention of the drought during Ahab's reign. As was noted above, Josephus, at the same time, shows himself rather critical regarding the accuracy of the passage of Herodotus adduced by him.

e) *"Connective Additions"*: A large group of Josephus' additions in 8,212-420 consist of items which, in some way or other, make connections with other portions of his work, thereby enhancing the cohesion of the whole. Within this group, one may further distinguish between reminiscences of earlier episodes and foreshadowings of subsequent ones. To begin with the former category, I would note the following instances of *Rückverweise* interjected by Josephus: Baasha's house is exterminated *à la* that of Jeroboam "as we have narrated" (8,309 referring back to 8,289). Elijah goes to Sinai "where Moses is said to have received the laws from God" (8,349). The reference to Ramoth Gilead's "having been taken" from Israel by the father of "Adados" (8,399) recalls the Syrian king's mention of the Israelite cities seized by his father (1 Kings 20,34a // 8,387), just as the promise of the 400 prophets (8,402) that Ahab's projected campaign will result in his subduing the Syrians "as before" alludes back to his victory over them as described in 8,383-384 (// 1 Kings 20,29-30). Finally, in Josephus' account of Ahab's death (8,398-420), note the references to the earlier initiatives of the prophets Elijah and "Jadōn" which he places on the lips of Zedekiah in 8,407-408.

As for Josephus' "foreshadowings", some of these involve explicit prior announcements of upcoming events which he will relate, see, e.g., the *Vorspiel* of the eventual end of the Northern Kingdom which he appends to his account of Jeroboam's illicit initiatives (8,225-229 // 1 Kings 12,25-31) in 8,229b: "this [Jeroboam's measures] was the beginning of the Hebrews' misfortunes and led to their being defeated in war by other races and to their falling captive. But of these things we shall write in their proper place [see 9,277ff.]". Others are more implicit/allusive. E.g., in 8,258-259 Josephus embellishes 2 Chron 12,9b's brief notices on Shisak's seizure/despoliation of Jerusalem with items which parallel features of subsequent assaults on Jerusalem as he will relate these. Again, Josephus' sequence concerning the prophecies of Elijah and Micaiah which, given their seeming discrepancy, are disbelieved by a king (Ahab), but nevertheless are both finally fulfilled (8,407-409.417-

418) adumbrates a similar sequence concerning the prophecies of Jeremiah and Ezekiel regarding king Zedekiah.

f) *Evaluative additions*: On several occasions, Josephus introduces explicitly evaluative comments concerning characters where the Bible leaves readers to form their own judgments. Right from the start, e.g., he designates Jadōn's Bethelite antagonist as a "wicked false prophet" (8,236, cf. 1 Kings 13,18), later calling him "a wicked and impious man" (8,243) as well. In the same line the 400 who advise Ahab are "false prophets" (8,402, cf. 409) as is their leader, Zedekiah (8,406).

g) *Psychologizing additions*: In general Josephus' Biblical sources have little to say about the psychic states underlying characters' words and deeds. The historian, on the contrary, makes a regular point of filling this lacuna by inserting references to the feelings which prompt his personages to speak and act as they do or to the inner affects of another character's initiatives upon a given figure. In most instances these psychologizing additions are made *en passant*, via a brief phrase. From among many possible examples, I note the following: the people return to Rehoboam "excited and anxious to hear what the king might say..." (8,218). Rehoboam himself, seeing the stoning of Adoram, is "afraid that he might suffer the same dreadful fate..." (8,221). Jadōn's words against the Bethel altar cause Jeroboam to be "roused to fury" (8,233), whereas the same king is "overjoyed" to have his hand restored (8,234). God's intimation of victory for Judah over the Ethiopians evokes "joy" on the part of Asa (8,294) who, subsequently, "fears" Baasha's assault (8,304).

On two occasions within 8,212-420, however, Josephus does go into somewhat greater detail concerning the affects of a character's experiences upon that character. In both instances, the character in question is a woman, i.e., the wife of Jeroboam responding to Ahijah's announcement concerning the imminent death of her son (8,273a, compare 1 Kings 14,17) and Elijah's hostess confronted with the "demise" of her son (8,325, compare 1 Kings 17,18). Elsewhere, Josephus offers extended disquisitions on the (religious) psychology operative in a defection from right behavior (or the persistence therein despite warnings), see 8,251-253 (the underlying causes for the apostasy of Rehoboam and his people) and 301-302 (reflection on Baasha's (negative) response to Jehu's word of doom). Under this heading too might be cited the historian's psychologically insightful portrayals of "false prophets" manipulating kings, i.e. the Bethelite Jeroboam (8,243-245) and Zedekiah Ahab (8,406b-409), see too the masterfully persuasive address which Josephus develops for Jeroboam in 8,227-228.

h) *Moral-theological additions*: The final category of Josephan additions to be distinguished comprises the (politico-)moral and theological
reflections which the historian works into his presentation over the
course of 8,212-420. As with the preceding category, this class involves
both longer and shorter passages. Josephus' shorter reflections typically
take the form of parenthetical comments within the body of a given
narrative, see, e.g., 8,216 (God prompts Rehoboam to disregard the
elders' counsel, cf. also 8,217) and 8,409 ("Fate" inspires Ahab to heed
the false prophets rather than Micaiah). Longer reflections, on the
other hand, generally appear as prefaces or appendixes to a narrative.
Among the extended moral/theological additions within our segment,
the following stand out: 8,313-314 (observations on the contrast in
behavior and fate between the Northern and Southern kings) and 418-
420 (lessons to be drawn from Ahab's disastrous end). Under this
rubric too, reference might be made to Josephus' overall accentuation
of the explicitly political-reflective element in his version of the North-
South split (8,212-224 // 1 Kings 12,1-24 // 2 Chron 10,1-11,4) via, e.g.,
his introduction of Hellenistic kingship terminology and the insights on
the ruler-subject relationship he attributes to the "elders" (8,215).

D. Final Comparison and Evaluation

Having treated Josephus' rewriting techniques in the preceding section, I now turn to a consideration of a final question: how ultimately
and overall does Josephus' presentation in 8,212-420 compare with its
Biblical sources and what estimate of Josephus as a redactor of the
Biblical story (at least as far as our segment is concerned) is in order?
   In response to the above query, I begin by noting that, as far as its
basic content goes, Josephus' account in 8,212-420 largely corresponds
to that given by the sources; readers come away with a picture of
events that is generally in keeping with the one(s) put forward in Kings
and/or Chronicles. In this segment of *AJ* at any rate then there is
considerable justification for the historian's controverted claim at the
opening of his work: "the precise details of our Scripture records will
then be set forth, each in its place, as my narrative proceeds... neither
adding nor omitting anything" (1,17)[1832]. Indeed, in my view, the only
instance of real contentual "distortion" of the Biblical data within our
segment occurs in Josephus' treatment of the circumstances of Asa's
end (8,314). Josephus may then, in 8,212-420 at least, be called a
faithful reteller of the Biblical story.
   At the same time, as our discussion of his various rewriting techniques makes clear, Josephus is a redactor who allows himself considerable freedom to modify the sources' presentation on matters of detail.

1832. On this formulation, see FELDMAN, *Mikra*, pp. 466-470.

How then should one characterize the result of such an approach vis-à-vis its models? Perhaps, one does best to view 8,212-420 as (what is intended to be) an improved version of the Biblical account(s). So many of the above-cited omissions, rearrangements, modifications and additions do, in fact, seem motivated by the desire to provide readers with a narrative that is smoother-reading, as well as more readily comprehensible, unambiguous and unproblematic than the original(s). To this end, e.g., Josephus introduces transitional and closing formulae. Obscure, metaphorical expressions receive prosaic "translations"; indeterminate designations ("man of God") yield to definite ones ("prophet"). Elements that raise difficulties in one or other respect ("mistakes", theologically offensive items) are reworked or excised entirely. Right from the start questions as to how characters like the Bethelite prophet or Zedekiah and his colleagues are to be viewed are resolved. Examples of all these "tendencies" have been given above. At the same time, it should, however, be kept in mind that Josephus is by no means consistent in his application of these. Josephus, the faithful, if free redactor, is also a somewhat haphazard, spasmatic one.

Even more specifically, one might speak of Josephus' version as a Hellenized improvement of the originals. Many particular features of the historian's rewriting give evidence of his intent to compile just such a work. He replaces "Semitic" parataxis with the hypertaxis more in accord with Greek style. Terms used in the LXX with peculiar Hebraicizing meanings (e.g., διαθήκη) are replaced by more current ones. Unfamiliar place names, etc. receive elucidations. Greek authors are cited. On occasion at least, Greek concepts (e.g., Fate) are substituted for Biblical ones (the monocausality of God). Items likely to prove uninteresting to Hellenized readers are reduced or eliminated, whereas more congenial material, e.g., accounts of political and military developments are accentuated. Finally, the interpolation of reflective passages serves to remind Gentile readers that the Jewish story does have lessons to teach reminiscent of those propounded by the Greek classics (e.g., concerning the operation of fate and the prosperity-hubris-punishment cycle, see Josephus' remarks on the defection of Rehoboam and his people, 8,251-253).

There remain to note various overarching differences and commonalities between Josephus and his sources. With regard to the former, the historian's presentation is, clearly, more overtly didactic and reflective than its Biblical counterpart(s); Josephus is less inclined than were his sources to let readers form their own judgments on characters or identify the lessons of history for themselves. At the same time, his presentation is also obviously more permeated with explicit psychologizing and attention to characters' emotions than is the Biblical record; Josephus does not share Scripture's own sobriety on such matters. On the other hand, Josephus' account is not substantially more "apologetic" than that of his sources in the sense that he does not attempt to cover over or conceal (in our segment anyway) the many failings of both kings and people as a whole (his treatment of Asa's end is an exception in this regard). His narrative is likewise not notably less theological or "miraculous" than the Bible's; in fact, on one or other occasion Josephus seems to accentuate these dimensions of the narrative. This finding is particularly worthy of note given the "de-theologizing" and rationalizing tendencies which scholars have identified as operative in various (other) contexts of AJ[1833].

A final word. I conclude my study of Josephus' rewriting of Scripture in AJ 8,212-420 with a large measure of respect for the care and intelligence he brought to his task. In this sequence at least, he contrives, successfully, in my view, to make his people's history accessible to a Gentile-Hellenistic audience while at the same time remaining basically faithful to the content and underlying theological thrusts of the Biblical record[1834]. Having said this, I can only acknowledge, conversely, that Josephus' version is, ultimately, "no improvement" on the original, much of whose depth, vividness, provocative ambiguity and ironic bite gets lost in his "translation"[1835]. But in that Josephus' endeavor is merely at one with 2000 years worth of commentaries on and reformulations of the Bible's own story.

1833. On this point, see FELDMAN, *Mikra*, pp. 503-507.

1834. Thus for 8,212-420 I would subscribe to the judgment of FRANXMAN, *Genesis*, p. 289 on Josephus' version of Genesis: "On the surface his version... has some of the ungoverned, creative and slightly erratic aura about it which one frequently perceives in the general style and approach of the Pseudepigraph. This, however, is but an impression deriving from less acquaintance with our author than this investigation has allowed us to continue to have. Beneath the surface of Jos.'s style we have found a far more careful author who is toeing the line of the text of his original quite faithfully and whose alterations may represent exegetical traditions much better thought out than has been heretofore supposed".

1835. See the general characterization of AJ by J. Weill, *Josèphe*, I, p. i: "... n'est qu'un abrégé de la Bible à l'usage des lecteurs païens, rendu fade à notre goût par l'abus d'une rhétorique banale, le manque de naïveté, sinon de fait, l'absence de sentiment poétique...".

212 (viii. 1) Μετὰ δὲ τὴν Σολομῶνος τελευτὴν
διαδεξαμένου τοῦ παιδὸς αὐτοῦ τὴν βασιλείαν
Ῥοβοάμου, ὃς ἐκ γυναικὸς Ἀμμανίτιδος ὑπῆρχεν
αὐτῷ γεγονὼς Νοομᾶς τοὔνομα, πέμψαντες εὐθὺς
εἰς τὴν Αἴγυπτον οἱ τῶν ὄχλων ἄρχοντες ἐκάλουν
τὸν Ἱεροβόαμον. ἀφικομένου δὲ πρὸς αὐτοὺς εἰς
Σίκιμα πόλιν καὶ Ῥοβόαμος εἰς αὐτὴν παραγίνεται·
δέδοκτο γὰρ αὐτὸν ἐκεῖσε συνελθοῦσι τοῖς Ἰσραη-
213 λίταις ἀποδεῖξαι βασιλέα. προσελθόντες οὖν οἵ
τε ἄρχοντες αὐτῷ τοῦ λαοῦ καὶ Ἱεροβόαμος παρ-
εκάλουν λέγοντες ἀνεῖναί τι τῆς δουλείας αὐτοῖς καὶ
γενέσθαι χρηστότερον τοῦ πατρός· βαρὺν γὰρ ὑπ'
ἐκείνῳ ζυγὸν αὐτοὺς ὑπενεγκεῖν· εὐνούστεροι δὲ
ἔσεσθαι πρὸς αὐτὸν καὶ ἀγαπήσειν τὴν δουλείαν
214 διὰ τὴν ἐπιείκειαν ἢ διὰ τὸν φόβον. ὁ δὲ μετὰ
τρεῖς ἡμέρας εἰπὼν αὐτοῖς ἀποκρινεῖσθαι περὶ ὧν
ἀξιοῦσιν ὕποπτος μὲν εὐθὺς γίνεται μὴ παραχρῆμα
ἐπινεύσας αὐτοῖς τὰ πρὸς ἡδονήν, πρόχειρον γὰρ
ἠξίουν εἶναι τὸ χρηστὸν καὶ φιλάνθρωπον καὶ ταῦτ'
ἐν νέῳ, ἐδόκει δ' ὅμως καὶ τὸ βουλεύσασθαι τῷ
μὴ παραυτίκα ἀπειπεῖν ἀγαθῆς ἐλπίδος ἔχεσθαι.
215 (2) Συγκαλέσας δὲ τοὺς πατρῴους φίλους ἐσκο-
πεῖτο μετ' αὐτῶν ποδαπὴν δεῖ ποιήσασθαι τὴν ἀπόκρισιν πρὸς τὸ πλῆθος. οἱ δ', ἅπερ εἰκὸς τοὺς
εὔνους καὶ φύσιν ὄχλων εἰδότας, παρῄνουν αὐτῷ
φιλοφρόνως ὁμιλῆσαι τῷ λαῷ καὶ δημοτικώτερον
ἢ κατὰ βασιλείας ὄγκον· χειρώσεσθαι γὰρ οὕτως
εἰς εὔνοιαν αὐτόν, φύσει τῶν ὑπηκόων ἀγαπώντων
τὸ προσηνὲς καὶ παρὰ μικρὸν ἰσότιμον τῶν βασι-
216 λέων. ὁ δ' ἀγαθὴν οὕτως καὶ συμφέρουσαν ἴσως
πρὸς τὸ πᾶν, εἰ δὲ μή, πρός γε τὸν τότε καιρὸν
ὅτ' ἔδει γενέσθαι βασιλέα γνώμην ἀπεστράφη τοῦ
θεοῦ ποιήσαντος, οἶμαι, κατακριθῆναι τὸ συμφέρον
ὑπ' αὐτοῦ· καλέσας δὲ μειράκια τὰ συντεθραμμένα
καὶ τὴν τῶν πρεσβυτέρων αὐτοῖς συμβουλίαν εἰπών,
217 τί δοκεῖ ποιεῖν αὐτοῖς ἐκέλευσε λέγειν. τὰ δέ,
οὔτε γὰρ ἡ νεότης οὔτε ὁ θεὸς ἠφίει νοεῖν τὰ

κρείττω, παρήνεσαν ἀποκρίνασθαι τῷ λαῷ τὸν
βραχύτατον αὐτοῦ δάκτυλον τῆς τοῦ πατρὸς
ὀσφύος εἶναι παχύτερον καί, εἰ σκληροῦ λίαν
ἐπειράθησαν ἐκείνου, πολὺ μᾶλλον αὐτοῦ λήψεσθαι
πεῖραν δυσκόλου· καὶ εἰ μάστιξιν αὐτοὺς ἐκεῖνος
ἐνουθέτει, σκορπίοις τοῦτο ποιήσειν αὐτὸν προσ-
218 δοκᾶν. τούτοις ἡσθεὶς ὁ βασιλεὺς καὶ δόξας προσήκειν τῷ τῆς ἀρχῆς ἀξιώματι τὴν ἀπόκρισιν, ὡς
συνῆλθεν ἀκουσόμενον τὸ πλῆθος τῇ τρίτῃ τῶν
ἡμερῶν, μετεώρου τοῦ λαοῦ παντὸς ὄντος καὶ
λέγοντος ἀκοῦσαί τι τοῦ βασιλέως ἐσπουδακότος,
οἰομένου δέ τι καὶ φιλάνθρωπον, τὴν τῶν μειρα-
κίων αὐτοῖς συμβουλίαν, παρεὶς τὴν τῶν φίλων,
ἀπεκρίνατο. ταῦτα δ᾽ ἐπράττετο κατὰ τὴν τοῦ
θεοῦ βούλησιν, ἵνα λάβῃ τέλος ἃ προεφήτευσεν
Ἀχίας.

219 　(3) Πληγέντες δ᾽ ὑπὸ τῶν λόγων καὶ ἀλγήσαντες ὡς ἐπὶ πείρᾳ τοῖς εἰρημένοις ἠγανάκτησαν
καὶ μέγα πάντες ἐκβοήσαντες οὐκέτι οὐδὲν αὐτοῖς
εἶναι συγγενὲς πρὸς Δαυίδην καὶ τοὺς ἀπ᾽ αὐτοῦ
μετ᾽ ἐκείνην ἔφασαν τὴν ἡμέραν· παραχωρεῖν δ᾽
αὐτῷ μόνον τὸν ναὸν ὃν ὁ πάππος αὐτοῦ κατ-
220 εσκεύασεν εἰπόντες καταλείψειν ἠπείλησαν. οὕτως
δ᾽ ἔσχον πικρῶς καὶ τὴν ὀργὴν ἐτήρησαν, ὡς
πέμψαντος αὐτοῦ τὸν ἐπὶ τῶν φόρων Ἀδώραμον,
ἵνα καταπραΰνῃ καὶ συγγνόντας τοῖς εἰρημένοις,
εἴ τι προπετὲς ὑπὸ νεότητος καὶ δύσκολον ἦν
ἐν αὐτοῖς, ποιήσῃ μαλακωτέρους, οὐχ ὑπέμειναν,
221 ἀλλὰ βάλλοντες αὐτὸν λίθοις ἀπέκτειναν. τοῦτ᾽
ἰδὼν Ῥοβόαμος καὶ νομίσας αὐτὸν βεβλῆσθαι τοῖς
λίθοις, οἷς τὸν ὑπηρέτην ἀπέκτεινεν αὐτοῦ τὸ
πλῆθος, δείσας μὴ καὶ ἔργῳ πάθῃ τὸ δεινὸν ἐπιβὰς
εὐθὺς ἐπὶ ἅρματος ἔφυγεν εἰς Ἱεροσόλυμα. καὶ
ἡ μὲν Ἰούδα φυλὴ καὶ ἡ Βενιαμῖτις χειροτονοῦσιν

αὐτὸν βασιλέα, τὸ δὲ ἄλλο πλῆθος ἀπ᾽ ἐκείνης
τῆς ἡμέρας τῶν Δαυίδου παίδων ἀποστὰν τὸν
Ἱεροβόαμον ἀπέδειξε τῶν πραγμάτων κύριον.
222 Ῥοβόαμος δὲ ὁ Σολομῶνος παῖς ἐκκλησίαν ποιήσας
τῶν δύο φυλῶν, ἃς εἶχεν ὑπηκόους, οἷός τε ἦν
λαβὼν ὀκτωκαίδεκα παρ᾽ αὐτῶν στρατοῦ μυριάδας
ἐπιλέκτους ἐξελθεῖν ἐπὶ τὸν Ἱεροβόαμον καὶ τὸν
λαόν, ὅπως πολεμήσας ἀναγκάσῃ δουλεύειν αὐτῷ.
223 κωλυθεὶς δ᾽ ὑπὸ τοῦ θεοῦ διὰ τοῦ προφήτου
ποιήσασθαι τὴν στρατείαν, οὐ γὰρ εἶναι δίκαιον
τοὺς ὁμοφύλους πολεμεῖν οὗτος ἔλεγε καὶ ταῦτα
κατὰ τὴν τοῦ θεοῦ προαίρεσιν τῆς τοῦ πλήθους
224 ἀποστάσεως γεγενημένης, οὐκέτ᾽ ἐξῆλθε. διηγήσομαι δὲ πρῶτον, ὅσα Ἱεροβόαμος ὁ τῶν Ἰσραηλιτῶν βασιλεὺς ἔπραξεν, εἶτα δὲ τούτων ἐχόμενα
τὰ ὑπὸ Ῥοβοάμου τοῦ τῶν δύο φυλῶν βασιλέως
γεγενημένα δηλώσομεν· φυλαχθείη γὰρ ἂν οὕτως
ἄχρι παντὸς τῆς ἱστορίας τὸ εὔτακτον.
225 (4) Ὁ τοίνυν Ἱεροβόαμος οἰκοδομήσας βασίλειον
ἐν Σικίμῃ πόλει ἐν ταύτῃ τὴν δίαιταν εἶχε, κατεσκεύασε δὲ καὶ ἐν Φανουὴλ πόλει λεγομένῃ. μετ᾽
οὐ πολὺ δὲ τῆς σκηνοπηγίας ἑορτῆς ἐνίστασθαι
μελλούσης λογισάμενος ὡς ἐὰν ἐπιτρέψῃ τῷ πλήθει
προσκυνῆσαι τὸν θεὸν εἰς Ἱεροσόλυμα πορευθέντι
καὶ ἐκεῖ τὴν ἑορτὴν διαγαγεῖν, μετανοῆσαν ἴσως
καὶ δελεασθὲν ὑπὸ τοῦ ναοῦ καὶ τῆς θρησκείας τῆς
ἐν αὐτῷ τοῦ θεοῦ καταλείψει μὲν αὐτόν, προσχωρή-
σει δὲ τῷ πρώτῳ βασιλεῖ, καὶ κινδυνεύσει τούτου
γενομένου τὴν ψυχὴν ἀποβαλεῖν, ἐπιτεχνᾶταί τι
226 τοιοῦτον· δύο ποιήσας δαμάλεις χρυσᾶς καὶ οἰκοδομήσας ναΐσκους τοσούτους ἕνα μὲν ἐν Βηθήλῃ
πόλει, τὸν ἕτερον δὲ ἐν Δάνῃ, ἣ δ᾽ ἐστὶ πρὸς ταῖς
πηγαῖς τοῦ μικροῦ Ἰορδάνου, τίθησι τὰς δαμάλεις
ἐν ἑκατέρῳ τῶν ἐν ταῖς προειρημέναις πόλεσι
ναΐσκων, καὶ συγκαλέσας τὰς δέκα φυλὰς ὧν
αὐτὸς ἦρχεν ἐδημηγόρησε τούτους ποιησάμενος
227 τοὺς λόγους· " ἄνδρες ὁμόφυλοι, γινώσκειν ὑμᾶς

νομίζω τοῦτο, ὅτι πᾶς τόπος ἔχει τὸν θεὸν καὶ οὐκ
ἔστιν ἓν ἀποδεδειγμένον χωρίον ἐν ᾧ πάρεστιν,
ἀλλὰ πανταχοῦ τε ἀκούει καὶ τοὺς θρησκεύοντας
ἐφορᾷ. ὅθεν οὔ μοι δοκεῖ νῦν ἐπείγειν ὑμᾶς εἰς
Ἱεροσόλυμα πορευθέντας εἰς τὴν τῶν ἐχθρῶν
228 πόλιν μακρὰν οὕτως ὁδὸν προσκυνεῖν· ἄνθρωπος
γὰρ κατεσκεύακε τὸν ναόν, πεποίηκα δὲ κἀγὼ
δύο χρυσᾶς δαμάλεις ἐπωνύμους τῷ θεῷ καὶ τὴν
μὲν ἐν Βηθήλῃ πόλει καθιέρωσα τὴν δ' ἐν Δάνῃ,
ὅπως ὑμῶν οἱ τούτων ἔγγιστα τῶν πόλεων κατ-
ῳκημένοι προσκυνῶσιν εἰς αὐτὰς ἀπερχόμενοι τὸν
θεόν. ἀποδείξω δέ τινας ὑμῖν καὶ ἱερεῖς ἐξ ὑμῶν
αὐτῶν καὶ Ληουίτας, ἵνα μὴ χρείαν ἔχητε τῆς
Ληουίτιδος φυλῆς καὶ τῶν υἱῶν Ἀαρῶνος, ἀλλ' ὁ
βουλόμενος ὑμῶν ἱερεὺς εἶναι προσενεγκάτω μόσχον τῷ θεῷ καὶ κριόν, ὃ καὶ τὸν πρῶτον ἱερέα
229 φασὶν Ἀαρῶνα πεποιηκέναι." ταῦτ' εἰπὼν ἐξηπάτησε τὸν λαὸν καὶ τῆς πατρίου θρησκείας
ἀποστάντας ἐποίησε παραβῆναι τοὺς νόμους.
ἀρχὴ κακῶν ἐγένετο τοῦτο τοῖς Ἑβραίοις καὶ τοῦ
πολέμῳ κρατηθέντας ὑπὸ τῶν ἀλλοφύλων αἰχμαλωσίᾳ περιπεσεῖν. ἀλλὰ ταῦτα μὲν κατὰ χώραν
δηλώσομεν.

230 (5) Ἐνστάσης δὲ τῆς ἑορτῆς ἑβδόμῳ μηνὶ βουλόμενος καὶ αὐτὸς ἐν Βηθήλῃ ταύτην ἀγαγεῖν,
ὥσπερ ἑώρταζον καὶ αἱ δύο φυλαὶ ἐν Ἱεροσολύμοις,
οἰκοδομεῖ μὲν θυσιαστήριον πρὸ τῆς δαμάλεως,
γενόμενος δὲ αὐτὸς ἀρχιερεὺς ἐπὶ τὸν βωμὸν ἀνα-
231 βαίνει σὺν τοῖς ἰδίοις ἱερεῦσι. μέλλοντος δ' ἐπιφέρειν τὰς θυσίας καὶ τὰς ὁλοκαυτώσεις ἐν ὄψει
τοῦ λαοῦ παντὸς παραγίνεται πρὸς αὐτὸν ἐξ Ἱεροσολύμων προφήτης Ἰάδων ὄνομα τοῦ θεοῦ πέμψαντος, ὃς σταθεὶς ἐν μέσῳ τῷ πλήθει τοῦ βασιλέως
ἀκούοντος εἶπε τάδε πρὸς τὸ θυσιαστήριον ποιού-
232 μενος τοὺς λόγους· " ὁ θεὸς ἔσεσθαί τινα προλέγει

ἐκ τοῦ Δαυίδου γένους Ἰωσίαν ὄνομα, ὃς ἐπὶ σοῦ
θύσει τοὺς ψευδιερεῖς τοὺς κατ' ἐκεῖνον τὸν καιρὸν γενησομένους καὶ τὰ ὀστᾶ τῶν λαοπλάνων
τούτων καὶ ἀπατεώνων καὶ ἀσεβῶν ἐπὶ σοῦ καύσει.
ἵνα μέντοι γε πιστεύσωσιν οὗτοι τοῦθ' οὕτως ἕξειν,
σημεῖον αὐτοῖς προερῶ γενησόμενον· ῥαγήσεται τὸ
θυσιαστήριον παραχρῆμα καὶ πᾶσα ἡ ἐπ' αὐτοῦ
233 πιμελὴ τῶν ἱερείων ἐπὶ γῆν χυθήσεται." ταῦτ'
εἰπόντος τοῦ προφήτου παροξυνθεὶς ὁ Ἱεροβόαμος
ἐξέτεινε τὴν χεῖρα κελεύων συλλαβεῖν αὐτόν. ἐκ-
τεταμένη δ' ἡ χεὶρ εὐθέως παρείθη καὶ οὐκέτ' ἴσχυε
ταύτην πρὸς αὐτὸν ἀναγαγεῖν, ἀλλὰ νεναρκηκυῖαν
καὶ νεκρὰν εἶχεν ἀπηρτημένην. ἐρράγη δὲ καὶ τὸ
θυσιαστήριον καὶ κατηνέχθη πάντα ἀπ' αὐτοῦ,
234 καθὼς προεῖπεν ὁ προφήτης. μαθὼν δὲ ἀληθῆ τὸν
ἄνθρωπον καὶ θείαν ἔχοντα πρόγνωσιν παρεκάλεσεν
αὐτὸν δεηθῆναι τοῦ θεοῦ ἀναζωπυρῆσαι τὴν δεξιὰν
αὐτῷ. καὶ ὁ μὲν ἱκέτευσε τὸν θεὸν τοῦτ' αὐτῷ παρασχεῖν, ὁ δὲ τῆς χειρὸς τὸ κατὰ φύσιν ἀπολαβούσης
χαίρων ἐπ' αὐτῇ τὸν προφήτην παρεκάλει δειπνῆσαι
235 παρ' αὐτῷ. Ἰάδων δ' ἔφησεν οὐχ ὑπομένειν εἰσελθεῖν πρὸς αὐτὸν οὐδὲ γεύσασθαι ἄρτου καὶ ὕδατος
ἐν ταύτῃ τῇ πόλει· τοῦτο γὰρ αὐτῷ τὸν θεὸν ἀπειρηκέναι καὶ τὴν ὁδὸν ἣν ἦλθεν ὅπως μὴ δι' αὐτῆς
ποιήσηται τὴν ἐπιστροφήν, ἀλλὰ δι' ἄλλης ἔφασκεν·
τοῦτον μὲν οὖν ἐθαύμαζεν ὁ βασιλεὺς τῆς ἐγκρατείας,
αὐτὸς δ' ἦν ἐν φόβῳ, μεταβολὴν αὐτοῦ τῶν πραγμάτων ἐκ τῶν προειρημένων οὐκ ἀγαθὴν ὑπονοῶν.
236   (ix.) Ἦν δέ τις ἐν τῇ πόλει πρεσβύτης πονηρὸς
ψευδοπροφήτης, ὃν εἶχεν ἐν τιμῇ Ἱεροβόαμος ἀπατώμενος ὑπ' αὐτοῦ τὰ πρὸς ἡδονὴν λέγοντος.
οὗτος τότε μὲν κλινήρης ἦν διὰ τὴν ἀπὸ τοῦ γήρως
ἀσθένειαν, τῶν δὲ παίδων αὐτῷ δηλωσάντων τὰ
περὶ τοῦ παρόντος ἐξ Ἱεροσολύμων προφήτου καὶ
237 τῶν σημείων τῶν γενομένων, καὶ ὡς παρεθεῖσαν
αὐτῷ τὴν δεξιὰν Ἱεροβόαμος εὐξαμένου πάλιν
ἐκείνου ζῶσαν ἀπολάβοι, δείσας μὴ παρευδοκι-

μήσειεν αὐτὸν ὁ ξένος παρὰ τῷ βασιλεῖ καὶ πλείονος
ἀπολαύοι τιμῆς, προσέταξε τοῖς παισὶν εὐθὺς ἐπι-
στρῶσαι τὸν ὄνον ἕτοιμον πρὸς ἔξοδον αὐτῷ παρα-
238 σκευάσαι. τῶν δὲ σπευσάντων ὃ προσετάγησαν
ἐπιβὰς ἐδίωξε τὸν προφήτην καὶ καταλαβὼν ἀνα-
παυόμενον ὑπὸ δένδρῳ δασεῖ καὶ σκιὰν ἔχοντι
δρυὸς εὐμεγέθους ἠσπάσατο πρῶτον, εἶτ’ ἐμέμφετο
μὴ παρ’ αὐτὸν εἰσελθόντα καὶ ξενίων μεταλαβόντα.
239 τοῦ δὲ φήσαντος κεκωλῦσθαι πρὸς τοῦ θεοῦ γεύσασθαι παρά τινι τῶν ἐν ἐκείνῃ τῇ πόλει, " ἀλλ’
οὐχὶ παρ’ ἐμοὶ πάντως," εἶπεν, " ἀπηγόρευκέ σοι
τὸ θεῖον παραθέσθαι τράπεζαν· προφήτης γάρ εἰμι
κἀγὼ καὶ τῆς αὐτῆς σοι κοινωνὸς πρὸς αὐτὸν
θρησκείας, καὶ πάρειμι νῦν ὑπ’ αὐτοῦ πεμφθεὶς
240 ὅπως ἀγάγω σε πρὸς ἐμαυτὸν ἐστιασόμενον." ὁ
δὲ ψευσαμένῳ πεισθεὶς ἀνέστρεψεν· ἀριστώντων δ’
ἔτι καὶ φιλοφρονουμένων ὁ θεὸς ἐπιφαίνεται τῷ
Ἰάδωνι καὶ παραβάντα τὰς ἐντολὰς αὐτοῦ τιμωρίαν ὑφέξειν ἔλεγεν καὶ ποδαπὴν ἐδήλου· λέοντα
γὰρ αὐτῷ κατὰ τὴν ὁδὸν ἀπερχομένῳ συμβαλεῖν
ἔφραζεν, ὑφ’ οὗ διαφθαρήσεσθαι καὶ τῆς ἐν τοῖς
241 πατρῴοις μνήμασι ταφῆς ἀμοιρήσειν. ταῦτα δ’
ἐγένετο οἶμαι κατὰ τὴν τοῦ θεοῦ βούλησιν, ὅπως
μὴ προσέχοι τοῖς τοῦ Ἰάδωνος λόγοις Ἱερόβοαμος
ἐληλεγμένῳ ψεύδει. πορευομένῳ τοίνυν τῷ Ἰάδωνι
πάλιν εἰς Ἱεροσόλυμα συμβάλλει λέων καὶ κατασπάσας αὐτὸν ἀπὸ τοῦ κτήνους ἀπέκτεινε, καὶ
τὸν μὲν ὄνον οὐδὲν ὅλως ἔβλαψε, παρακαθεζόμενος
δ’ ἐφύλασσε κἀκεῖνον καὶ τὸ τοῦ προφήτου σῶμα,
μέχρις οὗ τινες τῶν ὁδοιπόρων ἰδόντες ἀπήγγειλαν
242 ἐλθόντες εἰς τὴν πόλιν τῷ ψευδοπροφήτῃ. ὁ δὲ
τοὺς υἱοὺς πέμψας ἐκόμισε τὸ σῶμα εἰς τὴν πόλιν
καὶ πολυτελοῦς κηδείας ἠξίωσεν ἐντειλάμενος τοῖς
παισὶ καὶ αὐτὸν ἀποθανόντα σὺν ἐκείνῳ θάψαι,
λέγων ἀληθῆ μὲν εἶναι πάνθ’ ὅσα προεφήτευσε
κατὰ τῆς πόλεως ἐκείνης καὶ τοῦ θυσιαστηρίου
καὶ τῶν ἱερέων καὶ τῶν ψευδοπροφητῶν, ὑβρι-

σθήσεσθαι δ' αὐτὸς μετὰ τὴν τελευτὴν οὐδὲν σὺν
ἐκείνῳ ταφείς, τῶν ὀστῶν οὐ γνωρισθησομένων.
243 κηδεύσας οὖν τὸν προφήτην καὶ ταῦτα τοῖς υἱοῖς
ἐντειλάμενος πονηρὸς ὢν καὶ ἀσεβὴς πρόσεισι τῷ
Ἱεροβοάμῳ καὶ "τί δήποτ' ἐταράχθης," εἰπών,
"ὑπὸ τῶν τοῦ ἀνοήτου λόγων;" ὡς τὰ περὶ τὸ
θυσιαστήριον αὐτῷ καὶ τὴν αὐτοῦ χεῖρα διηγήσαθ'
ὁ βασιλεύς, θεῖον ἀληθῶς καὶ προφήτην ἄριστον
ἀποκαλῶν, ἤρξατο ταύτην αὐτοῦ τὴν δόξαν ἀνα-
λύειν κακουργῶν καὶ πιθανοῖς περὶ τῶν γεγενημένων χρώμενος λόγοις βλάπτειν αὐτῶν τὴν
244 ἀλήθειαν. ἐπεχείρει γὰρ πείθειν αὐτὸν ὡς ὑπὸ
κόπου μὲν ἡ χεὶρ αὐτῷ ναρκήσειε βαστάζουσα
τὰς θυσίας, εἶτ' ἀνεθεῖσα πάλιν εἰς τὴν αὐτῆς
ἐπανέλθοι φύσιν, τὸ δὲ θυσιαστήριον καινὸν ὂν
καὶ δεξάμενον θυσίας πολλὰς καὶ μεγάλας ῥαγείη
καὶ πέσοι διὰ βάρος τῶν ἐπενηνεγμένων. ἐδήλου
δ' αὐτῷ καὶ τὸν θάνατον τοῦ τὰ σημεῖα ταῦτα
προειρηκότος ὡς ὑπὸ λέοντος ἀπώλετο· "οὕτως
οὐδὲ ἓν οὔτ' εἶχεν οὔτ' ἐφθέγξατο προφήτου."
245 ταῦτ' εἰπὼν πείθει τὸν βασιλέα, καὶ τὴν διάνοιαν
αὐτοῦ τελέως ἀποστρέψας ἀπὸ τοῦ θεοῦ καὶ τῶν
ὁσίων ἔργων καὶ δικαίων ἐπὶ τὰς ἀσεβεῖς πράξεις
παρώρμησεν. οὕτως δ' ἐξύβρισεν εἰς τὸ θεῖον καὶ
παρηνόμησεν ὡς οὐδὲν ἄλλο καθ' ἡμέραν ζητεῖν ἢ
τί καινὸν καὶ μιαρώτερον τῶν ἤδη τετολμημένων
ἐργάσηται. καὶ τὰ μὲν περὶ Ἱεροβόαμον ἐπὶ τοῦ
παρόντος ἐν τούτοις ἡμῖν δεδηλώσθω.
246 (x. 1) Ὁ δὲ Σολομῶνος υἱὸς Ῥοβόαμος ὁ τῶν
δύο φυλῶν βασιλεύς, ὡς προειρήκαμεν, ᾠκο-
δόμησε πόλεις ὀχυράς τε καὶ μεγάλας Βηθλεὲμ
καὶ Ἠταμὲ καὶ Θεκωὲ καὶ Βηθσοὺρ καὶ Σωχὼ
καὶ Ὀδολλὰμ καὶ Εἰπὰν καὶ Μάρισαν καὶ τὴν
Ζιφὰ καὶ Ἀδωραὶμ καὶ Λάχεις καὶ Ἀζηκὰ καὶ
247 Σαρὰμ καὶ Ἠλὼμ καὶ Χεβρῶνα. ταύτας μὲν ἐν
τῇ Ἰουδαίᾳ φυλῇ καὶ κληρουχίᾳ πρώτας ᾠκο-
δόμησε, κατεσκεύασε δὲ καὶ ἄλλας μεγάλας ἐν τῇ

Βενιαμίτιδι κληρουχία, καὶ τειχίσας φρουράς τε
κατέστησεν ἐν ἁπάσαις καὶ ἡγεμόνας, σῖτόν τε
πολὺν καὶ οἶνον καὶ ἔλαιον τά τε ἄλλα τὰ πρὸς
διατροφὴν ἐν ἑκάστῃ τῶν πόλεων δαψιλῶς ἀπέθετο,
πρὸς δὲ τούτοις θυρεοὺς καὶ σιρομάστας εἰς πολλὰς
248 μυριάδας. συνῆλθον δὲ οἱ παρὰ πᾶσι τοῖς Ἰσραηλίταις ἱερεῖς πρὸς αὐτὸν εἰς Ἱεροσόλυμα καὶ
Ληουῖται καὶ εἴ τινες ἄλλοι τοῦ πλήθους ἦσαν
ἀγαθοὶ καὶ δίκαιοι, καταλιπόντες αὐτῶν τὰς
πόλεις, ἵνα θρησκεύσωσιν ἐν Ἱεροσολύμοις τὸν
θεόν· οὐ γὰρ ἡδέως εἶχον προσκυνεῖν ἀναγκαζόμενοι τὰς δαμάλεις ἃς Ἱεροβόαμος κατεσκεύασε·
καὶ ηὔξησαν τὴν Ῥοβοάμου βασιλείαν ἐπ᾽ ἔτη
249 τρία. γήμας δὲ συγγενῆ τινα καὶ τρεῖς ποιησάμενος ἐξ αὐτῆς παῖδας ἤγετο ὕστερον καὶ τὴν ἐκ
τῆς Ἀψαλώμου θυγατρὸς Θαμάρης Μαχάνην
ὄνομα καὶ αὐτὴν οὖσαν συγγενῆ· καὶ παῖς ἐξ
αὐτῆς ἄρρην αὐτῷ γίνεται, ὃν Ἀβίαν προσηγό-
ρευσεν. τέκνα δὲ εἶχεν καὶ ἐξ ἄλλων γυναικῶν
πλειόνων, ἁπασῶν δὲ μᾶλλον ἔστερξε τὴν Μαχάνην.
250 εἶχε δὲ τὰς μὲν νόμῳ συνοικούσας αὐτῷ γυναῖκας
ὀκτωκαίδεκα παλλακὰς δὲ τριάκοντα, καὶ υἱοὶ μὲν
αὐτῷ γεγόνεισαν ὀκτὼ καὶ εἴκοσι θυγατέρες δ᾽
ἑξήκοντα. διάδοχον δὲ ἀπέδειξε τῆς βασιλείας τὸν
ἐκ τῆς Μαχάνης Ἀβίαν καὶ τοὺς θησαυροὺς αὐτῷ
καὶ τὰς ὀχυρωτάτας πόλεις ἐπίστευσεν.

251 (2) Αἴτιον δ᾽ οἶμαι πολλάκις γίνεται κακῶν καὶ
παρανομίας τοῖς ἀνθρώποις τὸ τῶν πραγμάτων
μέγεθος καὶ ἡ πρὸς τὸ βέλτιον αὐτῶν τροπή· τὴν
γὰρ βασιλείαν αὐξανομένην οὕτω βλέπων Ῥοβόαμος εἰς ἀδίκους καὶ ἀσεβεῖς ἐξετράπη πράξεις, καὶ
τῆς τοῦ θεοῦ θρησκείας κατεφρόνησεν, ὡς καὶ τὸν
ὑπ᾽ αὐτῷ λαὸν μιμητὴν γενέσθαι τῶν ἀνομημάτων.
252 συνδιαφθείρεται γὰρ τὰ τῶν ἀρχομένων ἤθη τοῖς
τῶν ἡγεμόνων τρόποις, καὶ ὡς ἔλεγχον τῆς ἐκείνων
ἀσελγείας τὴν αὐτῶν σωφροσύνην παραπέμποντες
ὡς ἀρετῇ ταῖς κακίαις αὐτῶν ἕπονται· οὐ γὰρ

ἔνεστιν ἀποδέχεσθαι δοκεῖν τὰ τῶν βασιλέων ἔργα
253 μὴ ταῦτα πράττοντας. τοῦτο τοίνυν συνέβαινε
καὶ τοῖς ὑπὸ Ῥοβοάμῳ τεταγμένοις ἀσεβοῦντος
αὐτοῦ καὶ παρανομοῦντος σπουδάζειν μὴ προσκρούσωσι τῷ βασιλεῖ θέλοντες εἶναι δίκαιοι. τιμωρὸν δὲ τῶν εἰς αὐτὸν ὕβρεων ὁ θεὸς ἐπιπέμπει
τὸν Αἰγυπτίων βασιλέα Ἴσωκον, περὶ οὗ πλανηθεὶς Ἡρόδοτος τὰς πράξεις αὐτοῦ Σεσώστρει
254 προσάπτει. οὗτος γὰρ ὁ Ἴσωκος πέμπτῳ ἔτει
τῆς Ῥοβοάμου βασιλείας ἐπιστρατεύεται μετὰ
πολλῶν αὐτῷ μυριάδων· ἅρματα μὲν γὰρ αὐτῷ
χίλια καὶ διακόσια τὸν ἀριθμὸν ἠκολούθει, ἱππέων
δὲ μυριάδες ἕξ, πεζῶν δὲ μυριάδες τεσσαράκοντα.
τούτων τοὺς πλείστους Λίβυας ἐπήγετο καὶ
255 Αἰθίοπας. ἐμβαλὼν οὖν εἰς τὴν χώραν τῶν
Ἑβραίων καταλαμβάνεται τὰς ὀχυρωτάτας τῆς
Ῥοβοάμου βασιλείας πόλεις ἀμαχητὶ καὶ ταύτας
ἀσφαλισάμενος ἔσχατον ἐπῆλθε τοῖς Ἱεροσολύμοις.
   (3) Ἐγκεκλεισμένου τοῦ Ῥοβοάμου καὶ τοῦ
πλήθους ἐν αὐτοῖς διὰ τὴν Ἰσώκου στρατείαν καὶ
τὸν θεὸν ἱκετευόντων δοῦναι νίκην καὶ σωτηρίαν,
256 οὐκ ἔπεισαν τὸν θεὸν ταχθῆναι μετ' αὐτῶν· ὁ δὲ
προφήτης Σαμαίας ἔφησεν αὐτοῖς τὸν θεὸν ἀπειλεῖν
ἐγκαταλείψειν αὐτούς, ὡς καὶ αὐτοὶ τὴν θρησκείαν
αὐτοῦ κατέλιπον. ταῦτ' ἀκούσαντες εὐθὺς ταῖς
ψυχαῖς ἀνέπεσον καὶ μηδὲν ἔτι σωτήριον·ὁρῶντες
ἐξομολογεῖσθαι πάντες ὥρμησαν ὅτι δικαίως αὐτοὺς
ὁ θεὸς ὑπερόψεται γενομένους περὶ αὐτὸν ἀσεβεῖς
257 καὶ συγχέοντας τὰ νόμιμα. κατιδὼν δ' αὐτοὺς
ὁ θεὸς οὕτω διακειμένους καὶ τὰς ἁμαρτίας ἀνθ-
ομολογουμένους οὐκ ἀπολέσειν αὐτοὺς εἶπε πρὸς
τὸν προφήτην, ποιήσειν μέντοι γε τοῖς Αἰγυπτίοις
ὑποχειρίους, ἵνα μάθωσι πότερον ἀνθρώπῳ δου-
258 λεύειν ἐστὶν ἀπονώτερον ἢ θεῷ. παραλαβὼν δὲ
Ἴσωκος ἀμαχητὶ τὴν πόλιν, δεξαμένου Ῥοβοάμου
διὰ τὸν φόβον, οὐκ ἐνέμεινε ταῖς γενομέναις συνθήκαις, ἀλλ' ἐσύλησε τὸ ἱερὸν καὶ τοὺς θησαυροὺς

ἐξεκένωσε τοῦ θεοῦ καὶ τοὺς βασιλικούς, χρυσοῦ
καὶ ἀργύρου μυριάδας ἀναριθμήτους βαστάσας
259 καὶ μηδὲν ὅλως ὑπολιπών. περιεῖλε δὲ καὶ τοὺς
χρυσοῦς θυρεοὺς καὶ τὰς ἀσπίδας, ἃς κατεσκεύασε
Σολομὼν ὁ βασιλεύς, οὐκ εἴασε δὲ οὐδὲ τὰς χρυσᾶς
φαρέτρας, ἃς ἀνέθηκε Δαυίδης τῷ θεῷ λαβὼν παρὰ
τοῦ τῆς Σωφηνῆς βασιλέως, καὶ τοῦτο ποιήσας
260 ἀνέστρεψεν εἰς τὰ οἰκεῖα. μέμνηται δὲ ταύτης
τῆς στρατείας καὶ ὁ Ἁλικαρνασεὺς Ἡρόδοτος
περὶ μόνον τὸ τοῦ βασιλέως πλανηθεὶς ὄνομα, καὶ
ὅτι ἄλλοις τε πολλοῖς ἐπῆλθεν ἔθνεσι καὶ τὴν
Παλαιστίνην Συρίαν ἐδουλώσατο λαβὼν ἀμαχητὶ
261 τοὺς ἀνθρώπους τοὺς ἐν αὐτῇ. φανερὸν δ᾽ ἐστὶν
ὅτι τὸ ἡμέτερον ἔθνος βούλεται δηλοῦν κεχειρω-
μένον ὑπὸ τοῦ Αἰγυπτίου· ἐπάγει γὰρ ὅτι στήλας
κατέλιπεν ἐν τῇ τῶν ἀμαχητὶ παραδόντων ἑαυτοὺς αἰδοῖα γυναικῶν ἐγγράψας· Ῥοβόαμος δ᾽
αὐτῷ παρέδωκεν ὁ ἡμέτερος βασιλεὺς ἀμαχητὶ
262 τὴν πόλιν. φησὶ δὲ καὶ Αἰθίοπας παρ᾽ Αἰγυπτίων
μεμαθηκέναι τὴν τῶν αἰδοίων περιτομήν· '' Φοίνικες γὰρ καὶ Σύροι οἱ ἐν τῇ Παλαιστίνῃ ὁμολογοῦσι παρ᾽ Αἰγυπτίων μεμαθηκέναι.'' δῆλον
οὖν ἐστιν ὅτι μηδένες ἄλλοι περιτέμνονται τῶν ἐν
τῇ Παλαιστίνῃ Σύρων ἢ μόνοι ἡμεῖς. ἀλλὰ περὶ
μὲν τούτων ἕκαστοι λεγέτωσαν ὅ τι ἂν αὐτοῖς
δοκῇ.
263   (4) Ἀναχωρήσαντος δὲ Ἰσώκου Ῥοβόαμος ὁ
βασιλεὺς ἀντὶ μὲν τῶν χρυσέων θυρεῶν καὶ τῶν
ἀσπίδων χάλκεα ποιήσας τὸν αὐτὸν ἀριθμὸν παρ-
έδωκε τοῖς τῶν βασιλείων φύλαξιν. ἀντὶ δὲ τοῦ
μετὰ στρατηγίας ἐπιφανοῦς καὶ τῆς ἐν τοῖς πράγμασι λαμπρότητος διάγειν ἐβασίλευσεν ἐν ἡσυχίᾳ
πολλῇ καὶ δέει πάντα τὸν χρόνον ἐχθρὸς ὢν Ἱερο-
264 βοάμῳ. ἐτελεύτησε δὲ βιώσας ἔτη πεντήκοντα
καὶ ἑπτά, βασιλεύσας δ᾽ αὐτῶν ἑπτακαίδεκα, τὸν
τρόπον ἀλαζὼν ἀνὴρ καὶ ἀνόητος καὶ διὰ τὸ μὴ
προσέχειν τοῖς πατρῴοις φίλοις τὴν ἀρχὴν ἀπ-

ὀλέσας· ἐτάφη δ' ἐν Ἱεροσολύμοις ἐν ταῖς θήκαις
τῶν βασιλέων. διεδέξατο δ' αὐτοῦ τὴν βασιλείαν
ὁ υἱὸς Ἀβίας, ὄγδοον ἤδη καὶ δέκατον ἔτος Ἱερο-
265 βοάμου τῶν δέκα φυλῶν βασιλεύοντος. καὶ ταῦτα
μὲν τοιοῦτον ἔσχε τὸ τέλος· τὰ δὲ περὶ Ἱεροβόαμον
ἀκόλουθα τούτων ἔχομεν πῶς κατέστρεψε τὸν βίον
διεξελθεῖν· οὗτος γὰρ οὐ διέλιπεν οὐδ' ἠρέμησεν εἰς
τὸν θεὸν ἐξυβρίζων, ἀλλὰ καθ' ἑκάστην ἡμέραν ἐπὶ
τῶν ὑψηλῶν ὀρῶν βωμοὺς ἀνιστὰς καὶ ἱερεῖς ἐκ
τοῦ πλήθους ἀποδεικνὺς διετέλει.
266 (xi. 1) Ταῦτα δ' ἔμελλεν οὐκ εἰς μακρὰν τά σε-
βήματα καὶ τὴν ὑπὲρ αὐτῶν δίκην εἰς τὴν αὐτοῦ
κεφαλὴν καὶ πάσης αὐτοῦ τῆς γενεᾶς τρέψειν τὸ
θεῖον. κάμνοντος δ' αὐτῷ κατ' ἐκεῖνον τὸν καιρὸν
τοῦ παιδός, ὃν Ὀβίμην ἐκάλουν, τὴν γυναῖκα
αὐτοῦ προσέταξε τὴν στολὴν ἀποθεμένην καὶ
σχῆμα λαβοῦσαν ἰδιωτικὸν πορευθῆναι πρὸς Ἀχίαν
267 τὸν προφήτην· εἶναι γὰρ θαυμαστὸν ἄνδρα περὶ
τῶν μελλόντων προειπεῖν· καὶ γὰρ περὶ τῆς βασιλείας αὐτῷ τοῦτον δεδηλωκέναι· παραγενομένην δ'
ἐκέλευσε περὶ τοῦ παιδὸς ἀνακρίνειν ὡς ξένην, εἰ
διαφεύξεται τὴν νόσον. ἡ δὲ μετασχηματισαμένη, καθὼς αὐτῇ προσέταξεν ὁ ἀνήρ, ἧκεν εἰς
268 Σιλὼ πόλιν· ἐκεῖ γὰρ διέτριβεν ὁ Ἀχίας. καὶ
μελλούσης εἰς τὴν οἰκίαν αὐτοῦ εἰσιέναι τὰς ὄψεις
ἡμαυρωμένου διὰ τὸ γῆρας, ἐπιφανεὶς ὁ θεὸς ἀμφό-
τερα αὐτῷ μηνύει τήν τε Ἱεροβοάμου γυναῖκα
πρὸς αὐτὸν ἀφιγμένην καὶ τί δεῖ περὶ ὧν πάρεστιν
269 ἀποκρίνασθαι. παριούσης δὲ τῆς γυναικὸς εἰς τὴν
οἰκίαν ὡς ἰδιώτιδος καὶ ξένης ἀνεβόησεν '' εἴσελθε,
ὦ γύναι Ἱεροβοάμου· τί κρύπτεις σαυτήν; τὸν
γὰρ θεὸν οὐ λανθάνεις, ὃς ἀφιξομένην τέ μοι φανεὶς
ἐδήλωσε καὶ προσέταξε τίνας ποιήσομαι τοὺς
λόγους. ἀπελθοῦσα οὖν πρὸς τὸν ἄνδρα φράζε
270 αὐτὸν ταῦτα λέγειν· ' ἐπεί σε μέγαν ἐκ μικροῦ
καὶ μηδενὸς ὄντος ἐποίησα καὶ ἀποσχίσας τὴν
βασιλείαν ἀπὸ τοῦ Δαυίδου γένους σοὶ ταύτην

ἔδωκα, σὺ δὲ τούτων ἠμνημόνησας καὶ τὴν ἐμὴν
θρησκείαν καταλιπὼν χωνευτοὺς θεοὺς κατασκευά-
σας ἐκείνους ἐτίμας, οὕτω σε πάλιν καθαιρήσω
καὶ πᾶν ἐξολέσω σου τὸ γένος καὶ κυσὶ καὶ ὄρνισι
271 βορὰν ποιήσω γενέσθαι. βασιλεὺς γὰρ ἐξεγείρεταί
τις ὑπ᾽ ἐμοῦ τοῦ λαοῦ παντός, ὃς οὐδένα ὑπολείψει
τοῦ Ἱεροβοάμου γένους· μεθέξει δὲ τῆς τιμωρίας
καὶ τὸ πλῆθος ἐκπεσὸν τῆς ἀγαθῆς γῆς καὶ διασπαρὲν εἰς τοὺς πέραν Εὐφράτου τόπους, ὅτι τοῖς
τοῦ βασιλέως ἀσεβήμασι κατηκολούθησε καὶ τοὺς
ὑπ᾽ αὐτοῦ γενομένους προσκυνεῖ θεοὺς τὴν ἐμὴν
272 θυσίαν ἐγκαταλιπόν.᾽ σὺ δέ, ὦ γύναι, ταῦτ᾽ ἀπαγγελλοῦσα σπεῦδε πρὸς τὸν ἄνδρα. τὸν δὲ υἱὸν
καταλήψῃ τεθνηκότα· σοῦ γὰρ εἰσιούσης εἰς τὴν
πόλιν ἀπολείψει τὸ ζῆν αὐτόν. ταφήσεται δὲ
κλαυσθεὶς ὑπὸ τοῦ πλήθους παντὸς κοινῷ τιμηθεὶς
πένθει· καὶ γὰρ μόνος τῶν ἐκ τοῦ Ἱεροβοάμου
273 γένους ἀγαθὸς οὗτος ἦν.᾽᾽ ταῦτ᾽ αὐτοῦ προφητεύσαντος ἐκπηδήσασα ἡ γυνὴ τεταραγμένη καὶ
τῷ τοῦ προειρημένου παιδὸς θανάτῳ περιαλγής,
θρηνοῦσα διὰ τῆς ὁδοῦ καὶ τὴν μέλλουσαν τοῦ
τέκνου κοπτομένη τελευτὴν ἀθλία τοῦ πάθους
ἠπείγετο κακοῖς ἀμηχάνοις καὶ σπουδῇ μὲν
ἀτυχεῖ χρωμένη διὰ τὸν υἱὸν αὐτῆς (ἔμελλε γὰρ
αὐτὸν ἐπειχθεῖσα θᾶττον ὄψεσθαι νεκρόν), ἀναγ-
καίᾳ δὲ διὰ τὸν ἄνδρα. καὶ παραγενομένη τὸν μὲν
ἐκπεπνευκότα καθὼς εἶπεν ὁ προφήτης εὗρε, τῷ
δὲ βασιλεῖ πάντα ἀπήγγειλεν.

274 (2) Ἱεροβόαμος δ᾽ οὐδενὸς τούτων φροντίσας
πολλὴν ἀθροίσας στρατιὰν ἐπὶ τὸν Ῥοβοάμου
παῖδα τῶν δύο φυλῶν τὴν βασιλείαν τοῦ πατρὸς
διαδεξάμενον Ἀβίαν ἐξεστράτευσε πολεμήσων·
κατεφρόνει γὰρ αὐτοῦ διὰ τὴν ἡλικίαν. ὁ δὲ
ἀκούσας τὴν ἔφοδον τὴν Ἱεροβοάμου πρὸς αὐτὴν
οὐ κατεπλάγη, γενόμενος δ᾽ ἐπάνω καὶ τῆς νεότητος τῷ φρονήματι καὶ τῆς ἐλπίδος τοῦ πολεμίου,

στρατιὰν ἐπιλέξας ἐκ τῶν δύο φυλῶν ἀπήντησε
τῷ Ἱεροβοάμῳ εἰς τόπον τινὰ καλούμενον ὄρος
Σαμαρῶν καὶ στρατοπεδευσάμενος ἐγγὺς αὐτοῦ
275 τὰ πρὸς τὴν μάχην εὐτρέπιζεν. ἦν δ' ἡ δύναμις
αὐτοῦ μυριάδες τεσσαράκοντα, ἡ δὲ τοῦ Ἱεροβοάμου στρατιὰ διπλασίων ἐκείνης. ὡς δὲ τὰ
στρατεύματα πρὸς τὰ ἔργα καὶ τοὺς κινδύνους
ἀντιπαρετάσσετο καὶ συμβαλεῖν ἔμελλε, στὰς ἐφ'
ὑψηλοῦ τινος Ἀβίας τόπου καὶ τῇ χειρὶ κατασείσας, τὸ πλῆθος καὶ τὸν Ἱεροβόαμον ἀκοῦσαι
276 πρῶτον αὐτοῦ μεθ' ἡσυχίας ἠξίωσε. γενομένης δὲ
σιωπῆς ἤρξατο λέγειν· " ὅτι μὲν τὴν ἡγεμονίαν ὁ
θεὸς Δαυίδῃ καὶ τοῖς ἐκγόνοις αὐτοῦ κατένευσεν
εἰς ἅπαντα χρόνον, οὐδ' ὑμεῖς ἀγνοεῖτε· θαυμάζω
δὲ πῶς ἀποστάντες τοὐμοῦ πατρὸς τῷ δούλῳ
Ἱεροβοάμῳ προσέθεσθε καὶ μετ' ἐκείνου πάρεστε
νῦν ἐπὶ τοὺς ὑπὸ τοῦ θεοῦ βασιλεύειν κεκριμένους
πολεμήσοντες καὶ τὴν ἀρχὴν ἀφαιρησόμενοι τὴν
ὑπάρχουσαν· τὴν μὲν γὰρ πλείω μέχρι νῦν Ἱερο-
277 βοαμος ἀδίκως ἔχει. ἀλλ' οὐκ οἶμαι ταύτης
αὐτὸν ἀπολαύσειν ἐπὶ πλείονα χρόνον, ἀλλὰ δοὺς
καὶ τοῦ παρεληλυθότος δίκην τῷ θεῷ παύσεται
τῆς παρανομίας καὶ τῶν ὕβρεων, ἃς οὐ διαλέλοιπεν
εἰς αὐτὸν ὑβρίζων καὶ ταὐτὰ ποιεῖν ὑμᾶς ἀναπε-
πεικώς, οἳ μηδὲν ἀδικηθέντες ὑπὸ τοὐμοῦ πατρός,
ἀλλ' ὅτι μὴ πρὸς ἡδονὴν ἐκκλησιάζων ὡμίλησεν,
ἀνθρώπων πονηρῶν συμβουλίᾳ πεισθείς, ἐγκατ-
ελίπετε τῷ μὲν δοκεῖν ὑπ' ὀργῆς ἐκεῖνον, ταῖς δ'
ἀληθείαις αὐτοὺς ἀπὸ τοῦ θεοῦ καὶ τῶν ἐκείνου
278 νόμων ἀπεσπάσατε. καίτοι συνεγνωκέναι καλῶς
εἶχεν ὑμᾶς οὐ λόγων μόνον δυσκόλων ἀνδρὶ νέῳ
καὶ δημαγωγίας ἀπείρῳ, ἀλλ' εἰ καὶ πρός τι
δυσχερὲς ἡ νεότης αὐτὸν καὶ ἡ ἀμαθία τῶν πραττομένων ἐξῆγεν ἔργον, διά τε Σολομῶνα τὸν πατέρα καὶ τὰς εὐεργεσίας τὰς ἐκείνου· παραίτησιν

γὰρ εἶναι δεῖ τῆς τῶν ἐκγόνων ἁμαρτίας τὰς τῶν
279 πατέρων εὐποιίας. ὑμεῖς δ' οὐδὲν τούτων ἐλογίσασθε οὔτε τότε οὔτε νῦν, ἀλλ' ἧκε στρατὸς ἐφ'
ἡμᾶς τοσοῦτος· τίνι καὶ πεπιστευκὼς περὶ τῆς
νίκης; ἢ ταῖς χρυσαῖς δαμάλεσι καὶ τοῖς ἐπὶ τῶν
ὀρῶν βωμοῖς, ἃ δείγματα τῆς ἀσεβείας ἐστὶν ὑμῶν
ἀλλ' οὐχὶ τῆς θρησκείας; ἢ τὸ πλῆθος ὑμᾶς
εὐέλπιδας ἀπεργάζεται τὴν ἡμετέραν στρατιὰν
280 ὑπερβάλλον; ἀλλ' οὐδ' ἡτισοῦν ἰσχὺς μυριάδων
στρατοῦ μετ' ἀδικημάτων πολεμοῦντος· ἐν γὰρ
μόνῳ τῷ δικαίῳ καὶ πρὸς τὸ θεῖον εὐσεβεῖ τὴν
βεβαιοτάτην ἐλπίδα τοῦ κρατεῖν τῶν ἐναντίων
ἀποκεῖσθαι συμβέβηκεν, ἥτις ἐστὶ παρ' ἡμῖν τετηρηκόσιν ἀπ' ἀρχῆς τὰ νόμιμα καὶ τὸν ἴδιον θεὸν
σεβομένοις, ὃν οὐ χεῖρες ἐποίησαν ἐξ ὕλης φθαρτῆς
οὐδ' ἐπίνοια πονηροῦ βασιλέως ἐπὶ τῇ τῶν ὄχλων
ἀπάτῃ κατεσκεύασεν, ἀλλ' ὃς ἔργον ἐστὶν αὐτοῦ
281 καὶ ἀρχὴ καὶ τέλος τῶν ἁπάντων. συμβουλεύω
τοιγαροῦν ὑμῖν ἔτι καὶ νῦν μεταγνῶναι καὶ λαβόν-
τας ἀμείνω λογισμὸν παύσασθαι τοῦ πολεμεῖν καὶ
τὰ πάτρια καὶ τὸ προαγαγὸν ὑμᾶς ἐπὶ τοσοῦτον
μέγεθος εὐδαιμονίας γνωρίσαι.''
282 (3) Ταῦτα μὲν 'Αβίας διελέχθη πρὸς τὸ πλῆθος·
ἔτι δὲ αὐτοῦ λέγοντος λάθρα τινὰς τῶν στρατιω-
τῶν 'Ιεροβόαμος ἔπεμψε περικυκλωσομένους τὸν
'Αβίαν ἔκ τινων οὐ φανερῶν τοῦ στρατοπέδου
μερῶν. μέσου δ' αὐτοῦ περιληφθέντος τῶν πολεμίων ἡ μὲν στρατιὰ κατέδεισε καὶ ταῖς ψυχαῖς
ἀνέπεσεν, ὁ δ' 'Αβίας παρεθάρρυνε καὶ τὰς ἐλπίδας ἔχειν ἐν τῷ θεῷ παρεκάλει· τοῦτον γὰρ οὐ κε-
283 κυκλῶσθαι πρὸς τῶν πολεμίων. οἱ δὲ ὁμοῦ πάντες ἐπικαλεσάμενοι τὴν παρὰ τοῦ θεοῦ συμμαχίαν
τῶν ἱερέων τῇ σάλπιγγι σημανάντων ἀλαλάξαντες
284 ἐχώρησαν ἐπὶ τοὺς πολεμίους· καὶ τῶν μὲν ἔθραυσε
τὰ φρονήματα καὶ τὰς ἀκμὰς αὐτῶν ἐξέλυσεν ὁ
θεός, τὴν δὲ 'Αβία στρατιὰν ὑπερτέραν ἐποίησεν·
ὅσος γὰρ οὐδέποτ' ἐμνημονεύθη φόνος ἐν πολέμῳ

γεγονέναι οὔθ᾽ Ἑλλήνων οὔτε βαρβάρων, τοσούτους
ἀποκτείναντες τῆς Ἱεροβοάμου δυνάμεως θαυμαστὴν καὶ διαβόητον νίκην παρὰ τοῦ θεοῦ λαβεῖν
ἠξιώθησαν· πεντήκοντα γὰρ μυριάδας τῶν ἐχθρῶν
κατέβαλον καὶ τὰς πόλεις αὐτῶν διήρπασαν τὰς
ὀχυρωτάτας ἑλόντες κατὰ κράτος, τήν τε Βηθήλην
καὶ τὴν τοπαρχίαν αὐτῆς καὶ τὴν Ἰσανὰν καὶ τὴν
285 τοπαρχίαν αὐτῆς. καὶ Ἱεροβόαμος μὲν οὐκέτι
μετὰ ταύτην τὴν ἧτταν ἴσχυσεν ἐφ᾽ ὅσον Ἀβίας
περιῆν χρόνον. τελευτᾷ δ᾽ οὗτος ὀλίγον τῇ νίκῃ
χρόνον ἐπιζήσας ἔτη βασιλεύσας τρία, καὶ θάπτεται
μὲν ἐν Ἱεροσολύμοις ἐν ταῖς προγονικαῖς θήκαις,
ἀπολείπει δὲ υἱοὺς μὲν δύο καὶ εἴκοσι θυγατέρας
δὲ ἑκκαίδεκα. πάντας τούτους ἐκ γυναικῶν δεκα-
286 τεσσάρων ἐτεκνώσατο. διεδέξατο δ᾽ αὐτοῦ τὴν
βασιλείαν ὁ υἱὸς Ἄσανος· καὶ ἡ μήτηρ τοῦ νεανίσκου Μαχαία τοὔνομα. τούτου κρατοῦντος εἰρήνης ἀπέλαυεν ἡ χώρα τῶν Ἰσραηλιτῶν ἐπὶ ἔτη
δέκα.

287 (4) Καὶ τὰ μὲν περὶ Ἀβίαν τὸν Ῥοβοάμου τοῦ
Σολομῶνος οὕτως παρειλήφαμεν. ἐτελεύτησε δὲ
καὶ Ἱεροβόαμος ὁ τῶν δέκα φυλῶν βασιλεύς,
ἄρξας ἔτη δύο καὶ εἴκοσι. διαδέχεται δ᾽ αὐτὸν ὁ
παῖς Νάβαδος δευτέρου ἔτους ἤδη τῆς βασιλείας
Ἀσάνου διεληλυθότος. ἦρξε δὲ ὁ τοῦ Ἱεροβοάμου παῖς ἔτη δύο, τῷ πατρὶ τὴν ἀσέβειαν καὶ
288 τὴν πονηρίαν ἐμφερὴς ὤν. ἐν δὲ τούτοις τοῖς
δυσὶν ἔτεσι στρατευσάμενος ἐπὶ Γαβαθῶνα πόλιν
Παλαιστίνων οὖσαν πολιορκίᾳ λαβεῖν αὐτὴν προσ-
έμενεν· ἐπιβουλευθεὶς δ᾽ ἐκεῖ ὑπὸ φίλου τινὸς
Βασάνου ὄνομα Σειδοῦ δὲ παιδὸς ἀποθνήσκει,
ὃς μετὰ τὴν τελευτὴν αὐτοῦ τὴν βασιλείαν παρα-
289 λαβὼν ἅπαν τὸ Ἱεροβοάμου γένος διέφθειρε. καὶ
συνέβη κατὰ τὴν τοῦ θεοῦ προφητείαν τοὺς μὲν ἐν
τῇ πόλει τῶν Ἱεροβοάμου συγγενῶν ἀποθανόντας
ὑπὸ κυνῶν σπαραχθῆναι καὶ δαπανηθῆναι, τοὺς

δ' ἐν τοῖς ἀγροῖς ὑπ' ὀρνίθων. ὁ μὲν οὖν Ἱεροβοάμου οἶκος τῆς ἀσεβείας αὐτοῦ καὶ τῶν ἀ-
νομημάτων ἀξίαν ὑπέσχε δίκην.

290   (xii. 1) Ὁ δὲ τῶν Ἱεροσολύμων βασιλεὺς Ἄσανος
ἦν τὸν τρόπον ἄριστος καὶ πρὸς τὸ θεῖον
ἀφορῶν καὶ μηδὲν μήτε πράττων μήτ' ἐννοούμενος
ὃ μὴ πρὸς τὴν εὐσέβειαν εἶχε καὶ τὴν τῶν νομίμων
φυλακὴν τὴν ἀναφοράν. κατώρθωσε δὲ τὴν αὐτοῦ
βασιλείαν ἐκκόψας εἴ τι πονηρὸν ἦν ἐν αὐτῇ καὶ
291 καθαρεύσας ἁπάσης κηλῖδος. στρατοῦ δ' εἶχεν
ἐπιλέκτων ἀνδρῶν ὡπλισμένων θυρεὸν καὶ σιρομάστην ἐκ μὲν τῆς Ἰούδα φυλῆς μυριάδας τριάκοντα, ἐκ δὲ τῆς Βενιαμίτιδος ἀσπίδας φορούντων
292 καὶ τοξοτῶν μυριάδας πέντε καὶ εἴκοσι. ἤδη δὲ
αὐτοῦ δέκα ἔτη βασιλεύοντος στρατεύει μεγάλῃ
δυνάμει Ζαραῖος ἐπ' αὐτὸν ὁ τῆς Αἰθιοπίας βασιλεὺς ἐνενήκοντα μὲν πεζῶν μυριάσιν ἱππέων δὲ
δέκα τριακοσίοις δ' ἅρμασι. καὶ μέχρι πόλεως
Μαρίσας, ἔστι δ' αὕτη τῆς Ἰούδα φυλῆς, ἐλάσαντος
αὐτοῦ μετὰ τῆς οἰκείας δυνάμεως ἀπήντησεν
293 Ἄσανος, καὶ ἀντιπαρατάξας αὐτῷ τὴν στρατιὰν
ἔν τινι φάραγγι Σαφαθὰ λεγομένῃ τῆς πόλεως
οὐκ ἄπωθεν, ὡς κατεῖδε τὸ τῶν Αἰθιόπων πλῆθος,
ἀναβοήσας νίκην ᾔτει παρὰ τοῦ θεοῦ καὶ τὰς
πολλὰς ἑλεῖν μυριάδας τῶν πολεμίων· οὐδὲ γὰρ
ἄλλῳ τινὶ θαρσήσας ἔλεγεν ἢ τῇ παρ' αὐτοῦ βοηθείᾳ δυναμένῃ καὶ τοὺς ὀλίγους ἀπεργάσασθαι
κρείττους τῶν πλειόνων καὶ τοὺς ἀσθενεῖς τῶν
ὑπερεχόντων ἀπαντῆσαι πρὸς μάχην τῷ Ζαραίῳ.
294   (2) Ταῦτα λέγοντος Ἀσάνου νίκην ἐσήμαινεν ὁ
θεός, καὶ συμβαλὼν μετὰ χαρᾶς τῶν προδεδηλωμένων ὑπὸ τοῦ θεοῦ πολλοὺς ἀποκτείνει τῶν
Αἰθιόπων καὶ τραπέντας εἰς φυγὴν ἐδίωξεν ἄχρι
τῆς Γεραρίτιδος χώρας. ἀφέμενοι δὲ τῆς ἀναιρέσεως ἐπὶ τὴν διαρπαγὴν τῶν πόλεων (ἥλω
γὰρ ἡ Γεράρων) ἐχώρησαν καὶ τῆς παρεμβολῆς

αὐτῶν, ὡς πολὺν μὲν ἐκφορῆσαι χρυσὸν πολὺν δὲ
ἄργυρον λείαν τε πολλὴν ἀπαγαγεῖν καμήλους τε
295 καὶ ὑποζύγια καὶ βοσκημάτων ἀγέλας. Ἄσανος
μὲν οὖν καὶ ἡ σὺν αὐτῷ στρατιὰ τοιαύτην παρὰ
τοῦ θεοῦ νίκην λαβόντες καὶ ὠφέλειαν ἀνέστρεφον
εἰς Ἱεροσόλυμα, παραγενομένοις δὲ αὐτοῖς ἀπήντησε κατὰ τὴν ὁδὸν προφήτης Ἀζαρίας ὄνομα.
οὗτος ἐπισχεῖν κελεύσας τῆς ὁδοιπορίας ἤρξατο
λέγειν πρὸς αὐτοὺς ὅτι ταύτης εἶεν τῆς νίκης παρὰ
τοῦ θεοῦ τετυχηκότες, ὅτι δικαίους καὶ ὁσίους
ἑαυτοὺς παρέσχον καὶ πάντα κατὰ βούλησιν θεοῦ
296 πεποιηκότας. ἐπιμένουσι μὲν οὖν ἔφασκεν ἀεὶ
κρατεῖν αὐτοὺς τῶν ἐχθρῶν καὶ τὸ ζῆν μετ' εὐδαιμονίας παρέξειν τὸν θεόν, ἀπολιποῦσι δὲ τὴν
θρησκείαν ἅπαντα τούτων ἐναντία συμβήσεσθαι
καὶ γενήσεσθαι χρόνον ἐκεῖνον, "ἐν ᾧ μηδεὶς
ἀληθὴς εὑρεθήσεται προφήτης ἐν τῷ ὑμετέρῳ
297 ὄχλῳ οὐδὲ ἱερεὺς τὰ δίκαια χρηματίζων, ἀλλὰ καὶ
αἱ πόλεις ἀνάστατοι γενήσονται καὶ τὸ ἔθνος κατὰ
πάσης σπαρήσεται γῆς, ἔπηλυν βίον καὶ ἀλήτην
βιωσόμενον." καιρὸν δ' αὐτοῖς ἔχουσι συνεβούλευεν ἀγαθοῖς γίνεσθαι καὶ μὴ φθονῆσαι τῆς εὐμενείας αὐτοῖς τοῦ θεοῦ. ταῦτ' ἀκούσας ὁ βασιλεὺς καὶ ὁ λαὸς ἐχάρησαν καὶ πολλὴν πρόνοιαν
ἐποιοῦντο κοινῇ τε πάντες καὶ κατ' ἰδίαν τοῦ δι-
καίου· διέπεμψε δ' ὁ βασιλεὺς καὶ τοὺς ἐν τῇ
χώρᾳ τῶν νομίμων ἐπιμελησομένους.

298 (3) Καὶ τὰ μὲν Ἀσάνου τοῦ βασιλέως τῶν δύο
φυλῶν ἐν τούτοις ὑπῆρχεν. ἐπάνειμι δ' ἐπὶ τὸ
πλῆθος τῶν Ἰσραηλιτῶν καὶ τὸν βασιλέα αὐτῶν
Βασάνην τὸν ἀποκτείναντα τὸν Ἱεροβοάμου υἱὸν
299 Νάβαδον καὶ κατασχόντα τὴν ἀρχήν. οὗτος γὰρ
ἐν Θαρσῇ πόλει διατρίβων καὶ ταύτην οἰκητήριον
πεποιημένος εἴκοσι μὲν ἐβασίλευσεν ἔτη καὶ τέσ-
σαρα, πονηρὸς δὲ καὶ ἀσεβὴς ὑπὲρ Ἱεροβοάμου
καὶ τὸν υἱὸν αὐτοῦ γενόμενος, πολλὰ καὶ τὸ
πλῆθος κακὰ διέθηκε καὶ τὸν θεὸν ἐξύβρισεν· ὃς

αὐτῷ πέμψας Ἰηοῦν τὸν προφήτην προεῖπε διαφθερεῖν αὐτοῦ πᾶν τὸ γένος καὶ τοῖς αὐτοῖς οἷς καὶ
τὸν Ἱεροβοάμου κακοῖς περιέβαλεν οἶκον ἐξολέσειν,
300 ὅτι βασιλεὺς ὑπ' αὐτοῦ γενόμενος οὐκ ἠμείψατο
τὴν εὐεργεσίαν τῷ δικαίως προστῆναι τοῦ πλήθους
καὶ εὐσεβῶς, ἅπερ αὐτοῖς πρῶτον τοῖς οὖσι τοιούτοις ἀγαθά, ἔπειτα τῷ θεῷ φίλα, τὸν δὲ κάκιστον
Ἱεροβόαμον ἐμιμήσατο καὶ τῆς ψυχῆς ἀπολομένης
τῆς ἐκείνου ζῶσαν αὐτοῦ τὴν πονηρίαν ἐνεδείξατο·
πεῖραν οὖν ἕξειν εἰκότως τῆς ὁμοίας συμφορᾶς
301 αὐτὸν ἔλεγεν ὅμοιον αὐτῷ γενόμενον. Βασάνης
δὲ προακηκοὼς τὰ μέλλοντα αὐτῷ συμβήσεσθαι
κακὰ μεθ' ὅλης τῆς γενεᾶς ἐπὶ τοῖς τετολμημένοις
οὐ πρὸς τὸ λοιπὸν ἡσύχασεν, ἵνα μὴ μᾶλλον
πονηρὸς δόξας ἀποθάνῃ καὶ περὶ τῶν παρῳχημένων ἔκτοτε γοῦν μετανοήσας συγγνώμης παρὰ
302 τοῦ θεοῦ τύχῃ, ἀλλ' ὥσπερ οἱ προκειμένων αὐτοῖς
ἄθλων ἐπὰν περί τι σπουδάσωσιν οὐ διαλείπουσι
περὶ τοῦτο ἐνεργοῦντες, οὕτω καὶ Βασάνης προειρηκότος αὐτῷ τοῦ προφήτου τὰ μέλλοντα ὡς ἐπ'
ἀγαθοῖς τοῖς μεγίστοις κακοῖς ὀλέθρῳ γένους καὶ
οἰκίας ἀπωλείᾳ χείρων ἐγένετο, καὶ καθ' ἑκάστην
ἡμέραν ὥσπερ ἀθλητὴς κακίας τοῖς περὶ ταύτην
303 πόνοις προσετίθει. καὶ τελευταῖον τὴν στρατιὰν
παραλαβὼν πάλιν ἐπῆλθε πόλει τινὶ τῶν οὐκ
ἀφανῶν Ἀραμαθῶνι τοὔνομα σταδίους ἀπεχούσῃ
Ἱεροσολύμων τεσσαράκοντα, καὶ καταλαβόμενος
αὐτὴν ὠχύρου προδιεγνωκὼς καταλιπεῖν ἐν αὐτῇ
δύναμιν, ἵν' ἐκεῖθεν ὡρμημένοι τὴν Ἀσάνου βασιλείαν κακώσωσι.

304 (4) Φοβηθεὶς δὲ Ἄσανος τὴν ἐπιχείρησιν τοῦ
πολεμίου καὶ λογισάμενος ὡς πολλὰ διαθήσει
κακὰ τὴν ὑπ' αὐτῷ βασιλευομένην ἅπασαν ὁ κατα-
λειφθεὶς ἐν Ἀραμαθῶνι στρατός, ἔπεμψε πρὸς τὸν

Δαμασκηνῶν βασιλέα πρέσβεις καὶ χρυσὸν καὶ
ἄργυρον, παρακαλῶν συμμαχεῖν καὶ ὑπομιμνῄσ-
κων ὅτι καὶ πατρῷα φιλία πρὸς ἀλλήλους ἐστὶν
305 αὐτοῖς. ὁ δὲ τῶν χρημάτων τὸ πλῆθος ἀσμένως
ἐδέξατο καὶ συμμαχίαν ἐποιήσατο πρὸς αὐτόν, διαλύσας τὴν πρὸς τὸν Βασάνην φιλίαν, καὶ πέμψας
εἰς τὰς ὑπ' αὐτοῦ βασιλευομένας πόλεις τοὺς
ἡγεμόνας τῆς ἰδίας δυνάμεως ἐκέλευσε κακοῦν
αὐτάς. οἱ δὲ τὰς μὲν ἐνεπίμπρασαν τὰς δὲ διήρπασαν πορευθέντες, τήν τε Αἰῶνα λεγομένην
306 καὶ Δάνα καὶ Ἀβελλάνην καὶ ἄλλας πολλάς. ταῦτ'
ἀκούσας ὁ τῶν Ἰσραηλιτῶν βασιλεὺς τοῦ μὲν
οἰκοδομεῖν καὶ ὀχυροῦν τὴν Ἀραμαθῶνα ἐπαύσατο,
μετὰ δὲ σπουδῆς ὡς βοηθήσων τοῖς οἰκείοις
κακουμένοις ἀνέστρεψεν, ὁ δ' Ἄσανος ἐκ τῆς
παρεσκευασμένης ὑπ' αὐτοῦ πρὸς οἰκοδομίαν ὕλης
πόλεις ἀνήγειρεν ἐν αὐτῷ τῷ τόπῳ δύο καρτεράς,
307 ἡ μὲν Γαβαὰ ἐκαλεῖτο, ἡ δὲ Μασφά. καὶ μετὰ
ταῦτα καιρὸν οὐκ ἔσχεν ὁ Βασάνης τῆς ἐπὶ τὸν
Ἄσανον στρατείας· ἐφθάσθη γὰρ ὑπὸ τοῦ χρεών,
καὶ θάπτεται μὲν ἐν Θαρσῇ πόλει, παραλαμβάνει
δ' αὐτοῦ τὴν ἀρχὴν παῖς Ἤλανος. οὗτος ἄρξας
ἐπ' ἔτη δύο τελευτᾷ φονεύσαντος αὐτὸν ἐξ
ἐπιβουλῆς Ζαμβρίου τοῦ ἱππάρχου τῆς ἡμι-
308 σείας τάξεως· κατευωχηθέντα γὰρ αὐτὸν παρὰ τῷ
οἰκονόμῳ αὐτοῦ Ὡσᾶ τοὔνομα πείσας ἐπιδραμεῖν
τῶν ὑφ' αὐτὸν ἱππέων τινὰς ἀπέκτεινε δι' αὐτῶν
μεμονωμένον τῶν περὶ αὐτὸν ὁπλιτῶν καὶ ἡγε-
μόνων· οὗτοι γὰρ ἅπαντες περὶ τὴν πολιορκίαν
τῆς Γαβαθώνης ἐγίνοντο τῆς Παλαιστίνων.
309 (5) Φονεύσας δὲ τὸν Ἤλανον ὁ ἵππαρχος
Ζαμβρίας αὐτὸς βασιλεύει καὶ πᾶσαν τὴν Βασάνου
γενεὰν κατὰ τὴν Ἰηοῦ προφητείαν διαφθείρει·
τῷ γὰρ αὐτῷ τρόπῳ συνέβη τὸν οἶκον αὐτοῦ
πρόρριζον ἀπολέσθαι διὰ τὴν ἀσέβειαν, ὡς καὶ τὸν

310 Ἱεροβοάμου διαφθαρέντα γεγράφαμεν. ἡ δὲ πολιορκοῦσα τὴν Γαβαθώνην στρατιὰ πυθομένη τὰ
περὶ τὸν βασιλέα καὶ ὅτι Ζαμβρίας ἀποκτείνας
αὐτὸν ἔχει τὴν βασιλείαν καὶ αὐτὴ τὸν ἡγούμενον
αὐτῆς Ἀμαρῖνον ἀπέδειξε βασιλέα, ὃς ἀπὸ τῆς
Γαβαθώνης ἀναστήσας τὸν στρατὸν εἰς Θαρσὴν
παραγίνεται τὸ βασίλειον καὶ προσβαλὼν τῇ πόλει
311 κατὰ κράτος αἱρεῖ. Ζαμβρίας δὲ τὴν πόλιν ἰδὼν
ᾑρημένην συνέφυγεν εἰς τὸ μυχαίτατον τῶν βασιλείων καὶ ὑποπρήσας αὐτὰ συγκατέκαυσεν ἑαυτὸν
βασιλεύσας ἡμέρας ἑπτά. διέστη δ' εὐθὺς ὁ τῶν
Ἰσραηλιτῶν λαὸς καὶ οἱ μὲν αὐτῶν Θαμαναῖον
βασιλεύειν ἤθελον, οἱ δὲ τὸν Ἀμαρῖνον. νικήσαντες
δ' οἱ τοῦτον ἄρχειν ἀξιοῦντες ἀποκτείνουσι τὸν
Θαμαναῖον, καὶ παντὸς βασιλεύει ὁ Ἀμαρῖνος τοῦ
312 ὄχλου. τριακοστῷ δὲ ἔτει τῆς Ἀσάνου βασιλείας
ἦρξεν ὁ Ἀμαρῖνος ἔτη δώδεκα· τούτων τὰ μὲν ἓξ
ἐν Θάρσῳ πόλει, τὰ δὲ λοιπὰ ἐν Σωμαρεῶνι λεγομένῃ πόλει ὑπὸ δὲ Ἑλλήνων Σαμαρείᾳ καλου-
μένῃ. προσηγόρευσε δ' αὐτὴν οὕτως Ἀμαρῖνος
ἀπὸ τοῦ τὸ ὄρος ἀποδομένου αὐτῷ ἐφ' ᾧ κατ-
313 εσκεύασε τὴν πόλιν Σωμάρου. διέφερε δ' οὐδὲν
τῶν πρὸ αὐτοῦ βασιλευσάντων ἢ τῷ χείρων αὐτῶν
εἶναι· ἅπαντες γὰρ ἐζήτουν πῶς ἀποστήσωσιν ἀπὸ
τοῦ θεοῦ τὸν λαὸν τοῖς καθ' ἡμέραν ἀσεβήμασι καὶ
διὰ τοῦτο δι' ἀλλήλων αὐτοὺς ὁ θεὸς ἐποίησεν
ἐλθεῖν καὶ μηδένα τοῦ γένους ὑπολιπεῖν. ἐτελεύτησε δὲ καὶ οὗτος ἐν Σαμαρείᾳ, διαδέχεται δ'
αὐτὸν ὁ παῖς Ἄχαβος.

314 (6) Μαθεῖν δ' ἔστιν ἐκ τούτων ὅσην τὸ θεῖον
ἐπιστροφὴν ἔχει τῶν ἀνθρωπίνων πραγμάτων, καὶ
πῶς μὲν ἀγαπᾷ τοὺς ἀγαθούς, μισεῖ δὲ τοὺς πονη-
ροὺς καὶ προρρίζους ἀπόλλυσιν· οἱ μὲν γὰρ τῶν
Ἰσραηλιτῶν βασιλεῖς ἄλλος ἐπ' ἄλλῳ διὰ τὴν παρανομίαν καὶ τὰς ἀδικίας ἐν ὀλίγῳ χρόνῳ πολλοὶ
κακῶς διαφθαρέντες ἐγνώσθησαν καὶ τὸ γένος

αὐτῶν, ὁ δὲ τῶν Ἱεροσολύμων καὶ τῶν δύο φυλῶν
βασιλεὺς Ἄσανος δι᾽ εὐσέβειαν καὶ δικαιοσύνην
εἰς μακρὸν καὶ εὔδαιμον ὑπὸ τοῦ θεοῦ προ-
ήχθη γῆρας καὶ τεσσαράκοντα καὶ ἓν ἄρξας ἔτος
315 εὐμοίρως ἀπέθανε. τελευτήσαντος δ᾽ αὐτοῦ διεδέξατο τὴν ἡγεμονίαν ὁ υἱὸς Ἰωσαφάτης ἐκ
γυναικὸς Ἀβιδᾶς τοὔνομα γεγενημένος. τοῦτον
μιμητὴν Δαυίδου τοῦ προπάππου κατά τε ἀνδρείαν
καὶ εὐσέβειαν ἅπαντες ἐν τοῖς ἔργοις ὑπέλαβον.
ἀλλὰ περὶ μὲν τούτου τοῦ βασιλέως οὐ κατεπείγει
νῦν λέγειν.

316   (xiii. 1) Ὁ δὲ Ἄχαβος ὁ τῶν Ἰσραηλιτῶν βασιλεὺς κατῴκει μὲν ἐν Σαμαρείᾳ, τὴν δ᾽ ἀρχὴν κατέσχεν ἕως ἐτῶν εἴκοσι καὶ δύο, μηδὲν καινίσας
τῶν πρὸ αὐτοῦ βασιλέων, εἰ μὴ ὅσα γε πρὸς τὸ
χεῖρον καθ᾽ ὑπερβολὴν πονηρίας ἐπενόησεν, ἅπαντα
δ᾽ αὐτῶν τὰ κακουργήματα καὶ τὴν πρὸς τὸ θεῖον
ὕβριν ἐκμιμησάμενος καὶ μάλιστα τὴν Ἱεροβοάμου
317 ζηλώσας παρανομίαν· καὶ γὰρ οὗτος τὰς δαμάλεις
τὰς ὑπ᾽ ἐκείνου κατασκευασθείσας προσεκύνησε
καὶ τούτοις ἄλλα παράδοξα προσεμηχανήσατο.
ἔγημε δὲ γυναῖκα θυγατέρα μὲν Ἰθωβάλου τοῦ
Τυρίων καὶ Σιδωνίων βασιλέως Ἰεζαβέλην δὲ
ὄνομα, ἀφ᾽ ἧς τοὺς ἰδίους αὐτῆς θεοὺς προσκυνεῖν
318 ἔμαθεν. ἦν δὲ τὸ γύναιον δραστήριόν τε καὶ τολ-
μηρόν, εἰς τοσαύτην δ᾽ ἀσέλγειαν καὶ μανίαν
προύπεσεν, ὥστε καὶ ναὸν τῷ Τυρίων θεῷ ὃν
Βελίαν προσαγορεύουσιν ᾠκοδόμησε καὶ ἄλσος
παντοίων δένδρων κατεφύτευσε· κατέστησε δὲ καὶ
ἱερεῖς καὶ ψευδοπροφήτας τούτῳ τῷ θεῷ· καὶ
αὐτὸς δ᾽ ὁ βασιλεὺς πολλοὺς τοιούτους περὶ αὐτὸν
εἶχεν ἀνοίᾳ καὶ πονηρίᾳ πάντας ὑπερβεβληκὼς
τοὺς πρὸ αὐτοῦ.

319   (2) Προφήτης δέ τις τοῦ μεγίστου θεοῦ ἐκ
πόλεως Θεσβώνης τῆς Γαλαδίτιδος χώρας προσελθὼν Ἀχάβῳ προλέγειν αὐτῷ τὸν θεὸν ἔφασκε
μήθ᾽ ὕσειν αὐτὸν ἐν ἐκείνοις τοῖς ἔτεσι μήτε

δρόσον καταπέμψειν εἰς τὴν χώραν, εἰ μὴ φανέντος
αὐτοῦ. καὶ τούτοις ἐπομόσας ἀνεχώρησεν εἰς τὰ
πρὸς νότον μέρη, ποιούμενος παρὰ χειμάρρῳ τινὶ
τὴν διατριβήν, ἐξ οὗ καὶ τὸ ποτὸν εἶχε· τὴν γὰρ
τροφὴν αὐτῷ καθ' ἡμέραν κόρακες προσέφερον.
320 ἀναξηρανθέντος δὲ τοῦ ποταμοῦ δι' ἀνομβρίαν εἰς
Σαρεφθὰ πόλιν οὐκ ἄπωθεν τῆς Σιδῶνος καὶ
Τύρου (μεταξὺ γὰρ κεῖται) παραγίνεται τοῦ θεοῦ
κελεύσαντος· εὑρήσειν γὰρ ἐκεῖ γυναῖκα χήραν,
321 ἥτις αὐτῷ παρέξει τροφάς. ὢν δ' οὐ πόρρω τῆς
πύλης ὁρᾷ γυναῖκα χερνῆτιν ξυλιζομένην· τοῦ δὲ
θεοῦ δηλώσαντος ταύτην εἶναι τὴν μέλλουσαν αὐτὸν διατρέφειν, προσελθὼν ἠσπάσατο καὶ κομίσαι
ὕδωρ παρεκάλεσεν, ὅπως πίῃ, καὶ πορευομένης
μετακαλεσάμενος καὶ ἄρτον ἐνεγκεῖν ἐκέλευσε.
322 τῆς δ' ὁμοσάσης μηδὲν ἔχειν ἔνδον ἢ μίαν
ἀλεύρου δράκα καὶ ὀλίγον ἔλαιον, πορεύεσθαι δὲ
συνειλοχυῖαν τὰ ξύλα, ἵνα φυράσασα ποιήσῃ αὐτῇ
καὶ τῷ τέκνῳ ἄρτον, μεθ' ὃν ἀπολεῖσθαι λιμῷ
δαπανηθέντα μηκέτι μηδενὸς ὄντος ἔλεγεν, " ἀλλὰ
θαρσοῦσα," εἶπεν, " ἄπιθι καὶ τὰ κρείττω προσδοκῶσα, καὶ ποιήσασα πρῶτον ἐμοὶ βραχὺ κόμισον·
προλέγω γάρ σοι μηδέποτ' ἐπιλείψειν ἀλεύρων
ἐκεῖνο τὸ ἄγγος μηδ' ἐλαίου τὸ κεράμιον, μέχρις
323 οὗ ἂν ὕσῃ ὁ θεός." ταῦτ' εἰπόντος τοῦ προφήτου
παραγενομένη πρὸς αὐτὴν ἐποίησε τὰ εἰρημένα
καὶ αὐτῇ τε ἔσχε καὶ τῷ τέκνῳ χορηγεῖν τὴν
διατροφὴν καὶ τῷ προφήτῃ, ἐπέλιπε δ' οὐδὲν
αὐτοὺς τούτων, ἄχρις οὗ καὶ ὁ αὐχμὸς ἐπαύσατο.
324 μέμνηται δὲ τῆς ἀνομβρίας ταύτης καὶ Μένανδρος
ἐν ταῖς 'Ιθωβάλου τοῦ Τυρίων βασιλέως πράξεσι
λέγων οὕτως· " ἀβροχία τ' ἐπ' αὐτοῦ ἐγένετο ἀπὸ
τοῦ 'Υπερβερεταίου μηνὸς ἕως τοῦ ἐχομένου ἔτους
'Υπερβερεταίου, ἱκετείαν δ' αὐτοῦ ποιησαμένου
κεραυνοὺς ἱκανοὺς βεβληκέναι. οὗτος πόλιν Βότρυν
ἔκτισε τὴν ἐπὶ Φοινίκῃ καὶ Αὖζαν τὴν ἐν Λιβύῃ."
καὶ ταῦτα μὲν δηλῶν τὴν ἐπ' 'Αχάβου γενομένην

ἀνομβρίαν (κατὰ γὰρ τοῦτον καὶ Ἰθώβαλος ἐβα-
σίλευε Τυρίων) ὁ Μένανδρος ἀναγέγραφεν.

325   (3) Ἡ δὲ γυνὴ περὶ ἧς πρὸ τούτων εἴπομεν,
ἡ τὸν προφήτην διατρέφουσα, τοῦ παιδὸς αὐτῇ
καταπεσόντος εἰς νόσον, ὡς καὶ τὴν ψυχὴν ἀφεῖναι
καὶ δόξαι νεκρόν, ἀνακλαιομένη καὶ ταῖς τε χερσὶν
αὐτὴν αἰκιζομένη καὶ φωνὰς οἵας ὑπηγόρευε τὸ
πάθος ἀφιεῖσα κατῃτιᾶτο τῆς παρ᾽ αὐτῇ παρουσίας
τὸν προφήτην ὡς ἐλέγξαντα τὰς ἁμαρτίας αὐ-
326 τῆς καὶ διὰ τοῦτο τοῦ παιδὸς τετελευτηκότος.   ὁ
δὲ παρεκελεύετο θαρρεῖν καὶ παραδοῦναι τὸν υἱὸν
αὐτῷ· ζῶντα γὰρ αὐτὸν ἀποδώσειν. παραδούσης
οὖν βαστάσας εἰς τὸ δωμάτιον, ἐν ᾧ διέτριβεν
αὐτός, καὶ καταθεὶς ἐπὶ τῆς κλίνης ἀνεβόησε πρὸς
τὸν θεὸν οὐ καλῶς ἀμείψεσθαι τὴν ὑποδεξαμένην
καὶ θρέψασαν, τὸν υἱὸν αὐτῆς ἀφαιρησόμενον,
ἐδεῖτό τε τὴν ψυχὴν εἰσπέμψαι πάλιν τῷ παιδὶ
327 καὶ παρασχεῖν αὐτῷ τὸν βίον. τοῦ δὲ θεοῦ κατοικτείραντος μὲν τὴν μητέρα, βουληθέντος δὲ καὶ
τῷ προφήτῃ χαρίσασθαι τὸ μὴ δόξαι πρὸς αὐτὴν ἐπὶ
κακῷ παρεῖναι, παρὰ πᾶσαν προσδοκίαν ἀνεβίωσεν.
ἡ δ᾽ εὐχαρίστει τῷ προφήτῃ καὶ τότε σαφῶς ἔλεγε
μεμαθηκέναι ὅτι τὸ θεῖον αὐτῷ διαλέγεται.

328   (4) Χρόνου δ᾽ ὀλίγου διελθόντος παραγίνεται πρὸς
Ἄχαβον τὸν βασιλέα κατὰ βούλησιν τοῦ θεοῦ,
δηλώσων αὐτῷ τὸν γενησόμενον ὑετόν. λιμὸς δὲ
τότε κατεῖχε τὴν χώραν ἅπασαν καὶ πολλὴ τῶν
ἀναγκαίων ἀπορία, ὡς μὴ μόνον ἀνθρώπους ἄρτων
σπανίζειν, ἀλλὰ καὶ τὴν γῆν μηδ᾽ ὅσα τοῖς ἵπποις
καὶ τοῖς ἄλλοις κτήνεσι πρὸς νομήν ἐστι χρήσιμα
329 διὰ τὴν ἀνομβρίαν ἀναδιδόναι.   τὸν οὖν ἐπιμελόμενον αὐτοῦ τῶν κτημάτων ὁ βασιλεὺς καλέσας
Ὠβεδίαν, ἀπιέναι βούλεσθαι πρὸς αὐτὸν εἶπεν ἐπὶ
τὰς πηγὰς τῶν ὑδάτων καὶ τοὺς χειμάρρους, ἵν᾽ εἴ
που παρ᾽ αὐτοῖς εὑρεθείη πόα ταύτην εἰς τροφὴν
ἀμησάμενοι τοῖς κτήνεσιν ἔχωσι. καὶ περιπέμψαντα κατὰ πᾶσαν τὴν οἰκουμένην τοὺς ζητήσοντας

τὸν προφήτην Ἠλίαν οὐχ εὑρηκέναι· συνέπεσθαι
330 δ' ἐκέλευσε κἀκεῖνον αὐτῷ. δόξαν οὖν ἐξορμᾶν
αὐτοῖς, μερισάμενοι τὰς ὁδοὺς ὅ τε Ὠβεδίας καὶ
ὁ βασιλεὺς ἀπῄεσαν ἕτερος ἑτέραν τῶν ὁδῶν.
συνεβεβήκει δὲ καθ' ὃν Ἰεζαβέλη ἡ βασίλισσα
καιρὸν τοὺς προφήτας ἀπέκτεινε τοῦτον ἑκατὸν
ἐν τοῖς ὑπογείοις σπηλαίοις κρύψαι προφήτας καὶ
τρέφειν αὐτοὺς ἄρτον χορηγοῦντα μόνον καὶ
331 ὕδωρ. μονωθέντι δ' ἀπὸ τοῦ βασιλέως Ὠβεδίᾳ συνήντησεν ὁ προφήτης Ἠλίας· καὶ πυθόμενος παρ'
αὐτοῦ τίς εἴη καὶ μαθὼν προσεκύνησεν αὐτόν· ὁ
δὲ πρὸς τὸν βασιλέα βαδίζειν ἐκέλευσε καὶ λέγειν
332 ὅτι παρείη πρὸς αὐτόν. ὁ δὲ τί κακὸν ὑπ' αὐτοῦ
πεπονθότα πρὸς τὸν ἀποκτεῖναι ζητοῦντα καὶ
πᾶσαν ἐρευνήσαντα γῆν πέμπειν αὐτὸν ἔλεγεν·
ἢ τοῦτ' ἀγνοεῖν αὐτὸν ὅτι μηδένα τόπον κατέλιπεν,
εἰς ὃν οὐκ ἀπέστειλε τοὺς ἀνάξοντας εἰ λάβοιεν
333 ἐπὶ θανάτῳ; καὶ γὰρ εὐλαβεῖσθαι πρὸς αὐτὸν
ἔφασκε, μὴ τοῦ θεοῦ φανέντος αὐτῷ πάλιν εἰς
ἄλλον ἀπέλθῃ τόπον, εἶτα διαμαρτὼν αὐτοῦ,
πέμψαντος τοῦ βασιλέως, μὴ δυνάμενος εὑρεῖν
334 ὅπου ποτ' εἴη γῆς ἀποθάνῃ. προνοεῖν οὖν αὐτοῦ
τῆς σωτηρίας παρεκάλει τὴν περὶ τοὺς ὁμοτέχνους
αὐτοῦ σπουδὴν λέγων, ὅτι σώσειεν ἑκατὸν προφήτας Ἰεζαβέλης πάντας τοὺς ἄλλους ἀνῃρηκυίας,
καὶ ἔχοι κεκρυμμένους αὐτοὺς καὶ τρεφομένους
ὑπ' αὐτοῦ. ὁ δὲ μηδὲν δεδιότα βαδίζειν ἐκέλευε
πρὸς τὸν βασιλέα δοὺς αὐτῷ πίστεις ἐνόρκους ὅτι
πάντως κατ' ἐκείνην Ἀχάβῳ φανήσεται τὴν
ἡμέραν.
335 (5) Μηνύσαντος δὲ τῷ βασιλεῖ Ὠβεδίου τὸν
Ἠλίαν ὑπήντησεν ὁ Ἄχαβος καὶ ἤρετο μετ'
ὀργῆς εἰ αὐτὸς εἴη ὁ τὸν Ἑβραίων λαὸν κακώσας
καὶ τῆς ἀκαρπίας αἴτιος γεγενημένος. ὁ δ' οὐδὲν
ὑποθωπεύσας αὐτὸν εἶπεν ἅπαντα τὰ δεινὰ πεποιηκέναι καὶ τὸ γένος αὐτοῦ, ξενικοὺς ἐπεισενηνοχότας
τῇ χώρᾳ θεοὺς καὶ τούτους σέβοντας, τὸν δ' ἴδιον

αὐτῶν, ὃς μόνος ἐστὶ θεός, ἀπολελοιπότας καὶ
336 μηδεμίαν ἔτι πρόνοιαν αὐτοῦ ποιουμένους. νῦν
μέντοι γε ἀπελθόντα ἐκέλευε πάντα τὸν λαὸν εἰς
τὸ Καρμήλιον ὄρος ἀθροῖσαι πρὸς αὐτὸν καὶ τοὺς
προφήτας αὐτοῦ καὶ τῆς γυναικός, εἰπὼν ὅσοι τὸν
ἀριθμὸν εἴησαν, καὶ τοὺς τῶν ἀλσῶν προφήτας ὡς
337 τετρακοσίους τὸ πλῆθος ὄντας. ὡς δὲ συνέδραμον
πάντες εἰς τὸ προειρημένον ὄρος Ἀχάβου δια-
πέμψαντος, σταθεὶς αὐτῶν ὁ προφήτης Ἠλίας
μεταξύ, μέχρι πότε διῃρημένους αὐτοὺς τῇ διανοίᾳ
καὶ ταῖς δόξαις οὕτως βιώσειν ἔφασκε· νομίσαντας
μὲν γὰρ τὸν ἐγχώριον θεὸν ἀληθῆ καὶ μόνον,
ἕπεσθαι τούτῳ καὶ ταῖς ἐντολαῖς αὐτοῦ παρῄνει,
μηδὲν δὲ τοῦτον ἡγουμένους ἀλλὰ περὶ τῶν ξενικῶν
ὑπειληφότας ὡς ἐκείνους δεῖ θρησκεύειν αὐτοῖς
338 συνεβούλευε κατακολουθεῖν. τοῦ δὲ πλήθους μηδὲν
πρὸς ταῦτ' ἀποκριναμένου ἠξίωσεν Ἠλίας πρὸς
διάπειραν τῆς τε τῶν ξενικῶν θεῶν ἰσχύος καὶ τῆς
τοῦ ἰδίου, μόνος ὢν αὐτοῦ προφήτης ἐκείνων δὲ
τετρακοσίους ἐχόντων, λαβεῖν αὐτός τε βοῦν καὶ
ταύτην θύσας ἐπιθεῖναι ξύλοις πυρὸς οὐχ ὑφαφθέντος, κἀκείνους ταὐτὸ ποιήσαντας ἐπικαλέσασθαι
τοὺς ἰδίους θεοὺς ἀνακαῦσαι τὰ ξύλα· γενομένου
γὰρ τούτου μαθήσεσθαι αὐτοὺς τὴν ἀληθῆ φύσιν
339 τοῦ θεοῦ. ἀρεσάσης δὲ τῆς γνώμης ἐκέλευσεν
Ἠλίας τοὺς προφήτας ἐκλεξαμένους βοῦν πρώτους
τε θῦσαι καὶ τοὺς αὐτῶν ἐπικαλέσασθαι θεούς.
ἐπεὶ δ' οὐδὲν ἀπήντα παρὰ τῆς εὐχῆς καὶ τῆς
ἐπικλήσεως θύσασι τοῖς προφήταις, σκώπτων ὁ
Ἠλίας μεγάλῃ βοῇ καλεῖν αὐτοὺς ἐκέλευε τοὺς
340 θεούς· ἢ γὰρ ἀποδημεῖν αὐτοὺς ἢ καθεύδειν. τῶν
δ' ἀπ' ὄρθρου τοῦτο ποιούντων μέχρι μέσης ἡμέρας
καὶ τεμνόντων αὐτοὺς μαχαίραις καὶ σιρομάσταις
κατὰ τὸ πάτριον ἔθος, μέλλων αὐτὸς ἐπιτελεῖν τὴν
θυσίαν ἐκέλευσε τοὺς μὲν ἀναχωρῆσαι, τοὺς δ'
ἐγγὺς προσελθόντας τηρεῖν αὐτόν, μὴ πῦρ λάθρα
341 τοῖς ξύλοις ἐμβάλῃ. τοῦ δὲ ὄχλου προσελθόντος

λαβὼν δώδεκα λίθους κατὰ φυλὴν τοῦ λαοῦ τῶν
Ἑβραίων ἀνέστησεν ἐξ αὐτῶν θυσιαστήριον καὶ
περὶ αὐτὸ δεξαμενὴν ὤρυξε βαθυτάτην, καὶ συνθεὶς
τὰς σχίζας ἐπὶ τοῦ βωμοῦ καὶ κατ' αὐτῶν ἐπι-
θεὶς τὰ ἱερεῖα, τέσσαρας ἀπὸ τῆς κρήνης· ὑδρίας
προσέταξε πληρωθείσας ὕδατος κατασκεδάσαι τοῦ
θυσιαστηρίου, ὡς ὑπερβαλεῖν αὐτὸ καὶ τὴν δεξαμενὴν ἅπασαν γεμισθῆναι ὕδατος ὡς πηγῆς ἀνα-
342 δοθείσης. ταῦτα δὲ ποιήσας ἤρξατο εὔχεσθαι τῷ
θεῷ καὶ παρακαλεῖν αὐτὸν ποιεῖν τῷ πεπλανημένῳ
πολὺν ἤδη χρόνον λαῷ φανερὰν τὴν αὐτοῦ δύναμιν.
καὶ ταῦτα λέγοντος ἄφνω πῦρ ἐξ οὐρανοῦ, τοῦ
πλήθους ὁρῶντος, ἐπὶ τὸν βωμὸν ἔπεσε καὶ τὴν
θυσίαν ἐδαπάνησεν, ὡς ἀνακαῆναι καὶ τὸ ὕδωρ καὶ
ψαφαρὸν γενέσθαι τὸν τόπον.

343 (6) Οἱ δ' Ἰσραηλῖται τοῦτ' ἰδόντες ἔπεσον ἐπὶ
τὴν γῆν καὶ προσεκύνουν ἕνα θεὸν καὶ μέγιστον
καὶ ἀληθῆ μόνον ἀποκαλοῦντες, τοὺς δ' ἄλλους
ὀνόματα ὑπὸ φαύλης καὶ ἀνοήτου δόξης πεποιη-
μένα· συλλαβόντες δ' αὐτῶν καὶ τοὺς προφήτας
ἀπέκτειναν, Ἠλία τοῦτο παραινέσαντος. ἔφη δὲ
καὶ τῷ βασιλεῖ πορεύεσθαι πρὸς ἄριστον μηδὲν ἔτι
φροντίσαντα· μετ' ὀλίγον γὰρ ὄψεσθαι τὸν θεὸν
344 ὕοντα. καὶ ὁ μὲν Ἄχαβος ἀπηλλάγη, Ἠλίας δ'
ἐπὶ τὸ ἀκρωτήριον τοῦ Καρμηλίου ἀναβὰς ὄρους
καὶ καθίσας ἐπὶ τῆς γῆς προσηρείσατο τοῖς γόνασι
τὴν κεφαλήν, τὸν δὲ θεράποντα ἐκέλευσεν ἀνελθόντα
ἐπί τινα σκοπὴν εἰς τὴν θάλασσαν ἀποβλέπειν,
κἂν ἴδῃ νεφέλην ἐγειρομένην ποθέν, φράζειν αὐτῷ·
μέχρι γὰρ τότε καθαρῷ συνέβαινε τῷ ἀέρι εἶναι.
345 τοῦ δὲ ἀναβάντος καὶ μηδὲν πολλάκις ὁρᾶν φήσαντος, ἕβδομον ἤδη βαδίσας ἑωρακέναι μελαινόμενον
εἶπέ τι τοῦ ἀέρος οὐ πλέον ἴχνους ἀνθρωπίνου. ὁ
δὲ Ἠλίας ταῦτ' ἀκούσας πέμπει πρὸς τὸν Ἄχαβον

κελεύων αὐτὸν εἰς τὴν πόλιν ἀπέρχεσθαι πρὶν ἢ
346 καταρραγῆναι τὸν ὄμβρον. καὶ ὁ μὲν εἰς Ἰεζά-
ρηλαν πόλιν παραγίνεται· μετ' οὐ πολὺ δὲ τοῦ
ἀέρος ἀχλύσαντος καὶ νέφεσι καλυφθέντος πνεῦμά
τε λάβρον ἐπιγίνεται καὶ πολὺς ὄμβρος. ὁ δὲ προφήτης ἔνθεος γενόμενος τῷ τοῦ βασιλέως ἅρματι
μέχρι τῆς Ἰεζαρήλας πόλεως συνέδραμε.
347   (7) Μαθοῦσα δὲ ἡ τοῦ Ἀχάβου γυνὴ Ἰεζαβέλη
τά τε σημεῖα τὰ ὑπὸ Ἠλία γενόμενα καὶ ὅτι τοὺς
προφήτας αὐτῶν ἀπέκτεινεν, ὀργισθεῖσα πέμπει
πρὸς αὐτὸν ἀγγέλους ἀπειλοῦσα δι' αὐτῶν ἀποκτείνειν αὐτόν, ὡς κἀκεῖνος τοὺς προφήτας αὐτῆς
348 ἀπολέσειε. φοβηθεὶς δ' ὁ Ἠλίας φεύγει εἰς πόλιν
Βερσουβεὲ λεγομένην (ἐπ' ἐσχάτης δ' ἐστὶν αὕτη
τῆς χώρας τῶν τῆς Ἰούδα φυλῆς ἐχόντων τὰ κατὰ
τὴν Ἰδουμαίων γῆν) καταλιπὼν δ' ἐκεῖ τὸν θεράποντα εἰς τὴν ἔρημον ἀνεχώρησεν· εὐξάμενος δ'
ἀποθανεῖν, οὐ γὰρ δὴ κρείττων εἶναι τῶν πατέρων,
349 ἵνα ἐκείνων ἀπολωλότων αὐτὸς ζῆν γλίχηται,
κατεκοιμήθη πρός τινι δένδρῳ· διεγείραντος δ'
αὐτόν τινος ἀναστὰς εὑρίσκει παρακειμένην αὐτῷ
τροφὴν καὶ ὕδωρ· φαγὼν δὲ καὶ συλλεξάμενος ἐκ
τῆς τροφῆς ἐκείνης τὴν δύναμιν εἰς τὸ Σιναῖον
καλούμενον ὄρος παραγίνεται, οὗ Μωυσῆς τοὺς
350 νόμους παρὰ τοῦ θεοῦ λέγεται λαβεῖν. εὑρὼν δ'
ἐν αὐτῷ σπήλαιόν τι κοῖλον εἴσεισι καὶ διετέλει
ποιούμενος ἐν αὐτῷ τὴν μονήν. ἐρομένης δέ τινος
αὐτὸν φωνῆς ἐξ ἀδήλου τί παρείη καταλελοιπὼς
τὴν πόλιν ἐκεῖσε, διὰ τὸ κτεῖναι μὲν τοὺς προφήτας τῶν ξενικῶν θεῶν, πεῖσαι δὲ τὸν λαὸν ὅτι
μόνος εἴη θεὸς ὁ ὤν, ὃν ἀπ' ἀρχῆς ἐθρήσκευσαν,
ἔφησε· ζητεῖσθαι γὰρ ἐπὶ τούτῳ πρὸς τιμωρίαν
351 ὑπὸ τῆς γυναικὸς τοῦ βασιλέως. πάλιν δὲ ἀκούσας
προελθεῖν εἰς τὸ ὕπαιθρον τῇ ἐπιούσῃ (γνώσεσθαι
γὰρ οὕτως τί δεῖ ποιεῖν), προῆλθεν ἐκ τοῦ σπηλαίου
μεθ' ἡμέραν καὶ σεισμοῦ τε ἐπακούει καὶ λαμ-
352 πρὰν πυρὸς αὐγὴν ὁρᾷ. καὶ γενομένης ἡσυχίας

φωνὴ θεία μὴ ταράττεσθαι τοῖς γινομένοις αὐτὸν
παρακελεύεται, κρατήσειν γὰρ οὐδένα τῶν ἐχθρῶν
αὐτοῦ, προσέταξέ τε ὑποστρέψαντα εἰς τὴν οἰκείαν
ἀποδεῖξαι τοῦ πλήθους βασιλέα Ἰηοῦν τὸν Νεμεσαίου παῖδα, Δαμασκοῦ δὲ τῶν Σύρων Ἀζάηλον·
ἀντ᾽ αὐτοῦ δὲ προφήτην Ἐλισσαῖον ὑπ᾽ αὐτοῦ
γενήσεσθαι ἐκ πόλεως Ἀβέλας· " διαφθερεῖ δὲ τοῦ
ἀσεβοῦς ὄχλου τοὺς μὲν Ἀζάηλος τοὺς δὲ Ἰηοῦς."
353 ὁ δ᾽ Ἠλίας ὑποστρέφει ταῦτ᾽ ἀκούσας εἰς τὴν
Ἑβραίων χώραν καὶ τὸν Σαφάτου παῖδα Ἐλισσαῖον καταλαβὼν ἀροῦντα καὶ μετ᾽ αὐτοῦ τινας
ἄλλους ἐλαύνοντας ζεύγη δώδεκα προσελθὼν ἐπ-
354 έρριψεν αὐτῷ τὸ ἴδιον ἱμάτιον. ὁ δ᾽ Ἐλισσαῖος
εὐθέως προφητεύειν ἤρξατο καὶ καταλιπὼν τοὺς
βόας ἠκολούθησεν Ἠλίᾳ. δεηθεὶς δὲ συγχωρῆσαι
αὐτῷ τοὺς γονεῖς ἀσπάσασθαι, κελεύοντος τοῦτο
ποιεῖν, ἀποταξάμενος αὐτοῖς εἵπετο καὶ ἦν Ἠλίου
τὸν ἅπαντα χρόνον τοῦ ζῆν καὶ μαθητὴς καὶ
διάκονος. καὶ τὰ μὲν περὶ τοῦ προφήτου τούτου
τοιαῦτα ἦν.
355. (8) Νάβωθος δέ τις ἐξ Ἰεζαρήλου πόλεως
ἀγρογείτων ὢν τοῦ βασιλέως παρακαλοῦντος αὐτὸν
ἀποδόσθαι τιμῆς ὅσης βούλεται τὸν πλησίον αὐτοῦ
τῶν ἰδίων ἀγρόν, ἵνα συνάψας ἓν αὐτὸ ποιήσῃ
κτῆμα, εἰ δὲ μὴ βούλοιτο χρήματα λαβεῖν ἐπι-
τρέποντος ἐκλέξασθαι τῶν ἀγρῶν τινα τῶν ἐκείνου,
τοῦτο μὲν οὔ φησι ποιήσειν, αὐτὸς δὲ τὴν ἰδίαν
καρπώσεσθαι γῆν, ἣν ἐκληρονόμησε τοῦ πατρός.
356 λυπηθεὶς δ᾽ ὡς ἐφ᾽ ὕβρει τῷ μὴ τἀλλότρια λαβεῖν
ὁ βασιλεὺς οὔτε λουτρὸν προσηνέγκατο οὔτε
τροφήν, τῆς δ᾽ Ἰεζαβέλης τῆς γυναικὸς αὐτοῦ
πυνθανομένης ὅ τι λυπεῖται καὶ μήτε λούεται μήτε
ἄριστον αὐτῷ παρατίθεται μήτε δεῖπνον, διηγήσατο
αὐτῇ τὴν Ναβώθου σκαιότητα καὶ ὡς χρησάμενος
ἐπιεικέσι πρὸς αὐτὸν λόγοις καὶ βασιλικῆς ἐξουσίας
357 ὑποδεεστέροις ὑβρισθείη μὴ τυχὼν ὧν ἠξίου. ἡ
δὲ μὴ μικροψυχεῖν ἐπὶ τούτοις παρεκάλει, παυ-

σάμενον δὲ τῆς λύπης ἐπὶ τὴν συνήθη τρέπεσθαι
τοῦ σώματος πρόνοιαν· μελήσειν γὰρ αὐτῇ περὶ
358 τῆς Ναβώθου τιμωρίας. καὶ παραχρῆμα πέμπει
γράμματα πρὸς τοὺς ὑπερέχοντας τῶν Ἰεζαρηλιτῶν ἐκ τοῦ Ἀχάβου ὀνόματος νηστεῦσαί τε
κελεύουσα καὶ ποιησαμένους ἐκκλησίαν προκαθίσαι
μὲν αὐτῶν Νάβωθον (εἶναι γὰρ αὐτὸν γένους ἐπιφανοῦς), παρασκευασαμένους δὲ τρεῖς τολμηρούς
τινας τοὺς καταμαρτυρήσοντας αὐτοῦ, ὡς τὸν θεόν
τε εἴη βλασφημήσας καὶ τὸν βασιλέα, καταλεῦσαι
359 καὶ τούτῳ διαχρήσασθαι τῷ τρόπῳ. καὶ Νάβωθος
μέν, ὡς ἔγραψεν ἡ βασίλισσα, οὕτως καταμαρτυρηθεὶς βλασφημῆσαι τὸν θεόν τε καὶ Ἄχαβον
βαλλόμενος ὑπὸ τοῦ πλήθους ἀπέθανεν, ἀκούσασα
δὲ ταῦτα Ἰεζαβέλη εἴσεισι πρὸς τὸν βασιλέα
καὶ κληρονομεῖν τὸν Ναβώθου ἀμπελῶνα προῖκα
360 ἐκέλευσεν. ὁ δὲ Ἄχαβος ἥσθη τοῖς γεγενημένοις
καὶ ἀναπηδήσας ἀπὸ τῆς κλίνης ὀψόμενος ἧκε τὸν
ἀμπελῶνα τὸν Ναβώθου. ἀγανακτήσας δ᾽ ὁ θεὸς
πέμπει τὸν προφήτην Ἠλίαν εἰς τὸ Ναβώθου
χωρίον Ἀχάβῳ συμβαλοῦντα καὶ περὶ τῶν πεπραγμένων ἐρησόμενον ὅτι κτείνας τὸν ἀληθῆ
δεσπότην τοῦ χωρίου κληρονομήσειεν αὐτὸς ἀδίκως.
361 ὡς δ᾽ ἧκε πρὸς αὐτόν, εἰπόντος τοῦ βασιλέως ὅ τι
βούλεται χρήσασθαι αὐτῷ (αἰσχρὸν γὰρ ὄντα ἐπὶ
ἁμαρτήματι ληφθῆναι ὑπ᾽ αὐτοῦ), κατ᾽ ἐκεῖνον
ἔφη τὸν τόπον ἐν ᾧ τὸν Ναβώθου νεκρὸν ὑπὸ
κυνῶν δαπανηθῆναι συνέβη, τό τε αὐτοῦ καὶ τὸ
τῆς γυναικὸς χυθήσεσθαι αἷμα καὶ πᾶν αὐτοῦ τὸ
γένος ἀπολεῖσθαι, τοιαῦτα ἀσεβῆσαι τετολμηκότος
καὶ παρὰ τοὺς πατρίους νόμους πολίτην ἀδίκως
362 ἀνῃρηκότος. Ἀχάβῳ δὲ λύπη τῶν πεπραγμένων
εἰσῆλθε καὶ μετάμελος, καὶ σακκίον ἐνδυσάμενος
γυμνοῖς τοῖς ποσὶ διῆγεν οὐχ ἁπτόμενος τροφῆς
ἀνθομολογούμενός τε τὰ ἡμαρτημένα καὶ τὸν θεὸν
οὕτως ἐξευμενίζων. ὁ δὲ ζῶντος μὲν αὐτοῦ πρὸς
τὸν προφήτην εἶπεν ὑπερβαλεῖσθαι τὴν τοῦ γένους

τιμωρίαν ἐπεὶ ἐπὶ τοῖς τετολμημένοις μετανοεῖ,
τελέσειν δὲ τὴν ἀπειλὴν ἐπὶ τῷ υἱῷ τοῦ Ἀχάβου.
καὶ ὁ μὲν προφήτης ταῦτ᾽ ἐδήλωσε τῷ βασιλεῖ.

363 (xiv. 1) Τῶν δὲ περὶ τὸν Ἄχαβον ὄντων τοιούτων
κατὰ τὸν αὐτὸν καιρὸν ὁ τοῦ Ἀδάδου υἱὸς βα-
σιλεύων τῶν Σύρων καὶ Δαμασκοῦ δύναμιν ἐξ
ἁπάσης τῆς χώρας συναγαγὼν καὶ συμμάχους
τοὺς πέραν Εὐφράτου βασιλέας ποιησάμενος τριά-
364 κοντα καὶ δύο, ἐστράτευσεν ἐπὶ τὸν Ἄχαβον. ὁ δ᾽
οὐκ ὢν ὅμοιος αὐτῷ τῇ στρατιᾷ πρὸς μάχην μὲν
οὐ παρετάξατο, πάντα δ᾽ εἰς τὰς ὀχυρωτάτας
πόλεις ἐγκλείσας τὰ ἐν τῇ χώρᾳ αὐτὸς μὲν ἔμεινεν
ἐν Σαμαρείᾳ· τείχη γὰρ αὐτῇ λίαν ἰσχυρὰ περιεβέβλητο καὶ τὰ ἄλλα δυσάλωτος ἐδόκει· ὁ δὲ Σύρος
ἀναλαβὼν τὴν δύναμιν ἧκεν ἐπὶ τὴν Σαμάρειαν
καὶ περικαθίσας αὐτῇ τὸν στρατὸν ἐπολιόρκει.
365 πέμψας δὲ κήρυκα πρὸς Ἄχαβον ἠξίου πρεσβευτὰς
δέξασθαι παρ᾽ αὐτοῦ, δι᾽ ὧν αὐτῷ δηλώσει τί
βούλεται. τοῦ δὲ τῶν Ἰσραηλιτῶν βασιλέως
πέμπειν ἐπιτρέψαντος ἐλθόντες οἱ πρέσβεις ἔλεγον
κατ᾽ ἐντολὴν τοῦ βασιλέως τὸν Ἀχάβου πλοῦτον
καὶ τὰ τέκνα αὐτοῦ καὶ τὰς γυναῖκας Ἀδάδου
τυγχάνειν· ἂν δ᾽ ὁμολογήσῃ καὶ λαβεῖν αὐτὸν τούτων ὅσα βούλεται συγχωρήσῃ, τὴν στρατιὰν ἀπάξει
366 καὶ παύσεται πολιορκῶν αὐτόν. ὁ δ᾽ Ἄχαβος τοῖς
πρέσβεσιν ἐκέλευσε πορευθεῖσι λέγειν τῷ βασιλεῖ
αὐτῶν ὅτι καὶ αὐτὸς καὶ οἱ ἐκείνου πάντες κτήματά
367 εἰσιν αὐτοῦ. ταῦτα δ᾽ ἀπαγγειλάντων πέμπει
πάλιν πρὸς αὐτὸν ἀξιῶν ἀνωμολογηκότα πάντα
εἶναι ἐκείνου δέξασθαι τοὺς πεμφθησομένους εἰς
τὴν ἐπιοῦσαν ὑπ᾽ αὐτοῦ δούλους, οἷς ἐρευνήσασι
τά τε βασίλεια καὶ τοὺς τῶν φίλων καὶ συγγενῶν
οἴκους ἐκέλευε διδόναι πᾶν ὅ τι ἂν ἐν αὐτοῖς εὕρωσι
κάλλιστον, "τὰ δ᾽ ἀπαρέσαντα σοὶ καταλείψου-
368 σιν." Ἄχαβος δ᾽ ἀγασθεὶς ἐπὶ τῇ δευτέρᾳ πρεσ-
βείᾳ τοῦ τῶν Σύρων βασιλέως, συναγαγὼν εἰς
ἐκκλησίαν τὸ πλῆθος ἔλεγεν ὡς αὐτὸς μὲν ἑτοίμως

εἶχεν ὑπὲρ σωτηρίας αὐτοῦ καὶ εἰρήνης καὶ γυναῖκας τὰς ἰδίας προέσθαι τῷ πολεμίῳ καὶ τὰ
τέκνα καὶ πάσης παραχωρῆσαι κτήσεως· ταῦτα
γὰρ ἐπιζητῶν ἐπρεσβεύσατο πρῶτον ὁ Σύρος.
369 '' νῦν δ' ἠξίωκε δούλους πέμψαι τάς τε πάντων
οἰκίας ἐρευνῆσαι καὶ μηδὲν ἐν αὐταῖς καταλιπεῖν
τῶν καλλίστων κτημάτων, πρόφασιν βουλόμενος
πολέμου λαβεῖν, εἰδὼς ὅτι τῶν μὲν ἐμαυτοῦ δι'
ὑμᾶς οὐκ ἂν φεισαίμην, ἀφορμὴν δ' ἐκ τοῦ περὶ
τῶν ὑμετέρων ἀηδοῦς πραγματευόμενος εἰς τὸ
370 πολεμεῖν· ποιήσω γε μὴν τὰ ὑμῖν δοκοῦντα.'' τὸ
δὲ πλῆθος μὴ δεῖν ἀκούειν τῶν κατ' αὐτὸν ἔλεγεν,
ἀλλὰ καταφρονεῖν καὶ πρὸς τὸ πολεμεῖν ἑτοίμως
ἔχειν. τοῖς οὖν πρεσβευταῖς ἀποκρινάμενος λέγειν
ἀπελθοῦσιν ὅτι τοῖς τὸ πρῶτον ἀξιωθεῖσιν ὑπ'
αὐτοῦ καὶ νῦν ἐμμένει τῆς τῶν πολιτῶν ἀσφαλείας
ἕνεκα πρὸς δὲ τὴν δευτέραν ἀξίωσιν οὐχ ὑπακούει,
ἀπέλυσεν αὐτούς.
371 (2) Ὁ δ' Ἄδαδος ἀκούσας ταῦτα καὶ δυσχεράνας
τρίτον ἔπεμψε πρὸς Ἄχαβον τοὺς πρέσβεις ἀπειλῶν
ὑψηλότερον τῶν τειχῶν οἷς καταφρονεῖ χῶμα τούτοις ἐπεγείρειν αὐτοῦ τὴν στρατιὰν κατὰ δράκα γῆς
λαμβάνουσαν, ἐμφανίζων αὐτῷ τῆς δυνάμεως τὸ
372 πλῆθος καὶ καταπληττόμενος. τοῦ δ' Ἀχάβου
μὴ καυχᾶσθαι δεῖν ἀποκριναμένου καθωπλισμένον
ἀλλὰ τῇ μάχῃ κρείττω γενόμενον, ἐλθόντες οἱ
πρέσβεις καὶ δειπνοῦντα καταλαβόντες τὸν βασιλέα
μετὰ τριάκοντα καὶ δύο βασιλέων συμμάχων
ἐδήλωσαν αὐτῷ τὴν ἀπόκρισιν· ὁ δ' εὐθέως τοῦτο
προσέταξε καὶ περιχαρακοῦν τὴν πόλιν καὶ χώματα
βάλλεσθαι καὶ μηδένα τρόπον ἀπολιπεῖν πολιορκίας.
373 ἦν δ' Ἄχαβος τούτων πραττομένων ἐν ἀγωνίᾳ δεινῇ
σὺν παντὶ τῷ λαῷ· θαρρεῖ δὲ καὶ τῶν φόβων ἀπολύεται προφήτου τινὸς αὐτῷ προσελθόντος καὶ
φήσαντος αὐτῷ τὸν θεὸν ὑπισχνεῖσθαι ποιήσειν τὰς
τοσαύτας τῶν πολεμίων μυριάδας ὑποχειρίους.
374 πυθομένῳ δὲ διὰ τίνων ἂν ἡ νίκη γένοιτο, '' διὰ

τῶν παίδων," εἶπε, " τῶν ἡγεμόνων, ἡγουμένου
σου διὰ τὴν ἀπειρίαν ἐκείνων." καλέσας δὲ τοὺς
τῶν ἡγεμόνων υἱούς, εὑρέθησαν δ' ὡς διακόσιοι
καὶ τριακονταδύο, μαθὼν τὸν Σύρον πρὸς εὐωχίαν
καὶ ἄνεσιν τετραμμένον, ἀνοίξας τὰς πύλας ἐξ-
375 έπεμψε τοὺς παῖδας. τῶν δὲ σκοπῶν δηλωσάντων
τοῦτο τῷ Ἀδάδῳ πέμπει τινὰς ὑπαντησομένους,
ἐντειλάμενος, ἂν μὲν εἰς μάχην ὦσι προεληλυθότες,
ἵνα δήσαντες ἀγάγωσι πρὸς αὐτόν, ἂν δ' εἰρηνικῶς,
376 ὅπως ταὐτὸ ποιῶσιν. εἶχε δ' ἑτοίμην Ἄχαβος
καὶ τὴν ἄλλην στρατιὰν ἐντὸς τῶν τειχῶν. οἱ δὲ
τῶν ἀρχόντων παῖδες συμβαλόντες τοῖς φύλαξι
πολλοὺς αὐτῶν ἀποκτείνουσι καὶ τοὺς ἄλλους ἄχρι
τοῦ στρατοπέδου διώκουσιν. ἰδὼν δὲ τούτους
νικῶντας ὁ τῶν Ἰσραηλιτῶν βασιλεὺς ἐξαφίησι
377 καὶ τὴν ἄλλην στρατιὰν ἅπασαν. ἡ δ' αἰφνιδίως
ἐπιπεσοῦσα τοῖς Σύροις ἐκράτησεν αὐτῶν, οὐ γὰρ
προσεδόκων αὐτοὺς ἐπεξελεύσεσθαι, καὶ διὰ τοῦτο
γυμνοῖς καὶ μεθύουσι προσέβαλλον, ὥστε τὰς
πανοπλίας ἐκ τῶν στρατοπέδων φεύγοντας καταλιπεῖν καὶ τὸν βασιλέα διασωθῆναι μόλις ἐφ'
378 ἵππου ποιησάμενον τὴν φυγήν. Ἄχαβος δὲ πολλὴν ὁδὸν διώκων τοὺς Σύρους ἤνυσεν ἀναιρῶν
αὐτούς, διαρπάσας δὲ τὰ ἐν τῇ παρεμβολῇ (πλοῦτος
δ' ἦν οὐκ ὀλίγος, ἀλλὰ καὶ χρυσοῦ πλῆθος καὶ
ἀργύρου), τά τε ἅρματα τοῦ Ἀδάδου καὶ τοὺς
ἵππους λαβὼν ἀνέστρεψεν εἰς τὴν πόλιν. τοῦ δὲ
προφήτου παρασκευάζεσθαι φήσαντος καὶ τὴν δύναμιν ἑτοίμην ἔχειν, ὡς τῷ ἐπιόντι πάλιν ἔτει
στρατεύσοντος ἐπ' αὐτὸν τοῦ Σύρου, ὁ μὲν Ἄχαβος
πρὸς τούτοις ἦν.

379   (3) Ὁ δὲ Ἄδαδος διασωθεὶς ἐκ τῆς μάχης μεθ'
ὅσης ἠδυνήθη στρατιᾶς συνεβουλεύσατο τοῖς αὑτοῦ
φίλοις, πῶς ἐπιστρατεύσηται τοῖς Ἰσραηλίταις.
οἱ δ' ἐν μὲν τοῖς ὄρεσιν οὐκ ἐδίδοσαν γνώμην συμβαλεῖν αὐτοῖς· τὸν γὰρ θεὸν αὐτῶν ἐν τοῖς τοιούτοις
δύνασθαι τόποις καὶ διὰ τοῦτο νῦν ὑπ' αὐτῶν νε-

νικῆσθαι· κρατήσειν δὲ ἔλεγον ἐν πεδίῳ ποιησα-
380 μένους τὴν μάχην. συνεβούλευον δὲ πρὸς τούτῳ
τοὺς μὲν βασιλέας οὓς ἐπηγάγετο συμμάχους ἀπολῦσαι πρὸς τὰ οἰκεῖα, τὴν δὲ στρατιὰν αὐτῶν
κατασχεῖν, ἀντ᾽ ἐκείνων σατράπας καταστήσαντα·
εἰς δὲ τὴν τῶν ἀπολωλότων τάξιν στρατολογῆσαι
δύναμιν ἐκ τῆς χώρας τῆς αὐτῶν καὶ ἵππους καὶ
ἅρματα. δοκιμάσας οὖν ταῦτα εἰρῆσθαι καλῶς
οὕτως διεκόσμησε τὴν δύναμιν.

381   (4) Ἀρξαμένου δὲ ἔαρος ἀναλαβὼν τὴν στρατιὰν
ἦγεν ἐπὶ τοὺς Ἑβραίους, καὶ γενόμενος πρὸς πόλει
τινί, Ἀφεκὰ δ᾽ αὐτὴν καλοῦσιν, ἐν μεγάλῳ στρατοπεδεύεται πεδίῳ. Ἄχαβος δ᾽ ἀπαντήσας αὐτῷ
μετὰ τῆς δυνάμεως ἀντεστρατοπεδεύσατο· σφόδρα
δ᾽ ἦν ὀλίγον αὐτοῦ τὸ στράτευμα πρὸς τοὺς πο-
382 λεμίους ἀντιπαραβαλλόμενον. τοῦ δὲ προφήτου
προσελθόντος αὐτῷ πάλιν καὶ νίκην τὸν θεὸν αὐτῷ
διδόναι φήσαντος, ἵνα τὴν ἰδίαν ἰσχὺν ἐπιδείξηται
μὴ μόνον ἐν τοῖς ὄρεσιν ἀλλὰ κἂν τοῖς πεδίοις
ὑπάρχουσαν, ὅπερ οὐκ εἶναι δοκεῖ τοῖς Σύροις,
ἑπτὰ μὲν ἡμέρας ἀντεστρατοπεδευκότες ἡσύχαζον,
τῇ δὲ ὑστάτῃ τούτων ὑπὸ τὸν ὄρθρον προελθόντων
ἐκ τοῦ στρατοπέδου τῶν πολεμίων καὶ παραταξαμένων εἰς μάχην ἀντεπεξῆγε καὶ Ἄχαβος τὴν
383 οἰκείαν δύναμιν. καὶ συμβαλὼν καρτερᾶς τῆς
μάχης γενομένης τρέπεται τοὺς πολεμίους εἰς
φυγὴν καὶ διώκων ἐπέκειτο. οἱ δὲ καὶ ὑπὸ τῶν
ἁρμάτων καὶ ὑπ᾽ ἀλλήλων ἀπώλοντο, ἴσχυσαν δ᾽
ὀλίγοι διαφυγεῖν εἰς τὴν Ἀφεκὰ πόλιν αὐτῶν.
384 ἀπέθανον δὲ καὶ αὐτοὶ τῶν τειχῶν αὐτοῖς ἐπιπεσόντων ὄντες δισμύριοι ἑπτακισχίλιοι. διεφθάρησαν δ᾽ ἐν ἐκείνῃ τῇ μάχῃ ἄλλαι μυριάδες δέκα.
ὁ δὲ βασιλεὺς τῶν Σύρων Ἄδαδος φεύγων μετά
τινων πιστοτάτων οἰκετῶν εἰς ὑπόγειον οἶκον
385 ἐκρύβη. τούτων δὲ φιλανθρώπους καὶ ἐλεήμονας
εἶναι φησάντων τοὺς τῶν Ἰσραηλιτῶν βασιλέας
καὶ δυνήσεσθαι τῷ συνήθει τρόπῳ τῆς ἱκετείας

χρησαμένους τὴν σωτηρίαν αὐτῷ παρ' Ἀχάβου
λαβεῖν, εἰ συγχωρήσειεν αὐτοῖς πρὸς αὐτὸν ἀπ-
ελθεῖν, ἀφῆκεν· οἱ δὲ σάκκους ἐνδυσάμενοι καὶ
σχοινία ταῖς κεφαλαῖς περιθέμενοι (οὕτως γὰρ τὸ
παλαιὸν ἱκέτευον οἱ Σύροι), πρὸς Ἄχαβον παρεγένοντο καὶ δεῖσθαι τὸν Ἄδαδον σῴζειν αὐτὸν
ἔλεγον, εἰς ἀεὶ δοῦλον αὐτοῦ τῆς χάριτος γενησό-
386 μενον. ὁ δὲ συνήδεσθαι φήσας αὐτῷ περιόντι καὶ
μηδὲν ἐν τῇ μάχῃ πεπονθότι, τιμὴν καὶ εὔνοιαν
ἣν ἄν τις ἀδελφῷ παράσχοι κατεπηγγείλατο.
λαβόντες δὲ ὅρκους παρ' αὐτοῦ μηδὲν ἀδικήσειν
φανέντα προάγουσι πορευθέντες ἐκ τοῦ οἴκου ἐν
ᾧ ἐκέκρυπτο καὶ προσάγουσι τῷ Ἀχάβῳ ἐφ'
ἅρματος καθεζομένῳ· ὁ δὲ προσεκύνησεν αὐτόν.
387 Ἄχαβος δὲ διδοὺς αὐτῷ τὴν δεξιὰν ἀναβιβάζει
ἐπὶ τὸ ἅρμα καὶ καταφιλήσας θαρρεῖν ἐκέλευε καὶ
μηδὲν τῶν ἀτόπων προσδοκᾶν, Ἄδαδος δ' εὐχαρίστει καὶ παρ' ὅλον τὸν τοῦ ζῆν χρόνον ἀπομνημονεύσειν τῆς εὐεργεσίας ὡμολόγει καὶ τὰς πόλεις
τῶν Ἰσραηλιτῶν, ἃς ἀπήνεγκαν οἱ πρὸ αὐτοῦ
βασιλεῖς, ἀποδώσειν ἐπηγγείλατο καὶ Δαμασκὸν
ὥστε ἐξελαύνειν εἰς αὐτήν, καθὼς καὶ οἱ πατέρες
αὐτοῦ εἰς Σαμάρειαν εἶχον τοῦτο ποιεῖν, ἀνήσειν.
388 γενομένων δ' αὐτοῖς ὅρκων καὶ συνθηκῶν πολλὰ
δωρησάμενος αὐτῷ Ἄχαβος ἀπέπεμψεν εἰς τὴν
ἰδίαν βασιλείαν. καὶ τὰ μὲν περὶ τῆς Ἀδάδου τοῦ
Σύρων βασιλέως στρατείας ἐπὶ Ἄχαβον καὶ τοὺς
Ἰσραηλίτας τοιοῦτον ἔσχε τὸ τέλος.

389 (5) Προφήτης δέ τις τοὔνομα Μιχαίας προσελθών τινι τῶν Ἰσραηλιτῶν ἐκέλευεν αὐτὸν εἰς τὴν
κεφαλὴν πλῆξαι· τοῦτο γὰρ ποιήσειν κατὰ βούλησιν τοῦ θεοῦ. τοῦ δὲ μὴ πεισθέντος προεῖπεν
αὐτῷ παρακούσαντι τῶν τοῦ θεοῦ προσταγμάτων
λέοντι περιτυχόντα διαφθαρήσεσθαι. συμβάντος
τούτου τἀνθρώπῳ, πρόσεισιν ἑτέρῳ πάλιν ὁ προ-

390 φήτης ταὐτὸ προστάσσων. πλήξαντος δ' ἐκείνου
καὶ θραύσαντος αὐτοῦ τὸ κρανίον, καταδησάμενος
τὴν κεφαλὴν προσῆλθε τῷ βασιλεῖ λέγων αὐτῷ
συνεστρατεῦσθαι καὶ παραλαβεῖν ἐπὶ φυλακῇ τινα
τῶν αἰχμαλώτων παρὰ τοῦ ταξιάρχου, φυγόντος
δ' αὐτοῦ κινδυνεύειν ὑπὸ τοῦ παραδεδωκότος
ἀποθανεῖν· ἀπειλῆσαι γὰρ αὐτόν, εἰ διαφύγοι ὁ
391 αἰχμάλωτος, ἀποκτείνειν. δίκαιον δὲ φήσαντος
'Αχάβου τὸν θάνατον εἶναι, λύσας τὴν κεφαλὴν
ἐπιγινώσκεται ὑπ' αὐτοῦ Μιχαίας ὁ προφήτης ὤν.
ἐκέχρητο δὲ σοφίσματι πρὸς αὐτὸν τῷ γενομένῳ
392 πρὸς τοὺς μέλλοντας λόγους· εἶπε γὰρ ὡς ὁ θεὸς
ἀφέντ' αὐτὸν διαδρᾶναι τὴν τιμωρίαν "Αδαδον τὸν
βλασφημήσαντα εἰς αὐτὸν μετελεύσεται καὶ ποιήσει
αὐτὸν μὲν ἀποθανεῖν ὑπ' ἐκείνου, τὸν δὲ λαὸν ὑπὸ
τῆς στρατιᾶς αὐτοῦ. παροξυνθεὶς δ' "Αχαβος πρὸς
τὸν προφήτην τὸν μὲν ἐγκλεισθέντα φυλάττεσθαι
ἐκέλευσε, συγκεχυμένος δ' αὐτὸς ἐπὶ τοῖς Μιχαίου
λόγοις ἀνεχώρησεν εἰς τὴν οἰκίαν.
393   (xv. 1) Καὶ "Αχαβος μὲν ἐν τούτοις ἦν· ἐπάνειμι
δὲ ἐπὶ τὸν Ἱεροσολύμων βασιλέα Ἰωσάφατον, ὃς
αὐξήσας τὴν βασιλείαν καὶ δυνάμεις ἐν ταῖς πόλεσι
ταῖς ἐν τῇ τῶν ὑπηκόων χώρᾳ καταστήσας οὐδὲν
ἧττον ταῖς ὑπὸ 'Αβία τοῦ πάππου καταληφθείσαις
τῆς 'Εφραΐμου κληρουχίας Ἱεροβοάμου βασι-
394 λεύοντος τῶν δέκα φυλῶν, φρουρὰς ἐγκαθίδρυσεν
ἀλλ' εἶχεν εὐμενές τε καὶ συνεργὸν τὸ θεῖον, δίκαιος
ὢν καὶ εὐσεβὴς καὶ τί καθ' ἑκάστην ἡμέραν ἡδὺ
ποιήσει καὶ προσηνὲς τῷ θεῷ ζητῶν. ἐτίμων δ'
αὐτὸν οἱ πέριξ βασιλικαῖς δωρεαῖς, ὡς πλοῦτόν
τε ποιῆσαι βαθύτατον καὶ δόξαν ἄρασθαι μεγίστην.
395   (2) Τρίτῳ δ' ἔτει τῆς βασιλείας συγκαλέσας τοὺς
ἡγεμόνας τῆς χώρας καὶ τοὺς ἱερεῖς ἐκέλευε τὴν
γῆν περιελθόντας ἅπαντα τὸν λαὸν τὸν ἐπ' αὐτῆς

διδάξαι κατὰ πόλιν τοὺς Μωυσέος νόμους καὶ
φυλάσσειν τούτους καὶ σπουδάζειν περὶ τὴν θρησκείαν τοῦ θεοῦ. καὶ ἤσθη πᾶν τὸ πλῆθος οὕτως,
ὡς μηδὲν ἄλλο φιλοτιμεῖσθαι μηδὲ ἀγαπᾶν ὡς τὸ
396 τηρεῖν τὰ νόμιμα. οἵ τε προσχώριοι διετέλουν
στέργοντες τὸν Ἰωσάφατον καὶ πρὸς αὐτὸν εἰρήνην
ἄγοντες· οἱ δὲ Παλαιστῖνοι τακτοὺς ἐτέλουν αὐτῷ
φόρους καὶ Ἄραβες ἐχορήγουν κατ' ἔτος ἄρνας
ἑξήκοντα καὶ τριακοσίους καὶ ἐρίφους τοσούτους.
πόλεις τε ὠχύρωσε μεγάλας ἄλλας τε καὶ βάρεις·
καὶ δύναμιν στρατιωτικὴν καὶ ὅπλα πρὸς τοὺς
397 πολεμίους ηὐτρέπιστο. ἦν δὲ ἐκ μὲν τῆς Ἰούδα
φυλῆς στρατὸς ὁπλιτῶν μυριάδες τριάκοντα, ὧν
Ἐδναῖος τὴν ἡγεμονίαν εἶχεν, Ἰωάννης δὲ μυριάδων
εἴκοσι. ὁ δ' αὐτὸς οὗτος ἡγεμὼν κἀκ τῆς Βενιαμίτιδος φυλῆς εἶχε τοξοτῶν πεζῶν μυριάδας εἴκοσι,
ἄλλος δ' ἡγεμὼν Ὀχόβατος ὄνομα μυριάδας ὁπλιτῶν ὀκτωκαίδεκα τὸ πλῆθος τῷ βασιλεῖ προσένειμε
πάρεξ ὧν εἰς τὰς ὀχυρωτάτας διέπεμψε πόλεις.
398 (3) Ἠγάγετο δὲ τῷ παιδὶ Ἰωράμῳ τὴν Ἀχάβου
θυγατέρα τοῦ τῶν δέκα φυλῶν βασιλέως Ὀθλίαν
ὄνομα. πορευθέντα δ' αὐτὸν μετὰ χρόνον τινὰ εἰς
Σαμάρειαν φιλοφρόνως Ἄχαβος ὑπεδέξατο καὶ τὸν
ἀκολουθήσαντα στρατὸν ἐξένισε λαμπρῶς σίτου τε
καὶ οἴνου καὶ θυμάτων ἀφθονίᾳ, παρεκάλεσέ τε
συμμαχῆσαι κατὰ τοῦ Σύρων βασιλέως, ἵνα τὴν ἐν
399 τῇ Γαλαδηνῇ πόλιν Ἀραμαθὰν ἀφέληται· τοῦ γὰρ
πατρὸς αὐτὴν τοῦ αὐτοῦ πρῶτον τυγχάνουσαν
ἀφῃρῆσθαι τὸν ἐκείνου πατέρα. τοῦ δὲ Ἰωσαφάτου
τὴν βοήθειαν ἐπαγγειλαμένου (καὶ γὰρ εἶναι δύναμιν
αὐτῷ μὴ ἐλάττω τῆς ἐκείνου) καὶ μεταπεμψαμένου
τὴν δύναμιν ἐξ Ἱεροσολύμων εἰς Σαμάρειαν, προ-
εξελθόντες ἔξω τῆς πόλεως οἱ δύο βασιλεῖς καὶ
καθίσαντες ἐπὶ τοῦ ἰδίου θρόνου ἑκάτερος τοῖς
οἰκείοις στρατιώταις τὸ στρατιωτικὸν διένεμον.
400 Ἰωσάφατος δ' ἐκέλευσεν εἴ τινές εἰσι προφῆται
καλέσαντ' αὐτοὺς ἀνακρῖναι περὶ τῆς ἐπὶ τὸν Σύρον

ἐξόδου, εἰ συμβουλεύουσι κατ᾽ ἐκεῖνον τὸν καιρὸν
αὐτῷ ποιήσασθαι τὴν στρατείαν· καὶ γὰρ εἰρήνη τε
καὶ φιλία τότε τῷ Ἀχάβῳ πρὸς τὸν Σύρον ὑπῆρχεν
ἐπὶ τρία ἔτη διαμείνασα, ἀφ᾽ οὗ λαβὼν αὐτὸν αἰχ-
μάλωτον ἀπέλυσεν ἄχρις ἐκείνης τῆς ἡμέρας.

401   (4) Καλέσας δὲ Ἄχαβος τοὺς αὐτοῦ προφήτας
ὡσεὶ τετρακοσίους τὸν ἀριθμὸν ὄντας ἐκέλευσεν
ἔρεσθαι τὸν θεόν, εἰ δίδωσιν αὐτῷ στρατευσαμένῳ
ἐπὶ Ἄδαδον νίκην καὶ καθαίρεσιν τῆς πόλεως, δι᾽
402 ἣν ἐκφέρειν μέλλει τὸν πόλεμον.   τῶν δὲ προφητῶν συμβουλευσάντων ἐκστρατεῦσαι, κρατήσειν
γὰρ τοῦ Σύρου καὶ λήψεσθαι ὑποχείριον αὐτὸν ὡς
καὶ τὸ πρῶτον, συνεὶς ἐκ τῶν λόγων Ἰωσάφατος
ὅτι ψευδοπροφῆται τυγχάνουσιν, ἐπύθετο τοῦ
Ἀχάβου εἰ καὶ ἕτερός τίς ἐστι προφήτης τοῦ θεοῦ,
" ἵνα ἀκριβέστερον μάθωμεν περὶ τῶν μελλόντων."
403 ὁ δ᾽ Ἄχαβος εἶναι μὲν ἔφη, μισεῖν δ᾽ αὐτὸν κακὰ
προφητεύσαντα καὶ προειπόντα ὅτι τεθνήξεται
νικηθεὶς ὑπὸ τοῦ Σύρων βασιλέως καὶ διὰ ταῦτα
ἐν φυλακῇ νῦν αὐτὸν ἔχειν· καλεῖσθαι δὲ Μιχαίαν,
υἱὸν δ᾽ εἶναι Ἰεμβλαίου · τοῦ δ᾽ Ἰωσαφάτου κελεύσαντος αὐτὸν προαχθῆναι, πέμψας εὐνοῦχον ἄγει
404 τὸν Μιχαίαν.   κατὰ δὲ τὴν ὁδὸν ἐδήλωσεν αὐτῷ
ὁ εὐνοῦχος πάντας τοὺς ἄλλους προφήτας νίκην τῷ
βασιλεῖ προειρηκέναι.   ὁ δὲ οὐκ ἐξὸν αὐτῷ καταψεύσασθαι τοῦ θεοῦ φήσας, ἀλλ᾽ ἐρεῖν ὅ τι ἂν αὐτῷ
περὶ τοῦ βασιλέως αὐτὸς εἴπῃ, ὡς ἧκε πρὸς τὸν
Ἄχαβον καὶ λέγειν αὐτῷ τἀληθὲς οὗτος ἐνωρκίσατο,
δεῖξαι τὸν θεὸν αὐτῷ φεύγοντας τοὺς Ἰσραηλίτας
ἔφη καὶ διωκομένους ὑπὸ τῶν Σύρων καὶ διασκορπιζομένους ὑπ᾽ αὐτῶν εἰς τὰ ὄρη, καθάπερ ποιμένων
405 ἠρημωμένα ποίμνια.   ἔλεγέ τε σημαίνειν τοὺς μὲν
μετ᾽ εἰρήνης ἀναστρέψειν εἰς τὰ ἴδια, πεσεῖσθαι
δ᾽ αὐτὸν μόνον ἐν τῇ μάχῃ.   ταῦτα φήσαντος τοῦ
Μιχαία, πρὸς Ἰωσάφατον ὁ Ἄχαβος " ἀλλ᾽ ἔγωγε

μικρὸν ἔμπροσθεν ἐδήλωσά σοι τὴν τἀνθρώπου,"
φησί, "πρός με διάθεσιν, καὶ ὅτι μοι τὰ χείρω
406 προεφήτευσε." τοῦ δὲ Μιχαία εἰπόντος ὡς προσῆκεν αὐτῷ πάντων ἀκροᾶσθαι τῶν ὑπὸ τοῦ θεοῦ
προλεγομένων, καὶ ὡς παρορμήσειαν αὐτὸν οἱ
ψευδοπροφῆται ποιήσασθαι τὸν πόλεμον ἐλπίδι
νίκης, καὶ ὅτι δεῖ πεσεῖν αὐτὸν μαχόμενον, αὐτὸς
μὲν ἦν ἐπ' ἐννοίᾳ, Σεδεκίας δέ τις τῶν ψευδοπροφητῶν προσελθών, τῷ μὲν Μιχαίᾳ μὴ προσέχειν
407 παρῄνει· λέγειν γὰρ αὐτὸν οὐδὲν ἀληθές· τεκμηρίῳ
δ' ἐχρήσατο οἷς Ἠλίας προεφήτευσεν ὁ τούτου
κρείττων τὰ μέλλοντα συνιδεῖν· καὶ γὰρ τοῦτον
ἔλεγε προφητεύσαντα ἐν Ἰεζαρήλα πόλει ἐν τῷ
Ναβώθου ἀγρῷ τὸ αἷμα αὐτοῦ κύνας ἀναλιχμήσεσθαι προειπεῖν, καθὼς καὶ Ναβώθου τοῦ δι'
408 αὐτὸν καταλευσθέντος ὑπὸ τοῦ ὄχλου. "δῆλον
οὖν ὅτι οὗτος ψεύδεται, τῷ κρείττονι προφήτῃ
τἀναντία λέγων, ἀπὸ ἡμερῶν τριῶν φάσκων τεθνήξεσθαι. γνώσεσθε δ' εἴπερ ἐστὶν ἀληθὴς καὶ
τοῦ θείου πνεύματος ἔχει τὴν δύναμιν· εὐθὺς γὰρ
ῥαπισθεὶς ὑπ' ἐμοῦ βλαψάτω μου τὴν χεῖρα, ὥσπερ
Ἰάδαος τὴν Ἱεροβοάμου τοῦ βασιλέως συλλαβεῖν
θελήσαντος ἀπεξήρανε δεξιάν· ἀκήκοας γὰρ οἶμαι
409 πάντως τοῦτο γενόμενον." ὡς οὖν πλήξαντος αὐτοῦ τὸν Μιχαίαν μηδὲν συνέβη παθεῖν, Ἄχαβος
θαρρήσας ἄγειν τὴν στρατιὰν πρόθυμος ἦν ἐπὶ τὸν
Σύρον· ἐνίκα γὰρ οἶμαι τὸ χρεὼν καὶ πιθανωτέρους
ἐποίει τοῦ ἀληθοῦς τοὺς ψευδοπροφήτας, ἵνα λάβῃ
τὴν ἀφορμὴν τοῦ τέλους. Σεδεκίας δὲ σιδήρεα
ποιήσας κέρατα λέγει πρὸς Ἄχαβον ὡς θεὸν αὐτῷ
σημαίνειν τούτοις ἅπασαν καταστρέψεσθαι τὴν
410 Συρίαν. Μιχαίαν δὲ μετ' οὐ πολλὰς ἡμέρας
εἰπόντα τὸν Σεδεκίαν ταμιεῖον ἐκ ταμιείου κρυβόμενον ἀμείψειν ζητοῦντα φυγεῖν τῆς ψευδολογίας
τὴν δίκην, ἐκέλευσεν ὁ βασιλεὺς ἀπαχθέντα φυλάττεσθαι πρὸς Ἀχάμωνα τὸν τῆς πόλεως ἄρχοντα

καὶ χορηγεῖσθαι μηδὲν ἄρτου καὶ ὕδατος αὐτῷ
περισσότερον.

411 (5) Καὶ Ἄχαβος μὲν καὶ Ἰωσάφατος ὁ τῶν
Ἱεροσολύμων βασιλεὺς ἀναλαβόντες τὰς δυνάμεις
ἤλασαν εἰς Ἀραμάθην πόλιν τῆς Γαλαδίτιδος. ὁ
δὲ τῶν Σύρων βασιλεὺς ἀκούσας αὐτῶν τὴν στρατείαν ἀντεπήγαγεν αὐτοῖς τὴν αὐτοῦ στρατιὰν καὶ
412 οὐκ ἄπωθεν τῆς Ἀραμάθης στρατοπεδεύεται. συνέθεντο δὲ ὅ τε Ἄχαβος καὶ Ἰωσάφατος ἀποθέσθαι
μὲν τὸν Ἄχαβον τὸ βασιλικὸν σχῆμα, τὸν δὲ τῶν
Ἱεροσολύμων βασιλέα τὴν αὐτοῦ στολὴν ἔχοντα
στῆναι ἐν τῇ παρατάξει, κατασοφιζόμενοι τὰ ὑπὸ
τοῦ Μιχαία προειρημένα. εὗρε δ᾽ αὐτὸν τὸ χρεὼν
413 καὶ δίχα τοῦ σχήματος· ὁ μὲν γὰρ Ἄδαδος ὁ τῶν
Σύρων βασιλεὺς παρήγγειλε τῇ στρατιᾷ διὰ τῶν
ἡγεμόνων μηδένα τῶν ἄλλων ἀναιρεῖν, μόνον δὲ τὸν
βασιλέα τῶν Ἰσραηλιτῶν. οἱ δὲ Σύροι τῆς συμβολῆς γενομένης ἰδόντες τὸν Ἰωσάφατον ἑστῶτα
πρὸ τῆς τάξεως καὶ τοῦτον εἰκάσαντες εἶναι τὸν
414 Ἄχαβον ὥρμησαν ἐπ᾽ αὐτόν, καὶ περικυκλωσάμενοι ὡς ἐγγὺς ὄντες ἔγνωσαν οὐκ ὄντα τοῦτον,
ἀνεχώρησαν ὀπίσω πάντες, ἀρχομένης δ᾽ ἠοῦς
ἄχρι δείλης ὀψίας μαχόμενοι καὶ νικῶντες ἀπέκτειναν οὐδένα κατὰ τὴν τοῦ βασιλέως ἐντολήν,
ζητοῦντες τὸν Ἄχαβον ἀνελεῖν μόνον καὶ εὑρεῖν οὐ
δυνάμενοι. παῖς δέ τις βασιλικὸς τοῦ Ἀδάδου
Ἀμανὸς ὄνομα τοξεύσας εἰς τοὺς πολεμίους τιτρώσκει τὸν βασιλέα διὰ τοῦ θώρακος κατὰ τοῦ
415 πνεύμονος. Ἄχαβος δὲ τὸ μὲν συμβεβηκὸς οὐκ
ἔγνω ποιῆσαι τῷ στρατεύματι φανερὸν μὴ τραπείησαν, τὸν δ᾽ ἡνίοχον ἐκέλευσεν ἐκτρέψαντα τὸ
ἅρμα ἐξάγειν τῆς μάχης· χαλεπῶς γὰρ βεβλῆσθαι
καὶ καιρίως. ὀδυνώμενος δὲ ἔστη ἐπὶ τοῦ ἅρματος
ἄχρι δύνοντος ἡλίου καὶ λιφαιμήσας ἀπέθανε.
416 (6) Καὶ τὸ μὲν τῶν Σύρων στράτευμα νυκτὸς
ἤδη γενομένης ἀνεχώρησεν εἰς τὴν παρεμβολήν,
καὶ δηλώσαντος τοῦ στρατοκήρυκος ὅτι τέθνηκεν

"Αχαβος ἀνέζευξαν εἰς τὰ ἴδια, κομίσαντες δὲ τὸν
417 Ἀχάβου νεκρὸν εἰς Σαμάρειαν ἐκεῖ θάπτουσι. καὶ
τὸ ἅρμα ἀποπλύναντες ἐν τῇ Ἰεζαρήλα κρήνῃ (ἦν
δὲ καθημαγμένον τῷ τοῦ βασιλέως φόνῳ) ἀληθῆ
τὴν Ἠλία προφητείαν ἐπέγνωσαν· οἱ μὲν γὰρ κύνες
ἀνελιχμήσαντο αὐτοῦ τὸ αἷμα, αἱ δὲ ἑταιριζόμεναι
ἐν τῇ κρήνῃ τὸ λοιπὸν λουόμεναι τούτῳ διετέλουν.
ἀπέθανε δ' ἐν Ἀραμάθῃ Μιχαία τοῦτο προειρη-
418 κότος. συμβάντων οὖν Ἀχάβῳ τῶν ὑπὸ τῶν δύο
προφητῶν εἰρημένων μέγα δεῖ τὸ θεῖον ἡγεῖσθαι
καὶ σέβειν καὶ τιμᾶν αὐτὸ πανταχοῦ, καὶ τῆς ἀληθείας μὴ τὰ πρὸς ἡδονὴν καὶ βούλησιν πιθανώτερα
δοκεῖν, ὑπολαμβάνειν δ' ὅτι προφητείας καὶ τῆς
διὰ τῶν τοιούτων προγνώσεως οὐδέν ἐστι συμφορώτερον, παρέχοντος οὕτω τοῦ θεοῦ τί δεῖ φυ-
419 λάξασθαι, λογίζεσθαί τε πάλιν ἐκ τῶν περὶ τὸν
βασιλέα γεγενημένων στοχαζομένους προσῆκε τὴν
τοῦ χρεὼν ἰσχύν, ὅτι μηδὲ προγινωσκόμενον αὐτὸ
διαφυγεῖν ἔστιν, ἀλλ' ὑπέρχεται τὰς ἀνθρωπίνας ψυχὰς ἐλπίσι κολακεῦον χρησταῖς, αἷς εἰς τὸ
420 πόθεν αὐτῶν κρατήσει περιάγει. φαίνεται οὖν καὶ
"Αχαβος ὑπὸ τούτου τὴν διάνοιαν ἀπατηθείς, ὥστε
ἀπιστῆσαι μὲν τοῖς προλέγουσι τὴν ἧτταν, τοῖς δὲ
τὰ πρὸς χάριν προφητεύσασι πεισθεὶς ἀποθανεῖν.
τοῦτον μὲν οὖν ὁ παῖς Ὀχοζίας διεδέξατο.

BIBLIOGRAPHY

I. TEXTS, TRANSLATIONS, TOOLS

I. BEKKER, *Flavii Josephi Opera Omnia*, Leipzig, 1855-1856.

H. BENGSTON (ed.), *Die Staatsverträge des Altertums*, II, München, 1975².

A.E. BROOKE, N. MACLEAN, H.ST.J. THACKERAY (eds.), *The Old Testament in Greek according to the Text of Codex Vaticanus*. II/II: *I and II Kings*, Cambridge, 1930; II/III *I and II Chronicles*, 1932.

K. BRUGMANN and A. THUMB, *Griechische Grammatik*, München, 1913⁴.

F. BUFFIÈRE (ed. and trans.), *Héraclite, Allégories d'Homère*, Paris, 1962.

E. CARY (ed. and trans.), *The Roman Antiquities of Dionysius of Halicarnassus* (LCL), London-Cambridge, MA, 1937-1950.

F.H. COLSON and G.H. WHITAKER (eds. and trans.), *Philo* (LCL), London-Cambridge, MA, 1929-1963.

R. LE DÉAUT and J. ROBERT (eds. and trans.), *Targum des Chroniques*, I-II (AnBib, 51), Roma, 1971.

L. DELATTE, *Les traités de la royauté d'Ecphante, Diotogène et Sthénidas*, Paris, 1942.

G. DIERCKS, *Luciferi Calaritani Opera Quae Supersunt* (CC, Series Latina, 8), Turnhout, 1978.

G. DINDORF, *Flavii Josephi Opera*, Paris, 1845-1847.

K. ELLIGER and W. RUDOLPH (eds.), *Biblia Hebraica Stuttgartensia*, Stuttgart, 1977.

I. EPSTEIN (ed.), *The Babylonian Talmud*, London, 1935-1952. '

L.H. FELDMAN, *Josephus and Modern Scholarship (1937-1980)*, Berlin - New York, 1984.

—, *Josephus: A Supplementary Bibliography*, New York - London, 1986.

N. FERNÁNDEZ MARCOS et J.R. BUSTO SAIZ (eds.), *Theodoreti Cyrensis Quaestiones in Reges et Paralipomena. Editio critica* (TECC, 32), Madrid, 1984.

—, *El texto antioqueno de la Biblia Griega*. I: *1-2 Samuel* (TECC, 50) Madrid, 1989; II: *1-2 Reyes* (TECC, 53), 1992.

H. FREEDMAN and M. SIMON (eds.), *The Midrash Rabbah*, London, 1977.

L. GINZBERG, *The Legends of the Jews*, Philadelphia, 1909-1925.

A.D. GODLEY (ed. and trans.), *Herodotus*, I (LCL), London-Cambridge, MA, 1920-1925.

D.J. HARRINGTON and A.J. SALDARINI (trans.), *Targum Jonathan on the Former Prophets* (The Aramaic Bible, 10), Wilmington, DE, 1987.

J. HUDSON and S. HAVERCAMPUS, *Flavii Josephi Opera Omnia*. I-II, Amsterdam, 1726.

G. KITTEL and G. FRIEDRICH (eds.), *TWNT*, Stuttgart, 1933-1973.

P. DE LAGARDE (ed.), *Librorum V.T. Canonicorum Graece pars prior*, Göttingen, 1883.

H.G. LIDDELL, R. SCOTT and H.S. JONES, *A Greek-English Lexicon*, Oxford, 1968.

S.A. NABER (ed.), *Flavii Josephi Opera omnia*, Leipzig, 1888-1896.

B. NIESE (ed.), *Flavii Josephi Opera. Editio maior*, Berlin, 1885-1895.

—, *Flavii Josephi Opera. Editio minor*, Berlin, 1888-1895.

E. NODET (ed.), *Flavius Josèphe, Les Antiquités juives. I: A. Livres I à III. Introduction et texte; II: B. Traduction et notes*, Paris, 1990.

W.A. OLDFATHER (ed. and trans.), *Epictetus* (LCL), London-Cambridge, MA, 1925.

A. PELLETIER (ed. and trans.), *Lettre d'Aristée à Philocrate* (SC, 89), Paris, 1962.

T. REINACH, *Textes d'auteurs grecs et romains relatifs au Judaïsme*, Paris, 1895.

—, J. WEILL et al. (trans.), *Œuvres complètes de Flavius Josèphe*, Paris, 1900-1932.

K.H. RENGSTORF (ed.), *A Complete Concordance to Flavius Josephus*, Leiden, 1973-1983.

A. SCHALIT (trans.), *Joseph ben Mattityahu Kadmoniot ha-jehudim*, I-III, Jerusalem, 1944-1963.

—, *Namenwörterbuch zu Flavius Josephus* (A Complete Concordance to Flavius Josephus, Supplement I), Leiden, 1968.

A. SCHLATTER, *Die hebräischen Namen bei Josephus* (BFCT, 17:3), Gütersloh, 1913.

H.H. SCHMITT (ed.), *Die Staatsverträge des Altertums*, III, München, 1969.

A. SPERBER, *The Bible in Aramaic*, II. *The Former Prophets according to Targum Jonathan*, Leiden, 1959.

J.M. STAHL, *Kritisch-historische Syntax des griechischen Verbums der klassischen Zeit*, Heidelberg, 1907.

M. STERN (ed.), *Greek and Latin Authors on Jews and Judaism* I, Jerusalem, 1974.

H.ST.J. THACKERAY, R. MARCUS, A. WIKGREN and L.H. FELDMAN (eds. and trans.), *Josephus* (LCL), London-Cambridge, MA, 1926-1965.

C. VERCELLONE, *Variae Lectiones Vulgatae Latinae Bibliorum Editionis* II, Romae, 1864.

R. WEBER, *Les anciennes versions latines du deuxième livre des Paralipomènes* (CBL), Rome, 1945.

G.A. WEVERS (trans.), *Sanhedrin Gerichtshof*, in M. HENGEL et al. (eds.), *Übersetzung des Talmud Yerushalmi* IV/4, Tübingen, 1981.

II. STUDIES

A. AEJMELAEUS, *Parataxis in the Septuagint. A Study of the Renderings of the Hebrew Coordinate Clauses in the Greek Pentateuch* (AASF Dissertationes Humanorum Litterarum, 31), Helsinki, 1982.

L.C. ALLEN, *The Greek Chronicles*, I-II (VTSup, 25), Leiden, 1975.

N. ALLEN, *Jerusalem and Shechem*, in *VT* 24 (1974) 353-357.

B.H. AMARU, *Land Theology in Josephus' Jewish Antiquities*, in *JQR* 71 (1980-1981) 201-221.

A. ARAZY, *The Appellations of the Jews (Ioudaios, Hebraios, Israel) in the Literature from Alexander to Justinian*, Diss. New York University, 1977.

K.C. ATKINSON, *Some Observations on Ptolemaic Ranks and Titles*, in *Aegyptus* 32 (1952) 204-214.

H.W. ATTRIDGE, *The Interpretation of Biblical History in the* Antiquitates Judaicae *of Flavius Josephus* (HDR, 7), Missoula, MT, 1976.

—, *Josephus and his Works*, in M.E. STONE (ed.), *Jewish Writings of the Second Temple Period* (CRINT 2/2), Assen, 1984, pp. 185-232.

D.E. AUNE, *The Use of ΠΡΟΦΗΤΗΣ in Josephus*, in *JBL* 101 (1982) 419-421.

E. BAMMEL, φίλος τοῦ καίσαρος, in *TLZ* 77 (1952) 205-210.

J. BARR, *Seeing the Wood for the Trees? An Enigmatic Ancient Translation*, in *JSS* 13 (1968) 11-20.

D. BARTHÉLEMY, *Les Devanciers d'Aquila* (VTSup, 10), Leiden, 1963.

W.W. GRAF BAUDISSIN, *Kyrios als Gottesname im Judentum und seine Stelle in der Religionsgeschichte*, II (ed. O. EISSFELDT), Giessen, 1929.

A. BAUMANN, *Naboths Fasttag und Josephus*, in *Theokratia* 2 (1970-2) 26-44.

C.T. BEGG, *The Death of Josiah: Josephus and the Bible*, in *ETL* 64 (1988) 157-163.

—, *The "Classical Prophets" in Josephus' Antiquities*, in *LS* 13 (1988) 341-357.

—, *Josephus' Zedekiah*, in *ETL* 65 (1989) 96-104.

—, *"This Thing I Cannot Do" (1 Kings 20,9)*, in *SJOT* 2 (1989) 23-27.

—, *The Death of King Ahab According to Josephus*, in *Ant* 64 (1989) 225-245.

J. BEHM, διαθήκη, in *TWNT* 3, 1938, 106-137.

—, θύω κτλ, in *TWNT* 3, 1938, 189-190.

—, καρδία κτλ, in *TWNT* 3, 1938, 609-619.

E. BEN-ZVI, *The Authority of 1-2 Chronicles in the Late Second Temple Period*, in *JSP* 3 (1988) 59-88.

G. BERTRAM - K.L. SCHMIDT, ἔθνος, in *TWNT* 2, 1935, 362-370.

E. BEST, *The Use and Non-use of Pneuma by Josephus*, in *NovT* 3 (1959) 218-225.

O. BETZ, *Offenbarung und Schriftforschung in der Qumransekte* (WUNT, 6), Tübingen, 1960.

—, φωνή κτλ, in *TWNT* 9, 1973, 272-302.

—, *Das Problem des Wunders bei Flavius Josephus im Vergleich zum Wunderproblem bei den Rabbinen und im Johannesevangelium*, in O. BETZ, K. HAACKER, M. HENGEL (eds.), *Josephus-Studien. FS O. Michel*, Göttingen, 1974, 23-44.

—, *Miracles in the Writings of Flavius Josephus*, in L.H. FELDMAN and G. HATA (eds.), *Jesus, Judaism and Christianity*, Detroit, 1987, 212-235.

W. BEYER, διακονέω κτλ, in *TWNT* 2, 1935, 81-93.

—, ὕβρις κτλ, in *TWNT* 8, 1969, 295-307.

E. BIKERMAN, *Instituts des Seleucides*, Paris, 1938.

P. BILDE, *Flavius Josephus between Jerusalem and Rome* (JSPSup, 2), Sheffield, 1988.

B. BLACKBURN, *Theios Anēr and the Markan Miracle Traditions* (WUNT, 2/40), Tübingen, 1991.

J. BLENKINSOPP, *Prophecy and Priesthood in Josephus*, in *JJS* 25 (1974) 239-263.

H. BLOCH, *Die Quellen des Flavius Josephus in seiner Archäologie*, Leipzig, 1879.

P.-M. BOGAERT, *Le repentir d'Achab d'après la Bible hebraïque (1 R 21) et d'après la Septante (3 Règnes 20)*, in G.F. WILLEMS (ed.), *Élie le Prophète. Bible, Tradition, Iconographie* (Publications de l'Institutum Iudaicum), Leuven, n.d. 39-58.

S.P. Brock, *The Recensions of the Septuagint Version of 1 Samuel*, Diss. Oxford, 1966.

B. Brüne, *Flavius Josephus und seine Schriften in ihrem Verhältnis zum Judentume, zur griechisch-römischen Welt und zum Christentume*, Gütersloh, 1913.

F. Büchsel, εἰμί, ὁ ὤν, in *TWNT* 2, 1935, 396-398.

R. Bultmann and D. Lührmann, φαίνω κτλ, in *TWNT* 9, 1973, 1-11.

C.F. Burney, *Notes on the Hebrew Text of the Book of Kings*, London, 1903 (rpt. New York, 1970).

J.R. Busto Saiz, *On the Lucianic Manuscripts in 1-2 Kings*, in C. Cox (ed.), *VI Congress of the International Organization for Septuagint and Cognate Studies* (SBL SCS, 23), Atlanta, 1987, 305-310.

—, *El Texto Lucianico en el Marco del Pluralismo textual. Estado de la Cuestion y Perspectivas*, in *EstEcl* 65 (1990) 3-18.

A. Catastini, *1 Re 13:1-10 e la Redazione delle Tradizioni su Geroboamo I*, in *Egitto e Vicino Oriente* 10 (1987) 109-121.

S.J.D. Cohen, *Josephus in Galilee and Rome. His Vita and Development as a Historian* (Columbia Studies in the Classical Tradition, 8), Leiden, 1979.

J.N. Collins, *Diakonia. Reinterpreting the Ancient Sources*, Oxford - New York, 1990.

S. Daniel, *Recherches sur le vocabulaire du culte dans la Septante* (Études et commentaires, 61), Paris, 1966.

E. Danielius, *The Sins of Jeroboam Ben-Nabat*, in *JQR* 58 (1967-68) 95-114, 204-223.

R. Le Déaut, φιλανθρωπία *dans la littérature grecque jusqu'au Nouveau Testament (Tite III,4)*, in *Mélanges E. Tisserant*, I (Studi e Testi, 231), Vatican City, 1964, 255-294.

G. Delling, ΜΟΝΟΣ ΘΕΟΣ, in *TLZ* 77 (1952) 469-472.

—, *Josephus und das Wunderbare*, in *NovT* 2 (1958) 291-309.

S.J. De Vries, *1 Kings* (WBC, 12), Waco, TX, 1985.

E.K. Dietrich, Recension of S. Rappaport, *Agada*, in *Philologische Wochenschrift* 51 (1931) 465-470.

—, *Die Umkehr (Bekehrung und Busse) im Alten Testament und in Judentum*, Stuttgart, 1936.

R.B. Dillard, *2 Chronicles* (WBC, 15), Waco, TX, 1987.

H. Donner, *Der "Freund" des Königs*, in *ZAW* 73 (1961) 269-277.

F.G. Downing, *Redaction Criticism: Josephus' Antiquities and the Synoptic Gospels* (I), in *JSNT* 8 (1980) 46-65; (II) 9 (1981) 29-48.

H. Drüner, *Untersuchungen über Josephus*, Marburg, 1896.

S. Ek, *Herodotismen in der Jüdischen Archäologie des Josephus und ihre textkritische Bedeutung* (Kungl. Humanistiska Vetenskapssamfundet i Lund, Årsberåtellelse 1945-1946), Lund, 1946, 27-62, 213.

W.A.E. Elmslie, *The Book of Chronicles* (CBC), Cambridge, 1916.

K. Eriksson, *Das Präsens historicum in der nachklassischen griechischen Historiographie*, Diss. Lund, 1943.

L.H. Feldman, *Josephus as an Apologist to the Greco-Roman World: His Portrait of Solomon*, in E. Schüssler Fiorenza (ed.), *Aspects of Religious Propaganda in Judaism and Early Christianity*, Notre Dame, 1976, 69-88.

—, *Josephus' Portrait of Saul*, in *HUCA* 53 (1982) 45-99.

—, *Flavius Josephus Revisited: The Man, his Writings, and his Significance*, in H. TEMPORINI and W. HAASE (eds.), *ANRW* II:21:2, Berlin-New York, 1984, 763-862.

—, *Josephus as a Biblical Interpreter: the 'AQEDAH*, in *JQR* 75 (1985) 212-252.

—, *Josephus' Portrait of Deborah*, in A. CAQUOT et al. (eds.), *Hellenica et Judaica*. FS V. Nikiprowetzky, Leuven-Paris, 1986, 115-128.

—, and G. HATA (eds.), *Jesus, Judaism and Christianity*, Detroit, 1987.

—, *Use, Authority and Exegesis of Mikra in the Writings of Flavius Josephus*, in M.J. MULDER and H. SYSLING (eds.), *Mikra* (CRINT, 2:1), Assen, 1988, 455-518.

—, *Josephus' Version of Samson*, in *JSJ* 19 (1988) 171-214.

—, *Josephus' Portrait of Noah and its Parallels in Philo, Pseudo-Philo's Biblical Antiquities and Rabbinic Midrashim*, in *PAAJR* 55 (1988) 31-57.

— and G. HATA (eds.), *Josephus, The Bible and History*, Leiden, 1989.

—, *Josephus' Portrait of Jacob*, in *JQR* 79 (1989) 101-151.

—, *Josephus' Portrait of David*, in *HUCA* 60 (1989) 129-174.

—, *Josephus' Portrait of Joshua*, in *HTR* 82 (1989) 351-376.

—, *Prophets and Prophecy in Josephus*, in *JTS* 41 N.S. (1990) 386-422.

—, *Josephus*, in D.N. FREEDMAN (ed.), *The Anchor Bible Dictionary*, Vol. 3, New York, 1992, 981-998.

—, *Josephus' Portrait of Moses*, in *JQR* 82 (1992) 285-328.

—, *Josephus' Portrait of Joseph*, in *RB* 99 (1992) 379-417; 504-528.

—, *Josephus' Portrait of Ahab*, in *ETL* 67 (1992) 67-78.

N. FERNÁNDEZ MARCOS, *The Lucianic Text in the Book of Kingdoms: From Lagarde to the Textual Pluralism*, in A. PIETERS and C. COX (eds.), *De Septuaginta*. FS J.W. Wevers, Mississauga, Ont., 1984, 161-174.

—, *En Torno al Texto Hexaplar de 1 Re 14,1-20*, in *Sef* 46 (1986) 177-190.

—, *Literary and Editorial Features of the Antiochene Text in Kings*, in C. COX (ed.), *VI Congress of the International Organization for Septuagint and Cognate Studies* (SBL SCS, 23), Atlanta, 1987, 287-304.

—, *Some Reflections on the Antiochian Text of the Septuagint*, in D. FRAEN-KEL et al. (eds.), *Studien zur Septuaginta*. FS Robert Hanhart (MSU 20), Göttingen, 1990, 219-229.

M.J. FIEDLER, Δικαιοσύνη *in der diaspora-jüdischen und intertestamentlichen Literatur*, in *JSJ* 1 (1970) 120-143.

W. FOERSTER, ἔξεστιν κτλ, in *TWNT* 2, 1935, 557-572.

T.W. FRANXMAN, *Genesis and the "Jewish Antiquities" of Flavius Josephus* (BibOr, 35), Rome, 1979.

V. FRITZ, *The "List of Rehoboam's Fortresses" in 2 Chr 11:5-12 – A Document from the Time of Josiah*, in *ErIs* 15 (1981) 46-53.

J.G. GAMMIE, *Herodotus on Kings and Tyrants: Objective Historiography or Conventional Portraiture?*, in *JNES* 45 (1986) 171-195.

G. GARBINI, *Gli "Annali di Tiro" e la Storiografia Fenica*, in R.Y. EBIED and M.J.L. YOUNG (eds.), *Oriental Studies*. FS B.S.J. Isserlin, Leiden, 1980, 114-127.

G. GERLEMAN, *Studies in the Septuagint. II: Chronicles*, Lund, 1946.

J.G. GIBBS and L.H. FELDMAN, *Josephus' Vocabulary for Slavery*, in *JQR* 76 (1986) 281-310.

D.W. GOODING, *Ahab according to the Septuagint*, in *ZAW* 76 (1964) 269-280.
—, *Problems of Text and Midrash in the Third Book of Reigns*, in *Textus* 7 (1969) 1-29.
J. GRAY, *I and II Kings* (OTL), London, 1970².
W. GRUNDMANN, ἐγκράτεια κτλ, in *TWNT* 2, 1935, 338-340.
—, θαρρέω (θαρσέω), in *TWNT* 3, 1938, 25-27.
—, μέγας κτλ, in *TWNT* 4, 1942, 535-550.
W. GUTBROD, Ἰσραήλ κτλ, in *TWNT* 3, 1938, 356-394.
A. VON GUTSCHMID, *Kleine Schriften* IV (ed. F. RÜHL), Leipzig, 1893.
H. HANSE, ἔχω κτλ, in *TWNT* 2, 1935, 816-832.
—, *"Gott Haben"*. *In der Antike und im frühen Christentum. Eine religionsgeschichtliche und begriffsgeschichtliche Untersuchung* (Religionsgeschichtliche Versuche und Vorarbeiten, 27), Berlin, 1939.
F. HAUCK-S. SCHULZ, πόρνη, in *TWNT* 6, 1959, 579-595.
R.S. HAUPERT, *The Relation of Codex Vaticanus and the Lucianic Text in the Book of Kings from the Viewpoint of the Old Latin and Ethiopic Versions*, Philadelphia, 1930.
F. HAUPTVOGEL, *Welche Handschriften sind für eine Ausgabe der lateinischen Übersetzung des ἀρχαιλογία des Josephus besonders wertvoll?*, in *Programm des k.k. Deutschen Stadtsgymnasiums der Kleinseite in Prag 1913-1914*, Prag, 1914, 1-9.
M. HENGEL, *Die Zeloten* (AGJU, 1), Leiden, 1961.
B. HELLER, *Die Scheu vor Unbekannten in Agada und Apokryphen*, in *MGWJ* 83 (1939) 170-193.
P. HERRMANN, *Der römische Kaisereid* (Hypomnemata, 20), Göttingen, 1968.
A. HILHORST, *"Servir Dieu" dans la terminologie du judaïsme hellénistique et des premières générations chrétiennes de langue grecque*, in A.A. BASTIAENSEN et al. (eds.), *Fructus Centesimus. FS G.J.M. Bartelink* (Instrumenta Patristica, 19), Steenbrugis, 1989, 177-192.
G. HÖLSCHER, *Josephus*, in *PW* 9², Stuttgart 1916, cc. 1934-2000.
L.P. HOGAN, *Healing in the Second Temple Period* (NTOA, 21), Freiburg-Göttingen, 1992.
J. HOLDER, *The Presuppositions, Accusations and Threats of 1 Kings 14:1-18*, in *JBL* 107 (1988) 27-38.
C.H. HOLLADAY, *Theios Aner in Hellenistic Judaism* (SBL MS, 40), Missoula, MT, 1977.
W. HORNBORSTEL, *De Flavii Josephi Studiis Rhetoricis Quaestiones Selectae*, Halle, 1912.
J. HORST, *Proskynein. Zur Anbetung im Urchristentum nach ihrer religionsgeschichtlichen Eigenart* (Neutestamentliche Forschungen, 2), Gütersloh, 1932.
E. JAHN, *Observationes criticae in Flavii Josephi Antiquitatibus Iudaicis*, Erlangen, 1891.
A. JAUBERT, *La notion d'alliance dans le Judaïsme aux abords de l'ère chrétienne*, Paris, 1963.
S. JELLICOE, *The Septuagint and Modern Study*, Oxford, 1968.
J. JEREMIAS, ἄνθρωπος - ἀνθρώπινος, in *TWNT* 1, 1933, 365-367.
M. JOHANNESSOHN, *Das biblische καὶ ἐγένετο und seine Geschichte*, in *ZVS* 53 (1925) 161-212.

J. JÜTHNER, *Hellen und Barbaren. Aus der Geschichte des Nationalbewusstseins*, Leipzig, 1923.

P.E. KAHLE, *The Cairo Geniza*, London, 1941.

H.J. KATZENSTEIN, *The History of Tyre*, Jerusalem, 1973.

H.P. KINGDOM, *The Origins of the Zealots*, in *NTS* 19 (1972-1973) 74-81.

G. KITTEL, ἀκολουθέω κτλ, in *TWNT* 1, 1933, 210-219.

M. KRENKEL, *Josephus und Lukas*, Leipzig, 1894.

G.N. KNOPPERS, *Rehoboam in Chronicles: Villain or Victim?*, in *JBL* 109 (1990) 423-440.

H. KÖSTER, φύσις, in *TWNT* 9, 1973, 246-271.

F. KREBS, Recension of B. NIESE, *Flavii Josephi Opera II*, in *Wochenschau für klassische Philologie* 3 (1886) 1094-1098.

J.L. LIEZENBERG, *Studia Flaviana. Observationes criticae in Flavii Josephi Antiquitates Judaicas*, Schiedami, 1899.

A.B. LLYOD, *Herodotus Book II Commentary 99-182*, Leiden, 1988.

U. LUCK, φιλανθρωπία κτλ, in *TWNT* 9, 1973, 107-111.

D. LÜHRMANN, *Epiphaneia. Zur Bedeutungsgeschichte eines griechischen Wortes*, in G. JEREMIAS *et al.* (eds.), *Tradition und Glaube. FS K.G. Kuhn*, Göttingen, 1971, 185-199.

J. LUST, *A Gentle Breeze or a Roaring Thunderous Sound?*, in *VT* 25 (1975) 110-115.

M. MACH, *Entwicklungsstadien des jüdischen Engelglaubens in vorrabbinischer Zeit* (Texte und Studien zum antiken Judentum, 34), Tübingen, 1992.

M. MACNAMARA, *The New Testament and the Palestinian Targum to the Pentateuch* (AnBib, 27), Rome, 1966.

G.W. MACRAE, *Miracle in the Antiquities of Josephus*, in C.F.D. MOULE (ed.), *Miracles. Cambridge Studies in their Philosophy and History*, London, 1965, 129-147.

A. MARMORSTEIN, *The Doctrine of Merits in Old Rabbinic Literature*, New York, 1968 (rpt.).

S. MASON, *Flavius Josephus on the Pharisees: A Composition-critical Study* (SPB, 39), Leiden, 1991.

G. MAYER, *Josephus Flavius*, in *TRE* 17, Berlin - New York, 1988, 258-264.

L. MAZOR, *The Origin and Evolution of the Curse upon the Rebuilder of Jericho – A Contribution of Textual Criticism to Biblical Historiography*, in *Textus* 14 (1988) 1-26.

S.L. MCKENZIE, *The Source for Jeroboam's Role at Shechem (1 Kgs 11:43–12:3,20)*, in *JBL* 106 (1987) 297-300.

—, *The Trouble with Kings. The Composition of the Book of Kings in the Deuteronomistic History* (VTSup, 42), Leiden, 1991.

B.M. METZGER, *Chapters in the History of New Testament Text Criticism* (NTTS, 4), Leiden, 1963.

K. METZLER, *Der griechische Begriff des Verzeihens untersucht am Wortstamm συγγνώμη von den ersten Belegen bis zum vierten Jahrhundert n. Chr.* (WUNT, 2/44), Tübingen, 1990.

H.E. FABER VAN DER MEULEN, *Das Salomo-Bild im Hellenistisch-Jüdischen Schrifttum*, Diss. Kampen, 1978.

A. MEZ, *Die Bibel des Josephus untersucht für Buch V-VI der Archäologie*, Basel, 1895.

W. MICHAELIS, ὁράω κτλ, in *TWNT* 5, 1954, 315-381.

O. MICHEL, O. BAUERNFEIND and O. BETZ, *Der Tempel der goldenen Kuh (Bemerkungen zur Polemik im Spätjüdentum)*, in *Gott und die Götter*. FS E. Fascher, Berlin, 1958, 56-67.

H.R. MOEHRING, *Rationalization of Miracles in the Writings of Flavius Josephus*, in E.A. LIVINGSTONE (ed.), SE VI = TU 112 (1973) 376-383.

J.A. MONTGOMERY, *The Religion of Flavius Josephus*, in *JQR* 11 N.S. (1920-1921) 277-305.

— and H.S. GEHMAN, *A Critical and Exegetical Commentary on the Book of Kings* (ICC), Edinburgh, 1951.

A. MORENO HERNÁNDEZ, *Glosas inéditas de Vetus Latina en manuscritos españoles: aportaciones para la reconstrucción de* 1 Re 20, in *Sef* 48 (1988) 343-356.

O. MURRAY, *Aristeas and Ptolemaic Kingship*, in *JTS* 68 (1967) 337-371.

S.A. NABER, *Observationes criticae in Flavium Josephum*, in *Mnemosyne* 13 (1885) 252-399.

J.H. NEYREY, *"Without Beginning of Days or End of Life" (Hebrews 7:3): Topos for a True Deity*, in *CBQ* 53 (1991) 439-455.

E. NODET, *Le texte des Antiquités de Josèphe (l. 1-10)*, in *RB* 94 (1987) 323-375.

—, *Pourquoi Josèphe?*, in *Naissance de la méthode critique. Colloque du centenaire de l'École biblique et archéologique française de Jérusalem* (Patrimoines, Christianisme), Paris, 1992, 99-106.

E. NORDEN, *Agnostos Theos*, Leipzig-Berlin, 1923².

M.A.O'BRIEN, *The Deuteronomistic History Hypothesis: A Reassessment* (OBO, 92), Freiburg-Göttingen, 1989.

C. OBSOMER, *Les campagnes de Sésostris dans Hérodote*, Bruxelles, 1989.

A.T. OLMSTEAD, *Source Study and the Biblical Text*, in *AJSL* 30 (1913) 1-35.

A. PAUL, *Flavius Josephus' "Antiquities of the Jews": An Anti-Christian Manifesto*, in *NTS* 31 (1985) 473-480.

E. PAX, *ΕΠΙΦΑΝΕΙΑ. Ein religionsgeschichtlicher Beitrag zur biblischen Theologie* (MTS, 10), München, 1955.

—, *Epiphanie*, in *RAC* 5, Stuttgart, 1962, 832-909.

A. PELLETIER, *Flavius Josèphe, adaptateur de la Lettre d'Aristée*, Paris, 1962.

E. PETERSON, *ΕΙΣ ΘΕΟΣ. Epigraphische, formgeschichtliche und religionsgeschichtliche Untersuchungen* (FRLANT, 41), Göttingen, 1926.

S. PISANO, *Additions or Omissions in the Books of Samuel* (OBO, 57), Freiburg-Göttingen, 1984.

A. POZNANSKI, *Über die religionsgeschichtliche Anschauungen des Flavius Josephus*, Halle, 1887.

H. PREISKER, ἐπιείκεια-ἐπιεικής, in *TWNT* 2, 1935, 585-587.

I.W. PROVAN, *Hezekiah and the Book of Kings* (BZAW, 172), Berlin - New York, 1988.

G. QUELL and G. SCHRENK, δίκη, in *TWNT* 2 (1935) 176-229.

— and W. FOERSTER, κύριος κτλ, in *TWNT* 3 (1938) 1038-1098.

C. RAAB, *De Flavii Josephi Elocutione Quaestiones criticae et observationes grammaticae*, Erlangen, 1890.

A. RAHLFS, *Septuaginta-Studien. III. Lucians Rezension der Königsbücher*, Göttingen, 1911.

T. RAJAK, *Josephus and the "Archaeology" of the Jews*, in *JJS* 33 (1982) 465-477.

S. RAPPAPORT, *Agada und Exegese bei Flavius Josephus*, Wien, 1930.

—, Recension of H.ST.J. THACKERAY, *Josephus*, in *REJ* 92 (1932) 100-112.

W.L. REED, *The Aserah in the Old Testament*, Fort Worth, TX, 1949.

J. REILING, *The Use of ψευδοπροφήτης in the Septuagint, Philo and Josephus*, in *NovT* 13 (1971) 147-156.

H. REMUS, *Does Terminology Distinguish Early Christian from Pagan Miracles?*, in *JBL* 101 (1982) 531-541.

G.A. RENDSBURG, *The Mock of Baal in 1 Kings 18:27*, in *CBQ* 50 (1988) 414-417.

K.H. RENGSTORF, μαθητής, in *TWNT* 4, 1942, 392-466.

—, σημεῖον, in *TWNT* 7, 1964, 199-268.

—, τεράς, in *TWNT* 8, 1969, 113-127.

G. RICCIOTTI, *Il testo della Bibbia in Flavio Giuseppe*, in *Atti del XIX Congresso Internazionale degli Orientalisti*, Roma, 1938, 464-470.

J. RIBERA, *El Profetismo segun el Targum Jonatan y el Targum Palestinense*, in D. MUÑOZ LEÓN (ed.), *Salvación en la Palabra. Targum-Derash-Berith. Memorial A. Díez Macho*, Madrid, 1986, 489-502.

E. RIGGENBACH, *Der Begriff der διαθήκη im Hebräerbrief*, in *Theologische Studien Theodor Zahn dargebracht*, Leipzig, 1908, 291-316.

K.O. SANDES, *Paul – One of the Prophets? A Contribution to the Apostle's Self-Understanding* (WUNT, 2/43), Tübingen, 1991.

A. SCHALIT (ed.), *Zur Josephus-Forschung* (Wege der Forschung, 84), Darmstadt, 1973.

J.D. SCHENKEL, *Chronology and Recensional Development in the Greek Text of Kings* (HSM, 1), Cambridge, MA, 1968.

A. SCHLATTER, *Wie Sprach Josephus von Gott?* (BFCT, 14:1), Gütersloh, 1910.

—, *Der Evangelist Matthäus*, Stuttgart, 1929.

—, *Die Theologie des Jüdentums nach dem Bericht des Josephus* (BFCT, 2. Reihe, 26), Gütersloh, 1932.

G. SCHMIDT, *De Flavii Iosephi Elocutione Observationes criticae*, in *Jahrbücher für classische Philologie, Supplementband* 20 (1894) 345-550.

K.L. SCHMIDT, ἔθνος κτλ, in *TWNT* 2, 1935, 362-370.

H. SCHRECKENBERG, *Einige Vermutungen zum Josephustext*, in *Theokratia* 1 (1967-1969) 64-75.

—, *Rezeptionsgeschichtliche und textkritische Untersuchungen zu Flavius Josephus* (ALGHJ, 10), Leiden, 1977.

G. SCHRENK, ἐντέλλομαι κτλ, in *TWNT* 2, 1935, 541-553.

W. SCHUBERT, *Das hellenistische Königsideal nach Inschriften und Papyri*, in *APF* 12 (1937) 1-26.

—, *Das Gesetz und der Kaiser in griechischen Urkunden*, in *Klio* 30 (1937) 54-66.

R.J.H. SCHUTT, *Studies in Josephus*, London, 1961.

—, *The Concept of God in the Works of Flavius Josephus*, in *JJS* 31 (1980) 171-189.

S. SCHWARTZ, *Josephus and Judean Politics* (Columbia Studies in the Classical Tradition, 18), Leiden, 1990.

J. VAN SETERS, *In Search of History*, New Haven - London, 1983.

C. Spicq, *La Philanthropie hellénistique, vertu divine et royale*, in *ST* 12 (1958) 161-191.

—, *Notes de lexicographie néo-testamentaire* I (OBO, 22/1), Freiburg-Göttingen, 1978; II (OBO, 22/2), 1978; III, Supplément (OBO, 22/3), 1982.

V. Spottorno, *Some Remarks on Josephus' Biblical Text for 1-2 Kings*, in C. Cox (ed.), *VI Congress of the International Organization for Septuagint and Cognate Studies* (SBL SCS, 23), Atlanta, 1987, 277-285.

—, *Flavio Josefo. Técnicas de adaptación del texto bíblico (1 Re 3,16-28)*, in *Sef* 52 (1992) 227-234.

L.R. Stachowiak, *Chrestotes. Ihre Biblisch-Theologische Entwicklung und Eigenart* (SF N.F., 17), Freiburg, 1957.

G. Stählin, *Das Schicksal im NT und bei Josephus*, in O. Betz, K. Haacker, M. Hengel (eds.), *Josephus-Studien. FS O. Michel*, Göttingen, 1974, 319-343.

G.E. Sterling, *Historiography and Self-Definition. Josephos, Luke-Acts and Apologetic Historiography* (NovTSup, 64), Leiden, 1992.

P.D. Stern, *The ḥerem in 1 Kgs 20,42 as an Exegetical Problem*, in *Bib* 71 (1990) 43-47.

H.-J. Stipp, *Elisha-Propheten-Gottesmänner. Die Kompositionsgeschichte des Elishazyklus und verwandter Texte, rekonstruiert auf der Basis von Text-und Literarkritik zu 1 Kön 20.22 und 2 Kön 2–7* (ATSAT, 24), St. Ottilien, 1987.

M.L. Strack, *Griechische Titel im Ptolemäerreich*, in *Rheinisches Museum für Philologie* 55 N.F. (1900) 162-190.

H. Strathmann, λάος, in *TWNT* 4, 1942, 29-39.

S.P. Swinn, ἀγαπᾶν *in the Septuagint*, in T. Muraoka (ed.), *Melbourne Symposium on Septuagint Lexicography* (SBL SCS, 28), Atlanta, 1990, 49-82.

Z. Talshir, *The Duplicate Story of the Division of the Kingdom (LXX 3 Kingdoms xii 24a-z)* (Jerusalem Biblical Studies), Jerusalem, 1989 (Hebrew).

—, *Is the Alternative Tradition of the Division of the Kingdom (3 Kgdms 12:24a-z) Non-Deuteronomistic?*, in G.J. Brooke and B. Lindars (eds.), *Septuagint, Scrolls and Cognate Writings* (SBL SCS, 33), Atlanta, 1992, 599-621.

B.A. Taylor, *The Lucianic Manuscripts of 1 Reigns*. Volume I: *Majority Text* (HSM, 50), Atlanta, 1992.

H.St.J. Thackeray, *The Septuagint and Jewish Worship*, London, 1923[2].

—, *Josephus, the Man and the Historian*, New York, 1929.

R. Then, *"Gibt es keinen mehr unter den Propheten? Zum Fortgang der alttestamentlichen Propheten in frühjüdischer Zeit* (BEAAJ, 22), Frankfurt/M, 1990.

B. Thérond, *Discours au style indirect et discours au style direct*, in A. Caquot et al. (eds.), *Hellenica et Judaica. FS V. Nikiprowetzky*, Leuven-Paris, 1986, 139-152.

E.R. Thiele, *The Mysterious Numbers of the Hebrew Kings*, Chicago, 1951.

E. Tov, *Lucian and Proto Lucian. Towards a New Solution of the Problem*, in *RB* 79 (1972) 101-113.

J.C. Trebolle Barrera, *Salomon y Jeroboan. Historia de la recensión y redacción de 1 Reyes 2-12,14* (Bibliotheca Salmanticensis Dissertationes, 3), Salamanca-Jerusalem, 1980.

—, *Centena in Libros Samuelis et Regum* (TECC, 47), Madrid, 1989.
—, *Critica textual de 1 Re 22,35. Aportación de una neuva lectura de la Vetus Latina*, in *Sef* 52 (1992) 235-243.
N. TURNER, *A Grammar of New Testament Greek*. III. *Syntax*, Edinburgh, 1963.
E.C. ULRICH, *The Qumran Text of Samuel and Josephus* (HSM, 19), Missoula, MT, 1978.
—, *Josephus' Biblical Text for the Books of Samuel*, in L.H. FELDMAN and G. HATA (eds.), *Josephus, the Bible and History*, Leiden, 1989, 81-96.
W.C. VAN UNNIK, *Het Godspredikaat "Het Begin en het Einde" bij Flavius Josephus en in de Openbaring van Johannes* (Mededelingen der Koninklijke Nederlandse Akademie van Wetenschappen, Afd. Letterkunde N.R. 39:1), Amsterdam, 1970.
—, *Josephus' Account of the Story of Israel's Sin with Alien Women in the Country of Midian (Num 25:1ff.)*, in M.S.H.G. VAN VOS et al. (eds.), *Travels in the World of the Old Testament*. FS M.A. Beek, Assen, 1974, 241-261.
—, *Flavius Josephus als historischer Schriftsteller* (Franz Delitzsch Vorlesungen, N.F.), Heidelberg, 1978.
F. VATTIONI, *3 (1) Re 12,10; 2 Par (Cr) 10,10 e Teodoreto di Ciro*, in *Aug* 31 (1991) 475-477.
R. DE VAUX, *Les Philistins dans la Septante*, in J. SCHREINER (ed.), *Wort, Lied und Gottesspruch. Beiträge zur Septuaginta*. FS J. Ziegler (FzB, 1), Würzburg, 1972, 185-194.
P. VILLALBA I VARNEDA, *The Historical Method of Flavius Josephus* (ALGHJ, 19), Leiden, 1986.
H. VAN VLIET, *No Single Testimony. A Study of the Adoption of the Law of Deut. 19:15 Par. into the New Testament*, Utrecht, 1958.
B.Z. WACHOLDER, *Nicolaus of Damascus*, Berkeley - Los Angeles, 1962.
—, *Josephus and Nicolaus of Damascus*, in L.H. FELDMAN and G. HATA (eds.), *Josephus, the Bible and History*, Leiden, 1989, 147-172.
M. WEINFELD, *The Loyalty Oath in the Ancient Near East*, in *UF* 8 (1976) 379-414.
—, *The Counsel of the "Elders" to Rehoboam and its Implications*, in *Maarav* 3 (1982) 27-52.
—, *The King as Servant of the People: The Source of the Idea*, in *JJS* 33 (1982) 189-194.
H.F. WEISS, *Pharisäismus und Hellenismus. Zur Darstellung des Judentums im Geschichtswerk des jüdischen Historikers Flavius Josephus*, in *OLZ* 74 (1979) 421-433.
K. WEISS, χρηστός, in *TWNT* 9, 1973, 472-481.
J.W. WEVERS, *Exegetical Principles Underlying the Septuagint Text of 1 Kings ii 12-xxi 43*, in *OTS* 8 (1951) 300-322.
—, *Principles of Interpretation Guiding the Fourth Translator of the Kingdoms (3 K. 22:1–4 K. 25:30)*, in *CBQ* 14 (1952) 40-56.
M.J. WILKINS, *The Concept of Disciple in Matthew's Gospel* (NovTSup, 59), Leiden, 1988.
H.G.M. WILLIAMSON, *1 and 2 Chronicles* (NCB), Grand Rapids, 1982.
T.M. WILLIS, *The Text of 1 Kings 11:43–12:3*, in *CBQ* 53 (1991) 37-44.

INDEXES

ABBREVIATIONS

I. *Ancient Writings, Manuscripts, Editions*

A	Codex Alexandrinus of LXX
AJ	*Antiquitates Judaicae*
Ap	*Contra Apionem*
B	Codex Vaticanus of LXX
BHS	*Biblia Hebraica Stuttgartensia*
BJ	*Bellum Judaicum*
Bk	I. Bekker, ed. of Josephus
codd	(all) Greek codices of Josephus
E	Epitome, *AJ*
Ed.pr.	Editio princeps of Josephus
Esth. Rab.	*Esther Rabbah*
Exc	Excerpta Peiresciana, *AJ*
Df	G. Dindorf, ed. of Josephus
Gen.Rab.	*Genesis Rabbah*
h.p.	historic present
Hud	J. Hudson, ed. of Josephus
L	Codex Laurentianus, *AJ*
LA	*Letter of Aristeas*
Lat	Latin version, *AJ*
Lev.Rab.	*Leviticus Rabbah*
Luc	(proto) Lucianic recension of LXX
LXX	Greek version of OT
M	Codex Marcianus, *AJ*
Mar	R.Marcus, ed.-trans., *AJ*
Meg.	Tractate *Megillah*, Babylonian Talmud
Midr.	*Midrash* (on a Biblical book)
MT	Masoretic Text
N	B. Niese, editio maior of Josephus
N*	B. Niese, editio minor of Josephus
Na	S.A. Naber, ed. of Josephus
O	Codex Oxoniensis, *AJ*
P	Codex Parisinus, *AJ*
Par	Paralipomenon
R	Codex Regius (Parisinus), *AJ*
Rgns	(I-IV) Reigns
S	Codex Vindobonensis, *AJ*
Šabb.	Tractate *Šabbat*, Babylonian Talmud
Sanh.	Tractate *Sanhedrin*, Babylonian Talmud
Sc	A. Schalit, trans., *AJ*
TC	Targum on Chronicles
t.e.	textus emendatus

TJ	Targum Jonathan on the Former Prophets
t. Sanh.	*Tosefta Sanhedrin*
V	Codex Vaticanus, *AJ*
VL	Vetus Latina
W	J. Weill, trans., *AJ*
y. Sanh.	Tractate *Sanhedrin*, Jerusalem Talmud
y. Sukk.	Tractacte *Sukka*, Jerusalem Talmud
Z	Zonaras, *Chronicon*

II. *Journals, Monograph Series, Dictionaries*

AASF	Annales Academiae Scientiarum Fennicae
AGJU	Arbeiten zur Geschichte des antiken Judentums und des Urchristentums
AJSL	*American Journal of Semitic Languages and Literature*
ALGHJ	Arbeiten zur Literatur und Geschichte des hellenistischen Judentums
AnBib	Analecta Biblica
ANRW	*Aufstieg und Niedergang der römischen Welt*
Ant	*Antonianum*
APF	*Archiv für Papyrusforschung*
ATSAT	Arbeiten zu Text und Sprache im Alten Testament
Aug	*Augustinianum*
BEATAJ	Beiträge zur Erforschung des Alten Testaments und des antiken Judentums
BFCT	Beiträge zur Förderung christlicher Theologie
Bib	*Biblica*
BibOr	Biblica et orientalia
BZAW	Beiträge zur *ZAW*
CBC	Cambridge Bible Commentary
CBL	Collectanea Biblica Latina
CBQ	*Catholic Biblical Quarterly*
CC	Corpus Christianorum
CRINT	Compendia rerum iudaicarum ad Novum Testamentum
ErIsr	Eretz Israel
EstEcl	*Estudios eclesiásticos*
ETL	*Ephemerides Theologicae Lovanienses*
ETS	Erfurter Theologische Studien
FB	Forschung zur Bibel
FRLANT	Forschungen zur Religion und Literatur des Alten und Neuen Testaments
HDR	Harvard Dissertations in Religion
HSM	Harvard Semitic Monographs
HTR	*Havard Theological Review*
HUCA	*Hebrew Union College Annual*
ICC	International Critical Commentary
JNES	*Journal of Near Eastern Studies*
JBL	*Journal of Biblical Literature*

JETS	*Journal of the Evangelical Theological Society*
JJS	*Journal of Jewish Studies*
JQR	*Jewish Quarterly Review*
JSJ	*Journal for the Study of Judaism in the Persian, Hellenistic and Roman Periods*
JSNT	*Journal for the Study of the New Testament*
JSOT	*Journal for the Study of the Old Testament*
JSP	*Journal for the Study of the Pseudepigrapha*
JSPSup	Journal for the Study of the Pseudepigrapha, Supplement Series
JTS	*Journal of Theological Studies*
LCL	Loeb Classical Library
LS	*Louvain Studies*
LSJ	Liddell-Scott-Jones, *Greek-English Dictionary*
MGWJ	*Monatsschrift für Geschichte und Wissenschaft des Judentums*
MTS	Münchener Theologische Studien
MSU	Mitteilungen des Septuaginta Unternehmens
NCB	New Century Bible
NovT	*Novum Testamentum*
NovTSup	Novum Testamentum, Supplements
NTS	*New Testament Studies*
NTOA	Novum Testamentum et Orbis antiquus
NTTS	New Testament Tools and Studies
OBO	Orbis biblicus et orientalis
OLZ	*Orientalische Literaturzeitung*
OTL	Old Testament Library
OTS	*Oudtestamentische Studiën*
PAAJR	*Proceedings of the American Academy of Jewish Research*
PW	Pauly-Wissowa, *Real-Encyclopädie der klassischen Altertumswissenschaft*
RAC	Reallexikon für Antike und Christentum
RB	*Revue biblique*
REJ	*Revue des études juives*
SBL MS	SBL Monograph Series
SBL SCS	SBL Septuagint and Cognate Studies
SC	Sources chrétiennes
SE	Studia evangelica
Sef	*Sefarad*
SF	Studia Freiburgensia
SJOT	*Scandinavian Journal for the Old Testament*
SPB	Studia postbiblica
ST	*Studia Theologica*
TECC	Textos y Estudios "Cardenal Cisneros"
TLZ	*Theologische Literaturzeitung*
TRE	Theologische Realenzyklopädie
TU	Texte und Untersuchungen
TWNT	G. Kittel and G. Friedrich (eds.), *Theologisches Wörterbuch zum Neuen Testament*
UF	*Ugarit-Forschungen*
VT	*Vetus Testamentum*

VTSup Vetus Testamentum, Supplements
WBC Word Biblical Commentary
WMANT Wissenschaftliche Monographien zum Alten und Neuen Testament
WUNT Wissenschaftliche Untersuchungen zum Neuen Testament
YCS *Yale Classical Studies*
ZAW *Zeitschrift für die alttestamentliche Wissenschaft*
ZVS *Zeitschrift für vergleichende Sprachforschung*

MODERN AUTHORS

JOSEPHAN PASSAGES

Antiquitates Judaicae (AJ)

1,1–11,296	2 3	137	125	273	51
1,1–10	1	140	153	279	33 159
1,3	70	142	215	283	126
14	62 148	146	38	294	159
15	175	154	159	298	33
17	284	155	151	303	48
19	175	157	120	309	215
20	173	159	125	311	133
31	223	167	49	319	102
37	153	175	225	323	159
43	54	177	221	325	15
46	15	181	75	327	124
49	167	183	24	337	159
54	43	184	37 159	340	219
55	46	185	192	341	178
56	46	186	39 48		
58	178	187	159	**2,6**	18
61	15	188	48	7	99 106
64	15	190	133	12	69
65	116 181	191	53	13	71
69	20	196	52	15	48
72	266	199	48 67	24	35
75	147	200	197	28	101
85	114	202	89 204	39	50
89	157	203	52	41	181
91	158	207	122	42	71
98	147	208	69	49	55
99	75 116 147	209	222	54	94
101	118	212	190	66	15
103-119	70	222-236	154	69	48
103	218	222	239	73	20
108	82	223	53 147 174	80	15 267
109	70	227	21	85	172
110	159	228	43 179 257	87	49
111	126	232	15	89	49
113	153	237	115 264	91	51
115	99	245	181	92	172
118	71	250	75	106	228
123	145	256	109	108	207
124	145	259	122 159	113	164
126	70 145	263	15	125	174
129	15 238	268	48	126	48

127	25	296	70	95	191		
128	132	299	126	100	191		
129	54 90	303	180	101	99		
136	132	304	233	102	48 228		
141	151	308	43	114	223 264		
146	175	310	33	129	153		
148	151	320	208	180	59		
159	21	322	54	186	145		
160	181	323	59 191 221	189	238		
164	48	331	218	190	101		
168	124	332	224	203	186		
170	218	333	90	207	43 182		
173	136	334	48	212	191		
175	218	335	100	217	145		
184	48	341	126 217	219	76	126	219
185	48 194	345	23		223		
189	126 157	348	82	222-223	239		
192	200	349	191	222	191 240		
196	109			223	38 239		
201-202	39	3,1	182 191	227	179		
202	136	3	3 261	228	43 178		
205	88	6	48	231	37 43 46 240		
214	106	7	100 218	233	43		
217	106	9	182	235	178		
224	71	10	176	238	178		
226	20	20	14	242	144		
235	55	21	169	243	43 46		
237	257	22	185	246	103		
238	181	25	59	250	43		
239	72 161	26	157	251	37		
242	130	27	157	257	43		
252	49 226	32	48	266	51		
253	171	35	87	269	178		
259	179	36	185	271	102		
262	49	45	107	273	86		
265	87	46	124	274	133		
267	33	62	191	281	167		
270	104	65	49	286	191		
272	257	71	67 223	295	191		
274	46 54	73	181	296	93		
276	121 131 192	75	181	298	87		
277	196	76	87 191	299	87 233		
280	104	81	82 198	301	99		
283	46 191 192	83	185	306	218		
	194	87	125	308	258		
284	191	88	192	309	99		
286	98	89	164	310	21 48 183		
291	191 231	90	192	314	218		
293	48 147	93	48 253	317-322	239		

317	88	132	55	292	151
		137	93 172	302	102
4,1	18 24	138	152	305	36 87
3	48 54	139	187	306	118 239
4	121	140	70	308	43
5	218	142	133	309	38
7	98	143	252	310	126
12	107	144	67	311	254
18	37	151	70	312	52
19	101	152-154	183	318	239 266
23	201	153	108 187	322	95
24	25 33	154	70	323	99
31	100 178	156	46	329	253
36	19	158	82		
41	15	159	239	**5**,5	5
43	191 192	161	260	7	20
46	159	165	159	8	89
47	233	167	132	27	99
48	181	168	218	31	154
49	67	172	41	33	90
55	159	173	245	39	75 92
58	51	176	257	43	151
61	116 239	177	24	45	56 225
63	215	184	48	52	221
67	37	188	232	53	20
70	43	191	18 239	60	225
75	43 182	192	87	64	218
76	102	202	203	65	120 159 218
78	264	205	36 167	66	225
84	115	207	203	68	89 153
86	102	209	30	70	89
87	247	210	239	72	89 215
93	115	214	37	74	223
96	174	216	19 181	76	33
97	115 136 142	222	36	79	89
102	52 136 137	224	136	87	65
104	59 93	233	25	90	92 177
105	88	234	48	93	215
108	256	239	126	96	122
109	132	241	43 178	97	48
112	159	242	93 200	98	218
116	52	243	239	101	172
120	102	246	254	107	172 177
122	164	248	153	108	102
123	73 178	257	214	111	87
125	20	262	252	112	15
126-155	187	266	25	113	227
129	124	269	175	114	178
131	136	286	90	117	109

118	99	285	123	44	229
123	90 132	286	267	47	25 134
124	264	287	170	48	25
133	46	292	89	49	47 89
143	49	294	170	50	121
144	223	295	46	54	22
145	102	299	228	56	102 186
147	162	306	39 265	58	69
149	133	307	49	59	214
150	89	309	232	60	91 138 267
151	25 248	314	59	61	151
158	48	317	49 264	64	48
159	48 73 224	330	99	66	257
170	89	336	260	67	134
173	126	338	248	68	130
175	256	339	74	78	228
178	33 93	342	134	79	220 221
179	15 266	343	89	80	195
180	108	344	48	81	22 48 102
182	153	345	42 48	82	73 224
183	142	346	104	84	197
184	86	347	76	86	23 156
186	248	354	88	88	229
188	99	357	89	89	44
192	55 231	358	164	90	121
197	86 130	359	130	91	11 181
201	47	361	37	92	61
204	218			93	67
205	186	**6,2**	31	94	223
206	120 225	5	15	97	72
213	126 181	7	121	101	178
216	120	8	258	107	218
222	15	10	76 171	113	121 180 220
225	107	13	228	115	88
229	122	21	67 218	116	220
230	159	22	138	119	220
232	109	24	48 74	120	261 264
235-236	100	25	245	122	248
236	51	26	225	129	72 77
240	208	31	223	130	106
244	217	32	190	131	11 44
246	190	35-36	126	132	39 130
254	130	35	11 134	133	76
266	178	38	87	135	72 142 225
270	109	39	22	136	116 231
271	140	40	11	138	147
276	48	41	122	139	159
277	141	42	14 48 106 116	141	48 248
280	48 141	43	22	142	24

143	22 208	255	22 88	7	22 247
145	49 73 224	257	228	8	11
147	67	260	121	9	11
148	37 173	263	35	11	212
151	54 178	265	147	13	225
153	67	268	181	17	107
154	31	271	72 121	19	54
155	134 183 262	272	89	24	11 228
157	170	273	48	26	33
158	52	275	267	27	101
160	147 149	277	89	30	16 244
165	231	278	87	40	94 207 227
166	196 256	284	25 140	42	162
172	257	290	134	43	214
174	33	291	108 171	44	126
178	153	292	51 115	45	86
179	257	293	264	46	262
181	4 120	294	132	48	59
183	75	300	164	50	116 132
184	181	303	24	51	228
187	203	305	258	52	102
191	107	306	86	56	37
192	76 137	307	74 102	58	76
199	69 174	311	22	61	217
205	226	316	22	62	217
206	257	317	132 214	66	137
208	102	321	244	70	69
212	102	329	74 106	71	11
213	121	331	102	72	45
218	233	334	74 183	73	260
219	259	338	52 228	74	267
220	134	339	108 159	76	223 247
222	196	341	132	77	122 220
223	257	342	252	82	22
224	102	343	152 258	85	223
229	185 193	345	253	88	33
230	174	355	72 229	89	39 154
231	226	356	108	92	24 53 159 170
233	255, 256	358	232		264
234	229	360	158	93	100 228
235	56 118	362	220 221	95	126
237	102	366	267	96	166
239	252	368	225	99	76 77
244	66 75	369	106 115	100-105	78
249	66	377	158 264	100-103	211
250	16	378	86	100	78 211 212
251	34 257			101-103	78
252	101	**7,1**	222	101	248
253	230	2	95	103	136 211 212

8,212-420

346	10 134 186 189 192
347-354	6 **189-198** 202
347-349	**189-191**
347	183 185 189 192 194 232 272
348	197 281
349	10 197 198 275 276 282
350-352	**191-195**
350	22 67 72 183 192
351	24 194 197 202
352	11 123 124 194 195 198 212
353-354	**195-197**
353	224
354	196 197
355-362	6 **199-210**
355-356	**199-201**
355	186 204 254 274
356	201 207
356-360	**201-204**
357	207
358-359	209
358	23 153 185 203 204 206 209 233 255 276
359	201 203 204 233 255 274
360-362	**204-209**
360	24 185 239
361	116 205 207-209 255 265
362	24 74 75 208 209 227 280
363-392	6 **211-235** 274
363-378	**211-221**
363	27 211 217 223
364	213 217 223 225
365	213 227 229 261 263
366	214 215
367	16 101 123 185 214 215
368-369	123 **215-216** 235
368	216
369	216
371-378	216
371	213 218
372	223 234
373-382	231
373	75 218 224 230 256
374	33
375	185
376	121 220
377	221 222
378-384	**222-226**

378	224 230 234
379	16 222 224 226 233
380	224
381	11 **223-22**5 230 256 259 262
382	25 73 224 225 230 233 247
383-384	282
383	225
384-392	**226-234**
384	228 234
385	207 213 227 229 234 281
386	102
387	164 234 245 248 256
388	27
389	231-233
390	233
391	**232-233**
392	46 203 233-235 249 252 258 265
393-397	6 **236-242** 271
393-394	**236-238**
393	25-27 117 130 149 237
394	17 104 128 238 240 243
395	65 105 126 127 **238-239** 242 277
396-398	**239-241**
396	240-242
397	241
398-420	6 **243-269** 271 274 277 278 281
398-400	269
398-399	**243-246**
398	26 244 246
399	245 254 259
400-410	**246-258**
400	88 249 279
401	73 224 247 260
402	50 123 248 250
403	249 250 252 265
404	249 252 254 264 281
405	33 121 233 252 257 261 264 265
406	45 50 60 252 256 265 267 269 283
406-409	283
407-409	282
407-408	123 **255-256** 269 282
407	206 255 264
408	**256-257** 264 265

182	108	273	37 178	62	37 239
183	48 57	274	37	63	67 239
187	239	275	248	64	15 48
188	99	277-282	39	65	172
189	25 45	277	46	66-67	58
190	25	278	26 108	66	50 172
193	172	280	166	67	20 25 45 58
194	91	281-282	39	68	60 156
195	45	281	38	70	240
196	61	282	11 116	71	37
198	267	283-287	162	72	178 239
199	60 257	288	152 156 172	73	86
200	141	289	156	74-77	263
203	115	290	67	75	213 263
204	86 114			76	60 257 263
205	105 114	**10**,1	26 108	77	54 57 94
208	24 84	2-4	75	81	7 114
211	156 248	2	102 171	83	136
214	47	4	98	84	140
215	7 109 114	9	217	86	260
216	67	11	48	87	119
222	105	12	47	89	125
225	193	15	211	91	130
227	140	16	167	92	88 248
228	115	17	166	93	21 102 202
234	115	18	71 181	96-97	75
236	104	19	71 213	98	7
237	48 147 213	22	218	100-101	75
239	44	23	7 114	100	228
243	38 74 84 87	24	178	102	11
244	136	26	48	103	140
246	26 67	27	24 44 88	104	50
249	116 223	28	54	106	255
251	223	32	267	108	101
253	108	33	45	110	213 220
255	93 172	37	7	111	50
256	91	39	44 61	117	132
257	43	41	47 223 226	123	208
258	22	42	175	124	50
260	22 33 36 67	43	178	131	217
	104 267	46	86 109	137	225
261	93 100	47	115	138	33
262	36	49	152	141-142	267
263	43	50	147	141	266
266	75	52	56 172	143	86 130
268	240	53	43	144	75
269	31 36	56	181	145	75 76
271	178	59	38 86 92 239	147	45
272	109	60	38 75	152	114

275	102	119	17	287	121 213
276	59	122	22	289	212
287	50	126	151 172	291	102
297	43	127	80	293	223
299	107	130	98	300	48 107 253
301	33	131	80 229	304	121
302	86 114	133	101	307	214 225
305	141	143	161	312	195
310	87	153	126	313	46 118
317	208	161	216	314	181
321	140	164	102	315	213
326	37	165	164	316	37 73 102 224
327	22	172	89	328	213
333	31	179	51	342	267
335	24	187	89	343	72 213
339	177	188	136	344	121
344	196	189	181	350	213
		195	69	351	260
12,6	64	196	51	355	98
7	80	199	166	357	75 95 162
8	228	203	70 149	358	75
11-118	28	204	46 181	359	86
13-15	13	212	11 267	361	11
19	33	219	214	363	217
25	13	222	121	364	22 38,
28	141	226	25	367	213
32	67	228	144	372	98 107
42	104	241	80	374	86 142
44	33	244	135	376	169 228
46	140	250	76	378	167
47	76 238	251	37	379	181
48	168	252	22 59 256	381	175
49	238	253	67 178	382	136 228
51	10	255	177	384	38 74
54	132	257	156	385	38 59 74
55	20	259	161	386	248
56	147	263	222	389	135
57	238	265	211	392	125
77	120	269	38 93	394	246
91-93	13	271	152 177	395	22
92	33	272	213	396	228
95	227	273	59	398	15 267
98	219	274	56	401	102 169
102	10 13	275	101	403	22 181 248
107	20	278	93 248	405	56
108	13	279	162	407	48
109	181	280	177	409	104 225
110	13 48	281	214	410	220
113	207	285	109 181	419	137

426	212	123	46 213	324	213
427	107	128	100	334	137 213
428	56	137	56	335	137
429	220	141	121 220	337	108 213
430	162	144	248	347	181
		148	212	353	166
13,4	15	156	217 228	356	121
6	236	165	258	357	72 108
9	213	166	126	363	141
13	181	168	37 73	365	115
16	212	170	137 244	366	7
26	212	173	20	369	248
31	195	174	212	370	191
32	137	186	212	371	253
33	37	187	20	373	250
34	59	188	145	375	221
37	213	196	212	378	115
41	151 191	198	100	385	204
43	169	201	15	386	50 86
45	137	214	124	393	212
46	30 212	219	22	394	195
50	100	220	32	397	177
54	239	223	50 137 213	398	162
55	102	225	241	406	33
58	212	227	137	411	257
59	225	235	121	421	267
64	156	237	186	422	15
65	120 156	241	30		
67	196	243	74	**14,3**	267
68	45	250	24 137	4	248
73	37	252	250	6	33
74	239	253	7 114	11	22 101 130
75	33	261	137	12	33
77	168	264	137	16	221
78	33 49 147	269	142	19	141
79	239	273	136	20	101
80	147	279	239	22	157 158 161
81	48	283	181		181
83	50	289	197 244	28	71 181
91	46	299	101 117	32	101
92	253	300	23 47 88	33	56 119
97	56	301	121	38	213
100	252	303	55	41	14
106	164	304	162	48	159
108	54 90 169	308	255	51	244 267
110	137	311	88	55	106
114	215	316	61 90	61	217
116	137	319	80	73	43
119	86	322	251	94	99

Contra Apionem (Ap)

Bellum Judaicum (BJ)

458	11	**2**,2	164	406	203
459	262	3	11	434	217
460	214	7	252	443	252
464	102	11	22	447	252
467	262	13	142	451	229
478	88	27	202	453	230
483	204	47	225	455	102
490	7 87 114	52	101	468	32
501	101 102	74	227	469	164 240
502	257	82	214	490	102
503	164	104	15	492	22
506	133	120	49	497	164
515	15 50	123	118	500	241
519	32 88 136	128	104	503	138
527	141	133	49	504	137
529	153	138	49	515	72
537	126	139	207	528	161
538	201 214	145	37	529	20
542	267	152	267	531	141
544	162	156	71	539	24
550	22 223	157	54	552	225
553	204	174	38	587	151
556	95	185	236	590	153
559	262	195	38 177	592	136
566	267	197	236	602	74
567	104	199	126	606	212
571	214	201	134 237	612	144
572	94	202	239	617	51
580	115	213	267	619	33
582	162	218	87 212	624	263
584	233	223	114	650	15
585	89	230	61	654	98
596	56	232	260		
606	215	259	46 251	**3**,2	17
620	214	261	50	8	212
625	74	263	260	22	32
628	101	264	168	26	213
630	35	266	236	27	144
631	233	276	267	61	213
632	11	280	221	68	241
633	254	290	260	69	196
637	151	299	176	70	49
639	102	302	225	86	201
644	94	309	211	100	32
646	11 238	310	141	132	73
649	56	324	216 228	143	248
660	95	345	240	145	213
664	121	347	15	157	213
665	11 95	393	38	186	87
668	11	394	120	193	87

315	15	113	108	342	133
318	229	139	70	362	141
329	248	163	134	369	253
330	104	165	104	370	213
339	108	173	212	371	39
345	229	176	179 213	378	133
349	104	199	141	392	169
353	137	201	94	403	107
356	229	239	216	406	49
378	229	247	69	407	203
387	228	252	114 212	410	266
395	84	255	214	411	134
411	91	260	126	413	104
426	250	264	52	416	87
436	71	269	151	424	177
442	238	270	133	428	151
		276	212	431	229
7,43	168	278	180	443	17
44	75	304	126	444	258
71	15	305	52	447	163
77	248	319	107	449	258
82	214	323	75 173	451	87
84	87 116	327	132 267	455	267
85	70	333	116		

Vita

23	87	152	20	298	46
45	46	155	101	301	171
62	126	158	141	306	248
63	195	160	18 126 239	308	20
74	126	161	245	310	195
77	126	171	25	314	101
78	228	172	54	321	25
79	118	173	196	327	225
82	248	184	51 126	339	163
83	90	193	73	342	54
87	101	207	169	343	102
88	101	222	49	356	151
92	99	224	80	369	175
99	222	227	132	375	256
107	20	252	232	378	25
123	101	261	258	380	233
124	101	270	157	383	46
126	18	271	101 248	393	20
130	233	280	215	404	22
134	239	290-303	199	414	20
144	195	290	181	416	232 248
149	267	292	248	424	92

BIBLICAL REFERENCES

18,5	166 167
18,6	168
18,7-8	169
18,7	168 169 171
18,8	169
18,9-14	169
18,9-11	170
18,9	169
18,10	167-168 169
18,11	169
18,12	53 168-171 187
18,13	171 187
18,14	171
18,15	171
18,16	171
18,17-40	**171-183**
18,17	171 172
18,18	172 187
18,19	153 154 172-174
18,20	173
18,21	173-175
18,22-24	174
18,22	174 187
18,23-24	174
18,23	174 175
18,24	175 176
18,25	175-176 187
18,26	176 177
18,27	176-177 187
18,28	177 187
18,29	177-178 181 184 187
18,30-35	181
18,30-32	187
18,30	178 187
18,31	24 179 197
18,32-38	179
18,32	178 179 275
18,33-34	176
18,33	179-180
18,34-35	180
18,34	180 187
18,35	180
18,36-37	180-181
18,36	181 184
18,37	181
18,38	181-182 188

18,39	182-183 187 192 195
18,40	10 180 183 189
18,41-46	**184-186**
18,41-42	185
18,41	184
18,42	184 187
18,43	184-185 190
18,44	185
18,45-46	185
18,45	185-186 275
18,46	186 187
19,1-21	6 158 **189-199** 209 234
19,1-9	**189-191**
19,1	189
19,2	189 198
19,3-4	190
19,3	197 272 281
19,4	190
19,5-8	190 198 276
19,5	190-191 197
19,6-8	190 198 275
19,6	191
19,7	197
19,8	191
19,9-18	189 **191-195**
19,9-10	198
19,9	24 191-192 194
19,10	192
19,11-12	193 198
19,11	193 197
19,12	193 194
19,13	191 193 194 198
19,13-14	198
19,14	194
19,15-18	123
19,15-16	193 194 198
19,15	194
19,16	194-195
19,17-18	198
19,17	195
19,18	195
19,19-21	189 **195-197**
19,19	195-196
19,20	196 198

19,21	196-198
20 (LXX 21),1-43	6 **211-235** 247 269 274 281
20,1-21	**211-221**
20,1-9	211
20,1	211-213
20,2-3	213 214
20,2	213
20,3	213 215
20,4	214
20,5-6	123 214
20,5	214
20,6	16 214 215
20,7-9	214
20,7	215 216
20,8	216
20,9	216
20,10-18	216
20,10	216-217 234 277
20,11	217
20,12	217-218 220 234
20,13-14	219
20,13	218-219 224 231
20,14	33 219
20,15	219 220
20,16-17	219
20,16	219-221
20,17-18	220
20,17	220
20,18	220
20,19-21	216
20,19	219 220
20,20	220 221
20,21	221 234
20,22-30	**222-226**
20,22-25	222
20,22	222-224 231
20,23-25	222
20,23	16 222-224
20,24-25	222
20,24	222-223
20,25	223 224
20,26-30	223
20,26	223

OTHER ANCIENT WRITINGS

BIBLIOTHECA EPHEMERIDUM THEOLOGICARUM LOVANIENSIUM

LEUVEN UNIVERSITY PRESS / UITGEVERIJ PEETERS LEUVEN

SERIES I

* = Out of print

*1. *Miscellanea dogmatica in honorem Eximii Domini J. Bittremieux,* 1947.

*2-3. *Miscellanea moralia in honorem Eximii Domini A. Janssen,* 1948.

*4. G. PHILIPS, *La grâce des justes de l'Ancien Testament,* 1948.

*5. G. PHILIPS, *De ratione instituendi tractatum de gratia nostrae sanctificationis,* 1953.

6-7. *Recueil Lucien Cerfaux. Études d'exégèse et d'histoire religieuse,* 1954. 504 et 577 p. FB 1000 par tome. Cf. *infra,* n°s 18 et 71 (t. III).

8. G. THILS, *Histoire doctrinale du mouvement œcuménique,* 1955. Nouvelle édition, 1963. 338 p. FB 135.

*9. *Études sur l'Immaculée Conception,* 1955.

*10. J.A. O'DONOHOE, *Tridentine Seminary Legislation,* 1957.

*11. G. THILS, *Orientations de la théologie,* 1958.

*12-13. J. COPPENS, A. DESCAMPS, É. MASSAUX (ed.), *Sacra Pagina. Miscellanea Biblica Congressus Internationalis Catholici de Re Biblica,* 1959.

*14. *Adrien VI, le premier Pape de la contre-réforme,* 1959.

*15. F. CLAEYS BOUUAERT, *Les déclarations et serments imposés par la loi civile aux membres du clergé belge sous le Directoire (1795-1801),* 1960.

*16. G. THILS, *La «Théologie œcuménique». Notion-Formes-Démarches,* 1960.

17. G. THILS, *Primauté pontificale et prérogatives épiscopales. «Potestas ordinaria» au Concile du Vatican,* 1961. 103 p. FB 50.

*18. *Recueil Lucien Cerfaux,* t. III, 1962. Cf. *infra,* n° 71.

*19. *Foi et réflexion philosophique. Mélanges F. Grégoire,* 1961.

*20. *Mélanges G. Ryckmans,* 1963.

21. G. THILS, *L'infaillibilité du peuple chrétien «in credendo»,* 1963. 67 p. FB 50.

*22. J. FÉRIN & L. JANSSENS, *Progestogènes et morale conjugale,* 1963.

*23. *Collectanea Moralia in honorem Eximii Domini A. Janssen,* 1964.

24. H. CAZELLES (ed.), *De Mari à Qumrân. L'Ancien Testament. Son milieu. Ses Écrits. Ses relectures juives* (Hommage J. Coppens, I), 1969. 158*-370 p. FB 900.

*25. I. DE LA POTTERIE (ed.), *De Jésus aux évangiles. Tradition et rédaction dans les évangiles synoptiques* (Hommage J. Coppens, II), 1967.

26. G. THILS & R.E. BROWN (ed.), *Exégèse et théologie* (Hommage J. Coppens, III), 1968. 328 p. FB 700.

27. J. COPPENS (ed.), *Ecclesia a Spiritu sancto edocta. Hommage à Mgr G. Philips,* 1970. 640 p. FB 1000.

28. J. COPPENS (ed.), *Sacerdoce et célibat. Études historiques et théologiques,* 1971. 740 p. FB 700.

29. M. Didier (ed.), *L'évangile selon Matthieu. Rédaction et théologie*, 1972. 432 p. FB 1000.
*30. J. Kempeneers, *Le Cardinal van Roey en son temps*, 1971.

Series II

31. F. Neirynck, *Duality in Mark. Contributions to the Study of the Markan Redaction*, 1972. Revised edition with Supplementary Notes, 1988. 252 p. FB 1200.
32. F. Neirynck (ed.), *L'évangile de Luc. Problèmes littéraires et théologiques*, 1973. *L'évangile de Luc – The Gospel of Luke*. Revised and enlarged edition, 1989. x-590 p. FB 2200.
33. C. Brekelmans (ed.), *Questions disputées d'Ancien Testament. Méthode et théologie*, 1974. *Continuing Questions in Old Testament Method and Theology*. Revised and enlarged edition by M. Vervenne, 1989. 245 p. FB 1200.
34. M. Sabbe (ed.), *L'évangile selon Marc. Tradition et rédaction*, 1974. Nouvelle édition augmentée, 1988. 601 p. FB 2400.
35. B. Willaert (ed.), *Philosophie de la religion – Godsdienstfilosofie. Miscellanea Albert Dondeyne*, 1974. Nouvelle édition, 1987. 458 p. FB 1600.
36. G. Philips, *L'union personnelle avec le Dieu vivant. Essai sur l'origine et le sens de la grâce créée*, 1974. Édition révisée, 1989. 299 p. FB 1000.
37. F. Neirynck, in collaboration with T. Hansen and F. Van Segbroeck, *The Minor Agreements of Matthew and Luke against Mark with a Cumulative List*, 1974. 330 p. FB 900.
38. J. Coppens, *Le messianisme et sa relève prophétique. Les anticipations vétérotestamentaires. Leur accomplissement en Jésus*, 1974. Édition révisée, 1989. xiii-265 p. FB 1000.
39. D. Senior, *The Passion Narrative according to Matthew. A Redactional Study*, 1975. New impression, 1982. 440 p. FB 1000.
40. J. Dupont (ed.), *Jésus aux origines de la christologie*, 1975. Nouvelle édition augmentée, 1989. 458 p. FB 1500.
41. J. Coppens (ed.), *La notion biblique de Dieu*, 1976. Réimpression, 1985. 519 p. FB 1600.
42. J. Lindemans & H. Demeester (ed.), *Liber Amicorum Monseigneur W. Onclin*, 1976. xxii-396 p. FB 1000.
43. R.E. Hoeckman (ed.), *Pluralisme et œcuménisme en recherches théologiques. Mélanges offerts au R.P. Dockx, O.P.*, 1976. 316 p. FB 1000.
44. M. de Jonge (ed.), *L'Évangile de Jean. Sources, rédaction, théologie*, 1977. Réimpression, 1987. 416 p. FB 1500.
45. E.J.M. van Eijl (ed.), *Facultas S. Theologiae Lovaniensis 1432-1797. Bijdragen tot haar geschiedenis. Contributions to its History. Contributions à son histoire*, 1977. 570 p. FB 1700.
46. M. Delcor (ed.), *Qumrân. Sa piété, sa théologie et son milieu*, 1978. 432 p. FB 1700.
47. M. Caudron (ed.), *Faith and Society. Foi et Société. Geloof en maatschappij. Acta Congressus Internationalis Theologici Lovaniensis 1976*, 1978. 304 p. FB 1150.

48. J. KREMER (ed.), *Les Actes des Apôtres. Traditions, rédaction, théologie*, 1979. 590 p. FB 1700.
49. F. NEIRYNCK, avec la collaboration de J. DELOBEL, T. SNOY, G. VAN BELLE, F. VAN SEGBROECK, *Jean et les Synoptiques. Examen critique de l'exégèse de M.-É. Boismard*, 1979. XII-428 p. FB 1400.
50. J. COPPENS , *La relève apocalyptique du messianisme royal. I. La royauté – Le règne – Le royaume de Dieu. Cadre de la relève apocalyptique*, 1979. 325 p. FB 1000.
51. M. GILBERT (ed.), *La Sagesse de l'Ancien Testament*, 1979. Nouvelle édition mise à jour, 1990. 455 p. FB 1500.
52. B. DEHANDSCHUTTER, *Martyrium Polycarpi. Een literair-kritische studie*, 1979. 296 p. FB 1000.
53. J. LAMBRECHT (ed.), *L'Apocalypse johannique et l'Apocalyptique dans le Nouveau Testament*, 1980. 458 p. FB 1400.
54. P.-M. BOGAERT (ed.), *Le Livre de Jérémie. Le prophète et son milieu. Les oracles et leur transmission*, 1981. 408 p. FB 1500.
55. J. COPPENS, *La relève apocalyptique du messianisme royal. III. Le Fils de l'homme néotestamentaire*, 1981. XIV-192 p. FB 800.
56. J. VAN BAVEL & M. SCHRAMA (ed.), *Jansénius et le Jansénisme dans les Pays-Bas. Mélanges Lucien Ceyssens*, 1982. 247 p. FB 1000.
57. J.H. WALGRAVE, *Selected Writings – Thematische geschriften. Thomas Aquinas, J.H. Newman, Theologia Fundamentalis*. Edited by G. DE SCHRIJVER & J.J. KELLY, 1982. XLIII-425 p. FB 1400.
58. F. NEIRYNCK & F. VAN SEGBROECK, avec la collaboration de E. MANNING, *Ephemerides Theologicae Lovanienses 1924-1981. Tables générales. (Bibliotheca Ephemeridum Theologicarum Lovaniensium 1947-1981)*, 1982. 400 p. FB 1600.
59. J. DELOBEL (ed.), *Logia. Les paroles de Jésus – The Sayings of Jesus. Mémorial Joseph Coppens*, 1982. 647 p. FB 2000.
60. F. NEIRYNCK, *Evangelica. Gospel Studies – Études d'évangile. Collected Essays*. Edited by F. VAN SEGBROECK, 1982. XIX-1036 p. FB 2000.
61. J. COPPENS, *La relève apocalyptique du messianisme royal. II. Le Fils d'homme vétéro- et intertestamentaire*. Édition posthume par J. LUST, 1983. XVII-272 p. FB 1000.
62. J.J. KELLY, *Baron Friedrich von Hügel's Philosophy of Religion*, 1983. 232 p. FB 1500.
63. G. DE SCHRIJVER, *Le merveilleux accord de l'homme et de Dieu. Étude de l'analogie de l'être chez Hans Urs von Balthasar*, 1983. 344 p. FB 1500.
64. J. GROOTAERS & J.A. SELLING, *The 1980 Synod of Bishops: «On the Role of the Family». An Exposition of the Event and an Analysis of its Texts*. Preface by Prof. emeritus L. JANSSENS, 1983. 375 p. FB 1500.
65. F. NEIRYNCK & F. VAN SEGBROECK, *New Testament Vocabulary. A Companion Volume to the Concordance*, 1984. XVI-494 p. FB 2000.
66. R.F. COLLINS, *Studies on the First Letter to the Thessalonians*, 1984. XI-415 p. FB 1500.
67. A. PLUMMER, *Conversations with Dr. Döllinger 1870-1890*. Edited with Introduction and Notes by R. BOUDENS, with the collaboration of L. KENIS, 1985. LIV-360 p. FB 1800.

68. N. LOHFINK (ed.), *Das Deuteronomium. Entstehung, Gestalt und Botschaft / Deuteronomy: Origin, Form and Message*, 1985. XI-382 p. FB 2000.

69. P.F. FRANSEN, *Hermeneutics of the Councils and Other Studies*. Collected by H.E. MERTENS & F. DE GRAEVE, 1985. 543 p. FB 1800.

70. J. DUPONT, *Études sur les Évangiles synoptiques*. Présentées par F. NEIRYNCK, 1985. 2 tomes, XXI-IX-1210 p. FB 2800.

71. *Recueil Lucien Cerfaux*, t. III, 1962. Nouvelle édition revue et complétée, 1985. LXXX-458 p. FB 1600.

72. J. GROOTAERS, *Primauté et collégialité. Le dossier de Gérard Philips sur la Nota Explicativa Praevia (Lumen gentium, Chap. III)*. Présenté avec introduction historique, annotations et annexes. Préface de G. THILS, 1986. 222 p. FB 1000.

73. A. VANHOYE (ed.), *L'apôtre Paul. Personnalité, style et conception du ministère*, 1986. XIII-470 p. FB 2600.

74. J. LUST (ed.), *Ezekiel and His Book. Textual and Literary Criticism and their Interrelation*, 1986. X-387 p. FB 2700.

75. É. MASSAUX, *Influence de l'Évangile de saint Matthieu sur la littérature chrétienne avant saint Irénée*. Réimpression anastatique présentée par F. NEIRYNCK. *Supplément: Bibliographie 1950-1985*, par B. DEHANDSCHUTTER, 1986. XXVII-850 p. FB 2500.

76. L. CEYSSENS & J.A.G. TANS, *Autour de l'Unigenitus. Recherches sur la genèse de la Constitution*, 1987. XXVI-845 p. FB 2500.

77. A. DESCAMPS, *Jésus et l'Église. Études d'exégèse et de théologie*. Préface de Mgr A. HOUSSIAU, 1987. XLV-641 p. FB 2500.

78. J. DUPLACY, *Études de critique textuelle du Nouveau Testament*. Présentées par J. DELOBEL, 1987. xxvii-431 p. FB 1800.

79. E.J.M. VAN EIJL (ed.), *L'image de C. Jansénius jusqu'à la fin du XVIIIe siècle*, 1987. 258 p. FB 1250.

80. E. BRITO, *La Création selon Schelling. Universum*, 1987. XXXV-646 p. FB 2980.

81. J. VERMEYLEN (ed.), *The Book of Isaiah – Le Livre d'Isaïe. Les oracles et leurs relectures. Unité et complexité de l'ouvrage*, 1989. X-472 p. FB 2700.

82. G. VAN BELLE, *Johannine Bibliography 1966-1985. A Cumulative Bibliography on the Fourth Gospel*, 1988. XVII-563 p. FB 2700.

83. J.A. SELLING (ed.), *Personalist Morals. Essays in Honor of Professor Louis Janssens*, 1988. VIII-344 p. FB 1200.

84. M.-É. BOISMARD, *Moïse ou Jésus. Essai de christologie johannique*, 1988. XVI-241 p. FB 1000.

85. J.A. DICK, *The Malines Conversations Revisited*, 1989. 278 p. FB 1500.

86. J.-M. SEVRIN (ed.), *The New Testament in Early Christianity – La réception des écrits néotestamentaires dans le christianisme primitif*, 1989. XVI-406 p. FB 2500.

87. R.F. COLLINS (ed.), *The Thessalonian Correspondence*, 1990. XV-546 p. FB 3000.

88. F. VAN SEGBROECK, *The Gospel of Luke. A Cumulative Bibliography 1973-1988*, 1989. 241 p. FB 1200.

89. G. THILS, *Primauté et infaillibilité du Pontife Romain à Vatican I et autres études d'ecclésiologie*, 1989. XI-422 p. FB 1850.

90. A. VERGOTE, *Explorations de l'espace théologique. Études de théologie et de philosophie de la religion,* 1990. XVI-709 p. FB 2000.
91. J.C. DE MOOR, *The Rise of Yahwism: The Roots of Israelite Monotheism,* 1990. XII-315 p. FB 1250.
92. B. BRUNING, M. LAMBERIGTS & J. VAN HOUTEM (eds.), *Collectanea Augustiniana. Mélanges T.J. van Bavel,* 1990. 2 tomes, XXXVIII-VIII-1074 p. FB 3000.
93. A. DE HALLEUX, *Patrologie et œcuménisme. Recueil d'études,* 1990. XVI-887 p. FB 3000.
94. C. BREKELMANS & J. LUST (eds.), *Pentateuchal and Deuteronomistic Studies: Papers Read at the XIIIth IOSOT Congress Leuven 1989,* 1990. 307 p. FB 1500.
95. D.L. DUNGAN (ed.), *The Interrelations of the Gospels. A Symposium Led by M.-É. Boismard – W.R. Farmer – F. Neirynck, Jerusalem 1984,* 1990. XXXI-672 p. FB 3000.
96. G.D. KILPATRICK, *The Principles and Practice of New Testament Textual Criticism. Collected Essays.* Edited by J.K. ELLIOTT, 1990. XXXVIII-489 p. FB 3000.
97. G. ALBERIGO (ed.), *Christian Unity. The Council of Ferrara-Florence: 1438/39 – 1989,* 1991. X-681 p. FB 3000.
98. M. SABBE, *Studia Neotestamentica. Collected Essays,* 1991. XVI-573 p. FB 2000.
99. F. NEIRYNCK, *Evangelica II: 1982-1991. Collected Essays.* Edited by F. VAN SEGBROECK, 1991. XIX-874 p. FB 2800.
100. F. VAN SEGBROECK, C.M. TUCKETT, G. VAN BELLE & J. VERHEYDEN (eds.), *The Four Gospels 1992. Festschrift Frans Neirynck,* 1992. 3 volumes, XVII-X-X-2668 p. FB 5000.

SERIES III

101. A. DENAUX (ed.), *John and the Synoptics,* 1992. XXII-696 p. FB 3000.
102. F. NEIRYNCK, J. VERHEYDEN, F. VAN SEGBROECK, G. VAN OYEN & R. CORSTJENS, *The Gospel of Mark. A Cumulative Bibliography: 1950-1990,* 1992. XII-717 p. FB 2700.
103. M. SIMON, *Un catéchisme universel pour l'Église catholique. Du Concile de Trente à nos jours,* 1992. XIV-461 p. FB 2200.
104. L. CEYSSENS, *Le sort de la bulle Unigenitus. Recueil d'études offert à Lucien Ceyssens à l'occasion de son 90e anniversaire.* Présenté par M. LAMBERIGTS, 1992. XXVI-641 p. FB 2000.
105. R.J. DALY (ed.), *Origeniana Quinta. Papers of the 5th International Origen Congress, Boston College, 14-18 August 1989,* 1992. XVII-635 p. FB 2700.
106. A.S. VAN DER WOUDE (ed.), *The Book of Daniel in the Light of New Findings,* 1993. XVIII-574 p. FB 3000.
107. J. FAMERÉE, *L'ecclésiologie d'Yves Congar avant Vatican II: Histoire et Église. Analyse et reprise critique,* 1992. 497 p. FB 2600.
108. C. BEGG, *Josephus' Account of the Early Divided Monarchy (AJ 8, 212-420). Rewriting the Bible,* 1993. IX-377 p. FB 2400.

109. J. BULCKENS & H. LOMBAERTS (eds.), *L'enseignement de la religion catholique à l'école secondaire. Enjeux pour la nouvelle Europe*, 1993. XII-260 p. FB 1250

110. C. FOCANT (ed.), *The Synoptic Gospels. Source Criticism and the New Literary Criticism*, 1993. XXXIX-670 p. FB 3000.

GRUZSI LLATE. F. B. 4.. N. 200 1. book.

THE UNITED LIBRARY
2121 Sheridan Road
Evanston, IL 60201

ORIENTALISTE, P.B. 41, B-3000 Leuven

THE UNITED LIBRARY
2121 Sheridan Road
Evanston, IL 60201